DATE DUE

Deeper Shades of GREEN

The Rise of Blue-Collar and Minority Environmentalism in America

Jim Schwab

Sierra Club Books

San Francisco

To John Erickson, who always had faith that this would happen.

———

The Sierra Club, founded in 1892 by John Muir, has devoted itself to the study and protection of the earth's scenic and ecological resources— mountains, wetlands, woodlands, wild shores and rivers, deserts and plains. The publishing program of the Sierra Club offers books to the public as a nonprofit educational service in the hope that they may enlarge the public's understanding of the Club's basic concerns. The point of view expressed in each book, however, does not necessarily represent that of the Club. The Sierra Club has some sixty chapters coast to coast, in Canada, Hawaii, and Alaska. For information about how you may participate in its programs to preserve wilderness and the quality of life, please address inquiries to Sierra Club, 730 Polk Street, San Francisco, CA 94109.

Copyright © 1994 by Jim Schwab

Library of Congress Cataloging in Publication Data
Schwab, James.
    Deeper shades of green : the rise of blue-color and minority environmentalism in America / by Jim Schwab.
      p.   cm.
    Includes bibliographical references and index.
    ISBN 0-87156-462-9
    1. Green movement–United States. 2. Environmentalism–United States. 3. Environmental protection–United States–Case studies.
    I. Title.
GE197.S3 1994
363.7'00973–dc20   93-29848
                                                   CIP

Production by Janet Vail
Jacket design by Laurie Dolphin
Book design by Amy Evans

Contents

Acknowledgments   iv

Preface   ix

Foreword   xi

Introduction   xvii

1. Robbins: Desperate for Development   1

2. California: The Politics of Life and Breath   44

3. Cleveland: Accidents Will Happen   77

4. East Liverpool: Landfill in the Sky   104

5. The Calumet Region: Industrial Prosperity to Crash
   Landing   160

6. Louisiana: Meandering Rivers of Justice   207

7. Appalachia: Defending the Land   283

8. Indian Country: Defending Mother Earth   321

9. A Place at the Table   383

10. Detoxifying America   394

11. The Future of the Movement   410

Appendix A: Record of Interviews Conducted and
   Meetings/Conferences Attended   421

Appendix B: Bibliographic Guide   433

Appendix C: Principles of Environmental Justice   441

Notes   445

Index   480

Acknowledgments

It is repetitive, but it must be said. No one writes this kind of book without drawing on the resources and assistance of a wide variety of friends, institutions, and colleagues. My experience is no different, except perhaps more so, for I must take the opportunity to thank the hundreds of people who took time to talk to me. Because the list is so long, I have separated the interviewees into a special list in an appendix. I will reserve my acknowledgments here for those who offered other types of assistance without which this book would have been, at the least, deficient in its documentation, and might well have proven impossible to complete.

First, there are those who supplied documents, ranging from copies of newspaper articles to whole reports, books, and, in some cases, entire boxes of information. Barry Neal, vice president for project development at the Reading Energy Corporation, was one of the first to supply a hefty packet of material concerning his firm's proposed incinerator in Robbins, Illinois. Matthew Dunn, of the Illinois attorney general's office, was equally helpful in supplying copies of materials pertaining to his agency's lawsuits over both the Robbins incinerator and the Chemical Waste Management facility in Chicago. Various people in the Chicago Greenpeace office also supplied information concerning the Robbins facility, as did Kevin Greene, research director at Citizens for a Better Environment.

The members of the Concerned Citizens of South Central plied me with news clippings about the LANCER incinerator, and Lupe Vela of the Los Angeles Integrated Waste Management Office supplied information about the city's recycling-market development plans.

Terri Swearingen and Connie Stein of the Tri-State Environmental Council supplied numerous packages of widely varying materials concerning the WTI facility. Niaz Dorry of the Chester, West Virginia, field office of Greenpeace also supplied a profusion of news clippings. Gary Peters provided some last-minute assistance in East Liverpool by double-checking some local newspaper references, as did the reference librarians in the Cleveland Public Library's newspaper section. In Cleveland, Lisa Casini, Katherine and Robert Chaney, and Sharon Fields supplied me with similarly substantial files of information regarding GSX. The Ohio EPA staff was responsive to my request to examine files and promptly copied and mailed to me the documents I requested concerning both GSX and WTI. In that regard, Shelby Thurman-Jackson, the agency's public-involvement coordinator, was particularly friendly and helpful. The U.S. EPA press office also supplied materials pertaining to the May 1993 announcement of an incinerator moratorium.

In the Chicago area, James E. Landing, professor of geography at the University of Illinois, and Marc Bouman, professor of geography at Chicago State University, both supplied me with valuable documentation about issues concerning the Calumet region of Southeast Chicago and Northwest Indiana. In addition, the staff of PAHLS, an Indiana citizens' organization, kept me informed of their activities by sending me their newsletters. Dorreen Carey of the Grand Calumet Task Force also supplied some useful material. Mike Wright of the United Steelworkers of America Safety Division in Pittsburgh supplied a raft of material dealing with worker health and safety in steel plants. The Burns Harbor Port Authority provided some materials and a videotape about its operations. Finally, Gary Westefer and Diana Gountanis at the U.S. EPA Region V headquarters in Chicago were very gracious in extending themselves to supply documents concerning the Chemical Waste Management incinerator in Southeast Chicago. Mary Ryan and Chuck McDermott of Waste Management Inc. both supplied papers pertaining to their company's operations and their views on the issue of environmental equity.

In Louisiana, the help in acquiring documents was extensive, starting with Marylee Orr and her staff at the Louisiana Environmental Action Network, who gave me free rein to peruse and copy their files. It included substantial assistance from William Fontenot of the Louisiana Justice Department, without whose help no one could fully explore that state's environmental movement; from Zack Nauth at the Louisiana Coalition for Tax Justice; from Tom Estabrook, while he was still with the Oil, Chemical, and Atomic Workers Local 4-620 in Baton Rouge; from Peggy Frankland of the Calcasieu League for Environmental Action Now; from Audrey Evans at the Tulane University Environmental Law Clinic; from David Czernik and Bill Temmink at the Injured Workers Union; and from Paul Templet, former secretary of the Louisiana Department of Environmental Quality, who has now returned to teaching at Louisiana State University. On the other side of the fence, Richard Kleiner supplied materials pertaining to the activities and programs of the Louisiana Chemical Association, and Guy Barone supplied material pertaining to Dow USA. On no particular side of the fence, Mark Schliefstein and James O'Byrne, reporters for the *New Orleans Times-Picayune*, supplied me with clippings of their past articles.

Joe Szakos and other members of Kentuckians for the Commonwealth, specifically including Susan Shoulders, Patty Wallace, and Tyler Fairleigh, supplied me with copious quantities of materials about that state's environmental problems. Charlie Cray of Greenpeace supplemented that with specific information about Calvert City. Dianne Bady and Barbara Christian supplied reports, videotapes, and news clippings, among other things, concerning the Ohio Valley Environmental Coalition's battle with Ashland Oil Company. In Charleston, West Virginia, Paul Hill, executive director at the National Institute for Chemical Studies, supplied a number of useful documents on the chemical industry. Norm Steenstra, executive director of the West Virginia Citizen Action Group, did likewise on the chemical, mining, and waste-management industries. Billie Elmore of NC-WARN supplied me with a healthy array of news clippings and reports on the status of waste-management projects in North Carolina.

Christine and Ronald Valandra, leaders of the Good Road Coalition on the Rosebud Sioux Indian Reservation in South Dakota, provided me with a package of news clippings and contracts documenting the history of their people's struggle to block a landfill on Sioux lands. Johna Rodgers, of the *Meridian Star* in Meridian, Mississippi, supplied me with a complete package of the printed news coverage of the aborted plan to locate an incinerator on the Choctaw reservation near Philadelphia, Mississippi. Annette Rasch, an activist in Seymour, Wisconsin, supplied me with materials pertaining to mining and other environmental issues in Wisconsin. Both free-lance writer Debra Schwartz and former interim tribal vice chairman Nicholas A. Alvarez supplied news clippings and other materials about the Chemehuevi Indian reservation and the proposed Ward Valley nuclear-waste dump. Susan Dawson, Chellis Glendinning, Lila Bird, and Anna Rondon supplied newsletters, clippings, and documents pertaining to uranium-mining issues. Lila Bird and Grace Thorpe of Yale, Oklahoma, supplied material pertaining to the storage of high-level nuclear waste on Indian reservations.

All of the people above supplied information primarily related to one of the local issues detailed in this book. However, there is a second list of people who helped by supplying other kinds of printed or video information of a general nature or pertaining to local struggles other than those discussed in the first eight chapters. These people, in no particular order, include Robert Ginsburg, an independent environmental consultant in Chicago; Mary O'Connell, editor of the *Neighborhood Works* at the Center for Neighborhood Technology in Chicago; Lois Gibbs and her staff at the Citizen's Clearinghouse for Hazardous Waste; James Quigley and Tom Webster of the Center for the Biology of Natural Systems at Queens College in New York; Peter Montague, editor of *Rachel's Hazardous Waste News* at the Environmental Research Foundation; Fred Millar of Friends of the Earth; Charles Lee at the United Church of Christ's Toxics and Minorities Project; Ken Westlake of the U.S. EPA in Chicago; and Sharon Pines at Greenpeace in Chicago. I may well have missed some people, and if so, I offer my apologies for not keeping better track along the way.

Finally, there are a few people who rendered steady and faithful service in the editorial process. Deborah Griffin-Pittenger did yeoman's work in transcribing dozens of tape-recorded interviews so that I would find them more readily useful. Larry Barr did some library research. Marianne Salcetti, Michael F. Sheehan, James

Quigley, Carolyn Kennedy, Jeri Parish, James Hecimovich, Alex L. Bailey, Dorreen Carey, James F. Berry, Joe Szakos, Oannes Pritzker, Lori Goodman, Chas Wheelock, Lila Bird, Burl Self, Tom Goldtooth, Paul Templet, Pat Bryant, and Marylee Orr all read various portions of the manuscript and supplied feedback and insights on potential improvements. And there is my literary agent, Malaga Baldi, who labored hard to find an appropriate publishing home for this project. Her steady optimism was invaluable as I slugged my way through a project that often felt like a literary marathon. In that same regard, I owe a debt of gratitude to Sierra Club Books editor Erik Migdail for his steady confidence in and support of this project, especially in its sometimes hectic closing days.

I must also add here a short comment on the use of source materials for this book. By its nature, a book-length exploration into a highly diverse grass-roots movement depends heavily on oral sources as well as the use of organizational newsletters and clippings from local newspapers, often supplied by local people. Some of these sources are very local indeed, including newspapers not regularly indexed or readily available, if at all, in libraries. Wherever possible, I have endeavored to include page numbers as well as issue dates for newspaper listings, even when they reached me as incompletely labeled photocopies or original clippings. In some cases, however, this was not possible even though it was clear that the material was pertinent. In most cases, interview information supplemented this wealth of printed material. If, as some claim, journalism is the first draft of history, then it is essential that this draft be as accurate and complete as the sources available will allow. There is no question that the stories of grass-roots movements such as the one for environmental justice have received insufficient attention in the past.

Preface

Every author starts with a premise, and if the topic of the book is at all related to his or her life experience, it is inevitable that experience will influence and shape the perspective the author presents. I am no different, and I think the reader deserves some insight into the road that I have traveled in coming to write this book—not all the fine details, but the broad philosophical path.

My father spent most of his working life in a Cleveland chemical plant as a truck mechanic. In a sense, he was better off than most in that plant because he had a set of distinct mechanical skills that set him apart from those who had to work in the various production departments, such as antimony, uranium, and cuprous chloride. I did work in all those areas, and more, as a college student earning good union wages during summers and winter breaks to earn my way through Cleveland State University. I saw 50-year-old men who looked as though they were 80. I saw injured workers. And I knew that workplace safety and environmental protection were not issues to be taken lightly, nor were these workers' needs for jobs and employment issues of small concern. They were there because they had to be, even if it killed or maimed them.

While in college taking economics classes, I heard professors tell us in lectures that the environment was an "amenity," mostly of recreational value to the middle class, that consumers could choose to buy just as they bought other goods and services. Environmental quality was thus dependent on our willingness to pay. The people in the industrial neighborhoods in Cleveland had no means to pay, and the paint peeled on the sides of their pollution-stained houses, and they breathed dirty air because they thought that was the way it had to be. And I knew that these professors had never spent a day in a chemical plant. They were, to be blunt, full of crap when it came to understanding the equity factors involved in environmental protection.

Over the years, that awareness festered like a sore as I worked with environmental groups on a variety of issues, and as I later took up my career as a combination of journalist and urban planner, specializing in environmental-planning issues. As book ideas are wont to do, some time in early 1990 the ticking time bomb went off, and this book was born.

I still had a lot to learn, and I traveled a long road to learn it. I am still learning. And this book is the temporary product of that sojourn.

Jim Schwab
Chicago, June 1993

Foreword

Throughout American history there have been many movements of peoples' struggle for justice. People fighting for what is fair, what is right, and for what belongs to them; not only for what is legally theirs, but also ethically and morally theirs.

Deeper Shades of Green is about the struggle for a better environment at home, in our communities. The heroes of this struggle are people of every walk of life, every income bracket, every color, who have banded together to protect their neighborhoods. These under-funded citizen alliances have done an astonishing amount of good work. And they continue a fight that is one of the brightest aspects of American life—the struggle for dignity, self-esteem, and respect.

The people and organizations discussed throughout this book define environment differently than is traditional. Their environment is the place they live, work, and play. Issues of drugs, violence, and poverty are as much a part of their struggle as a proposed incinerator or landfill. Residents living in communities described in this book are people who are fighting for their basic right to participate in decisions about their environment. People want a say in what risks they take and what risks are totally unacceptable. *Deeper Shades of Green* is about a new social justice movement made up of people who, for the most part, have never been politically active before. It describes how people with little formal education quickly learn about very technical issues, and debate them masterfully with more highly educated opponents.

Like the civil rights, labor, and women's movements, this new movement has been created out of need and for survival. It is a movement that goes by many names, but focuses always on justice. This new movement, like the great social movements in our history, is being driven by local, community-based fights and victories, which are leading our society to achieve social change on a larger-than-local level. Many national movements evolved through the activities of local activists who stood up in their communities to make their voices heard and achieve change, and the environmental justice movement is no different. *Deeper Shades of Green* captures these voices and tells story after story of local people, with few or no resources, waging David and Goliath battles. These stories are moving descriptions of courageous women and men, workers in the factories and workers in the fields. This book reveals the history of entire cultures that have fought for generations to protect and reclaim both what they have lost and what has been taken away from them. It brings this history full circle, showing the important role this country's different cultures play in today's movement and in shaping our future.

This new movement is evolving and following in the footsteps of other such struggles in our history. Ella Baker, an organizer in the civil rights movement, once said, "My basic sense of it has always been to get people to understand that in the long run they themselves are the only protection they have . . . people have to be made to understand that they cannot look for salvation anywhere but in themselves." If we were to recount the history of the Montgomery bus boycott and the civil rights movement, we would remember that they were spurred on by the simple local action of Rosa Parks, who refused to give up her seat on the bus. Similarly, *Deeper Shades of Green* describes a young woman, Robin Cannon of Concerned Citizens of South Central Los Angeles (CCSC), who, like Rosa Parks, took a stand.

In a low-income, urban area, Robin mobilized her neighbors out of fear that their already unhealthy environment would become worse; they were determined to stop an incinerator from being built. "We brought out more than 1,000 black people. They [a city council committee] had never seen so many black folks and didn't know what we were there for." Robin and members of CCSC let them know not only why they were there, but also that the community was not going to stand by while someone else decided it was okay to poison their air. CCSC was ultimately successful, but it wasn't easy.

South Central, 52 percent African American and 44 percent Latino, was a community with few financial resources. The corporation that wanted to build the incinerator offered a $10 million "Community Betterment Fund" as an enticement, to be used to build a needed community center, which was to be named after the wife of a popular local politician. CCSC was forced to spend 18 hours a day to create the pressure needed to stop this incinerator. Their funds were derived from passing the hat in an inner-city neighborhood. The CCSC's courage and resourcefulness are common features of the fight for social justice.

When we look back at the history of the labor movement, the force that beat the giant auto manufacturers was the strength of thousands of workers who sat down in local factories until their demands to reduce the work day from 12 hours were met. Kentuckians for the Commonwealth (KFTC) was forced to take a similar stand. *Deeper Shades of Green* tells of the struggle that families living on the coal fields had to undertake to protect their homes from destruction by the mining companies. The coal companies said they had the right to extract the mineral in any way they chose from beneath land where families had their homes. Homes, pastures for grazing, and large areas of timber were totally and needlessly destroyed by the coal companies, without any concern for the residents' needs. It was a long fight, and when the courts ruled against the local people and in favor of the coal companies, KFTC and local activists went directly to the voters of the state of Kentucky. In a democracy, if enough people get involved justice can be had. That's exactly what happened in Kentucky. KFTC mobilized two-thirds of the voting population to amend the state's constitution.

Deeper Shades of Green not only tells us about people's struggles, but also places those battles in the context of history—how do yesterday's events fit into what's happening today? It gives us some understanding of different cultures and how cultural differences enrich us all. One chapter in the book describes how the Navajo contribution to the U.S. military was indispensable to our victory in the Pacific war against Japan. It was the Navajo "code talkers" who devised a secret code from their language to transmit safely information about Japanese troop and naval movements. That was yesterday.

Today the corporations are trying to build waste disposal facilities on Native American lands. The reward for Navajo service in World War II ought not to be toxic incursions, and by remembering their sacrifices we become motivated to come to their defense.

You will learn through this book how a determined group of community activists, worried about their families' health and their biggest investments—their homes—joined with workers from the local petro-chemical plant. It happened in the Deep South in Louisiana. Organized union workers were locked out of the BASF plant after their contract had expired. Workers walked the picket line for eight months outside the gates as temporary contract workers ran the plant. Because these temporary workers were neither familiar with the plant nor properly trained, the safety of the plant came into question. Locked-out workers began to investigate the plant's record since the lockout and found increasing incidence of safety violations. Local residents also had serious complaints about BASF, its chemical discharges, and general pollution emanating from the plant. This led the workers to find their natural allies in the local community. Working together, hand in hand, this coalition of workers and community leaders won their battle with BASF. People said this type of coalition could not be built—especially in the South—and, if built, would never survive. *Deeper Shades of Green* tells the story of how it was built and why the coalition succeeded.

Historian Lawrence Goodwyn once wrote, "One cannot construct what one cannot imagine. Citizens must be aware not only that problems exist, but that possibilities to diminish these problems exist as well. Citizens must be able to imagine what can happen when people try to make change." *Deeper Shades of Green* is an important tool in demonstrating what can happen if people get involved, and how people living in a democracy can obtain justice—but only when people work together collectively.

As a leader in this movement since 1978, I am continually amazed at what groups of people, with few resources, limited formal education, and opposing some of the most powerful people and corporations, are able to accomplish. There is no limit to what we can do as a society to right the wrongs, to work toward a sustainable society, and to protect our children's future health, environment, and economic base. What is needed is a willingness by people to take a stand and make their voices heard.

A small blue-collar community of 900 families at Love Canal in Niagara Falls, New York, brought to the nation's attention the problems of hazardous wastes. As a result, a major piece of federal legislation was written and passed; called Superfund, it will help future Love Canals that are poisoned by toxic waste dumpsites. At Love Canal, all 900 families were evacuated from their contaminated community, with the president of the United States traveling to the neighborhood to sign the legislative bill that appropriated the funds to move people. This was my backyard. I, like my neighbors, had little money and no more than a high school education. However, what the Love Canal families demonstrated is that a small group of dedicated people can achieve significant change.

Now there are over 7,500 grass-roots groups in our network at the Citizens' Clearinghouse for Hazardous Wastes. These groups literally have halted the building of commercial hazardous waste dumps across the United States. This network helped to pass federal laws like the Right to Know, giving everyone access to information on toxic releases, storage, and transportation. At the state and county levels, protective laws are being passed at a steady rate—laws like the Bad Actor law, which forbids corporations with felonies to operate in the legislating state or county. Bans have also been passed to stop the use of polystrene foam in fast-food restaurants, religious institutions, schools, and state houses. The changes don't end there— mandatory recycling and waste reduction programs have been implemented in towns, cities, and entire states. Finally, there have been several campaigns that have moved us as a society closer to consumer protection. The Alar-in-apples campaign, championed by Mothers and Others, and Earth Island Institute's dolphin-free tuna campaign are two powerful examples. Alar is no longer used on apples, and tuna-fishing techniques have changed dramatically.

Yet this is just the beginning of this new movement's accomplishments. As we forge ahead we will continue to encounter many obstacles similar to those described in this book. The advantage we have over others who fought for justice is our rich history of their struggles, showing us what worked and what didn't. We have a unique opportunity to learn from our brothers and sisters who came before us. *Deeper Shades of Green* gives us insight into some of this history, details some of the obstacles faced, and provides us with some understanding of the pathways to success. This book also gives us a sense of hope for our future and that of our children. Throughout the book, you'll find profiles of some of the most skilled, dedicated, courageous, and caring people our country possesses. And if you look as far as your own backyard, your own community, you'll see that there are people just like the activists in this book, waiting to get involved.

Lois Gibbs, Executive Director,
Citizens' Clearinghouse for Hazardous Wastes

Introduction

Great movements for social and political change invariably arise out of deeply felt injustices that society has left unredressed or unresolved for extended periods of time. The issue of slavery, for instance, festered in the United States for more than 200 years before the Civil War erupted. Even then, the war was not solely about slavery, and many of its participants, even on the Union side, had no particular interest in truly bringing about racial equality. With the issue of slavery settled, then, the issue of true legal equality through civil rights festered for another century before erupting anew, somewhat more peacefully, in the civil-rights movement of the 1950s and 1960s. Other longstanding social grievances—those of the agrarian populists, of women suffragists, and of organized labor—took decades and much toil, sweat, and suffering to emerge as major items on the nation's political agenda.

The conservation movement of the early twentieth century likewise had deep roots. It matured politically under the administration of President Theodore Roosevelt simply because a formerly weak voice—a voice in the wilderness, if John Muir will pardon the pun—had finally gained enough strength to reach the halls of Congress and the White House, much as the abolitionist voice had finally reached those halls a generation earlier.

Sometimes it is possible to see where these great movements have intersected and to trace how previously distinct voices and issues found common ground. For various reasons, and for an ever-so-brief period before Jim Crow snuffed it out, agrarian populism with its powerful cry for economic justice reached out to southern African-Americans with their cry for racial justice, and together the two launched a brief but wildly successful experiment in third-party politics. In the 1890s, the People's Party managed to unnerve deeply the Democratic Party chieftains of the Deep South, electing congressmen from Alabama and Georgia and mounting viable campaigns in Texas and Louisiana. In reaction to this potent coalition of poor white and African-American farmers, Jim Crow became the violent means of repression that forced the civil-rights rebellions of the 1960s.

Now a new merger of movements is aborning. African-Americans, who had largely ignored much of the environmental movement as irrelevant to their primary social and economic concerns, became increasingly aware that racial discrimination can take the form of environmental injustice. Workers, long accustomed to the adage that jobs are more important than preserving the environment, have discovered that they were often sold a bill of goods. In many deindustrializing communities, African-Americans have lost their jobs but are still holding the toxic bag of abandoned waste dumps and poisoned rivers, lakes, groundwater, and air. The fact is that traditional environmental organizations have had few members from these communities. Thus these organizations have exhibited little immediate interest in the impact of environmental crises on the daily lives of these communities, which has forced minority and blue-collar neighborhoods to develop their own resources and fight their own fights when they have unearthed environmental injustices.

In the process, these groups have found each other. They have become America's newest, most radical, and most committed environmentalists. Radical, not because they adhere to esoteric theories about humankind's ecological crimes against the biosphere, but because they have discovered a mother's passion for true family values when her child's life or health is in danger. Committed, not because they believe deeply in a particular political philosophy, for most come from fairly unremarkable backgrounds, but because they are America's real communitarians. They believe that neighborhoods matter and that government should be in the business of protecting, not destroying, our sense of community.

In that commitment, many have rediscovered a cause almost forgotten in middle America: the survival of Native American culture. No one has been fighting for the survival of community longer than our Native American tribes, who face a new threat from the desire of waste companies to site garbage dumps, incinerators, and nuclear-waste repositories on their land. Thus, African-Americans, Hispanics, Native Americans, Asian-Americans, and blue-collar whites have begun to find common cause in an environmental revival that is on the verge of shaking American politics at its roots. This book is their story. It is, necessarily, an unfinished story. But it is imperative that everyone understand it—now.

The first widely visible burst of publicity surrounding this new movement came in its infancy during the late 1970s. The cradle was Love Canal. The organizer was Lois Gibbs, a young homemaker married to a chemical worker. She and her husband had two children, and they lived in a modest bungalow in Niagara Falls, New York. Most of the story is by now familiar to environmentalists. Their children and many others attended a neighborhood school built at the edge of a former dump site for hazardous chemicals, yet they were told the school was safe. Gibbs began to suspect otherwise when her son developed asthma and seizures, common reactions to toxic chemicals. She began to investigate. When she asked to have him transferred to another school, school officials refused. From that refusal, a neighborhood organization was born. As the denials and refusals accumulated, Gibbs and her neighbors grew bolder, overcoming handicaps of limited education and previous political passivity to challenge city hall, the state of New York, and ultimately the White House in a quest for answers. In the end, it was the government that gave ground, moving the residents, passing the historic 1980 Superfund law, and cleaning up the Love Canal site. After a struggle of several years, a blue-collar neighborhood had challenged toxic pollution and won, not quietly, but in front of national television cameras.

The response from similarly afflicted blue-collar and minority communities across the country was contagious. People suffering like to know that someone in similar or worse straits has won. Lois Gibbs, once too shy to give a book report in school, became a national spokeswoman for an emerging cause and moved to Arlington, Virginia, to launch the Citizens' Clearinghouse for Hazardous Wastes, a resource group that networks with and supports grass-roots organizations fighting toxic-waste problems across the country. Over the last decade, Gibbs has become a speaker in demand, appearing in hundreds of communities. Her group has a network of regional coordinators sharing basic organizing lessons with their constituents.

The new movement reached a second milestone in 1983. African-American citizens in North Carolina smelled racism in the air when the state chose predominantly African-American Warren County as the site for a landfill to store polychlorinated biphenyls (PCBs), a hazardous organochlorine compound with a variety of toxic effects on humans and wildlife. The state's plan was to dispose of soil collected along long stretches of highway where the material had been dumped illegally.

They enlisted the services of the Reverend Leon White, director of the North Carolina–Virginia field office of the United Church of Christ's (UCC) Commission on Racial Justice. The protests he helped mobilize eventually led to the arrests of more than 500 activists who employed a campaign of nonviolent civil disobedience to block the trucks that entered the site. Among them was the Reverend Benjamin Chavis, the UCC Commission's national executive director. Where Love Canal had served to merge the agendas of environmentalists and blue-collar neighborhoods, Warren County served to merge the civil-rights and environmental agendas. In a clear sign of the poignancy of this issue, Chavis ten years later was chosen the executive director of the NAACP.

Those mergers were furthered tragically just three years later in the aftermath of the Union Carbide leak of methyl isocyanate from its plant in Bhopal, India, killing thousands and injuring tens of thousands more. The distant accident startled the world with the stark severity of the consequences of industrial-chemical accidents. American workers soon learned as well that it *could* happen here. The Bhopal plant had an identical twin in the African-American town of Institute, West Virginia, along the Kanawha River that flows through Charleston. A year later, it too suffered a leak, sending 135 people to the hospital. Shocked out of complacency that existing laws might be adequate, Congress responded by passing the landmark 1986 Superfund Amendments and Reauthorization Act.

SARA included the Emergency Planning and Community Right-to-Know Act that granted, for the first time in federal legislation, the public's right to know what chemicals are being stored or produced at all manufacturing sites and what their potential health impact might be. It is a tool that has significantly empowered environmental activists ever since.

By now the merger of three movements was nearing consummation. The UCC, following up on its Warren County experiences, continued to explore the relationships between race and exposure to toxic waste. In 1987, it released a study directed by Charles Lee, the director of its toxics and minorities project. *Toxic Wastes and Race* proved to be just what civil-rights groups had been waiting for as they reassessed earlier attitudes toward the environmental movement. With elaborate statistical regressions using nationwide demographic data, the report proved that race, even more than socioeconomic status, was the major determinant of the location of toxic-waste facilities in the United States. The report became a virtual bible within the fast-growing African-American environmental-justice movement.

Native Americans, because of their wide variety of cultures and often isolated geographic locations, have had less exposure for their own battles in the environmental arena. But throughout the 1980s, they have led much of the emerging movement, bringing the experience of centuries of repression and discrimination to bear on the analysis of why racial minorities in America were the object of environmental injustice.

They, too, however, have had their moments of epiphany. A classic case was the 1988 gathering of the Gwich'in elders in Arctic Village, Alaska. The Gwich'in, a northern Athabaskan tribe that follows the caribou herds of the Porcupine River through the Yukon Territory and Alaska, hold a general meeting only when their nation is in danger. In 1988, they had not gathered in more than a century, but the proposals for drilling oil in the Arctic National Wildlife Refuge stirred their fears. What emerged from that gathering was a new people taking command of their political and environmental future and refusing to let larger coalitions speak for their unique needs and concerns. The Gwich'in, a people almost invisible to most Americans, became a force for oil interests to reckon with and a rallying point for Native American involvement in environmental issues.

All of these interests finally came together in one path-breaking weekend in Washington, D.C., in October 1991. Organized with the help of the UCC, the First National People of Color Environmental Leadership Summit drew more than 600 activists, combining the colors of the rainbow in one giant sharing and strategizing meeting that has literally and permanently changed the complexion of the U.S. environmental movement. Networks took hold that had never existed between African-Americans and Native Americans, between Hispanic farmworkers and Asian-American computer-chip makers, between white and nonwhite environmentalists. There were still, somewhere outside the hotel, white middle-class environmental professionals and activists who did not grasp the significance of that weekend, but their numbers were dwindling. The leaders of the large, old mainstream conservation organizations were under assault for their failure to reach out to minorities and to hire minority applicants for staff positions. There was a new set of players at the table. This is their book and their story. And these are their milestones.

ROBBINS

Desperate for Development

In March 1990, Robbins, Illinois, was a decidedly testy place. On March 7, an Illinois Environmental Protection Agency hearing drew some 700 people, 100 of whom were left outside in the cold. The Keller Elementary School gymnasium was not big enough to hold them. Because many in the crowd were angry about a proposed municipal waste incinerator in the south Chicago suburb, the hearing also attracted a combined force of 50 state and local police, who marched dogs across the stage whenever they perceived that the audience was becoming unruly. While many hoisted their "Ban the Burn" signs, Mayor Irene Brodie urged opponents to "go home."[1]

She did not mean around the corner. She meant home to the other suburbs from which, she charged, most of them had come. Robbins, founded as the North's first all-African-American town in 1917,[2] would not tolerate the opposition of outsiders to its plans. "We have the right to progress," Brodie declared.

But if the crowd's dissident elements were all from somewhere else, it was news to Gloria Scott and Julia Hartsfield, two sisters who, with the Reverend Adolph Coleman and some friends, had called or visited virtually every Robbins household in the local telephone book to rally opposition to the facility. In the town of 7,000, they had already collected hundreds of petition signatures opposing the new facility, which would burn area garbage to generate electricity. Their reward had been an arrest citation.[3]

It was not Scott's first encounter with the Robbins police over a seemingly legal activity. "The first time I was nearly arrested, I was in front of the post office," she said. "I was running out of flyers and ready to go in. The mayor wanted to know, 'What are you doing? Don't you know there are jobs being brought into town?' She called me crazy and a troublemaker." The police station, she noted, was just a block and a half away, and "four squad cars came to tell us we couldn't pass out flyers. . . . They told us there was an ordinance." Having nearly exhausted her supply of flyers, Scott chose to leave.[4]

But her second encounter, during the weekend prior to the hearing, led to an arrest. She and her sister, she noted, were collecting signatures in a neighborhood where the village trustees lived. As they had done before, both were wearing "Ban the Burn" sandwich boards. "We went to the police station and got there about ten to six. They called my mother and Reverend Coleman. Then we sat in the station for about three hours while they verified who we were. When we finally did get recognized, it turned out my mother and Reverend Coleman had been sitting there all that time. Neither of us knew the other was there."

When Scott and Hartsfield appeared in court on April 6, the judge asked what they had been doing at the time of the arrest. Upon learning that they had been collecting petition signatures, he had just one word to add: "Dismissed."

When it was founded in 1917, Robbins, named after a supportive white developer, became the first city in the North governed by African-Americans. Later, it hosted the first airport in the nation managed by African-Americans. Today, however, it is full of small, old clapboard houses with front yards nearly as narrow as the cracked sidewalks that abut them. The water mains break because of the aging infrastructure. Robbins ranks among the nation's poorest communities. The public till is nearly always empty; as of 1990, the city was $6 million in debt. Its annual budget was $1.6 million, but the local property-tax base produced only $250,000. The Philadelphia-based Reading Energy Company's new facility was to bring jobs and economic recovery, including nearly $1 million yearly in royalties, lease fees for the site, and taxes.[5] Few places in the Chicago area needed all of the above more than Robbins.

The idea, in fact, had not originally come from Reading. Village officials, seeking to lift their community out of its economic morass, had first broached the idea of an energy park in the late 1970s. In their concept, a solid-waste incinerator generating electricity from burning garbage—known in the industry as a waste-to-energy incinerator or resource-recovery plant—would be the hub of this new park, attracting ancillary businesses that could somehow benefit from its presence. The village board had chosen a 16-acre site across the Calumet Sag Channel from a Clark Oil refinery and zoned it industrial. It did the same with a second 16-acre site adjacent to the intended incinerator location.

But the plan languished because the village was too poor to pursue its own dream and lacked the necessary resources to attract outside developers. The idea also had drawbacks. Electric power in the area was cheaper than any that could be produced from such a facility, and waste-disposal rates for area landfills were still lower than those required to make an incinerator viable. As the proposal waited, Robbins decayed and businesses fled. Between 1970 and 1990, the village lost one-third of its population, whose average income stagnated at $7,000 per capita.

Thus, when Reading Energy officials accepted the village's invitation in late 1987 to discuss the possibility of developing the facility, Barry Neal, vice president for project development, could barely believe his ears. Working in an industry that seems to breed public distrust, the young executive fully expected some doubt and skepticism about his company's intentions. Instead, village leaders welcomed him with open arms. "A number of people were shaking our hands and saying, 'We want this project. We've tried to do this for a number of years,' " he recalled.

Thanks to a 1981 Illinois law, the energy production side of the economic equation had changed. Public Act 82-782 had created an indirect public subsidy for electricity generation by municipal waste incinerators by allowing such facilities to sell their power to the electric utilities at retail rates, and then allowing the utility to charge off the difference from its own wholesale rates on its state taxes. In Reading Energy's case, the higher power rates would yield an estimated $150 million over the 20-year life of the project. In the meantime, due to decreasing landfill capacity, tipping fees at area disposal sites had climbed some 25 percent per year, making the incinerator's projected tipping fees look more competitive. Reading, after conducting its own feasibility analyses, sought and won village approval for the Calumet Sag Channel site in December 1988. Another Illinois law gave counties and municipalities the authority for siting waste-disposal facilities. The Illinois EPA (IEPA) may only consider air-quality and construction-permit applications after siting has been approved.

At the village siting hearing, no one objected.[6] Gloria Scott claimed from the beginning that neighbors had never received the required notification.

Reverend Coleman did not learn of the plan until October 1989, when he received a flyer promoting the idea. The pastor of the West Pullman Church of God, on Chicago's nearby South Side, had not moved to Robbins until 1986. After he heard about the proposal, Coleman recalled, he "did extensive study on incinerators before telling the mayor I would oppose this." Coleman learned that another incinerator had been proposed just a mile away in nearby Crestwood. There, two more incinerator opponents, Jean and Joseph Golf, had also upset a strong-willed mayor and been arrested for their protests. In a suburb with mostly decaying streets but one curious newly paved stretch of highway along Kedzie Avenue, some 150 to 200 trucks would be hauling garbage into town daily. Within a few blocks of the site sat a housing project, a senior-citizen home, and a medical center.

Coleman quickly took the lead in organizing community opposition. But, as he recalled, local churches and schools were largely unwilling to provide meeting space for a group opposed to the incinerator. Undeterred, he organized a meeting at a Pentecostal church in neighboring Blue Island. Lacking local organizational resources, he solicited the aid of People for Community Recovery (PCR), an environmental group based in Chicago's Altgeld Gardens public-housing project. By the time Illinois EPA officials arrived, Coleman's group had mailed some 800 letters to Robbins residents asking them to voice their opposition. PCR volunteers also gathered some 3,000 signatures on petitions opposing the incinerator. When the IEPA hearing was over, Coleman, Scott, and Hartsfield went to work creating links with the opponents from neighboring suburbs who had joined them that night.[7]

Blue Island is largely a Chicago working-class bungalow suburb. The city of 22,000 is immediately adjacent to Robbins on the east, but somewhat more prosperous. It is about 90 percent white, with small but growing percentages of African-Americans and Hispanics. Along its western border with Robbins lies California Gardens, a largely African-American enclave of apartments and trailer homes with its own community center. That is where Reverend Coleman would have preferred to hold the "Ban the Burn" rally on April 7, which marked the close of the Illinois EPA's 30-day public-comment period following the Robbins hearing.

Instead, it took place in the Dwight D. Eisenhower High School gymnasium, in a predominantly white area of Blue Island. "You take help wherever you can get it," Coleman noted, "but we'd have had a better turnout in the black neighborhood." Mayor Brodie, he said, had been "poisoning the people" against the interference of "outsiders." Coleman, Hartsfield, and Scott were all welcoming the crowd as some 200 African-American, white, and Asian-American people filed into the gymnasium. The Reverend David Scott, like Coleman an African-American Church of God pastor, was the emcee. He had been instrumental in defeating three different proposed incinerators in Harvey, a racially mixed suburb south of Blue Island.

"Dear Father," Scott began his invocation, "We thank you for this gathering. We ask you to let your spirit enter this meeting here today in the words that are spoken. Let them be truthful, and faithfully dedicated to your people, and let us be on fire, to destroy these incinerators that are coming into our communities. We implore you in Jesus' name. Amen."

"Amen!" came a shout from the audience.

After a short talk about his total opposition to incinerators, Scott introduced Coleman. "Incinerators," Coleman began, "compete for recyclable material and would harm recycling efforts. . . . Children are six times more likely to suffer from air pollution than adults. . . . Incinerator proponents pick areas where people are less likely to resist. We're a low-income area, but I want them to know when they came to Robbins, they grabbed a tiger by the tail because we won't stand for this!" Applause rattled the bleachers. Adults howled and whistled; children with signs proclaiming slogans such as "Ban the Burn" and "Over Our Dead Bodies" pounded the seats with their sticks.

Coleman plunged ahead. "Anyone living within a 30-mile radius of an incinerator will be adversely affected. . . . There is no system in which heavy metals cannot get out. . . . It's ludicrous to place this within four blocks of a senior citizen home." Coleman geared up for his climax, referring to Mayor Brodie's denunciation of incinerator protesters as "outsiders."

"You're not the outsiders. The real outsiders are the people who propose these things and don't live here!" The bleachers resounded again with raucous echoes of approval.

A member of U.S. Rep. Marty Russo's staff followed Coleman to the microphone, reading a letter Russo had sent to the Illinois EPA, expressing support for extending the deadline for public comment. It was not enough. As he began to leave the gymnasium, a chant rippled through the crowd: "Take a stand! Take a stand!"

Scott calmly informed the audience that he had talked to Russo, a Democrat whose district included Robbins, a few days earlier, telling him that at some point he would have to make a decision. He criticized politicians who "wait to see how many people are on each side. We want honest politicians."

Then he introduced Lu Palmer, an announcer for African-American radio station WVON. Palmer had led voter-registration drives for the late Chicago Mayor Harold Washington. After Harold Washington was elected in 1983, Palmer ran in the Democratic primary for Washington's vacant First District congressional seat. He lost to Rep. Charles Hayes, a prominent African-American trade unionist whom Washington had endorsed over Palmer.

Palmer knows well how to rankle conservative white audiences.

But it was his birthday, as Scott noted, and at this rally he was a consummate crowd pleaser.

"I don't live in Robbins," he began, "but whenever my people are at risk and I'm invited to help solve that problem, I come. That's why I deal with the issue of South Africa. This issue is a false fight between economic and health issues. My investigation shows me that few economic benefits will come to the residents of Robbins from that incinerator. Whatever benefits might come cannot outweigh the health risks not only to the people in Robbins, but to you who live in the neighborhoods around Robbins.

"I'm being told that this fight is being masterminded by outside white people." Scattered boos punctuated his talk. "But pollutants in the air don't care what color you are or what race you are." Rousing cheers erupted. "Talk to me about white outsiders—the people who want to build this are white outsiders! They'll make a whopping profit, a lot of money. The people who are running this insane country have gotten to the point they don't care whether black or white people die, but how much money they'll make. Stop these incinerators!"

The bleachers vibrated again with bouncing signs. Hands clapped in thunderous applause. Scott introduced Robert Starks, an African-American political-science professor at Northeastern Illinois University, who further ignited the audience: "I, too, live on the South Side of Chicago, and I am here today to tell you this: These incinerators are economic and environmental apartheid for the South Side of Chicago!"

The crowd had not yet completely lost its reserve. It was time now for Sharon Pines, a young white lawyer who headed the Midwest office of Greenpeace. They knew her as the tough organizer whose expertise had made their battles credible. Pines was Chicago's leading champion of blue-collar and people-of-color environmental causes. In the mid-1980s, while the late Harold Washington was mayor, she had worked for Alderman Bobby Rush, a former Black Panther who then chaired the city council's environmental committee. If these working people had previously believed that Greenpeace was solely devoted to "saving the whales," Pines had dramatically reshaped their perceptions and made of them committed Greenpeace fans. They were here in part to show their appreciation and affection.

Pines was not about to disappoint them. She turned her fire on the consultants whom incinerator developers employed to obtain advice about siting their facilities. "Those consultants told them . . . you go to the white ethnic, blue-collar communities, and go to African-American, Hispanic, and Native American communities. And that is the shame of this industry, my friends. This is what they're doing across this country." Waves of applause crashed against the gymnasium walls.

"The industry thinks that you folks do not, cannot, and will not fight back," Pines declared, listing all the communities she had helped organize. "The message is: Boys, you're in a whole lot of trouble." The waves crashed higher. "These people are saying no to an increased risk of asthma. The American Public Health Association says there is no way incinerators should be built in an area that is already heavily polluted like the south suburbs. . . . You all are saying no to the 1,000 pounds of lead and 4,400 pounds of mercury a year that will come belching out of this facility. . . . You're also saying no to the threat to taxpayers. Because these technologies are unproven, there will be constant expenses. . . . Your taxes are going to go up and up and up to pay for rising maintenance costs.

"You're saying yes to public participation in the decision-making process. . . . You're saying yes to recycling. You're saying no to candy bars wrapped in triple layers of plastic, and yes to recoverable packaging. . . . EPA has a goal of 25 percent recycling. That means 75 percent incineration. You tell them you want 75 to 80 percent recycling. . . . Don't let anyone tell you they have a draft permit locked up. Folks, it ain't over till it's over! Tell them you want to ban the burn! Incineration no, recycling yes!"

Valerie Johnson, of People for Community Recovery, followed Pines. Under an agreement between the Illinois EPA and Chemical Waste Management, a subsidiary of Waste Management, Inc., following a series of pollution violations, Johnson became a paid citizen watchdog at the firm's hazardous-waste incinerator on the heavily industrial Southeast Side of Chicago. Her neighborhood, she told the audience, has the highest cancer rate in the United States.

She personally had had a miscarriage "because of my work. But if I won't do it, who will? I'd rather die than let 10,000 others suffer."

Other speakers followed, from Citizens for a Better Environment, Suburbs United to Reclaim the Environment, and the Chicago Lung Association. State Rep. Clem Balanoff, a maverick Democrat from the Southeast Side, was one of the few politicians this audience liked. Elected on an environmental platform, he had adhered to his promise to oppose incinerators.

After his talk, the audience dwindled slowly. Other public officials spoke, mostly mayors and village trustees from surrounding communities. As one lectured the audience, Pines, visiting with members of the crowd, whispered, "They like to hear the sound of their own voices." A suburban alderman admonished the audience to give its public officials alternatives and not just oppose things. Pines smirked, then added to no one in particular, "If it doesn't come from them, it doesn't count." The audience continued to drift away. By the time the last official was finished, only half the crowd remained. The meeting had lasted too long. There had been too many speakers. "If they had hired a bus," Pines observed ruefully, "they could have gotten more people here from Robbins."[8]

By that spring, enough southern suburbs had fought enough battles against enough incinerator proposals to make talk of a broad coalition possible. But few opponents had much organizing experience. The opponents in Robbins, Reverend Coleman noted after the Blue Island rally, were still unsure how to counter effectively the mayor's vocal criticisms of "outsiders." In view of the town's considerable political apathy, opponents were not at all sure they had any hope of stopping the incinerator. Few other African-American clergy in Robbins were willing to speak up, Coleman noted, because "leadership gets bought out. But they're not taking the pulse of the people." He would like to have a rally in Robbins, he said, but "we get harassed so much we get locked out of any place to have it."

But he was far from pessimistic. Proposed incinerators had already been shelved in the south suburbs of Stickney, Harvey (three times), Crestwood, Dolton, and Ford Heights, the latter the indisputably poorest and financially shakiest community in the entire metropolitan area.[9] Another proposal, for Bedford Heights, was facing an equally rocky public reception.[10] The long series of fights had made its mark on the South Suburban Mayors and Managers Association (SSMMA), which then included 38 municipalities. In April 1989, the SSMMA had adopted a policy statement opposing the construction of any facilities not needed to handle waste generated solely among those communities. Its forthcoming study of area solid-waste management needs was expected to propose just one facility to do that job, and no more. The southern suburbs, Reverend Coleman had declared in Blue Island, were determined not to "become a garbage dump."

But incinerator opponents were also developing a preventive strategy against even one incinerator—persuading their communities not to send their waste to any such facility. They would lobby their suburbs not to sign contracts, as they put it, to "feed the monster." Without long-term contracts to bring garbage to the incinerator from neighboring communities, Reading Energy's financial picture might look less promising, short of importing garbage from other states. It would mean that the "outsiders" Mayor Brodie had excoriated were not cooperating.

Some of the proposed incinerators that had been blocked were for medical waste, and some others had been for hazardous waste. But in Robbins, the proposal was to burn household or "municipal" waste collected from residential areas. The facility was to include a recycling plant to remove such nonburnable trash as aluminum and ferrous metals.

Opponents fought in part because of fears about stack emissions, especially dioxins and furans, highly carcinogenic substances that escape in small quantities with the flue gases. The chemicals are actually an entire family of hydrocarbons that first came to prominence as a byproduct of petroleum-derived herbicides.[11] Dioxins conjure up negative images even for those with no scientific background. They have been implicated in such highly publicized calamities as the use of Agent Orange as a defoliant in Vietnam and the creation of a ghost town in Times Beach, Missouri, where a mixture of dioxin and waste oil had been sprayed for dust control. Scientific attention focused on the compound after its accidental discharge in Seveso, Italy, following a 1976 explosion at a plant manufacturing the herbicide 2,4,5-T. Some 600 animals were destroyed in the aftermath, and many of the 700 local residents who were evacuated suffered from chloracne, a disfiguring skin rash traceable to dioxin exposure.[12]

The point at which dioxins and furans are created during the incineration process has been the subject of furious debate between industry scientists and opponents like Dr. Barry Commoner, director of the Center for the Biology of Natural Systems at New York's Queens College. The industry view has been that dioxins and furans can be reduced or removed from the process with a high combustion efficiency that destroys them during the incineration of the paper and plastics that provide the chlorine that forms a base for dioxin molecules. In this view, dioxin emissions can be prevented with proper engineering systems built into the plant. Commoner, however, has argued that dioxins cannot be destroyed in the incineration process because they are actually synthesized as hot combustion gases cool in the stack, at which time certain carbon compounds, broken down from lignin, a constituent of wood and paper, attach themselves to fly-ash particles. In that process, the carbon compounds could react with chlorine to create dioxins and furans. If Commoner is right, the incinerator industry has no good answer for dioxin emissions other than to shut down. It is not hard to see why Commoner's thesis has won precious little acceptance among industry experts.

Heavy-metal emissions have produced their own share of incinerator controversy. Mercury, lead, and cadmium emissions have all helped to inspire protest because of their toxicity and the difficulty of tracing some of their detrimental impacts. The history of mercury as a central-nervous-system contaminant dates back to the nineteenth century, when Lewis Carroll popularized the image of the "mad hatter" in *Alice in Wonderland*. The occupational hazard involved was no fantasy. Workers used mercury to soften fur for felt hats, suffering permanent brain damage from the exposure. More modern horror stories have included mercury-in-tuna scares and Japan's outbreak of Minamata disease in the 1950s, ultimately traced to the accumulation of dimethylmercury sediments resulting from emissions from the Chisso Corporation's plastics plant on Minamata

Bay.[13] The disease, which killed about 1,000 victims and injured thousands more, poisons the central nervous system.

Mercury finds its way into the waste stream because of its common use in chemicals and chlorinated plastics. Incinerator opponents charge that failure to control mercury emissions from Florida plants is causing the poisoning of the endangered Florida panther, a charge industry has tried to refute by demonstrating that contamination occurred from other sources. While natural sources of mercury in the atmosphere include phenomena like volcanoes, recent research has indicated that three-fourths of the atmospheric mercury today comes from human sources.[14] Who are the two biggest culprits? Coal-burning power plants and solid-waste incinerators.[15] Eventually, like any other particulate matter, atmospheric mercury finds its way back to the ground, often entering bodies of water. As a result, freshwater fish supplies have become heavily contaminated and have begun to pose serious health risks.

Lead is also implicated in brain degeneration, but of a different sort. Its primary sin lies in retarding mental development, and its prevalence in inner-city housing has been associated with the mental retardation of young children in such areas. That link was so strong even in the early 1970s that it induced Congress to mandate the introduction of unleaded gasoline as a means of partially detoxifying dangerously polluted inner-city air. The last thing poor children need, incinerator opponents note, is another potent source of lead in their bloodstreams. Yet incinerators, for obvious reasons, tend to be in urban areas. In 1991, despite this evidence, the Council on Competitiveness, chaired by Vice President Quayle, squelched a proposed EPA regulation to require the removal of lead-acid batteries from the waste stream entering municipal solid-waste incinerators.

Cadmium, another frequent pollution concern of incinerator opponents, has been linked to emphysema and kidney damage. In Japan, cadmium poisoning produced the first known cases of "itai-itai" disease (meaning literally "ouch-ouch"), a form of bone deterioration.[16]

The incinerator industry has worked hard to find ways to control these emissions, in part because failure to appease opponents can only lead to the kind of deadly political and regulatory stalemate

that stalled the nuclear-power industry—an analogy of which critics
and supporters alike are painfully aware. But a basic law of physics—
that matter does not simply disappear—continues to vex the industry. Potential emissions trapped by pollution-control measures end
up instead in either the fly ash or the bottom ash, thus rendering
either or both of these potentially toxic. This issue is critical to the
industry's future because the cost of incinerator-ash disposal rides on
whether or not regulators deem this material hazardous. Non-
hazardous ash can be disposed of, like household garbage, at an ordinary sanitary landfill. (There just is no way to escape the landfill in
this cycle.) Burning waste typically reduces its volume by about 90
percent, and its weight by about 60 percent, but there is still a landfill tipping fee for the resulting ash, a serious cost of doing business.
That cost escalates dramatically, however, when the ash must be
taken not to a normal sanitary landfill, but to a special hazardous-
waste landfill. The difference can be as much as $200 per ton. (In a
case that the U.S. Supreme Court accepted on appeal, the city of
Chicago sought to overturn a Seventh Circuit Court of Appeals decision that held that incinerator ash was hazardous under the Resource Conservation and Recovery Act. This overturned a federal
district court ruling that favored the city, whose Northwest Waste-
to-Energy Facility was storing its ash in an ordinary Michigan landfill for about $23 per ton. The city estimated that storage in a
hazardous-waste landfill would cost $210 per ton, or nine times as
much. See *Chicago v. Environmental Defense Fund*, No. 92-1639, accepted for hearing in June 1993.) In short, the better the air-pollution control, the more toxic the resulting ash.

One way around part of the problem, of course, is to drastically
reduce the volume and number of contaminants reaching the incinerator. In mass-burn incinerators, where trucks simply dump garbage
into the burners indiscriminately, there is little effort to do this. Aluminum cans and newspapers all find their way to the same incinerator grates. But Reading Energy had planned a refuse-derived-fuel
(RDF) facility. Its RDF plant would first sort glass, aluminum, and
ferrous metals for potential recycling before compacting the remaining waste into pellets. There was even consideration of sorting some
types of recyclable plastics, though this was not guaranteed in either

the permit application or plant design. By thus eliminating some of the sources of heavy metal before the waste is burned, the plant could reduce much of its potential problem. Still, today's waste stream is complex, and the preliminary recycling step in the Robbins plant would not eliminate every potential environmental toxin before it found its way into the plant's fuel. Simple items of garbage, like common plastic tools and packages, not to mention batteries, inks, pesticides, and rubber toys, are shot through with constituents that form troublesome pollutants during incineration.

Predictably, these common criticisms of incinerators were the main currency of Reading's critics. Kevin Greene, research director for Citizens for a Better Environment, noted at the IEPA hearing in Robbins that "the best way to ensure compliance is through continuous monitoring of stack emissions." Of course, when there are literally hundreds of potential organic compounds in the stack emissions, such monitoring is not only infeasible but, to the extent it is even attempted, prohibitively expensive. The alternative, Greene noted, is a stack test "conducted at the incinerator soon after construction to determine the actual concentrations of these pollutants in the air emissions." But old incinerators, like old cars, Greene added, tend not to work as well in controlling emissions as when they are new. In any event, such early tests are indicative only of an incinerator's peak performance.[17]

In addition, mercury poses a special dilemma for air-quality control because, as Greene noted, it and a compound, mercury chloride, gasify at lower temperatures than other metals (the very quality that makes it so useful as a liquid in thermometers). Thus, at stack temperatures that cause other metals to condense onto fly ash, mercury is simply escaping into the atmosphere in its gaseous form. Reading attempted to remedy this problem by including a baghouse in its emission-control system. A baghouse traps many of the particulates to which mercury molecules would attach themselves during combustion, thus lowering the volume of mercury emitted. Reading officials maintained, however, that this effort was another example of the "redundancy" built into the emission controls on their plant, even though scrubbers, the other key emission-control feature, are notoriously poor at trapping mercury.

Finally, critics were aghast that the IEPA would even consider the company's proposal to truck the Robbins ash to the mixed-waste Woodland landfill in northwest suburban South Elgin, instead of requiring its disposal in a "monofill," a special facility designed to handle only incinerator waste. The presence of the Woodland landfill, which was not even equipped with plastic liners to control leaching of pollutants into groundwater, had already helped to fuel protests against a proposed balefill (a landfill containing baled, as opposed to loosely dumped, waste) in the neighboring township of Bartlett.[18]

The awareness of a common link between the unloved landfills of northwestern Cook County and the positively hated incinerator proposals of southern Cook County suggests the potential breadth of organizational ties available to the activists fighting the Robbins incinerator. But in the spring of 1990, their primary organizational work lay far closer to home. Before regional or statewide links could make much sense, the Robbins opponents needed to weave a disparate collection of community opposition groups into a single coalition capable of influencing the waste-disposal priorities of the SSMMA, which was busy establishing its own South Suburban Solid Waste Agency to hire a consultant to study the problem.

On the surface, at least, neither the residents of the south suburbs nor their municipal officials had enough in common to suggest the potential for much unity. The communities involved ranged from the relatively affluent, like Tinley Park and Flossmoor, to the desperately poor and nearly bankrupt, like Robbins and another largely African-American community, Ford Heights (which had changed its name from East Chicago Heights in an effort to revamp its tattered image).[19] Ford Heights officials had also dreamed of using an incinerator to advance their town's prospects for economic development. They were less fortunate, however, in their choice of vendors. In 1987, the village watched in dismay as its New York underwriter for $500 million in tax-free municipal bonds, Matthew & Wright, Inc., abandoned its role amid an international scandal over its handling of such bonds for a number of communities.[20] Undaunted, Ford Heights officials a year later enlisted Ogden Martin Systems, Inc., one of the nation's major engineering firms, to propose a new facility that would be underwritten by untainted Smith Barney, Harris Upham & Co., Inc.[21]

Residents who had already watched Chicago's nearby Southeast Side become a haven for landfill operators, both legal and illegal, became alarmed at the growing competition to turn the southern suburbs into a haven for incinerators. Suddenly, old ethnic, racial, and class divisions seemed to matter less than the need for a united citizens' front to halt what many saw as an invasion of the newest fad in waste disposal—one that aroused deep suspicions concerning public health and safety. Each new proposal spawned one more committee opposed to incineration. In search of technical information and cogent arguments with which to browbeat aldermen and village trustees, each group eventually touched base with the available— and always helpful—local environmental resource groups, such as the Chicago Lung Association, Citizens for a Better Environment, and the Chicago-based Midwest office of Greenpeace. In addition, they found a handful of college professors and technical professionals who sympathized with their goals and advised them on their testimony before village boards and county and state regulatory authorities.

Some also encountered the radicalizing experience of being snubbed or ignored, particularly by village or city officials. Most of them, being newcomers, were truly angered and offended by this behavior, which came all too naturally to those area mayors and village trustees who had enjoyed long and largely unchallenged tenure in their positions.

Helen Cuprisin, of Evergreen Park, emerged as one of those newly minted activists. She first attended a village board meeting in January 1990, as she said, "just asking innocently enough, 'Why don't we have curbside recycling in Evergreen Park?' And they said, 'Because there's no money in it.'" Cuprisin described her reception among the trustees as "really hostile and uncooperative," causing her to wonder why they would battle her over "such a sensible idea." A month later, she said, when Mayor Anthony Vacco announced that interested parties should attend the March 7 incinerator-permit hearing in Robbins, she got her answer. A long-time inactive contributor to Greenpeace, she called Sharon Pines, to "start getting my money's worth" from the groups she had supported. Pines put her in touch with Robert Shannon of Dolton, who had launched Suburbs United to Reclaim the Environment, which had modeled itself on a Chicago Southeast Side group, Citizens United to Reclaim the Environment.

Shannon, a high-school biology teacher, plied Cuprisin not only with names of additional contacts but with detailed information about recycling and incinerator operations, much of which he had already been supplying to various suburban mayors. Turning into a quick study, Cuprisin attended the March 7 hearing and began to meet a bevy of opponents, such as Reverend Coleman and Charlie Orr, a South Side restaurateur, who inspired her to challenge her village officials. Her first opportunity to do so arose that very night when she spotted two of them talking to Reading Energy officials, one of whom told her the incinerator was a "marvelous idea." But at that hearing, she also discovered what some opponents in the adjacent Chicago neighborhoods of Beverly and Morgan Park also learned—that they were within the primary fallout area for particulate matter from the incinerator. "My God, that's going to be falling on my house!" she recalled a neighbor exclaiming. When Cuprisin and her neighbors returned home, they began a multipronged attack on the incinerator through telephone calls to officials and letters to the editors of local newspapers.

That exposure led to new connections. Seeing Cuprisin's name in the news so often, Mary Martin, a previously uninvolved resident of Morgan Park, called her, asking if she would like to join a group Martin was organizing at her home. Having quickly taken note of the limitations of Shannon's information-intensive approach to the issue, Cuprisin was ready. As she put it:

> I had been telling Bob Shannon all along, "We're struggling here in Evergreen, there's Mary in Crestwood, Jean and Joe Golf, and Marcia's in Midlothian, and whatever." I said, "We should all be working together to present a united front. You'd be much more effective." But it was like, Bob was so overwhelmed with all the stuff he had, he didn't seem to be able to coordinate anything.

The eventual product of the meetings at Martin's home was the creation of the South Cook County Environmental Action Coalition (SCCEAC), which has become the organizational vehicle for opponents of the Robbins incinerator. But while the germ of the coalition idea developed during the summer, Cuprisin and others still needed to build an effective environmental constituency within their own communities. Cuprisin herself assiduously courted support within Evergreen Park, a suburb of nearly 23,000 people. She visited PTA and school board meetings, and ". . . everywhere I went there were obstacles. Well, we can't do this, the PTA says we can't get involved. We called the PTA in Springfield [the state capital], they say don't get involved. . . . Then I tried churches. Shouldn't the priest or minister be concerned about the health of his flock? That was the worst, dealing with the priests in our community."

Cuprisin, an active Roman Catholic, squarely faced off with the male power structure within her church, growing steadily more militant with every encounter. She noted that the mayor and three trustees attended the same church, Holy Redeemer. The priest, she noted, had "eased out one of the other priests because he envisioned him as being a little too liberal." At a meeting of the ladies' guild, she said, one member told her, "Well, we have to see what the men think on the parish council." But through Citizens for a Better Environment, Cuprisin had finally found another activist woman within the guild. At that meeting, she recalled, "Father Divine walks in and says, 'I don't know why you're wasting your time discussing the incinerator because everybody's for it.' "

Cuprisin encountered similar attitudes at the village hall, where, she said, some members of the environmental commission suggested that, instead of speaking to the village board herself, she bring a man. She bowed to reality for one meeting and brought in Kevin Greene, who "gave a nice speech," but the condescension of village officials and parish priests helped to create a merciless and relentless critic. Like other new environmentalists throughout the area, Cuprisin had rapidly shed her earlier trust in both the system and its public officials. By the fall of 1990, her group had prodded city hall to initiate curbside collection of recyclables. The following spring, Cuprisin angrily confronted Mayor Vacco and the trustees at a preelection village board meeting, demanding over Vacco's gavel that the trustees state their position on any potential flow-control agreement with the Robbins incinerator. The board's only woman, Carol Kyle, drew a huge round of applause when she alone announced her opposition to the incinerator. No other trustee was willing to state a clear position.[22]

The Beverly and Morgan Park neighborhoods, meanwhile, were breeding the leadership of the evolving coalition. Ironically, those leaders were, for the most part, political newcomers in one of Chicago's most powerful wards. Beverly, far back into the nineteenth century, had always attracted Irish Catholics who had "made it" and looked down on those working-class Irish who remained behind in less prosperous neighborhoods like former Mayor Richard J. Daley's Bridgeport. Perhaps not accidentally, hilly, tree-lined Beverly sits atop the highest point in the city. One of the few middle-class areas of the South Side, it has only recently begun to attract African-Americans. Those who have arrived are themselves part of the middle class. Beverly's well-maintained single-family housing demanded such credentials. Morgan Park, in contrast, had hosted a number of African-American residents since before World War I.[23]

The Democratic organization in the 19th Ward, which includes Beverly and Morgan Park, boasted a number of political heavyweights, including State Senator Jeremiah Joyce and Alderman Michael Sheahan, who later that year ousted a Republican incumbent (in a race that was dirty even by Chicago standards) to become Cook County sheriff. It is the kind of Chicago ward organization whose leaders know everyone, and just about everything, that matters in the ward.

They did not seem to know, however, that a serious environmental rebellion was brewing right under their noses. In large part, that was because the organizers were, as the coalition's public-affairs chairman, Jeff Tangel, later put it, "a bunch of nobodies in the 'hood."

They were, however, ambitious nobodies. Mary Martin, who lives in Morgan Park, recalled incurring monthly telephone bills of up to $100, calling other members of the coalition five to ten times daily to confer on the progress of efforts to attract new people to meetings for a new neighborhood group, Beverly-Morgan Park Citizens Opposed to Incineration. The upshot, Tangel noted, is that "we now all

have answering machines." Taking advantage of an IEPA extension
of the comment period for the Robbins incinerator proposal, the new
group's leaders organized a May rally at a Methodist church in Morgan Park. From nowhere, it seemed, flyers appeared on school walls,
and letters appeared in all the weekly neighborhood and suburban
newspapers.

The rally drew 500 people, including most of the key Robbins opponents. Within days, the group was meeting with local politicians
anxious to discover who had organized this previously unnoticed
uprising. None of them had taken the rally seriously enough beforehand to appear, although a few sent aides. After all, as Martin noted,
they were each getting about 20 calls a day. The turnabouts in attitude were dramatic. State Rep. James Keane's aide was remembered
unfondly as having "a real attitude." Before the week was out, Keane
announced his opposition to the Robbins incinerator.

Alderman Sheahan's aide, Terry McDermott, was the only political crowd pleaser of the evening, echoing most of their concerns.
The group followed up successfully with pressure on Sheahan to introduce a resolution, which passed, stating that Chicago would not
contract with Reading to ship its garbage to the Robbins incinerator. That involved no small element of hypocrisy, for the city has
long operated an incinerator of its own that has violated a number of
pollution limits over the years. But it was nonetheless one more small
victory for an organization learning to assert itself.

Perhaps the most significant coup came after the group's visit to
State Sen. Jeremiah Joyce, a long-time power broker within the Cook
County legislative delegation. Martin and four others met him at his
office to ask him to issue a formal statement against the incinerator.
Joyce and his visitors quickly clashed. Martin advised him that the
group would be issuing a press release outlining where area politicians stood on the matter, but, said Martin, when she asked him to
state his position, he replied, "Frankly, I don't care what you write in
the press release."

"Fine," Martin told him, "We'll write that—that you don't care
what we write." Martin and her friends walked out.

The next day, Joyce called to say that he would be issuing a statement announcing his opposition to the incinerator. Now, Tangel

noted, Joyce "speaks to people about us with high regard." The deciding factor, according to Tangel, was Joyce's perception that "these people are very serious, they live and breathe this stuff." The key, he added, is that "We are at their functions, we are at their fundraisers, we are in their face, we are on their phones, we come see them."

Access to politicians like Joyce opened a series of doors for the Robbins opponents. It was an election year, and Joyce had the ear of Illinois Attorney General Neil Hartigan, who was then running an uphill race for governor as the Democratic nominee. Hartigan proved to be an important asset as the activists prepared a major protest for June 11, four days before the Illinois EPA was scheduled to issue a decision on the Reading Energy permit application. The opponents planned to hold the rally outside the huge State of Illinois Building in downtown Chicago, hauling busloads of protesters from towns like Robbins. Hartigan, who was originally scheduled to speak, was in the hospital on the day of the rally, but his staff was instrumental in helping the environmentalists set up the platforms and microphones and line up political speakers. Hartigan had not only aligned himself with the protesters against the Robbins incinerator, but was steadily moving to a general position against any incineration as a waste-disposal option.

At noon on a hot summer day, television, radio, and print media all arrived for a political spectacle. Meanwhile, a handful of Robbins residents, including Gloria Scott, grew suspicious of their village officials as they waited for a chartered bus that never came. Village police did show up, Scott recalled, to see how many people were waiting for the bus. The 15 activists she had rounded up—far from enough to satisfy her—eventually made it to the rally, late, after they found a city bus.

At about 3:00 p.m., roughly an hour and a half after the rally was over, Jeff Tangel got a call at his Loop office, where he worked on the trading floor of the Mercantile Exchange. Had he heard the news? U.S. Rep. Marty Russo, from the South Side district that includes Robbins and the Beverly-Morgan Park area, told Tangel that the Illinois EPA had just issued the permit for the incinerator that afternoon.[24]

———

A month later, in July, Attorney General Hartigan kept his promise to the demonstrators. He filed an appeal of the state agency's decision to the U.S. Environmental Protection Agency. Most federal environmental legislation allows the U.S. EPA to delegate the administration of programs to state environmental agencies, provided they meet EPA criteria. State administration of these programs, such as air quality, hazardous-waste management, and water-pollution control, is voluntary; the state need not apply to manage its own program. The desire for state sovereignty, however, impels most to do so. For one thing, a state wishing to impose stricter criteria, as California has often done, may then use its own legislation and regulations. Nonetheless, the federal agency retains final review power to ensure that its own minimum standards are met. Hartigan's appeal, therefore, essentially challenged the presumption that the Illinois EPA had met those standards in granting the permit.

One basis on which the attorney general's office filed for review was its allegation that the Illinois EPA had failed to properly analyze the available technologies for controlling emissions of mercury. U.S. EPA rules require the use of the "best available control technology," a term of art that basically means that if there is a more effective way to control a particular pollutant it must be used, and less effective technologies may not be substituted. The essential purpose of this regulatory device is to ratchet up the expected efficacy of pollution-control devices. If someone invents a better mousetrap, the rest of the industry, until an even better one is invented, is expected to use it in any new facilities.

As far as opponents were concerned, the better mousetrap existed for controlling mercury. The Illinois EPA permit would allow about eight ounces of mercury emissions per hour, while two other states then allowed just four percent of that amount. Better mercury-control equipment already existed in Germany but was not required. Still, the Illinois EPA made some "judgment calls" in the company's favor. In practice, it was also unlikely that Hartigan's appeal would succeed. Very few such appeals succeed, and those that do almost always make news.

Hartigan's appeal did have one practical effect. Reading Energy could not begin construction until U.S. EPA Administrator William

Reilly ruled on the petition, and it might be harder for the company to line up financing until the matter was resolved. Most EPA appeals take from six months to a year, depending on the backlog of cases.[25]

Little of that, however, fazed Reading Energy Vice President Barry Neal. The delay, as far as he was concerned, was simply one that the company had anticipated, although he expressed frustration at "the political nature" of the appeal. Site clearance, the one activity in which Reading could engage, would begin the following summer. Neal combatively noted that preparing the site benefited the village of Robbins because the company was reclaiming a site that was otherwise being used by illegal dumpers. Bechtel Corporation, which would build the plant, would participate in underwriting the project with its own equity capital, just as it had "made these sorts of guarantees" with other projects around the country.[26]

There was another agency in the picture, and it had not been moving very swiftly, either. In order to confront the political hot potato of garbage disposal, the South Suburban Mayors and Managers Association had hired Envirodyne Engineers, a Chicago firm, to prepare a solid-waste plan for the region. A 1988 Illinois law, the Solid Waste Planning and Recycling Act, required every county to develop a 20-year waste-management plan. Cook County was required to submit its plan by March 1, 1991. County officials allowed the SSMMA and other suburban-area associations to plan for their regions with the intent of incorporating all such plans into the county plan. For that to happen, SSMMA needed to finish its study by January.

The result may have proven the aphorism that haste makes waste, for the study, especially when compared to some of the more sophisticated waste-management plans that other jurisdictions have devised, was transparently mediocre. It produced an obviously skewed recommendation in favor of the Robbins incinerator. One major flaw, clearly delineated in the Envirodyne report, was that the firm did not include the development costs of any of its alternatives (landfills, composting, recycling, etc.). Clearly, the highest development costs are associated with an incinerator, whereas a recycling program incurs its greatest costs for labor and implementation. The executive summary for the study merely hinted at the reason for this crucial decision in estimating costs by referring to them as "potential fees," a strange term in view of the certainty of their occurrence. Further, the study basically never presented, among its six alternatives, a serious high-percentage recycling option, but largely compared varying percentages of waste dedicated to either landfill disposal or incineration.[27]

The SSMMA hearing process that ensued, whether conceived thoughtfully or in fear of the environmental coalition's rabble-rousing skills, served only to exacerbate the mistrust between activists and public officials. Using a process borrowed from the Illinois Department of Transportation, SSMMA held its hearings on the Envirodyne plan in a high school in Richton, a small suburb at the southern extremity of the far-flung region that the association's 39 member suburbs covered. The late afternoon hearings required the use of multiple rooms that effectively divided the few people who attended. Citizens testified individually, sans audience, before a court reporter who recorded their comments. The net result was that, although enterprising activists could read the transcript of someone else's testimony, they could not hear it when it was being given. Even a husband and wife, Jeff Tangel recalled, were isolated from each other in this process. In another room, however, citizens could talk in small groups to the technical experts who had prepared the study. Finally, in an adjacent room, they could likewise informally discuss the matter with elected officials from the SSMMA.

But it should have been small wonder that the SSMMA by now seemed very much at sea in dealing with its half-million area citizens. In March 1989, a suburban attorney with a practice in Palos Hills had been elected mayor of the small village of East Hazel Crest (pop. 1,360). Tom Brown had not previously held elective office. But in July, he was suddenly handed the chairmanship of the SSMMA's new South Suburban Solid Waste Agency, a subsidiary entity created to handle the solid-waste planning mandated by state law. The more experienced mayors of larger towns had clearly recognized a political hot potato and steered the job to a neophyte. Brown, the earnest mayor of one of the SSMMA's tiniest villages, was a convenient choice for colleagues who viewed the job primarily as an opportunity to anger constituents.

Brown was also somewhat handicapped. The SSMMA had already hired Envirodyne by the time he took over the reins of the new solid-waste agency. The planning deadline loomed just months away. It would become Brown's job to publicly defend both the firm's work product and the SSMMA's antiseptic "public" hearing procedures.

Brown was not averse to the latter job. In fact, he later defended it to me with relish, criticizing the format of previous municipal hearings where "twelve members of Mr. Tangel's group started screaming and would not let us say a thing." The Richton hearings, in his view, offered a certain solemnity that Tangel and his friends did not want. "Everyone had a right to make written comments. We felt it worked out better. When we had our final public hearing at Richton South High School, we had a classroom with 40 to 50 chairs in it. People signed up to talk to municipal officials; we had 15 to 20 people at any given time. When one asked a question, the other 19 could listen. A lot of people at public hearings will say more gets accomplished that way. All the people who came through seemed satisfied that they could talk in a real normal voice. It's a better way than mass protest."

What Brown clearly saw in the SSMMA hearing procedure was not the stifling of public participation that Jeff Tangel and Mary Martin had described. Brown saw a small victory over mob rule. In the coalition's view, the hearings were poorly attended by design, drawing, by Brown's estimates, from 45 to 50 people, one-third of whom supported the plan, probably a higher percentage than would have been the case with a larger turnout. Brown was a foot soldier in the battle for representative democracy, a system in which public officials could be trusted to make wise decisions, as opposed to the environmental coalition's vision of forcing public accountability for indifferent or even arrogant mayors and aldermen. "I've asked people what they think of the Robbins facility," he said. "Ninety-five percent say *you* figure out where it goes. Out of 600,000 people in our area, very few come out." Brown understood the concern of those who would live close to the Robbins incinerator, but, "I've traveled, and people near incinerators in Sweden and Japan don't even know they are there."

Finally, Brown, by the summer of 1991, had become somewhat

embittered by the cauldron of controversy into which he had been thrown. "I tried to point out to those groups that this is not an easy decision for me to make. I would not have run for mayor if I had known I would be thrown into this spotlight. I have had death threats and vandalism on my house." And there was a certain inevitability that seemed to bar him from opposing the train of progress. "Where does Cook County look to put its waste? Robbins had a permitted facility. Do we ignore it or use it? They can get waste from anywhere they want. They may as well use *our* garbage."[28]

In a legal sense, Brown was right. The U.S. Supreme Court had ruled that waste was an item in interstate commerce, and thus any state ban against its importation was unconstitutional.[29] If Reading Energy did not get enough garbage from the Chicago area, it was free to bring it in from Indiana, Ohio, or even the East Coast if necessary. With the Long Island garbage barge still a recent memory, the importation of massive quantities of municipal solid waste was a very real possibility.

Mayor Brown also suggested that health concerns related to incineration could not be the overriding factor in choosing solutions to Cook County's waste-disposal crisis. But public-health officials and even private hospitals were beginning to take exception to that assumption. In early 1990, the American Public Health Association, in a lengthy resolution, announced support for a construction ban on all garbage incinerators in areas that were not yet meeting federal Clean Air Act standards.[30] Chicago was such an area. The association, founded in 1872 to represent public-health disciplines and professionals, laid out a litany of concerns about incineration that echoed those of many scientific critics and called on the federal government, and EPA specifically, to plan for comprehensive alternatives such as recycling, composting, and product substitution to achieve a reduction in solid waste. It was a serious blow to the prestige of the incinerator industry.

But it did not hurt Reading Energy nearly as much as another blow much closer to home. Around Christmas of 1990, St. Francis Hospital, located in Blue Island just one mile from the proposed incinerator site, issued a denunciation of the Robbins facility on public-health grounds.[31] The statement caught Reading officials off guard and sent its president, Thomas Cassel, into a rage. Tangel and other coalition leaders wasted little time in exploiting this new blow to Reading's credibility. Cassel wasted little time in confronting the hospital's administrators to demand a retraction. The company was not shy about pointing out that hospitals—St. Francis not excepted—have long resorted to incineration as a means of disposing of infectious medical waste. With the predominance of disposable plastic syringes, medical packaging, and even food containers in hospital cafeterias, no hospital could claim innocence on the question of burning dioxin-generating plastics. St. Francis announced a long-planned waste-reduction program, but it did not stop Reading Energy from complaining about institutional "hypocrisy." A public-relations war was underway.

The charges and countercharges that flew in either direction set the stage for some hot confrontations before the city council waste-management committee in Oak Lawn, a suburb of 70,000 people outside the SSMMA. In its search for secure, large sources of fuel, Reading Energy had approached the village about contracting for garbage disposal at the Robbins incinerator. Because of its size, Oak Lawn was a potential pacesetter for the decisions of surrounding communities, making it particularly important for Reading, which needed to enlist a significant flow of garbage to fill its incinerator's planned capacity. The committee planned its hearings for two cold nights in late January 1991.

Smelling an opportunity to draw blood, the environmental coalition quickly mobilized. It invited Reading Energy to debate Dr. Paul Connett, a chemistry professor at St. Lawrence University in Canton, New York. Connett is precisely the sort of mercurial, passionate, humorous, and caustic critic that industries love to hate. Operating on a shoestring plus the subscriptions of fellow critics and citizens' groups, Connett and his wife, Ellen, have since 1988 produced a weekly newsletter, *Waste Not*, which bills itself as the "weekly reporter for rational resource management." It is a merciless stream of attacks on the incinerator industry intended to inspire and inform incinerator opponents. A busy fax machine and a busy telephone keep the Connetts up to date on developments in dozens of incinerator battles across the country, while Paul travels to international scientific symposiums in Sweden, Japan, and elsewhere to document what he perceives as the depredations of the industry and the technology on human health and the natural environment. He is not shy about labeling industry apologists "liars" or ridiculing their attempts to defend accident-prone corporate track records. Like his close friend and ally, Dr. Barry Commoner, Connett has a gift rare among scientists for restating complex technical concepts in plain English, often using amusing analogies. It is the kind of skill that galvanizes accusations of distortion and oversimplification.

Reading Energy immediately refused the coalition's invitation. Just as predictably, Connett came anyway. On Friday, January 18, the coalition used both an afternoon press conference in Oak Lawn and an evening speech at St. Xavier College on Chicago's South Side to rejuvenate and educate its forces. Connett was his entertaining best, describing how the overwhelming majority of American garbage could be composted or recycled. Landfills could then fill a modest need to handle an irreducible but safe fractional remainder of the nation's waste. Incinerators could be eliminated.

With its message in hand, the coalition marched its forces to Oak Lawn for the first waste hearing at 8:00 p.m. on Monday, January 28. Reading Energy had refused to share a forum with its opponents, so the solid-waste committee had scheduled anti and pro arguments for two successive nights. Nearly 300 incinerator opponents encountered a situation tailor-made for the politics of confrontation.

Committee chairman Ronald Stancik, a stern-looking politician with strong, tightly set jaw and sharp, recessed eyes, had either not considered the possibility of an overflow audience or did not care. The council chambers seat 135. Stancik refused to move the meeting, and most of the coalition activists stood on the front porch of the village hall.

The weather, while not bitterly cold that night, was distinctly chilly with a hint of snow—just enough to aggravate the festering sense of political abuse that had animated many of the incinerator critics in the past. A few leaders who had arrived early, like Tangel and coalition treasurer Robert Goebel, a politically conservative IRS employee, served as information shuttles between the packed chambers and the crowd outdoors. At the same time, coalition leaders like chairperson Mary Martin were stranded outdoors, though she chose to make the most of the organizing opportunity.

Early in the evening, Tangel spoke to the audience at some length, mentioning the American Public Health Association position on incineration. Tangel reported gleefully that Reading Energy had referred to the St. Francis position paper as "a bunch of crap" and that Cassel was "ripping mad."

(Even as a writer, I had my own trouble gaining entrance until Goebel vouched for me to the local police. Until then, they had refused to accept my business card as a press badge. At one time, the card said "assistant editor." A few months before, I had been promoted to "senior research associate," not an obvious reference to any sort of reportorial position. Even when I did finally enter, it was partly with the encouragement of the crowd outside, which felt that it was more important to let the news media witness what they considered a travesty of public access than to get one more activist through the door.)

But at that moment, oddly, the meeting was still being conducted with considerable decorum, as though there were no large crowd outside. Kevin Greene, research director of Citizens for a Better Environment, was testifying calmly that the village should target all parts of its waste stream for recycling or composting, with Stancik reassuring him that a recycling plan was a license condition for any haulers contracting with the city. After a few minutes, Stancik thanked the earnest Greene for his informative testimony, and indicated the committee would follow up on the recycling issue during its regularly scheduled meeting the following month.

Having just heard the last speaker who had prepared a presentation beforehand, Stancik opened the hearing to citizen comments. In a foretaste of what was to come, Jim Lee, an Oak Lawn resident, stepped to the microphone to "represent the people outside. This is the third time I've come here that people were denied access." He asked the committee to relocate the second night's hearing, when Reading Energy would make a presentation, to a location that could accommodate the crowd. The chambers erupted in applause.

Stancik, who takes a dim view of such outbursts, was annoyed.

"Tomorrow night," he reminded the audience, "is the other side of the coin." As for tonight's hearing, "We need a controlled environment," in order for the committee to glean the most useful information for making a decision. When Lee persisted with his argument, Stancik pointedly noted, "Maybe you're not hearing me."

"Very arrogant, degrading," one woman in a middle aisle said to her neighbors.

"Police state!" yelled a woman from the back of the hall.

Another village trustee more sympathetic to the audience's concerns, Harold Mozwecz, tried to advance the prospect of finding an alternative site for the second night of the hearing. Stancik would have none of it. The meeting would stay where he had scheduled it.

A former trustee, Jay Bergamini, spoke next, attacking the incinerator plan and suggesting that area mayors and city managers meet with its critics to reconsider their plan.

As citizens continued to seize the microphone, Stancik gradually lost the iron grip on the proceedings he had so clearly coveted. He repeatedly reprimanded an elderly man who spoke away from the microphone toward the audience, ignoring the chair. He sought to refute another man's suggestion that a face-to-face debate with Reading Energy would be more likely to ferret out the truth. "We have a reputation of being pretty fair people," Stancik replied.

Tangel jumped up in the back of the audience. "Reading Energy refused to debate Paul Connett a week ago," he yelled.

A stream of women began to move toward the microphone, testifying about existing and potential air-pollution maladies such as bronchitis, about how the incinerator could affect the health of their children, or about a husband dying of leukemia. One mother represented Parents of Asthmatic Children. A man who had worked with dioxins noted that they can be spread when you touch your face with your hands, and then ridiculed Stancik as a candidate "for cancer because he is always touching his face." Stancik had lost control. Women began shouting their comments from the rear of the chambers, concluding with Gloria Scott, testifying from behind a video camera she was using to tape the hearings: "Our officials (in Robbins) have sold us out. It's too late for us. Don't sell your people out."

Finally, Mozwecz pleaded with the audience to see the other side.

"I fought to shut down the Westinghouse incinerator on Route 83. We want to stop the state and federal government from dumping problems on our laps. I have proposed a $4 deposit on lead-acid batteries. But we would have no control over this incinerator if we didn't send garbage and they got their burnables from who knows where. Where would that leave us? We want a committee of various suburbs that would have a say-so over what went on there. We're not your enemies. Please don't feel that we are. We're trying to gather the facts. No decisions will be made without more input from you people." As Mozwecz finished, a member of the audience shouted out a proposal for an Oak Lawn citizens task force.

The following night, the second hearing took place in the same crowded council chambers with one small accommodation to the South Cook County Environmental Action Coalition's consistent drawing power—a closed-circuit television hookup in a nearby room. Stancik did not want to see the overflow, but he had agreed to accommodate it.

There were, however, enough incinerator critics again to dominate the audience, despite construction-trade union attempts to pass out pro-incinerator information packets and to fill seats with supporters. From the beginning, Reading Energy president Cassel had a certain ulcerated, nervous look in his eyes. He deferred regularly to Stancik's preference for personally chastising the audience whenever the situation required.

Cassel introduced a team of Reading experts to testify that night following his own slide presentation, which led the audience through the essentials of Illinois solid-waste legislation, the crisis in landfill capacity, and the nation's trends in garbage generation. The 1,600-ton-per-day facility would relieve the area of some two-thirds of its daily garbage load. Yet even that was but a small dent in the Chicago metropolitan area's overall daily generation of more than 20,000 tons of solid waste. Cassel noted that while just two percent of the state's trash was being burned, 92 percent was still going to landfills, whose numbers had dwindled from 1,200 in 1980 to just 126 by 1989, thanks to shrinking capacity and new environmental regulations. Reading, however, was offering an "integrated solution to the trash problem," emphasizing not only incineration but the ability to recycle one-fourth of the trash delivered to the Robbins plant. And, Cassel noted, incineration was a coming trend in which Illinois would follow European practices, where Switzerland incinerated 75 percent of its waste, Sweden half, and Germany about one-third. Even the public was coming around, with increasing percentages of Americans telling pollsters they supported it as a solid-waste solution.

It was a slick, well-oiled presentation, but Cassel was nonetheless visibly angry. In a sharp voice, he attacked "materials distributed last night" that were "inaccurate and provided disinformation." The plant, he declared, would save the area money. He pointedly added that his firm had demanded and anticipated a retraction from St. Francis Hospital. "We visited St. Francis two weeks after their statement," he said. "They acknowledged they have not performed a study. They admitted they have never looked at the emissions data."

It was the beginning of a tense night of cat and mouse among Cassel's Reading Energy team, one skeptical trustee, and a largely hostile audience. Trustee Harold Mozwecz began to quiz Cassel. Would all of the promised 25-percent reduction in burned volume[32] at the plant be recycled or would some of it go to a landfill? Cassel replied that, "assuming markets," all of it was "potentially recyclable" material.

Mozwecz shifted gears: "Could someone brief us on what comes out of the stack?" David Minot, Reading's air-quality specialist and vice president of energy resources, replied that the incinerator would generate a variety of pollutants in small quantities resulting from the combustion of waste. These would include trace metals and trace organic compounds, but the important point was that the "amounts are very small."

If the ploy was to let a vague but technical-sounding answer suffice, it failed. "Be more concise and direct," Mozwecz demanded.

"Trace quantities of mercury," Minot replied.

"I hear one to two tons of mercury per year," Mozwecz persisted. In fact, the permit allowed 4,400 pounds.

"If you saw 10 percent of that allowable emissions figure, I'd be surprised," Minot countered.

"It's a specific number. It will be small," Cassel added. "I don't have the specific number."

"I'd be happier with figures in tons," said Mozwecz.

"I don't have precise tonnage figures with me," Minot answered.

Mozwecz was losing patience. "You have permits, but you don't know what's coming out of the stack?"

Standing in the middle of the audience, Jeff Tangel loudly offered to supply Cassel's figures for him. "We know the figures," he suggested on behalf of the coalition. Stancik, who as chairman seemed more concerned with decorum than with precise answers, sternly reminded Tangel that his side had had its turn the night before.

Minot sought to assure Mozwecz and the crowd that the permit limits were set by "competent scientists and epidemiologists. We will get those figures for you." Mozwecz pressed on, asking for figures on dioxin. Cassel replied that the permit procedure had lasted for 18 months, the "most rigorous we had ever seen, with reams of documents." Later, replying to another Mozwecz question on health problems, Cassel again talked of standards set by scientists "with pregnant mothers and babies all in mind," but again without specific figures.

Cassel introduced Dr. Bertram Carnow, a University of Illinois professor of medicine who had just joined Reading's consulting team for the project. Carnow has a long pedigree as a public-health specialist dating back to work with the U.S. EPA in the 1970s. In general terms, Carnow sought to reassure the trustees, if not the audience, that "the body removes toxic materials as it takes them in up to a certain point." This was "true also of mercury. When you go beyond that point, you accumulate." The levels of pollutants at the Reading plant, he said, "are not levels which will affect human health."

Again, Mozwecz persisted, asking whether Carnow's assurances accounted for "the total air package we breathe."

"I'm not familiar with those other sources," Carnow replied, but EPA had measured them.

"Would it still then keep it far below what our bodies can get rid of on a daily basis?"

"Yes," Carnow insisted.

The coalition forces had already been grumbling in the back of the room. Carnow, despite his credentials, was rapidly becoming a key target of the environmentalists' effort to discredit Reading's claims. His testimony was a lightning rod for audience criticism despite Stancik's efforts to remind them that they had had their turn the night before.

One local activist, Louise Gasior, a longtime thorn in Stancik's side, yelled out her objections. Stancik directed the police to remove her from the room. "Why are you singling me out," she screamed, "when Stancik objected to people clapping when a man in the audience accused Cassel of dancing around the issue?"

"You're just angry with her because she comes in here to tell you the truth," her husband shouted.

Another local woman vocally noted that St. Francis Hospital, contrary to Cassel's statement, was not retracting its position. Cassel tartly replied that retracting its position before doing a study would be an admission by the hospital of ethical irresponsibility. Answering persistently shouted demands for a debate, Cassel noted that company officials had appeared in televised debates with Greenpeace in two other suburbs, but that Connett was too emotional.

The meeting ended as police ejected Gasior from the room while she shouted, "Am I being *arrested?*"[33]

Spring, once every four years, is municipal-election season in Illinois. The quadrennial date arrived in 1991, just after the Oak Lawn confrontation. In Chicago, Mayor Richard M. Daley was coasting to an encore performance where his late father, Richard J., had left off some 16 years before. In an election virtually devoid of suspense, Daley destroyed the campaigns of two African-American competitors, one inside the Democratic primary and one from the independent Harold Washington Party. Former Mayor Jane Byrne, seeking a dramatic comeback, was buried alive with a minuscule four percent of the vote.

In the suburbs, many entrenched incumbents were seeking to steamroller their own opponents with Daley-like victories. In an oddity of Illinois politics, many of them used party labels unique to their own suburbs, as did their adversaries. Thus, ballots were peppered with slate names like the People's Party, Mayor's Reform Coalition, and New Leadership Party. The devices served a number of purposes, including one discovered long ago by the mayor of suburban Niles to the north—denying opponents the opportunity to challenge his slate in a primary by changing the party name in each election.

Despite the historically high tolerance of Chicagoans—even suburbanites—for what many citizens elsewhere might regard as dirty pool, the South Cook County Environmental Action Coalition concluded that spring that its best strategy was to challenge directly those politicians its members had come to believe were their biggest obstacle in stopping the Robbins incinerator. If they would not listen to the people, they would have to be taught that there was a price to pay.

With 39 suburbs in the SSMMA, plus other nearby suburbs like Oak Lawn discussing contracts with Reading Energy, inflicting that punishment seemed to require political logistics beyond the capabilities of neophytes who had coalesced into an effective unit only within the previous nine months. Tangel and Martin were not deterred. They had, after all, shown that sheer doggedness and numerical strength could spook even veteran Chicago politicians. And they did not see that they had any choice.

Tangel and Martin led the coalition in drafting an aggressive questionnaire for city-council and mayoral candidates throughout the area, querying their positions on solid-waste management and the Robbins incinerator. They mailed it out; most never came back. Some candidates, in fact, protested to reporters that they resented such pressure tactics (as if they were really all that new in the Chicago area, which they are not). The protests mostly served notice that many candidates did not take the coalition seriously as a factor in their own communities' elections.

Indeed, it is hard to see why the issue would take on a life-or-death status in many of the smaller, more affluent suburbs that were more distant from the incinerator site. Even the coalition's rhetoric about the distribution of air pollutants had little resonance in areas that were clearly not downwind. Robbins, after all, happened to be on the northern fringe of the south suburban area. Only the South Side of Chicago and an inner ring of towns could reasonably expect some political fallout from the projected air-pollution fallout. These were also the more blue-collar, industrial areas of the entire region, where the issue resonated against a background of historical air-pollution abuses.

In Alsip, the Alsip People's Party challenged what coalition leaders regarded as the authoritarian regime of 20-year mayor Arnold Andrews, whose party symbol manages to serve as the artwork for the city vehicle-fee sticker that shows that car owners have paid a municipal car tax. Despite having its headquarters shut down a few days before the election because of alleged building-code violations, the opposition, which had adopted a position against the incinerator, came within five percent of ousting the Andrews slate, the narrowest margin in years.[34]

In Blue Island, Mayor Donald Peloquin preempted the opposition when the city council passed a resolution opposing the plant.[35] Shortly after the April 7 election, Peloquin and members of the Blue Island Chamber of Commerce launched a bitter attack on Reading Energy President Cassel at a luncheon in the chamber offices, questioning Cassel's assurances that incinerator fees would remain lower than those at area landfills. Peloquin was also vocal in challenging the assumption that the incinerator would not hurt area recycling efforts, while some chamber members challenged the accompanying Dr. Carnow about emissions of heavy metals like lead and mercury. A mile downwind of Robbins, the Blue Island business community was beginning to sound like an echo of the skeptical citizens at the Oak Lawn hearings.[36]

In a few other scattered suburbs, for varying reasons and with varying degrees of emphasis on the issue, incinerator foes won seats on city councils. In Oak Lawn, some incumbents bore self-inflicted wounds into the fray. Joseph Vogrich lost his seat to Marjorie Joy, one of two challengers who opposed the project, mostly because he had created a flap much earlier with highly publicized comments that smacked of racism and prompted one flamboyant West Side Chicago alderman to threaten a water embargo unless the village board censured him, which it did. Quinn Mucker, a noncommittal member of the solid-waste committee, lost his seat to Robert Streit, a vocal incinerator opponent.[37] It seemed likely that the new Oak Lawn village board would temper any previous enthusiasm for the plant.

But time was running out fast for the coalition, and the election results seriously affected only a handful of the communities involved in the SSMMA or its south suburban waste agency. The SSMMA held its last round of hearings on the solid-waste plan in late April, in preparation for a May 2 vote by its mayors on endorsing the plan. To mount opposition, the coalition leaders resorted to a familiar tactic. Frustrated with the SSMMA's hearing process, they staged their own hearing at a hotel in Midlothian. The attendance, more than 150, was similar to that in Blue Island nearly a year before. The rhetoric—and even some of the speakers—were also much the same.[38]

On May 2, with representatives of 22 of the SSMMA's 39 member municipalities voting, the SSMMA adopted a resolution authorizing negotiations with Reading Energy on a master contract for garbage disposal at the Robbins facility. Seventeen members backed the plan, many of them among the smaller towns in the region. One of the five opposing votes was cast by Thomas Murawski, mayor of Midlothian and chairman of the SSMMA.

Summer approached in 1991 with incinerator foes and supporters on the South Side awaiting the decision by the U.S. EPA on the appeal filed a year earlier by the Illinois attorney general's office. Rumors circulated, often originating from coalition leaders and heatedly denied by Reading Energy Vice President Barry Neal, that Reading was facing financial difficulties and might be looking for a corporation with "deep pockets" to salvage its delayed project. Such talk was largely premature, however, for appeals to the U.S. EPA administrator's office often take from six months to a year to be resolved. Reading found itself on the long end of the spectrum, but Neal insisted that that presented no problem.[39]

For Reading, the wait proved worthwhile, even if company officials resented what they considered the "political nature" of the appeal. On August 6, EPA Administrator William Reilly ruled, first, that Hartigan's office had had no standing to file such an appeal and had not, in any event, filed it in a timely manner. But having disposed of the appeal on technical grounds, Reilly went on to defend the incinerator in a 14-page opinion, calling its health effects "negligible."[40]

At the Illinois attorney general's office, Matthew Dunn, chief of the environmental-control division, was terse, noting that further appeal was unlikely.[41] Later, however, the attorney general's office filed suit to invalidate the original rezoning on grounds that affected neighbors had not been properly notified, a prerequisite for establishing the village's jurisdiction to conduct siting hearings. Attorney General Roland Burris, who had succeeded Hartigan, was forced to defend himself against accusations by incinerator proponents of obstructionism.[42]

The coalition, which that very same day was holding a seminar at St. Xavier College on Chicago's Southwest Side with UCLA urban-planning professor Robert Gottlieb, coauthor of *War on Waste*, was back to square one. It had opposed the Robbins facility through the system, even enlisting the aid of key state officials, and lost. Reading Energy, with its Illinois EPA permit cleared, was at last free to begin construction on the site, where it had previously been limited to site-preparation activities, such as grading and demolition removal. Now, according to Neal, the company could look forward to completing its project and beginning operation by 1995.[43]

For the opponents, the choices were stark. They could gear up to lobby at least 39 communities—and probably more—not to contract with Reading Energy for their garbage disposal, knowing all the while that Reading could always go farther afield to find its trash. Or they could throw in the towel.

Within the SSMMA, where the contract was likely to be offered for acceptance or rejection by member communities within a 60- or 90-day period, there was a high probability that the issue could be settled in a lightning blitz of lobbying and contract votes. But it might also lead to a hodgepodge of mixed results.

The dawning of 1992 thus set the stage for one of the most politically complex battles any incinerator had ever faced. SCCEAC geared up for a form of protracted political guerrilla warfare, taking potshots at an adversary sometimes poorly equipped to anticipate where the next citizen uprising over the issue might occur. By April, the coalition could announce some success, with the village board of Matteson (pop. 10,000) voting unanimously to withdraw from the SSMMA Solid Waste Agency and not to use the Robbins incinerator. Officials began contacting other nonparticipating towns to form an alternative solid-waste agency.[44] By midsummer, Blue Island, Merrionette Park, and Oak Forest had been enlisted for the new agency. Oak Forest, pushed by a strong resident recycling lobby, adopted a curbside recycling program with volume-based disposal rates to encourage waste reduction.[45] Meanwhile, Reading Energy began to evince some of the financial strains from its delayed project when the huge Bechtel Corporation withdrew its participation, leaving Foster Wheeler Corporation to move into the void.[46]

Suddenly, as if out of nowhere, lightning struck for the opponents. On July 17, Cook County Circuit Court Judge Everette A. Braden ruled the original village siting permit invalid in a lawsuit filed in late 1991 by Illinois Attorney General Roland Burris. Amid considerable criticism that he was being obstructionist, Burris had alleged a pattern of failure by Reading Energy to notify about 90 percent of the property owners within 250 feet of the incinerator site, as required by law. Braden's ruling forced Reading back to square one, reapplying for the siting permit as an alternative to waiting and hoping for a favorable appeal. Worse, the judge affirmed Burris's contention that, if the siting permit was invalid, so too was the Illinois EPA construction permit. Reading *might* have to reapply for that as well.

By September, Reading opted to pursue both alternatives at once. Undoubtedly aware that the law required a hearing within 90 to 120 days after an application is filed, Reading reapplied on September 21. The village board then obliged the company by scheduling its hearing for December 22 in the hope that the holidays would discourage a large turnout.

Early on a damp, drizzly, and dark Tuesday night, cars from throughout the south suburbs began to converge on the poorly marked side street where they found the Robbins Recreation and Training Center. Police waved flashlights to direct them down the road to any parking place they could find. Well over 300 people showed up just two nights before Christmas Eve. The environmental

coalition had mailed out a newsletter asking members to "attend the
. . . hearing as a holiday gift to the environment and your family."[47]

They were beaten to the punch. By 6:00 p.m., local incinerator
supporters, backed by area construction workers, had occupied the
front seats in the gymnasium for a rally preceding the hearing. Dozens of supporters had made themselves especially visible in the audience by wearing white work caps with blue letters that read, "Yes, In
My Back Yard." State Rep. William Shaw harangued them with powerful, though clearly untrue, demagoguery, asserting that people from
surrounding suburbs opposed the Robbins Resource Recovery Center because they could see it meant money and jobs, and they wanted
to take it away for themselves. The Reverend John Cook, a local
minister who headed an interfaith council supporting the project,
backed up Shaw's rhetoric with the charge that opponents wanted
to "deny Robbins a chance."[48]

Incredibly, to most outsiders, the proceedings then segued quickly
into a legally constituted public hearing on the same stage. The village attorney introduced Mayor Brodie for some opening remarks.
Somewhat more mellow and perhaps chastened by three years of controversy surrounding her project, she was more conciliatory than in
the past, promising that the village board would "listen to all the
evidence" and approach the new siting hearing, the result of what
she called a "technicality," with an "open mind." In the wake of the
rally, the promise of impartiality convinced no one.

The hearing began with a panel ascending the stage to present
Reading's case for the incinerator. Little had changed in Robbins
from the very first hearing. For local supporters, the men were economic saviors. For opponents like Gloria Scott, the lack of diversity
among the ten white men up front spoke volumes about the project
itself. For two hours, these men testified, one after another, each presenting his own credentials for his own area of expertise, saying essentially what had already been said at many other hearings before.
David Minot testified about air quality, Dr. Bertram Carnow about
health effects with the same glibness that raised doubts at the Oak
Lawn hearing. None of the emissions, he asserted, were adequate to
cause any health impacts whatsoever. Not lead, not mercury, not
dioxin. The amounts of all of them that would be emitted would be

"incredibly small." Others followed, on real-estate values, compliance with floodplain rules, hazardous-waste problems, and traffic flows generated by the plant.

After a break, the hearing resumed to allow the village attorney to read audience cross-questions of the panel from forms filled out during the evening. Another hour and a half passed, and it was nearly 11:30 p.m. before the panel finished. The village attorney called for another break. The crowd was thinning quickly. Finally, annoyed citizen critics of the plant, many from surrounding suburbs, got their chance to testify for five minutes apiece. It was nearing midnight. With just a rump caucus remaining, the Robbins officials had succeeded in blunting the force of the opposition. The hearing dragged on with the remaining SCCEAC members insisting on presenting their testimony that night. A weary hearings officer had suggested that the hearing could reconvene at 10:00 a.m. Opponents angrily rejected that overture. "We sat through five hours of your crap," one yelled. "We're staying." Long after midnight, the last environmentalist testified.

On February 10, the Robbins village board did the expected. It voted to grant a new siting permit to Reading Energy to build an incinerator at West 135th Street and Kedzie Avenue. In response, the village board of Oak Lawn unanimously voted to oppose any incinerator within five miles of its community and to back proposed state legislation disallowing any incinerator within five miles of a school.[49]

For Mayor Irene Brodie, little had changed from the beginning of her tenure. Reading Energy remained the knight in shining armor of her economic-development dreams for the village. Time and experience had mellowed her only slightly. "Strangely enough," she said in an interview during the hearing, "the opposition was good in that it assured us that the best possible equipment would be installed to control pollutants that we might have overlooked." Now, however, it was time to get on with the project. "Those of us who have lived here know that we have tried other kinds of businesses." Even after turning to the incineration option, "we went through many companies. Unless something new and disturbing is uncovered during these hearings, I would have a hard time saying no to the site."

It was both a generational and a class division. Brodie related to the older African-American professionals who had made a commitment to stay in Robbins. She had filled her citizens advisory committee with these people, "chemists and such," like Rudolf Bouie, an Argonne Laboratory scientist, because she respected them. Together, they had fought to "reconfigure our basket of benefits" from the incinerator because "I knew the money was out there." And no one had shown her a better way.[50]

Where Brodie's mission was clear, the SSMMA's goals seemed merely opportunistic. The SSMMA planning process, SCCEAC's grass-roots lobbying, and Reading Energy's spirited attempt to enlist suburbs for its disposal contract all missed the most essential point. The putative vision behind the state's 1988 mandate to counties to prepare comprehensive solid-waste plans was a holistic one. Its initial recycling and waste-reduction goals, though modest by environmentalists' standards, were designed as moveable targets that could grow over time as communities gained experience and sophistication in analyzing their waste streams. Counties were chosen to submit the plans so that solid-waste planning would emphasize regional needs over more parochial community concerns.

The opposite happened in Robbins. Aided by some current and former municipal officials with business ties to the project, a small, neglected, and poverty-stricken community stole the march on its more affluent neighbors. It sited a privately owned and operated incinerator, paving the way for its state permit, before the SSMMA ever formulated the basic questions it should have asked about regional waste management in the south suburbs. Faced with a *fait accompli*, SSMMA leaders took the easy path, building their planning process around a presumed solution, rather than first defining the problem. When pressured, they pleaded helplessness, noting that the Robbins facility would be built whether they liked it or not. Therefore, better it should burn their garbage than someone else's. The Robbins village board had backed an entire regional planning agency into abdicating its planning responsibilities. Instead, neighboring towns focused their efforts on winning some control over a facility that one community had courted and approved unilaterally.

As the spring and summer of 1993 approached, however, the facade of unity erected earlier to support this *fait accompli* began to crumble. The tiny village of East Hazel Crest and its mayor, Tom Brown, who had chaired the negotiations with Reading, suddenly withdrew, declaring in a letter, ". . . it now appears to us that a satisfactory agreement is not possible."[51] A growing list of suburbs was passing resolutions opposing the incinerator, although in October 1993, one affluent community, Country Club Hills, did finally approve a contract with Reading Energy. One village board member voted against the contract in part because of concern that it involves bringing more toxics into a minority community. Robbins and Reading Energy plug along, seeking more contracts to fuel the project's financial viability.[52]

In the end, the SSMMA approach did not so much resemble planning as it did a bizarre twist on the famous line from *Field of Dreams*: "If you build it, we will come, so that others will not."

And then many of its own began to turn away.

CALIFORNIA
The Politics of Life and Breath

William Ruckelshaus, the Chief Executive Officer of Browning Ferris Industries, the nation's second-largest waste-management firm, had just finished a keynote address to the first annual conference of the Society of Environmental Journalists in Boulder, Colorado, in October 1991. The former U.S. EPA administrator under two presidents, Richard Nixon and Ronald Reagan, had discussed the future of recycling and environmental regulation. The first questioner asked about the future of solid-waste incineration.

"We currently incinerate about 14 percent of our solid waste in this country," Ruckelshaus replied. "There are a number of plants under construction. Most people who step back and look at the trends say the trend is up for incineration, down for landfills, and sharply upward for recycling. Public opposition will slow those upward trends for incineration. We only build incinerators now where building a landfill is an even worse alternative."

In less than a minute, Ruckelshaus, generally respected for his honesty even by many who disagreed with his policies as EPA chief, had summarized the political changes that have swept over the waste industry like a tidal wave. The public distaste for landfills had given the incineration industry an incredibly brief opening through which to push forward its agenda before it, too, aroused a wave of public hostility. In the process, public opinion had quickly mobilized around recycling as an alternative to a continued emphasis on either land-fills or incineration. But, as Ruckelshaus had forcefully noted in his speech, recycling ultimately must entail major shifts in lifestyles and in the value system of American society if it is to function as a com-prehensive solution to the nation's solid-waste crisis. The crux of the political crisis, as Ruckelshaus had also noted, was that public support for recycling, like its antipathy for the waste industry's con-ventional solutions, went "well beyond the understanding of public officials."

Few situations have more clearly demonstrated this trend than the one in California. Los Angeles, long derided for its dirty air, has been blending air-pollution issues with recycling initiatives to create a new community-organizing focus on air cleanup. The fight began in what traditional environmentalists would have regarded as a most unlikely place, one both without a serious history of environmental activism and with a lengthy agenda of social problems—South Cen-tral Los Angeles, the scene of *Boyz 'N the Hood*, a movie about teen-age gangs, and of the vastly destructive April 1992 riots that followed the acquittal of four policemen accused in the videotaped beating of Rodney King. South Central, just north of Watts but unscathed by the 1960s riots, suffers an average of one murder a day. Once almost entirely African-American, the gritty industrial neighborhood, whose precincts former Mayor Tom Bradley once patrolled as a young policeman, is now 52 percent African-American and 44 per-cent Latino. Many in the Latino portion of the community neither vote nor speak up about their lot in life, as they are illegal aliens. With a median income of just $7,500 and 33 percent unemployment, South Central has never been the kind of place where the Sierra Club recruits its members.[1] Yet its environmental problems merit sig-nificant attention from the environmental movement. A *San Fran-cisco Examiner* investigation, for instance, found that South Central's one-square-mile 90058 ZIP-code area was California's most toxic neighborhood, with 18 companies discharging 33 million pounds of waste chemicals in 1989, five times as much as the state's runner-up ZIP code in Orange County.[2]

Charlotte Bullock and Robin Cannon, two middle-aged women who work as data-entry clerks at city hall, both remember finding the same letter in their mailboxes when they arrived at home one night in 1985.[3] Cannon found hers first after being dropped off by Bullock. But by the time she tried to telephone her longtime friend, Bullock was already on the telephone herself, telling other friends about the letter and its accompanying flyer, which informed them of a meeting the following Saturday in which the Los Angeles Bureau of Sanitation would discuss an incinerator it proposed to locate in the neighborhood.

Sheila Cannon, Robin's sister, already had two children suffering from asthma. Children in Los Angeles were already known to suffer disproportionately from the city's air. A 1984 study by the University of Southern California (which borders parts of South Central) had shown that children in the South Coast air basin had 10 to 15 percent less lung capacity than those living in Houston, the most polluted city in Texas.[4] Furthermore, newborns and infants suffer a far greater intake of particulate matter in their lungs, up to 10 times the adult concentration, because they breathe far more air in relation to their body weight than do adults.[5] As residents of the most polluted neighborhood in the city with the nation's most polluted air, South Central's children were surely suffering the most. Bullock and Cannon were not interested in adding an incinerator to their neighborhood's existing inventory of problems.

The pair showed up at the local community room girded for battle. The Los Angeles Bureau of Sanitation presented a film that mentioned that the Los Angeles City Energy Recovery Project (LANCER), which would burn some of the city's huge daily haul of solid waste, would produce dioxins and furans as byproducts that, as Cannon paraphrases it, "would be nothing to worry about." The film also told them that a filter system would draw away odors. Afterward, South Central's city-council member, Gilbert Lindsay, compared the proposed facility to Forest Lawn, a beautiful suburban area, saying that it would be so pristine that residents could hold weddings there. As for financing, the city's municipally owned water and power company would buy the electricity that would be generated by burning the garbage.

Cannon and Bullock fired away with an arsenal of questions. The facility would use 800,000 gallons of water daily, of which 100,000 gallons would be wastewater. But there had been a recent fire in the Baldwin Hills area just three miles to the west. Would there be adequate water pressure? They had learned through the grapevine that employees would need malaria shots. Was it really a healthy workplace? The neighborhood's main street, Washington Boulevard, was already heavily congested during the day. What would happen when 250 trucks per day rumbled down those streets to deliver garbage? The two struck a nerve with the skeptical audience in a neighborhood that had few positive dealings with city hall. Throughout the meeting, vocal opponents were busy exchanging telephone numbers.

Cannon recalled that "they were shocked that we knew so much." The city officials gave her the project's environmental impact statement, which normally would have cost her $25, "to allay my fears." They may have thought the thick volume would deter her curiosity. Instead, she took it home and began reading it that night. By 10:00 p.m., she was more than halfway through. She called her sister, Sheila Cannon, and said, "They are trying to kill us here."

The opponents who had exchanged phone numbers were quickly in touch with each other and booked a room at the Central Avenue library for the following Saturday. In short order, they formed the Concerned Citizens of South Central Los Angeles (CCSC) and pledged to "stay together whether we defeated LANCER or not."

During most of Southern California's booming growth after World War II, notes Robert Gottlieb, solid waste was a middle-class issue. Gottlieb has studied Southern California's waste problems as an instructor in UCLA's graduate program in urban and regional planning, where he has co-authored the book *War on Waste* and contributed to an American Planning Association report on waste management. Throughout the 1940s and 1950s, and even into the 1960s, Los Angeles and other jurisdictions sited their landfills in outlying areas. But as the suburbs spread toward the mountains and into the desert, those sites became prime real estate. The environmental issue surrounding landfills resulted largely from the problem of moving middle-class housing into areas where garbage had previously been dumped. Such constituencies, however, tend to be sufficiently powerful and knowledgeable to militate for effective solutions by local government.[6]

Increasingly, incineration became a regional garbage-disposal option. Several facilities were proposed outside Los Angeles, though just one actually got built, in the industrial enclave of the City of Commerce, where the municipal population is in the very low three figures but the tax base is substantial.[7] It is one of several incorporated municipalities in the area devoted primarily to using a small residential population to legitimize the land-use needs of resident industries. They are, in effect, the California equivalent of England's "rotten boroughs" in the early days of the Industrial Revolution.

As Los Angeles County's development, in particular, began to bump up against the ring of mountains that surrounds the region, landfill space grew scarce, even as the region generated a geometrically expanding mountain of daily garbage. Two major existing landfills, Toyon I and Lopez Canyon, were rapidly exhausting their capacity.[8] New solutions were a necessity, and, as Gottlieb also notes, the Los Angeles Bureau of Sanitation had long been committed to a "one-stop solution" to the problem of waste disposal.[9] During the 1970s, city sanitation officials came to feel that incineration offered that promise.

A number of factors came together to push their thinking in that direction. In 1976, Congress had passed the Resource Conservation and Recovery Act, which imposed a variety of new restrictions on landfilling and encouraged the development of waste-to-energy incineration projects as an alternative. The city of Los Angeles, in fact, had successfully applied for a U.S. EPA grant to study the feasibility of a central-city incinerator. Then, in 1981, as this study was being completed, President Ronald Reagan succeeded the more environmentally oriented Carter administration and essentially eliminated the funding Carter had targeted for research into new waste recycling and reduction technologies. The Bureau of Sanitation conceived its new strategy involving three waste-to-energy facilities, each capable of burning 1,600 tons per day, eventually handling about 70 percent of the city's solid-waste-disposal problem. The second and third units were to be built in the San Fernando Valley and on the city's liberal West Side, where Mayor Bradley had the support of white environmentalists.[10] The first was slated for South Central because, according to Gottlieb, "If you went to a poor neighborhood, environmentalism was something 'out there' and you could talk about the vast number of jobs the facility would bring. They figured out that, if opposition developed later to the second and third units, they could argue that racism was involved because of the lack of opposition to LANCER 1."[11] In short, the order of development of the three units was designed to neutralize environmental opposition. Bradley wanted to put an end to the divisiveness that was plaguing the city through its bitter garbage debates.

By 1984, the Los Angeles City Council was buying into the project. It established a LANCER steering committee in February. The Bureau of Sanitation searched for a site, finally securing 13.3 acres at the corner of Alameda and 41st Street before announcing its plans.[12] That same year, a consulting firm, Cerrell Associates, produced a report commissioned by the California Waste Management Board, examining how various kinds of communities respond to the siting of waste-to-energy facilities.[13] Whether or not its findings significantly influenced city officials in their search for the first LANCER site, the "Cerrell Report" has subsequently become infamous among grass-roots environmental activists because it essentially told state waste officials that not all communities are alike in their ability to generate or sustain resistance to an incineration project. The most accepting, in the final analysis, would be rural, low-income neighborhoods, with older, poorly educated residents. While South Central was anything but rural, it met all the other criteria. In any event, Los Angeles had no rural sites left within a reasonable distance.

If one sets aside the moral issues and examines only the strategic problems facing the incineration industry, the Cerrell analysis, in view of the history of siting waste-to-energy plants, made sense. But for reasons that escaped even mainstream environmental groups, many of whom took a pass on the LANCER fight in South Central, it was a siting strategy that quickly blew up in the city's face. The explosion terminated energy-recovery facilities as a politically viable waste-management option in the city of Los Angeles.

The fight over LANCER in South Central reflected, in part, a generational divide in the way the African-American community viewed such projects. Gilbert Lindsay, the octogenarian chairman of the city council's Public Works Committee, seems to have given little thought to LANCER's environmental and health impacts and a good deal of thought to playing "Let's Make a Deal." A $10 million "Community Betterment Fund" would help to finance needed community projects, including a community center to be named after Lindsay's wife. As to the Bureau of Sanitation's preselected site, which violated the usual environmental-assessment procedure of first considering alternative sites to determine that the location was in fact the best available, Lindsay's opinion was simple. It seemed only fair that he accept the first LANCER facility in his own backyard, and, in any event, it would bring badly needed jobs to a neighborhood with the highest unemployment rate in the city.[14]

Concerned Citizens saw the tradeoffs in a dramatically different light. Proposed dioxin emissions were 170 times higher than the allowable limit in Sweden, whose Environmental Protection Agency had a reputation for being particularly conscientious in setting standards. Crowded neighborhood streets would groan under the daily impact of 224 diesel trucks hauling garbage into the new facility, as well as others hauling toxic ash out, all the while aggravating the already poor air quality in an area heavily polluted by downtown freeway traffic.[15] In any event, Cannon noted, the $10 million fund was a fraud because it would be spread over ten years, with about $750,000 going to street improvements "that should have been done anyway." She added, "I didn't see why we should accept a bribe for our health."

If reports like that from Cerrell Associates had led sanitation officials to believe siting an incinerator in South Central would be a simple, noncontroversial matter, Concerned Citizens was about to disabuse them of that impression. Within days after the first library meeting, which became a weekly Saturday morning ritual, Bullock had begun collecting files, checking with the city clerk's office for any available information on LANCER's progress. She and Cannon added their names to the bureau's mailing list so that they could attend every hearing. When they attended, they invariably found more people interested in joining their fight.

By October 1985, the group discovered from a Bureau of Sanitation letter that the project needed a conditional-use permit because the land was zoned for residential and light manufacturing use, and the incinerator required a heavy manufacturing classification. Bullock and Cannon discovered that their group could file an appeal of the permit for $60, and quickly passed the hat at CCSC's next meeting to raise the money. CCSC members then canvassed the blocks surrounding the LANCER site to inform the facility's future neighbors and urge them to carpool to city hall for the hearing. "We brought out more than 1,000 black people. They had never seen so many black folks and didn't know what we were there for. Lindsay said this small group of people will never sway his opinion or that of others," Cannon recalled.

Such bravado simply spurred Cannon to widen her organizing net. CCSC members spread out across the city, seeking allies who could influence crucial city-council votes. Finding another traditional bastion of Bradley's support, they sold their case to a West Side growth-control advocacy group, Not Yet New York, on the city's liberal, environmentally conscious West Side, by pointing out that LANCER 1 would be followed by two more facilities there and in the San Fernando Valley. But aside from such newly discovered self-interest, Cannon recalled, "most affluent white areas didn't want to hear us," viewing the matter in purely parochial terms. Nonetheless, with their new friends on the West Side came news-media access that the South Central residents had never previously enjoyed. CCSC also won the backing of an anti-incineration coalition from the San Gabriel Valley, the California Alliance in Defense of Residential Environments (CADRE).[16]

Meanwhile, another member, Omawale Fowles, who had prepared CCSC's appeal of the permit, urged the group to find out whether the city had ever prepared a health-risk assessment. When it turned out that no such document existed, Fowles urged the group to lobby for one and insist that it be subjected to peer review by other scien-

tists. The city quickly agreed to a 15-member peer-review committee, even though CCSC would have settled for seven. The committee was soon bombarded with new citizen concerns. What were the
short-term health impacts, the long-term impacts, the synergistic
(i.e., resulting from chemical interactions) and compound impacts?
Would the model used reflect not a hypothetical "average" person,
as many do, but the actual health of the people in the affected community? This latter point was critical because the area, largely due to
its poverty, was already exhibiting below-normal health statistics and
would be more vulnerable to pollution impacts than a healthier
population. Any realistic assessment had to account for this.

The city also created a LANCER advisory committee of 23
people, including five CCSC leaders. As the number of hearings and
meetings grew, another member, Wilson Smith, became a one-man
canvass team, walking the streets with leaflets and "swelling meetings." The leaders of Concerned Citizens, despite their jobs, spent
most of their 18-hour days on the telephone, on the streets, poring
over documents, or attending meetings in an increasingly testy fight
to stop LANCER.[17]

Help poured in from other directions. Louis Armand, a CCSC
member who was then a UCLA graduate student, suggested that they
propose a study of the project to the university's graduate program in
urban planning, which had a history of researching planning issues
involving social equity. The group presented a proposal to Gottlieb,
who happened to be Armand's professor. Gottlieb agreed to the idea,
and his students eventually produced a report so devastating to the
LANCER program[18] that it won a national award from the American Planning Association.[19]

But 1986 was also an election year, and Bradley was the Democratic challenger to Governor George Deukmejian, who was seeking
reelection. The South Central activists saw an Achilles' heel for Bradley and dogged the mayor's campaign. They staged marches in the
neighborhood protesting LANCER. Bradley had committed himself
to spending a day in the community. Through their newsroom contacts, the opponents learned the mayor's campaign itinerary. One
morning, a reporter called to ask if they knew that Bradley would be
spending an entire day in South Central. Sheila Cannon arrived at a

local McDonald's with friends wearing gas masks, causing Bradley to flee to the men's room, asking the restaurant manager to remove her. The manager refused on the grounds that he could not ask a customer to leave. Later in the afternoon, the mayor was at Brotherhood Crusade. At the press conference, Charlotte Bullock managed to ask what made Bradley any better than the governor, who was being challenged to clean up the state's water. Bradley exploded, Cannon and Bullock recalled, replying, "I will not mention LANCER!" Bullock had not even specifically referred to the project.

At a church later in the day, another member, Assata Umoja, who pretended not to be part of Concerned Citizens, asked a generic question about community decision-making power concerning facility siting. Again, Bradley declared that he would not discuss LANCER. When church members took umbrage at Umoja's question for upsetting Bradley, she simply responded by calling the mayor an "Uncle Tom." Meanwhile, another CCSC member was blowing up balloons containing index cards telling area residents to call Mayor Bradley and ask about LANCER. The balloons had just enough helium to float at arm's reach so that people could grab them. According to Bullock, "[The mayor's] phone was lit up that day."

As the group learned to play electoral hardball, a new strategy emerged. The real votes affecting the fate of LANCER were on the city council, and elections for even-numbered districts would take place in June 1987. Bullock decided to look into the campaign contributions council members might be getting from LANCER vendors, such as the Ogden Martin Corporation, one of the bidders for the first LANCER construction project. When the *Los Angeles Times* investigated, it found that money from potential vendors was flooding into campaign coffers for both the mayor and his city-council supporters. Leading the parade was Smith Barney, which hoped to earn money the old-fashioned way through the lucrative bond-underwriting contract. It had given Bradley $60,000 and council members another $11,800. Running a distant second was E.F. Hutton, which also wanted people to listen, supplying $18,350 to the mayor and $11,300 to council members.[20] The campaign even attracted a political heavyweight from New York City, former sanitation commissioner Norman Steisel, who co-founded the California Waste-to-Energy Council to lobby for the LANCER program. Steisel, who already in 1982 had been named president of the National Resource Recovery Association, a pro-incineration wing of the U.S. Conference of Mayors, later extended his revolving-door career by returning to public office as New York's first deputy mayor, under David Dinkins. His appointment prompted cries of betrayal from environmentalists who had supported Dinkins for mayor in 1989 because of his promise to oppose incinerators.[21]

Other revelations continued to pound nails into LANCER's coffin. The city, CCSC revealed, would need to waive its South Africa divestiture policy if Ogden Martin were to build the facility. Although the company had terminated its ties with that country in November 1986, city law required a 12-month waiting period after divestiture before a company doing business in South Africa could resume doing business with the city. The Los Angeles County Medical Association and a UCLA panel attacked the findings of a University of California-Berkeley consultant, hired by the city, who minimized the health risks from LANCER.

By June 6, the issue became a costly one for the council members involved. Council president Pat Russell lost to the more environmentally oriented Ruth Galanter, while another LANCER supporter also succumbed to the growing voter discontent over the city's garbage policy. The city's most marginal citizens had sparked a voter uprising that would permanently alter the politics of garbage in Los Angeles. By June 17, the mayor, with Gilbert Lindsay at his side, announced that the project was dead.[22]

But it was not too late for the opponents to have one last round of fun. Again, a reporter called to tell the group about Bradley's intentions. When the group arrived at the press conference where Bradley was to concede the defeat of LANCER, the Sierra Club and Citizens for a Better Environment, two groups that Cannon very specifically does not recall as offering help "until the very last minute," appeared on the mayor's press release, taking credit for the environmental victory. Cannon recalled that "the reporter asked me where these people were when we were fighting it. They had not participated." Greenpeace, she said, was the "only major group at the forefront. The others didn't deem it an environmental issue." Deeming the mayor's failure to mention Concerned Citizens an accidental over-sight, Cannon and her friends simply decided to include themselves in the mayor's photo opportunity, in which he joined environmen-talists who were taking credit for what her group had wrought.

Nonetheless, the late arrivals to the party achieved a payoff that has eluded CCSC and its allies. The local Environmental Federa-tion, composed of the mainstream groups, got itself listed for free on a payroll-deduction plan at city hall. The federation had neglected to invite the participation of the South Central group. When chal-lenged by Charlotte Bullock, a spokesman for the federation indi-cated that, for a $5,000 up-front fee, the group would be welcome to apply. Concerned Citizens has never had that much money lying around.

While the activists of South Central were launching their campaign against the LANCER incinerator, another poverty-stricken neigh-borhood was organizing to express its grievances. The issue in East Los Angeles, however, at first did not appear to portend the emer-gence of another environmental group. The target of the residents' wrath was a new prison proposed in 1985 by Governor Deukmejian. To the largely Hispanic population of East L.A., about three miles from downtown, the planned prison symbolized everything that was wrong with the state's attitude toward minority neighborhoods. More than two-thirds of the adults in East L.A. had never finished high school, compared to 30 percent countywide,[23] yet schools were poorly funded and the war on drugs was at best a bad joke. Nonetheless, the state could find tens of millions of dollars to incarcerate those who failed to become productive adults. The mothers of East L.A. quickly mobilized to express their anger over the governor's plan.

Juana Gutierrez thinks that her neighborhood group's later emer-gence as a force on toxic-waste issues was a perfectly natural evolu-tion. Like many other minority environmentalists, she hastens to point out that in minority and working-class neighborhoods the "en-vironment" is the entire physical and social setting in which people live every day, not just something "out there," away from home and family and workplace. Drugs, violence, and poverty are as much a part of the inner-city environment, in this view, as the lead paint on tenement walls and the toxic fumes from nearby factories. All these factors contribute to a general degradation of the quality of life that breeds the despair that feeds crime rates and overcrowded prisons. In ways that the conservative Republican governor was never able to perceive, his proposed prison came to symbolize the environmental crisis in East L.A.

It was a local priest, Father Moretta from Resurrection Church, who suggested the name "Mothers of East L.A." (MELA) to the group that organized against the prison.[24] Eventually, the group claimed fathers and children in its membership, but initially, according to Gutierrez, about 100 mothers came together. Most were probably much like Gutierrez, a grandmother who lives in a modest home along a narrow street whose pavement shows signs of age and decay. Despite the neighborhood's poverty, the home's well-maintained interior shows clear signs of Mexican working-class pride. The reputation of East L.A. notwithstanding, Deukmejian had offended many families' pride in a neighborhood they still felt was worth defending.

Assemblywoman Gloria Molina, who represented the area, had alerted her constituents to Deukmejian's plan. In May 1985, having sounded out her district, she brought petitions to Sacramento bearing 1,500 signatures of prison opponents. Meanwhile, activists like Gutierrez, who co-founded Mothers of East L.A., began working to inform the community about the plan through the most universally available network in the neighborhood—people streaming out of Sunday morning Mass. The group used these crowds to advertise for weekly Monday marches against the prison. Fathers like Juana's husband, Ricardo, laughed off their apparent exclusion from the group's name. Often, they made the signs and organized the march, claiming to be the mothers' "chauffeurs." Taking partial credit for the success of the marches, Ricardo added, "One reason the TV was there all the time was because the signs were always different." For two years, the group marched every Monday at noon, steadily expanding until the last march drew nearly 3,500 mothers, fathers, and children. In the face of this growing and relentless uprising over his proposal, Deukmejian eventually flew the white flag of surrender. The prison plan was dropped.

In many neighborhoods, that might also have spelled the end of

the group. But East Los Angeles faced so many other threats that the triumphant mothers hardly had time to celebrate before two state legislators from the area, Assemblywoman Lucille Roybal-Allard and Senator Art Torres, brought news of a planned hazardous-waste incinerator in the neighboring municipality of Vernon (pop. 100).[25] Having already lent its support to the fight against LANCER in South Central, MELA decided to challenge California Thermal Treatment Service (CTTS), the owner of the proposed facility. The firm had already obtained city permits from Vernon, another of those peculiar California municipalities incorporated almost entirely for the purpose of accommodating industrial development. MELA members were considerably more distressed that the company had also managed to get permits from the California Health Department and the U.S. EPA.

Within the year, MELA had mobilized to file a lawsuit against CTTS and every agency that had granted the firm a permit. Joel Reynolds, a Natural Resources Defense Council lawyer who had represented Concerned Citizens of South Central against LANCER, took the case. But the Mothers already had their own powerful modus operandi. While they sued, they marched. This time, they drew support from a wide range of Hispanic and environmental activists across the state, some of whom had faced similar challenges in their own communities. In November 1988, nearly 1,000 of them came to a rally outside Resurrection Parish Church, driving from places like Casmalia, in northern California, which had suffered from a leaking toxic-waste dump.[26] Or from Richmond, in the Bay Area, which had also contended with toxic-waste issues. Or Kettleman City, in the Central Valley, where People for Clean Air and Water later filed a suit against Chemical Waste Management, a subsidiary of Waste Management, Inc., of Oak Brook, Illinois, the nation's largest waste hauler, alleging a nationwide pattern of racial discrimination in its choice of sites for hazardous-waste incinerators. Kettleman City is 95-percent Hispanic.

From the church, the protesters marched more than a mile to the gates of the $29 million project, which was slated to burn 125,000 pounds of toxic waste per day. As they marched down the cordoned boulevard, they chanted, *"El pueblo parará el incinerador!"* (The people will stop the incinerator.) Aurora Castillo, who co-founded MELA with Gutierrez, denounced politicians' and corporations' assumptions that the people would not fight. The crowd responded: *"Pueblo que lucha triunfa!"* (People who fight win.)[27]

As the marches continued, the lawsuit dragged on. By the summer of 1991, after more than four years of jousting with MELA, CTTS threw in the towel, proclaiming its proposed project "too expensive." The city of Vernon also gave up. MELA had scored another major victory.

Once again, the organization had little time to celebrate, for more battles had emerged even during the Vernon fight. On the East Los Angeles side of Slauson Avenue, across the street from Vernon, another firm, Chemclean, had proposed to treat toxic waste. This proposal had disturbed Ricardo Gutierrez even more than the Vernon facility because of its location. Not only were there "people living close by, but they had to pass through the largest food-producing area in the city of L.A. They had to turn past Farmer Jones, Oscar Mayer, and Happy Hot Dog." Chemclean's assurances that it would only use the local roads at night failed to assuage his fears because most of the food producers worked around the clock. Chemclean offered to move away from Slauson to the site of the defeated Vernon incinerator. That, too, failed to satisfy MELA, which threatened to launch another lawsuit. Finally, Chemclean also pulled out. Throughout the incinerator battles, MELA also fended off a planned oil pipeline through the neighborhood, forcing a consortium of oil companies to settle for replacing an existing line. A neighborhood that had once been known as a political patsy—many of its residents are "illegals," and even many Hispanics who are citizens do not regularly vote—was acquiring an unrivaled reputation for toughness in protecting its environmentally degraded turf.

But MELA could not win everything. Its most frustrating battle centered on California's peskiest insect—the Mediterranean fruit fly, popularly known as the "Medfly." At the behest of its powerful agricultural interests, the state had responded to Medfly infestations with widespread spraying of malathion, a pesticide that has engendered extensive controversy because of its potential impacts on the human nervous system, skin, and eyesight. East L.A. is clearly not an agricultural area, but state agricultural officials feared that unchecked urban infestations could spread to the state's rich, irrigated orchards in the San Joaquin Valley and elsewhere. Residents were warned to take their animals indoors and to cover their cars during the spraying, as well as to cover ponds and swimming pools to keep the poison out of the water. To no avail, MELA protested the entire plan, noting that, while pets might be indoors, homeless people would be sleeping outside. Homeless people, in fact, joined the protests against the spraying. MELA found medical experts to make its case, including Dr. Jorge R. Mancillas of the UCLA Medical Center, who told residents that the Medfly had actually been a relatively constant presence in the Los Angeles area for some 40 years, coming and going over time but incapable of crossing the mountains to infect the precious San Joaquin Valley. Mancillas noted that the flies would find their way into traps located almost anywhere in the city simply because the insects had never been eradicated. But MELA's experts did not convince state officials. The spraying proceeded.

Garbage and hazardous-waste incinerators aside, nothing symbolizes the deterioration of Los Angeles's air quality more than the ubiquitous and indispensable automobile. Ever since a consortium led by General Motors bought and dismantled the city's private commuter train systems in the 1930s, cars have been the undisputed leading source of regional air pollution. Southern California's climate, with warm ocean breezes bucking up against inland mountains, virtually constitutes a natural laboratory for smog formation. Photochemical smog generation of the type prevalent in Los Angeles requires volatile organics, oxides of nitrogen, and particulate matter reacting with the energy provided by the sun. To many outsiders, it would seem that the car is so deeply rooted in the California culture as to make the air-quality problem insoluble.

In the early 1980s, workers at the General Motors plant in Van Nuys, a Los Angeles neighborhood north of Santa Monica, mounted a protest of the company's plans to shut the plant. The Labor/Community Strategy Center, based in Van Nuys, materialized from that struggle. The campaign focused on building a multiracial coalition to back the workers in a way that would transform a labor-management dispute into a community issue that focused on jobs and corporate responsibility. It was, however, anything but an environmental campaign. Most environmentalists, says founder Eric Mann, probably would have viewed the death of an auto plant as essentially a good thing.[28] After all, Southern California's central environmental problem was that it had been choking in smog because automobiles had so long dominated the region's transportation system.

That the Labor/Community Strategy Center has subsequently taken the driver's seat in constructing the regional environmental agenda says a great deal not only about what has happened to environmentalism in Los Angeles in the last decade, but also about the shortcomings in the organizing perspectives of mainstream environmental organizations, whose failure to build a multiracial movement that included blue-collar workers allowed the Center to fill a massive void. Southern California today, after all, is one massive mosaic of ethnic groups and racial minorities—all of them seeking their rightful place in California's political sun.

Mann has understood the racial component of Southern California politics for a long time. He articulates a vision of progressive politics that is explicitly critical of many in the progressive movement who fail to conceptualize labor and minority issues as interwoven parts of the same agenda. One need only examine the makeup of many Los Angeles labor unions to see that, in many cases, neither the collars nor the skin colors are white. During the peak of the Van Nuys campaign, from 1982 to 1986, Mann noted, the movement behind the workers was predominantly Latino and African-American. Some labor leaders like Mark Masaoka, a unit chairman for United Auto Workers Local 645, were part of L.A.'s growing Asian community. It was not hard to find support among these ethnic communities. The hardest part, Mann noted, was simply "getting workers to believe they had the power to keep the plant open." Many, he recalled, were conditioned "to justify General Motors' right to close the plant."

Mann's first serious encounter with the questions about the auto industry posed by the environmental movement came at a Greens conference in 1985, where he was asked to conduct a workshop about the Van Nuys campaign. He recalled confronting "young white kids" who wanted to know, "What's so good about keeping the Van Nuys plant open? It will poison the air and the people." Offended by their attack on his defense of workers' jobs, Mann counterattacked. "I said, 'Half the people in L.A. are building military stuff, and we're not killing anybody.' They were very arrogant."

Two people siding with Mann that day were Tony Mazzocchi, vice president of the international Oil, Chemical, and Atomic Workers Union, and Richard Grossman, a longtime writer and activist on labor issues. They, too, emphasized the arrogance of the young Greens in so casually dismissing the importance of the Van Nuys issue for workers. But they also had something to tell Mann. After the workshop, they pulled him aside. Mazzocchi told Mann that he had not the faintest idea what he was talking about concerning the environment.

"Tony said, 'I have to talk to our members about the dangers of oil and nuclear technology, and you have to talk to your people about transportation and the environment,'" Mann recalled. For Mann, the advice was an eye-opener, mostly because it came from fellow labor leaders, people whom he deeply respected. Mazzocchi, in particular, had been leading the labor movement far beyond its traditional concerns to deal with far-reaching questions of reducing the impact of toxic chemicals in industrial production and equipping workers for a transition to less environmentally damaging modes of production— even when that meant their current jobs might disappear. Grossman had written about the environmental hazards of the modern workplace. Mann began to integrate their ideas with those of Barry Commoner, who has also addressed questions of job preservation and creation in an environmentally sustainable economy. The environment began to assume a more central place in Mann's thinking about the components of a progressive economic strategy.

As it happened, Mann's conversion to a focus on the environment coincided with the emergence of the incinerator issues in South Central and East Los Angeles. The strategy center could suddenly take into account an environmental fight that not only *included* people of color, but was actually initiated and led by them. In addition, the group had the benefit of input from Cynthia Hamilton, an African-American professor of political science at California

State University who was directly involved with the South Central LANCER fight. Hamilton was primarily known in progressive circles for her contributions on issues of community economic development, particularly in the African-American community. The environment began to emerge in Mann's mind as a way for working-class people of all colors to address true life-and-death issues that required the resolution of other clearly defined questions of social equity. And, especially in light of the issues posed by the incinerators, no question was more urgent in Los Angeles than that of air quality.

Air pollution, in fact, soon proved to be an issue of amazing political synergy. Air, far more than any other component of the environment, moves around, often quickly. Airborne pollutants literally travel around the globe, and most certainly within a day can be dispersed throughout a large metropolitan region, even one that suffers air inversions as often as Southern California, whose mountains trap breezes blown inland from the coast. Thus, opponents of projects initially deemed harmful to minority neighborhoods could easily make the case that at least *some* of the dioxins, benzene, or particulate matter from an undesirable incinerator or refinery would contaminate the air of more affluent downwind areas.

At the same time, dispersion is dilution, so the greatest impact occurs in the area immediately downwind. Low-income neighborhoods adjacent to industrial areas, such as South Central and East L.A., tend to be downwind of concentrations of freeway interchanges. Industrial pollutants also tend to be concentrated around sources located in low-income barrios and ghettos. East Los Angeles is crowded with small metal-plating and auto-body repair shops that produce a variety of air toxins, including chromium, lead, and nickel in the former case, and toluene, methyl chloride, and xylene in the latter.[29] The cumulative health impact is sobering. Exposure to toluene, for example, induces such symptoms as fatigue, dizziness, skin irritations, headaches, and insomnia. In the longer term, kidney damage can result. (Toluene is a key ingredient in the model glue that has produced nerve malfunctions and death in some teenagers who have intentionally sniffed it for a dangerous form of "high.")[30] Xylene has similar chemical and toxicological properties.

In many cases, these were marginal businesses that could not afford adequate pollution-control equipment and employed minimally skilled workers with little understanding of the health impacts of the materials they were using. The pattern dated back to the 1920s, exacerbated by a frequent city-council tendency to forego the buffer zoning practiced in other residential areas because the area was largely populated by immigrants. A UCLA student study commissioned by MELA described the result as a "minefield of environmental hazards."[31]

This situation allowed the development of an enlightened multiracial, multiclass movement around the issue of air pollution. As Mann states, the issue affects everyone, but not equally. In fact, for some pollutants, such as ozone, the impact is arguably more severe in some middle-class areas like Glendora and Pasadena than in downtown Los Angeles. Only in more expensive coastal areas are ozone levels remotely comparable to those in almost any other metropolitan area in the United States.[32] But the solutions to the problems created by traffic congestion opened the way for a free-ranging discussion of alternative modes of transportation, including the equity issues involved in investment in mass transit. Another factor had made the air-pollution issue politically feasible for community organizing: The state had conveniently created a system of regional air-quality policymaking authority that gave environmental organizers a target for effecting change. Once the issue was clear, the Strategy Center necessarily focused its energies on the South Coast Air Quality Management District.

The evolution of the South Coast Air Quality Management District (AQMD) reflects California's growing awareness that air pollution is a regional and not a purely local issue. It also reveals Southern Californians' acceptance of the notion that, as much as they often decry the influence of government on their lives, they had created a critical situation that forced them to make a fundamental choice. Because the air pollution created by government neglect of environmental policy touched their daily lives and their health in such a radical fashion, the area's residents came to accept what they hoped was the more benign though extensive influence of a single regional regulatory agency to combat it. The AQMD, driven by state and federal air-quality standards as well as local demands for change, is reaching deeply into everyday life in the South Coast in a highly visible effort to clean the air.

The AQMD began as a city pollution-control agency in Los Angeles in the 1940s and evolved into a county agency in the following decade. In 1976, the state's Lewis Air Quality Act consolidated the county air-pollution-control districts for Los Angeles, Orange, and Riverside counties and the urbanized, nondesert portion of San Bernardino County, empowering the new agency to enact regulations with the force of state law to implement air-quality plans throughout the area. As of 1992, the AQMD employed a staff of nearly 1,200, including technicians, community-outreach specialists, air-quality scientists, and engineers. In its quest for talent during the 1980s, the agency also attracted Dr. James M. Lents, whose previous accomplishment had been a dramatic improvement in the air quality of urban Denver while chief of its pollution-control efforts.

If Lents was looking for a challenge, the South Coast air basin was surely it. Because of the combination of climate, geography, and rapidly growing population, no other place in the United States faces the same set of challenges in cleaning up its air. The AQMD's 13,350-square-mile region contains more than 12 million residents, whose number is projected to grow to more than 17 million by 2010.[33] While the population has grown, state and federal ambient air-quality standards have been tightened. Together these two forces have acted like a vise to clamp down on pollution privileges once taken for granted, affecting everything from auto emission standards to future land-use patterns to the right merely to grill meat in an open-pit barbecue. Virtually no real or potential source of air pollution, however small, seems untouched by regulations, yet the region's air quality, while improving, remains the nation's worst. The South Coast is facing enormous costs for environmental regulation and praying for enormous health and economic benefits to materialize from the whole labyrinthine process.

The origin of the problem is as simple as it is intractable. Even the original inhabitants, the Shoshone Indians, observed that the South Coast created a natural air-pollution stew when they called it the

"Valley of Smoke" because the mountains trapped the emissions from their campfires.[34] Los Angeles sits at the bottom of a bowl of flatland surrounded by mountains on three sides and the Pacific Ocean to the west. It is the classic scenario for air inversions, where warm ocean breezes are trapped beneath a layer of cold air with no route of escape until a new front pushes it over and above the mountains. To make matters worse, the stagnant air bakes in the hot California desert sun while it waits. The heat provides a perfect chemical laboratory for reactive organic gases, oxides of nitrogen, and particulate matter to react with solar energy to generate photochemical smog, a key component of which is ozone. Combined in turn with the massive emissions of carbon monoxide and particulates from automotive traffic, the result is the famous brown cloud that passes for sky. Of all the nation's major metropolitan areas, only Los Angeles experiences brown-cloud days that surpass federal ozone standards more than 120 times per year. No other city even comes close.

In fact, in 1989, the region exceeded federal standards on four of the six criteria pollutants used in establishing ambient air-quality standards. It met those standards only for lead, a problem virtually eliminated everywhere by the mandated switch to unleaded gasoline, and for sulfur dioxide, a precursor of acid rain. California's reliance on oil, rather than coal, for electric-power generation facilitated meeting the sulfur-dioxide standards. The region violated standards for ozone by more than 150 percent, for carbon monoxide by nearly 100 percent, for particulate matter by 75 percent, and just barely violated the standards for nitrogen dioxide. None of these standards addressed another problem on the minds of both public and politicians: air toxins, the dozens of compounds and toxic elements poured into the air daily from factories, gasoline pumps, trucks, power plants, and oil refineries. In the last few years, federal, state, and AQMD regulations have begun to reflect those concerns as well, and the air-quality bureaucracy has grown again as a result.

At the top of the list of industrial air polluters emitting air toxins, according to 1989 state statistics, was the very same General Motors Van Nuys plant that Mann and his allies had fought to keep open. Its sheer volume of air emissions, totaling more than 4.27 million pounds including methyl chloroform, xylene, and acetone, easily eclipsed runner-up Douglas Aircraft Company in Long Beach, which emitted little more than one-fourth that amount.[35]

Barry Commoner, a biologist well known for his environmental writings and advocacy, in his review of *L.A.'s Lethal Air*, the Labor/Community Strategy Center's manifesto for the fight against air pollution, noted that its slogan might well be, "Think locally, act locally." While there assuredly are global consequences for some environmental problems, Commoner essentially said, the consequences that matter most to residents of East Los Angeles are local. Commoner suggested the slogan as a revision of the popular E.F. Schumacher admonition, "Think globally, act locally." What does that slogan mean, Commoner asked, in East L.A.?[36]

Juana Gutierrez's answer was a direct affront to the very values and priorities of the AQMD. At a meeting called by the AQMD to discuss the district's air-quality management plan and the Latino community, she challenged the traditional planners' ideal of a "jobs-housing balance," in which air pollution from mobile sources would be reduced because people lived in close proximity to their jobs. Her community indeed has such a balance, but the jobs—in furniture factories, metal-plating shops, and auto-body repair shops—produce fumes that sicken the community's children. "We need jobs, but we need our health as well," Gutierrez noted.[37] In short, East L.A.'s short-haul commuters were paying a stiff price for their generous, if unintentional, contribution to reducing the region's overall air pollution.

Moreover, the nature of the jobs that employed most East Angelenos took an additional toll on the health of the workers themselves. Two UCLA planners, Paul Ong and Evelyn Blumenberg, studied the relationship of race and environment and found minority workers in California disproportionately represented in the deadliest and most hazardous jobs. They found that Spanish surnames accounted for 44 percent of the state's registry of lead-poisoning victims.[38] Even for minority small-business owners, many of whom opt for enterprises with low barriers to entry, such as dry cleaning, there are health threats. Dry cleaners, for instance, tend to use large quantities of solvents such as perchloroethylene, a suspected carcinogen that is also listed as a neurotoxin, a substance capable of damaging the nervous system.

The problem with the jobs-housing balance, as pinpointed by Gutierrez, is pervasive in the South Coast. While only about one-third of whites are estimated to live in the areas with the most polluted air, half of all Latinos and 71 percent of all African-Americans do.[39] It is one thing to discuss that balance when the commute is from a middle-class home in Pasadena to a nearby office building housing insurance companies and travel agencies. It is quite another to live in a highly polluted neighborhood and walk to a job where one sprays paint on car bodies all day long. The latter reality is one that regulators and land-use planners have seldom addressed adequately.

An influential oasis of progressive thinking has emerged, however, at the UCLA planning school. The study done by graduate students for CCSC has become one in a growing series. Another group of students, under instructor Stephanie Pincetl, undertook a double study for the Mothers of East L.A. and the Santa Fe Springs City Employees Association. The latter group worked at a city hall directly across the street from the troublesome Powerine oil refinery, where odors and toxic air emissions led the city workers to initiate complaints and seek assistance.

A key point of the MELA study, which the students produced in both English and Spanish, was that small-business owners, such as the auto-body repair and paint shops that dot East L.A. like industrial chicken pox, frequently lack the technical knowledge and the capital to engineer many of the renovations that would prevent or reduce pollution at the source. The problem is especially severe for minority business owners, for throughout the South Coast basin the AQMD can probably count at least 30 native languages other than English among entrepreneurs subject to its rules. If the district's regulations are to have any impact other than forcing such people out of business, the AQMD needs to reach out in ways that cater to their special needs. Realistically, however, the report recognized that some of the most problematic industrial land uses in East L.A. might need simply to be phased out over time.[40]

Two initiatives resulted from pressures generated by these concerns. By the end of September 1991, the AQMD had created an ethnic advisory council to provide input on issues affecting minorities.[41] The following year, the Small Business Office began establishing new outreach programs for reviewing permit needs and pollution-prevention options with small-business owners on an informal basis prior to their permit applications.[42]

The Labor/Community Strategy Center, which also refers to itself as "the Watchdog," has also worked with county employees to counter what it considers class-biased economic solutions to L.A.'s air-quality problem. Conservative economists in recent years have succeeded in mounting a major push to bring market mechanisms into play in addressing environmental problems. Rather than rely purely on technological mandates, the argument goes, society should also—and preferably—employ economic incentives to induce people and industries to behave in more environmentally sound ways. If, for instance, people paid the true cost of automotive transportation, they would be more likely to resort to mass transit as an option. This thinking was certainly behind H. Ross Perot's proposal in the 1992 presidential debates for a 50-cent-per-gallon gasoline tax to finance transportation infrastructure improvements, and it has been instrumental in winning congressional approval for the idea of "marketable" permits in air-pollution credits, wherein companies can "sell" their permit rights to emit a certain volume of air pollution to others. In the latter idea, regulators would gradually ratchet down the overall number of units of pollution allowed, thus driving up the price and making it cheaper for some companies to clean up than to continue polluting. For more conservative environmentalists, the idea seems ingenious. For others, the very idea of being able to buy and sell rights to pollute the air is morally offensive, calling to mind Chief Seattle's famous question about how it could be possible to own the land, any more than one could own the air and the water.

From the perspective of a billionaire like Perot, all the economic tradeoffs between cars, mass transit, and other modes of transportation make perfect sense. So long as one has access to all the alternatives, it is simply a matter of rational behavior.

The problem begins when some of the alternatives are missing.

For poor and working-class people in car-dependent Los Angeles, many of the essential alternatives have been missing for a long time—ever since the General Motors consortium tore up the railroad tracks. Thus, when the Los Angeles County Board of Supervisors decided to "implement" one of the AQMD's pet strategies for increasing carpooling and transit use, county employees rebelled.

The AQMD's Regulation XV requires employers with more than 100 workers to develop plans to increase carpooling and reduce employee auto use. There are many ways to implement such a mandate, including the use of company vans and subsidization of bus passes. The county board, however, simply chose to impose a tax of $70 to $120 per month on employee parking privileges despite the fact that Service Employees International Union (SEIU) Local 660 had negotiated free parking as an employee benefit. Many of those affected were clerical and secretarial workers earning up to $1,500 per month, for whom the new fee was at least as much a form of economic punishment as an incentive to reduce car use. The AQMD, which had initially opposed the county's plan, approved it under pressure from the county before the union had a chance to negotiate the matter.

Union researcher Kimberly Kyle, however, discovered documents that showed that the county actually wanted to incorporate the parking lots into larger land packages for deals with developers who would pay ground rents to build high rises and hotels that would increase car usage four times over, clearly the opposite of the intent of the pollution-reduction goal. Moreover, the AQMD's own policy exempted parking benefits that were part of a collective-bargaining agreement. Nonetheless, the AQMD maintained its support of the county's plan when SEIU and the Strategy Center presented this evidence. Furthermore, Mann noted, AQMD officials said their mandate was to reduce vehicle use regardless of questions of social equity. But Mann did not attribute this response to callousness, noting that one strongly anti-union county supervisor, Mike Antonovich, also served on the AQMD board and regularly attacked the agency as "out of control." The county finally imposed its parking tax in December 1990.

The Watchdog decided it was time to strike back at a more fundamental level, organizing a broad-based coalition behind a social equity amendment to Regulation XV. The AQMD agreed to an informational hearing on March 1, 1991, to review the proposed rule:

> Any employer plans to comply with Regulation XV and to increase average vehicle ridership: 1) Cannot interfere with workers' rights to bargain collectively; 2) Cannot impose undue hardship on workers; and 3) Cannot have racially or gender-based discriminatory impacts.

The Watchdog's supporters on this issue, beyond the SEIU, included other unions, MELA, CCSC, minority and women's groups, the Sierra Club, and a disabilities-rights organization. Before the hearing, they demonstrated in front of AQMD; inside they testified for two hours. The AQMD agreed to a public hearing that fall, and finally, by December 1991, the Watchdog and its allies secured their victory. In the meantime, the county had backed off on the parking charges. The lesson to Mann was obvious: The AQMD was caught in crossfire between powerful corporations and environmentalists or, as Mann put it, between a rock and a soft place, for the latter had too often been no match for the former. The role of the Watchdog, in bringing new and militant constituencies into the environmental arena, was to strengthen the backbone of the counterforce to corporate power. The AQMD, as a regulatory agency, even with some sympathetic staff members, could not be expected to initiate social-equity policies on its own.[43]

The entire debate over county employees' parking privileges also pointed out a larger, more intractable inequity. Using pricing tools to induce changes in commuter behavior is fair only if government provides a workable alternative. Los Angeles's mass-transit system, as presently constituted, cannot in any way pass for a reasonable alternative. By the time the parking-fee fight was over, Mann and his coworkers had done some serious thinking about the Watchdog's priorities. He indicated that the group would be getting its own transportation planner to look into environmentally sound forms of public transportation. The group was working with United Auto Workers (UAW) dissident Jerry Tucker on his New Directions Movement platform for his race for the UAW international presidency, including attempts to persuade auto workers to support the controversial corporate average fuel-efficiency standards.[44]

Mann—and the unionists allied with him—had come a long way in their thinking since the first days of the Van Nuys anti-shutdown campaign. With the issues that still loom on the Southern California environmental scene, a long road ahead still awaits them.

Spurred by the Concerned Citizens of South Central and the defeat of LANCER, the city of Los Angeles has traveled a long way in its thinking about garbage. Recycling is a part of that rethinking, but the name of the new city program for brainstorming solutions to the waste crisis suggests an even more comprehensive approach: Integrated Solid-Waste Management. In fact, the office's name is in part a response to state legislation that requires integrated waste-management planning by municipalities and counties.[45] California, as a whole, has been forced to rethink much of its strategy on waste.

One of the policymakers involved in that reassessment has no explicit environmental background. Lupe Vela is, instead, a Latina who happens to be an industrial-development expert but also has a background as a community activist. It has come to this: Waste is now a resource, and California plans to use it to create jobs and a new tax base. A 1991 law even empowered the state's Integrated Waste Management Board to authorize the creation of a sort of "green" enterprise zone, offering tax incentives for businesses using or producing recycled products to locate in designated areas. Vela's job is as simple as it is challenging—to find the markets for recyclables in order to complete the circle that was started by the decision to recycle as much municipal solid waste as possible, instead of landfilling or incinerating it. Without the markets, as many municipal recycling programs are learning the hard way, the circle is merely a broken arc that stops in the middle of nowhere. Unsalable materials end up in the landfill in spite of the best intentions, and a cynical public begins to question the whole point of the recycling exercise.

In an interview I conducted in January 1992, Vela described her job as a three-pronged attack on waste through policy changes, technical assistance, and cooperative ventures. To examine her task is to peer into the creative future that was salvaged from the scrap heap when CCSC blocked the Bureau of Sanitation's all-too-easy one-stop solution of incineration. Los Angeles, if the program succeeds, will be mining "urban ore," a term coined by David Morris, the founder of the Institute for Self-Reliance in Washington, D.C. By 1990, the city had already achieved a 21-percent overall recycling rate.

Vela was quick to note that "the industrial areas are all located in East L.A." When one talks about designing and integrating waste processing into all communities, she noted, "There's a debate because small-scale facilities must be close to the areas where the waste is generated. Otherwise, with large-scale facilities, because of zoning or the cost of land, you end up going back to minority areas." Large-scale recycling facilities, she said, "are setting up shop in East L.A. without mitigating their impacts." Only after she and Joan Edwards, director of the Office of Integrated Solid-Waste Management (City of Los Angeles), began to discuss these equity impacts did public-works engineers begin to consider mitigation.

Vela has introduced a sensitivity to minority viewpoints that has not always been present in L.A.'s garbage policy. "Everybody wants to do set formats of recycling," she noted. But what works in affluent West L.A. may be a disaster in poverty-stricken East L.A. "Low-income families have always been doing recycling. Maybe each community should design its own recycling program for itself," she suggested. "Many of the new curbside recycling programs are generating lower rates from low-income areas. Why? It takes away from street people trying to earn some money."

The challenge of diversity, if not heeded, could easily overwhelm L.A.'s incipient program in ways that suburbanites might never grasp. According to Vela, the city has more than 200 waste haulers serving the private sector, which generates two-thirds of the waste stream. The other third, collected by the city, simply involves single families or housing stock of up to four units. In other words, the city's direct impact in redirecting its waste is limited.

The leverage for what Vela does, however, is so straightforward that it is a wonder that it is not more obvious to most city officials. The city of Los Angeles, she noted, spends billions of dollars on joint development ventures with major corporations. "You would think the city would be able to use the impact on residents to direct manufacturers to use recycled products in their feedstocks [the raw materials from which products are formed]."

"We have decided to look at every material as a commodity," she stressed. The goal is to connect economic development and recycling, which is as much an attitudinal challenge as an economic one. But Vela's office is afloat in ideas. For instance, large volumes of waste paper are shipped overseas—to become raw material for Asian industries. "L.A. could probably use smaller manufacturers making hand-made paper and smaller feedstock production. You need a smaller amount of capital investment than paper mills, and you can direct that feedstock away from overseas." The office was developing two legal tools, she said. One required 50-percent public participation in Department of Public Works contracts, thus bringing in nonprofits and for-profit enterprises. The other was a procurement ordinance then under development. "The city of Los Angeles handles several hundred million dollars of foreign contracts," she noted. "We'll give more preference to those who use the maximum amount of recycled feedstock."[46]

Another example of the city's new creativity is to be found at Los Angeles International Airport. The city found that 14 percent of the airport's waste consisted of airplane pillowcases, used once and thrown away. After finding a mill to accept the paper pillowcases if they were all the same color, Ellyn Hae, the chief consultant for the airport waste study, convinced the airlines to standardize their pillowcases nationwide, reducing their own disposal costs. Hae also found that wooden pallets for forklift delivery were generally not reused. Unbroken used pallets became fair game for anyone who wanted to use them, and broken pallets went into a special recycling area along with broken cargo boxes.[47]

The strength of the staff constructed by Edwards and Vela is simple: They are nontraditional recyclers, with expertise in industries like garment manufacturing and printing. They understand the problems they will face, the retooling required, and how to combine different resources. They can sit down with industry representatives to discuss specific plans for each manufacturing sector. It is the next stage of recycling: beyond rhetoric, beyond a pure focus on environmental virtue. Now that inner-city residents have kept the residues of the city's garbage out of their polluted air, it is time to improve their economic environment. It is time to use recycling to bring home the jobs. CCSC and MELA still have an agenda before them.

Minority interest in environmental issues has spread through the rest
of California like a wildfire. South Central and East L.A. are no
longer alone, no longer unique portents of a movement still in the
making. African-Americans in the Bay Area have been vocal on
environmental issues. In Richmond, north of Berkeley, for instance,
the West County Toxics Coalition (WCTC) has been doing battle
with such companies as Chevron over toxic air pollution from its
refinery. Henry Clark, the coalition's director, organized door-to-
door canvassing and media campaigns to win the right to negotiate
with company officials. Those meetings, in turn, produced a phase-
out of the use of chlorine, a community early-warning system for accidents, and the relocation of some ammonia storage tanks.[48] It was
not the first time Chevron had been the target of community pressure. A lawsuit by the Bay Area office of Citizens for a Better Environment had induced the company to pursue pollution-prevention
techniques in ferreting out the source of chromium and nickel discharges into Bay waters, where they are toxic to aquatic organisms
even in tiny amounts. Chevron had contributed 35 percent of all
chromium and half of all nickel from major point sources into the
northern part of the Bay in 1986. The company found it was able to
reduce various heavy metal discharges by between 67 and 97 percent.[49]

With some valuable organizing lessons in hand, WCTC pushed
for the use in the Richmond area of a state law allowing a 10-percent
tax on hazardous-waste handling facilities. The community, according to Clark, was the first to get a commitment from a proposed facility for a 10-percent contribution for community services and
health-care concerns. But Clark noted that "money is not going to
eliminate health risk concerns. But if you have to have a facility, it
helps to get the mitigation in place. No one ethnic group should
have to bear the burden of having it in their community. There has
to be some fair-share principle."

At least, he noted, Contra Costa County is responding to his
group. Clark was appointed to the county's Hazardous Materials
Commission, where his group could help to draft the county's state-
mandated hazardous-waste management plan. Along with other

linkages for Clark and coalition members to various county and municipal planning bodies, the coalition has proven once more that a well-organized blue-collar and minority voice can penetrate the environmental decision-making process.[50]

Perhaps the most forgotten and powerless of California's residents are its largely Hispanic farmworkers. For them, air pollution has taken on a particularly nasty dimension. Pesticides attack from the air, often while they are still in the fields, often while children, who are especially vulnerable, accompany their parents outdoors. The malathion spraying in East L.A. was a minor dose of what threatens many farmworkers' health on a daily basis.

For many, there is no alternative but to suffer. Even legal farmworkers often lack the skills to seek other employment, and starvation is not a viable alternative to the backbreaking poverty of picking grapes, lettuce, and apples. For illegal aliens, the alternatives are even grimmer—arrest and deportation. To complain is to buy a one-way ticket home.

In Kettleman City, however, Chemical Waste Management (CWM) encountered history-making resistance from local Mexican-American farmers and farmworkers. Joe and Esperanza Maya organized their neighbors to resist a proposed hazardous-waste incinerator in the 95-percent Hispanic community in the San Joaquin Valley. CWM had already acquired a dump site at the same rural location in 1979. The Mayas farm 2,700 acres of lettuce, tomatoes, and melons and feared the pollution would damage crops. What particularly incensed them was the failure of Kings County officials to publish public-hearing notices in Spanish despite the community's overwhelming ethnic makeup and the fact that many residents speak no English. Moreover, the county board itself refused to hold hearings before its vote, which took place just four days before two new supervisors were to take office.[51] In January 1991, the company won the board's approval (3-to-1) to build California's first commercial toxic-waste incinerator, which would burn an estimated 100,000 tons yearly and generate $25 million in revenue.

In May, the Mayas and their organization, People for Clean Air and Water, filed suits in state and federal courts against the company, the state, and Kings County, charging a violation of their civil rights. The suit, filed by Luke Cole, a lawyer for California Rural Legal Assistance, alleged a pattern of discrimination by CWM in siting facilities. It noted that its three other incinerators were located in communities with large minority populations: Chicago's South Side, 72 percent African-American and 11 percent Hispanic; Sauget, Illinois, 73 percent African-American; and Port Arthur, Texas, 40 percent African-American and six percent Hispanic. CWM replied that it had never sited these facilities, but acquired them as existing operations of smaller firms.[52] It also defended the proposed site's geological merits. Dennis Eymil, counsel for Kings County, sought to deride the suit, calling it "make-work" and noting that the charge of environmental racism was "a very, very sexy thing right now." The suit was "the first where they're going to try to make something of it."[53]

Early the following year, however, the Mayas and their neighbors made history. Judge Jeffrey Gunther of Sacramento Superior Court ruled that the county's failure to translate notices and testimony into Spanish indeed had violated the plaintiffs' civil rights and invalidated the county's approval of the plant. The decision did not touch upon the broader issue of discriminatory siting practices, which awaited decision in a related suit in a federal court in Fresno.[54]

That legal victory was more likely to delay than to stop Chem Waste's plans. The firm simply geared up to repeat the process. Nonetheless, it tied up the project while Chem Waste appealed, and the federal case was held in abeyance until the state appeals court ruled, something that was not expected until late 1993.[55] For the national environmental movement of people of color, however, it was a stirring wake-up call. A little town in rural California had become the mouse that roared. Minority environmental rights had at last been vindicated in a U.S. court of law.

CLEVELAND
Accidents Will Happen

"I have my theories about what draws hazardous waste to Ohio," said Rick Sahli, as we talked in his office at the Ohio Environmental Council in Columbus. "I think it's the wheeler-dealers."[1]

Sahli is personally familiar with Ohio's wheeler-dealers. In January 1991, when Republican Governor George Voinovich succeeded Democratic Governor Richard Celeste, Sahli took a 50-percent pay cut to become the council's executive director. His experience—first as an assistant attorney general for the state and then as the Ohio Environmental Protection Agency's deputy director for legal affairs and legislative policy—made it feasible for him to pursue a more lucrative position, but Sahli's priorities lay elsewhere. "I couldn't sit back and watch Ohio's environment go down the drain," he said bluntly.

He may also have had a score to settle with some of the wheeler-dealers. The powerful speaker of Ohio's House of Representatives, Democrat Vern Riffe, took a dislike to him when he was the Ohio EPA's chief lobbyist. Riffe manages to control many of his colleagues by sharing some of the $1 million he raises at $400-per-person fundraisers. His semiannual galas at Columbus's Aladdin Shrine Temple are attended by virtually every Ohio industrial lobbyist who matters. With some pointed hints about the damage the agency's budget might suffer if Sahli stayed on, Riffe forced Ohio EPA Director Richard L. Shank to remove him from his duties at the capitol, even though lobbying was specifically part of his job description.[2]

Riffe is so powerful (and so well entrenched with fellow power bro-
kers), Sahli noted, that former four-term Republican governor James
Rhodes endorsed his unsuccessful bid for the governorship in 1990
despite the fact that Riffe is a Democrat.

Rhodes, as governor, had coined the motto, "Profit is not a dirty
word in Ohio." Given the tone that his long reign set for state politics, many environmentalists concluded that Rhodes meant that environmental concerns would never be allowed to stand in the way of
profit. Celeste, who took office in 1983, improved the situation. Certainly, according to Sahli, enforcement was stronger. In the free-
wheeling days of the Rhodes administration, the Ohio EPA referred
on average just two cases per year to the attorney general's office for
legal action. Under Celeste, this number grew to 20 per week. But
Celeste's own mixed record helped set the stage for Ohio's epic
battles over hazardous waste.

For far more than a century, Ohio has been the nation's foundry. It
remains so today, even in an era of Rust Belt decline. The state has
long been dominated by heavy industry, including steel, chemicals,
and even the remnant of John D. Rockefeller's oil trust, Sohio, which
is now owned by British Petroleum as BP America. In recent years,
the toxic chickens of that industrial heritage have been coming
home to roost. They have laid most of their nests in blue-collar
neighborhoods whose residents never used to see themselves as environmentalists. Those residents, however, made a remarkably rapid
conversion to the cause in the late 1980s, reshaping it in their own
image.

Perhaps it is small wonder. Industry used to dispose of most of its
hazardous waste cheaply and on site—through the air, the water,
and on the ground. Ohio paid a heavy price for that sort of careless
disposal. In 1970, Cleveland suffered national ridicule after the
Cuyahoga River, steeped in unspeakable industrial filth, caught fire
and burned. For generations, smoggy, gray skies hung relentlessly
over mill towns like Youngstown, Akron, and Warren.

With the advent of federal environmental legislation and the creation of the U.S. Environmental Protection Agency in 1970, the
noose began to tighten on the uncontrolled release of toxic sub-

stances into the environment. The noose tightened further on hazardous waste with the tracking requirements of the federal Resource Conservation and Recovery Act (RCRA) of 1976, whose licensing provisions created a sizeable and burgeoning market for treatment, storage, and disposal facilities. That law, for the first time, defined what constituted a hazardous waste, although it took the U.S. EPA until 1980 to issue regulations enumerating the specific chemicals that met the definition and fell under RCRA's requirements.[3]

Ohio's large industrial base made it an attractive location for treatment-facility operators. Eventually, as landfill regulations in eastern states became increasingly stringent, Ohio, with cheaper land, became a magnet for landfills handling waste from New York, New Jersey, and New England. But landfills face serious problems as storage sites for hazardous waste, including potential contamination of underlying groundwater. Incineration gained favor with federal and state regulators as a disposal option. Again, Ohio looked good, and profit was not a dirty word. By 1992, Ohio had acquired almost one-fourth of the nation's hazardous-waste-incineration capacity, with only Texas drawing a larger share.

This chapter and the next tell the story of two ventures, one in Cleveland and one in East Liverpool, that ran the gauntlet of state and federal environmental regulations to build their facilities. (Neither ever agreed to the author's requests for interviews.) In the end, both generated fierce opposition from citizens. The first did so only after generating a track record of carelessness over several years of operation. The second obtained its permits but languished on the back burner for several years. When its owners finally began to build, they ignited a firestorm of controversy that culminated in civil disobedience and congressional investigations. Between them, the facilities dramatize a failure of public policy on what has become Ohio's primary environmental concern. Ohio has reached a crossroads. If the state cannot come to grips with the issue of hazardous waste, the rest of its environmental agenda may never matter.

The casual visitor to Cleveland would never see the building at 7415 Bessemer Avenue. Nothing is left but the shuttered hulk of a facility that, until the fall of 1990, was storing and treating a variety of hazardous wastes. While serving Ohio's numerous heavy industries, the plant also handled wastes from Virginia, Alabama, New Jersey, and other states.

The only major highway near the site is Interstate 77, which begins near downtown Cleveland in the Flats, the home of the city's deteriorating Rust Belt steel mills and chemical plants in the Cuyahoga River Valley. On its way south, I–77 traverses the Appalachians through the center of West Virginia, slices through western North Carolina to Charlotte, and finally terminates outside Columbia, South Carolina. Columbia houses the headquarters of Laidlaw Environmental Services, formerly GSX Chemical Services. GSX bought the treatment facility in 1988 from Alchem-Tron, a local Cleveland outfit. Laidlaw, a Canadian firm, acquired GSX in early 1990, using its new U.S. subsidiary to secure its place as North America's second-largest hazardous-waste hauler, behind Waste Management, Inc. But neither owner could keep the plant out of trouble with Ohio authorities, and Laidlaw ultimately settled a lawsuit by agreeing to close it.

The companies had little reason to expect a major confrontation with the Cleveland plant's neighbors, in spite of their frightening proximity. A public housing project, Garden Valley Estates, lay just a quarter-mile to the north. About 10,000 people lived within a one-mile radius. On their way to the plant, trucks meandered through a series of aging commercial and residential streets on Cleveland's southeast side. Access from I–77 was by way of a special ramp to East 55th Street, a road lined with industrial plants, a few blocks south to Truscon Avenue. One block down Truscon, the trucks turned south onto East 61st Street, again turning east within a block onto Roland Avenue. Two blocks later, another turn south onto East 65th Street, and a block later east on Bessemer. Finally, a half-mile down Bessemer, trucks reached the plant. The entire twisting path beyond East 55th Street consisted of two-lane city streets.

Along many of the side streets lining that path are small frame bungalows, some with torn screen doors and worn steps, others looking as pristine as their proud owners can keep them. Even few Clevelanders ever see or visit this lusterless area, tucked away behind steel mills, railroad tracks, and, to the west, the winding but navigable Cuyahoga. But until recently, like Chicago's Back of the Yards, its unionized industrial jobs gave hope and a solid paycheck to generations of working-class immigrants and their descendants. Many have moved up in the world and left for the suburbs. But those who have stayed behind are fiercely territorial. Slogans like "Don't Mess with Broadway" are not meant to be playful. They portend a fight for those who tread on the neighborhood's pugnacious pride.

It is not hard to notice the largely Slavic character of the Broadway area. East 71st Street, south of Broadway, bears such storefront signs as "Slavic Village Medical Center," "Slavic Village Association," "Orzech's Tavern," "Polish Inn," and "Alliance of Poles of America Auditorium." Broadway residents have worked in the mills since at least the turn of the century and are not easily alarmed by industrial pollution and toxic waste. But their territoriality is intensely personal, oriented to their families, children, and homes. Deep beneath a studied indifference to industrial hazards lies a smoldering suspicion that the neighborhood has unnecessarily been dumped on by its longtime employers, who include LTV Steel, Republic Steel, and, to the southwest in the industrial suburb of Newburgh Heights, a string of chemical plants that serve the needs of Cleveland's steel and auto makers. The neighborhood's air quality is indisputably the worst in the metropolitan area. Residents could tolerate this unredressed indignity as long as no one rubbed it in their faces or insulted their intelligence. In time, the owners of the Bessemer Avenue facility succeeded in doing exactly that. When the area's citizens mobilized to fight back, GSX and Laidlaw paid the price.

Regulatory trouble builds slowly at hazardous-waste facilities. After opening in 1981, Alchem-Tron's Bessemer Avenue plant operated for seven years before attracting serious attention from the neighborhood. During that time, it racked up a series of violations of its state hazardous-waste permit conditions, year after year, not only on Bessemer Avenue but at a second facility on Train Avenue, which it closed in 1988. The company's repeated failure to correct some of the violations resulted in legal action that led to a 1985 consent decree. The company then managed to violate the consent decree as well as its permit requirements, leading the Ohio EPA director to ask the state attorney general to seek contempt citations. Finally, in 1990, the state simply sued in a state trial court to shut down the entire operation.

Why did all this go on so long? Neither state nor federal environmental agencies can afford round-the-clock regulatory vigilance at every treatment plant subject to their jurisdiction. They have neither the budget nor the inspection staff to sustain such monitoring. The budgetary commitment varies widely among the states, and Ohio, with its many industrial plants, can hardly afford to inspect every permitted facility as often as it would like. Even with facilities as dangerous as those handling hazardous wastes, on-site inspections may be as infrequent as once a year. Only the largest operations, because of their potential for catastrophe as well as their ability to support substantial permit fees, attract full-time, on-site Ohio EPA inspectors. Almost always, such an arrangement stems from a special permit condition under which the firm agrees to pay for the cost of the inspector's presence at the plant.

With a plant of modest size and just a few dozen employees, Alchem-Tron's Bessemer location was not one of those sites. In the beginning, it attracted only routine annual review by an EPA field inspector.

It was also an advantageous time for some entrepreneurs to enter the hazardous-waste treatment business. Federal regulations were just beginning to force industrial-waste generators to account more carefully for the disposal of their chemical wastes, creating a growing market for firms like Alchem-Tron. The firm's letterhead slogan, "Pollution Control Through Chemistry," testified to the owners' awareness of these new opportunities. At the same time, they could count on loose state oversight from the Rhodes administration, never known for an aggressive regulatory stance on environmental issues. Finally, the local scene had to be encouraging for new businesses. Just a year before Alchem-Tron sought its permit, Rhodes's lieutenant governor, George Voinovich, had returned home to run for mayor of Cleveland. In the fall of 1979, he handily defeated one-term Mayor Dennis Kucinich, who had regularly chastised the city's financial leaders, taken the city into default on its bonds as he fought to retain a municipal electric system, and barely survived a recall vote. After the city's brief flirtation with populist turmoil under a young and egotistical Democratic mayor, Voinovich seemed to offer the city's business leaders a sort of long-term Pax Republicana. The voters, apparently relieved by the lack of bickering that followed, rewarded Voinovich with a full decade in office before he moved to the governor's mansion in 1990.

Alchem-Tron's three-year installation-and-operation permit from the Ohio Hazardous Waste Facility Board (HWFB) was also a routine matter. Issued in October 1981, it allowed the company to store and treat hazardous waste. No incineration was involved. The treatment activities were to include sludge mixing, fixation, and solidification; the storage would be in tanks and containers. The permit specifically did not include ignitable chemicals.[4]

The board, however, was at that time a new entity in state government, strangely constructed and still finding its mission and establishing its own mode of operation. Its legal responsibility is to approve the siting and operating permits for all hazardous-waste facilities in the state. Composed of five members from designated state agencies, it is an adjudicatory body that is chaired, by law, by the director of the Ohio EPA. Sahli, who chaired the board from June 1988 to January 1991 as EPA Director Shank's designated surrogate, notes that the board's legal structure places the chairman in an awkward position, for it is his own staff that evaluates a company's application. That was Shank's reason for appointing Sahli, his deputy director for legal affairs and legislative policy, to replace him.[5] Shank wanted to be free to advocate before the board, but advocacy for the chief of a board sitting in judgment on permit applications would have posed an obvious conflict of interest. In fact, the agency's legal counsel had advised Shank that discussion with his own staff about the status of a pending application would constitute an illegal *ex parte* communication, the same sort of taboo that applies to judges meeting privately with parties to a case they are hearing.[6] Once Shank had designated Sahli, his deputy then had to observe the legal strictures while Shank gained a freer hand. Shank is the only Ohio EPA director who has chosen to untie his own hands in this way.

The board is an odd regulatory duck among state permitting agencies. In the federal system and in most states, the environmental agency issues the permits as an administrative action after determining that the application satisfies the relevant agency requirements and policies. Adjudication takes place only later, if the permit is challenged or a denial is appealed. In the Ohio system, however, the permit has, in effect, been adjudicated from the outset. It is unquestionably a more cumbersome procedure, one that, according to Sahli, "environmentalists love and the U.S. EPA and industry hate."[7]

Once the board has fashioned a permit, with all the attendant conditions it chooses to impose, it is up to Ohio EPA to inspect the facility and enforce the permit conditions. At the time, this was limited to enforcing state hazardous-waste laws. The U.S. EPA handles federal hazardous-waste law, mostly through the provisions of RCRA, unless it has delegated such authority to the state. It did not delegate RCRA authority to Ohio until 1990. Consequently, Alchem-Tron also acquired a federal permit from the U.S. EPA's Region V office in Chicago.

In the summer of 1983, Ohio EPA inspectors initiated a long series of citations against the firm for violations of state laws and permit conditions at Bessemer Avenue. In late August, an inspection revealed violations of a dozen state regulations. The problems involved manifests, waste-analysis plans, accident preparedness, deficiencies in personnel training, recordkeeping, waste piles, and inadequacies in the plant's financial assurance for closure of the facility and in its liability coverage. Closure plans are designed to ensure that, in the event the facility is shuttered, the company will remain financially responsible for the site.

These citations, referred to the attorney general for action, followed a May 13 letter in which Ohio EPA Director Robert H. Maynard warned Alchem-Tron President Inderjit S. Soni of possible legal proceedings concerning an odor release caused by the treatment of sludge which, Ohio EPA inspector Deborah Berg found, contained ignitable substances that the company had been accepting for six months but was not authorized to handle. That violation came to light when the Cleveland Fire Department and Division of Air Pollution Control responded to an odor complaint.

The air division cited Alchem-Tron over its failure to control volatile gases and cover the area in which it dried paint sludges by allowing those substances to evaporate. It won a court decree requiring such coverage but agreed to let the firm control its emissions by installing a sludge dryer system with an afterburner incinerator.[8] The materials would essentially pass through an oven that would dry them out prior to their being burned. Gases would pass through a scrubber to remove pollution before being vented out a 75-foot stack. That system, however, required a modification of Alchem-Tron's RCRA permit from the U.S. EPA.

By December, Berg returned to inspect the facility for corrections of its August violations. She cited the company for numerous additional violations. The following March, this fast-accumulating track record was again referred to the attorney general's office, whose workload of problems to resolve only grew with September 1984 inspections at both Bessemer and Train avenues that resulted in even more violations, among them unlawful waste-storage practices, incorrect waste evaluations, and more problems with personnel training, as well as with contingency plans, labeling of waste containers, and security. A pair of inspections at each facility in July 1985 added to the list. The attorney general's pending and growing action against the company in the Cuyahoga County Court of Common Pleas finally led to an October 9, 1985, consent decree that required numerous corrective efforts by Alchem-Tron to achieve compliance and assessed a $144,000 penalty.[9]

The consent decree failed to reverse Alchem-Tron's pattern of noncompliance. Inspections over the next two years continued to turn up additional violations, not only of state regulations but of the consent decree itself, leading eventually to contempt actions against the company. In addition, the company at some undetermined date installed and began to use a cyanide destruction tank for which it had no permits. Only later did it seek permission from Ohio EPA to treat hazardous wastes containing cyanide.

By the time GSX Chemical Services, a South Carolina firm, acquired Alchem-Tron in February 1988, its new facility had already become an object of heightened suspicion at Ohio EPA's Northeast District Office in Twinsburg, a suburb of nearby Akron. As the violations grew, Mike Savage, manager of the agency's surveillance and enforcement section, said, "We began to question whether these people were in the right business." Explaining that all hazardous-waste facilities are inherently dangerous, Savage noted that "a compliant operator gives you a sense of security." But Ohio EPA inspectors ceased to view Alchem-Tron in this light. Instead, he said, "Our level of comfort eroded."[10]

All that remained was for newly awakened activists to raise the plant's profile in Columbus and at Cleveland City Hall as well. GSX, which retained the existing plant management, soon found itself circling its wagons as the neighborhood attacked.

On April 29, 1988, two months after GSX Chemical Services, Inc., bought 100 percent of Alchem-Tron's stock, a U.S. EPA hearing took place at the Cleveland Public Library concerning GSX's request for a permit modification to include the spray dryer that the Cleveland Division of Air Pollution Control had agreed would improve the company's sludge-drying operations. Few people attended, and only two spoke for local environmental groups: Alan Kuper for the Sierra Club, and Nancy Martt for the Northern Ohio Lung Association. Peter Butol, president of Kosack Consultants, an environmental-management firm, testified on behalf of GSX, as did Anthony DePillo, manager of environmental safety and health care for GSX Chemical Services of Ohio, the GSX subsidiary set up to run the Bessemer Avenue facility. The following exchange took place after the initial presentations:

> Mr. Kuper: First I want to say that Mr. DePillo has been very helpful to us in discussing this whole operation. And I think that I would like to make sure that when the community generally is confronted by these kinds of decisions to raise questions, somebody's got to do it, and we feel that as an environmental organization, we should do it . . . although obviously, it should be EPA that should also consider these questions and answer them. This really isn't—certainly is not an adversary relationship.
>
> Mr. DePillo: No, sir, not at all.[11]

Neither Kuper nor Martt lived in the neighborhood. As the transcript suggests, their concern was rather casual, almost apologetic. It

was one of the last public forums in which GSX officials would receive such friendly treatment. In June, GSX received its federal permit. It had but one obstacle: a state siting permit for the incinerator
from the Ohio HWFB.

Few people attended the HWFB siting hearing in November 1988,
either. Robert Castro, who owned a hardware store around the corner from the GSX plant, heard about it through the wife of a customer and neighboring businessman, who had learned of it from
reading a legal notice in the newspaper. He visited the plant manager, Thomas Smith, who handed him a copy of the firm's 98-page
siting proposal. He took it home and read it, and, he said, "Bells and
whistles went off. I read of 100 million tons being treated, etc."[12]
   Word spread as others learned belatedly about the HWFB hearing. Anger built over how something so dangerous nearly could have
been approved without neighborhood input, although it is not apparent that the company ever disguised the nature of its operations.
But Castro was a member of the board of directors of University
Settlement, a community-service organization, and took the siting
report to its director, Mary Sanders. Sharon Fields, Sanders's administrative assistant, became involved after the owner of Aluminum
Coatings, whose property abutted the GSX lot, persuaded her to read
his copy of the siting report. She complained vocally one day to her
Avon lady, who put her in touch with Cynthia D'Agostino, who
became a valuable housewife-researcher. Tony Hobson, an organizer
for Citizens to Bring Broadway Back (CBBB), a neighborhood group,
took the lead in developing an action agenda and holding the group
to it. Marge Grevatt, executive director of the Center for Cooperative Action, a low-income neighborhood assistance group on
Cleveland's West Side, also learned of the GSX application and offered help to the organizers. She prevailed on the Legal Aid Society's
Joseph Meissner to attend a meeting at University Settlement in late
1988 that pulled together a dozen community activists to discuss
strategy. Those present divided the tasks: community outreach, legal
research, checking the history of the facility, and finding pressure
points. Meissner reluctantly agreed to file a lawsuit on behalf of the
Neighborhood Environmental Coalition, a long-dormant entity con-

sisting of two churches and seven environmental and community groups that had won an air-pollution case against Republic Steel in the late 1970s.

The group quickly found that, because of the courtesy of Michael Shapiro, the HWFB's acting executive director, they still had time to appeal the siting decision. "He could have said we had our public hearing" in November, Castro recalled. "But he said if we can find enough interested people in the next 30 days, he'd hold another hearing." The group petitioned for another hearing and organized an informational meeting for the community in late January 1989. Fields cranked out mailings to the University Settlement's lists of neighborhood residents. She even visited Garden Valley Estates, a predominantly African-American housing project just north of GSX, winning support of project residents, she said, largely by demonstrating that she cared enough to show up at a meeting in the projects at night.[13]

Meanwhile, five council members, led by the Broadway-area council member, Edward Rybka, introduced a resolution asking the city health director to object to GSX's proposed state permit. It also asked the city's law director to file legal action against the permit. The city was already busy hiring a consultant to evaluate the facility.[14]

GSX officials still assumed that a friendly and cooperative attitude would win over suspicious neighbors. Smith, in particular, remained open to the area's residents, providing tours of the plant to relieve their fears. For the most part, the strategy was unproductive. Castro and his allies became convinced that the facility, and particularly a hazardous-waste incinerator, simply did not belong in a densely populated neighborhood.

Moreover, one young activist couple that had joined the opposition, Robert ("Rob") Lee and Katherine ("Katie") Chaney, had begun to pick apart the company's siting application. Rob worked as a paralegal for the major downtown law firm of Baker, Hostetler and Patterson. The pair found holes, particularly concerning the plant's proximity to its neighbors. In 1984, the Ohio General Assembly had passed a law requiring any hazardous-waste facilities not already licensed to be located at least 2,000 feet from any residence or school, unless the facility owners could show good cause why a lesser distance would still be safe. The GSX application stated that the closest residence was 0.45 miles, or more than 2,300 feet, away.[15] Fields, for one, knew better. She lived little more than a block away.[16]

The misleading siting information alone generated a tidal wave of mistrust toward GSX, though other strange developments throughout the year continued to fuel the neighborhood's rumor mill and its rage. With the kind of timing only a community organizer could pray for, the California attorney general on January 19 filed charges against GSX for conspiracy to eliminate competition, in part through a bid-rigging scheme.[17] But local occurrences also built suspicion. Fields says she was once called to a midnight meeting with the Broadway area's Ward 12 council member, Edward Rybka. A contractor, after demanding anonymity from those present, provided them with copies of specifications that showed that the eight-inch concrete driveway base atop polyurethane that GSX had described in its application had less than eight inches of concrete and no polyurethane. The purpose of those specifications was to prevent seepage of toxic chemical leaks into the underlying soil.

Even stranger, however, was the hot day in July when a man wearing a ski mask showed up at Fields's office. After asking for a pen and paper, he wrote a note: "GSX incinerator PLAN: SUN FREE FREEZE-DRIED TOXIC/NUCLEAR WASTE TREATMENT IF NECESSARY THEN—Councilman Rybka . . . FROM R2D2 to SHARON." Fields guessed that the man was most likely a GSX employee who did not want to be identified but wanted somehow to warn that the company had plans to burn nuclear waste.[18] There is, however, no record of their having done so.

The protest gathered momentum so quickly that numerous local politicians hastened to jump on board. The bandwagon included state senators Charles Butts and Michael White, city-council members Rybka and Preston Terry (whose ward included Garden Valley), and eventually Mayor Voinovich. The political support was visibly biracial, representing both ethnic whites to the south of the plant and African-Americans to the north. White and Terry are African-American; Butts and Rybka are white. But some political leaders soon found they had visible tracks to cover. Both White and Rybka had written letters to the U.S. EPA in support of GSX's permit application.[19] Although there was nothing sinister about that—they were the types of letters public officials often write in support of new businesses locating in their districts—the mood of the neighborhood was such that both men needed to make their newfound opposition even more visible to compensate for the suspicions that their earlier support had generated.

White invited Fields to meet with him prior to the January meeting. She had never met him before, though he became increasingly important to her efforts later in the year. (Mayor Voinovich chose not to run for reelection. White ran and won.) In the meeting, White gave her a half-hour to make her case. Fields said she did it in ten minutes. As she recalled, it was an emotionally intense ten minutes:

> I told him about growing up on 49th Street, which is right down here where the steel mills were operating, when there were no regulations. On a hot day like this, you'd be walking down the street, you'd feel rain drops and it'd be black. You couldn't hang your clothes out, the houses were ruined. And not only were we getting that shit, Route 21, I lived right by Route 21, so we were getting all the fumes from the cars also. I told him about how there was two respiratory intensive care units in Cleveland and, oddly enough, one's at St. Alexis, the other's at Metro Hospital, and we're in between them. Does that tell you something about our neighborhood?
>
> I've seen a lot of people with asthma, lot of people with lung diseases, emphysema, people die of cancer that never smoked a cigarette in their life, throat cancer. And you can't tell me, you can never convince me it wasn't caused from the steel mills or all the environmental problems that we had in this neighborhood. And I says for one thing, I've lived here my whole life, and I'm tired of us being the dumping ground.
>
> And we're fed up. We're not taking no more. I don't trust this company; they lied to get their permit. I says, I did some investigation, they're not a reputable company, and they do not have my safety in mind. And until they convince me that they care about my life, then they're not going to burn that incinerator in my neighborhood. If I have to go over there and take it apart brick by brick, they're not going to do it.[20]

White promised to investigate and, if he had been wrong about the company, to hold a press conference to say so. Four days later, White invited Fields to his press conference. He reversed course and backed her efforts to shut down GSX.

With politicians behind them and the press trailing them, the Broadway crew was still not totally prepared for what happened when January 25 arrived. University Settlement overflowed with 500 people—the elderly, the young, working men and women, business-men in suits, and nuns. Castro raised fears about a projected increase in truck traffic and potential accidents. Mayor Voinovich pledged that the city would "not become the dumping ground for hazardous waste." GSX facility director Thomas Smith tried to quiet fears that the firm would transport or burn radioactive waste, dioxins, or Agent Orange, the defoliant used in Vietnam, even noting that he himself was a Vietnam veteran.

All to no avail. Mary Sanders pounded away about the danger to homebound citizens in the event of an accident. A string of council members and state legislators attacked the company at length until citizens demanded time to speak for themselves—which they did.[21]

"It was a media event, but we didn't understand that at the time," said Castro. It was also a political success. Shapiro scheduled a new hazardous-waste board hearing for April 13.[22]

New allies swelled the size of the coalition opposing GSX. Tawny Ratner, a liberal member of the wealthy Ratner family of Shaker Heights, owners of the Forest City Lumber Company and other long-time Cleveland enterprises, "became consumed by the issue and or-ganized around it." A middle-aged mother concerned about the future of her children's environment, she led a suburban group called Families Insisting on a Toxic-free Environment (FITE). Living just east of Cleveland and the GSX plant, they became the "downwind" objectors. Never seeking the limelight, which Ratner always believed belonged to the Broadway residents, her group instead applied the kinds of quiet influence more familiar to liberal suburban profession-als. As Ratner recalled, "We assigned committees to write letters. We met with the governor. We met with whoever we needed to meet with."[23] Among the volunteers was a young Shaker Heights lawyer named Eric Fingerhut, who would examine the legal requirements for affecting policy in state agencies. His work helped him build a powerful rapport with suburban environmentalists on Cleveland's east side. A year later, he was elected the district's new state senator when Lee Fisher, the incumbent, won a statewide race to become attorney general.

Among the Broadway activists, an unlikely synergy emerged. Groups that tended to be jealously territorial—Citizens to Bring Broadway Back, University Settlement, and Southeast Clevelanders Together—learned to work with each other and divide responsibilities within a cause whose emotional resonance seemed to overwhelm and transcend them all. Personality differences that ordinarily would have separated Katie and Rob Chaney, Fields, and Castro instead allowed them to complement each other for a time. The Chaneys haunted the Ohio EPA's Northeast District office in nearby Twinsburg as well as the Columbus headquarters, copying documents and searching for evidence of corporate environmental malfeasance. Alone, they would never have generated the media attention or inspired the crowds that moved the issue along. Fields supplied the media and her neighbors with the personable, longtime neighborhood resident whose voice they would respect. Her rapport with her neighbors was best capsulized by the *Plain Dealer*'s Tom Breckenridge, who described this "brash, blocky woman" as the "hard-edged, soft-hearted embodiment of the Broadway neighborhood."[24] Castro, ever a media hound but also a technical mind, filled in the gaps in her descriptions of the company's sins and wrongdoings. Amid it all, Hobson kept the group's organizing mission on track. The Chaneys and D'Agostino would soon grow to hate and distrust Castro, whose newsmongering instincts clashed with their own reticence about speaking to reporters. But the flood of enthusiasm that carried the movement along managed to focus their attention on GSX and away from personal differences.

Fearing a public-relations debacle, GSX officials threatened to boycott the HWFB hearing, charging the board with violating its own rules by even holding the hearing. The original public-comment hearing had expired on December 19, but Shapiro was stretching it in deference to public opinion. Smith, the facility manager, felt that he and his company were being wronged.

"Let them boycott," Ratner told reporters. "Let them also fold up their tent and go away."[25]

When the meeting began at 7:00 p.m. at Our Lady of Lourdes Church, somewhere between 600 and 1,000 people filled the gymnasium. The GSX officials, looking grim, mostly stood at the back of the hall, listening to an avalanche of verbal punishment. They had circulated a statement beforehand by plant manager Smith to the effect that GSX would accept questions only in writing, to be answered afterward in writing. Smith objected to the board's failure to bring technical experts who could verify GSX's answers to questions from the audience.

The meeting got a raucous start with Castro imitating the heroine of *Norma Rae*, the movie about a southern textile-union organizer, by merely rotating silently in the front of the hall with a simple sign: "Stop GSX; No Toxic Waste Incinerator in Cleveland." The idea came from Fields, and it was brilliant. An ecstatic audience applauded nonstop for ten minutes.[26]

The Catholic church's pastor, the Reverend Frank Masek, played to the crowd with an irreverent imitation of the new president: "Read my lips: No new toxins." As if on cue, a laundry list of politicians paraded before the microphone to attack GSX.

"GSX should be shut down totally," Rybka declared. "Why does the inner city always get dumped on?"

Mayor Voinovich told the board, chaired by Sahli, that GSX was violating the law, having installed the proposed incinerator in violation of city building and zoning codes and within 2,000 feet of homes, schools, and hospitals.

State Senator Vermel Whalen charged that the incinerator was "something that was sneaked into our community." She called it a "toxic time bomb."

Finally, Ralph Temple, the GSX operations manager, felt he had had enough. He counterattacked from the rear of the hall, noting that he had taken Rybka and White on tours of the plant. "What are we covering up?" Temple demanded.

But the residents and the suburban environmentalists got their turn, and the attack never abated. A Cleveland Heights epidemiologist had collected signatures from medical professionals opposing the facility. An eighth-grade student read a statement from her class objecting to its presence in the neighborhood. Susan Hyatt, the daughter of Ohio's Senator Howard M. Metzenbaum, called the meeting "democracy in action" and read a statement from her father charging that approving the permit would undercut efforts to find more environmentally sound methods of disposing of hazardous waste.[27]

On and on the denunciations continued, with Rob Chaney finally wrapping up the testimony at about 3:00 a.m., in a droning presentation that attempted to cover any points left untouched by eight hours of previous speakers.[28] At that point, only the Chaneys could have determined what those remaining points could possibly be.

Four days later, on April 17, local residents repeated the scene when the Ohio EPA held its own hearing to receive public comment on the GSX application. Although the matter had to be resolved by the HWFB, the EPA staff reviews pending applications and can provide information and advice to the board.

In the days following those tumultuous meetings, the Cleveland news media discovered its voice on a major community issue. The *Plain Dealer*, the Cleveland area's sole daily newspaper, chided both GSX and the public for trying to "have it both ways," accusing the company of double talk and the public of wanting industrial plants without industrial waste. Noting the increasingly adamant tone of the political rhetoric surrounding the GSX issue, the newspaper reminded public officials that "[n]ot meeting with GSX officials is a mistake because both sides may become too entrenched to work out any solution."[29]

That was not a problem for Rybka. In his next column in the *Neighborhood News*, a weekly for the Broadway area and nearby suburbs, he exulted that "this community turned out for a public meeting like never before." The city council, he noted, had unanimously approved his resolution requesting that all GSX permits be denied.[30]

Throughout the spring and summer of 1989, GSX officials found their company increasingly on the defensive. The county hired a law firm to pursue legal action against the company.[31] In June, under intense pressure from citizen activists, Ohio EPA director Shank reversed a January staff decision that added 83 chemicals to the list officially approved for treatment by GSX, 26 of which were to be permitted for burning in the new incinerator. The Ohio EPA staff had the power to approve minor amendments to the company's permit. Shank's action automatically referred the matter to the HWFB by reclassifying the change as a substantive amendment to the permit. Shank referred to specific and recent citations against the company for violating state hazardous-waste laws. The company, following a surprise inspection, had agreed to pay $90,800 while challenging $800,000 in other fines.[32]

Meanwhile, the opponents, particularly the Chaneys and D'Agostino, were probing the company's performance elsewhere. They found a variety of critics in the south, particularly in South Carolina and Florida. A GSX incinerator in Roebuck, South Carolina, had encountered regulatory trouble with that state's Department of Health and Environmental Control, following complaints from neighbors about burning eyes, sore throats, odors, and contaminated groundwater. Its Pinewood, South Carolina, landfill also attracted concern, expressed in part by five members of Citizens Asking for a Safe Environment who were arrested for blocking access to the site. They were all acquitted after arguing that they were preventing a greater harm to society, the first time a "necessity" defense had been used successfully in South Carolina.[33] As if that publicity were not bad enough, the landfill also fell under the effect of a state legislative ban on importation of chemical waste, which took effect March 1. The site had been accepting 135,000 tons of hazardous wastes yearly. Although the U.S. Supreme Court was likely to overrule such a ban as a violation of the U.S. Constitution's interstate-commerce clause, as it has done before, Tucker Askew, an aide to Governor Carroll Campbell, announced, "We want to send a signal, to put pressure on these [other] states to get their own houses in order." South Carolina, at the time, was importing some 120,000 tons of hazardous waste per year.[34]

The increased attention failed to deter GSX from undermining its own credibility. In July, a fire broke out among containers of hazardous waste at the Bessemer Avenue plant. The materials were marked only with the word "nasty," accompanied by a skull and crossbones. More than 50 different unlabeled chemicals had spent 16 months in storage without being analyzed, a clear violation of hazardous-waste regulations. Sixteen people were given medical attention, including three Cleveland firefighters and two emergency medical personnel. Four GSX employees were admitted to the hospital for smoke inhalation. Those exposed to the smoke disrobed and were hosed down in the parking lot.[35] Within days, the Ohio EPA won a court order suspending operations at Bessemer Avenue for at least a week, until Common Pleas Judge Lillian J. Greene could hold a full hearing on prolonging the shutdown.[36] By July 27, however, after contentious hearings that did not particularly convince residents that the state's attorneys were well prepared, Greene lifted her injunction and allowed GSX to reopen. Greene still needed to decide what size fines she would impose. The Ohio EPA was asking for retroactive fines of $10,000 per day from the time GSX acquired the facility. Castro, ever ready with a quick quote, was unimpressed: "It's pocket change to them, just the cost of doing business." During the shutdown, according to Smith, his plant had suffered a loss of $700,000.[37]

Unfortunately for Smith, the plant's new difficulties had drawn the governor to Cleveland to meet with residents. Whether he had actually planned to do so of his own accord is unclear. But Fields cornered him during a suburban gathering, with the media in tow, to find out when and where he would talk to the Broadway residents. Celeste, who knew Fields, conceded easily and scheduled the meeting for August 2.[38]

Celeste was greeted at University Settlement with dead flowers. He wasted no time revealing that he had decided to support a permanent closure of the facility. The 200 residents attending, sensing an explosion of their newfound political clout, erupted in enthusiastic applause. Celeste, who had ridden a local tour vehicle, "Lolly the Trolley," through the truck route, and had seen the homes and housing project within short distances of the plant, expressed a firsthand appreciation of the neighborhood's safety predicament. He seconded forceful complaints presented at the meeting by Fields and Castro.[39]

Meanwhile, GSX also attracted federal regulatory scrutiny. A few days after the Celeste visit, the U.S. EPA's Region V office in Chicago proposed a $120,000 fine and a withdrawal of the plant's RCRA permit. William Muno, the region's hazardous-waste enforcement chief, noted the agency's inability to prevent GSX from operating waste piles where it was also treating hazardous materials, an issue that had already caused the agency to file suit in 1986. That case was still pending, despite the fact that the agency had approved a new RCRA operating permit in 1988.[40] By mid-August, Ohio Attorney General Anthony J. Celebrezze, Jr., added to the firm's growing legal bills by filing additional contempt charges for its alleged violations of the earlier consent decree. Investigations following the July fire, Celebrezze charged, had revealed storage of hazardous waste in an unauthorized area, unlabeled drums, inaccurate records, and failure to separate stored incompatible wastes.[41]

Then the city's Zoning Board of Appeals piled on, ruling in a 3-to-2 vote that GSX had violated zoning regulations by never obtaining a certificate of occupancy for its sludge-treatment building. It also ruled that incineration was not among the permitted uses in the zone where the plant was located. Instead of building it while waiting for a state permit, the company should have applied for a variance. GSX lawyers argued that the city itself had required the incinerator, but to no avail. They also submitted a list of other companies that operated incinerators in general-industry zones, but board chairman Richard Jablonski would not allow testimony on this point. A former air-pollution-control commissioner simply replied that the city's earlier agreement did not relieve the company of the responsibility to submit its incinerator plans to meet building and zoning regulations.[42]

The company soon challenged the ruling in the county Common Pleas Court. GSX did trigger one result that probably differed from its real intent. The city launched an investigation of other industrial incinerators that might be violating city zoning regulations. GSX facility manager Smith had questioned whether there were "two sets of rules, one for GSX and one for everyone else?" All of the companies on the GSX list, including a medical waste burner just 500 feet away from the GSX plant, had valid city air-pollution permits.[43]

Encouraged by this continuing onslaught of legal, political, and regulatory activity, the anti-GSX coalition turned on the pressure. They chose October 8, the fifth anniversary of the expiration of the facility's original three-year HWFB permit, for a demonstration in front of the plant on Bessemer Avenue. The plant had been operating on interim status ever since, now awaiting the board's decision following its extended hearings on the GSX application. Rybka was there. Members of CBBB, of the Greater Cleveland Environmental Coalition, and of a new group organized by the Chaneys, People Out to Win Environmental Rights (POWER), carried picket signs.[44] By now, the Chaneys had broken with CBBB president Castro. They had also begun to make a crusade of pointing out what they regarded as deficiencies in the GSX permits.[45]

Three weeks later, CBBB and Southeast Clevelanders Together returned with a treat for the television cameras—a Halloween protest. While elderly men and women carried more sedate placards, younger "toxic-waste survivors" sported gas masks and, in some cases, grotesque facial paint. In little more than ten months, the environmental coalition had learned how to become almost professionally telegenic. As 1990 dawned, GSX was no longer merely fighting public opinion in its immediate backyard. It was fighting a negative image that was being effectively disseminated throughout the entire metropolitan area.

The new year also found the company still pursuing its elusive permit from the HWFB. The coalition of opponents kept every violation and every conceivable issue affecting GSX relentlessly before the news media. Local news shows, such as WEWS-TV's "Morning Exchange," invited Fields, Castro, and others onto the show to elaborate on the reasons for their opposition to GSX. One question that must have puzzled many Cleveland viewers was how a blue-collar neighborhood with so many residents working in steel mills and chemical plants found itself on the environmental warpath with a chemical waste-treatment facility. Host Fred Griffith, in fact, asked Fields about the GSX employees who would lose their jobs if the facility were shut down. Fields replied that "the people they hire at GSX are minimum wage, untrained, uneducated. They prey on the poor—$4 an hour."[46]

Inexplicably, given the intense scrutiny the company already faced, GSX suffered additional accidents that brought it into the public eye. On March 12, an overpressurized tank popped open and sprayed solvent on a nearby foundry building and on cars in its parking lot about 50 yards away. Apparently, an employee had been pumping used solvent from a 55-gallon drum into a tank that contained incompatible materials.[47] The incident also manifested a continuing capacity on Fields's part to show up on the scene when accidents occurred, often before police and fire officials arrived. This uncanny skill surely nettled GSX officials, who may have been unaware that her father operated an auto-body repair shop across the street.[48]

It was time for another white knight. GSX was acquired by Laidlaw Inc., of Burlington, Ontario, a Canadian railroad firm that had moved into the waste-hauling business. Laidlaw also acquired Tricil, a Canadian waste firm, and combined the two subsidiaries into Laidlaw Environmental Services, with 45 plants in the two countries. Increasingly, the Bessemer Avenue facility, doing about $20 million in annual business, was a small potato on a large corporate farm. The overall combination made Laidlaw the largest hazardous-waste management operation in North America. Implied in the merger was the promise that the parent company's resources would guarantee an upgrade in the besieged Cleveland facility.[49]

That promise never came true. By July, the state attorney general was already filing 14 new contempt-of-court charges against Laidlaw for violations of the 1985 consent decree.[50] The same month, Shank finally fulfilled Celeste's threat by revoking Laidlaw's state operating permit, though Laidlaw was allowed to remain open while appealing the action before an Ohio EPA appeals board.[51] The next month, Mayor White announced that the city had filed its own suit seeking a court order to shut the plant down as a health nuisance. A few days before, the plant had been evacuated after an acid spill, and just two days later some nitric-acid waste emitted a "poisonous orange vapor," causing another evacuation.[52] For Laidlaw, it seemed, bad news just could not happen fast enough.

In a contentious courtroom, again before Judge Greene, Laidlaw attorney Louis E. Tosi, of the Toledo law firm of Fuller and Henry, argued strenuously that the company had things under control. A spokesman for Laidlaw reassured the court that the company was planning to improve its training and equipment. According to Marge Grevatt, Tosi, who later told me that the neighborhood opponents were "not a factor in the case from a lawyer's point of view," exuded precisely the kind of arrogance that motivated the residents to push their fight to the limits.[53] Tosi, in fact, would question whether the organizations opposing Laidlaw "were really representative of the neighborhood."[54] But Tosi did not win his argument that day. For the second time in a year, Judge Greene ordered a temporary shutdown of the facility.

A week later, a city housing court also found the company guilty of failure to report its March 12 accident to the city's air-pollution-control division. Laidlaw unsuccessfully argued that when the lid had popped, it was functioning as it should have, preventing a rupture of the tank itself. The jury still felt an accident was an accident, and should have been reported.[55]

By now, the regulatory apparatus was in such full swing that the role of the organizers had largely become one of kibitzing the federal, state, county, and city lawyers' efforts to shut down Laidlaw. Within the Ohio EPA, the negotiations between the agency and Laidlaw attorneys, particularly Tosi, grew strained.[56] The shutdown was increasingly expensive, especially when Greene, in early September, extended it to October 11. At that time, state lawyers planned to ask for a permanent shutdown until regulatory agencies decided the fate of the company's permits.[57]

It became obvious that the plant's closing was merely a matter of time. The Neighborhood Environmental Coalition (NEC), sensing imminent victory, turned down concessions the company offered in order to settle the organization's lawsuit. Finally proffering too little too late—or perhaps hoping to divide the opposition—Laidlaw offered to set up an advisory committee and close three of its treatment operations. NEC stood firm, refusing to accept the deal and citing the company's compliance record as its primary reason for not wanting a settlement. In fact, Reverend Timothy Crouch, a co-chair of NEC, noted that the state had already shut down one of the three treatment operations, the one for solidification of liquid wastes, the previous spring. NEC's only interest was in a schedule for closure.[58]

As October 1990 dragged on, it became a rough month for Laidlaw's attorneys and plant executives. Environmentalists staged a conference on October 13 that began with a mock funeral at the plant's gates. The meeting attracted South Carolina activist Marilyn Ayers, who had fought the Pinewood landfill as president of Citizens Asking for a Safe Environment and had become director of the Palmetto Alliance, a statewide environmental network. Her speech, a highlight of the program, detailed the role of Bill Stillwell, who had issued the landfill's permit while employed by the South Carolina Department of Health and Environmental Control. Three days later, she told her audience, he was hired by SCA Services, the landfill's original owner; he remained with Laidlaw as president of its hazardous-waste operations after it acquired SCA.[59]

A political scandal was also brewing in South Carolina. It erupted three months later, when a federal grand jury indicted state House Speaker Pro Tem Jack Rogers on charges of taking more than $23,000 from lobbyists, including $13,500 from a GSX representative between 1988 and 1990. During that period, the legislature had been considering hazardous-waste measures that included the possible closure of a GSX landfill.

Meanwhile, the company was being chewed up in court. Cleveland Fire Department officials said employees had been uncooperative and appeared untrained. Laidlaw employees testified about various accidents, followed by the Ohio EPA personnel who had investigated them.[60] Finally, on October 23, almost anticlimactically and for reasons none of the environmentalists proclaimed to understand, Laidlaw's representatives signed a consent decree in which they agreed to shut down the Bessemer Avenue facility and pay civil penalties of $450,000.[61] From that point forward, the only activity at the site would be remedial cleanup and closure.

Few things better exemplified the differences in style among the Laidlaw opponents than their response to the news of the settlement. The Chaneys speculated that the consent decree may have resulted from something Laidlaw attorneys saw in their files on the company. Four days earlier, Laidlaw attorneys had visited the Chaney household to examine those files under a discovery procedure.[62] Sharon

Fields bemoaned the loss of jobs for those working at Laidlaw and visited the plant, hugging plant manager Michael Baker when he came down the front steps. She then entered the plant to address the plant employees, promising to help them find jobs through University Settlement. Robert Castro met with the EPA to ask that the fines be split among the neighborhood groups, a request that Fields fought, arguing that University Settlement would rather see the money used to help the dislocated employees.[63] Before long, Citizens to Bring Broadway Back was in financial trouble. Castro, who had closed his hardware store because the GSX fight became too time-consuming, moved on to become a professional community organizer.[64] FITE, having lost its most dramatic cause, shrank, but continued to choose smaller issues that would keep its smaller core of activists occupied.[65]

Marge Grevatt found it fascinating that Laidlaw's backing of the troubled plant did not outlast the citizen coalition that hounded it. "It was always an unstable, fragile coalition," she observed later. "The wonder of it all is that it came together just long enough to achieve its objective. And then it fell apart."[66]

Election day followed the consent judgment by less than two weeks, and many of the politicians involved in the Laidlaw/GSX struggle also moved on. Former State Senator Lee Fisher, who represented the district in which FITE operated, succeeded Celebrezze as attorney general, while Eric Fingerhut, the volunteer FITE attorney, won Fisher's seat in the Ohio Senate. State Senator Michael White, of course, had become mayor a year earlier. Mayor George Voinovich, whose brother was in the hazardous-waste business, ran for governor, handily defeating Attorney General Celebrezze, who, in Rick Sahli's view, ran an inept campaign that let Voinovich look like the better environmentalist, even though Celebrezze had a respectable track record on the issue. Voinovich then raised eyebrows among environmentalists by naming Grant Wilkinson as the Ohio EPA's general counsel. Wilkinson had been a protege of Louis Tosi.

Vern Riffe, who had ousted Sahli from his lobbying position on behalf of the Ohio EPA, remained, as ever, the Speaker of the Ohio House. But with a new administration, Sahli had to move on. The

Ohio Environmental Council was becoming more overtly political after years of avoiding the legislative trenches, and its board chose Sahli as its new executive director. Pleasantly surprised that such a high former state official would take the job, it was not long before the people from East Liverpool came calling.[67]

EAST LIVERPOOL

Landfill in the Sky

During the fall gubernatorial campaign in 1990, work began on the construction of a $140 million hazardous-waste incinerator in East Liverpool. A lame-duck Celeste administration was unprepared and unwilling to scrutinize the facility's permits and plans. The new Voinovich administration took until April to appoint Ohio EPA career employee Donald Schregardus to head the agency, operating during the interim with an acting director. By then, the project was well underway.

Angry area residents immediately reacted to the incinerator as a real-life nightmare. East Liverpool, a town of 12,000 people, sits on the northern bank of the Ohio River, across from Chester, West Virginia, and near the tri-state border with Pennsylvania. The incinerator sits on property that Waste Technologies Industries (WTI) leased from the Columbiana County Port Authority. Beneath the property sit two aquifers that provide a source of drinking water in the valley. WTI has built the incinerator atop a concrete base that raises it just barely above the 100-year floodplain, the maximum level to which the river is projected to rise in the worst flood likely in a century. It sits at the bottom of a ravine that rises about 50 feet, at the top of which, some 400 feet away, sits a row of modest wood-frame houses on a narrow street. It is the East End, East Liverpool's working-class district, which has housed generations of pottery and steel workers. Across the street, just 1,100 feet from the incinerator, sits an elementary school. Adjacent to it is a business college. Beyond, in the distance, more hills and more houses rise above the river in a series of terraces. The entire valley's terrain consists of such terraces, steep cuts, and winding highways.

The region is famous in the technical literature on air pollution. In 1948, in nearby Donora, Pennsylvania, along the Monongahela River, a tributary of the Ohio River, an air inversion trapped a suffocating pall of industrial pollution for seven days, during which 18 people died, and 10 percent of the 14,000 residents became seriously ill.[1] (In an air inversion, cooler air is confined beneath a stagnant ceiling of warmer air.) The incident became classic among meteorological and air-pollution-control professionals and helped to advance the cause of federal intervention in the problem of air pollution. The valley around East Liverpool suffers atmospheric inversions at least 200 days per year.

Of course, inversions alone did not make the valley's air a health hazard. Nature does not normally provide the pollutants that kill. But from Cincinnati to Pittsburgh, the Ohio River Valley has for more than a century supported much of the nation's heavy industry, especially steel, with all its attendant jobs, odors, and respiratory illnesses. East Liverpool, which at its peak claimed more than 20,000 residents, had been the "pottery capital of the world," shaping and baking cookery from the red clay of the river's hillsides. By the 1920s, the steel industry provided, if not a breath of fresh air, at least an economic lifeline to East Liverpool when its pottery mills declined. By the 1970s, however, the prosperity the mills had sustained was also vanishing, and no one else seemed interested in a quaint, hilly, out-of-the-way mill town. By the time John Payne became mayor, determined to prevent his town's demise, he was prepared to seize any lifeline that came near the community.

In 1979, an old high-school friend showed up from Arkansas with just such a proposition for his home town. Sensing that there was a fortune waiting to be made in handling hazardous waste, an Arkansas investment banker, Jackson T. Stephens, organized the firm called Waste Technologies, Inc. The firm hired Don Brown, who, like Payne, had graduated from East Liverpool High School in 1964.

Also, like Payne, he had initially become a teacher. Unlike Payne, who then found his way into hometown politics, Brown became in-volved in waste-management studies for Battelle Memorial Institute in Columbus, where he attracted the attention of the Stephens firm. After signing on, Brown chose to be East Liverpool's angel of mercy. He knew well that it had everything WTI was looking for—good transportation access in the midst of a heavily industrialized area.

Brown, however, did not emphasize hazardous waste in his early descriptions of the plant, which was pitched as a means of convert-ing industrial waste to power for local industries. For Payne, it was a small matter. Unemployed men idled their time on downtown streets, which suffered disrepair because of the city's $750,000 in un-paid bills. Anything that promised to alter the town's dismal eco-nomic outlook was a blessing. And the new facility had all the sound and sophistication of progressive new technology. What more could a desperate mayor want?

At a series of meetings beginning in 1980, Brown introduced WTI personnel like President Arch Pettit to Payne and other city offi-cials. All the news sounded good. A safe, new, state-of-the-art incin-erator already tested in Europe would handle 230,000 tons of waste yearly, cost $80 million to build, provide 200 construction jobs, gen-erate 100 permanent jobs, and yield $1.25 million in property taxes and $265,000 in city payroll taxes, jacking up municipal revenue by about one-third. All the grateful city would have to do was say yes. Business leaders in the beleaguered community lined up to endorse the idea.[2] Like the people in Cleveland's Broadway neighborhood, they saw industry as a familiar friend. The enemy was unemploy-ment, which hovered then at around 17 percent.

Still, there were doubters. Unlike the Clevelanders, they moved into gear long before the WTI incinerator ever had a single permit. One of them, Bob Cheeks, had also graduated with Payne and Brown before going into electronics. But he, like many others in town, even-tually found himself unemployed. He also became enormously suspi-cious of his two friends' proposal after reading the plans in the local library. Having turned to a strict religious philosophy, he began to see the issue in moral terms, denouncing the whole scheme in a long series of letters to public officials and bureaucrats. He also promised his old friend that he would do everything in his power to remove him from office.

Others developed their doubts through more typical channels. The Ohio EPA at one point suggested that WTI develop plans for a landfill for the 30,000 tons of hazardous residue the plant would generate yearly in the form of slag, filter-cake, and wastewater. The company sent agents into the Columbiana County countryside to test the soil for an appropriate site and found none—the soil was too sandy and porous. The company then contracted instead to send its ash to a Clermont County landfill operated by CECOS International.[3] In the process, however, many area farmers failed to get what they considered straight answers about the company's intentions, and the first serious seeds of doubt about WTI's integrity began to surface. Farmers began to organize an opposition group, the Citizens Protection Association.

Town residents soon had their own organization as well, Save Our County (SOC). Its president, Alonzo Spencer, a retired African-American steelworker, did not initially oppose the incinerator. He had watched Crucible Steel Company, the last vestige of East Liverpool's industrial salad days, close its doors. Jobs were good. But he had always harbored an instinctive distrust of the local power structure, born of labor and civil-rights struggles. Spencer was a past president of the local National Association for the Advancement of Colored People (NAACP). He and other labor activists knew that, in the past, local industrialists concerned about wage rates had resisted the introduction of new industries that might compete for the local labor pool, and their stance had contributed to the city's predicament. Their enthusiastic support for WTI gave him pause. The Chamber of Commerce, he said, had never before done anything that was beneficial for the community. Why would they start now? Further, Payne, whom Spencer regarded as a friend, had solicited his support for WTI but neglected to tell him it would burn hazardous waste. Spencer began to attend hearings and meetings and read everything he could find on the subject, including *Laying Waste*, a book by Michael Brown, the reporter who had broken the Love Canal story.[4]

The opposition grew, and so did the tension between opposing camps. From jewelers to car dealers, businesses supporting WTI became the target of powerful boycotts. Payne's dream of an economic miracle was turning to dust while the incinerator plans awaited regulatory action.

On the Monday afternoon of November 8, 1982, Ohio EPA hearing officer Lily Aaron rapped her gavel to call a public hearing to order at the Westgate Elementary Building in East Liverpool. The object of the hearing was to gather input for a preliminary staff determination on issuing WTI a permit to install its incinerator. In essence, this was to be an approval of WTI's pollution-control technology, with its siting to be handled later by the new Hazardous Waste Facilities Board.

From the beginning, speakers politely but firmly took officials to task for even considering the idea. The very first suggested that "a time of economic stress can easily cloud the judgment of those who believe that they must grasp at straws for the benefit of the moment no matter what the long-term price."[5] Demonstrating the hours they had spent at the East Liverpool Public Library, opponents attacked the location and distinguished it from other incinerators to which the WTI operation was being compared, such as one in Burnside, Louisiana, in the midst of swamps, and another in Nyborg, Denmark, which had the advantage of occupying a narrow peninsula where winds blew pollution across a 12-mile-wide strait. Perry Ross, the new mayor of Chester, West Virginia, feared the inadequacy of disaster planning, noting that no one could guarantee his town that an accident would not happen.[6] The Columbiana County health commissioner expressed some of the medical community's earliest concerns with the facility. John Wargo, a state representative and former county recorder, noted concerns about declining property values and potential contamination of downstream water sources from permitting hazardous waste to be sited on the Ohio River.[7] And Rebecca Tobin, a social worker and the wife of a local judge, made her first appearance at a public hearing, targeting an issue that would eventually symbolize the community's eroding faith in WTI's corporate integrity.

"The way the laws are now," she charged, responsibility for an accident "can conveniently be shuffled back and forth from WTI to other business partners they have such as Koppers" to local and state officials, to federal officials, to truckers, and "back to WTI."[8] Waste Technology Industries had become a consortium of four partners, whose names would change over time as Von Roll, a Swiss firm involved in European hazardous-waste burning, acquired a major interest in the project while the Stephens banking empire withdrew.

The issue of shifting and shirking responsibility arose quietly at first. Ohio EPA issued its permit in February 1983. That same year, the U.S. EPA was considering the company's application for a Resource Conservation and Recovery Act (RCRA) permit. EPA regulations for RCRA permits, issued in 1980, had specified that such applications must contain authorized signatures on behalf of both the operator of the licensed facility and the landowner, if the two entities were not the same.[9] There was no mystery behind the existence of such a rule. The intent of Congress in enacting RCRA was to establish strict lines of responsibility for the storage, transportation, and disposal of hazardous waste. Holding both parties responsible was clearly a means of foiling the elaborate corporate shell games often used by waste-hauling companies, particularly those that were tainted by the influence of organized crime. In the case of WTI, this meant that the application needed the endorsement of the Columbiana County Port Authority, which had acquired the land through the Ohio Department of Transportation (ODOT) on the presumption that it intended to develop a riverfront port facility. The lease, however, predated the ODOT's purchase of the property on the port authority's behalf. In effect, the port authority leased its land to WTI before it ever owned it.[10]

But the port authority never co-signed WTI's application. Despite that omission, the U.S. EPA's Region V office in Chicago approved the permit in June 1983. It allowed WTI to burn 176,000 tons of hazardous waste yearly, emitting up to 9,400 pounds of lead, 2,560 pounds of mercury, nearly 100 tons of sulfur dioxide (a precursor of acid rain), and almost 80 tons of particulate matter.[11] Some of those limits struck opponents as suspiciously close to the legal limits that, if exceeded, would have made the furnace a major source of air pollution under Clean Air Act provisions regarding the Prevention of Significant Deterioration (PSD) of air quality in more rural areas. That would have required a more elaborate permitting process.[12]

The only remaining regulatory hurdle at that point for WTI was the state's hazardous-waste board, which had inaugurated its existence by aggressively processing hundreds of permit applications with minimal investigation. The board had hired Richard Brudzynski, a former Ohio EPA attorney, as its sole hearing examiner. Brudzynski respected the technology WTI intended to use but expressed serious doubts about the company's forthrightness about the details of its operations. He recommended a denial of the permit until WTI supplied the missing information.[13]

Richard Sahli recalls being in the room the day the board considered WTI's permit. In one of his first cases as an assistant state attorney general, he was involved in another case, a minor permit regarding on-site disposal of hazardous waste for Pittsburgh Plate and Glass. The vote on WTI, he observed in retrospect, could have "gone either way." When the vote was called, he remembers, "the other four members turned and looked at the chairman, Bob Maynard," who was then the Ohio EPA director. "He said he'd vote for it," in effect overturning Brudzynski's recommendation. It was the board's first big case, Sahli said, and the board members "just deferred to Bob Maynard."[14] Maynard later left the Ohio EPA to join a major Columbus law firm, lobbying on behalf of many of Ohio's leading corporate clients.

By June 1984, WTI's new siting permit from the HWFB may have seemed a pyrrhic victory. Certainly, it was for Payne, who spent the latter half of his mayoral term combating a growing restiveness about the project among city-council members. Originally compliant, they had begun to rebel. In February 1983, 20-year-old councilman James Scafide instigated a successful vote to censure Payne through a letter instructing him to cease backing WTI when he testified as a representative of the community. The rationale: His opinion no longer coincided with the majority sentiment of East Liverpool voters.[15]

It was the opening shot in a political war that brought about Payne's demise. Although he won some skirmishes, particularly when law director David Buzzard told the council it could not tell Payne what he could say, the war of attrition relentlessly ground him down. In November, the voters unceremoniously dumped him, like so much garbage in a landfill. The man who had dreamed of saving his home town had instead come to be perceived as a traitor. With little political future, he moved on to selling cars for a Chevy dealership whose previous owner, Lou Greenburg, had backed Payne's plan. Greenburg had then sold the business and retired after suffering sizeable losses from a boycott led by incinerator opponents.[16]

Time now seemed to work against WTI. Opponents challenged the waste-board permit in the Ohio Court of Appeals and then in the Ohio Supreme Court, losing both times. The company never lost legally but never seemed to progress, either. In late 1984, the Ohio General Assembly enacted its new siting criteria for hazardous-waste-treatment units, requiring a minimum distance of 2,000 feet from schools and residences, but exempted those facilities whose permits had already been granted—WTI being the most obvious case in point.

Yet a construction date continued to elude the company while the cost of waiting escalated. Brown, the would-be hometown economic hero, tired of the delays and moved to another hazardous-waste firm in New Hampshire. By 1987, WTI announced that Chemical Waste Management, Inc. (CWM), of Oak Brook, Illinois, a subsidiary of Waste Management, Inc., had signed an agreement to acquire the consortium, previously owned by four partners— Stephens Inc. of Arkansas, Mustang Fuel of Oklahoma, Environmental Elements of Maryland, and Von Roll Inc. of Switzerland. Environmental Elements, the agreement said, would continue construction using the Von Roll technology. CWM would be an experienced firm, already operating two hazardous-waste burners in Chicago and Sauget, Illinois.

As before, promises were made. The firm would stringently control the wastes that entered its plant. It already had a remedial-action division that specialized in cleaning up contaminated sites. CWM would know what it was doing.[17]

It was not to be. Opponents immediately objected that a change of ownership constituted a modification of the permit, thus necessitating new hearings. Ohio EPA Director Warren Tyler rejected that argument, however, ruling in May 1987 that the change in ownership did not alter the arrangements for the incinerator. SOC appealed that decision to the Ohio EPA's Environmental Board of Review, the only agency body empowered to review the director's decisions. But the CWM involvement underscored WTI's need for financing for the project.

Unfortunately for WTI, Richard Shank, who succeeded Tyler, overturned that ruling, forcing WTI to file a request for a permit change. And in late 1987, the Ohio legislature enacted a so-called "bad boy" law, a measure that requires a background check of any person or firm wishing to acquire or license a hazardous-waste facility of any kind in the state. Other states, like New Jersey, had also turned to such laws to weed out bad actors in a business that has long been reputed to attract lawbreakers, sloppy operators, and underworld criminals. SOC sought just such a disclosure for CWM.[18] Waste Management, Inc., had been convicted of bid rigging and fined numerous times for environmental violations and might well have failed to pass the background check, but it may never be known what influence that had on its evaluation of the WTI project.[19] In June 1989, CWM withdrew its planned participation, forcing WTI to search anew for the financing it needed in order to go forward.

WTI had languished for so long that many people assumed the whole idea had simply died. It was merely dormant. So, too, was much of the opposition, though the groups fighting WTI had evolved and matured. SOC had absorbed most of the members of the earlier, competing Columbiana County group, the Citizens Protective Association, which withered in the face of legal defeats.[20] In West Virginia, Save Our State (SOS) had led the struggle from Wheeling, while the Stewartville-Weirton Area Against Incineration (SWAI) worked farther upriver. Chester residents organized Let's Improve Valley Environment (LIVE). Pennsylvania hatched the Southwestern Pennsylvania Alliance for a Clean Environment (SPACE), with the Pittsburgh area adding its own group, Pittsburgh Against Toxic Incineration (PATI). To coordinate their efforts, these organizations formed an umbrella coalition, the Tri-State Environmental Council. WTI ceased to be primarily an Ohio issue; Tri-State members were now writing and calling officials in three states, demanding action to block the incinerator.

The emerging regional coalition had also, at long last, begun to get the attention of national environmental groups. In April 1989, SOC held a "leadership conference," attracting Lois Gibbs, the co-founder of the Citizens' Clearinghouse for Hazardous Wastes (CCHW), and her husband, Steven Lester, a toxicologist. CCHW, based in Arlington, Virginia, is the grass-roots assistance network that grew out of Gibbs's experience in organizing her Love Canal neighborhood in Niagara Falls, New York, after it was discovered to be contaminated by hazardous waste buried years before by the Hooker Chemical Company. Peter Montague, the editor of the weekly newsletter *Rachel's Hazardous Waste News*, also spoke. Greenpeace, too, began to supply money and advice.

Although it was unclear why WTI was taking so long to line up financing for the project, environmentalists had to regard no news as good news. Anyone familiar with construction projects knows that lengthy delays increase costs, and environmentalists have won many battles across the nation simply because delays caused development projects to become financially untenable. The same scenario *might* happen in East Liverpool. On the other hand, CWM had withdrawn because of its own unique problems, and the steeply rising cost of hazardous-waste disposal could well make this project appear *more* profitable over time. Environmentalists would be confident that WTI was dead only when the company announced that it was canceling its plans. Instead, it simply sought and won permit extensions. A project with valid permits was always susceptible to resuscitation.

The environmentalists' cold shower arrived in September 1990, in the midst of the contest between former Cleveland Mayor George Voinovich and state Attorney General Anthony Celebrezze to succeed Governor Celeste. The owners announced that a banking consortium of J.P. Morgan and the Union Bank of Switzerland would underwrite what was now a $128 million project. Rust International Corporation of Birmingham, Alabama, which had experience with some municipal waste incinerators, would be the general contrac-

tor.[21] Just a month before, Von Roll, the Swiss firm in the WTI consortium, had acquired the interests of its remaining partners, ending
the role of Stephens Inc., which had initiated the entire venture.
Von Roll had already acquired Environmental Elements (Ohio) Inc.,
another Environmental Elements group, and the U.S. licensing
rights that Environmental Elements Corporation had held on the
application of Von Roll's rotary-kiln incineration technology. In the
new acquisition, because Von Roll had already been involved in
WTI, the Ohio EPA decided that new permits would not be required.[22]

The cold shower was a particularly powerful wake-up call for Terri
Swearingen, a relatively introverted registered nurse who worked
mostly as a dental technician for her husband, Lee Swearingen, a
dentist. The couple lived quietly and comfortably in a large house
atop a hill in Chester that afforded beautiful views of the countryside below. From that lofty perch, Swearingen, a Republican who
opposed the WTI plant, had blithely assumed that "the government
wouldn't allow anything that would hurt us."[23] The realization that
WTI was now under construction and *would* operate unless stopped
by citizen action transformed the pipefitter's daughter almost overnight into a full-time volunteer activist whose obsessive research, in
turn, transformed the movement she joined. Another longtime Republican dilettante in Chester, Sally Riley, emerged from obscurity
as a housewife to become mayor, an office she used relentlessly as a
tool of opposition. Both women acquired the breathless commitment
of those who sense that time is running out because they may have
waited too long. Nonstop activism became their road to atonement.

The confrontations resulting from the onset of construction materialized rapidly. WTI requested a modification of its permit to incorporate a spray-dryer system, intended to reduce emissions.
Tri-State members requested a local hearing, which the Ohio EPA
granted. By late November, with newly elected Governor George
Voinovich preparing to take office, the agency held an informational
meeting to explain its planned hearing to nearly 200 local residents.
Public-involvement coordinator Shelby Thurman-Jackson attempted vainly to explain that the hearing would consider only the
spray dryer, not WTI's previously granted construction permit. A

five-member panel of agency experts responded to questions, only to draw howls of laughter when air-quality specialist Robert Hodanbosi noted that 78 tons of yearly pollution "may seem like a lot, but the average car emits half a ton per year." At least with a car one knows what is emitted, one opponent yelled.[24]

The informational meeting was a mere shadow of what would ensue. Opponents built the tempo of protest rapidly. In December, they delivered a brown and green "toxic" birthday cake to the U.S. EPA office in Wheeling, West Virginia. Now that the agency was 20 years old, they declared, "the party's over."[25] Telephones rang and flyers spread through town. On January 17, at 6:30 p.m., when the Ohio EPA hearing began in the auditorium of the East Liverpool Middle School, more than 350 people filled the room.

Among them were experts both sides had imported. For WTI, under European ownership, there was nothing unusual about the presence of Dr. Peter Schoener, technical director of the Hesse Industrial Waste Company in Germany, who told the Ohio EPA that Von Roll's spray-dryer technology had worked with two German incinerators since 1981 with no problems and no increase in heavy-metal concentrations in nearby soil.[26]

But war was underway in the Persian Gulf. Bombs were bursting over the skies of Kuwait, Iraq, and Saudi Arabia. Many in the audience had relatives serving in reserve units, and the atmosphere in the crowded hearing room was full of comparisons between Saddam Hussein's vaunted poison gas and the chemicals that WTI would incinerate. It was the perfect setting for an insurrection, and the Tri-State Environmental Council had laid a trap for state officials. They, too, had paid travel expenses for visiting experts, and dozens of opponents had signed up to testify with the sole intent of yielding their time. Ohio EPA rules allotted five minutes to each speaker, hardly enough to make any significant points on a complex topic—unless these times were piled on repetitively.

Paul Connett, the chemistry professor from upstate New York's St. Lawrence University who produces a bombastic weekly newsletter, *Waste Not*, beloved by opponents of incineration, got the first shot when Michael Stein, an SOS member from Wheeling, yielded to him. Starting politely, he noted that he had been involved in "600 presentations in 44 states" during six years of involvement in the waste-management issue. He had visited communities with hazardous-waste incinerators. This, he emphasized, was the "worst site that I have ever seen in terms of protecting the health of the population in this area. It is an absolute disgrace."

But the hearing was not about siting. Connett knew this. That issue had been decided almost seven years earlier before the hazardous-waste board. He turned his attention to the spray dryer with a mocking voice and formal accent emblematic of his unique style. He noted that company literature portrayed the spray dryer as resulting "in only an increase in the quantity of warm vapor leaving the stack." "That is scientifically untrue, and if that is the quality of their science, these people shouldn't be allowed to operate a bus, let alone a hazardous-waste incinerator," he scoffed.

But scoffing would score no points with regulators, nor would it educate opponents. Connett, the educator, had a huge classroom before him, and he was ready with charts and diagrams and pointer. The original arrangement for the plant would have sent liquid waste to a sewage treatment plant, eventually finding its way to the Ohio River. "Needless to say, people did not take kindly to that," he noted, and the company concocted the spray-dryer "notion."

The spray dryer would spray the liquid waste with hot gases that would evaporate through the stacks where scrubbers would remove airborne pollutants. The solids would fall out, reducing a larger quantity of liquid waste to two daily truckloads of solid waste taken to a landfill. Less mess, less pollution—everyone should be happy.

But not according to Connett. The WTI report said the hot gases would enter at 700 degrees F. and exit at 320 degrees F. Volatile material collected in the dry scrubber system, including chlorinated organic material, dioxins, fluorines, and mercury, would also evaporate and loop back through the electrostatic precipitator (which electrically "zaps" particulate matter before it can leave the smokestack) and the wet scrubber. This system, however, would not trap these materials. They would join more volatile material entering the system, with a minimal amount escaping through the stack. The quantity thus increased, the cycle would repeat itself. Eventually, all the volatile material would escape through the stack.

As a sort of mocking intelligence test for the state officials, Connett asked the audience if it understood what he had just explained. People applauded.

Connett then challenged the Ohio EPA to reconsider the original permit, quoting from federal regulations that the location of a facility may not be reconsidered during a modification of the permit "unless new information or standards indicate that a threat to human health or to the environment exists which was unknown at the time of permit issuance."

It was a perfect opening for every speaker who followed, and none was bashful about using it. After some denunciations of the track records of operating hazardous-waste incinerators elsewhere, Connett was reminded of his time limit. Staff attorney Karen Haight, who was conducting the hearing, did not want "one person dominating the hearing."

"Madam," Connett replied, "I've come a long way and I've got a lot of information that these people need to hear, and I don't think you are going to stop me."

After some verbal contretemps with the audience, Haight called another speaker. That speaker yielded her time to Connett, who continued. After another audience disruption, Haight testily noted, "You don't have to have this hearing at all." She was promptly reminded from the floor that the protesters were concerned with "what is going on in the democracy when you ram these things down their throats." A proponent suggested that the hearing was being turned into a "three-ring circus." Seeking to regain control, Haight indicated that the current speaker could yield to Connett, but the next could not.

Connett made his arguments as to why new health information that had emerged justified reconsidering the entire permit, drawing from his wide travels to incinerator sites worldwide. "Nobody, nobody, in 1991," he concluded, "would sanction the building of a hazardous-waste incinerator here. . . . You have to find a way of denying this permit."

Haight called other speakers, and a new pattern began—revolving experts. Up and down they went, in and out of their seats in five-minute intervals as people yielded time to their favorite witness. At one point, the situation became so amusing that Hugh Kaufman, the whistleblower chief of the U.S. EPA's hazardous-waste division, responded to an unexpected five-minute bonus by yelling, "Hells bells! I should have bought one of those lottery tickets."

Kaufman, who had written most of the tough federal regulations on hazardous waste, had come from Washington, D.C. An engineer, he had done the investigative work on Love Canal as the EPA's chief investigator on hazardous sites in the 1970s. Acknowledging Haight's admonitions about focusing on the spray dryer, Kaufman objected that, because the detailed technical information on the system was confidential, "the public does not have the opportunity to have technical experts to review the technical information and give you adequate responses." Given that problem, he insisted, "I don't see how you can go ahead with the regulatory process, unless this is a sham. . . ."

Matt Petrovick, a former U.S. EPA employee from Raleigh, North Carolina, told of his research in the neurotoxicology division before he left to earn a living from music while engaging in environmental activism.

Finally, Michael McCawley, a civil-engineering professor teaching air-pollution courses at West Virginia University in Morgantown, criticized shortcomings in the Ohio EPA review process, the most glaring being the lack of a safety analysis in order to detect mistakes in the company's engineering design. He was accompanied by a colleague, Robert Diener, a professor of waste management at WVU, who simply described incineration as "the wrong way to dispose of waste." He charged that the WTI emission controls, which would find criteria pollutants like carbon dioxide, sulfur dioxide, and nitrates, would nonetheless be "powerless" to control chlorinated hydrocarbons and gasified heavy metals in the stack. He condemned the hilly floodplain location, noting that "in the presence of an inversion y'all understand that you could have a Bhopal condition here in East Liverpool."

Haight followed Diener's testimony with a reminder to the audience that clapping only took time away from the speakers, who continued to be Connett, Kaufman, Petrovick, and McCawley, until she clamped a lid on the proceedings by insisting no one else would be allowed to yield time. The hour was getting late, and Haight was losing patience.

"You set a precedent already. You can't change your mind," someone yelled from the floor.

"Sir, I'm sorry, but we're not going to be able to conclude this hearing if you keep going on the same way," she replied.

"You can't do that," came another yell amid cheers and clapping.

"Sir," Haight replied indignantly, "I can do anything I want. This is my meeting."

The audience thought otherwise, and from that point forward, nearly every time Haight called another speaker, bedlam interrupted the proceedings. Haight repeatedly suggested that she did not even have to continue the hearing, but would do so if the audience behaved. By dominating the testimony through sheer numbers and using their time to advantage by incessantly yielding it to their invited guests, the opponents had won a psychological victory. Never again would the Ohio EPA confront the public with any degree of self-confidence. It would always be a war of nerves to sway public opinion. It would become a protester's battleground where, for the most part, the U.S. and Ohio EPAs could only lose.

In the months that followed, the WTI opponents matured through their own research efforts into articulate proponents of an alternate vision of waste management for not only Ohio, but the nation. Their increasingly affectionate ties to experts like Connett, McCawley, Kaufman, and another U.S. EPA whistleblower, William Sanjour, provided them not only with a steady stream of data but also with an education about waste-reduction alternatives to incineration that often took on moral dimensions.

From people like Peter Montague, the gentle, gray-haired editor of *Rachel's Hazardous Waste News* at the Environmental Research Foundation, in Washington, D.C., they learned that the U.S. and Ohio EPAs could not honestly tell them the exact volume and nature of the hundreds of hazardous pollutants that would spew from the incinerator once it was in operation. What the EPA could and did say was that WTI would conduct a test burn before its facility ever went on line and that that test burn would serve as an indicator of the types of pollutants the plant might generate. But on a daily basis, the agency's best measure consisted of monitoring a handful of criteria pollutants to determine the incinerator's destruction and removal efficiency (DRE), which supposedly would be around 99.99 percent. In other words, the furnace would emit less than 1/10,000 of the amount of these monitored pollutants that came into the plant. As industry and EPA officials see it, these criteria pollutants serve as surrogates for the thousands of others being burned. The assumption is that their emission rates serve as valid indicators of the efficiency with which the fire is consuming the entire range of chemicals subjected to incineration.

Critics have charged that this assumption casts a blind eye to some serious shortcomings in the technology of incinerating hazardous waste. For one thing, although a 99.99 percent DRE sounds to the uninitiated like a remarkable achievement in making hazardous waste disappear into thin air, the reality falls far short of alchemy. As much as nine percent of the original volume of liquid hazardous waste, and up to 29 percent of the original volume of solid hazardous waste, remains as ash that still requires burial in a special landfill designed for such wastes—the very reason WTI had engendered suspicion in trying to test the soil on nearby farmlands. One U.S. EPA report indicated that in 1987 hazardous-waste incinerators in the U.S. were producing 148 million pounds of such residue.[27]

But the critics charged that even the DRE itself was a fantasy based on skimpy science. For one thing, the DRE merely measures the stack emissions of a specific list of chemicals against the quantities that initially entered the furnace. Even a test burn yields data only for those chemicals selected for the test. But hazardous-waste incinerators emit an undetermined number of unburned chemicals that have never been identified. Some of these are totally new recombinants created by the combustion process itself, in part because different chemicals will burn at different temperatures, and those temperatures themselves will vary in different parts of the burner and stack. In other words, the unit-for-unit ratio reflected in the DRE says nothing about the quantity of unburned chemical compounds emitted because they never existed before the combustion process triggered the chemical reactions that produced them. There simply is no reliable information on these chemicals, known to engineers as products of incomplete combustion (PICs). Claims to the contrary indicate far more about a particular project's public-relations needs than they do about the state of scientific knowledge concerning the process of hazardous-waste incineration.

Even internal U.S. EPA studies raised questions about the true reliability of incineration technology. Several years earlier, the agency had contracted with the Energy and Environmental Research Corporation of Irvine, California, to analyze the failure of incinerators to fully destroy hazardous wastes. The study revealed that "current technology has difficulty meeting the licensing regulations" for destruction of waste streams that represented less than 1,000 parts per million of the feedstock entering the incinerator. Dioxins and chlorophenol-contaminated pesticides were among the wastes typically found in such low concentrations.[28] The agency chose not to publish the study until 1989. Three years later, Sylvia Lowrance, EPA's director of solid waste, issued a memorandum to regional directors confirming this finding relating to dioxin in response to concerns they had raised about a study by Greenpeace researcher Pat Costner showing poor destructive efficiency by an incinerator in Jacksonville, Arkansas.[29]

The opponents learned more than science from their technical allies. They also learned an even deeper mistrust of government than the vague sense they had previously shared that something was not quite right if something like WTI could happen to them. They learned that both government and company officials could deliberately mislead them. For example, in June 1991, Alfred Sigg, an engineer at Von Roll's U.S. headquarters in Norcross, Georgia, virtually parroted Paul Connett's critique of the proposed spray-dryer addition at an annual meeting of the Air and Waste Management Association in Vancouver, British Columbia.[30] Connett noted that, to accommodate his criticism, the company had installed an activated charcoal system to capture the volatilized chemicals, like mercury, whose emissions would otherwise be increased. The company, he charged, did this as quietly as possible so that the Ohio EPA could avoid classifying the change as a major modification of the permit, which would necessitate new hearings.[31]

Certainly, some double talk ensued concerning Connett's critique. Both Ohio and U.S. EPA officials have maintained at various times that Connett and McCawley failed to submit any scientific documentation to support their statements, even though both agencies had confirmed in various ways that they had received such material not only from Connett but from local opponents who resubmitted Connett's material. Throughout 1991, the grass-roots activists became increasingly savvy in taking their message to elected officials, winning sympathy in West Virginia from Governor Gaston Caperton, Senators Robert Byrd and Jay Rockefeller, and Representative Allan Mollohan, and in Ohio from Senator Howard Metzenbaum, among others. In the blizzard of correspondence that followed, as these officials sought answers to their constituents' questions, U.S. EPA officials began to contradict themselves. Swearingen and another activist, Connie Stein from Wheeling, West Virginia, were relentless in poring over every word of every letter to every interested party. Finally, they snared U.S. EPA Region V Director Valdas Adamkus in this web. In a letter to Byrd, Adamkus stated that his agency had "not received scientific documentation from Dr. Connett and Dr. McCawley to support their claims."[32] Earlier, however, Adamkus had written to Jane Massey, a resident of East Liverpool, noting that "the U.S. EPA has received a copy" of Connett's written statement to the Ohio EPA.[33] Swearingen pointed this out to Byrd, calling Adamkus a liar.[34] Even if this double talk resulted purely from ineptitude, it did nothing to enhance either agency's credibility with the public.[35]

Winter left, spring arrived, and the shape of the new Voinovich administration in Columbus became clear. It was not good news for WTI's opponents or for environmentalists generally. Whatever sympathy for the opposition existed at the Ohio EPA under Shank and Sahli disappeared as Republicans filled key jobs. Sahli, now at the Ohio Environmental Council, was on the outside looking in but free to criticize where once his hands had been tied by his chairmanship of the hazardous-waste board. By May, the incinerator was about 25 percent complete. Voinovich made clear that he would not intervene in the agency's dealings with WTI, drawing sharp criticism from his counterpart in West Virginia, who declared himself "very much with the people who are fighting WTI."[36]

Meanwhile, WTI began to make plans for installing a second incinerator upon completion of the first. The company had previously said it planned to build only one of the two units for which it had received permits unless a market for additional capacity developed. Now, apparently, the firm had mustered the market and cash flow to proceed.[37]

WTI opponents decided to mount a special appeal to the governor by marching to Columbus. Outside help began pouring in. Greenpeace co-sponsored the march. Actor Martin Sheen, an Ohio native who was working in Pittsburgh on a new movie, spoke at area rallies to inaugurate the event.[38] WTI predictably blasted Sheen for not attempting to hear its side of the story first.[39]

For the first time, the WTI opponents were merging their concerns with those of a larger, statewide coalition. Marchers were to converge on Columbus by June 29 from three points: Steubenville, the starting point for WTI opponents from the tri-state area; Nova, the north-central Ohio site of a hazardous-waste incinerator proposed by Ohio Technologies; and Fairborn, near Dayton, the site of an operating cement kiln burning hazardous waste, owned by Southdown Inc. of Texas.[40] Notably absent from this list was the town of Grafton, the site of a peculiarly noncontroversial hazardous-waste incinerator owned by the local Ross family.

The demands developed for the march also showed a new maturity in the opposition movement, which was beginning to articulate issues far broader than those affecting only the WTI incinerator. The marchers sought at least a five-year moratorium on all new or expanded incineration and new legislation mandating reduction of the use of toxic chemicals in industry, the latter as a means of reducing the need for incineration capacity.[41] The marchers were fostering a growing awareness of Ohio as a dumping ground not only for its own, but for the nation's, excessive production of hazardous waste. The protesters were no longer thinking locally or even regionally. They were fast becoming part of a national strategy on the issue of toxics.

Their aggressive campaign began to attract noteworthy allies. West Virginia Attorney General Mario Palumbo appealed WTI's permit modification to the Ohio EPA's Environmental Board of Review.[42] The Ohio State Medical Association joined the Columbiana County Medical Society's earlier opposition to the plant.[43] During the march, the Pittsburgh City Council passed a resolution opposing the plant and asking for state and county analyses of the incinerator's impact on the city's air and water quality.[44] Reinforcing Pittsburgh-area sentiments against WTI, the Allegheny County Board of Commissioners added its own resolution requesting a halt to WTI's construction.

WTI mounted a public-relations counterattack, seeking first to neutralize medical-community opposition by donating $10,000 to East Liverpool City Hospital, which was planning an $8.7 million renovation. More important, WTI pledged $1 for every ton of waste treated at its facility during the first 10 years, or about $60,000 per year just from the first unit.[45] Von Roll America President D.J. Blake Marshall became more personally vocal, telling reporters that the plant would be meeting standards "10 years from now because we are so far ahead of anything that's being planned."[46] Plant manager Sam Kasley invited local opponents to a private breakfast to discuss their differences. They refused, calling the breakfast a bribe and insisting that any meeting be open to the news media. WTI rejected that arrangement.[47]

WTI also hired an Atlanta public-relations firm, Cookerly & Co., to step up its efforts.[48] But one WTI brochure backfired when it was discovered that "Part of the Solution" included as supporters of hazardous-waste incineration the names of organizations that either did not support incineration or had no position on the issue. In August, WTI withdrew the brochures amid accusations by opponents that it would never have done so but for their diligent research.[49] Von Roll also unfurled, in a 20-foot banner adorning its plant, a new slogan, "Don't Waste the Earth. Support WTI," accompanied by the negation symbol overlying a barrel of hazardous waste.[50]

In the midst of the public-relations controversy, the Ohio EPA announced its tentative approval of the permit modifications WTI had sought earlier in the year.[51] In many siting controversies, that might have begun to bring closure to the issue. But in East Liverpool in 1991, it merely invited more debate, which produced the need for more studies. The city council had already contracted with Isaac Yomtovian, a consultant who headed STC Enviroscience, a Cleveland engineering firm, for an environmental impact study. That move produced its own public-relations difficulties because WTI offered $10,000 to help the city pay for the study, prompting charges that WTI was buying the results. City officials took umbrage at the suggestion, noting that the city, not WTI, chose Yomtovian, and that the money covered services that the city itself would otherwise have to cover. Mayor James Scafide expressed frustration at the city's inability to enact measures more stringent than state law, noting that, even if the city filed for an injunction to stop construction, it would have to post a bond of $5 million per week. A city-council liaison committee began to meet with WTI officials about the expenses the city incurred because of WTI's presence.[52]

Meanwhile, the University of Pittsburgh's Center for Hazardous Materials Research (CHMR), an academic think tank, undertook its own independent evaluation of the WTI facility, funded in part by a grant from the Pennsylvania Department of Environmental Resources.[53] The project also received $20,000 from Von Roll. Just six weeks later, CHMR released the study, which gave high marks to WTI but drew scathing criticism from environmentalists for its superficiality.[54] A great deal of the report did merely reiterate the previous statements of regulators and WTI officials as justifications for its conclusions.[55] CHMR's credibility with activists sank further when its president, Dr. Edgar Berkey, offered the trite declaration, "I would live next to this plant—absolutely."[56] East Liverpool had long since passed the point where such statements swayed public opinion.

The Ohio Department of Health fared little better. Governor Voinovich sought to mollify opponents by promising a study of health risks from the plant. The promise first surfaced indirectly through Mayor Scafide at a September 3 city-council meeting, where he described it as "the best thing that could happen for all of us."[57] Scafide's tidings were followed a day later by an announcement from Pennsylvania's Republican U.S. Representative Rick Santorum, representing a downwind district, who noted that "Ohio doesn't necessarily have the environmental stakes in it that Pennsylvania and West Virginia do."[58] For that reason, Santorum asked that the U.S. EPA, rather than the Ohio EPA, conduct the study. It also quickly became apparent that the two studies would somehow be done in conjunction, and that Region V Director Adamkus had initially suggested that WTI and the Ohio EPA perform the study with U.S. EPA oversight, an arrangement certain to incense wary environmentalists. Ohio EPA spokesman Shelby Thurman-Jackson quickly ruled that out.[59]

But the posturing mattered mostly to politicians and bureaucrats. For opponents, it completely missed the point, as Governor Voinovich soon learned. On September 18, after demonstrating outside his office and insisting on a meeting, a group of protesters spoke with Voinovich, who told them that WTI had survived several legal challenges and that he lacked any authority to revoke or delay its permits. He then reaffirmed his promise of a health study in which nearby residents' blood samples, cancer rates, and birth weights would be monitored before and after WTI began operations to determine whether the facility actually posed a health threat. If there were any permit violations, Mike Dawson, the governor's aide, reassured them, "Of course we'll shut it down." But Dawson described the health study as a "unique opportunity."

"He's asking us to be guinea pigs. We don't want to be part of a major experiment," Terri Swearingen replied. Vincent Eirene, a Pittsburgh opponent, added, "There's nothing left but massive civil disobedience."

The most incendiary language came from Connie Stein. If WTI opened, she promised, "All hell is going to break loose in East Liverpool."[60]

Stein's comment, above all, galvanized both sides in the debate. D.J. Blake Marshall reacted hotly to the prospect of civil disobedience, calling it a "cowardly act" for people who use modern conveniences and help to generate hazardous waste. He promised that WTI would beef up its security to handle such a contingency.[61]

In opposition, a new organizing effort took root in Weirton, West Virginia, just 10 miles south of East Liverpool, under the leadership of a local resident, Carol Hicks. When Hancock County officials expressed some doubts about the political efficacy of civil disobedience, Alonzo Spencer drew upon his civil-rights experience to reassure the audience that it would help to build the movement. "We're going to be very peaceful and nondestructive," he said.[62]

Rick Sahli became more vocal, noting that if he had been chairman when WTI came before the hazardous-waste board, "We would have laughed the proposal out of the room." He also cited chapter and verse from the Ohio code to make his case that both Voinovich and the Ohio EPA had discretionary authority to review the permits for WTI in view of technological changes since the permit was issued. He called on the EPA to send the issue back to the board. Sahli took the position that no facility like WTI should be located anywhere within a quarter-mile, preferably a half-mile, of the Ohio River because of the possibility of fallout from an explosion.[63] He wrote to Ohio EPA Director Schregardus to point out the relevant code section but, he claims, never received a reply.[64] The Ohio EPA, in Sahli's view, had become a mere vassal of its federal partner, which very much wanted WTI licensed. Facing a hostile public, the Ohio EPA withdrew ever further into the U.S. EPA's protective cocoon.

Region V, however, was also under attack, in no small part because of its role in handling the Chemical Waste Management incinerator in southeastern Chicago. Swearingen and Spencer claim that, in a September 10 meeting between Region V officials and local opponents in East Liverpool, William Muno, the regional hazardous-waste director, cited the CWM unit as a model incinerator.[65] Just a few days before, Illinois State Representative Clem Balanoff held a joint press conference with Greenpeace in Pittsburgh to blast both incinerators. The Chicago incinerator was in his district and exploded in February 1991, resulting eventually in its permanent closure. Balanoff brought with him dramatic footage of the event from in-plant video cameras.[66] Those visuals made Muno's plaudits tragically laughable in the eyes of protesters.

Muno's recollection of the meeting sheds an even more fascinating light on the deteriorating relations between the regional office and East Liverpool citizens. In an interview,[67] Muno indicated that his goal in going to East Liverpool was "to establish a rapport rather than being an impersonal bureaucrat in Chicago." But he also wanted to "give them a sense of some of the statutory and regulatory limits that exist in EPA."

But once the EPA public-affairs staff had arranged the meeting, "word spread around. They brought in people with video cameras so the whole thing could be documented, and the whole thing became almost a media event. That was not my intent in having it. I wanted to talk one on one." Instead, "We walked in and, all of a sudden, there was a mike in my face." Angry that they had not gotten from regional director Valdas Adamkus the answers they wanted to questions they had submitted in writing, Michael and Connie Stein confronted Muno with demands that he discuss the issues in their letter to Adamkus.[68]

Nearly 100 protesters brought their best black humor to the East Liverpool Middle School on September 24. The U.S. and Ohio EPAs held a joint informational meeting concerning the proposed air-pollution-permit revisions for WTI. The protesters stood outside, chanting and discouraging others from entering. Only about 40 people entered the meeting, about a dozen of them asking questions of the officials. Occasionally, an elderly woman, walking with a cane, wandered in to yell, "Traitors! Traitors!"[69] A phalanx of state highway patrolmen and local police were present to guard the meeting, reportedly at Voinovich's request.

Protesters declared that "democracy is dead in America." Swearingen declared the plan to test children's blood "Governor Voinovich's sick experiment" and labeled the University of Pittsburgh study a "prostitution of science. Where is the peer review?"[70]

That same day, WTI plant manager Sam Kasley and Sarah Wilson, chair of the city-council liaison committee, signed an agreement in which WTI agreed to pay $10 per ton, or about $600,000 per year, to the city of East Liverpool to underwrite the costs of emergency training, infrastructure, and other municipal expenses in handling the WTI presence. Wilson was not sure the agreement would satisfy opponents, but suggested that "we will at least be able to address some of their concerns."[71]

The next night, the EPA officials returned for their official joint hearing on finalizing the proposed permit revisions. Protesters had staged a "mock funeral for democracy," placing an American flag in a coffin.[72] But there seemed to be no second boycott. Hundreds filled the hearing room. At 7:00 p.m., Ohio EPA public-involvement co-ordinator Shelby Thurman-Jackson called the meeting to order.

Terri Swearingen took a deep breath, then jumped up on her seat. She whipped out a small bullhorn and pressed it to her mouth. "The public hearing process is a sham! We demand democracy!" she shouted.

On cue, more than 600 opponents began to chant: "No more EPA. Safe jobs for Tri-State. We won't die for WTI." Placards swung back and forth. The shouting from ghostlike painted faces pounded eardrums from wall to wall for nearly half an hour. Perhaps 150 WTI supporters, including construction-trade unionists employed by contractors, waved countersigns that read "Welcome WTI," but to no avail. Plant manager Sam Kasley had brought written testimony he planned to present on the spray dryer. He could only sit in stunned silence. Jackson tried to regain the floor but was drowned out. Young protesters from Greenpeace had joined older citizens like 73-year-old Clare Stover and Alonzo Spencer's gang of retired steelworkers in sustaining the deafening roar. The EPA officials waited in vain for the bedlam to taper off. Finally, in abject frustration, they wheeled a blackboard onto the stage with a written announcement.

"Because the U.S. EPA and the Ohio EPA are not able to conduct the hearing on the proposed modifications of the WTI permit, this meeting is now adjourned. Please submit your comments in writing by Oct. 21 to U.S. EPA, 230 South Dearborn, Chicago, Ill., 60604," it read.

A victory cheer erupted. Then the shouting continued, the protesters turning the aborted public hearing into an impromptu opposition pep rally. When they were done, the leaders "resurrected" the American flag and held it aloft to a resounding cheer.

Sam Kasley distributed copies of his testimony to the press. He planned to mail it to the EPA.[73] At the Ohio EPA, Jackson, whose job is to manage public involvement, would never again have a kind word to say about the protesters in East Liverpool. She had tried to do her job, and they had thwarted her.

Alonzo Spencer complained that the demonstration had resulted from the EPA's failure to provide answers to opponents' questions. The group had instead received a five-page letter from the U.S. EPA that contained references to confidential memos. Spencer hinted that the agency was withholding information.[74]

In its first decade, the WTI proposal seemed to crawl so slowly that it was often presumed dead. By the fall of 1991, however, events had suddenly been jolted into fast-forward, and no day was without more news, more twists to the story, more complications. Activism became a full-time preoccupation, with overtime, for the entire core leadership of the Tri-State Environmental Council. They filled their days with telephone calls, correspondence, planning meetings, and poring over new documents either released or unearthed through a plethora of records requests to government Freedom of Information Act officers. WTI, which was bracing for the next protest, was now facing a nearly professional, if almost entirely unpaid, opposition staff. Many of those full-timers were spending hundreds of dollars monthly to support their cause.[75]

This commitment left politicians little room to maneuver. They were either for or against the WTI proposal, although city officials in East Liverpool faced hazards with either position. Opposition looked more and more like the wise choice. "You don't have to be a weatherman to tell which way the wind blows," Martin Sheen had said during the summer, quoting folk singer Bob Dylan.

On October 1, Yomtovian unleashed the STC Enviroscience consulting report. Yomtovian blasted the lack of public access to crucial documents that would have allowed citizens and local officials to judge the soundness of WTI's technology for themselves. Instead, he noted, WTI failed even to supply nonconfidential data that president D.J. Blake Marshall had already promised in writing.[76]

Yomtovian developed a laundry list of "concerns" about the WTI facility that loaded the opposition's verbal arsenal to overflowing.

Yomtovian warned, for instance, of the prevalent practice in the hazardous-waste-incineration industry of bypassing automatic cutoff systems that would shut down an incinerator in the event of an emergency or the burner's failure to perform to specifications. The point of an automatic cutoff is, quite simply, to prevent a malfunctioning incinerator from continuing to operate, but the U.S. EPA had discovered a common practice by operators of circumventing these systems. The city, Yomtovian suggested, "must have some type of monitoring system or working relationship with WTI/Von Roll that will ensure that *immediate cutoff* will occur."[77]

Yomtovian criticized the air-dispersion modeling done for the WTI application prior to 1984 as outdated and inadequate. Such modeling aims to predict how and where pollutants emitted from a stack will be distributed by wind patterns.[78] The report noted that the wind blows in the direction of the nearby elementary school 36 percent of the time.[79] Further, because of the local topography, "the top of the smoke stacks (elevation *50 feet* mean sea level) will be at or below the *floor level* of the majority of local homes, offices, and other buildings."[80]

On and on the questions went, for 181 pages. Yomtovian even suggested that the ownership of WTI merited further investigation, as activists had claimed.[81] He quoted state and national medical-association statements questioning the wisdom of incineration.[82] Yet he commended Governor Voinovich's plan for a health study, hinting, however, that the governor's aides had underestimated the true scope of such a task if it were properly conducted.[83]

Nonetheless, even as a consultant to the city, Yomtovian cut to the quick of the very question that had undermined citizens' confidence in their own local government. With reference to the spray-dryer controversy, Yomtovian noted that "elected officials signed a letter in complete support of changes and revisions made by WTI in their facility design" against the advice of their consultant.[84] Yomtovian also noted that the city could not afford to conduct "studies, surveys, professional and legal investigations, and other necessary activities" related to WTI "with its existing budget."

"Possible litigations by WTI/Von Roll against the City," the report added, "has forced the City officials not to take any action (such as adoption of pollution ordinance) at this time. Therefore, the City has been compelled to negotiate a solution to this problem."[85] In effect, the city's consultant said that fear of WTI's deep pockets for a legal battle had paralyzed city officials when they should have been acting to protect the health, safety, and welfare of their own citizens. Yomtovian proposed that fees on WTI be high enough to support a wide variety of health and safety services necessitated by the WTI presence.

Yomtovian seemed to anticipate that WTI would seek to downplay his credentials. He answered the question in his opening remarks, noting that his firm was "not expert in all areas," but could provide any needed outside experts to the city. On a specific point, the spray dryer, Yomtovian had commissioned as co-author of the report an engineer, Thomas Walsh, who had expertise on precisely this point.[86] Interestingly, Ohio EPA officials would observe the following summer that Yomtovian had seemed to be "floundering" in seeking agency information for his consulting study.[87]

The mayor's initial reaction to the final draft of the Yomtovian study was not to release it, based on advice from the liaison committee's private lawyer. It found its way to the public through the *Plain Dealer*, Cleveland's daily newspaper, which used Ohio's open-records law to obtain a copy.[88]

Depending on whose numbers one uses, somewhere between 700 and 1,000 people rallied in downtown East Liverpool on Sunday, October 13. Despite some rain the previous week, it was the type of cool but sunny autumn afternoon that makes Buckeye small towns with their colorful tree leaves postcard-perfect. Atop a large platform with a public-address system, Martin Sheen and Paul Connett strove to buck up the crowd's courage to challenge WTI more directly than ever before.[89]

Connett's indignation was in full bloom. He suggested that to understand the incinerator's illegality the governor needed only a ruler, "unless WTI could pay for someone to say that 1,100 feet is 2,000 feet." He ranted that local activists had sent EPA's Region V $200 for a stack of papers they were told was "this high" (holding his arms far apart) but had then received only a fraction of the documents they had paid for.

"How can you judge people?" he asked, noting that most people have no way of knowing "who is telling the truth." To answer the question, he excoriated WTI officials for their cowardice in refusing to debate publicly "a little old chemistry professor from upstate New York." (Actually, Connett is neither little nor old but middle-aged and physically both imposing and very healthy.) "What have they got to hide?" he asked. As the horn from a passing train interrupted his talk, he humored the audience. "It's probably bringing toxic waste from Florida."

Sheen prepared the audience for its march to the plant fence. "I will go all the way with you," he declared. "You all know what I do for a living. This is what I do to stay alive." Then, hinting at what was to follow, he added, "I always have to dig deeper and pray harder. There's no room for any violence or any anger."

The crowd marched down the street to the WTI site, with Sheen leading them in the Lord's Prayer, arm in arm, row upon row upon row. When they had prayed, they sang "Amazing Grace." Sheen, "moved by the Spirit," was the first to jump the chain-link fence and trespass on the WTI property. One by one, 32 others followed. Terri Swearingen. Paul Connett. Alonzo Spencer. Most had never been arrested in their entire lives. They knelt on the wet ground in prayer and waited for the police to respond.

A surprised but courteous police force handcuffed them, then called a station wagon to haul away the first carload. From the back seat, with the crowd of hundreds cheering from the other side of the fence, Connett, who at first had been nervous about compromising his status among scientific peers with this arrest, glanced out the back window. He held his cuffed hands aloft and waved. He no longer feared nor cared. His was a wave of triumph.

"I felt almost elated," he said later. "We were upholding the law, not breaking the law. Nobody should threaten children the way they were doing."[90]

At the jail that night, Connett, Sheen, and several others each posted a $250 bond for their release. Many local activists chose to

stay in jail until their Tuesday arraignment.[91] For Connett, this was
not a matter of breaking ranks. He believes passionately in not hurt-
ing his students by missing classes because of his activism. Nonetheless, following a hometown newspaper report that exaggerated the
legal threat facing Connett, a St. Lawrence University spokeswoman
had to downplay the possibility of his being fired because of the incident.[92]

On Monday, the police arrested a young Greenpeace activist from
Washington, D.C., who pitched his tent in the WTI driveway and
refused to move. About 30 protesters returned with a banner that
read, "Prevent Child Abuse, Impeach Voinovich."[93] In the evening,
demonstrators held candlelight vigils outside the jails. On Monday
morning, Becky Tobin left jail on a recognizance bond. She reported
that "the cockroaches in the jail were so bad we had to sit with our
feet up off the floor. We hardly slept all night."[94]

On Tuesday, a third protest occurred. Police arrested two more
people who lay down in front of the gate to block incoming traffic.
One was a Presbyterian pastor, the other a teacher.[95] Police Chief
Charles Coen began to express irritation at the continuing protests
and promised "more aggressive action" to deal with them.[96] WTI attorneys went to court seeking a restraining order to bar protesters
from blocking the gate to its plant. WTI safety director Scott Martin
even complained in his affidavit that one protester had brought her
young child into the WTI complex to use the bathroom.[97] The following day, Judge Douglas C. Jenkins granted WTI's request.[98]

Emboldened by their first brush with the law, Swearingen and Spencer dressed in prison garb to lead their fellow arrestees to Columbus
in a foiled attempt to meet with the governor about WTI. Spencer
was indignant over Voinovich's reported comment that most of the
protesters were "outsiders." Voinovich was in Iowa at the Midwest
Governors Conference. The group demanded that Voinovich visit
East Liverpool to learn about the incinerator firsthand.[99] He refused.[100] The protesters upped the ante, taking their next demonstration to his home in suburban Bexley. The governor exited a side
door and hopped into the back seat of a car. As the car backed out

the driveway, some called him a "wienie."[101] That epithet became an inspiration for yet another protest in late November. Returning to the governor's mansion, WTI foes donned hot-dog costumes and dubbed Voinovich a "wienie on waste" for his failure to take a strong stand on hazardous-waste reduction.[102]

At about the same time, Chester officials were taking some matters into their own hands. At Mayor Riley's request, the council passed an ordinance to require hazardous-waste haulers to notify the city and secure a police escort before coming through. For haulers entering East Liverpool from the eastern states, the Chester ordinance set up a gauntlet that could be circumvented only by crossing the Ohio River at far less convenient points and adding as much as 20 miles to the trip on secondary highways. The ordinance set other stringent standards, including a $10 million bond before the vehicle could be moved if a leak was discovered and a $20 million bond for the right to pass through the city at night.[103]

The biggest leak affecting WTI, however, was the deflation of its credibility. Investigative journalists like T.C. Brown of Cleveland's the *Plain Dealer* and Dan Hopey of the *Pittsburgh Press* had discovered WTI to be front-page material. They hacked away at the story relentlessly. Just before the Chester vote, Brown revealed that the Ohio EPA had bent its own rules regarding permit changes by allowing a major change in WTI's operating permit without a hearing. Ohio EPA memos revealed that WTI had threatened to cancel the entire project if forced to undergo a formal hearing because it feared that appeals by environmentalists would lead to "additional unacceptable delays."[104]

The drumbeat of protest and investigation took its toll on the governor. Conceding that "enough is enough" and that Ohio had done its "fair share" in accepting the burden of such facilities, Voinovich in early December called for a statewide moratorium on the construction of new commercial hazardous-waste incinerators. At 21 percent of the nation's capacity, Voinovich noted, the state was second only to Texas (29 percent) in hosting incinerators. This figure did not account for the use of cement kilns, which burn hazardous waste as a fuel source for mixing cement. Already, the Ross incinerator operating in Grafton, at 86,400 tons per year, exceeded by one-third the estimated capacity needs of Ohio industry. At double that size, WTI was actually adding import capacity. Ohio was becoming a magnet for hazardous waste in need of incineration.[105] The moratorium offered one sacrificial lamb on the altar of political expediency: the proposed incinerator in Nova, in the heart of heavily Republican farm country.

The moratorium proposal may have served to weaken the statewide coalition that environmentalists had built around the issue of hazardous-waste incineration. Certainly, Voinovich must have hoped it would be divisive, and Rick Sahli invested considerable time and effort in persuading the Nova opponents to stay with the larger cause rather than quitting simply because the toxic cup had passed them by.

Voinovich's moratorium did nothing, however, to soften the stance of East Liverpool opponents. Angry that the moratorium would still saddle them with the WTI facility while relieving others of their fears, they adopted increasingly militant and sarcastic protest tactics to make their point. First, they visited the governor's office with hot dogs wrapped in tin foil, leaving behind grade-school math books and flashcards to help him calculate Ohio's waste-burning capacity.[106] Then, just a week before Christmas 1991, they counterattacked.

Ohio EPA Director Donald Schregardus left the agency's downtown Columbus headquarters for a daylong series of meetings on Tuesday morning, December 17. Shortly after 11:00 a.m., nearly four dozen citizens arrived at the front desk, where a receptionist asked them to sign in. As the long line crawled forward, 12 members of the crowd suddenly bolted up the stairs, brushing past Schregardus's personal secretary and into his office, where they handcuffed themselves to each other after inserting their arms in metal tubes and circling Schregardus's desk chair. One cuffed herself to a flagpole.

Meanwhile, the other protesters began to roam the halls, "inspecting" and opening files, riding elevators, and handing out "pink slips" to employees who allegedly had failed to protect the public. Inside the director's office, the protesters ordered a vegetarian pizza. Security guards turned it away when the delivery man came. State police arrived and rounded up the wandering band, making them wait in a conference room on the first floor. Then, wearing latex gloves, they searched for explosives and stink bombs.

Upstairs, deputy director Gerry G. Ioannides offered coffee and water while asking the protesters to unchain themselves and "be civilized," a request that the group flatly rejected. Unaware of Schregardus's schedule, he suggested his boss could meet with them at 1:00 p.m. The meeting never happened because Schregardus would not return that day. Schregardus relayed a proposal to meet in a conference room, but the protesters refused to leave his office. They issued three demands: an immediate halt to processing the WTI permit; the release to the public of all files pertaining to WTI; and a written commitment by Schregardus to require industry to cut its use of toxics in half within five years (a goal similar to that in Massachusetts's Toxics Use Reduction Act).

The standoff dragged on into the early evening. Finally, after six hours, the state patrol moved into the office, severing the metal tubes and cuffs and arresting the 10 protesters who had stayed. Among them were Swearingen and Stein, Rebecca Tobin, and Beth Newman, a Greenpeace staff member who had set up an office in Chester.

Schregardus quickly issued a statement expressing his disappointment "in the deplorable tactics used today."[107]

A day later, the agency issued its revised permit to WTI.[108] At the end of the month, reflecting its heightened fear of public animosity, the Ohio EPA instituted tighter security, including employee identification badges and the placement of guards throughout the building.[109] Swearingen and the Tri-State Environmental Council welcomed the new year, in turn, by announcing that parents would oppose letting Voinovich "touch our children" through participation in the planned health study. Swearingen characterized the nature and timing of the study as "allowing the exposure, then studying the effects."[110]

In the first week of 1992, the wheels of government turned once again in their long, slow grind through the WTI affair as the Ohio Environmental Board of Review agreed to hear an appeal of the WTI permit by SOC and the state of West Virginia.[111] Alonzo Spencer expressed optimism despite the board's "rubber-stamp" image among environmentalists, but it was clear that opponents' faith in the system was eroding. Protesters, their ranks swelled by the newly vocal United Auto Workers Local 1714 from the General Motors plant in Lordstown, disrupted and then stomped out of a city-council meeting on January 6. Earlier in the meeting, Mayor Scafide had criticized the state's failure to consult with the city about the design of its health study.[112] Already, the opponents were looking for new ways to stop the plant. In response to their pleas, West Virginia's U.S. Representative Alan Mollohan requested an investigation by the General Accounting Office, Congress's auditing arm, of the adequacy of the U.S. EPA's review of WTI's permits.[113] Senator Jay Rockefeller joined the growing chorus of criticism from West Virginia politicians.

Judge Melissa Byers-Emmerling set the course for the entire trial of the "ELO (East Liverpool, Ohio) 33" when she allowed the protesters' attorneys to argue a necessity defense, a commonly used tactic in civil-disobedience cases. In essence, "necessity" is based on the concept of the lesser evil, of preventing a greater harm through a lesser but necessary violation of the law. In moral terms, it is precisely the opposite of the Nazi defense in the Nuremberg trials, where accused war criminals claimed that they were simply following orders in operating the concentration camps. Proponents of civil disobedience argue that *not acting* to prevent a likely harm represents a form of complicity. Thus, the defendants prepared to argue that, having exhausted their legal channels for stopping the WTI incinerator, they were forced to turn to extralegal but peaceful methods to make their point before it was too late.

Without that ruling, the trial in East Liverpool Municipal Court would have been short. No one denied jumping the fence, although Martin Sheen's lawyer unsuccessfully sought acquittal on grounds that jumping the fence was not illegal.[114] The prosecution's case was simple. Police Captain Michael McVay noted that a Greenpeace representative had assured him beforehand that the group was training protesters for a nonviolent sit-in at the gate and that his main concern was that 1,000 people would be marching down Highway 39. He was surprised when protesters began jumping the fence. WTI's security manager, Marty Scott, appeared uncomfortable as defense attorneys drew forth the concession that Police Chief Coen operated a private security firm that had been hired by WTI, effectively raising the specter of a conflict of interest. His discomfort may also have come from the rising temperatures on a crowded third floor, which eventually caused the judge to open the courtroom windows to the February cold outdoors. The prosecution's main attraction, however, was a videotape of the protest, showing the defendants jumping the fence, praying, and being led politely away in handcuffs.

But the defense, in proceedings that lasted a week, turned the courtroom into a studio for a televised debate, parading a series of expert witnesses before the jury to detail their reservations about incinerating hazardous waste. Greenpeace videotaped the entire trial, local television stations and newspaper reporters were in abundance, and New York's Courtroom Television Network, a cable channel, broadcast the spectacle nationwide. Martin Sheen, ignoring advice from his agent and attorney, sat with his fellow defendants throughout the trial, giving the cameras a celebrity focus.[115]

One by one, within their own clearly established areas of expertise, the expert witnesses laid the groundwork for proving that the defendants had a valid basis for their belief that they were acting to prevent a harm to the community great enough to justify their criminal trespass. Before even the first witness appeared, however, Paul Connett lost a philosophical argument with his attorneys. Connett argued that the defense should not rely solely on scientists and engineers to make its point, but should seek to highlight the practical experiences of people who had lived near other hazardous waste incinerators around the country.

Whether the court would have admitted such witnesses as experts is unclear, but Connett's strategy was a radical challenge to his attorneys' traditional notion of expertise. His resources for such a strategy, however, were substantial. Just a year earlier, the Chemical Waste Management facility on Chicago's southeast side had exploded. That facility was in the process of being closed permanently. In Lenoir, North Carolina, Dr. Marc Guerra had treated a variety of illnesses among 22 workers at the Caldwell Systems, Inc., incinera-

tor there. He attributed them to the facility's difficulties in comply-
ing with environmental regulations. That facility closed after a September 1989 chemical fire forced the evacuation and hospitalization
of nearby residents. In 1977, three storage tanks exploded at a New
Jersey facility owned by Rollins Environmental Services. Other
plants in Arkansas and Kentucky had showered problems on their
surrounding communities.[116] Connett's goal was to let the neighbors
of these facilities demonstrate to the jury and the community the
future that he felt East Liverpool faced if it allowed WTI to operate.
His strategy was tied intimately to his own central concept of what
constitutes valid science and thus valid evidence.[117]

If the defense limited its choice of evidence, its expert witnesses
at least rose eloquently to the occasion. Dr. David Ozonoff, a frequent adviser to citizens' groups concerned about hazardous-waste
sites, testified first. As a medical researcher at the Harvard University School of Public Health, Ozonoff had assisted the residents of
Woburn, Massachusetts, who had suffered from the effects of groundwater pollution from W.R. Grace Company. There, he had begun to
learn of the EPA's pattern of rigid resistance to accepting data from
medical surveys conducted by volunteers.[118] Ozonoff was well aware
that the sheer cost of professional surveys often made them impracti-
cal for neighborhood groups, thus limiting the availability of data
and disempowering citizens. For that very reason, volunteers could
often fill crucial gaps in the documentation of a public-health emergency. His view on this point is not popular among epidemiologists
but has made him an important figure in developing toxic-waste laws
and regulations in Massachusetts, where he was chairman of the
state's hazardous-waste advisory committee. Massachusetts has
moved to the forefront of pollution prevention in recent years with
the implementation of its Toxics Use Reduction Act, which seeks to
spur companies to find alternatives to using toxic materials in their
manufacturing processes.

The wastes that would be incinerated at WTI included more than
four dozen known or suspected carcinogens, Ozonoff testified. But
most compounds on WTI's long list of burnable substances had not
even been tested. What was important, he stressed, was to understand how cancer occurs.

A cell that becomes cancerous "begins to behave in a way that it didn't and crowds out other cells," Ozonoff explained. "Every time it divides, two daughter cells also behave that way, and so forth as they multiply. With the passage of time, you have not just millions but billions of cells behaving in this harmful way. The clue is that, as the cell divides, the reproduced cells have that inherited characteristic."

Cells contain a biochemical structure known as DNA that contains our genes, he continued. "When that's changed, that causes cancerous behavior. Carcinogens cause this alteration." Only about one percent of all chemicals have the capacity to cause these changes, Ozonoff noted, but on a hazardous-waste list an abnormal number of substances qualify. Further, it was not merely a question of how much exposure was required to trigger this reaction. "There is really no threshold because it only takes one abnormal cell. The amount [needed] can be just a few molecules. After the original change, your body is doing that destructive work for you." In other words, any exposure at all is like a random shot in a game of Russian roulette. The odds of damage simply increase with exposure, but the potential is always there.

The defense attorneys, having set up the scientific basis for this evaluation, then steered Ozonoff to the question of the site. Certainly, he answered, the nearby residents were at greater risk because of constant and prolonged exposure. "It is extraordinary in my experience to have a facility like this sited 1,100 feet from a school. The people in my department's eyes bugged out when they saw that, and they said, 'This is unbelievable.'" It was of "limited or no value," Ozonoff added, to shut the facility down when it was malfunctioning because the exposure would already have occurred. "We're talking about starting people on the road to cancer," he said, comparing the situation to someone who jumps from a fourteenth-floor window and yells as he passes the lower floors, "So far, so good."

Even more sarcasm was to follow. Asked about the impact on the siting of the area's problematic weather patterns, Ozonoff snapped, "It makes about as much sense as a transportation system for Death Valley that relies on ice skates." He offered the analogy of someone using a bucket of carbon tetrachloride, a deadly gas that biology students have used to stifle captured insects. "It makes a difference whether they use it in a closet or in a big room with the doors and windows open. The trouble is that meteorologically we're in a tiny little closed-off room." The region's air circulates beneath a 70-meter ceiling most of the time, thwarting the dilution of toxic pollutants. Worse, he said, "residences and schools are crowded in the closet with it." His teaching colleagues, he said, often used the area as an example of bad meteorology, along with nearby Steubenville, Ohio, and Donora, Pennsylvania.

So, the attorneys wanted to know, how had the Ohio Hazardous Waste Facility Board approved such a site? The board, Ozonoff replied, had looked at only a few pollutants like sulfur dioxide and total suspended particulates and decided that the plant would not add much to the region's existing pollution problems. Those pollutants were not the point, however, so much as a deadly gas like hydrogen cyanide, which still is used for execution in gas chambers. "It regularly kills landfill operators who mix incompatible wastes," he noted. Chlorine, lead, and other hazardous chemicals also went unexamined for their potential impacts. "They took an unbelievably narrow view," Ozonoff concluded. "It was a deliberate attempt to look in another direction."

"Can these chemicals cause problems other than cancer?" defense attorney Paul Boas asked. They affected reproduction, the ability of women to have babies born healthy, Ozonoff replied. There were effects on the central nervous and immune systems. "Why are these things called hazardous wastes? They are dangerous," he added. "It's not just a cancer problem."

Ozonoff noted that most wastes would arrive by truck, some by rail. "I called the Department of Transportation in Washington and talked to a man who prepares an annual report on hazardous materials on trucks. Ohio has one of the highest rates of hazardous materials spills in the nation." Most accidents, he added, "happen within a half-mile of your home. These vehicles will be converging on this plant. With 1,100 feet to an elementary school, it's astounding."

Boas saved his *coup de grace* for last. Ron Brown of WTI, he said, had spoken to the local Lions Club. Would it be true, as he said, that "only carbon dioxide, water vapor, and nitrogen would come from these stacks"?

"That's totally untrue," Ozonoff replied.

On cross-examination, the prosecution failed miserably, trying to quiz Ozonoff about his knowledge of other sources of air pollution in the valley. "It's hard to conceive of effects like these on this scale from any other source," Ozonoff insisted, "but I cannot comment on other specific sources."

Having questioned Ozonoff for more than an hour, Boas introduced Dr. Herbert Needleman, a specialist in psychiatry and pediatrics at the University of Pittsburgh who had investigated the health effects of low-level lead exposure for 20 years. He had written three books and more than 80 papers on the topic and worked for the removal of lead from gasoline in the early 1970s.

Boas noted that the permit allowed WTI to emit up to 4.7 tons of lead per year and asked about the effects of lead on children. "This is a rapidly growing field," Needleman said. "Forty years ago, it was assumed that a child suffering from lead poisoning either died or completely recovered." In the 1950s, however, researchers discovered an aftereffect of mental retardation. Elevated levels of blood lead increase the probability of brain disorders. "My study in 1979 in the *New England Journal of Medicine* showed lower IQ scores" for children with elevated levels of lead in their blood. Their high exposure levels later correlated with a "sevenfold increase in failure to complete high school." Moreover, "24 studies have shown similar effects."

As for the paths of exposure, lead can be absorbed through the lungs, Needleman added. Larger particles can be swallowed after being coughed up. Such particles can be as small as one-millionth of a meter in diameter. Some lead would fall as dust and be absorbed through dust. And, once again, proximity to the incinerator mattered. "Very good data," Needleman said, "shows that the closer you are to the emissions, the higher the level of blood absorption" that will occur. Having a school just 1,100 feet away created a "very high risk of substantial absorption of lead."

How did these problems manifest themselves in victims? "The bulk of studies have shown an inability to solve problems, speak well, sit still in class," and an impairment of physical growth, Needleman said. The bones of older people, who had absorbed lead over a lifetime, would begin to lose their mineral content. There was even evidence from a 1977 study in Boston of blood lead crossing a woman's placenta to affect a fetus. The outcome in follow-up studies was an increase in minor deformations at birth.

"Without a doubt," Needleman told the court, we do not understand all the ramifications of lead poisoning. "The more we study, the more we find."

Michael McCawley, a civil engineer who teaches air-pollution control and atmospheric science at West Virginia University, served on an advisory panel for Governor Gaston Caperton, for whom he performed an analysis of WTI. He was familiar with commercial hazardous-waste incinerator operations. He, too, described the area as one "well documented in the literature" of his field as "hallmarks of science for discoveries." He described how the terrain and meteorology combined to produce air inversions that kept warm air from rising above ground level and dispersing its pollutant loads. He, too, cited the famous instance of Donora, Pennsylvania, in 1948, which he said "could occur in the WTI setting today." The EPA models, he said, "assume it will always blow away, and that's just not true."

McCawley's points led inexorably to a simple conclusion. If there were no sources of air pollution in the valley, the air stagnation would not lead to any buildup of pollutants. The meteorological patterns only mattered as a health hazard "when things are injected. You're living in your own garbage." Furthermore, the EPA knew this. Its own regulations said that, "with an area of air inversions, you must have a model specific to this area. In West Virginia, we concluded that the WTI modeling was inadequate to begin with." The use of models that "would have likely underestimated" pollution during these inversion episodes was "violative of EPA's own standards."

Boas then listed the tonnages of permitted emissions from the WTI incinerator and asked McCawley whether any of the compounds were dangerous.

"All have known toxic effects," McCawley responded. "All are capable of being trapped in these inversions."

"What dangers," Boas then asked, "exist even within the limits of the permit?"

There were real possibilities of exceeding the area's ambient airquality standards for those pollutants, McCawley said. He noted that "site selection must be done unless there is no risk." The hazardous-waste board had decided there was no need to select alternative sites "because the WTI facility posed no environmental risk. The reason given was that it was a state-of-the-art facility. That term has no technical meaning. It doesn't mean that nothing can happen."

Gradually, Boas led McCawley into analogies to the risk analysis done for nuclear power plants, leading to an objection. A discussion of how East Liverpool, Ohio, could experience an accident akin to the pesticide gas leak in Bhopal, India, that killed thousands of residents also drew a sustained objection. Nonetheless, Boas found a new line of questioning that let McCawley describe how an invisible plume of incinerator air pollutants could become concentrated atop the hill above the river, possibly causing "acute effects from those gases."

"Were these taken into account in the air modeling?" Boas asked.

"No, they were not," McCawley insisted. "The study was not valid."

"Can you think of a worse location?" Boas continued.

"I can think of one or two similar locations, but probably none that were a whole lot worse. Part of the reason I am here is that I feel responsible to say some things to the court that I said to [the defendants] because what I said may be the reason for some of their actions that put them here."

McCawley proceeded to answer a question about products of incomplete combustion, explaining that "metals don't incinerate very well. Mercury will not burn very well. You hope to capture some of it downstream with pollution-control equipment. These sorts of incinerators," McCawley noted, "have been called 'landfills in the sky.' "

Hugh B. Kaufman was a special weapon for the defense. It was one thing to introduce to the jury an independent expert from academia. But Kaufman had never worked in academia. After a stint in Vietnam, the engineer had joined the U.S. EPA at its inception in 1971, starting its noise abatement and control office. He had been effective, persuading Congress to pass the 1973 Noise Abatement and Control Act.

That same year, he moved to the EPA's Office of Solid and Hazardous Waste, where he investigated all types of hazardous waste generated by U.S. industries. He then helped the agency develop a strategy for regulating solid and hazardous waste. The result was the passage in 1976 of the Resource Conservation and Recovery Act (RCRA), the nation's first attempt at comprehensive regulation of the storage, transportation, treatment, and disposal of hazardous waste. From 1975 to 1980, Kaufman was the EPA's chief hazardous-site investigator, tackling hundreds of cases across the U.S. In 1978, he testified before Congress about the environmental disaster at Love Canal. That research led to the passage in 1980 of the Comprehensive Environmental Response, Compensation, and Liability Act (CERCLA), known more commonly as the "Superfund law," which created a fund to expedite the cleanup of the nation's worst hazardous-waste dumps. Kaufman also had a hand in writing and commenting on the regulations developed to implement the nation's new hazardous-waste legislation.

It was WTI's compliance with, as well as the U.S. EPA's enforcement of, those regulations that became the focus of Kaufman's lightning-rod testimony. Kaufman was no longer leading the charge within the agency on these issues. During the Reagan years, as Rita Lavelle politicized and corrupted the hazardous-waste cleanup process, and as Anne Gorsuch diminished the agency's public credibility, Kaufman was relegated to the sidelines of the decision-making process. He became a whistleblower, and Gorsuch and Lavelle left the agency in disgrace. Kaufman increasingly turned to the new grassroots citizen activists as an alternative force to steer the EPA back toward aggressive enforcement. He had met with and advised Terri Swearingen, Becky Tobin, Alonzo Spencer, and others prior to the demonstration.

Despite occasional objections from the prosecution, Kaufman was able to discuss in considerable detail the May 19, 1980, *Federal Register* notice that contained final RCRA rules that he had written. They included a requirement that both the operator and owner of a hazardous-waste facility, as well as the owner of the land on which it sits, co-sign the facility's application for the RCRA Part B permit it must obtain before it can begin construction. The rationale for the requirement stemmed from Kaufman's experience in investigating waste sites, where often a shell company with no tangible assets posed as the owner of a site in order to protect the real owner from liability for an expensive cleanup. "This [rule] made them all jointly and severally liable for costs," Kaufman explained.

A central controversy concerning the WTI site was the land's continued ownership by the Columbiana County Port Authority. Was it true as listed on the permit application, Boas asked, that WTI was both the owner and operator?

"That's a lie," Kaufman flatly stated. In fact, he noted, in September 1981, the name on the application should still have been River Services Corporation, which owned the land prior to its acquisition by the Ohio Department of Transportation and subsequent transfer to the port authority. Standing by an easel with diagrams and blow-ups of property records, Kaufman noted that this deed transfer had not even happened by then. To underscore the seriousness of this alleged deception, Kaufman noted that "RCRA Section 308 states severe penalties of $50,000 per day and two years in prison for falsifying a permit application. There is no question," he continued, that in the event of an accident, "the state of Ohio and the port authority would have majority liability."

Correcting Boas, Kaufman added that "EPA does not have discretion to revoke this permit. They *have* to revoke this permit. . . . It's clear from the documents I've investigated that the federal government in this particular case has violated a number of criminal statutes, and the state has violated a number of criminal statutes." In this situation, he noted, "the ability to get a level playing field for the ordinary citizen is very difficult, if not impossible."

Kaufman had laid the groundwork for justifying civil disobedience by the defendants in the face of a corrupt system. Seeking to solidify this point, Boas asked, "Do you know of anything else these individuals could have done?"

"I don't," Kaufman replied with a firm gaze, "because the federal and state EPA have violated a number of statutes. To appeal to decision makers who have chosen to ignore the law after a while becomes meaningless."

The prosecution, on cross-examination, zeroed in on Kaufman far more than it had on any previous witness, sparring over the legality of the permit and Kaufman's credibility to make his assessment.

Kaufman stood by his insistence that the permits were blatantly illegal. The prosecution sniped at his seeming audacity. Was it WTI and not the defendants who were on trial?

"It's my understanding," Kaufman retorted, "that the judge is allowing information related to the necessity defense and that involves information about WTI activities. Whether you would say they are on trial, I don't know."

"Have the defendants filed a mandamus action?" city attorney Charles Payne demanded to know. A writ of mandamus, usually resulting from a citizen suit, orders a government official to perform a legally mandated action that he or she has refused to do. A mandamus action, however, requires the absence of discretionary power on the part of the official being sued.

"No, to my knowledge, they have not," Kaufman answered. But he could "understand and empathize with these people in their frustration in trying to go through these people with regard to the laws of the United States."

Finally, quizzed about the impact of the demonstration, Kaufman added, "I think the chain of events set in motion by the October 13 trespass case will result in government officials doing their job, and I hope that some officials not doing their job will be brought to justice."

The next morning, area newspapers quoted various U.S. EPA officials stating that Hugh Kaufman's views were his alone and were not those of his employer.[119]

"If I remain silent, my friends would die of shock," said Paul Connett, the first of many defendants to take the stand, unconcerned about potential self-incrimination. Like his scientific colleagues before him, he outlined his credentials and his involvement in hazardous-waste issues, and displayed his technical acumen, often reiterating points made by previous witnesses. He outlined his deeply held fears about the difference between the theory of incineration and its actual practice, and his inability to find any references to experience with the real-life performance of incinerators in EPA documents.

As was typical of Connett, however, the high point of his testimony was his defiant statement of personal principles. He had traveled to numerous cities in the U.S. and abroad to investigate incinerator performance, meeting with citizens who lived with breathing problems, odors, black smoke, accidents, fires, and explosions, and finding "nobody out there to help these people."

After extended discussion of his spray-dryer testimony, Connett inevitably focused on his reasons for joining the demonstrators himself.

"If you know something is going to happen to impact a kid, that kid's mine," he asserted. "This is my family. It's going to happen because it's only a matter of time before they mix the wrong chemicals in that plant. There needed to be some sort of shock tactic to get local and state and federal officials to take this seriously. I felt that, by becoming a victim myself, we could prevent the real victims from happening."

Normally a powerful speaker, Connett began to weep visibly, struggling to contain the emotional impact of his own testimony. Through a shield of tears, he credited Martin Sheen with maintaining the spiritual integrity of the protest by advising those who joined him that even the WTI officials "are not the enemy."

One more expert witness, Lynn Moorer, a policy consultant from Nebraska, followed Connett to the stand, along with a steady parade of defendants testifying about their "state of mind" in choosing civil disobedience as a strategy for stopping the incinerator. Swearingen and other local leaders discussed the dozens of books and government reports they had read in researching the issue of hazardous waste.

But the damage to the prosecution's case had already taken place in the minds of the jury. On Friday, February 14, after two-and-a-half hours of deliberation, eight jurors found all 29 remaining defendants not guilty. The news spread quickly through East Liverpool. So far as Judge Byers-Emmerling knew, it set a precedent as the first acquittal resulting from a necessity defense in the state of Ohio.[120]

The verdict of acquittal did not stop or even slow the WTI juggernaut. It did, however, attract national attention. WTI was no longer merely a local or even regional story, and its officials were increasingly hostile toward the media spotlight that focused on them. Hoping to undo some of the public-relations damage they had already suffered, the firm in late March announced plans to engage the University of Pittsburgh's Center for Hazardous Materials Research in developing a citizens advisory committee.[121] Unfortunately, it was an idea that came too late to entice any serious opponents to join. The effectiveness of such a committee requires a degree of mutual trust within the community. That bond had long ago been broken.

In the spring, congressional interest in the case quickened. Senator Howard Metzenbaum became a vocal opponent, questioning the permit-granting procedures in letters to U.S. EPA and WTI officials.[122] In April, Democratic presidential candidate Jerry Brown made East Liverpool a campaign stop, visiting the home of Bob and Sandy Estelle, whose backyard overlooks the incinerator.[123] In early May, the U.S. House Judiciary Committee opened investigative hearings on the permit approval for the WTI incinerator, calling Swearingen and Kaufman as witnesses. The hearing drew the attention of the New York Times as two officials of the U.S. EPA's Chicago office, under questioning by Representative Barney Frank, a Massachusetts Democrat, admitted that the agency had violated the law by issuing the 1983 permit even though the application was incomplete. In effect, they corroborated Swearingen's and Kaufman's central accusation. But they labeled the violation "minor and technical."[124] Later that month, Metzenbaum convinced the Senate Committee on Environment and Public Works, which was considering a reauthorization of RCRA, to back an amendment that would delay WTI's opening.[125] The RCRA bill itself, however, went nowhere in the midst of election-year politics.

Still, summer brought closer the prospect of a trial burn at the facility, a test that is designed to suggest to regulators how well the incinerator will perform in destroying certain substances. Regulations require that hazardous-waste incinerators achieve a destruction and removal efficiency (DRE) of 99.99 percent for most chemicals, permitting, in other words, no more than one in 10,000 parts of what came into the incinerator to escape unburned into the atmosphere. A trial burn cannot, of course, guarantee that the incinerator will always operate at the demonstrated efficiency, nor does it prove the absence of products of incomplete combustion, which are new compounds created through the chemical reaction generated either in the furnace or as gases cool in the smokestacks. As the latter have no precise basis for comparison to the materials that entered the incinerator, they are not factored into the DRE.

The Tri-State Environmental Council was determined to find a way to abort the trial burn, fearing that it would provide the ticket WTI needed for full-scale operation. In mid-July, after learning that Region V had granted permission for the trial burn, 20 protesters took their message to Washington by occupying the offices of U.S. EPA Administrator William Reilly. They left at 6:00 p.m. after negotiating throughout the day with Lewis Crampton, the EPA associate administrator for communications and public affairs, to obtain a pledge that WTI would delay the test for 10 days. The EPA promised to reexamine the issue during that time.[126] (Crampton raised environmentalists' hackles later in the year when he joined Waste Management, Inc., as a senior vice president for communications. It turned out that he had already been offered the job when the discussions with the protesters occurred. He also had had them arrested and jailed when they returned for a second protest after the 10 days expired.)[127]

When the 10 days had passed and nothing had changed, 25 incinerator opponents intensified their tactics by launching a hunger strike that lasted about five weeks. The tactic drew the attention of ABC's "Nightline," which sent a crew to East Liverpool and staged a debate between Terri Swearingen and Region V EPA administrator Valdas Adamkus. Swearingen, in the twenty-third day of her hunger strike, easily cornered and outargued the unfocused and vague Adamkus who, for the most part, offered assurances that he would do nothing to harm "the health and environment." Meanwhile, the hunger strikers managed to reveal the text of a letter from Von Roll America President D.J. Blake Marshall to Vice President Quayle, seeking help from his Council on Competitiveness in overcoming regulatory hurdles. They alleged a connection to WTI's receipt of permission for its trial burn, a charge the EPA denied.[128]

The state of Ohio, meanwhile, proved unwilling to test public opinion with another civil-disobedience trial. In Columbus, the protesters who had occupied the Ohio EPA headquarters won another ruling granting them the right to argue a necessity defense. Again, they had enlisted 12 expert witnesses to testify on their behalf. Anxious to avoid the spectacle, the state tried to settle the case. First, the charges would be dropped if the defendants agreed to enter the Ohio EPA offices only after scheduling an appointment. They rejected that offer. The state then backed down to merely asking that the defendants agree not to sue for false arrest. Again, they refused the offer. Finally, Ohio EPA public-information officer Patricia Madigan announced that the agency could not afford to use its officials' time in court to rebut a necessity defense. On August 30, the day before the trial was to begin, the state dropped all charges, depriving the defendants of their prime-time forum in the state capital.[129]

Also in August, the port authority, under growing pressure over its refusal to allow the EPA to add its name to the permit application as a retroactive correction, decided to opt out of its problem by abdicating its role as landowner. At an unruly meeting where public questions were barred and police were used to calm an angry crowd, the board voted to sell the 21 acres beneath the incinerator site to WTI for $5 million. Vice-chairman Carl Pelini declared that the money would be used to build a public riverport on 23 remaining acres. Alonzo Spencer accused the board of a desperate act to save an otherwise invalid permit.[130]

In late August, West Virginia Attorney General Mario Palumbo sought a preliminary injunction in federal district court to bar WTI from operating pending an investigation of the circumstances surrounding the permit. The city of Pittsburgh had earlier joined the case as an intervenor. Palumbo was seeking the order as part of his ongoing case seeking to bar WTI permanently from operating. But on July 9, the U.S. EPA had issued WTI a temporary authorization to finish construction and commence a "startup." In their briefs, both Palumbo and the city made liberal use of some elaborate research conducted by Tri-State Environmental Council volunteers, notably Swearingen, Stein, and Mick Casey, a small-town real-estate agent. Through record searches in Arkansas and Ohio, they mapped out changes in ownership and incorporation among the various WTI partners. In all, they showed, some 40 corporate entities and corporate names had participated in a vast paper shuffle, some involving

little more than adding or deleting a comma or parenthesis, allegedly so that regulators would not take notice, for instance, of the
difference between Waste Technologies, Inc. and Waste Technologies Inc. In view of Kaufman's testimony at the February trial, they
eyed these machinations suspiciously as an attempt to avoid liability
for potential accidents.[131] The briefs also questioned anew the legality of permits based on an application that had never been co-signed
by the Columbiana County Port Authority.[132]

The hunger strikers, finally seeing a credible path to a delay, called
off their strike. The legal opportunity proved an illusion. In November, Judge Frederick P. Stamp denied the injunction, allowing WTI
to proceed. In his ruling, Stamp largely relied on EPA's assurances
that the facility and its location were safe. This logic prompted Paul
Connett to denounce this "Catch-22" as a "rubber-stamping of injustice."[133]

This opened floodgates of anger among opponents. Anxiety over
health issues had grown when the state health department, shortly
after Labor Day, had released the preliminary results of its baseline
health study. Almost two-thirds of the tested children living near
the incinerator *already* had high blood-lead levels.[134] Dr. Ted Hill,
an osteopath who is Swearingen's brother, quickly marshalled support from 78 colleagues in the medical community for a stinging letter to the governor questioning the morality and fairness of
subjecting such a population to further exposure.[135]

During the week preceding Thanksgiving, opponents staged protests whose themes changed on a daily basis, ranging from "Nurses
and Doctors Day" to "Organized Labor Day." Each day selected protesters, most of them newcomers to civil disobedience, subjected
themselves to arrest. Hill, for the first time, joined the doctors and
nurses who were arrested. At week's end, the number of arrestees
had climbed to 125.[136] A handful of repeaters, including Swearingen
and Greenpeace staffer Beth Newman, were sentenced to jail terms
for violating previous court orders not to abet the trespassing. Some
sentences seemed designed to make a point. Greenpeace staffer Niaz
Dorry drew a 10-day sentence beginning December 21 and ending
on New Year's Eve.[137] On a personal level, Swearingen was entering
a precarious phase in her commitment to the cause. By her estimate,

she and her husband had already spent well over $20,000 fighting WTI. She was now surrendering holidays with her family as well.[138]

Finally, Vice-President-elect Al Gore waded into the fracas. Following up on a visit he and President-elect Clinton had made to the area during the campaign, he announced in early December that he and five other senators had asked the General Accounting Office, the auditing arm of Congress, to investigate WTI thoroughly, including the legality of its permits. Gore also announced that the new administration would not give WTI a test-burn permit until all questions posed in the investigation were answered satisfactorily.[139]

Gore's stance resolved nothing. Like all other political and legal moves in the case, it merely invited rejoinders from the other side. During Clinton's vaunted economic summit in Little Rock, WTI sponsored an advertisement in the *New York Times* and other newspapers, appealing to the president-elect to "Give Our Town Hope."[140] In January, the *Wall Street Journal* launched a series of sarcastic editorials concerning Gore's intervention, one of which suggested that Greenpeace had appeared to Gore "in a dream."[141] On January 8, obviously aware that the incoming Clinton administration had its doubts, the U.S. EPA issued a permit for a test burn.

The new president himself carried some environmental baggage that had given many activists pause during the primary campaign. Clinton's administration in Arkansas had approved the burning of abandoned pesticide waste at an incinerator in Jacksonville, often dubbed "Dioxinville" by critics, and that facility had been operating since September 1990. Hillary Clinton had been a partner in a Little Rock law firm and had represented a company controlled by the family of Jackson Stephens.[142] Yet the Clinton campaign had offered hints of a new policy against incineration. The new EPA administrator, Carol Browner, clearly had an activist background. At her very first meeting with the WTI opponents, however, she unexpectedly recused herself, turning the issue over to a holdover Bush appointee. Her husband worked for Citizen Action, a national group whose Ohio affiliate had signed a letter to Vice President Gore asking that he keep his campaign promise concerning WTI.[143] Connie Stein expressed the bewilderment of many of the WTI opponents at this sudden move, noting, "All these years we've been screwed by people with no ethics. It's refreshing to see somebody with real ethics, but now we get screwed by the ethics."[144]

Not content, however, to wait for a verdict from the new administration, environmentalists had filed new court cases in Ohio and Arkansas to halt incinerators. It was not their intent to take the heat off the White House, but it produced that effect by shifting the combat to the legal arena.

While U.S. District Court Judge Ann Aldrich held trial in Cleveland after granting a Greenpeace request for a stay of the U.S. EPA's trial-burn permit, another case proceeded in Arkansas, where environmentalists had filed suit against the Jacksonville facility. Vertac Site Contractors, a joint venture, was burning the 29,300 barrels of herbicide waste that the bankrupt Vertac Chemical Company had left behind after operating its plant from 1948 to 1987. After a long policy struggle and promises by the U.S. EPA that the ash would be free of toxics—a promise that turned out to be a lie—the environmentalists had sued, arguing that the plant could not meet the EPA's own emissions standards of 99.9999 percent destruction of dioxin. On February 12, 1993, Judge Stephen Reasoner in Little Rock ruled that no burning could continue until the government could prove that such a level of destruction of dioxin was actually occurring. Importantly, Reasoner found the use of substitute, or "surrogate," chemicals as efficiency tests in trial burns unacceptable.

At issue, in the view of environmentalists and Judge Reasoner, was the emergence of some of the U.S. EPA's internal, and dirty, scientific laundry. As far back as 1985, some EPA scientists had questioned the validity of using high-concentration principal organic hazardous constituents (POHCs) as surrogates for dioxin in trial burns, arguing that such tests had shown increasing destruction and removal efficiency (DRE) for such compounds with increasing concentration of the substances in the material being burned. Due to their extreme toxicity, dioxins are generally in very low concentrations in waste feed, so it was reasonable to infer that their DRE would be overstated by such tests.[145]

"We could have a burn in which dioxin was literally pouring out of the stack undestroyed," Reasoner said. If his opinion held elsewhere, WTI and every other incinerator burner would be forced to test every single poison of regulatory concern separately. The logic of chemical surrogacy would no longer have a viable legal foundation. That might shelve WTI forever.[146]

But WTI was tilting swords with Greenpeace closer to home. There, the issue involved another attack on EPA scientific methodology, again concerning dioxins. Lawyers for the Government Accountability Project, representing Greenpeace, introduced affidavits and testimony from a number of expert witnesses charging that EPA's risk analysis for cancer deaths from the WTI facility was grossly inadequate. EPA had focused exclusively on exposure from inhalation and found the risk to be beneath its threshold of 10 cancers per million people. These numbers, which relate to statistical probabilities rather than real people, meant that fewer than 10 people out of a million exposed over a 70-year lifetime to the projected dioxin emissions from operation of the WTI incinerator during that period would contract cancer as a result of that exposure. ·

But the Greenpeace experts controverted those assumptions by pointing out, in effect, that the emperor's calculations were naked because they had failed to account for exposure through the food chain. In effect, the calculations had "assumed" that the law of gravity did not apply to dioxins. Obviously, like any other solid matter, they eventually drift to earth, entering the food chain through absorption into vegetables, dairy products, and other foodstuffs. Their immediate concentration would lessen considerably with their dispersion from the incinerator, but once in the food chain, the risk could be distributed far and wide. .

Douglas Crawford-Brown, a professor of environmental science and policy at the University of North Carolina, argued in his affidavit that, using the EPA's own emissions data and exposure assumptions, including food-chain exposure would increase the estimated cancer risk by a factor of 10,000, to as many as 864 per million, far above the EPA threshold.[147] Barry Commoner and others substantiated this same point in Judge Aldrich's courtroom.

But the bombshell in the Cleveland case came on February 9, the third day of hearings on the requested preliminary injunction. A January 22 memorandum to Carol Browner by Richard Guimond, EPA's acting assistant administrator in the Office of Solid Waste and

Emergency Response, noted "very serious implications associated with adopting risk assessment procedures based on indirect exposure routes for air emission sources."[148] Just how serious those implications were was made plain when William Farland, the director of EPA's Office of Health and Environmental Assessment, testified that the health risk from ingestion during a one-year trial burn at WTI would reach 40 in one million. Farland, a national expert on risk assessment, had worked with Matthew Lorber, another EPA scientist, on a screening study that had determined that dioxin risks from beef and milk consumption were 1,000 times higher than EPA's determination the previous summer when processing the trial burn permit.[149]

After three weeks of deliberation, Aldrich delivered her expensive blow to WTI, which claimed it was losing $150,000 per day while it waited for permission to operate. The plant could proceed with its eight-day trial burn but could not proceed with commercial operation afterward while the EPA analyzed the results. Incinerators routinely go into operation after a trial burn because EPA's analysis can typically take a year or more. Aldrich ruled that "the approximately one-year post trial burn period of operation may cause imminent and substantial endangerment to health and the environment."[150]

But there was an unfortunate flaw in Aldrich's decision, and WTI's lawyers wasted no time in exploiting it. Aldrich ruled that, while conducting her hearing, she had also been holding her trial, a procedural error in that she had failed to indicate this to the parties beforehand, leaving the impression that a trial on the one count of public endangerment she had allowed was still forthcoming. Within two weeks, WTI had secured an emergency stay of Aldrich's decision from the Sixth Circuit Court of Appeals in Cincinnati, which was then poised to hold its own hearing—on whether to make its emergency stay permanent.[151] Meanwhile, Judge Reasoner's decision in Little Rock had also met a rocky reception in another federal appeals court in Missouri.[152]

In the aftermath of the Sixth Circuit decision, the Clinton administration announced that the courts had spoken and that there was nothing more it could do in the WTI case. Vice President Gore, formerly a vocal critic of WTI, took a dive for the nearest foxhole, refusing to comment or speak to reporters.[153] A colleague of Barry Commoner who had testified in the Cleveland hearing opined that Gore "had his legs chopped off."[154]

Nonetheless, the protesters did have an impact on the new administration. Never fully trusting that the White House would "do the right thing" without being pushed, they kept up the heat. They showed up at the White House posing as tourists, only to demand an audience with the president once inside. With the help of Greenpeace, they mimicked the style of the Clinton campaign by organizing a nationwide antitoxics bus tour that began in April in San Francisco and arrived in Washington, D.C., in time for the tenth-anniversary convention of the Citizens' Clearinghouse for Hazardous Wastes (CCHW) in mid-May.

In Chicago, the protesters held a mock trial of the U.S. EPA and at long last met with Region V Administrator Valdas Adamkus, who confessed, "Personally, in my heart, when I saw the location, I was shocked." To the dismay of the visitors, he suggested that the elementary school be bought out and moved, leaving unanswered the question of what ought to become of the rest of the community that lay close to WTI.[155]

When the CCHW convention was over, the WTI opponents promptly parked a truck in an awkward position on Pennsylvania Avenue, blocking the flow of traffic around the White House. They kept fire crews busy for most of a day, jackhammering the concrete blocks into which they had handcuffed themselves. Of more than 300 protesters, police arrested 56.[156] But EPA Administrator Carol Browner had already prepared a response: an 18-month freeze on new commercial hazardous-waste incinerators and a requirement that those already operating on interim status—some for as long as a decade—be forced to undergo the permanent licensing process. Browner opined that some would not meet the standards and would not get final permits. But the new rules did nothing about WTI.[157]

Peter Montague, the environmental-movement veteran and editor of *Rachel's Hazardous Waste News*, attended the press conference announcing the new policy, an affair from which Terri Swearingen and Joe Thornton, a Greenpeace researcher, were evicted. Upon returning to his office, he composed one of the most biting issues of his weekly newsletter that he had ever produced, dissecting what he described as three "large loopholes" of the new policy. First, it would not affect "remedial" incinerators, those that handle Superfund and other site cleanup wastes, such as toxic soil. Second, the moratorium applied only in the four states (Wyoming, Iowa, Alaska, and Hawaii) and four territories where the U.S. EPA had not already delegated authority to issue RCRA permits. Those states with delegated authority were free to go about their business—including Ohio. Finally, EPA officials said that even in the four states under direct EPA authority, incinerators that were already close to winning final permits would still be allowed to go forward. "The vaunted incinerator moratorium made headlines," Montague concluded, "but the substance is small."[158]

The bitter reality for the WTI opponents was that expensive plants already built tend to get the permits they need in order to operate. Closing the plant would engender bitterness among its workers and those who had supported it as a means of attracting badly needed local jobs. Keeping it open would compel opponents to choose between staying in town to wage an increasingly hopeless fight or moving on. Many had engaged in civil disobedience because they had already decided they could not live with WTI. In either case, East Liverpool would be a town divided for at least a generation. The community had been offered few choices over the last two decades, none of them truly desirable. No one in power locally or at the state level had articulated a new economic vision that would afford East Liverpool a way out of its toxic dilemma. The only dream ever offered had been a landfill in the sky.

THE CALUMET REGION

Industrial Prosperity to Crash Landing

In the spring of 1990, Chicago Mayor Richard M. Daley was brain-storming ways to leverage his city back into a debate that threatened to leave it behind. For years, while seeking to expand O'Hare International Airport, the city of Chicago had largely ignored suburban and downstate rumblings about the need for a third major airport serving the metropolitan area. Now the discussion was growing more serious, and a tri-state study committee was moving to consider alternative sites. If Chicago continued to boycott the discussion, it might end up with no voice in a decision that would enormously affect its economic future.

Daley examined the options, and only one seemed workable. He would bring the third airport back into Chicago's orbit by putting it inside the city at a location that everyone acknowledged was suffering long-term economic setbacks. Hegewisch, a small Polish-American enclave on the city's Southeast Side, would be the sacrificial lamb on the altar of economic progress.

Sandwiched between Lake Calumet, Wolf Lake, and the Grand Calumet River, Hegewisch seems like a world unto itself, isolated from the fabric of the city's larger pattern of development. It has the look and feel of a small midwestern town mysteriously transplanted into the midst of a huge industrial behemoth. Its 9,000 residents boast a tightly knit network of family and church relationships that have endured for generations. They have traditionally worked for the steel mills, paint plants, and related industries nearby, though an increasing number have been taking the commuter train downtown as those industries have declined. But those traditional employers were the industries that built the Calumet region, which extends from the southeastern corner of Chicago, across the state border, through Hammond and Gary, to the Indiana Dunes. Outsiders know the area best by the smelly air that induces Skyway motorists to roll up their windows.

While many other communities facing a bleak industrial future, like East Liverpool, were debating the desirability of landfills in the sky, Daley invited the Calumet region to ponder the sky itself as the source of its future. For a time, the prospect seemed so real that the main competition for Daley's Lake Calumet site was Indiana's desire to build the new airport in Gary instead. Daley thus began a political tug of war that mostly underscored just how desperately both states needed redevelopment in a region whose precipitous economic decline demanded radical solutions.

In order to understand fully both the appeal of the airport proposal and the fury it unleashed from those who felt betrayed, it is essential to understand the history of the entire region's industrial development and subsequent decline. That history is, above all else, a classic rebuttal to arguments that environmental concerns must yield to industrial development for the sake of jobs. Here, environmental concerns yielded, and many now wonder if any new development is still possible. Was an airport the only solution big enough for the Calumet region's festering problems?

Local Native American tribes gave us the names by which we know most of the southern end of Lake Michigan. At least by legend, Chicago took its name ("stinking onion") from a plant that grew in the prevalent wetlands that surrounded Lake Calumet and the nearby rivers. Calumet was an English corruption of the word for "peace pipe," which the Indians also used to describe the entire range of marshes and ridges throughout the region. White settlers adopted the place name repeatedly, for Lake Calumet, now in southern Chicago, and the Calumet River, as well as for the nearby suburbs of Calumet City and Calumet Park.

Little of what whites found has remained pristine. Some 10,000 years ago, when Lake Michigan was about 20 feet higher than it is now, the area was under water. The wind and other elements forged the dunes, marshes, and beaches as the lake retreated, leaving behind a wildly productive and varied ecosystem. In the last century and a half, geological change has been overtaken by the rapid pace of industrial change.

The Calumet River became the Grand Calumet and Little Calumet rivers after human hands rearranged its long, winding course. It had begun near present-day LaPorte, Indiana, and followed a course westward into Illinois, where it turned sharply northward and eastward, emptying into Lake Michigan on the east side of Gary. Before whites arrived, Native Americans had already tinkered with its hairpin curve in order to facilitate their access via canoe to Lake Michigan.[1] After the Civil War, the Calumet and Chicago Canal and Dock Company developed a drainage outlet that permitted the flow of ship traffic from Lake Michigan into Lake Calumet. The dredging cut off the river's bend. But by 1845, tinkering with the Calumet River's flow had weakened its resistance to the advancing siltation along the lakeshore, and sand had already plugged up the Calumet's natural outlet in Gary.[2] The stymied river reversed course, rejoining its other half in Chicago near what is now the O'Brien Locks and Dam. That project, built in 1964 by the Army Corps of Engineers, sent the combined river flow west through the Calumet Sag Channel (built in 1911, and along which the Robbins incinerator is to be built) into the Mississippi River watershed via the Des Plaines River—except during high water flows, when the gates open to let the two branches flow together into Lake Michigan.[3] But in 1909, the opening of the Indiana Harbor Canal in East Chicago created a new outlet to the lake, creating three current flows: one to the west at the western end, one to the east into the canal, and the westward flow to the canal from the cut-off original mouth.[4] The reversed river near the lake became the Grand Calumet; the branch that flows more or less naturally to the old hairpin curve is the Little Calumet. Together, they have come to symbolize the massive modern resculpting of the region's landscape.

The marshes and lakes also underwent transformations. Of some 22,000 acres of wetlands in the Illinois portion of the Calumet region, only some 500 remain today.[5] Dredging and filling and alterations of natural drainage patterns have destroyed the remainder, even wiping out two of the original lakes. Lake Calumet today occupies less than half of its original natural boundaries. From the 1880s on, railroads sliced through the area to support its industrial development, often built on high embankments to protect them from flooding. The very first, a line from Hammond, Indiana, to Irondale, now a south Chicago neighborhood, cut off the northeastern portion of Lake Calumet, part of the Van Vlissingen Prairie, an open space that continues to attract botanists.[6] The sturdy wetland ecology that remains still provides hunting and fishing recreation for many of the area's blue-collar residents.[7] The area is a haven for birdwatchers as well, who can observe substantial colonies of egrets, herons, and gulls.

Even the lakefront underwent such intense industrialization that few of its original features are readily discernible. To the north, partly under the influence of the famous Burnham plan, Chicago preserved most of its lakefront with an extensive park system, although much of it, too, sits atop landfill. But Gary lost its entire lakefront to the steel mills that built the city, acquiring beachfront parkland later only after annexing the adjacent town of Miller. The southern end of Chicago, annexed at the turn of the century, also lost much of its lakefront to the mills, particularly U.S. Steel's South Works, built in 1880 (originally by the Illinois Steel Company) at the mouth of the Little Calumet River. Whiting, Indiana, lost its lakefront to the Standard Oil Company refinery. East Chicago, Indiana, surrendered much of its lakefront to the Inland Steel Company.[8] And by 1889, Michigan City, Indiana, had opened a port that was sending 830 ships per year to other Great Lakes destinations.[9]

The southern terminus of Lake Michigan was attractive to industrial pioneers from the outset. It offered steelmakers a chance to use coal from southern Indiana and Illinois, and iron ore from such large midwestern deposits as Minnesota's Mesabi Range, and then to ship their finished product through the Great Lakes to manufacturers in Detroit and elsewhere. Midwestern agriculture found an outlet as well for its grains and meats. In the 1870s, George H. Hammond, who had engineered the early use of refrigerated railroad cars for shipping dressed beef, located a plant along the banks of the Grand Calumet River in Hammond, doing more than a million dollars worth of business yearly.[10] The environmental result was a river full of rotting offal, with nearly half of each beef carcass, including bones and heads, going to waste. Hammond's German butchers described the river's penetrating aroma as "nauseating to persons not accustomed to it."[11] A half-century later, after a number of other meatpackers had located in and around Chicago, H.L. Mencken respectfully dubbed the city the "abattoir by the lake."[12] By that time, however, the Chicago packers had gained a competitive advantage by learning to make far better use of the carcasses.

But Gary had been a special case, isolated from early development by the forbidding combination of sand and swamps and its nearly complete unsuitability for agriculture. Thus, by the turn of the century, it remained open land, awaiting the arrival of heavy industry to transform its rugged shoreline, whose primary land use until then had consisted of hunting lodges for wealthy visitors to the dunes.[13] Politics played a role too. U.S. Steel, which had joined other manufacturers in creating new land by filling the Illinois shoreline, was taking note of populist Governor John B. Altgeld's legal challenges to this practice. Indiana offered the company more of a free hand in shaping its environment.[14]

When U.S. Steel began to lay plans for its Gary Works in 1904, it employed a Chicago lawyer, A.F. Knotts, to acquire the land. He did so quietly and efficiently. He persuaded U.S. Steel's powerful chairman, Judge Elbert Gary of Chicago, after whom the city was named, that the company should also build a city to support the new plant's workers. Having represented the Pullman strikers in 1896, Knotts was able to overcome the general phobia most businessmen felt about company towns following that rebellion. The problem, he insisted, had been poor management and Pullman's greed, not the town itself. The town that Judge Gary built was to consist of freely owned properties and independent businesses.[15]

But there was a problem. Having been hired to develop such a city, Knotts undertook the task himself without the aid of any city planners such as Burnham, who had produced much of Chicago's urban design. No land along the lakefront was set aside for parks or public recreation. Everything revolved around the construction of the mill.[16] The resulting gap in city life led to several efforts to create a park, including an unsuccessful attempt to condemn land outside the city limits.[17] The city finally settled for land along the Little Calumet River.

Nonetheless, the new city grew rapidly around the most advanced steel factories of its time, reaching 100,000 people by the mid-1920s.[18] This industrial growth produced jobs and fed the families of tens of thousands of immigrants and their descendants. As a result of manpower shortages during World War I and subsequent needs for more unskilled labor, it gradually included jobs first for African-American migrants from the South, and then for Mexicans and Appalachian whites as well. Workers thus accepted and even welcomed the transformation of the landscape. Workers' complaints about their evolving environment during Gary's early days related primarily to overcrowded and unsanitary living conditions due to perennial housing shortages and to the company's paternalistic attitude toward workers, which led to a major failed strike in 1919. The ethnic prejudice directed at Slavic workers under the guise of the "Red Scare" during that struggle caused many to return in bitterness to their newly freed homelands.[19] U.S. Steel filled its ranks by encouraging the southern migration that eventually shifted Gary's racial balance. It was all part of a regional pattern one later resident described to folklorist Richard J. Dorson as the Law of the Latest Arrival: *In a given area, the residents of longest occupation demonstrate hostility toward the incoming group.*[20]

In an era of American dominance in steel, however, the opening of the St. Lawrence Seaway in 1959 expanded the expectations of workers and employers alike for new jobs through access to international shipping. The opportunity induced the Indiana Port Commission to open the modern Burns International Harbor in 1969, helping to make Indiana second among the states nationally today in per capita volume of international trade, exporting $9 billion worth of manufactured goods annually.[21]

One part of the Indiana lakefront, however, had become sacred— the dunes, a lengthy formation of windswept sand that rises to a peak of more than 200 feet on what is popularly known as Mount Baldy. The dunes have long been a primary source of outdoor recreation for area residents. Burns Harbor, developed in the heart of the dunes midway between Gary and Michigan City, seemed to portend their demise. The threat to their integrity, particularly amid the ecological awakening of the 1960s, opened floodgates of environmental activism in northern Indiana that have never been closed.

Lee Botts has made a career of protecting the lake for more than two decades. The founder of the Lake Michigan Federation now lives in a house overlooking the lake, which she purchased at the edge of the dunes in Miller. After World War II, she notes, "there was a big deliberate effort by Indiana politicians and economic interests literally to industrialize the shore all the way to Michigan City. National Steel had been buying up land, and Bethlehem too. They wanted a federal port built by federal dollars."[22]

Between Gary and Michigan City, however, stand the Indiana Dunes. Dorothy Buell, a resident of Ogden Dunes, Indiana, founded the Save the Dunes Council and fought to save them for a national park, an idea first advocated by President Theodore Roosevelt but delayed by the onset of World War I. Assistant Secretary of the Interior Stephen Mather had even conducted hearings in 1917, the same year in which a magnificent outdoor pageant in the dunes had excited the public imagination.[23] From the outset, organized labor was behind the campaign to preserve the dunes in a national park, in no small part because the unchecked development of the shore was seen as a corporate land grab. At the Mather hearings, Honore J. Jaxon spoke on behalf of the Chicago Federation of Labor and the Public Ownership League:

> For thirty years we have been cut off from the lakefront by railroad corporations, private hotels, private interests, and our voice has been suppressed and our protest has not been heard.[24]

By the 1960s, with the new Indiana port development underway, park advocates staged a huge, last-ditch battle. Already, the Burns Harbor development was accompanied by the National Steel and Bethlehem Steel plants and a Northern Indiana Public Service Company (NIPSCO) power plant. Finally, in 1966, with more damage already done than dunes proponents could stomach, the Indiana Dunes National Lakeshore Act was signed into law by President Lyndon Johnson. Interior Secretary Stewart Udall presided over a compromise that authorized 8,330 acres for a unique new park along the lake, some 35 miles from Chicago.[25] Later additions to the park brought its size to more than 13,000 acres.[26]

The dunes became the center of another epic environmental battle in 1970, when NIPSCO proposed to build the 685-megawatt Bailly nuclear power plant alongside its existing coal unit at Burns Harbor, just 800 feet from the new lakeshore park's western border. Despite numerous objections, including testimony before the Atomic Energy Commission (AEC) by Nathaniel P. Reed, Assistant Secretary of the Interior for Fish, Wildlife and Parks, the AEC granted a construction permit, and work began in 1974.[27] Steelworkers teamed up with environmentalists and coal miners to fight the plant, partly out of a desire to preserve the dunes and partly out of a sympathy for miners who feared losing jobs to nuclear power. The steelworkers also had legitimate safety concerns related to the impossibility of evacuating workers at the nearby Bethlehem plant, prompting United Steel Workers of America (USWA) Local 6787 (representing Bethlehem) to investigate. The union discovered that in an emergency 170 workers would be expected to remain at the plant to maintain the equipment. It learned also that AEC rules did not deem them "residents" for the purpose of calculating the adjoining area's population density.[28] United Steelworkers Local 1010, representing the Inland workers, helped in shaping the growing Bailly Alliance to lead the fight. The alliance included civil-rights activists and the city of Gary.[29] Finally, after massive protests and continued construction problems, NIPSCO canceled the project in 1981. The Bailly Alliance had united workers, environmentalists, and civil-rights activists in a way that few other environmental issues had done before anywhere in the country.

Although they won that fight, the steelworkers would soon be fighting hard to save their own jobs. The industrial economy of the region was about to take a nosedive.

The Calumet region's heyday lasted a century, roughly from 1880 to 1980. It left a toxic legacy that may last at least a century more. In its wake, there has arisen a human legacy of bitterness and shattered hopes, and a growing sense that the area's abandoned workers should not have to foot the bill for an expensive cleanup and restoration of the dumps and polluted rivers that industry has left behind. A new environmental militance fills the air, but to understand it, one must also understand how the region's environmental predicament came about.

Much of the region's industrial base was at the leading edge of America's post–Civil War industrial revolution. It developed at a time when pollution was not widely perceived as a legitimate concern. Wetlands, now a major environmental issue, were still called swamps and were something to be "reclaimed" by various kinds of fill. If some of the fill happened to be slag from steel furnaces, that was the price of progress. The marshes, accompanied by mosquitoes, were not deemed one of the region's greater assets.

Chicago's South Works, a now-closed U.S. Steel Company facility, offers a microcosm through which to view the region's industrial evolution. In 1880, the Illinois Steel Company broke ground for a new 73-acre steel plant that employed some 2,000 workers a year later, many of them Eastern European immigrants. The sign at the employment office was a testament to the ethnic melting pot that labored in the plant, bearing a notice to prospective employees in six languages. In 1901, U.S. Steel acquired the plant through a merger of Illinois Steel and 10 other companies. With the new ownership came expansion, including electric furnaces and the acquisition of more than 500 additional acres.

World War I brought Mexican workers to replace Americans gone to war. They were also used to break the 1919 strike. The community they established still thrives in Southeast Chicago and East Chicago, Indiana. The Great Depression produced labor strife that led to the famous Memorial Day massacre in 1937, in which 10 striking steelworkers were killed. U.S. Steel had recognized the Steel Workers Organizing Committee, later to become USWA Local 65. Although the strike involved nearby Republic Steel, no one escaped the animosity that permeated the polluted air.

With World War II came the greatest burst of prosperity. Employment at the South Works climbed to an all-time high of more than 20,000. African-Americans, like Mexicans before them, streamed in to absorb new jobs and to build their own community. The prosperity lasted two more decades, but the handwriting was on the wall. Japanese and German competition was overtaking the American steel industry. The U.S. dollar's strength in the early 1980s gave imports a significant competitive advantage, with the Japanese yen trading at 220 yen to the dollar in 1983, versus just 117 a decade later. Meanwhile, U.S. Steel spent $6 billion in 1982 to acquire Marathon Oil, a move that embittered union workers concerned about their future. Although the company said it spent $6.5 billion on modernization from 1970 to 1985, the biggest local beneficiary was the Gary Works, the company's "flagship" operation. The decline set in during the 1970s but took its greatest toll during the 1980s. Near the end, the South Works plant was reduced to just 700 workers. An employee buyout scheme surfaced, then failed. Finally, in early 1992, to no one's surprise, USX (no longer calling itself U.S. Steel) announced that South Works was history.[30] The announcement left the Lake Calumet area's unemployment at an unpromising 12 percent that year.[31] A year later, the only prospect on the horizon came from a Duluth, Minnesota, corporation, which was considering the use of a portion of the site for a stainless-steel minimill, part of a new wave of highly automated plants that are transforming the nature of the steel industry. The new mill would employ between 400 and 500 workers, a mere fraction of South Works's former labor force, making a fraction of the steel South Works had produced.[32]

South Works was not alone. Although the Calumet region still produced nearly one-fourth of the nation's steel,[33] its legacy of industrial prosperity was in tatters. Northwest Indiana was hit particularly hard by industrial decline. The once-mighty city of Gary had already experienced massive white flight to suburbs like Merrillville, inheriting broken dreams, broken families, and little in the way of resources with which to repair them. Even with its Gary Works still open, USX Corporation had reduced its northern Indiana workforce from 20,900 in 1980 to 7,500 by 1990. Inland Steel's workforce was cut from 21,000 to 14,700 in the same period; LTV Steel from 8,600 to 4,500; and Bethlehem Steel from 6,500 to 5,800.[34] The region lost population as well, but not nearly as fast, so unemployment plagued whole neighborhoods that had once been havens for blue-collar workers earning union wages. The work was hot and sweaty, but it had put many workers' children through college. But now the industrial base that supported the "city of big shoulders" had shrugged.

If any region's experience can make the case that waste disposal is an industry that preys on economic decline, Calumet is the place. The dumps did not, of course, start when industry left. They accompanied industry from the beginning, but at the turn of the century most people seemed oblivious to the dangers they posed, and urban environmental science was primitive at best.

Most of the early dumps were ancillary to the nearby industries and not commercial enterprises in their own right. In some cases, whole plants became liabilities, like the 176-acre Wisconsin Steel site, now the scene of an expensive Army Corps of Engineers cleanup that has uncovered such toxic contaminants as benzene, chromium, asbestos, lead, and polychlorinated biphenyls (PCBs). The overall toxic legacy of the area's industrial history is virtually unmeasurable, in part because many of the property records that would reveal these hazards are old or nonexistent and no one specifically monitored such details. It is not clear today—even with the attempts by city, state, and federal environmental agencies to map this legacy—that anyone really knows where all the historic dumps are, much less what chemical horrors they contain. But there are strong hints from the studies that have been done. A 1986 study by the Illinois Department of Energy and Natural Resources found 57 percent of the sediments in Lake Calumet highly toxic and the other 43 percent moderately toxic. The department labeled the lake a "severely disturbed ecosystem."[35]

Despite their numerous deficiencies, however, few of these are Superfund sites because, in the logic of the U.S. EPA's National Priority List (which ranks sites according to the public-health threat they pose), they do not pose a major threat to the drinking water of a large population. Many of the sites have contaminated nearby groundwater, but Chicago's three million people get their drinking water from Lake Michigan. Behind the point-scale logic of that ranking system, however, lies an acknowledged time bomb. If the poisons in the Calumet region's groundwater were to migrate into Lake Michigan, they could create a public-health disaster of major proportions.

And dumps tend to draw more dumps, in part because few other modern industries wish to locate in an area where they may incur heavy and unpredictable liabilities as new landowners. Federal law imposes strict joint and several liability on anyone involved with a contaminated property, a powerful deterrent to new investment in an area where guarantees of past purity are nearly impossible to provide. The Reverend Robert Klonowski, the activist minister of Hegewisch's century-old Lebanon Lutheran Church, calls the resulting pattern of land development in the area "toxic imperialism." Within a mile and a half of his church, he asserts, there exist no fewer than 46 toxic-waste dumps, most of them closed and awaiting cleanup.[36] The city's own studies for the proposed airport supported those estimates, showing roughly 60 heavily contaminated sites within the airport study area.[37] Chicago's Southeast Side contains one of the greatest concentrations of landfills on the North American continent.

Klonowski, a young pastor from a Polish Catholic family who came to his congregation in 1983, chooses his words carefully. He prefers "toxic imperialism" to the common movement phrase "toxic racism," he said, because his parishioners are mostly white ethnics. If the environmental movement's phraseology leaves them feeling like unacknowledged victims, he fears, they will find it hard to ally themselves with their natural allies in Hispanic and African-American neighborhoods. The Calumet region has long been prey to politicians who have exploited precisely those kinds of divisions.

On the other hand, Hazel Johnson, the founder and president of People for Community Recovery (PCR), uses the term "environmental racism" with full appreciation for the value of her white allies.

Her perspective is different. Sitting in the PCR office at Altgeld Gardens,[38] a public-housing complex just two miles west of Hegewisch, she sees its 10,000 residents at the center of a "toxic doughnut."[39] Her home is worlds away from the single-family bungalows of Klonowski's working-class neighborhood because few of the people are regularly employed. Many of its bedraggled units are boarded up. Taxi drivers shudder at the thought of entering the complex, whose only retail outlets are a liquor store and a beauty shop in a small building near the entrance to the complex. Nothing else is within walking distance. Police rarely patrol the area and seldom respond quickly. The forgotten complex, Johnson notes, is an easy mark for fly dumpers, who deposit waste—usually hazardous—illegally and surreptitiously in abandoned lots and along roadsides. The very term "fly dumpers" denotes the criminal, hit-and-run nature of those who dump "on the fly."

In the late 1940s, perhaps with the best intentions, Chicago Housing Authority built Altgeld Gardens atop the dump that railroad-car magnate George Pullman had used for human and industrial waste. Pullman Village, the scene of the famous Pullman strike of 1896, is just two miles to the north, but is worlds apart. In the 1960s, the Calumet Expressway (I–94) cut off Altgeld Gardens's contact with the city to the east. To the south lies the Little Calumet River and Maryland Manor, an old settlement of seven homes that, while part of Chicago, did not gain access to city water until 1986, largely after lobbying by PCR. Its residents had been relying on well water whose quality had probably become highly questionable given the surroundings.[40] To the west along 130th Street, the main arterial crossing the expressway, lies a string of heavy-industrial firms whose emissions fill the air that Johnson's constituents breathe daily. To the north lies a sewage treatment facility for the water-reclamation district, whose odors have made nearby workers ill, according to Johnson, and have been a constant source of contention with PCR. Finally, she added, the surrounding Riverdale neighborhood contains no fewer than 31 landfills, five of which are no longer active.

Hazel and her daughter, Cheryl, take all this personally. "My husband died of lung cancer," Johnson noted. "My younger daughter was five months pregnant and had an ultrasound. The baby didn't have a head or a behind. The majority of the birth deformities here are girls. We had a little girl three years old here who died of cancer. Another baby had a brain protruding through its head when it was born. It died at seven months. Another baby died at two months. Two years later, the coroner said she had died from breathing a paint solvent. We have hundreds of cases of asthma. They leave the area, according to Dr. Jackson, and will be in remission. They come back, and it starts all over again. A lot of cases of skin lesions. One little girl had circles as big as a nickel all over her chest and stomach."

Dr. Gloria Jackson Bacon operates a part-time health clinic. The nearest city clinic is in the Roseland neighborhood, about three miles to the northwest. Altgeld residents regularly complain about the quality and availability of health care in an area whose children are very much at risk. In the earliest days of PCR, hearing that the Southwest Side had some of the nation's highest cancer rates, Hazel Johnson contacted the Illinois EPA and the Chicago Health Department, who sent her complaint forms. She took them door to door, seeking to document the skin rashes, respiratory problems, birth deformities, and other illnesses affecting people.[41] It was another case of volunteer labor attempting to fill the gaps left by health-care professionals.

Predictably, in view of the lack of training for any of Johnson's volunteers, it drew criticism. Johnson's zeal and persistence in publicizing her findings have drawn harsh rebuttals from the waste industry and others. Mary Ryan, the community relations manager for Waste Management of North America, a Waste Management, Inc. subsidiary, told me in an interview, "If you want to hear some really outrageous stuff, go to the Southeast Side of Chicago. Hazel Johnson talks about stuff like babies without brains. Where's the proof?"[42] Curiously, Hazel Johnson later informed me that Waste Management has authorized a $3 million grant to Dr. Jackson's clinic, which will now operate full time.

Indeed, for many years, the proof seemed thin by official standards. PCR's volunteers had little idea of how to produce the kinds of proof that critics demanded, and few experts provided the necessary resources. Finally, however, in early 1993, Dr. Robert Ginsburg, a Chicago consultant on toxicological issues, and Vincent Champagne of the Clareitian Medical Clinic trained volunteers for a cooperative survey effort between PCR and the University of Illinois School of Public Health. The survey involved interviews with 197 residents of randomly selected apartments. In late summer, PCR released its findings. According to Dr. Herbert White, the regional medical director of occupational and environmental medicine at St. James Hospital in Chicago Heights, the most disturbing finding was that 51 percent of all pregnancies involved some abnormalities, including sick babies (7 percent), stillborns (7 percent), and premature births (12 percent). The survey also found that 66 percent of those who moved reported relief from symptoms they had experienced while living in the center of the toxic doughnut.[43]

Some of the militance of the blue-collar and minority environmentalism that has blossomed in the Calumet area since the early 1980s stems from the legendary aura that has surrounded many landfill operations. For many activists, it has become an avocation, a deadly serious game of citizen cops and robbers, of good guys and bad guys. In the case of the Paxton landfill, the scene of a 1983 armed standoff between company guards and Illinois state police seeking to search the dump for evidence, that figurative imagery was all too real. Not until 1992, after a lengthy legal battle, more than $2 million in proposed city fines, and extensive leakage of contaminants into groundwater, did the city succeed in shutting down the Paxton landfill.[44]

More often the basis for suspicion and rumor is far less dramatic. Even a walk through the woods and prairies of the Lake Calumet wetlands reveals old dumping grounds for abandoned cars, tires, and other effluvia of modern culture. The impossibility of tracing many of these activities feeds the local folklore that surrounds the area's dozens of dumps.

Occasionally, though, incidents break into the headlines that reinforce suspicions that the system is steeped in corruption. In 1986, for instance, a two-and-a-half-year FBI undercover investigation resulted in the indictment of several city council members. Among them was Alderman Clifford P. Kelley, who was charged with accepting bribes from Raymond Akers, Jr., a lobbyist for Waste Management, Inc. The matter involved the Metropolitan Sanitary

District's consideration of the company's proposal to expand its CID landfill, which straddles the line between Chicago and Calumet City, into land owned by the district.[45] The following year, Kelley pled guilty.[46] More recently, a former mayor of South Chicago Heights, Donald Prisco, left prison, where he was serving a sentence for corruption, to testify under oath that a later mayor, Charles Panici, had taken bribes in connection with landfill and garbage-hauling contracts.[47] In February 1993, Panici and two aldermen were convicted.[48] (That case did not involve Waste Management, Inc.) Against the backdrop of the larger history of corruption in Chicago-area local government, it would be surprising if citizens did not tend to suspect the worst when fighting proposals for waste facilities.

But outright corruption is simply the most extreme manipulation of the decision-making process. Chicago aldermen have never been particularly aggressive about enacting or enforcing ethics rules, and the waste industry has been generous with campaign contributions. Alderman Edward Vrdolyak's fabled Tenth Ward Democratic Organization (before he switched parties in 1988) was reputed to be a virtual vacuum cleaner for waste-industry contributions. However, as longtime neighborhood activist Marian Byrnes noted, it is almost impossible to construct a full picture of the waste industry's contributions because, to do so, one must know the name of virtually every individual involved. Simply looking for company names in the campaign finance reports yields a modest list of perfunctory donations. But even the longer list of individuals, she added, fails to reveal the number of businessmen "whose arms were twisted."[49] But regardless of whether the chicken or the egg came first, Vrdolyak endorsed the siting of numerous landfills on the Southeast Side.

The politics of landfills took a new turn temporarily during the administration of Mayor Harold Washington, beginning in the spring of 1983, largely because Vrdolyak led the city-council opposition throughout Washington's four-and-a-half years in office. (Washington died suddenly of a heart attack in November 1987.) As a candidate, Washington had asked Lee Botts, then working at Northwestern University's Center for Urban Affairs, for a briefing paper on waste issues. She advised him to look closely at the Southeast Side because traditional conservationists were uniting with labor organizations around landfill issues. Vrdolyak, in Botts's opinion, had "greased the wheels for Waste Management."

In August 1983, several months after Washington's inauguration, a meeting took place in the basement of St. Kevin's Catholic Church, which sits across the street from the Wisconsin Steel site. Its purpose was to let the new mayor meet with community groups. Botts attended along with Robert Ginsburg, a staff scientist for Citizens for a Better Environment, and Jerry Sullivan of the Audubon Society. The overflow crowd on that hot summer night reflected the Southeast Side's racial and ethnic diversity, Botts recalled: about one-third African-American, one-third white, and one-third Hispanic. People on the sidewalk watched and clapped through the windows. In the back of the hall, Botts said, stood "Ed Vrdolyak's boys . . . in pinstripe suits."

With Mary Ellen Montez, the leader of the United Neighborhood Organization (UNO), presiding, the groups presented their demands to Mayor Washington, the city's first African-American mayor. First, a moratorium on new landfills. Second, establishment of a task force to advise the city on ways of handling its solid-waste problems. Third, development of a citywide recycling program. Within two weeks, Vrdolyak announced his support for a landfill moratorium.[50]

The Washington administration set up a task force through the city planning department. An initial report, *Waste Management Options for Chicago*, appeared in January 1985, at which time the mayor appointed a citizens task force to continue the investigation. But the 1985 report set a tone that created some hope among environmentalists. Among its recommendations, embodied in ordinances backed by Washington, were a ban on all new sanitary landfills; stronger environmental review for expansion of existing landfills; the forbidding of any hazardous-waste disposal in sanitary landfills; the creation of an inventory and reporting system for all hazardous wastes produced by Chicago industries; increased indemnification for landfill and liquid-waste-facility operators; and zoning reforms to legitimize existing recycling centers in the city, many of which had been technically in violation of zoning ordinances. But the report went further, urging the city to move quickly toward investments in intensive recycling that would lessen demands on landfills in the future, in part as a matter of social equity for the neighborhoods whose residents had hosted these facilities in the past.[51] Those investments included diversion credits paid to nonprofit recyclers, in other words, tonnage fees paid for the amount picked up through curbside collections and diverted from landfills through recycling activities. The report also stressed increased reliance on incineration, an option that likely would have encountered political difficulty in the end.

Harold Washington, however, did not live to implement the plans. In the spring of 1987, he defeated Edward Vrdolyak and two other challengers in the mayoral race. Vrdolyak's brother Victor, a policeman, ran for and won his Tenth Ward council seat. Then Washington died suddenly of heart failure in November, setting off an ugly battle for succession that elevated Alderman Eugene Sawyer to the mayor's office, only to be defeated in a 1989 special election by Cook County State's Attorney Richard M. Daley, son of the former Mayor Daley. Where the Washington task force had advocated source separation as the key to successful recycling, Daley by 1990 introduced the notion of the "blue bag," a single plastic bag in which all recyclables would be commingled for later separation at a materials-recovery facility (MRF). Because the Daley plan seemed to cut the nonprofit recyclers out of the action in favor of large waste-hauling firms, while resulting in relatively poor-quality recycled materials, it engendered a firestorm of opposition from environmentalists. In late 1993, Waste Management won the contract to build an MRF.

Lee Botts still rues the outcome. "It took two years to issue the task force report in 1986," she said, "but it was a hell of a report. If Washington hadn't died, things would have been very, very different."

Eventually, the popular uproar over the politics of garbage on the Southeast Side led to the rise of a bombastic and argumentative challenger to the Vrdolyak machine—State Representative Clem Balanoff, whose mother, Marian, had once served as a reform alderman. Balanoff, first elected from the 35th district in 1988, has come to personify the Calumet region's blue-collar environmental revolt. His boyish looks, thin face, and lawyerly glasses belie the feisty character that either endears or alienates his constituents. He is a rarity in South Side Chicago politics—a candidate who honestly wishes he could build more interracial bridges through environmental politics, an interest that prompted him to file more than 50 bills in his first year in Springfield. For his followers, his duel with the Vrdolyak machine, most recently in his unsuccessful race against former Vrdolyak aide John Buchanan for the Tenth Ward aldermanic seat, is like Luke Skywalker fighting Darth Vader. There simply are no shades of gray.

In part, this is because Balanoff operates like no other state representative. He treats the job as a full-time organizing opportunity, rallying his troops in a series of crusades against local environmental evils. His staff reflects this penchant. His chief aide is Marian Byrnes, a longtime environmental activist before joining Balanoff, who puts the resources of his office at the disposal of virtually any serious community-organizing effort within his district. It is almost as if Saul Alinsky had been elected to the legislature on an environmental platform.

One epic battle pursued by Byrnes and Balanoff involved the Chemical Waste Management (CWM) incinerator in Southeast Chicago. U.S. EPA officials maintain that the plant, which burned PCBs, was a minor contributor to the region's overall air-pollution burden, and they were probably mathematically correct given the surrounding land uses. But the incinerator, owned by a major subsidiary of Waste Management, Inc., also came to symbolize industry's use of the Calumet region as a dumping ground. In time, CWM's performance at the facility also reinforced a perception that company management was cavalier at best in its attitude toward the hazards the facility posed for its neighbors.

The license to burn PCBs is a crucial factor in understanding the plant's importance to the U.S. EPA. PCBs are a family of organic chemicals first discovered in 1881, and produced exclusively in the United States after 1929 by Monsanto Chemical Company under the trade name Aroclor. Their value stemmed from their chemical composition as chlorinated hydrocarbons, in which up to 10 chlorine atoms can substitute for hydrogen in the molecular ring structure of biphenyls, producing 209 possible molecular structures, also known as isomers. Those varying combinations served a variety of industrial purposes in capacitors, transformers, hydraulic systems, and vacuum pumps. Their low flammability facilitated their use for insulating and cooling electrical equipment. In the environment, however, they have proven to be persistent toxic contaminants, making leakage a sufficient danger that many nonelectric uses were banned in 1972.[52] Nonetheless, PCBs have already been found in so many contaminated sites that they represent a major EPA cleanup priority, particularly at Superfund sites. Although work was already underway in the early 1980s on the use of PCB-degrading bacteria for decontamination, the cleanup technique EPA favored was incineration.

Like many facilities now owned by Waste Management or its subsidiaries, the Chemical Waste incinerator at 117th Street and Stony Island Avenue did not originally belong to the firm. Hyon, Inc., first operated the plant until SCA Chemical Services acquired it in 1981, in part because its location on the shores of Lake Calumet offered a buffer zone of open space (mostly dump sites) and heavy industry. The hills of a nearby landfill shielded the view. There was, however, one residential neighborhood within a half-mile and an elementary school about 1.4 miles downwind.[53]

Three years later, in the summer of 1984, Waste Management acquired a majority interest in SCA Chemical Services, and CWM took over responsibility for operating the incinerator, which burned some 350,000 tons of hazardous waste yearly, including PCBs and waste from federal Superfund cleanup sites. In the process, CWM also took responsibility for an ongoing permit process begun under SCA's ownership. Some aspects of that process have kept casual observers confused, so it is important to review its details before telling the story.

In 1976, Congress amended the Solid Waste Disposal Act by passing the Resource Conservation and Recovery Act (RCRA, commonly pronounced "Rick-ra"). The act established the nation's first attempt at comprehensive, or "cradle to grave," regulation of hazardous wastes through a permitting and tracking system that includes manifests for shippers. Facilities involved in treating, storing, or disposing (TSD in industry jargon) of hazardous waste were required to obtain federal permits to operate, but as with most federal environmental legislation, each state had the option of persuading U.S. EPA to delegate such authority to its own program if it met the minimum federal requirements. Illinois won such approval for RCRA permitting in January 1986, a year and a half after CWM had taken control of the SCA incinerator. The U.S. EPA retained authority in Illinois over permit provisions under a 1984 amendment, the Hazardous and Solid Waste Act, which contained new requirements, and so the two agencies acted together to permit aspects of TSD facilities under their respective jurisdictions. At that time, CWM still did not have a RCRA Part B permit, so the Illinois EPA became involved in permitting that aspect of CWM's operations.

Part B bestowed a final permit on hazardous-waste-facility operators and was all that new facilities, like WTI's East Liverpool plant, needed under RCRA. When Congress passed RCRA, however, it obviously could not expect existing facilities to shut down until they gained a final permit, so RCRA regulations set up two parts to permit applications. Because the EPA did not promulgate final RCRA regulations until 1980, facilities existing prior to November 19, 1980, had to notify the agency of their existence by submitting Part A of the application. So long as they met certain deadlines, they were then free to operate under interim status until they obtained a Part B permit. SCA had secured such interim status in 1983 and submitted a Part B application in August 1983. After a considerable round of technical-review comments from the state and federal agencies, as well as several updates and revisions by the applicant, the two agencies jointly announced their intention to issue a draft RCRA permit on May 22, 1987.[54]

In addition, the facility needed state and federal air-quality permits under the Clean Air Act, water-discharge permits from the state and the Metropolitan Sanitary District of Greater Chicago (for process water and stormwater runoff), and various industrial performance-standards permits from the city relating to the storage and handling of fuel oil, hazardous liquids, liquid waste, and flammable liquids. Finally, as one of only three plants in the country permitted to burn PCBs, the plant was subject to the requirements of the Toxic Substances Control Act through a permit it had obtained in September 1983. Like the WTI arrangement in Ohio, the plant leased land from the Illinois International Port District, which made the port authority a co-permittee with Waste Management—after it was added to the draft permit.

The drumbeat of opposition stoked by accidents and permit violations began at the CWM incinerator before Balanoff's ascension to the legislature. Marian Byrnes, long active on the Southeast Side, had already organized Citizens United to Reclaim the Environment (CURE), which at one point helped to organize Hazel Johnson's PCR. Byrnes and CURE dogged the incinerator operators' every step for several years. One of the ongoing violations that most grabbed their attention was a propensity by employees for disconnecting air-quality monitors.

CWM committed five violations of its 1986 Illinois EPA Clean Air Act operating permit between November 1986 and June 1987. Four of those five involved the disconnection of monitors measuring the concentration of carbon monoxide in the stack gas, an indication of the incinerator's thermal efficiency. The company notified the state of the violations in March 1988, and in June, the state entered into a consent decree. It provided that a citizen and expert oversight committee would keep regular hours at the site. PCR volunteers became part of the citizen oversight, helping to uncover 34 violations of the consent decree itself through July 1989. Nonetheless, in April 1989, the Illinois EPA issued a renewal air-quality operating permit.

In October, however, Illinois Attorney General Neil F. Hartigan entered the picture with a modification of the consent decree that extended the oversight committee for five years, to be paid for by CWM at a cost of $350,000 yearly. The new agreement also imposed a $340,000 civil penalty, or $10,000 per violation (the maximum), for those violations already uncovered by the oversight committee.[55]

In the midst of the RCRA permitting process with the state and federal environmental agencies, CWM found itself the target of a determined citizen organizing campaign. Letters and petitions poured into the offices of the U.S. EPA and Illinois EPA demanding that CWM be denied its permits. Balanoff, now a state representative, used his district office to organize and support the new 35th District Environmental Task Force, headed by his aide, Marian Byrnes. Organizational backers ranged from the Veteran's Park Improvement Association, a neighborhood group, to the Southeast Sportsmen's Club, a hunting and fishing club concerned about the potential poisoning of local wildlife.[56]

CWM officials insisted repeatedly that the violations that had aroused the surrounding area's citizenry were minor and did not threaten the public health. Often they suggested that they were largely matters of paperwork. But there had been other interpretations of CWM's impact as far back as 1985, when the *Wall Street Journal* reported that PCB levels at the downwind elementary school were 16 times higher than at another school two miles upwind.[57] Clearly, tracing the origins of these contaminants is always to some degree problematic, but in a case involving a single incinerator in the area licensed to burn PCBs, the finger of public suspicion inevitably pointed upwind.

Hartigan's action followed a series of public-relations debacles for CWM. In May, the U.S. EPA had proposed levying $4.47 million in fines for six violations involving improper recordkeeping, burning PCBs when the scrubbers in the smokestack were not operating, failure to monitor emissions, and failure to halt the feeding of PCB waste into the incinerator when stack monitors failed.[58] Eventually, the EPA and CWM settled on a $3.75 million fine. The fine, in Balanoff's view, was beside the point. He and his supporters wanted the facility shut down and saw no benefit in fines that allowed the plant to continue operating.[59] One of the most frequent refrains among environmental critics, in fact, is that for Waste Management such fines are merely a cost of doing business.

Significantly, a series of former employees had become whistleblowers, including Jack Tursman, a shift supervisor who insisted that operations manager Riad Alkhatib had ordered him to fill out a bogus form that falsified the extent of a major PCB spill. Tursman, who was fired in 1987 for allegedly mishandling a spill, also claimed the pollution monitors were often unplugged. Tursman sued for wrongful dismissal in state court.[60] Alkhatib was later fired after a transfer to another facility, but Tursman claimed he went public after determining that an internal investigation would be fruitless.[61]

Through the summer of 1989, the pressure of public opinion grew.

On August 5, PCR and CURE, aided by Greenpeace, staged a demonstration against the CWM facility that drew more than 200 protesters.[62] At the end of September, the Illinois EPA rejected the company's RCRA Part B application because of numerous deficiencies on a variety of safety issues, such as the risks of leaking drums.[63] CWM decided to redraft and resubmit its already delayed application. Meanwhile, in the legislature, Balanoff had introduced legislation drafted by Attorney General Hartigan to make tampering with monitors or temperature controls at hazardous-waste incinerators a felony. The measure passed, but Governor James Thompson, acting on the request of Daniel Webb, an attorney representing Waste Management, vetoed it on the grounds that it was clearly specific to one facility.[64]

On December 10, protesters took their opposition a step further. Hazel Johnson, Marian Byrnes, and several others including Greenpeace staffers chained themselves to three trucks they had parked horizontally across the front gate of the facility in an effort to block trucks from entering. Three people were chained inside each cab, while others handcuffed themselves to the axles. Throughout the day, according to Byrnes, a number of area residents visited in support of the action. Particularly gratifying to Byrnes was the police reaction after a protest that lasted most of the day before company officials finally requested arrests. Despite the fact that they had to cut people loose from the axles, Byrnes said, the police were "very polite and sympathetic. Many made remarks saying we were doing the right thing. The police at the booking desk said it's a shame they had to book us instead of them. 'When will they bring them in on charges?' "[65]

During the protest, many of the activists found it hard to believe that the state or federal EPA would ever act against Chemical Waste Management. Balanoff had echoed their sentiments several times, noting on one occasion, "It's the biggie, Waste Management. Everybody's afraid to go after the biggie, from the governor to the IEPA, all the way down the line."[66]

Barely two months later, though, the very accident that many feared finally came. Its consequences were minor compared to public fears, but the carelessness that set the stage for the event virtually guaranteed that state and federal officials would find the courage that Balanoff feared they lacked.

Shortly after midnight on February 13, 1991, workers at the plant fed a 16-gallon drum of mislabeled laboratory wastes, which turned out to be insufficiently diluted tetrazole, a combustible hazardous waste, into the incinerator. An explosion in the rotary kiln blew out two iron doors, letting ash from the incinerator escape into the atmosphere and onto the ground, where it caught fire and released a black smoke into the night air. The most pertinent violation of environmental regulations in this instance—because it was the immediate cause of the accident—involved burning waste whose character had not been clearly established first. Federal regulations require that hazardous-waste shippers include manifests properly describing their wastes and that facility operators check those manifests before disposing of the material. Furthermore, CWM had not previously burned tetrazole, and Illinois Pollution Control Board regulations required incinerator operators to analyze such new wastes for their heating value and explosive qualities.[67] For opponents, this lapse epitomized what they saw as a cavalier attitude on the part of management toward the entire operation.

The midnight explosion precipitated a broad-daylight explosion of public anger that in turn drove legal action against CWM by the state EPA, the U.S. EPA, and the Illinois attorney general. In mid-February, a grand jury began an investigation of mislabeling of wastes. The plant was shut down, at first on an interim and finally on a permanent basis. In June 1992, Assistant Illinois Attorney General Matthew J. Dunn presented in state court the details of a proposed consent decree that levied a record state fine of $3 million against the facility for falsifying inventory records and the sloppy practices that led to the explosion.[68] One of the most visible targets of environmentalists' wrath on Chicago's Southeast Side had met its end.

For Waste Management, however, it was not even close to the end. The facility, which had been one of 18 licensed hazardous-waste burners in the nation, had lasted in part because a federal ban on land disposal of many hazardous wastes drove the growth of incineration.[69] The U.S. EPA had largely ignored alternative treatment technologies during the 1980s in its implementation of RCRA.[70]

Although the loss of the Chicago facility was costly, the company had grown huge in the past 20 years, from a market value of $20 million in 1971, when it went public, to approximately $19 billion by the time of the explosion. It had taken a 12-percent share of the national garbage business, was twice the size of its nearest competitor, and was expected to grow. It had mustered an internal army of 80 lawyers and 22 Washington lobbyists, and had provided $1 million to political candidates in the previous four years while donating another $1.5 million to environmental and wildlife groups. That latter price it had paid to create a cleaner image—as well as sharp divisions within the environmental community over the propriety of accepting such donations—and it was minuscule in comparison to its $6 billion in 1990 revenues or even in relation to its fines.[71] Another troubled CWM incinerator continued to operate in Sauget, Illinois, outside St. Louis, and, though it was not licensed to burn PCBs, the company was poised to regain that business as well—through a new facility coming on line in Port Arthur, Texas.[72]

Landfill and incinerator issues provoked much the same public anger in Northwest Indiana that they did in southeast Chicago. Divided only by a state line, the region had generally become a huge dumping ground. Two other Balanoffs living in Hammond, James (Clem's uncle) and Betty (James's wife), are part of a community coalition fighting Rhone-Poulenc, a French chemical conglomerate, which plans to expand its chemical plant to include a hazardous-waste incinerator. Greenpeace drew regional attention to the issue when some of its members unfurled a banner after climbing to the top of Rhone-Poulenc's stacks. The plant sits across the street from a commuter transit station, an elementary school, and residential housing.

Environmental issues helped propel James Balanoff, the retired District 31 director of the United Steelworkers, into a successful 1983 race for the Hammond city council. Although he lost in 1987, the Rhone-Poulenc issue helped return him to the council in 1991, where he and another council member, Robert Golec, remain staunch advocates of strict municipal environmental controls. Golec, a Hammond fireman, chairs the council's environmental committee.[73] In December 1991, the two persuaded the council to pass an ordinance drafted by Ronald L. Novak, the city's director of environmental management, to place a full-time city inspector at the Rhone-Poulenc plant and charge the company for the expense. The following August, they also persuaded the council to pass an ordinance imposing strict regulations on boilers and industrial furnaces (BIF) despite the opposition of Mayor Tom McDermott, who later resigned to take charge of a private business commission. The inspector ordinance was unique in the nation, according to Golec. The BIF ordinance pushed Hammond further into experimental territory by creating a 15-member citizens advisory committee to monitor the facility. Community concerns were heightened when a California activist, Cathy Ivers, visited to describe a fire at a Rhone-Poulenc plant in Martinez that also recycles sulfuric acid and had applied for a hazardous-waste permit. In November 1992, the company challenged the city in a lawsuit seeking to invalidate the two ordinances, claiming that the inspector law violated constitutional protections against illegal search and seizure and that the BIF ordinance exceeded the city's regulatory powers.[74]

Perhaps the most significant group among many to emerge from the dozens of landfill and incinerator battles in Indiana, however, is People Against Hazardous Landfill Sites (PAHLS). Founded by Susan Lynch, it has become a resource group to train volunteer organizers in communities across the state on environmental issues. Lynch herself is almost a classic case study in the transformation of seemingly average women into powerful, committed activists through the catalyst of a threat to home and community. Formerly married to a local farmer in rural Wheeler, she had never gone far from home or even vacationed outside the state when she first became involved in fighting Waste Management, Inc., over its Wheeler landfill. The story of the Wheeler landfill sounds like many others. It is Lynch's evolution that is extraordinary.

At 37, she says, she had to step out of "a very small life." The Wheeler landfill had already been operating for nine years when she became involved in the issue because of odors emanating from the site. She discovered that the landfill, originally permitted to a local waste-hauling firm for municipal solid waste before being acquired by Waste Management, had become a disposal site for hazardous waste as well. Because of changes in environmental regulations, Waste Management needed a RCRA Part B permit to handle hazardous waste, and Lynch's new group fought the company vigorously, documenting alleged violations and calling them to the attention of state and county health officials. Eventually, the company withdrew its application for the permit, admitting that the decision resulted in part from community pressure.[75] PAHLS contended that trash was being deposited in open ponds of water that accumulated at the bottom of excavations at the landfill site. Its members feared potential contamination of groundwater beneath the surrounding farmlands. The Indiana Department of Environmental Management (IDEM) assured the group that its inspectors had checked and found no problem, according to Lynch. PAHLS was determined to see for itself.

At first, Lynch said, the company made a bid for public support by maintaining an open-door policy at the landfill, allowing visitors to observe operations. That soon changed. Lynch and other volunteers countered by spending six to seven hours per day at the back gate monitoring the operations inside. The company reacted to this uninvited oversight, she said, by building huge piles of soil to keep Lynch's friends from seeing in. Again, local citizens responded with ingenuity by climbing trees to shoot photographs to build evidence of poor waste-management practices. Waste Management erected a fence and sawed down the lookout post, according to Lynch. Having already become bolder than she ever believed possible, Lynch led a new effort to hire airplane pilots to take PAHLS members aloft to shoot aerial videotapes, slides, and still photographs. "IDEM can't refute that," she said, referring to the Indiana Department of Environmental Management.[76]

To say that this scenario produced tension between PAHLS and Waste Management would be a significant understatement, for Mary Ryan, community-relations manager for subsidiary Waste Management of North America, objected to virtually every claim that Lynch made. According to Ryan, only about one percent of the waste at the site is hazardous, though that is obviously due to the fact that Waste Management received its last shipment of such waste on January 24, 1983, and closed down that portion of the landfill in the middle of 1984. As the facility prepared to close in 1993, she noted, it was "filled to capacity."

But PAHLS, she maintained, never needed to resort to its aerial monitoring because "we're a high-profile company. We absolutely have an open-door policy at all of our facilities. The best way to demystify the handling of waste is to let people in. The thing that almost became sad is that Sue and her folks can't get headlines by going over there taking a tour. We had nothing to hide. Their environmental group, to have a cause and try to expand its membership base, in some instances, they had to resort to things that positioned their group as a headline grabber."[77]

Ryan was also anxious to confront claims by Lynch that the landfill had caused high levels of barium in local groundwater. "The residents would tell you that's not true," she replied. "They have historically had problems with septic systems and septic fields. The barium is in the geology itself." In fact, IDEM consistently supports Waste Management's position on this point, much to Lynch's distress. Tests conducted by IDEM in December 1990 sought evidence of tritium, a radioactive isotope of hydrogen whose presence would indicate that the age of the groundwater was less than that of the atomic tests initiated during the Cold War, which increased levels of tritium in the environment. The tests were conducted in shallow sand wells surrounding the landfill and found no tritium. The department concluded that the presence of barium in the groundwater predated World War II.[78] "Even faced with that kind of historic information, they find fault with the state agency and data," Ryan fumed. "Had the state agency concluded to the contrary, they would have absolutely embraced the results." Lynch held so firmly to her position that she signed up for courses in geology at the local college in order to bolster her skills in analyzing the IDEM data for flaws.

In the midst of such animosity, all sides suspect the others' motives. Sometime in early 1992, Ryan noted, a local nurse living in the area approached the firm about contributing to improved water quality in Wheeler, indicating that the residents she represented were "not looking to assess blame" but needed support from one of the few businesses still thriving in a dying town. "We debated for

many months," Ryan said. "If we do something, we will be accused of
having been guilty all along. We decided to let the chips fall where
they will." The company, she said, donated $600,000 to the White
Oak Conservancy District to provide water and sewer services to the
surrounding community, including a sewer hookup for the landfill
itself. The money supplemented state funds that apparently were not
quite adequate to accomplish the task.[79]

Lynch, for her part, makes no effort to disguise her contempt for
Waste Management. And Ryan makes an easy target because her
style, in the view of many environmentalists, exemplifies the
company's paternalistic manner in dealing with local residents. Ryan
can be both bombastic and dismissive in dealing with opponents'
questions, as when she responded in one public meeting to a question by State Representative Balanoff about the willingness of company officials to host a waste facility in their neighborhoods.

"I don't think that's relevant," she replied.[80] Case closed.

The most significant aspect of Lynch's experience was not Waste
Management's eventual decision to close down the site. It was
Lynch's ability to comprehend the frustrations of working-class
people confronted with the power of highly trained lawyers and engineers in hearings and permit proceedings that will determine the
future environmental quality of their communities. Since the early
1980s, that understanding has led hundreds of other Indiana citizens
to call upon PAHLS and Lynch to aid and train them for their own
local battles with a variety of environmental threats. Lynch has
worked upstate and downstate, with rural people and with citizens in
Gary, on problems relating both to the Gary Sanitary Landfill and to
Waste Management's attempt to site a competing facility across the
street in excavated wetlands. PAHLS is probably the group most responsible for inducing Senator Dan Coats, a Republican, to raise the
issue of allowing states to ban the importation of out-of-state wastes
to local landfills. Coats took up the matter after an Indiana law banning trash importation was struck down by federal courts as a violation of the U.S. Constitution's interstate-commerce clause. Similar
laws in Michigan and Alabama were struck down by the U.S. Supreme Court in June 1992.[81]

When I visited Lynch's Valparaiso office in December 1992 for an interview and tour of the region, it was a veritable beehive. One young woman, Jane Kammerer, who had moved to Indiana from New Zealand, was busy organizing a group, SOS, that was just three weeks old. It was dedicated to blocking plans by a company called SONAS to incinerate toxically contaminated dirt at the Burns International Harbor. Within six days, PAHLS had been able to help SOS rally 300 people for an organizational meeting. Another group, Hazard Alert, was fighting Magnetic Metals, Inland Steel's pickle-liquor recycling facility; according to Lynch, its problem was that it was sited on sand in Porter County. A young man who had been laid off from the steel mills was trying his hand at a new job for PAHLS, answering phones and doing basic research.

How long would all these people last? "Two years is the maximum for most people in the movement," Lynch replied. "It's too overwhelming." Perhaps recognizing that this made her a movement veteran, she added that she and her new husband, who is a criminal investigator for IDEM, "go out and hike at the dunes at least once a month. You have to remember what you're trying to protect." The stress of environmental organizing has taken its toll on Lynch, too. She cites it as the cause of her divorce from her first husband, who tired of the struggle.

Our trip took us across much of the bleak Calumet-Indiana landscape. It included the haunting small town of Westville, where Cam-Or, a former oil-recycling facility, awaited cleanup. The leakage into the soil was obvious and extensive. Oil had stained the concrete block above the ground for about a foot and a half, betraying the saturation that had occurred below. At the fence line along the road, the vegetation was black, having absorbed oil from the ground. Despite the clear need for immediate action, the front gate was locked and no one appeared to be inside. The buildings were dilapidated, rusting, falling apart.

I looked across the street. There, facing the Cam-Or site, in front of a handful of side streets in this small town with old houses, was a small building with a sign out front: Westville Chamber of Commerce.

Dorreen Carey also labors in the vineyards of grass-roots activism, but her focus is a river. A former instrumentation worker at U.S. Steel in Gary, she went to work for the Grand Calumet Task Force in 1990, when it needed a new executive director. Two other executive directors preceded Carey, who was laid off from the mill in 1983, when U.S. Steel eliminated half of her department. She decided to return to use her prior experience in photography and worked for two years for a local public-relations firm, which employed her in filming safety shows for steel mills. They also trained her in the use of video cameras to augment her still-photography skills.

That, in turn, led to the opportunity to make a videotape of the Grand Calumet River and show it to the task force. Soon she was working with the task force, and her experience with the film and "some intensive work on the Grand Cal," she said, made her "about as qualified as anybody that they knew at the time" to fill the post of executive director.

The task force began a decade earlier as a project of the Lake Michigan Federation. Steelworkers working at Inland Steel as water-process control operators had requested help to clean up and protect the Grand Calumet, a river so highly polluted that it posed a unique—and largely unquantified—threat to Lake Michigan itself. The Lake Michigan Federation staffed the Grand Calumet Task Force and helped organize a community-based board of directors, which applied for independent nonprofit status in 1986. The organization is now housed in a modest office at Calumet College, a Catholic institution in Whiting that, according to Carey, offered "reasonable rent and a supportive environment."

Starting at the beginning of the river in Gary, the task force has chosen to focus on neighborhoods adjacent to the river through the issues raised by the people who live there. In those forums, the task force and the community exchange concerns because, she said, "We realize that the people who are experiencing pollution and the effects of pollution firsthand may not see it the same way as somebody who's studying it from a distance." The aim, she added, is to develop demonstration projects that can be applied to river communities downstream in East Chicago and Hammond. Starting in Gary also meant that the initial focus was on people of color, primarily African-Americans but including some Hispanics, which meant that the task force "maintained an emphasis on needing clean and safe jobs as well as a clean and safe community." One such project involves the Gary neighborhood of Ambridge-Mann, which is seeking to reclaim a former little-league park along the riverfront that had become a haven for auto stripping and drug dealing. The task force and the community steering committee, at a community speakout at the park on October 24, 1992, announced plans to construct an environmental-education shelter where neighborhood children and adults could learn about river wildlife and regain pride in their surroundings. A workshop in December also helped residents develop organizing methods to link the health and safety concerns of residents and plant workers—some of whom are, after all, the same people.[82]

In short, the Grand Cal Task Force game plan has been to combine labor and community issues under the environmental banner. In Carey's view, "You're really talking about the sustainable community idea where you want to have jobs for people that are consistent with protecting the ecosystem, so that you're not using up your resources, your people, or the basic context in which you live."[83]

The extensive history of environmental abuse in the Calumet region almost makes the word "sustainable" seem out of place. We drove to the head of the Grand Calumet River to find a small lagoon in Gary's Marquette Park where the river once entered the lake. Now a trickle of water flows through a quarter-mile pipe beneath the USX facility's coke plant, amid acres of landfilled real estate created from wetlands and water through the disposal of industrial waste.

Most of Indiana's lakefront industry sits atop such filled land, but now the practice has stopped, except at Inland Steel's Indiana Harbor Works in East Chicago. There, four days a week, trucks continue to dump slag into the lake. In 1990, Inland poured some 39 million pounds of manganese compounds, 2.6 million pounds of zinc compounds, 1.3 million pounds of chromium compounds, 200,000 pounds of lead compounds, and 100,000 pounds of other toxins. According to a special investigative series in the Gary Post-Tribune, Inland's lake filling amounted to 9.8 percent of all on-site land disposal nationwide and 88.9 percent of the statewide total. But, the report added, "Mill officials insist it's neither economical nor necessary to remove the toxins before disposing of the slag in Lake Michigan."[84]

The Grand Calumet Task Force, Carey said, was planning to challenge Inland's right to continue filling the lake.[85] The federal government had already filed suit against Inland, Bethlehem Steel, and Federated Metals in October 1990 for violations of the Clean Water Act, Clean Air Act, Safe Drinking Water Act, and RCRA. On March 9, 1993, it announced a settlement under which Inland paid a $3.5 million civil fine and agreed to a package of cleanup projects estimated at over $50 million. About half of that money would be spent on correcting excessive air and water discharges.[86]

Most of the flow in the Grand Calumet these days is artificial, generated by the wastewater from the industries that line its banks (or culverts). The river never freezes because too much warm water enters from too many outfalls to allow it to happen. The Grand Calumet has been subjected to as much degradation as almost any river of its size in the nation. In 1990, Crain's *City & State*, reporting on the massive cleanup facing industry and government alike, headlined its article "The Rape of the Grand Calumet River." The magazine noted, among other problems, that the Gary Sanitary District had for years been dumping sludge containing toxic chemicals into the Ralston Street Sludge Lagoon, separated from the river by "a few yards of sandy soil." The district had for 13 years failed to comply with the Clean Water Act, dictates of the U.S. EPA and IDEM, and three federal-court consent decrees—after spending $118 million in federal and state grants to upgrade its treatment facility.[87] Yet Gary was not alone. The Hammond and East Chicago sewer districts also had a habit of pumping untreated wastewater into the Grand Calumet.[88] The magazine noted that, near the Hammond district's outfall pipes, the river sported two islands composed of excrements, whose fumes tended to gag nearby residents on hot summer days.[89] In the summer of 1980, some Chicago beaches were closed when fecal matter and grease balls washed ashore. They were traced to a Hammond pumping station.[90] Such miserable environmental performance by local government has done little to build trust among citizens. Betty and James Balanoff attribute the failure of the sanitary districts to their "management by hacks."[91]

Even if local government cleaned up its act, however, industrial practices of both the present and the past would continue to hamper the river's image. Dozens of dump sites, many of them from a bygone era and some of them Superfund sites, line the path of the river. Steel mills dump wastewater. The USX Gary Works alone pumped more than 250 tons of toxins into the river in 1990.[92] Like the Gary Sanitary District, they were not alone.

Dorreen Carey would be the first to concede that the Grand Calumet River is not a special problem in Northwest Indiana, but a symbol of what is wrong and a portent of the region's larger problems if things do not change. In 1990, Lake County, Indiana, the center of Northwest Indiana's heavy industry, ranked eighth in the nation in the volume of toxic chemicals released into the environment by local manufacturing industries. According to the U.S. EPA's Toxic Release Inventory (TRI), a system requiring mandatory reporting by industry under the 1986 Emergency Planning and Community Right-to-Know Act, Lake County industries pumped 67.7 million pounds of toxic waste into the air, land, and water. Just over the border, Cook County, Illinois, ranked tenth, with 66.6 million pounds.[93] But Lake County's 1990 total showed a real improvement over earlier industry practices. The county's 1988 TRI figure had been 91.3 million pounds.[94] The totals, however, understate the severity of the problem because the law does not cover nonmanufacturing industries, such as waste-management facilities and electric utilities.

The people of the region pay for this devastation in ways that have never been well monitored. Between 1983 and 1987, according to statistics of the National Cancer Institute and the National Institute of Health, cancer deaths were about 10 percent above the expected norm in all three Calumet-region counties in Indiana. Although cause and effect are almost impossible to trace in an environment with so many causal agents, Marc Lappé, a public-health professor at the University of Illinois at Chicago, described the community as "justifiably concerned" about the effects of chronic long-term exposure to industrial toxins.[95] But even the emphasis on cancer misses the point about the true long-term impacts of living in a polluted region. Many heavy metals, for instance, are potent neurotoxins, adversely affecting the central nervous system and creating behavioral and developmental disabilities in children that mortgage the future of communities whose resources are already strained by poverty and unemployment.

The toxic burden carried by Lake Michigan and its tributaries has also raised serious questions about bioaccumulation of such toxins in fish and resulted in a number of public-health advisories about the consumption of Great Lakes fish. In most of the Grand Calumet itself, aquatic life cannot survive. Documented historical and cultural patterns of fish consumption among minorities in the Great Lakes area, particularly African-Americans and Native Americans, have prompted concerns about disproportionate impacts on minority populations.[96]

Carey stressed that "nobody's ever done any health studies here, or any risk assessments. They haven't done any kind of epidemiological study. People don't want to admit it, and if there's no proof, it's easier to say I lived here all my life, I'm okay."[97]

If people in Northwest Indiana have had a hard time facing the reality of their environment, it has been even easier for the rest of Indiana to ignore the region's problems. It was only in 1990 that the state established a northwest regional office of IDEM in Gary, which regional director David Dabertin admitted remains understaffed. Under a long string of Republican governors, Dabertin said, predominantly Democratic and heavily minority-populated Northwest Indiana "could have dropped off the map" as far as downstaters were concerned. It was the election of Democratic Governor Evan Bayh that brought about a payback for the region through the regional offices of a few agencies like IDEM. Even so, it has not been easy to develop a rapport. Distrust of government is so high, and the organizational sophistication of grass-roots environmental groups is so poor, Dabertin said, that many cannot move beyond their entrenched suspicion of government to take advantage of opportunities that present themselves. Dabertin, himself a former activist, also complained that groups that want immediate action from IDEM refuse to support efforts to increase its staff and funding when the legislature is debating budgets. Nonetheless, he sees organizers like Carey and Lynch as "a step above" many others with whom he has been unable to build a productive relationship. Dabertin is well aware that the attitude many citizens harbor toward government is born of the corrupt and arm-twisting relationships they have experienced with local precinct bosses, "many of whom have ended up in prison." And he readily declared that the people of the region are "really suffering" because of its accumulation of environmental problems.[98]

If the community is at risk, workers are truly on the front lines. Carey, a former steelworker herself, has no trouble allying herself with labor unions on issues of worker health and safety. Many workers, in turn, have found common cause with groups like the Grand Calumet Task Force, PAHLS, or the Hoosier Environmental Council (HEC). Larry Davis, who chairs the environmental committee for USWA Local 6787, which represents workers at the Bethlehem Steel Burns Harbor plant, has done extensive volunteer work with all three groups. As a board member of HEC, he participated in the U.S. EPA's negotiated rulemaking on coke-oven standards under the 1990 Clean Air Act.

The issue of coke ovens, which burn coal as part of the process of making steel, has long been clear in Davis's view. He noted that, as far back as the eighteenth century, the British doctor Percival Potts had identified coal soot as a cause of scrotal cancer among chimney sweeps. "Those are the same byproducts produced in coking ovens," he observed. "We've known for a long time that the byproducts of coal had a carcinogenic nature."

Not everyone shares Davis's knowledge of industrial history and worker-safety regulations, which he has acquired through dogged persistence and spare-time scholarship. He is the type of union activist who infuriates company officials during negotiations by punching questions into a portable computer and generating instant refutations of their claims on a variety of pollution, safety, and regulatory issues. But neighbors of coking ovens have seldom needed more than noses, lungs, and smarting eyes to know that something is wrong. And those neighbors often have been steelworkers' families.

In Gary, coke-oven pollution was a potent local political issue as far back as 1970, when Richard Hatcher, the city's new African-American mayor, constructed an effective coalition of African-Americans and white environmentalists behind a proposed ordinance to regulate more strictly the air pollution from the mills. The only real target in town was the company that built Gary, U.S. Steel. Hatcher mined the deep discontent that African-Americans in the late 1960s felt toward U.S. Steel on a variety of social issues and brought attention to the public-health threat that steel-mill pollution posed to the minority communities that suffered the greatest exposure. At the same time, progressive clergy in white ethnic neighborhoods redirected unrest there away from racial fears toward air-pollution issues under the banner of the Calumet Community Congress. Hatcher's stance, which succeeded in tightening municipal environmental regulation in Gary, thus became an effective forerunner of other urban environmental coalitions more than a decade later. It began to crumble only after the collapse of the steel industry threatened workers' job security and undermined the local economy.[99]

The Gary initiative developed at about the same time that coke ovens emerged as a serious health and safety issue within the international headquarters of the United Steel Workers of America, according to Michael Wright, a veteran USWA safety official. Steelworkers, he noted, had long believed that the coke ovens were dangerous and produced a high rate of cancer. But until the *Journal of Occupational Medicine* published what became known as the "steelworker studies," he said, the union never had good evidence with which to negotiate. The studies, done by University of Pittsburgh researcher Carol Redmond Ciaccia, examined the medical histories of all steelworkers in the Pittsburgh area over a 30-year period, comparing mortality patterns of these tens of thousands of laborers by work areas—blast furnaces, coke batteries, and other plant areas. The studies showed major excesses of lung cancer among coke-oven workers, with those who worked atop the coke ovens being eight times as likely to develop cancer.

The studies also helped to highlight the degree to which race was tied to occupational exposure. The first industry response, Wright recalled, was to argue that the studies' results were somehow the result of special circumstances in Allegheny County, the only place where they were conducted. And then there was the ugly specter of race. "Some arguments went beyond dumb," Wright said. "They said that, since we see the excesses primarily among black rather than white coke-oven workers, there might be a racial factor involved in the susceptibility. We pointed out that the excess among white workers was just as great, but the numbers were not statistically significant." The reason: The steel companies historically had assigned far greater numbers of African-American workers to the dangerous coking ovens, while assigning white workers to other parts of the plant. The USWA instigated a lawsuit through the federal Equal Employment Opportunity Council, achieving a consent decree spanning the next 20 years. The decree "basically changed the way the seniority pools were calculated. People could transfer more equally between work areas. It made racial assignment between work areas illegal." Because of the long latency period for developing cancer, Wright noted, "the consent decree is just beginning to become effective" in altering exposure patterns among African-American and white workers.

Meanwhile, other medical researchers replicated the Pittsburgh steelworkers study and found similar results elsewhere. By 1974, the USWA began to attack the problem in negotiations by seeking contract language that allowed workers to strike over designated local issues while adhering to a national no-strike agreement that guaranteed three-percent annual increases plus a cost-of-living allowance. The union declared the coke-oven question a local issue despite its nationwide impact, and the locals began to negotiate health protections, armed with the new medical data. In 1974, the USWA also began to lobby the Occupational Safety and Health Administration (OSHA) for new coke-oven agreements.

Eula Bingham, now on the faculty of the University of Cincinnati, was the Assistant Secretary of Labor for OSHA who headed the hearings for the standards that were finally approved, "pretty much the way we wanted it," according to Wright. Those standards led to a legal challenge by the companies, who charged that they were so stringent that they would shut down the industry. That, however, never happened, and the court, which rejected the challenge, noted that if anyone had anything to lose in such an event, it was the steelworkers who had supported the new OSHA standards.

"With standards," Wright noted, "exposures on coke batteries came down enormously. You now see steam from quenching operations, but in the old days you could see black smoke for five miles." People in steel communities like Clairton (the site of a big USX mill in Allegheny County), he said, were worrying about what the pollution was doing to their own communities. In the face of this concern, he added, "The company does try to whip up some kind of split [between labor and environmentalists], but we do our best to make sure it's not successful."

In fact, the Clairton plant's pollution produced some local steelworker opposition called Group Against Smoke and Pollution (GASP), a leader in the steelworker-environmentalist coalition that entered a negotiated rulemaking in 1992, in which the U.S. EPA convened a number of interested parties to hammer out an agreement on new coke-oven standards under the 1990 amendments to the Clean Air Act. (The earlier OSHA standards dealt with worker health and safety. The EPA standards, concluded in early 1993, deal with air pollution.) One caucus at the rulemaking parley, according to Wright, consisted of the USWA, the Natural Resources Defense Council, and two local environmental groups—GASP and the Hoosier Environmental Council. On the other side were the industry trade groups. Ultimately, the only party not to sign on to the agreement was GASP, largely because the agreement required companies to install the best available technology, which by that time clearly seemed to be that employed by the Clairton USX plant. Thus, GASP may have felt shortchanged, Wright noted, though the pollution from the Clairton plant was complicated by the meteorology of Allegheny County, which resembles that around East Liverpool, Ohio, downriver from Pittsburgh. Nonetheless, Wright said, EPA estimated that the new standards would cut emissions by about 90 percent.[100]

For his part, Larry Davis, who represented HEC, was unimpressed with the industry stance, although he was moderately pleased with the resulting regulations. The environmental groups, steelworkers, and state and local air-pollution officials functioned well as a coalition, he said, while the industry representatives often seemed splintered, better able to react in a united way to environmental proposals than to offer a coherent counterproposal of their own. Almost wistfully, he wishes future negotiated rulemaking could be conducted in a less contentious atmosphere.

"I look forward to the day when everybody can identify the problem and cooperatively brainstorm and work together to find the best solution," he said.[101]

In the Calumet region, the best solution to most problems has long been elusive because of the deep social and political fault lines that crisscross the area. The two states often compete but seldom cooperate in planning for the area. City boundaries become green lines that separate, for instance, Hammond with a four-percent African-American population from Gary with its African-American majority. Even within cities, natural and manmade barriers separate white ethnic Hegewisch from African-American South Deering, and Altgeld Gardens is isolated from everything. And where no natural or political boundaries exist, the Law of the Latest Arrival has nonetheless historically separated neighborhoods along ethnic lines. Hard times have accentuated those divisions because there are fewer jobs and development prospects to share, and the bitter feeling lingers in many communities that the meager spoils are unevenly distributed. Environmental organizers have struggled against the odds to cement coalitions that cross these lines, but their task is overwhelming and their resources limited.

The Daley proposal for a Lake Calumet airport exposed and exploited all these fault lines.

From the moment the Daley plan took wings, contention filled the air. Community groups like the Grand Cal Task Force struggle to marshal political attention for their new visions of the region's economic future, but proposals on the scale of a new airport from the mayor of Chicago can dominate regional planning almost overnight. In fact, one prime complaint from Hegewisch businesspeople who opposed the plan was that it virtually froze all other investment plans for the area until the airport issue was resolved.[102]

In certain respects, Daley's proposal appealed to those who had long advocated redirecting industrial and commercial development to the urban core and away from the suburban fringe. Like many other American metropolises, the Chicago area has suffered from massive suburban sprawl in the late twentieth century. Since 1970, the area's population had grown a mere four percent while its developed land area had expanded by 50 percent. O'Hare International Airport was already at capacity, with landing rights restricted by the Federal Aviation Administration. The northwestern suburbs, concerned about noise and organized as the Suburban O'Hare Coalition, had fought the city in court to win an injunction against the development of any new runways. Chicago's first airport, the 640-acre Midway Airport, was hemmed in by a variety of neighborhoods and industrial uses and could not expand. A new airport at a "green-grass" site in exurban farmland would only complicate the problem of urban sprawl. On the other hand, a great deal of the ancillary transportation and public-works infrastructure to support a new airport already existed at Lake Calumet. An airport on the Southeast Side would directly create, according to the city's estimates, 46,000 jobs in an area whose industrial future seemed bleak and whose environmental cleanup demanded billions of dollars.[103] What better way to solve the region's problems, including cleanup of toxic dumps, than by attracting the huge investment required to build a new airport?

From the beginning, however, the airport proposal seemed ready to unravel. One obstacle, which Daley quickly overcame, was gaining representation for Chicago on a bi-state panel that already represented the states of Indiana and Illinois. Daley could not trust Illinois Governor James Edgar to pursue the Chicago site over competing downstate sites in Kankakee, Peotone, and the border town of Beecher. Indiana desperately wanted to sell the idea of expanding the existing Gary airport. Dealmaking was the order of the day. Daley quickly agreed to two key political tradeoffs. First, in order to accommodate flight-path problems that would otherwise result, Midway would close when the Lake Calumet airport opened. That created some opposition from the city's southwest neighborhoods, which would lose a valuable engine of their own economic development. Second, Daley agreed that the Lake Calumet airport would be under the control of a regional airport authority. Despite the loss of political control, he would be content to bring jobs and development into the city. In any event, Daley controlled the purse strings: U.S. Representative Daniel Rostenkowski, the city's powerful chairman of the House Ways and Means Committee, won passage of a measure that ensured that new passenger charges imposed at O'Hare could be used for development of the Lake Calumet site.[104] Previously, those funds had been restricted to improvements at the airport where they were collected.

But the Hegewisch neighborhood, which would be completely obliterated by the new airport, erupted in protest. The mayor's plan, which underwent some alterations, would have displaced 8,900 homes and 25,000 residents plus 137 businesses.[105] One of the businesses was the modern, retooled Ford Taurus assembly plant at the edge of Lake Calumet, which employed 3,200 people.[106] Owners of older businesses were concerned that the fair-market value they would receive for the condemnation of their aging plants would never pay for their relocation or reconstruction.[107] They would simply go out of business instead.

Of the residents to be relocated, 8,900 represented the entire population of Hegewisch. At one community meeting, city officials proposed creating a "new Hegewisch" at 103rd Street, near an incinerator and a freeway interchange. The offer was greeted with howls of disdain.[108] The largely Polish-American neighborhood also nursed a profound sense of betrayal as it watched Polish-American politicians like Rostenkowski and U.S. Representative William Lipinski do the mayor's bidding on the airport issue, as did Tenth Ward Alderman John Buchanan.

The other residents came from adjoining areas, including the largely African-American neighborhood of South Deering, just north of Lake Calumet, and most of Burnham, a suburb that lies along Chicago's southern border. In a nonbinding voter referendum in November 1990, residents of the Tenth Ward and Calumet City rejected the airport proposal by nearly a 2-to-1 margin.[109] Later, the opposition outside Hegewisch was weakened when the United Neighborhood Organization (UNO), largely representing Hispanics in South Deering and South Chicago, adopted a stance of cautious support. Hegewisch residents accused UNO leader Mary Ellen

Montez of selling out to the mayor after he appointed her to the Lake Calumet Advisory Commission, whose job was to lobby for the new airport. UNO members responded that their members needed jobs, and the airport might be a way to achieve that goal.[110]

In short order, opponents, who included State Representative Balanoff, began to marshal data that they felt proved the Lake Calumet site to be both unfeasible and unsound. One of those arguments was truly a double-edged sword. Consultants for the city and the bi-state panel vigorously debated the costs of the environmental cleanup and restoration that would inevitably be necessary to win federal approval. Even James Dermody, the division manager for the Federal Aviation Administration's Aviation Information office in Chicago, described Lake Calumet as "probably the biggest environmental challenge we've ever faced." The city's 1991 feasibility study identified 13 potential hazardous-waste sites, 15 landfill sites, 27 fly dumps, and 158 underground storage tanks in the area. It also noted the possibility of waste areas surrounding the extensive network of rail lines crossing the area, due to spills and leaks from rail cars and repair shops.[111] How much would this cleanup cost? Depending on the source, estimates ranged from a few hundred million dollars to nearly ten billion. These estimates became a primary weapon in the war of words over the total development cost at the various sites. TAMS Consultants, hired by the bi-state panel, estimated a 1991 cost of $17.4 billion to develop the Lake Calumet site, versus $9 billion for Gary and $4 billion for the most expensive rural site. Indiana officials insisted that the Gary site would cost only $6 billion.[112] Not surprisingly, Chicago put the figure for Lake Calumet at just under $10 billion, including less than $300 million for environmental remediation and mitigation.[113]

The issue for opponents was obvious. They wanted to see the area cleaned up. Daley was promising a source of money to do it. If the airport were not built, where would the money come from? But that issue served only to provoke outrage about the entire history that Klonowski labeled "toxic imperialism." Why, opponents asked, did the area get such attention only when the mayor wanted an airport? And in any event, since the city was anxious to prove that the Lake Calumet site was economically feasible, who could believe its figures? What sort of environmental cleanup could the city do for $300 million? The prevalent fear was that the cleanup would consist of merely capping the buried wastes beneath the tarmac.

Among the environmental costs were mitigation expenses for the disturbance of existing water and wetlands. The proposed site's 8,200 acres included 325 acres of open water that had to be filled and 329 acres of wetlands that would be affected by airport development. The plan involved altering (once again) the course of the Little Calumet and Grand Calumet rivers, with the airport site lying atop the Grand Cal's outlet to Lake Michigan from Lake Calumet.

The volatile combination of landfills and water, already a potent issue among the area's environmental activists, spurred a special protest from conservationists and sportsmen, some of whom were not always aligned on other issues. Both landfills and water attract birds. Birds pose a serious navigation hazard near airports. The region had long been a major migratory flyway because of its geography and topographical features, hosting nesting sites for 72 species, 25 of which were on the state's threatened or endangered species list.[114] The avian cornucopia included geese, ducks, herons, egrets, gulls, and cranes. The wildlife issue spurred the U.S. Fish and Wildlife Service to indicate that it would oppose the site as "without question, the most damaging."

Steve Sedam, the Great Lakes regional vice president for the Audubon Society in Columbus, Ohio, became a sarcastic critic of the city's plan, as did local naturalists like James Landing, a geography professor at the University of Illinois in Chicago and the founder of the Lake Calumet Study Committee. The local Sierra Club also dispensed some harsh criticism. Sedam noted that officials at New York's John F. Kennedy International Airport had ordered the shooting of 15,000 gulls in 1991 because of concerns about collisions between birds and airplanes, which had aborted 40 takeoffs since 1979.

But Michael Aniol, president of the Hegewisch Chamber of Commerce, which also opposed the Lake Calumet plan, offered perhaps the most graphic fear. Landfills generate methane gas as they decompose. The pipes that motorists see rising from the ground at Waste Management's CID landfill along I–94 are there to drain and flare off such gas to prevent hazardous accumulations beneath the

surface. Some landfills near the new airport would remain in operation. Most crashes occur during takeoffs and landings, which subject
aircraft to their greatest stress. Suppose, Aniol suggested, a jet
crashed into a landfill beyond the end of a runway. Would it ignite a
fireball of exploding gas?[115]

In the end, however, as had often happened in the past, most of
the arguments on either side were simply tools in the hands of powerful politicians wrestling for more power. Daley and Edgar, one an
urban Democrat, the other a downstate Republican, managed to join
forces behind the Lake Calumet site, but failed to overcome suburban opposition to the proposal. The state legislation Daley needed
for the new Lake Calumet airport authority failed to pass. Edgar
promised to try again.[116] Then suddenly, in the summer of 1992, almost as quickly as he had thrust the proposal onto the political stage,
Daley withdrew it. Expressing pique over the legislature's apparent
unwillingness to cooperate, Daley announced that henceforth the
city would concentrate on using its newly won passenger tax to improve operations at O'Hare and Midway. The city, he declared,
would not support a suburban airport site.[117]

Daley moved on to the advocacy of a downtown gambling casino
as his primary economic development mantra. The Calumet region
was cast back into obscurity, fending for itself amid a multitude of
newly forgotten problems. The Daley plan had ended in a crash landing.

During the battle over the airport, Chicago's Center for Neighborhood Technology (CNT) had quietly begun to construct a dialogue
on the Southeast Side about alternative economic-development scenarios. In the time it takes to build an airport, CNT founder Scott
Bernstein pointed out, other changes and plans could be conceived
and carried out. The area's abundance of used materials could be
transformed from a liability into an asset in a society that placed
greater value on efficiency in the use of its resources. Waste management, replaced by an emphasis on waste avoidance, could become a
relic of the past. Planners could shift the policy emphasis to create a
Lake Calumet Environmental Enterprise Zone, where rewards followed not only the creation of jobs but environmental improvements
as well.[118]

It is, however, far beyond the resources of a citizens group like the Grand Calumet Task Force to produce an economic plan for the Calumet region. Dorreen Carey knows that the only viable role for groups like hers is to act as catalysts for change. She is not about to wait for the planners and policymakers who, in her view, "will take anything they can get. The all-out polluters want to come here. And it's the people who are refusing the polluters and saying, 'We don't need more of that.' We need new kinds of industries. We need people that will come and give people jobs but aren't going to pollute the environment. And, of course, the Catch-22 is that nobody who has clean jobs wants to come here."

The answer to that dilemma, in the view of the task force, is to make a commitment to cleaning up the environment. Carey even envisions the possibility that the Calumet region could become a center for innovative environmental cleanup technology "as long as they don't truck in new waste from the rest of the country." Then, said Carey, "you need to offer people something for coming here and operating a clean business. You need a kind of enterprise zone that rewards people for being clean, not something that relaxes standards." As a means of making its point, the task force demanded a moratorium on the permitting of new toxic-waste-handling facilities.[119]

"Stop!" the task force seemed to be pleading with state and local officials. Stop your piecemeal, politically fragmented, business-as-usual nonsense long enough to develop a comprehensive vision for the region's future.

LOUISIANA

Meandering Rivers of Justice

Louisiana is the tip of a great funnel for America's natural resources. Its potential began to become clear only after the Louisiana Purchase, when a young nation opportunistically acquired the western half of the continent's most massive watershed. Though the Mississippi River was long ignored after its initial discovery by the Spanish explorer, Hernando de Soto, Americans quickly found a mission for it. By the time of Mark Twain, it was the busiest waterway in the world.

Louisiana is what half of the other states have made it. Long before the nation existed, long before Native Americans found their way to the Great River, half of the land that became the United States began pouring its soil and its water into a narrow channel that grew, over millennia, from what is now Baton Rouge into an unstable entrance to the Gulf of Mexico, 110 miles downriver from New Orleans. Over the millennia, the river has meandered, leaving in its restless wake vast stranded wetlands. The Atchafalaya Swamp, for instance, stretches over an ancient riverbed once occupied by the Mississippi before it shifted course.

That geological inheritance has made Louisiana, and particularly New Orleans, unlike any other place in the Deep South. In acquiring the Louisiana Territory, the United States also acquired, in its infancy, one of the New World's most distinctive cultures. The

Acadian French, popularly known as Cajuns, have thrived on the striking natural abundance of the state's semitropical wetland environment. Yet, while they lived in relative isolation along the swamps and bayous, Louisiana's cities thrived on river traffic that made them the cosmopolitan centers of the Gulf Coast. Midwestern states shipped grain and coal, while southern states sent cotton and rice. New Orleans remains the port of departure to foreign markets for midwestern corn, wheat, and soybeans. Grain silos dot the sides of the river near port facilities.

The oil companies have also discovered Louisiana. Like eastern Texas, Louisiana is afloat in oil, particularly offshore in the Gulf of Mexico. This resource, which drives so much of the modern American economy, has pulled Louisiana into the industrial revolution within a generation. Plastics manufacturers found cheap labor and an abundant petrochemical feedstock. By the late 1950s, the giants of the chemical industry began to set up shop, largely in the corridor between Baton Rouge and New Orleans, but elsewhere as well, around Lake Charles in the southwest and Shreveport in the north. Dow Chemical, Ciba-Geigy, Monsanto, Exxon, and a host of smaller refiners and manufacturers all took up residence.

Louisiana became the tip of the funnel for all the invisible environmental side effects of the American consumer's love affair with modern conveniences. Vinyl car seats, plastic credit cards, foam cushions, styrofoam cups, and the plastic casing on computer keyboards all emanate from petrochemical plants in Louisiana using feedstocks refined from Gulf Coast oil. This new industry has transformed the state's economy, producing 165,000 jobs and one of every three state tax dollars at its peak in 1982.[1]

But the state has paid a price, for it has absorbed the brunt of the toxic impacts of the nation's affluent lifestyle. When comparative data on corporate releases of toxic substances into the environment finally began to surface through the Toxic Release Inventory reporting requirements of the 1986 Emergency Planning and Community Right-to-Know Act, Louisiana promptly found itself at the top of the heap, leading the nation with more than 715 million pounds of annual toxic releases into the air, land, and water.[2] Operating for years in a laissez-faire state regulatory climate, the chemical companies had polluted the state's water, air, and land with virtual impunity until a modest environmental rebellion began to take root under Governor Buddy Roemer, elected in 1987. The state's discovery that it had paid a needlessly high price for attracting an industry that would have located in Louisiana anyway finally inflamed an environmental anger that had been smoldering for nearly a decade. Roemer's reform appointees at the Department of Environmental Quality (DEQ) set as their first priority getting Louisiana out of first place.

Like the headwaters of a thousand minor tributaries that feed into the Mississippi, these wellsprings of citizen discontent began to pour forth and merge into expanding streams of political activism. Across the state, grass-roots groups emerged, merged, fought their local chemical polluters, and learned vital political lessons.

William A. Fontenot is widely regarded as the grandfather of Louisiana environmentalism. But he might as easily be seen as the veteran smoke jumper of Louisiana's environmental conflagrations. Since former state Attorney General William J. Guste, Jr., hired him for a unique advocacy post in 1979, citizens have been calling his office for help in challenging local polluters. "Willie" always obliges. As head of the tiny Citizens Access Unit in the Louisiana Justice Department's Land and Natural Resources Division, he has traveled the state, meeting with concerned citizens, proffering organizing advice, pointing them to informational resources, teaching them research techniques, and accompanying them to public document rooms and to meetings with reluctant bureaucrats and company officials. One by one, slowly and carefully over more than a decade, a slew of grass-roots community environmental groups has grown up with Fontenot's constant encouragement, growing and merging into a statewide movement that is calling corporations and politicians to account in ways that Louisiana has never seen before. A biography of Willie Fontenot would almost suffice as a history of the Louisiana environmental movement.

The nature of Louisiana politics made it essential for someone like Fontenot to prod the development of a serious environmental movement. Education has always been a low priority in Louisiana, and few people who were educated ever showed much interest in using their skills to bring about political reform. Before the state began to industrialize, the Mississippi valley was lined with large sugar plantations, whose predominantly African-American workers had no effective political power. The high-powered career of Governor and Senator Huey Long, popularized in Robert Penn Warren's novel *All the King's Men*, typified the brand of strong-man politics that still infests the state today. Covering the 1991 campaign that brought former Governor Edwin Edwards back into power, *Wall Street Journal* reporter Dennis Farney described Louisiana as "not so much a state as a foreign country inexplicably washed up on the American shore." John Maginnis, a Louisiana political analyst, called it "America's last banana republic."[3]

Such politics cannot thrive in a strong participatory democracy. Instead, a veneer of southern gentility masks an almost inexplicable, naive faith in authority. The bane of Louisiana politics has been the folksy assumption, even among many African-Americans, that the government would never let "it" happen if "it" was bad. William Sanjour, a U.S. EPA scientist and whistleblower whom the Reagan and Bush administrations effectively removed from any power within the agency, has noted that this "it" is almost never clearly defined in the minds of those who maintain this faith in authority.[4] Lazy and unscrupulous local government officials, in turn, have often played on this faith to maintain that local scrutiny of a proposed industrial project is unnecessary because state and federal officials would surely scrutinize such projects before they become reality. This cop-out glosses over the obvious fact that even the best-intentioned environmental authorities have clearly defined legal limitations as to the kinds of protection they can offer. In Louisiana, it is a gross understatement to say that the legislature has been historically ungenerous in granting such powers to state bureaucrats.

Willie Fontenot has played the shepherd for many citizens who have begun to doubt. He has led them to the pastures of green populism and guided them through the valleys where the shadows of political and economic retaliation have lurked throughout Louisiana's history. And he has shown them, for more than a decade, that a promised land of environmental reform awaits them on the other side. It has been his unique genius to find the smallest seeds of Louisiana's environmental populist revolt and nurture them into a full-fledged rebellion.

Fontenot, by his own account, never expected to be a professional environmentalist. After graduating from college in 1970, he had returned to New Orleans with many of the environmental concerns other students had developed during the 1960s. He was working as a workers' compensation auditor for an insurance company, and the environment was a sideline interest.[5]

But the problems of Lake Pontchartrain and Louisiana's coastal wetlands grabbed his attention. He became the chairman of the local Sierra Club, now known as the Delta Chapter. He met a number of people from a variety of small groups in the area, all of whom were fighting either the U.S. Army Corps of Engineers, the Louisiana Department of Fish and Wildlife, or the state Highway Department over projects they considered harmful to the lake and its adjoining wetlands. Shell dredging by mining companies muddied the lake and destroyed the bottom-feeding clams and mussels that fed the lake's fish population. Leaking sewerage systems and septic tanks in parishes along the lengthy lakeshore poured bacterial filth into the lake, while storm drains doused it with a variety of chemical and organic toxins like motor oil and fertilizers. From area farms, agricultural runoff, including cow excrement, washed down tributaries like the Tangipahoa River into the lake.

The Audubon Society, the Sierra Club, and the Wildlife Federation were also fighting to stem coastal erosion and to block federal Soil Conservation Service efforts to channelize streams or drain wetlands to make more land available for agriculture. The loss of coastal wetlands, in particular, has become staggering, estimated at 50 square miles per year.[6] This, too, became an education for Fontenot, who noticed that these projects helped not family farmers but "large insurance companies, multinational corporations that were [using farms] as an investment." The small family farmer would suddenly "be competing with large holdings of 10,000- or 50,000-acre operations. They can just price you right out of the market." Fontenot was beginning to learn who pulled the strings for Louisiana's environmentally destructive pork-barrel projects.

But in the 1970s, Fontenot says, not much information existed about these issues. He was overjoyed on one occasion to find some editorials in the *New Orleans Times-Picayune* dealing with Lake Pontchartrain. Fontenot prepared some letters to the editor and went to the newspaper's offices to congratulate its staff for paying attention to the problem. There, he met with Louis Brumfield, an editor who shortly thereafter launched a regular environmental column. Still, he noticed, environmental news tended to be relegated to the back pages.

He also learned of the powerful role of chemical companies in contaminating the environment. In the early 1970s, a staff member of the state's water-quality division had called in the federal agency that is now the Centers for Disease Control to trace what he suspected was a strange virus that was killing thousands of Louisiana fish. He had tested the water and found nothing. The cause was not a virus. Using what was then advanced technology, a gas chromatograph mass spectrometer, the agency staff traced the problem to Velsico Chemical Company in Memphis, Tennessee, whose "sloppy operation" had been dumping pesticides such as endrin, DDT, and chlorinate through storm drains and other pipes directly into the Mississippi River, causing fish kills all the way downstream to the Gulf of Mexico. Before the poisoning began, Louisiana had nearly 50,000 brown pelicans. By the mid-1960s, they were extinct. Even by 1974, after a seemingly successful transplantation of some 300 Florida birds, 80 percent of the brown pelicans died again. The Department of Wildlife and Fisheries, which had been preparing a film, *The Brown Pelican: A Success Story*, quickly renamed it *The Brown Pelican: A Bird in Danger*.

In 1977, a liberal Democratic millionaire, William J. Guste, Jr., won the attorney general's office as a reformer. Fontenot, who had labored as an environmental volunteer for several years and already knew more people and more groups than any other activist in the state, was ready for a change. A friend recommended him to Guste, who hired him in June 1978, creating a special position that gave Fontenot virtually free rein as an advocate for environmental causes.

One of Fontenot's first calls came from Gay Hanks, a housewife in largely rural Vermilion Parish. Her father, a relatively wealthy white liberal, does some social work. According to Hanks, people would ask her father to "see what was going on."[7]

What was going on was a search by chemical waste-disposal companies for leases from local farmers, who were not making much money in a depressed local economy, to allow them to dump waste in pits. There was an obvious problem. Vermilion is a low-lying parish along the Gulf Coast where water tables—and the resulting potential for contamination—are very high. Neighbors of the willing farmers inevitably inquired about this new activity and, said Hanks, were usually paid off and became dependent on the waste firms.

Hanks attributed the almost incredibly bad choice of location to "ignorance, poverty, and the need for money." Residents paid a horrible price for their tenuous grip on prosperity, Hanks recalled. "People's clothes smelled like chemical pits. You could see the fumes rising over the pit." The shallow water wells, at only 300 to 400 feet in some places, were quickly poisoned by waste migrating through the porous ground. In excavating, Hanks claimed, the firms would often "break the clay barrier. You get a pit that's full one day and gone the next. Often they would illegally discharge into ditches. There was no limit to what the pits could take. One time after a 17-inch rain, every pit was overflowing. There's no doubt in my mind that it entered the food chain."

Years later, she said, cancer rates shot up, and victims became younger. It is a personal issue for Hanks. In 1968, she lost a daughter to leukemia. Doctors at St. Jude's Children's Hospital in Memphis told her they had "too many children in Louisiana coming in with this problem." Unaware of the potential causes at the time, Hanks said, she "had made a mental note."

With some organizing help from Fontenot, she fought back, with allies like Lloyd Campsie, an insurance agent, and Ernest Gerouard, a farmer with a Ph.D. As they called public attention to each new disposal site, opponents would surface. The group's numbers grew to nearly 400. Eventually, "the issue became so hot that people stopped leasing their lands." In a small town desperate for income, she said, "some people still glare at me. We made some enemies when we hurt some people in the pocketbook who wanted to lease their land."

More than a decade later, Hanks and her friends remain engaged in the fight to clean up Vermilion Parish. The fight has moved to the cleanup stage—some of the disposal sites are now federal Superfund sites facing costly cleanup expenses and protracted litigation. The federal Comprehensive Environmental Response, Compensation, and Liability Act (CERCLA), a law passed in 1980 to fund the cleanup of contaminated sites, imposes joint and strict and several liability on any party that may have contributed even partially to the contamination, including those who generated the waste that was shipped to the site. One Superfund site in Vermilion Parish, Gulf Coast Premix, involves 431 of these potentially responsible parties, some of them having barged in their waste from other states. But Fontenot was still aiding the activists' efforts, helping them to apply for technical assistance grants (TAG) under Superfund. The group received three $50,000 grants, allowing it to hire a technical adviser who could interpret the findings from monitoring well tests and other cleanup operations.

In his first prolonged effort, Fontenot encountered one of the most valuable allies he has acquired over the years—Wilma Subra, a laboratory technician who lives in New Iberia. In 1980 she was working for a quasi-governmental consulting firm, Gulf South Research, Inc. One feature of Subra's work bothered her, according to Fontenot. "She said she was in people's homes taking samples and was forbidden to tell them why she was taking samples or the significance of it and decided this was wrong." Once she left, said Fontenot, the two "helped organize 25 new groups in one year from scratch."

It took years for David Ewell to learn about or trust Willie Fontenot. Just north of Baton Rouge, in the winter of 1969–1970, pits at a chemical dump site owned by Petro Processors broke open and overflowed, pouring tons of toxic waste across a vast swamp. Much of the poisoned land belonged to Ewell, a local rancher, who sued ten corporations involved in the mess to clean up his land. The case went to trial in 1975, and Ewell's victory left him deeply embittered. Without ordering any cleanup of the property, the court awarded him compensation for his 150,000 acres and about 150 steers that had died. Not until 1980 did the Louisiana attorney general file suit under federal hazardous-waste laws to compel cleanup, which took even more years to begin. Fontenot noted that Ewell had become so distrustful of a system that seemed to take so long to accomplish so little that it took him nearly three years of contact with Fontenot to decide that Willie was for real.

Ewell was not the only victim who had trouble believing that someone like Fontenot could actually be working for the state of Louisiana. A few years later, as an EPA-supervised cleanup was progressing at the Petro Processors site, Fontenot took a 30-minute call from a worker who would not divulge his name. He said, however, that he worked at a plant and was getting sick from fumes, and described the situation without mentioning the plant or its neighbors.

"Well, from what you're describing," Fontenot replied, "you work at either Schuylkill or Reynolds." Both plants were literally across the street from Petro Processors where, Fontenot knew, the cleanup work was creating fumes that were sickening nearby workers.

"How do you know?" the stunned caller asked.

"Well," Fontenot said, "I'm familiar with the sites."

More accustomed to state inspectors whose familiarity with polluting plants was cursory at best, Ray Arnet revealed his identity. Within a few days, he brought a fellow worker, Gerald Tillman, a white Teamsters Union member, to Fontenot's office to discuss how to organize workers to respond to the situation. Fontenot directed them to Richard Miller, a progressive organizer for the Oil, Chemical, and Atomic Workers Local 4-620 in Baton Rouge. They also organized other workers, like Darnell Dunn, an African-American lead worker at Schuylkill, and residents, like E.W. Pate of the nearby Alsen neighborhood, an African-American subdivision on the northern outskirts of Baton Rouge.

For Tillman, the struggle that followed became a life-changing epic. A six-foot, two-inch Vietnam veteran, Tillman was not about to accept quietly the prospect of a "major Superfund site gassing us and nobody taking any initiative. Everybody was getting sick, throwing up, fever—you would get off from work and lay on the couch for three or four days and wonder why." The reason, apparently, was that the cleanup effort was mixing lime ash with between 61 and 100 unidentified chemicals, creating pervasive fumes. In addition, said Tillman, the drinking-water well for the Reynolds plant was just 500 feet from the Petro Processors site. Tillman set about organizing three local unions in the area plus the residents. For his troubles, he claimed, he suffered some harassment on his own job. He also has acquired a number of chemical sensitivities that have forced him onto a strict diet.[8]

The workers and residents spent the next year battling with the U.S. EPA and the Louisiana Department of Environmental Quality. According to Fontenot, the agencies were "telling workers and residents that they were just gonna have to put up with these odors, that it wasn't bad, that this was a court-ordered cleanup, it was EPA-supervised, and they'd just have to put up with these fumes." Fontenot's new friends decided otherwise and filed a nuisance suit to stop the cleanup. It succeeded, and work stopped for about two years.

Finally, by the spring of 1991, work started again. The state health department approached neighbors about conducting a health assessment of the effect of the Petro Processors site in the community. Fontenot attended a meeting with Dunn and Tillman, where health officials said they wanted only to deal with the impacts of the Petro Processors site.

"You can't do that," said Fontenot, applying the most important lesson he had learned in his years of advocacy. Dunn, he pointed out, worked at a secondary lead smelter and already carried a heavy burden of lead in his body. Health officials noted that he worked with a face mask. But Tillman, Fontenot noted, worked right across the street from the pits at Reynolds at a petroleum coke oven—which has its own "known cancer-causing problems"—and had no mask. In other words, for workers in the area who already had a critical level of exposure from their own facilities, it would be meaningless to study the impacts of the Petro Processors cleanup operation in isolation. It might, in fact, be precisely the slight added burden of toxic exposure that would "set it right off the chart." Further, Petro Processors was not the only off-site impact they were suffering. Nearby, another hazardous-waste treatment firm, Rollins Environmental Services, had already accumulated its own questionable track record.

"We only want to deal with Petro because the rest of this is so complicated," Fontenot recalled them saying. The statement galled him. "For the health department in 1991 not to be dealing with the complexity of the issue, or not to identify this as a problem, is ludicrous," he said. "So here we are, 20 years after the waste killed all these cattle, after the major lawsuits have been fought and successfully won through the courts—and the Louisiana health department, who's working on a contract with EPA, is unable to include in a health study or assessment a *real* health study or assessment. We haven't moved very far."[9]

If anyone in Louisiana understands the value of persistence in battling the system over environmental issues, it is Mary McCastle, one of Willie Fontenot's all-time folk heroes. An African-American woman in her seventies, McCastle has jousted with Rollins Environmental Services since 1976.[10] She is the undisputed leader of the Coalition for Community Action, the organization that has fought for the breathing rights of Alsen residents throughout that entire period. She makes feistiness run in her family. Her son, Roy, integrated the county sheriff's department by becoming its first African-American deputy.[11]

By any honest account, the residents of Alsen suffered through a nightmare for several years with little or no effective help from the city, state, or federal government. Residents complained of skin rashes, eye problems, and breathing problems. On one occasion, children in the elementary school began vomiting and had to be carried out of the building. Fumes from the Rollins facility were a constant problem. "You couldn't dare get out of your car without covering up your face," Roy McCastle recalls.[12]

The source of these fumes was the Rollins hazardous-waste landfill near the Mississippi River on the western side of Scenic Highway. Alsen is near the northern end of an 85-mile river corridor unaffectionately known to environmentalists as "Cancer Alley" because of the health impacts of pollution from petrochemical plants, refineries, and associated hazardous-waste treatment facilities. The Rollins landfill was the fourth largest in the nation, representing 11.3 percent of permitted hazardous-waste landfill capacity as of 1986.[13] As a disposal center for major companies along this corridor, including Exxon and BASF Wyandotte (a German chemical producer), Rollins played no small part in helping Louisiana achieve the dubious honor of hosting one-third of the nation's hazardous-waste landfill capacity by then.[14]

But establishing Rollins as the villain required a major effort to organize Alsen's 1,100 residents. Although somewhat better educated and more prosperous than the average African-American in Louisiana, many nonetheless were slow to accept Mary McCastle's faith that a large company like Rollins, whose annual revenue from the landfill exceeded $69 million,[15] could be challenged on environmental issues. In the 1970s, African-Americans in the South had almost no successful role models for such a struggle. Even Alsen's African-American political officials demurred. Mary's efforts to get the odors tested by state DEQ officials usually resulted in reports that their gauges had failed to show a problem.[16]

Fontenot, meanwhile, had his own nose in the air. Ever since moving to a neighborhood just a mile southeast of downtown Baton Rouge and the towering state capitol building, about three-and-a-half miles from Rollins, he had occasionally noticed a strange odor, "like something had died."[17] Because it was often mixed with paper-mill odors, he knew it came from the north, but he "walked all over the neighborhood" like an environmental Sherlock Holmes, unable to develop a clue as to the exact source.

One day in January 1980, shortly after a new environmental section had been set up in the attorney general's office, newly hired attorney Patricia Norton told Fontenot of a visitor from the day before. "This guy came in here, and his nose was all swollen and red, skin peelin' off," Fontenot recalled her saying. "Says he's taking cortisone shots in his nose 'cause the membrane is being eaten up by these chemicals comin' from someplace near Rollins. And he has petitions signed by 32 or 36 workers at Allied Signal, this guy was an electrician, and most of these guys were plumbers or electricians and signed a petition saying, 'We feel our health is being threatened by fumes by Rollins.' "

This is incredible, Fontenot thought. These guys are willing to put their jobs on the line. Even in 1980, it was virtually an article of faith within Louisiana labor circles that some environmental pollution was a necessary tradeoff for well-paid industrial jobs. Workers simply did not rebel over environmental issues.

Allied Signal lay just south of Rollins. And the man had the first smoking gun Fontenot had found in his search for the elusive "dead-horse" odors. Since October 1979, he had been keeping a diary. When the wind blew out of the south, things were okay. When the winds came from the north, the fumes were sometimes so powerful that workers had to don air packs in order to breathe. The man had come to the attorney general's office out of frustration with his inability to get his own company management to complain.

Fontenot called Catherine Ewell, a sister-in-law of David Ewell. She lived on the opposite side of the Rollins site. Because of the problems with Petro Processors, she, too, had been keeping a diary— since 1968. It recorded wind directions, the number of trucks that entered each site, and the types of odors fouling the air. Fontenot compared the two diaries. They matched. Each suffered the effects on days when the other was fine. The culprit lay in the middle.

Catherine Ewell referred Fontenot to Mary McCastle. He called. It took him nearly two weeks to arrange a meeting at her house. When he arrived around 7:00 p.m., nearly three dozen people were sitting in her living room. Fontenot, the only white person there, could "feel the tension." For the most part, despite their suffering with Rollins for nearly a decade and trying for four years to get someone to listen, the only whites they had seen in their neighborhood had been insurance salesmen and politicians—the latter only when they needed votes.

For nearly three hours, Fontenot tried to win their confidence, noting that a facility like Rollins would be chased out of *his* neighborhood. Two men sitting on either side of him asked, "Where do you live?"

"Near Government and 22nd."

"Where near Government and 22nd?" they demanded with a sudden excitement that sent a chill down Fontenot's spine.

The two, it turned out, delivered mail in the surrounding area and knew Fontenot's longtime carrier. I'd better do something good, he recalled thinking with a laugh, or I may start losing my mail.

"Are you gettin' these terrible fumes in here?" he asked.

"Oh, yeah," they answered, "the stuff'll come in, you gotta put wet towels over your head at night, you can't breathe, and you get tired all the time. They have flu-like symptoms and aching joints, and just feeling bad. Skin rashes."

"Well, you ever get any black dust?" Fontenot went on.

"Oh, yeah. That stuff sets in here, it's terrible! You gotta scrape it off your car."

"That's from the Reynolds coating manufacturing back there," Fontenot informed them. "Y'all ever get any white dust on ya?"

"Oh, yeah, yeah, we get that."

"Well, that's from Allied Signal. They make those styrofoam pellets," he told them. "That stuff'll blow out. You get that odor that smells like rotten eggs?"

Another affirmative.

"Well, that's from the two paper mills north of here. Do y'all ever get an odor that smells like somethin' died?"

"Oh, yeah! It comes in here horrible!"

"Well, that's Rollins." One problem, he told them, was that Rollins was land-farming the Exxon waste, a treatment technique that involved spreading it on the ground where certain types of bacteria would break down its chemical components. The reality, said Fontenot, is that most of it simply evaporated.

Fontenot got the cooperation he wanted—another set of diary keepers. Mary McCastle and a friend, Emma Johnson, were especially faithful in recording pollution incidents. They began calling him at all hours of the night and day when the worst odors occurred. Fontenot would drive to the scene to verify their observations. He got them to call the DEQ, which was later headed briefly by Norton, who made a notable personal visit that convinced her to take action against Rollins. In 1980, they also filed a lawsuit for damages from Rollins, enlisting Alsen residents as plaintiffs in a class action. They also began to call city hall. In all, said Fontenot, together they managed to verify 136 complaints about chemical fumes from Rollins.

Collectively, the diaries created damning evidence. Catherine Ewell, who had never before spoken in public, followed Carl Genn, the Allied Signal worker, to the stand in a January 1980 hearing by the state's Environmental Control Commission. What had begun as a minor agenda item resulted in a commission order for the Department of Natural Resources to perform a full inspection of Rollins, the first ever. The agency spent $60,000 and the full month of April on the investigation.

By April 23, the agency's report documented eight unpermitted discharges where waste was flowing off the site, with cyanide in virtually every sample. Alsen residents turned out at the meeting in force, and Rollins, ordered to do a massive cleanup, held an open house, complete with buses and tours, on May 22 and 23 to show off its progress.

Fontenot attended and was still disgusted. Parts of the site were still off limits, where waste was still pouring out of pits. The "state-of-the-art" pits he saw were "full of black liquids with barrels bobbing around." Around 5:00 p.m., while he was at Louisiana State University, Fontenot got a call from David Ewell. "Willie," he recalled Ewell saying, "you need to get up here 'cause they must have cut one of them pits open. It's the blackest I've ever seen it."

A group of civil- and environmental-engineering graduate students accompanied him to the site. While they were observing the discharge, a helicopter flew in carrying employees of the state water-quality division. It was the first time, he learned, that they had ever had access to a state helicopter. The pilot himself was excited to be doing genuine state business; he had always flown state officials for political appointments. Accompanying state environmental officials, they learned that the cyanide discharge had killed fish, turtles, and alligators in the swamp. The resulting melee from the exposure of this information forced the water-quality chief to back down on a positive report on the Rollins cleanup. Instead, the company was forced to shut down for a week. Worse yet, it had become a focal point for a newly empowered state environmental movement whose catalyst was Mary McCastle, a role model for a host of other African-American environmentalists who would surface in Louisiana in the decade that followed.

In their anger and with their new political savvy, Alsen residents retired some of the African-American politicians who had failed to take up their cause. New leaders, such as State Representative Kip Holden and State Senator Cleo Fields, emerged as key environmental advocates in the Louisiana legislature.

For Alsen residents, however, many bitter organizing lessons still followed. They did not achieve a settlement of their class-action suit until 1987, winning a meager $3,000 per plaintiff "just before Christmas."[18] In the interim, many residents, particularly the McCastles, lost faith in their lawyer.[19] The settlement shields Rollins from future health-effects claims, but many residents had wearied of the long fight. And they did not win the local health clinic they had wanted. Alsen residents must still drive into Baton Rouge for medical treatment. Finally, Rollins remained open, although its performance did improve.[20]

Rollins has suffered from the reputation it acquired. In 1989, the company sought a DEQ permit to triple the size of its facility, by installing new landfills and expanding its incineration units, in order to accept more out-of-state waste.[21] In a packed hearing room, the company heard little sympathy and intense criticism. Its hearing came little more than a month after an accident in which some hazardous chemicals reacted with water to create a poison gas that injured two contract workers, who claimed that they had not been warned of such hazards. An investigation by the federal Occupational Safety and Health Administration followed.[22] That accident prompted the U.S. EPA to suspend the company's authorization to receive or handle Superfund waste, a major source of income for hazardous-waste-treatment operators.[23] The same day, DEQ filed a suit challenging the U.S. EPA's planned disposal through Rollins of 1.7 million gallons of dinoseb, a banned pesticide linked to birth defects and male sterility that the company was to burn in its incinerator.[24] Later that spring, Attorney General Guste also moved to block U.S.

Department of Energy shipments of radioactive wastes to Rollins,[25] a topic that drew the investigative attention of *Baton Rouge Advocate* reporter Peter Schinkle in an extended series of articles over the next year. In all, the flurry of regulatory activity that attached itself to Rollins was a far cry from the minimal attention prior to 1980. The old order had begun to give way in Louisiana.

In its proximity to the capital, Alsen gained some advantages, however tenuous at times, that in the past have been completely unavailable to minority communities in more rural areas of Louisiana.

Herbert Rigmaiden, an African-American farmer from the Willow Springs area near Sulphur, in Calcasieu Parish, has learned the route from southwestern Louisiana to Baton Rouge, which still seems a world apart from his home. It became familiar during his neighbors' long battle with Browning Ferris Industries (BFI). As he told a congressional hearing on June 22, 1983, the state officials "hate to see us coming through the door."[26]

Rigmaiden made the statement during his first-ever trip to Washington, by way of his first-ever airplane flight, one he approached with the trepidation of the uninitiated. Willie Fontenot had arranged his testimony through Lois Gibbs, the veteran of the Love Canal neighborhood's fight with Hooker Chemical Company, who had gone on to found the Citizens' Clearinghouse for Hazardous Wastes (CCHW) in Arlington, Virginia. A local activist from the Lake Charles area drove Rigmaiden to the Houston airport, and Gibbs met him at Washington National Airport. Because Rigmaiden was a farmer of modest means from a community of even more modest means, the Subcommittee on Environment, Energy, and Natural Resources of the House Committee on Government Operations had agreed to pay for his travel. Representative Mike Synar (D-Oklahoma) was conducting hearings on groundwater contamination.

Whatever his educational deficits, Rigmaiden knew some very practical things about groundwater. He raised cattle and hay, and for years his family had benefited from the clear waters of the springs that lent the area its name. But for the last nine years, he had been trucking fresh water to his farm for drinking and cooking. His own wells were contaminated, and he blamed it on a hazardous-waste landfill that BFI developed in the late 1960s just 3,000 feet from his farm. Ironically, they called it the Willow Springs Landfill.

By all accounts, Rigmaiden stole the show, with reporters rushing to his side afterward, where he showed them a snapshot of a truck whose paint had peeled off because of chemical fumes. One reporter even startled him by asking for his address in order to send out a television crew.[27] Starting somewhat slowly, he told of fumes from the site that kept him from using his fans because they would pull the odors into his home. In 1978 and 1979, he "lost quite a few head of livestock in that stormwater let off on that site."[28] A doctor confirmed that the problem originated in water they were drinking from stormwater pits. "We never got paid for those," he added.[29]

In southwestern Louisiana's open prairie, farmers used "open range," in which cattle were allowed to wander at will. Some drank from contaminated water, "and those cattle got as wide as your automobile in front." Rigmaiden decided to open one of them, and "inside of her was just as green as you see paint lying on the ground." Another doctor arrived, who said the cow had died of pneumonia. State officials began to test water wells and found arsenic, lead, and other poisonous chemicals.[30]

In his most poignant note of the day, Rigmaiden brought the consequences of the site home to the subcommittee. "You gentlemen have got to remember that every time you throw a beefsteak or hamburger up to your face, you are eating that meat which comes off of that contaminated water underneath because I have no other way to water my cattle."[31]

"I appreciate that," responded Representative Craig. "I am a cattleman myself. I understand the importance."

Throughout the travail, Rigmaiden had noted, no one from BFI had spoken to him. "They brought it out there and said, 'Here it is'—I hope you will excuse me for this language—'you bunch of bastards, take it or leave it. Or die.' "[32]

People did, in fact, seem to be dying—or at least gasping for breath. Just before Rigmaiden's trip to Washington, the state had finally ordered the closure of the troubled landfill by the end of 1983. For many of his neighbors, it was too late.

To document its problems, the community around Willow Springs conducted its own health survey in 1984. It showed significant percentages of Willow Springs residents suffering from boils, rashes, and skin problems (84.9 percent); blood disorders (25.2 percent); headaches (59.2 percent); fatigue or exhaustion (49.6 percent); and respiratory problems (47 percent); among other ailments. As the numbers suggest, many residents exhibited multiple symptoms.[33]

The numbers were notably higher than those from another survey done just two years earlier under the auspices of the University of Texas Medical School at Galveston, which hired student interviewers from nearby McNeese State University. But Peggy Frankland, a white activist with the Calcasieu League for Environmental Action Now (CLEAN), said that some students were less than diligent, leaving behind interview forms at homes where people were illiterate when they should have conducted personal, on-site interviews. Another CLEAN activist, Ruth Shepherd, repeated that view in a separate conversation. "There never has been an adequate health study done of that area," Frankland said.[34]

Though such surveys are often readily dismissed as unscientific, they are no less meaningful than official community health studies, said Dr. Marvin S. Legator, a professor of toxicology at the nearby University of Texas Medical School in Galveston. Legator has long encouraged community groups to perform their own surveys, through such books as the *Health in Texas Handbook* and *Chemical Alert*. Legator, who has become somewhat cynical about government response to such communities, noting that "the adversary in most hazardous-waste sites is the government," said that most statistically valid community-health studies are inconclusive because the sample populations are too small to yield any statistical results. The question, he said, is why public-health officials continue to do such studies when such an outcome is clear from the numbers ahead of time. "We call them departments of reassurance, not departments of health," he said.

Citing a 1991 National Academy of Sciences monograph, *Epidemiology at Hazardous Waste Sites*, Legator said public officials need not wait for proof from such studies before acting. Instead, they should rely on just three preconditions to take preventive action: first, the existence of the exposure; second, the proof of what the chemicals involved are known to do in other settings; and third, the inference of what they are likely to do in the setting where the exposure is taking place.[35]

Legator's advice becomes particularly poignant where the victims are relatively powerless. Most of the residents within a mile of the Willow Springs site are poor African-American subsistence farmers. In the absence of BFI buying their property, an offer they said was never made or even discussed, they have nowhere else to go. Their property is virtually unsalable except for landfill expansion, an option that disappeared when the site was closed and eventually listed by the U.S. EPA for Superfund cleanup. It may be one of the most egregious examples of environmental racism ever perpetrated on a relatively powerless minority population.

Wilbert and Laberta Benoit live alongside the fence that separates their small house and yard from the BFI site. The fence was not always there, according to Frankland.[36] The neighbors' livestock frequently wandered onto the site, drank water from open pits, and returned. Inside the landfill, BFI merely dug the pits, poured in the poisons, and filled them up, with no real attempt to prevent the contaminants from leaching into groundwater or flowing out of their holes.

Frankland took me on a tour of Willow Springs. Chickens fell out of trees, Laberta said as we sat in the small, time-worn hovel that passed for a farmhouse. Trees died. "They sent us a big, old book practically denying everything." Laberta kept getting rashes, for which her doctor provided a lotion. Her cooking pots turned green from the water. The water was a sore point for Frankland, who noted that the parish had planned to exclude these people when it finally extended parish water lines to replace the contaminated groundwater wells. Parish officials deemed it too expensive to connect them, and the Benoits and their neighbors could not afford to pay. Only after Frankland had "lectured them" about their moral responsibilities to these people did they decide to include them.

Through a steady drizzle on an overcast day, Wilbert Benoit walked with me to the fence. On the other side, CECOS, a daughter company of BFI specializing in hazardous-waste disposal and cleanup,[37] now stored the waste below ground in sealed pits. There were warning signs posted above the pits inside the fence, but they were too far away, and the print was too small, to be readable from the boundary line. Wilbert showed me holes in the porous ground into which he poked a stick and retrieved crawfish. What was once an easy source of food had become highly suspect. The garden behind his house also used to sustain the family despite their meager income. Nothing grew there anymore.

Turk Vincent lived down the road, which is named after him. He had lost two wives to cancer, one of whom died at 58 with a tumor around her waist the size of an inner tube. A neighbor also died of cancer. Turk, who was in his eighties, had left the hospital earlier in the week, after suffering from high fever. Frankland noted that she and Mary Ellender, another CLEAN activist, had done their 1984 health survey to see if anything had changed after the University of Texas study. They surveyed more than 90 percent of the residents within a mile of the landfill, and virtually everyone was sick.

When they came to Turk Vincent's home, Frankland said, "Turk's wife had a handkerchief on his nose that was all bloody. There was an odor in the house from chemicals." For the parish water that replaced his contaminated groundwater "that stinks," he paid between $13 and $19 per month from his $309 Social Security check. He used to raise about 100 chickens, which helped make ends meet. They all died. Wilbert, who was with us, mentioned that a television news program from Alexandria two nights before had shown a picture of a frog someone had discovered with six legs, four in front and two in back.

Frankland noted that the elderly people in this community, although they could not afford "to telephone Washington or go to D.C. to tell them we have a problem," always participated in local meetings "when we need them." Nobody needed to ask the Reverend Joseph Bartlett to participate. The six-foot-four retired Baptist preacher, who lived away from the site, but not far enough away, was fighting mad. With his own hands, he had built his retirement dream home on 35 acres in the country. He had served in the pulpit of local churches for nearly 40 years. And since 1976, he had had to fight for his dream—through hearings, meetings, and a class-action lawsuit that dragged on for nearly a dozen years without ever going to trial. (It finally did go to trial in October 1993.)

To cut energy costs, he installed a ceiling fan in the house. Like Rigmaiden, he found himself unable to use it because it drew the fumes into his house.[38] He lost two horses to a respiratory ailment known as the "heaves." One day, he said, his herd of about 75 cattle all came to the house with their heads bowed, gasping for breathable air. A man who raised horses and loved the outdoors, he was often forced indoors—into an air-conditioned house—to escape chemical fumes so bad that on one occasion they knocked him to his knees, forcing him to crawl up the stairs.[39]

In the spring of 1991, he was declaring a partial victory. "I have not noticed fumes to the point of being ready to call somebody in a long time," he said. Frankland noted that people no longer referred to the environmentalists as "wildberries," or radicals, as they had 10 years earlier. Then, state officials would smoke or walk away when local activists began to speak during a hearing. Still, said Bartlett, it would only end "whenever you quit goin' to the meetings."

Between 1980 and 1986, BFI was cited 38 times for shortcomings in the operation of its Willow Springs landfill.[40] A 1982 state-financed study determined that chemicals were migrating from the site. Yet when I visited, a legal action brought against BFI in 1980 by some 200 neighbors, including Turk Vincent, was still dragging its way through the courts, struggling to meet the burden of proving that BFI's pollution was causing the illnesses suffered by area residents.[41]

To gain some perspective on what had happened at Willow Springs, I consulted Jeffery Hanor, a geology professor at Louisiana State University. Hanor's background is in sedimentary geochemistry; he has spent his career studying the origin and migration of fluids in rocks and minerals in the rocks. He has been involved in several permit hearings at the request of citizen groups on landfills and hazardous-waste injection wells.

Willow Springs, he said, was originally the site of a gas well, producing from the center of the site between 1958 and 1960. The company needed a place to dispose of the brine it was producing; it dug some pits and made some lagoons. The brine simply sat in those lagoons and leaked into two aquifers below. Eventually, the company converted the pits to refinery-waste disposal, simply pouring liquid wastes into the lagoons.

Commercial waste-disposal operations began in 1968, accepting waste from oil and gas drilling. Later, petrochemical wastes were added, including storage-tank bottoms, separator wastes, and waste plastics from refineries and chemical plants in the Lake Charles area as well as around the country. The unlined lagoons were in operation from 1968 until 1981 on the eastern two-thirds of the property. In 1977, the company secured a permit to dispose of industrial wastes in secure landfill cells, with excavation 35 feet into the ground, above a five-foot base of recompacted clay. Those operations were closed in 1984. In late 1982, organic chemical contamination was detected in a monitoring well. The state ordered investigations, and public hearings followed to discuss the results. Officials concluded that the subsurface contamination had come from the unlined lagoons. In 1976, the state granted a permit to convert the old gas well into a Class-I hazardous-waste injection well.

The U.S. Geological Survey office in Baton Rouge had taken on the Willow Springs site as a project. Hanor mapped the saline-brine plume in three directions. He also mapped out the dispersions of solvents and hazardous wastes in three directions from the subsurface. Some of the waters in the sands below the confining layer, he said, were saturated with respect to compounds like 1,2–dichloromethane. The waters contained from one to two percent dissolved organic chemicals.

Overall, Hanor said, there were two important things to know about southern Louisiana. First, the geology was far more complicated than people had previously recognized. This was because the geology was dominated by three processes. One was the transport of sediment by the Mississippi River and its streams and tributaries, which were constantly changing course. A second was large-scale oscillations in sea level in the Gulf of Mexico. The third was a continuous subsidence of land to the south, part of a natural geologic process.

The second point was that the thermal geometry of these sediments was extraordinarily complicated. (Thermal geometry refers to the temperature of the subsurface soils and waters at various levels and locations, a factor influenced by the geologic processes Hanor described.) Geologists had learned that the clays beneath southern Louisiana's soil leak. It was not, Hanor said, solid marine clay but was laid down by the region's rivers and coastal environments and was subjected to weathering that produced cracks and joints. The problem with all this was that waste disposal had been dealt with primarily in engineering terms. The details of the geology, Hanor said, had been neglected.[42]

In a separate interview earlier the same day, the Louisiana Geological Survey's Brad Hanson had been more blunt about the general problem. "There is no acceptable site for a landfill in southern Louisiana," he told me.[43]

African-Americans are not the only minority that has felt the sting of Louisiana's environmental racism. Kirby Verret, the chief of the Houma Indian Nation, knows it all too well. The United Methodist pastor in the small bayou town of Dulac, some 80 miles south of Baton Rouge along the Gulf Coast, attended a parochial high school only under the prodding of a friendly Roman Catholic priest. Well into the 1960s, the state's segregated educational system was so thoroughly racist that it simply did not accommodate Native Americans beyond the eighth grade. Their learning potential was further limited by the fact that most Houmas spoke broken French, the language they had adopted centuries before from their Cajun neighbors. The priest, new to the area, simply did not understand Verret's expectation of quitting school at that point. When Verret spelled it out for him, the priest broke into tears and insisted that he would find a way for him to finish. Verret's achievement was so unique for its time that when he then wanted to attend college, his father was willing to virtually bankrupt the family to send him. Verret would not let him. He insisted on earning his way, working with hot tar at the Delta Iron Works pipeyard.[44]

Despite the modest trailer he shares with his wife, Zoeanne, and four children near the Clanton United Methodist Church, amid the numerous shrimp boats that locals use to earn their livelihood, Verret represents a resurgence of the Houma nation both politically and culturally. He led the struggle to win federal recognition for a tribe once written off by officials as nearly extinct. A veteran of several industrial and business jobs before attending the seminary, he has also become one of the most powerful and knowledgeable spokespersons for environmental interests in Louisiana's southern bayou country. (Even the family trailer has become a symbol of the tenacity with which the Houmas cling to what remains of their land. The Verrets were forced out of this home by Hurricane Andrew in the fall of 1992. As of February 1993, the family was just preparing to reoccupy it with the help of federal disaster relief.)

The largely hidden history of the Houmas almost suggests, in a way that would fit Verret's way of thinking, that they had a providential destiny to become Louisiana's last voice of reason in saving the bayou. They first encountered whites through the French explorer Chevalier le Tonti in 1682, who deemed them "the bravest of all savages."[45] At the time, they were actually living upstream from Baton Rouge, which acquired its name from the "red stick" that designated their territory. Unfortunately, alliances between larger tribes and the English and Spanish later drove them south, beginning a series of migrations that ended at the southern tip of Terrebonne Parish.[46]

Their second migration, after being displaced by sugar growers, was to a village that is now Houma, the seat of Terrebonne Parish. After the Louisiana Purchase, they petitioned the new U.S. government to establish their land claim in the area, which was rejected in 1847. Because they had always moved peacefully, they had no written treaties granting them the land. They drifted into the marshes near the gulf, adapting to a new lifestyle much like the Cajun fishermen. Federal officials, who had little interest in following Indians into the swamp to count them, simply decided they were near extinction.[47] Although many proceeded to buy large amounts of local swampland, these individual properties did nothing to qualify the tribe for federal recognition or protection.[48] Over time, the Houmas suffered much the same kinds of racial discrimination that prevailed for African-Americans in the Deep South. Nonetheless, the tribe today still numbers some 15,000 members.

They live, however, in an area that is suffering most from the coastal erosion wrought by the "modern improvements" of agriculture and Army Corps of Engineers dredging projects. Flooding and saltwater intrusion threaten their homes and water supplies.[49] Saltwater intrusion will gradually kill the vegetation, including trees, that now holds back some of the floods. Artificial shipping canals were cut through their lands between the 1930s and 1962 to make shipping feasible from cities like Houma, ignoring the option of using Dulac as Houma's port.[50] Pollution and industrialization, including pipelines to serve the oil industry, threaten the continued viability of the shrimpers' livelihood. Nutrient overenrichment from sewage and agricultural runoff is stifling marine growth along the bayou bottoms.[51]

To protect themselves from the flooding, Terrebonne Parish officials planned a levee with flood gates. But reportedly because it would "cost too much" to include Dulac, they chose to locate the levee across the marshlands a quarter-mile north of Dulac, leaving the Houma settlement exposed to the elements—and probably more vulnerable than ever because of the floodwaters trapped behind the levee.[52] For Verret, it was the last straw in the fight for his people's survival.[53]

Verret was already an experienced advocate. He had fought a company whose plan for a hazardous-waste-treatment operation would have violated federal floodplain regulations by storing the waste in mud tanks at ground level. It was to be in a place where currents intermixed. It would have allowed caustic soda, he said, to settle into water bottoms where there was no current, disrupting oyster beds. The fishermen elected him spokesman. At the company's first public hearing, 50 shrimpers showed up. At another, a company official declared that a certain treated liquid was good enough to drink. Verret challenged him to do so, and he backed off.

Finally, having observed Verret's talent for rebutting such comments, officials placed him first on the list of speakers at a hearing where the conglomerate had brought in its leading executives and scientists, so that he could not first hear their proposal. Shrewdly, Verret examined their printed information, including the list of experts.

"You have the most outstanding and qualified people to do this work," he praised them. With his fishing friends suddenly fearing that Verret had been paid off, he added, "The interesting thing is that you belong to a huge corporation with large assets. With your qualifications, you can change jobs or go to another department. If you didn't get this job, you could go elsewhere, but fishermen have no other livelihood. If you destroy the seafood industry, there is nowhere else for them to go."

Verret was running for the parish council. During a break in the hearing, a powerful local businessman told Verret he was costing him money, warning that "on this bayou, I can get anybody to do anything I want."

"If I lose," Verret replied, "I have more time to fight this thing." He lost, and regards it as "the best thing that could have happened." Eventually, the company left town.

Verret was not against the hurricane-protection levee. With most of the barrier islands off the coast already destroyed, his tribe was living on vulnerable land. But none of the levee board's plans protected his community. Verret mobilized the area's churches, now led for the first time by a majority of Native American clergy, and took their case to the Louisiana Conference of Churches, winning the statewide body's support for moving the levee south of Dulac. The Houma people learned to hang together, finally forcing the levee board to consider at least a removable floodgate to alleviate the damage the original plan would cause.

In the summer of 1992, with the help of Senator Daniel Inouye (D-Hawaii), chairman of the Senate Indian Affairs Committee, Verret was seeking another victory for his people. Pursuing a fight that had dragged on since 1931, the Houma nation wanted federal recognition, which would make the tribe eligible for federal funds that could support development projects to reverse the effects of a long history of discrimination. For Verret, however, the primary benefit was not money, but pride. It did not happen under the Bush administration. But with the advent of the Clinton presidency, the tribe still hoped for a turnaround in federal policy that would at long last acknowledge that the invisible natives of the swamps had survived.

Esnard Gremillion knows the experience of "lost sheep" from another perspective. Organized labor has seldom enjoyed good times in
Louisiana, but his local of the Oil, Chemical, and Atomic Workers
International Union (OCAW) underwent one of the most intense
labor-management struggles in Louisiana history. In the end, it transformed Local 4-620 into one of the most environmentally progressive and innovative union locals in the nation.

Most of Local 4-620's members work at the BASF-Wyandotte
chemical plant in Geismar, downriver from Baton Rouge. Gremillion
had worked there since the early 1970s. Life seemed reasonably good.
Gremillion served on the local's negotiating committee and said the
union's 1981 contract with BASF was "pretty lucrative." Nonetheless, Gremillion had misgivings about the local president, Harold
Nickens, whom he accused of "more or less crawling in bed with the
company." Certainly, plant industrial-relations manager Francis Richard Donaldson claimed a good working relationship with Nickens
while viewing Gremillion as a militant.[54] Gremillion ran against
Nickens the following year and lost by three votes. Nickens resigned
in July 1983, and Gremillion was appointed the interim chairman
until December 1983. From that point on, Gremillion was regularly
reelected until he retired.[55]

Gremillion, popularly known among fellow workers as "Gremmy,"
immediately encountered a trial by fire. In June 1983, the company
demanded the rescission of a 10-percent increase due that month
under the contract. Donaldson also informed Gremillion that he
could no longer represent workers on company time and would have
to request time off for such business at least five days in advance.[56]
As a wave of such concessions had become the order of the day elsewhere in the aftermath of President Ronald Reagan's successful busting of the air-traffic controllers' union, Gremillion suspected that
worse was to come. The union held meetings for its membership during which the officers explained what they expected in 1984, when
the contract was up for renegotiation.[57]

What Local 4-620 members did not know was that BASF Corporation, the U.S. subsidiary of the German multinational BASF, was
on a union-busting spree across the country. BASF is huge, reporting

an international workforce of 130,000 in its 1985 annual report. It had acquired the Wyandotte Chemical Company in 1970, folding it into what became BASF Corporation's BASF Chemicals Division in 1986. The American subsidiary reported sales of almost $4 billion and a workforce of 21,000 in 1986. At the time of the negotiations, the Geismar plant, which had opened in 1957, employed 370. Originally manufacturing antifreeze, it had expanded to several other chemicals including Basagran herbicide, which comprised its largest production unit.

In 1979, Edwin Stenzel became president of BASF's U.S. corporation. With support from corporate headquarters in Germany, Stenzel unleashed a series of efforts to break unions at plants around the country.[58] In the 1984 negotiations, according to Gremillion, the company "came to the table with a contract that completely wiped out all the gains in our contract since 1959." In sum, the company specifically offered a series of wage cuts, major changes in the seniority system, and a reduction in its contribution to the employee health plan. The local demanded an eight-percent increase, improvements in the health plan, and renewal of the denied union-representation rights, which by then were on appeal. The courts, however, did not rule on that issue until September 1986, three years after Donaldson's decision.[59]

The contract expired without renewal on June 15, 1984. BASF management had a surprise in store for the workers, who had never struck in the plant's 27-year history. BASF locked the gates, claiming fear of union sabotage. The workers were in shock, "kind of like lost sheep," in Gremillion's recollection. For about eight months, they demonstrated at the plant, with virtually no media attention or community support. The company hired temporary workers and contracted out maintenance work. When Leslie Vann, who later succeeded Gremillion as the local's president, sarcastically suggested that the plant might blow up as a result of underskilled nonunion labor, a security guard misinterpreted his comment. Vann was barred from the plant as a suspected terrorist.[60]

Eventually, the international union headquarters in Denver recognized the need to provide some special assistance to the BASF workers. Richard Leonard, a special-projects director, arrived to advise the local and devise a new strategy to force BASF back to the bargaining table in good faith. Leonard taught members how to research every aspect of the company's record in a drive to make it pay a high public-relations price for its stance.[61] The union began to investigate BASF's environmental record and found not only ammunition but smoking guns. In September 1984, a truck hauling chemicals from the BASF plant to Rollins in Baton Rouge developed a leak. The resulting toxic steam release shut down Interstate 10. Expanding on that incident, union members began to examine the plant's safety record and found an increasing incidence of safety violations as a result of the company's hiring of nonunion replacement workers. By 1986, these resulted in $66,700 in fines imposed by the Louisiana DEQ.[62]

More important than any fines, though, which were inevitably small in relation to BASF profits, was the bridge the issue created between the union and the community. For the first time, the union had found an issue that bound members together in a common concern. Willie Fontenot aided the local in becoming involved with area environmental groups. Richard Miller arrived from the National Toxics Campaign (NTC) in Boston. Together, they helped Amos Favorite, a retired African-American aluminum worker who lived in Geismar, to establish an air-pollution watchdog group, the Ascension Parish Residents Against Toxic Pollution. Suddenly, by late 1985, the fight against the BASF lockout was becoming a community crusade.

The union's struggle also drew other environmentalists' attention to the Geismar area. The Delta Chapter of the Sierra Club began to study the general impact of pollution on local residents' health. The results were less than reassuring. Some 27 petrochemical plants are clustered in the Geismar–Dutchtown–St. Gabriel–Plaquemine stretch of the Mississippi River corridor between Baton Rouge and New Orleans, including Borden Chemical, Vulcan, Ciba-Geigy, Dow, Georgia-Gulf, Uniroyal, and Shell.[63] Their releases include benzene, chlorobenzene, carbon tetrachloride, chloroform, ethylene oxide, toluene, and vinyl chloride.[64] Moreover, their releases were not modest. On October 21, 1986, the Sierra Club released its study of permitted air releases at a press conference where community leaders also stepped forward to discuss their concerns about chemical pollution. The Sierra Club indicated that permits for the 18 plants on the eastern side of the river allowed total annual emissions of nearly 200 million pounds, or more than 46,000 pounds per person living in the study area.[65] In reality, state oversight was so poor that no one really knew the true level of emissions. Moreover, many of the companies had long been suspected of burning off loads of toxic waste in the dark of night, when residents would presumably be paying less attention. The flares function as a safety valve to prevent the buildup of excess pressure or what engineers call an "upset condition." Favorite had another way of describing its impact on the neighborhood. "Nighttime around here is like an evil dream," he told *Buzzworm*, one of many magazines that have interviewed him in the past few years.[66]

About the same time, Kay Gaudet, a local pharmacist, began to monitor miscarriages among women in the community. She spread the word of her search through her pharmacy and the Catholic church. She, too, came to some alarming conclusions. Within a year, her list of miscarriages in St. Gabriel (pop. 2,100) grew to 63. Approximately one-third of the pregnancies since 1983, she determined, had ended in fetal death.[67] Community members struggled with their disbelief at the magnitude of a problem that had previously been invisible, with individual women left to suffer their losses in silence and ignorance. The prevailing attitude had long been that the area's industrial development had been good for the state's underdeveloped economy. Now, it seemed, Gaudet was suggesting that the tradeoff had been Faustian in nature.

Gaudet first contacted the state DEQ and health department, asking them to conduct their own studies. Nothing happened. In January 1987, she asked the Louisiana Justice Department to write a letter. It did, but again nothing happened. Finally, the Sierra Club agreed to send Gaudet to Washington, D.C., to speak to members of Congress and hold a press conference. Within days, the state agencies at last contacted the community to learn what they could do to help.[68]

Ultimately, like the hero in Henrik Ibsen's play, *An Enemy of the People*, Gaudet and her husband paid a price for their persistence in spreading her troubling message. Some companies reportedly told their employees not to patronize the Gaudet pharmacy, a tactic that succeeded in driving them out of business. Gaudet today works for a chain pharmacy in Baton Rouge.[69] She also reported facing family pressures, telling the *Washington Post*, "My mom is always saying to me, 'Kay, shut up, didn't you ever see that Silkwood movie? If you're not worried about yourself, what about your kids?' And I say that's exactly what I'm worried about—my kids." The chemical industry also scoffed publicly at Gaudet's claims, with Fred Loy, a spokesman for the Louisiana Chemical Association, commenting to a student newspaper, "I could say they screw too much and that's the cause of the miscarriages. But then I would have no way to prove that."[70]

Gaudet was not alone in such frustrations. Favorite, too, braved a chorus of criticism from his own family. As late as 1991, he complained that he was still pleading with cancer victims to speak out about the community's health crisis, often to no avail. Relatives took him to task for even mentioning the nine cancer deaths the family had suffered by 1991, "as if it was something shameful. It's not like they died of a social disease." Favorite, however, was a tough opponent. As a young man, he had joined the Army in World War II to escape life on the sugar plantation where he was raised. Having been trained for chemical-warfare defense in the Pacific, he said, he did not come home to be poisoned in his own backyard. And since the Army had taught him to use a rifle (he was an antiaircraft gunner in fierce fighting at Saipan and Okinawa), he had used it to chase cross-burning Ku Klux Klan members off his property in the 1960s, when his daughter became the first African-American to integrate a previously all-white high school near their home. Whatever timidity existed elsewhere in Geismar or St. Gabriel, Amos Favorite and Kay Gaudet would have none of it.[71]

Perhaps the most revealing evidence of such family divisions occurred when I was interviewing Favorite at his home. At one point, he left to answer the telephone, and his gifted four-year-old granddaughter Jasmine—who had already learned how to read—wandered into the living room. "Some people say grampa shoots his mouth off," she told me with a smile.

If Gaudet had to travel to Washington in order to get a hearing, Gremillion and Leonard went even farther—to Ludwigshafen, Germany, the international headquarters of BASF. To support their trip and demonstrate solidarity, I.G. Chemie, the union that represented BASF workers in West Germany, contributed $10,000. At the stockholders' meeting, Gremillion was told that he had to speak German. Despite being effectively frozen out of the meeting, the two found an active support group in town. They learned that the union-busting tactics being applied to Local 4-620 in Louisiana would have been illegal in West Germany. In response to the workers' plight, two Green Party members of the West German parliament flew to Louisiana to meet with company officials in Geismar, but were turned back at the gate.[72] Their objective had been twofold, according to NTC's Miller. First, they wanted to inquire about labor-relations practices they had learned of that would have been impermissible in Germany, where lockouts were illegal. They also wanted to question the company's managers about the plant's environmental practices. Miller noted that "the Greens made better allies than the Social Democrats," one of whose Bundestag deputies, Hermann Rappe, was a former I.G. Chemie official who, he said, sought to stifle alliances with the American BASF workers. Interestingly, he added, Chancellor Helmut Kohl was a former BASF employee.[73]

New tactics began to emerge as the lockout stretched into its third year. Taking a cue from the striking P-9 local of the International Food and Commercial Workers of the Hormel plant in Austin, Minnesota, the local launched an "adopt-a-family" campaign within the community to support locked-out workers.[74] The union raised money from around the country and visited with others in similar straits, such as the striking coal workers in Pittston, Virginia. They traveled to Terre Haute, Indiana, to meet with civic and union groups about an incinerator BASF wanted to locate there. Still, the lockout exacted a personal toll on the members. Gremillion says about a dozen lost their homes, half that number suffered from broken marriages, and two committed suicide as a result of the stress.[75]

After three years, BASF began to wave a white flag. It recalled the OCAW operators in 1987, but still insisted on contracting its maintenance work. Two years later, BASF capitulated on that issue as well. After a period of retraining, the maintenance workers reappeared on the job in 1990. The 270-member workforce had shrunk by 100. Gremillion retired on sick pay. Workers like Vann continued to wear a union sticker on their hard hats. It demanded back pay.[76]

The BASF workers who returned were a radically changed group of people, no longer content to protect the company or believe its promises. By and large, they are grateful to an environmental community that, Gremillion says, "helped us to meet people." The revived local initiated a special $5 per month dues surcharge to support a special joint project with the National Toxics Campaign. Despite a bumpy experience that resulted in the dismissal of its first NTC project director, the local has continued to support organizing efforts in the surrounding community to monitor the environmental performance of all the petrochemical plants in the area. And some people in the Louisiana DEQ learned that they could trust the workers as whistleblowers who effectively aided enforcement.

Amos Favorite continued his organizing in the community with the local's support. The end of the lockout did not signal the end of Ascension Parish's staggering environmental problems. According to Toxic Release Inventory (TRI) figures for 1988, the parish still ranked second in the nation among counties in toxic chemicals emitted into the air, third for surface-water releases, and eighth in deep-well injection. The TRI numbers also showed an average of 2,397 pounds of toxic releases per person in the parish, 13 times the national average. BASF itself ranked twenty-second nationally in total releases, with 37.2 million pounds. And tiny Geismar (pop. 1,500) actually ranked in the top 50 cities nationwide with 93 million pounds of toxic chemical releases.[77] (The TRI is a mandatory annual disclosure by manufacturing companies of the nature and volume of toxic substances they release into the environment. Though imperfect, it gave communities vast amounts of new information about company operations.)

Ascension Parish's toxic releases loomed large even within the state of Louisiana, which led the nation. Total toxic-release figures for 1989 showed it second in the state with 26 percent of the state's overall releases. It actually led in air and water releases with 36 percent and 56 percent, respectively.[78]

But now companies faced some community opposition on issues like groundwater contamination. Residents who had depended on well water complained that their water, once pure and drinkable, had been ruined. They wanted the companies to pay for a new water system. Every plant expansion or permit renewal was subject to possible objections and citizen protests. Rubicon Chemical Company faced a hostile public-hearing crowd in June 1990 over its petition for an exemption from the EPA's pending land ban on disposal of hazardous wastes. Rubicon wanted to continue operating its hazardous-waste injection wells, claiming its wastes would remain within their injection zones for 10,000 years. Only one speaker at the hearing, who worked for another chemical company, spoke in favor of Rubicon. For the most part, doubt and fear filled the air.[79] BASF faced the same skepticism and scrutiny less than two years later when the Louisiana Department of Natural Resources (DNR) held a public hearing to review the company's appeal of the DNR's denial of its permit to continue operating a hazardous-waste injection well. Residents objected that BASF had the ability to neutralize the hydrochloric acid it was injecting in order to eliminate the threat it posed to their drinking water. They also noted that one of two wells BASF had been using since 1986 had been forced to shut down because of casing leaks, failed wellhead seals, and sand infiltration. In addition, they maintained, geological studies had uncovered the possibility of extensive faulting in the geologic formations beneath Geismar, allowing upward migration of wastes into well-water sources.[80]

By 1992, residents had reorganized their efforts under the banner of the Geismar/Dutchtown Residents for Clean Water and Air. Their executive committee was meeting actively with company representatives, and the group was lobbying the parish police jury (the equivalent of a county commission or board elsewhere) for a new piped water system that would utilize water from Baton Rouge.[81] In March 1992, the police jury appointed a waterworks board to plan for a newly designated waterworks district to serve the residents. One of the appointees was Amos Favorite, for a five-year term.[82] In response, the companies had learned to reach out as well, forming the

Ascension Parish Community Advisory Panel to represent a cross-section of community opinion.[83] All was not yet sweetness and light, but at least the "lost sheep" and their allies had found their voice and were being heard.

The spiritual transformation of Local 4-620 led to other initiatives. The union helped organize Louisiana Workers Against Toxic Chemical Hazards (LA-WATCH), an organization that involved Teamsters activist Gerald Tillman after Fontenot referred him to Richard Miller. Its aim was to organize and train workers around workplace-safety issues. LA-WATCH has faced more organizing hurdles than the community project in Ascension Parish, but it has raised some serious issues that the state of Louisiana has never addressed adequately. It has also been able to link up with two other organizations that have supported the notion that the welfare of workers, who serve on the front line of the chemical-pollution attack, is essential to any real effort to improve the environment (a notion that many environmentalists have yet to accept). One, the Injured Workers Union, fights for the compensation and job rights of workers injured by accidents on the job or suffering illnesses induced by occupational exposure. The other, the Institute of Human Relations (recently renamed the Louis J. Twomey Center for Peace through Justice) at Loyola University in New Orleans, has provided technical and organizational support for workers for more than four decades.

In 1991, when I visited his downtown Baton Rouge office, David Czernik was the sole staff person for both the Louisiana Consumers League and the Injured Workers Union. His office, at the top of an older small office building, was awash in books, reports, and legal paperwork. Czernik worked in a world of lost legal causes, tilting against a Louisiana legal system that catered to power and money. When the radicalized former Catholic seminarian talked about injured workers, his very being bristled with indignation.[84]

The Injured Workers Union, he said, sprang out of "the investigation we did on database blacklisting and the exposes that were run in the *Wall Street Journal* (in 1990). Several other national publications picked that up—where people are systematically discriminated against simply because they filed a workman's compensation claim.

"The big issue is that [companies] don't want to deal with the actual effects of unsafe work places. Either theirs or somebody else's. And they use the malingerer's excuse. Somebody who's been injured on the job is automatically a malingerer, and they don't want to have to deal with them because 'they'll file another claim if they work with us.'

"There's this concept I run into all the time when I deal with business people that there's this huge segment of the population that uses worker's compensation like public welfare, and it's a way not to have to work. They don't understand the system, and they don't understand the limitations in the system. All they know is that, from a business point of view, they pay a hell of a lot of money in premium. And they don't get much for it. And neither do the workers."

The insurance companies, Czernik insisted, were the magnets for money in this sorry scenario. But if anything elicited as much of Czernik's anger as the insurance companies, it was the legal system, which Czernik viewed as already weighted heavily against workers' interests. Its only merit, in his view, lay in generating new members for the Injured Workers Union. There were plenty of candidates, judging from the statistics. An LA-WATCH flyer listed the 1988 illnesses and injuries reported to the state labor department:

1,400 out of 26,800 chemical workers
20,900 out of 170,100 manufacturing workers
9,800 out of 84,100 construction workers[85]

One example he offered from the organization's brief experience involved a worker whose back, he said, had been torn apart when an I-beam swung across a platform on which he was working. The insurance company fought the claim on grounds that it was fraudulent, and at the hearing, the worker's attorney failed to appear, resulting in a malpractice suit. The injured worker, meanwhile, had gone deeply into debt and owed money to loan sharks. Faced with the dire prospect of waiting even longer to resolve his claim, Czernik said, the worker accepted the insurance company's offer of a $500 settlement on the spot. In the interim, "His wife left him, he lost his house, and he lost his car." Gerald Tillman, who knew him, saw him hitchhiking, picked him up, and gave him an LA-WATCH brochure. He called the group's toll-free number in New Orleans and then reached Czernik in Baton Rouge.

In another case, the Injured Workers Union teamed up with the Environmental Health Network, based in Harvey, Louisiana, to protest outside Texaco's main office in New Orleans on behalf of Deborah Hamby. The 39-year-old worker had suffered permanent brain damage from organic-phosphate poisoning during pesticide spraying of her office. Hamby, who was still awaiting payment of $168 in weekly compensation awarded her by the state in 1988, attended in a wheelchair. At this pre-Christmas 1990 demonstration, the protesters wore red-and-white Santa Claus suits and sang sarcastic parodies of popular Christmas carols.[86]

Alan Bernard was another recruit to the cause. He had been working in a New Orleans sugar plant. One Saturday morning, he said, he woke up with a sharp pain in his shoulder, which ultimately resulted in surgery to remove bone tips. He could not return to work, he said, because his employer had a policy against making "light duty" for disabled workers. He had lost his $135,000 home, he said. Since taking disability, he had been working with the Loyola institute and the Injured Workers Union, where I interviewed both him and William Temmink, the institute's director. Temmink indicated that Bernard had found his way to the institute through classes on the workers' compensation system. Bernard had begun to attend the institute's board meetings.

Bernard claimed that injured workers had become the object of discrimination within Louisiana's permissive pro-business environment. "We need something to speak to the suffering of injured workers," he said to explain what drove his involvement. "They refer to us as zombies, the living dead, no longer productive to the economy. Injured workers become the homeless, the derelicts, the alcoholics. Junkies taking pills for medication for injuries. Family breakups. Lost positions and suicides. I talked to one woman for almost six hours on the phone to keep her from committing suicide. She thought her family would get money from her death. . . . They treat our workers as a machine. If no parts are left that they can use, they junk it. That becomes a dangerous part of our society."[87]

A throwaway economy, these people seemed to be saying, inevitably generates throwaway workers. The same social malaise drives the waste of both environmental and human resources.

In Lafayette, where my pursuit of this issue next took me, Dr. Tom Callender has been treating workers' compensation patients for years. His clinic has specialized in environmental medicine, and he has developed some strong and vocal opinions on the topic. Removed from the daily struggle of organizing workers that faces Bernard, Czernik, and Temmink, he has dwelt more on the structural problems afflicting a system that generates the problems that they try to address. What he sees is a system that is undermining its own self-interest.

Callender, before all else, wanted me to know that he is no Luddite.[88] Formerly in the field of physics, he expressed an affection for the space program and aerospace technology. Without high technology, he noted, he would not have many of the medical tools he uses on a daily basis. The problem, he said, lay in a lack of "planning in depth" in this country.

"What I see as a physician in practice," he said, "is the consequences of what happens when planning really is not done or is done with the wrong priorities, when short-range profits are all that count. What's coming, I think, is economic ruin because a lot of people are getting sick in this country. And the people that say everything's okay either don't know or don't want to look."

It was in industry's best interest, he said, not to make environmental mistakes, "but there's a lot of attitude there. I think it's also issues of convenience and apathy." The issues that produced conflict between industry and the public, including workers, could be resolved in ways that would produce better and more productive industries, but "I see a system that I don't think is working too well. The government agencies that are supposed to regulate, the people who are supposed to be planning, just really aren't doing it." In the end, he suggested, we would all pay the price economically and environmentally with a growing list of Superfund sites, with all their attendant delayed cleanup costs.

"But what I see," he added, "is a steady stream of workers who are being injured who don't have to be." Very often, he said, even basic safety was not being implemented. Because of the number of injuries and the growing severity of the problem, and the fact that "medicine cannot cure everything," society faced a basic decision. "Do we cut service to the injured, do we provide those services and make sacrifices, or do we try to prevent injuries in the future? I see that the tendency is to provide less and less services. Somebody gets injured, the deal is, well, they're faking, they're malingering, they're trying to get something for nothing, and we're going to make it hard for them to get medical services. We're going to make it hard for them to get attorneys to represent them. And the bottom line is that there's a large number of people in this country that were blue-collar, salt-of-the-earth types that worked really hard. They never missed a day of work, they were the backbone of an industry. And when they get injured, they're automatically ejected like a piece of broken equipment that can't be fixed and they're ostracized by their fellow workers because of this stigma. It starts off this chain of events, and a lot of money is going into litigation that could be going into something more productive. You know it can't be good for industry."

Like little pieces of mercury, Callender said, these injured and displaced workers, "disenfranchised from the system," begin to coalesce. The resulting coalition would come to include the wider public as well. "I think the environmentalists are going to eventually merge or at least share a common interest with the workers. But the workers are usually the first guys to get poisoned, and they usually get the biggest brunt of it. But what goes over the fence affects the public too," he concluded.

The key issue for this worker-environmentalist coalition, in Callender's opinion, was simply to shift the burden of proof. "It's insane," he insisted, for a nation to conduct its business by insisting that victims prove chemicals harmful before the community can take action. He contrasted the millions of dollars spent in testing medical drugs before they are approved for the market with the ease with which new chemicals could be added to other consumer products.

"When somebody from industry says, well, I think everything's cool in Louisiana, when you realize what it takes to prove things to a scientific certainty, you realize that what they're doing is a joke because what they're saying is a joke because they know that nobody is going to put up the money and resources to prove it." Some 60,000 chemicals, he noted, are already in common industrial use. Each year, 2,000 more are invented. Testing each of those in different dose ranges for different races, sexes, age ranges, and medical problems at millions of dollars per project would clearly bankrupt the public treasury. Callender cited a rising incidence of asthma and other respiratory problems amid a decline in the percentage of smokers as a possible indication of the results of the massive national medical experiment taking place because of such assumptions.

To back up the points that he had made, Callender turned to his bookshelves, handing me a pile of photocopied materials. The topics covered the range of occupational exposures he had treated and, no doubt, some others for good measure: organic solvent neurotoxicity; neurologic symptoms among blue-collar women workers from long-term exposure to solvents; the neurobehavioral effects of solvents on construction painters; reduced memory and visual performance of seamen exposed to industrial solvents; neurasthenic complaints among rotogravure printers exposed to toluene; and so forth. The emphasis on neurotoxicity reminded me of the very first point Louisiana environmentalists had made to me as I arrived: Don't let the industry spokespeople pretend that the only issue is cancer.

In the end, Callender's concerns amounted to an argument for environmental democracy. The environmental and public-health problems of the failed communist system in the Soviet Union grew because the authorities "had nobody to tell 'em what they needed to hear. They took everybody who told them what they needed to hear and locked 'em up or executed 'em. They ridiculed and harassed 'em."

In Louisiana, it seemed, at least the latter part of that error-suppression system might still be intact.

Louisiana, traditionally one of the nation's poorer states, could at least fashion a rationale for its poor environmental policies if, in fact, it were gaining economically and wisely investing the new taxes that filled the public coffers. But another coalition operating out of Local 4-620's Baton Rouge offices contended that even that was not happening. The Louisiana Coalition/Citizens for Tax Justice (LCTJ)[89] maintained that industry not only had not paid its fair share but had

willfully robbed the state blind through a vast array of tax abatements that served no purpose but to beggar state and local government alike. Moreover, local government often had no say in the
matter. The tax abatements were and still are dispensed by a powerful state-level Board of Commerce and Industry (BCI), consisting of
11 members appointed by the governor.

From the standpoint of any rational economic-development strategy, the situation that led to the coalition's emergence in 1990 can
only be described as irrational and outrageous. The state's 1974 constitution empowered BCI to grant five-year property-tax exemptions,
with single five-year renewals, to manufacturing firms when BCI
deemed such an agreement to be "in the best interests of the state."[90]
The provision is no more nor less specific than that and obviously
left enormous room for discretion in a state already riddled with corruption, favoritism, and patronage.

During the decade from 1980 to 1989, according to the coalition's
major study of the state's tax system, *The Great Louisiana Tax Giveaway*, the state had forfeited more than $2.5 billion in parish prop-
erty taxes. In 1989 alone, taxpayers had foregone the collection of
$273 million from industrial firms.[91] The biggest chunk of tax breaks
made no sense at all. Utility companies pocketed some $922 million
in tax breaks during the 1980s.[92] Utilities clearly are not manufacturers, and no economic classification scheme in common use, including those of federal data-gathering agencies, has ever classified
them as such. Yet Louisiana Power and Light, Gulf States Utilities,
and Cajun Electric Power were the top three reapers of the state's
tax beneficence.[93]

The utility tax breaks were objectionable beyond their obvious
conflict with the clear constitutional language. Since the frequently
stated objective of such exemptions in Louisiana, as in most states,
was to create jobs, it made little sense to give tax breaks to those
industries that must locate in Louisiana anyway. Where else would a
Louisiana utility locate? It also made little sense to provide such incentives to a highly regulated public utility of any sort. Such entities
are generally expected by law to provide a public service as a regulated monopoly, with a rate of return on investment that is largely
guaranteed by the state's utility regulatory agency. From a job-cre-

ation standpoint, utilities are also terrible investments. Highly capital-intensive, they in fact showed the poorest rate of job creation per dollar of tax exemption, costing the state more than $100,000 per job created versus a $60,000 average for the entire tax-exemption program.[94] Finally, the utility tax breaks punished both the environment and consumers. By needlessly encouraging electric-utility investment in new power plants, BCI's generosity was discouraging utility efforts to foster energy conservation and efficiency, thus perpetuating and extending patterns of energy use that result directly in either air emissions or the radioactive-waste burdens of nuclear plants. Finally, consumers already suffering as taxpayers were forced to pay for new generating capacity at rates that, since the mid-1970s, had generally risen as new capacity was installed.

But what about the other $1.6 billion in foregone tax collections? There, too, serious questions could easily be raised about the value of such subsidies for industries that had powerful natural incentives to locate in Louisiana anyway. After all, the oil and chemical industry had come to Louisiana for just one reason, which had nothing to do with the quality of its infrastructure or educational system, both of which tended to be near the bottom of any national ranking. Louisiana was blessed with an abundance of natural resources, and when oil and gas were discovered earlier in the century, the petrochemical industry beat a path to Louisiana's door. Nonetheless, of the next seven top tax-exemption beneficiaries beyond the big three utilities, six were oil and chemical producers: Shell ($96 million); Exxon ($93 million); Texaco ($76 million); Dow ($61 million); Mobil ($56 million); and Citgo ($54 million).[95] Together, the oil-refining and chemical industries soaked up some $1.1 billion in taxpayer largesse during the 1980s.[96]

To compensate for all this, Louisiana maintained one of the highest sales-tax rates (including parish, city, and school-district sales taxes) in the nation. It is almost universally conceded by economists that the sales tax is among the most regressive revenue-collection schemes available. In other words, the poor got hit the hardest. In return, they got an educational system that was hopelessly underfinanced and ranked as one of the worst in the nation, guaranteeing that many of their children could not qualify for the very jobs

they were paying to create. The tax breaks for industry cost Louisiana schools $941 million during the study decade, while they ranked
dead last in high-school completion and the state ranked forty-sev-
enth in adult literacy.[97]

For all the power of these facts and arguments, another factor finally set off an epic political battle over industrial tax exemptions.
The very industries receiving the lion's share of BCI's virtually automatic dispensations were by and large the biggest polluters. The tax-
justice coalition could appeal easily to taxpayers with the notion that
environmental lawbreakers ought not to be rewarded. Many of the
companies receiving tax breaks had a long road to travel in cleaning
up their environmental track records. Exxon's Baton Rouge refinery,
for instance, suffered an explosion on Christmas Eve in 1989, killing
two workers and shaking the foundations of nearby homes.[98] Many
of the chemical companies receiving the largest share of tax breaks
had incurred some fines for state or federal environmental violations
in recent years.

The idea that rewarding polluters with tax breaks was unsound
public policy had surfaced as early as the debate in 1974 during the
constitutional convention that had crafted the tax-exemption provision. Governor Buddy Roemer had been a delegate to that convention and had expressed reservations about the whole scheme. The
system of industry tax breaks, he noted, had been abused often since
its inception in the 1930s under Governor Huey Long.[99] In 1982,
Republican State Representative Ben Bagert had introduced the idea
of a scorecard for environmental compliance that would limit exemptions for polluters. Industry pressure promptly killed the bill in
committee.[100] In 1986, Tulane University law professor Oliver
Houck had published a law-review article that proposed imposing
such conditions on future tax breaks.[101]

Finally, in December 1989, the new Tulane Environmental Law
Clinic filed a rulemaking petition with BCI to tie tax breaks to environmental compliance. Its 12 clients included the Sierra Club's Delta
Chapter, OCAW Local 4-620, CLEAN, Louisiana Environmental
Action Network (LEAN), and the Ascension Parish group. The petition cited a 1984 state supreme court ruling, *Save Our Selves v. Louisiana Environmental Control Commission* (commonly known as the

"IT" decision because it involved the IT Corporation) that held that all state agencies were responsible for implementing environmental protection.[102] It seemed obvious to the petitioners that BCI qualified as a state agency.

At that month's BCI meeting, Roemer aide Steve Cochran announced that the administration was developing a proposal to link environmental performance with tax breaks. The reaction from the audience of businesspeople was stunned silence. The board was caught flat-footed. For the citizen groups, it was the beginning of a crusade. For Governor Roemer, it triggered a siege of his administration by industry lobbyists that lasted until the end of his term.[103] Despite that reaction, it was never clear that the majority of the business community really supported the industry line. A poll by a local business magazine indicated that three-fourths of its readers agreed that tax exemptions should be tied to a company's environmental record.[104]

LCTJ gained its big public-relations coup the following summer. Its members had discovered that Citgo, which operated a big refinery in Lake Charles, had stated on its application for a $1.3-million sales-tax rebate under the state's enterprise-zone program that it had no pending citations for pollution violations. Louisiana DEQ records showed otherwise, and LCTJ brought this to the attention of the board, which deferred action until the August meeting. There, to the amazement of Calcasieu Parish labor and environmental activists who were in attendance, a Citgo spokesperson attempted to explain that the violations were actually committed by a separate company that just happened to be two-thirds owned by Citgo. DEQ Secretary Paul Templet requested a 30-day deferral to review the company's record and make a recommendation, but BCI refused to grant the deferral. The next day, Roemer angrily announced he was freezing all 111 pending tax-break applications.[105]

From there, the issue quickly escalated. Roemer, not even aware that the tax exemptions had required his approval, discovered that the Department of Economic Development had been signing the applications with a machine that mechanically reproduced his signature.[106] A Roemer task force fashioned a proposed environmental scorecard to base at least a portion of a firm's requested tax exemption on its record of compliance with environmental regulations. The scorecard that was eventually adopted allowed companies an automatic 50-percent exemption while conditioning 25 percent on environmental compliance. The other 25 percent was determined according to a formula that used a ratio of toxic emissions per job, with higher ratios resulting in lower tax exemptions.[107]

At first, seven of the eleven BCI members bucked the governor, asking him at their February 27, 1991, meeting to reconsider the proposed new scorecard. Because they were appointed to four-year terms, Roemer could do little about their resistance. But LCTJ members arrived at the board's March 28 hearing on the issue with brooms to conduct a "clean sweep" of what they considered obstinate board members. In the lobby outside the hearing room, the protesters chanted, "Hey, hey, ho, ho, the commerce board has got to go." Once inside, they waited about a half-hour before asking to speak. Chairman Mayson Foster granted permission, then suddenly rescinded it when he realized that the group was submitting a mock resignation letter in which BCI's seven scorecard opponents "apologized" to Roemer for causing him embarrassment through their February 27 vote. When the LCTJ spokesperson refused to yield the microphone, Foster called a recess and eight of nine board members exited the hearing room.[108]

The following month, somewhat chastened by the public and gubernatorial reaction, the board approved a revised version of the environmental scorecard.[109] The issue did not rest there. All the way through August, when the final rule was published in the state register, board members continued to introduce and approve weakening amendments, some of which Roemer accepted. At a board meeting in June 1991, according to the LCTJ study, some BCI members actually read proposed amendments off faxed messages they had received from the Louisiana Association of Business and Industry (LABI) the day before.[110] LCTJ counterattacked in the legislature, almost getting a measure passed that would have placed school property taxes off limits for industrial tax exemptions.[111] The issue also became part of the gubernatorial election, with both David Duke and former Governor Edwin Edwards campaigning against the scorecard. Edwards, in particular, reaped a huge measure of financial support

from industry lobbies for his stance. LABI and the Louisiana Chemical Association (LCA), which already despised Templet, clearly had
Roemer in their gun sights. He lost in the nonpartisan primary, placing third behind Edwards and Duke with 26 percent of the vote.

In early 1992, newly elected Governor Edwards fulfilled his campaign promise to industry. The new BCI promptly dismantled the
scorecard. His new DEQ secretary, Kai Midboe, argued that it was
not necessary to have another agency besides his penalizing polluters. "If our penalties are inadequate, we will ask the legislature for
more authority," he said.[112] At its first meeting under the new administration, the board first repealed the rule as an emergency measure, then approved a stack of 331 tax-exemption applications worth
$174 million in a six-hour session.[113] They had been kept in waiting
for the day when business returned to usual.

New Orleans Times-Picayune columnist James Gill had described
the process as "strictly lagniappe," a Cajun-French term that denotes
an extra or unexpected benefit akin to a "baker's dozen."[114] Lagniappe
was the essence of Louisiana's good ol' boy politics. It is the per-
petual illusion of a free lunch that drives the process.

Unfortunately, as one delegate to the 1974 constitutional convention had warned long before, there was no free lunch. Worse yet,
while industry continued to denude the coffers of local communities, some citizens, particularly those of African-American descent,
lost entire communities to the industrialization of the river corridor
they glumly called Cancer Alley.

Janice Dickerson grew up in the African-American community of*
Reveilletown, learning that her people's heritage was embodied in
its survival. The small, unincorporated settlement, just two miles
south of Plaquemine, was founded by freed slaves after the Civil War.
The church celebrated its centennial in the mid-1980s. Dickerson
was the fourth generation of her family to live on her property. The
community's continuity allowed her to trace her family back to her
great-great-grandmother, who was born in slavery.

But because of pollution problems that followed the arrival of a

*A version of the material on pages 253–261 first appeared in *The Neighborhood Works* magazine,
2125 W. North Ave., Chicago, IL 60647, (312) 278-4800.

chemical manufacturer, the historic town today no longer exists. Its residents have scattered throughout southern Louisiana. Dickerson became part of a core of six families that moved to the same Baton Rouge neighborhood. The town's ruin taught Dickerson some vital lessons about negotiating with corporate polluters when life nearby is no longer tenable.

In 1989, she began to apply those lessons as an organizer for the Gulf Coast Tenants Organization, which works with other communities based near large polluters. Increasingly, communities that had organized against companies because of toxic emissions were instead turning to a last-resort solution—buyouts—where the company paid the costs of relocating the residents of an entire community. Less drastic alternatives, residents said, might produce a generation of sick children and shortened lifespans for their parents because of health hazards associated with living near petrochemical plants. These communities had concluded that when it was clear a neighboring facility would not or could not clean up its act, it was time to get out.

In 1969, when the Georgia-Pacific Corporation built its plant within 300 feet of some Reveilletown homes, Dickerson said, the common perception was that "black folks aren't concerned about the environment." That perception never sat well with Dickerson, who first noticed problems with lawns and gardens when the company later added a vinyl-chloride unit. She recalled thinking, "If this stuff is killing grass and trees and vegetables, it's got to be doing something to people." Dickerson then organized Victims of a Toxic Environment United (VOTE United) to "raise hell with everybody we could."[115]

Often residents have no way of linking individual symptoms, such as the nausea, headaches, and respiratory problems experienced by Reveilletown residents, to an areawide problem, and relating that to plant emissions. For that reason, Dickerson said, "We decided we wanted health testing done." But "nobody had any vision of leaving Reveilletown."

Instead, VOTE United focused on enlisting plaintiffs for a class-action lawsuit it filed in 1984 against Georgia-Gulf Corporation, a Georgia-Pacific subsidiary that bought out the parent company. The suit, according to Ramona Stevens, an environmental consultant to the group, charged that the firm's toxic air emissions were damaging residents' health and sought monetary damages and relocation. VOTE United's struggle dragged on until the 1986 Superfund Amendments and Reauthorization Act created the Toxic Release Inventory, which provided the group with an effective new tool.[116]

TRI data are often rough estimates and not totally reliable. Nonetheless, as Dickerson noted, the data have provided a far better window into company operations than activists previously had. "Before 1986, we didn't know what the hell was going on over there," Dickerson said. The group had received some help from her brother and father, who had worked in the chemical industry. But after 1986, she said, "We started getting information on what was being produced over there and sharing it with people involved in the lawsuit."

The information produced a dramatic change of heart among the residents, who began for the first time to feel that moving was the only long-term way to protect their families' health.[117] The residents eventually settled out of court, but a court order sealed the records so that plaintiffs could not discuss the settlement or health findings, according to Stevens.[118]

"After we started doing research on the consequences of keeping our children in that kind of environment, one of our attorneys said Georgia-Gulf was willing to buy out the community," Dickerson said. "We resisted, but as the data started surfacing, we were placed in almost a no-win situation." With Ashland Chemical just three-fourths of a mile to the south, the village of 350 people "was surrounded." Noting that the residents expected little help at the time from Louisiana's notoriously lax regulatory agencies, Dickerson added, "We accepted that offer for our children."

But even after reconciling themselves to abandoning their historic community, Reveilletown residents learned how to hang tough. "We made a pact," Dickerson said. "If everybody didn't get what they wanted, nobody would move. No one would end up with a mortgage, and people would get some change for the kids."

Housing costs, however, were the easy part of the negotiations. Health issues proved stickier. "They were saying you could not in all honesty say the exposure to those chemicals caused that illness. Our biggest problem is getting health officials to link health conditions with specific exposures," Dickerson said.

But she was convinced that life had improved. "My mother took

Benadryl before and doesn't now," she said. "The kids don't have colds as frequently as they did. My general assessment is that if we had stayed, by now it may have been too late."[119]

The buyout issue was not confined to Louisiana. It became a more general Gulf-Coast and oil-patch problem. For instance, health effects were also an issue for Janis Terrell, who lived in the largely white, blue-collar Fairlea Subdivision in Port Arthur, Texas. Unlike Reveilletown, Fairlea grew up with the nearby Fina oil refinery, which was built in the 1930s. Few people in the strongly pro-union neighborhood ever questioned the value of having a refinery for a neighbor until early 1991, when Fina started up a new sulfur-recovery unit just 1,500 feet from the nearest house. Throughout the spring and summer, sporadic releases of hydrogen sulfide, which smells like rotten eggs, sent numerous residents to the hospital. According to Terrell, a spokesperson for Fairlea Residents Opposed to Noise and Toxins (FRONT), the emissions aggravated existing lung problems for some residents.[120]

Residents soon began keeping logs of air-pollution incidents, phoning them in to the Texas Air Control Board office in Beaumont and pleading with city officials for a crackdown on Fina. According to Dale L. Watson, the assistant city planner, Port Arthur had an industrial performance-standards agreement with Fina, which sits just beyond the city limits but within the city's zoning authority.[121]

As pollution episodes continued, residents' patience wore thin. Their interest in staying in the area also waned. For one thing, the persistent problem had made people aware that the L-shaped refinery property left the neighborhood, bounded on a third side by Sabine Lake, with only one route of escape in an emergency. That route involved three parallel roads that cross a railroad track. Residents realized, Terrell said, that "should we have to evacuate while a train is coming, we would be in a lot of trouble."

One man instigated a letter-writing campaign by distributing the address of the president of the Belgian company's U.S. subsidiary. When new problems arose in July 1991 with flaring and emissions of black smoke, residents showered letters on the executive at his firm's headquarters in Dallas, demanding a buyout of the neighborhood and relocation of its residents.

The local plant manager began to research the possibilities, and the company hired a real-estate group to negotiate an agreement. But Terrell noted that, at one point, the company attempted to bypass FRONT by approaching residents individually. The organization's firm stance in insisting on representing residents prevailed, however, and by February Fina was offering $4,000 in relocation assistance to each family. In addition, FRONT negotiated a valuation procedure in which each party could choose one appraiser from a list of 10 that Fina and FRONT jointly compiled. The total buyout cost for Fairlea's 211 households was expected to top $10 million and take up to eight years to complete. The neighborhood voted in late 1991 to let those who were sick move first.

Terrell also had plans for after the settlement. Learning from others' experiences, she wanted FRONT to maintain an ongoing directory of former residents in order to monitor long-term health effects. The group consulted with Dr. Marvin Legator, who, according to Terrell, told the group that proper testing of the effects, particularly in humans, of many industrial chemicals had never been done or was woefully inadequate.

Terrell said that one sticking point with Fina had been the company's insistence that residents sign a waiver releasing the company from any responsibility for future health problems. Terrell had other complaints about Fina's handling of the buyout. She wanted Fina to beef up its buyout budget to speed up the process and complained that the company was still being less generous than Conoco in Ponca City, Oklahoma, and Dow Chemical in Morrisonville, Louisiana, on the north end of Plaquemine.[122]

Dow had set the standard for corporate behavior in a buyout situation. Small wonder—Dow did not wait for the community to file a lawsuit or bang on its door demanding such a solution. It hired the same Prudential relocation team later employed by Fina to put together a package to initiate the proposal. For that, at least, it won some praise for its proactive stance. Its $10 million acquisition of Morrisonville, home to 250 residents, was a model of generosity and neighborly responsibility, at least in the eyes of chemical-industry observers. Whenever it announced a policy change that would result in a more generous offer to those who had not yet sold out, the company retroactively provided previous sellers the same benefits. Families living in small wooden shacks often ended up with more than $50,000.[123]

TRI data also showed that Dow had been making substantial progress in pollution prevention, reducing the plant's air emissions by 40 percent from 1989 to 1990. Dow appeared to have made substantial progress in reducing one major known carcinogen, benzene, cutting emissions by about 70 percent to 64,000 pounds.[124]

The company had experienced no major accidents at Morrisonville, and no one there was specifically organizing against Dow, but it did reduce its potential liability by millions of dollars. With no neighbors left, there would be far fewer victims to compensate in the aftermath of an accident.

Still, the move out of Morrisonville ended the heritage of one more historic African-American community, founded in the 1870s by freed slaves from a nearby plantation. Morrisonville had survived even when the government in 1932 ordered a relocation to higher ground for flood control along the Mississippi River. But as Dow expanded after opening its plant in 1958, the steady encroachment of noise and other impacts foreclosed the village's future. A few of the residents relocated to Morrisonville Estates, a cluster of homes and trailers that Dow built for them several miles down the road. Others, like many of Reveilletown's residents, simply dispersed to nearby cities. In the process, they lost forever their vegetable gardens, their fishing, their trees, and the landmarks that shaped a lifetime.

Even Dow USA spokesperson Guy Barone bemoaned the loss of heritage that came with buying out the historic community, noting only that "we tried to take a bad situation and make it as good as it could be." Referring to the original siting decision more than 30 years ago, he said that current company officials "had to work with the hand that history dealt us."[125]

Elizabeth Avants, a member of Alliance With and Action to Restore the Environment (AWARE), a Plaquemine environmental group that worked with Morrisonville residents, summed up the skepticism many of them still felt. "No amount of compensation can repay you for having lived next to one of these plants," she said. "They are cutting people's lives short for money."[126]

Health effects were a bone of contention in nearly every buyout. Dale Emmanuel was the plant manager for Placid Oil Refining Company, which in 1992 bought out the Sunrise community just north of Port Allen, across the Mississippi River from the state capitol in Baton Rouge. When Sunrise residents sued Placid to force a buyout based on health problems residents said were associated with living near the plant, Emmanuel said, his firm asked for proof of health impacts from the plaintiffs and never got any.[127]

Ada Mae Gaines, the president of Sunrise's VOTE United, organized by Dickerson and named after her Reveilletown organization, saw it differently. Gaines said her 12-year-old grandson had leukemia and another, 20 years old, had to have his sinuses drained periodically.[128] We were back to the problem Dr. Tom Callender had posed. Medical science often cannot pinpoint the cause of such illnesses, and demanding such proof requires victims and government agencies to establish an unwieldy and expensive system to test literally thousands of chemicals that often interact to create compound effects whose causes are virtually untraceable and unmeasurable.

Placid Oil, however, did agree to buy out its neighbors. In Baton Rouge, Exxon did not. For the most part, it chose to ignore the pleas of the Garden City Community Alliance (GCCA), whose vice president, Ledell J.R. Hannon, called Exxon's dealings with the neighborhood "one of the worst buyout situations in the nation. We are ready to move."[129]

As for pollution and its impacts, TRI data for 1989 and 1990 showed mixed results in pollution reduction at Exxon's chemical plant. Although benzene emissions were down by 60 percent to 165,000 pounds, methyl chloride, which has proven teratogenic (causes birth defects) in animal tests, rose by 45 percent to 680,000 pounds.[130] But the Baton Rouge chemical plant was also the one that experienced the December 1989 explosion, which left an indelible mark on the minds of its neighbors. Exxon later agreed in court to pay damages to 153 plaintiffs.[131]

Exxon community-affairs coordinator David Gardner said flatly that his company was not interested in buying the neighborhood. Exxon's property purchases were for the purpose of improving the area's safety and appearance, according to Gardner, who said that

GCCA was at odds with Exxon because it wanted the company to pursue a goal the company did not share.[132]

Hannon contended, however, that Exxon was undermining the area's stability. "When businesses move out," Hannon noted, "no one wants to move in. Vacancy rates rise, crime goes up, and drug pushers arrive."

In the summer of 1992, when both sides spoke to me, the bad blood extended also to the treatment of low-income homeowners desperate to move out of an area in which Exxon seemed to be the only available buyer. County records showed that one homeowner received only $6,000 for his house, far short of GCCA's modest demand for $37 per square foot, roughly in line with Dow's purchases. Hannon said that Exxon would not even discuss a relocation fee.[133] Gardner, for his part, suggested that the sellers had been happy with their transactions and that GCCA was "not really representative" of the neighborhood. In any event, Gardner said, Exxon was dealing strictly with individuals and not engaging in collective negotiations.

To Hannon, who was also the chair of LCTJ, the Exxon situation was a failure in corporate ethics. "Anybody should be able to buy property cheaply if they can," he said, "but we're talking about a problem they created. They're throwing small change in the faces of poor people."

The problem with all these situations, ultimately, was that Louisiana had no structured legal way of addressing them. As the number of buyouts grew, so too did talk of some form of statewide siting law, a measure long in use in many other states. Many of the plants, of course, had been built before the environment even surfaced as a political concern in Louisiana, but it was becoming ludicrous that, as the century drew to a close, Louisiana still had no regulatory mechanism for addressing the appropriateness of many industrial-plant locations.

Environmentalists and civil-rights activists were prone to charge that the practice of siting environmentally noxious plants primarily near or in African-American communities constituted environmental racism. In a sense, that charge was less relevant than the lack of a planning mechanism by which it could even be addressed. Industry spokespeople objected to charges of industrial racism, arguing that their criteria for selecting sites were strictly commercial and included access to rail and water transportation, the availability of large plots of land (such as plantations, but these usually were inhabited by African-Americans) for large-scale operations, and proximity to natural resources.[134] But many also saw no need for public hearings to regulate the process of siting their plants. In that sense, the charge of environmental racism was very relevant, for the objection to a siting law reflected a time-honored way of doing business in Louisiana: Keep 'em barefoot and pregnant. The fewer avenues for redressing grievances, the better. Even Dow's Guy Barone, who favored state-wide land-use planning, recognized his deviance from the ranks of industry. "Though I may catch flak for saying it," he acknowledged, state and local land-use planning must play a stronger role in helping to prevent buyout situations in the future.[135]

On December 1, 1990, half a world away from Louisiana, about 2,000 Taiwanese citizens gathered in front of that nation's Economics Ministry in Taipei to demonstrate against a chemical plant proposed for their village. Without knowing it, they were telegraphing a desperate message to citizens in St. John the Baptist Parish. Their target was Formosa Plastics, owned by Taiwanese magnate Y.C. Wang. For three years, they had stalled Formosa's plans for a plant in Ilan, 60 miles southeast of Taipei, disregarding the pleas of national officials not to interfere with Taiwan's economic development.[136]

It was not the first demonstration against Taiwan's largest corporation, which is also by far the world's biggest producer of polyvinyl chloride (PVC). The company's environmental track record, in a country that only began in the 1990s to pass and enforce serious pollution-control laws, has drawn fire repeatedly from the villagers victimized by nearby plants. On a small island, word has gotten around, and communities proposed as new locations for Formosa Plastics facilities have withdrawn the welcome mat. In January 1989, more than 1,000 people had protested near Taipei to block a 450,000-ton-per-year ethylene cracker and some related plants. (A cracker uses heat to break the organic structure of certain chemicals in order to reformulate them.) In June 1988, 500 residents had protested plans for a huge Formosa Plastics naphtha cracker near Tsaota, a village in northwestern Taoyuan County. Wang was getting the message: Look outside Taiwan for future investments. He had worn out his welcome in his native land.[137]

St. John the Baptist Parish council president Lester Millet, Jr., was undisturbed by these warnings. Protesters, after all, were a familiar sight in Louisiana, and he paid them little heed there. And a trip to Taiwan at the company's expense was undoubtedly an attractive way to learn more about Wang and the rayon plant that he wanted to build in Millet's parish. Wang had been courting parish officials for several months beforehand in 1989. At one point, according to the parish president's own correspondence, Wang presented him with a "beautiful clock" over dinner.[138] Millet had a reputation for making deals and loving to wield power. Shifting public funds around in strange ways was no problem if Millet knew what he wanted. At one point, he persuaded the parish council to allocate economic-development funds to pay for a jail expansion. "What's more economic development than keeping criminals in jail?" he asked. "We keep them out of the shopping centers and make it so other people aren't afraid to go out. Plus, who wants to come to an area where there's a lot of crime?" The money had come from a ⅜-cent sales tax approved by parish voters in 1988, ostensibly for economic-development purposes.[139]

Voters in 1987 had looked past Millet's 1976 conviction on federal extortion charges, for which he served a 4 ½-month sentence. For Millet, it had been a matter of forgiveness. In his 1991 reelection race, he noted, "A person has to have his slate wiped clean at some time." Charged with ruthlessness, he had replied, "Everybody's controversial. The only ones who are not are the ones who don't do anything."[140]

For Millet, bringing Formosa Plastics to St. John the Baptist Parish became one of those things he was determined to get done. But the way he tried to do it, combined with Formosa's track record and reasons for coming, locked him into one of Louisiana's epic environmental struggles.

The first small warning arrived on a beautiful spring day in 1990. Environmentalists had organized the Second Great Louisiana March Against Poisons, which lasted a week and took its participants from

New Orleans to Baton Rouge. About 50 people gathered for a rally on Wednesday, April 19, at the Whitney Plantation in Wallace, the planned site of the Formosa plant. The small town on the west bank of the Mississippi River was predominantly African-American, and the protesters had been organized by the Gulf Coast Tenants Organization, a statewide African-American association devoted to civil rights and environmental causes. Speakers found a parallel between the old plantations like Whitney and the new exploiters of the rural South. For them, it was no accident that such a plant would locate in a poverty-stricken minority community, and they challenged residents to fight back.

"Is it a crime," activist Carl Baloney, Jr., asked, "to retain your land? Is it a crime to ask questions?"[141]

Perhaps not, but before a larger evening rally in nearby Edgard materialized, Baloney and 22 other protesters, including Pat Bryant, the executive director of the Gulf Coast organization, were arrested for obstructing traffic when they chose to march down the River Road rather than follow a predetermined parade route. Later that year, charges were dropped against all but Bryant and Baloney, whom the sheriff regarded as the ringleaders. The two pleaded no contest.[142]

The night after the rally, tense and suspicious citizens filed into the 6:30 meeting of the parish council. On the agenda was Formosa's application for rezoning of 1,800 acres in Wallace from light-industrial and residential uses to heavy industry. Formosa had secured the 1,500-acre Whitney Plantation from its 13 fractious heirs and had added 300 more next to it.

Whitney, however, had not been its original choice. It had originally negotiated with Shell Oil Company for 2,200 acres at Willow Bend, an existing industrial site with the necessary zoning. Shell had wanted $17 million, but Formosa had assembled the alternate site in Wallace for about $9 million. The Willow Bend site already had river frontage, whereas the Wallace site required a dock. The South Louisiana Port Commission had come to the rescue by offering to spend $25 million in public money to build one. But what galled many opponents the most was how Formosa acquired Whitney—through Durel Matherne, a real-estate agent and friend of Millet, who earned a handsome commission for arranging the sales. According to Walter

Barnes, one of the family members who sold the Whitney Plantation, Millet had called to suggest Matherne as an agent, knowing the
family wished to sell.[143] Without the rezoning, the lucrative deal
would be worthless.

The vote that night came amid shouts and threats. Baloney hinted
at a recall effort against parish-council members and promised that
the opposition would persist. Haston Lewis, an African-American
whose council district included the site, angrily cited the west bank's
lingering poverty as a reason to proceed. Responding to arguments
about the health effects of chemical pollution, he said, "It's not how
long you live, it's how well you live and we haven't been living too
well over here."

Contractors in the area spoke up for the rezoning, noting their
need for new business. Alden Andre, a Formosa vice president, reassured the parish council that the new plant would get the newest
equipment for pollution control.

But opponents insisted that plants like Formosa were not the answer to the west bank's problems. "You, gentlemen, are the past,"
said Luke Fontana, a New Orleans attorney hired to represent an
environmental group, Save Our Wetlands. "We, gentlemen, are the
future." Fontana criticized Formosa's environmental track record and
declared the parish-council members "environmental scoundrels."

When the evening ended, the alleged "scoundrels" had carried
the day, approving Formosa's rezoning in a unanimous 8-to-0 vote.[144]
Within the month, Save Our Wetlands filed suit to overturn the
rezoning.[145] A few days later, the deficit-ridden parish school board
set off another controversy by approving a sales-tax exemption for
Formosa Plastics during construction of the plant, estimated to save
the firm $3 million. The three opponents on the 11-member board
argued, to no avail, that Formosa would come to the parish anyway,
and that the school board was simply throwing away badly needed
revenue.[146] The following year, after four new members won office,
the school board voted to retract the tax break, and rescinded its
retraction, sacrificing its credibility on all sides.

These moves underscored the historic powerlessness of the
west-bank residents. Louisiana's "river parishes" share borders that
crisscross the river in ways that seem to defy rationality, often incor-

porating small chunks of the historically poorer west bank, with a larger African-American population, at points where no bridges allow easy access to parish government on the other side. Wallace was only beginning to get the benefit of a new bridge as the Formosa deal materialized. The only other nearby crossing was by way of an undependable ferry. The originally intended result of this system was the effective disenfranchisement of the west bank's poor minority residents from any meaningful participation in local government.

One senior African-American state legislator who did not like the scenario that was evolving in St. John under these circumstances quickly introduced a bill that would effectively halt not only the Formosa plant, but any future plant sitings that would set the stage for future toxic buyouts such as those occurring elsewhere in Cancer Alley. State Representative Avery Alexander (D-New Orleans) drafted a measure requiring a one-mile buffer zone around any plant producing or emitting chemicals that the DEQ deemed harmful to human health. Backed by just three votes, two of them from fellow African-American legislators and one from the committee chairman, his bill died in the House Natural Resources Committee in June. Opponents of the bill charged it was too vague, but Alexander, who had amended it more than once to meet objections, saw a different explanation. "The industry is very strong," he said. "I guess they [the committee members] are suspect of anything a black presents." [147]

But the Formosa issue also typified a larger problem than the Alexander bill addressed. Like many rural parishes, St. John the Baptist had no planning department. In the midst of a highly industrialized area, there was no staff to perform environmental reviews before the parish council voted on land-use decisions. Parish officials simply saw that as the responsibility of state and federal officials, even though the siting decision clearly set the stage for the types of environmental impacts the DEQ and EPA would have to consider. Even more important, the lack of planning precluded the development of a more comprehensive vision for the parish's economic future. For politicians like Millet who loved splashy big deals, that was no problem. But a serious effort at economic development could have attracted many smaller, more committed companies producing at least as many jobs as the 1,000 that Formosa promised. Instead, a few powerful officials courted huge firms with major incentives that undermined the solvency of the public treasury. Beyond the school-board and port-commission inducements, Formosa had already won nearly $400 million in tax exemptions from the state Board of Commerce and Industry.

Yet the company's track record offered a classic example of precisely what the tax-justice campaign was decrying. Beyond the despoliation that led to protests in its native Taiwan, Formosa Plastics had attracted major regulatory attention in the United States. The firm's PVC plant in Baton Rouge had encountered a series of problems, starting with an EPA lawsuit in January 1984 over chronic emissions of vinyl chloride, known as causing liver, brain, and central-nervous-system cancers as well as having mutagenic (causing genetic mutations) properties; chronic exposure can cause a bone-loss disorder known as acroosteolysis.[148] On May 30, 1986, a line failure released 1,446 pounds of vinyl chloride, 902 pounds of hydrochloric acid, and 337 pounds of ethylene dichloride. Less than a month later, a ruptured line produced another spill of nearly four tons of vinyl chloride, creating what was described as "a large cloud of chemical moving toward the eastern base of the Old Mississippi bridge."[149]

Formosa's PVC facility in Delaware City, Delaware, raised even more questions about its ability or willingness to operate in an environmentally responsible manner. It purchased that facility from Stauffer Chemicals in 1981. In May 1984, the two companies agreed to a $1 million cleanup after tests of nearby wells showed high levels of vinyl chloride and ethylene dichloride. The state later acted against the company for illegal air releases of vinyl chloride. But the violations accumulated until October 1985, when the company took more than seven hours to report a vinyl-chloride leak, and then completely failed to report a more serious leak two days later that activated the plant's sprinkler system. An anonymous source reported the violation. The state Department of Natural Resources (DNR) moved to close the plant by revoking its permits, but company guards refused to admit state officials who came to serve notice. The DNR resorted to delivering the notice by dropping it on the office from a helicopter. The company challenged the revocation in court and lost. Six weeks later, the plant reopened after the firm completed a series of improvements.[150]

But Formosa had an excuse for those two plants: It had acquired the dated facilities from other companies. The excuse did not explain its performance in Point Comfort, Texas, where its record of violations was also extensive, even though it built the plant itself in 1982. Monitoring wells at that plant have shown high levels of contamination, including ethylene dichloride, vinyl chloride, chloroform, benzene, and trichloroethylene, in the groundwater around the plant.[151] In late 1991, the U.S. EPA settled a complaint against Formosa Plastics by imposing a $3.3 million fine, the largest for solid and hazardous-waste violations in its history.[152]

With this history, it is small wonder that environmentalists in Louisiana fully expected that Formosa's track record would be part of the U.S. EPA's deliberations in permitting the Wallace facility. That was not normal practice at the EPA, but it was permissible if the circumstances warranted. But the agency immediately attracted the same vitriol previously directed at parish officials when it announced that Formosa's environmental performance elsewhere would not be a factor in its environmental impact statement (EIS) for the Wallace site. By May, however, it was forced to reverse itself.[153]

The EPA hearings became verbal sparring matches. At the first, on January 3, Haston Lewis and other advocates promised an array of rosy futures for the west bank if approval of the $700 million rayon plant were forthcoming. Formosa officials promised 800 construction jobs for two years and 1,000 permanent jobs. Local foresters would have a market, since the plant would make its 2,000 metric tons of rayon per day by converting wood into the synthetic fiber. Pat Sellers, a local businessman, extolled progress by noting that "our forefathers ate their meat raw. We cook it."

But opponents saw themselves and their families as the raw meat waiting to be cooked. One housewife from St. James Parish asked that the area's high colon- and bladder-cancer rates be taken into consideration.

Another force appeared on the stage to suggest that there were economic losses, as well as gains, from industrializing the river corridor. James Coleman, Sr., spoke as an attorney on behalf of the 2,091-

acre Evergreen Plantation, which sat next to the Formosa site. Life alongside Formosa would make Evergreen impossible, he said. It would go out of business.[154]

The preserved plantations along the River Road were in fact the state's second-largest tourist attraction behind New Orleans, but who would want to visit an area where the putrid air induced headaches? Willie Fontenot, the state's veteran citizen organizer, was already suggesting the obvious—that along the river, tourism was an alternative to heavy industry as a form of economic development. An unlikely coalition began to emerge between the African-American environmentalists concerned about the quality of life in rural Louisiana and the historic preservationists whose interest lay in saving the plantations as tourist attractions. The coalition had a sense of urgency because the Evergreen Plantation's owners entered into purchase negotiations with Formosa shortly after the EPA hearings began.[155]

Further, the parish had contracted with the South Central Planning and Development Commission, based in Thibodaux, to conduct a survey of its 3,900 west-bank residents to find those interested in working for Formosa. In April, the commission presented its findings to Formosa and the school board. Of 687 people who had responded, about two-thirds indicated an interest in working at the plant. Half of those not interested were unemployed. Millet wasted little time in finding an endorsement of the plant in the survey results.

Fontenot thought otherwise. "All it shows," he told a reporter, "is that people would like to have a job. They work in those jobs because they don't have a lot of choices."

As the Save Our Wetlands lawsuit dragged on and eventually failed, much like an earlier, similar one against the parish over an Aristech Chemical plant in Mt. Airy, opponents turned up the political pressure to block the plant. The glare of the publicity they mustered around the Formosa plant even caught Governor Buddy Roemer in a bad light, forcing him to announce that he was returning $15,000 in donations Formosa had made to his reelection campaign.[156] Roemer's opponents used the incident to chip away at his reputation as an environmental champion. Meanwhile, historic preservationists steadily built the scaffolding of an effective coalition to block the plant, mustering support up and down the River Road. The Destrehan Plantation, opened in 1973 in adjacent St. Charles Parish, was drawing some 80,000 visitors annually, while the Ormond Plantation drew 25,000. They wanted new docks, too, but for riverboats, especially after Louisiana legalized riverboat gambling.[157] Down the road, the renovated Oak Alley Plantation's proprietor, Zeb Mayhew, became a spokesman for plantation tourism and denounced the threats posed by chemical pollution. In July 1991, their influence brought the state's Travel Promotion Association into the opposition tent, with a resolution stating that Formosa would ruin the Whitney Plantation and harm the nearby Evergreen, San Francisco, and Oak Alley plantations along what is known as the German Coast. Formosa's ploy to avert such criticism by promising a $1 million renovation of the Whitney into a museum and restaurant was failing miserably.[158] Evergreen Plantation owner Matilda Gray Stream, of Baton Rouge, reversed her attempt to sell and sued in May 1992 to block the Formosa plant as a nuisance to the enjoyment of her property.[159]

But if the preservationists were building the scaffolding, it was the residents of Wallace who were building the foundations of the coalition. Without them, the preservationists would have been one more group of white activists easily characterized by parish officials as outsiders unconcerned about the economic fortunes of local residents. The residents formed an opposition group, the River Area Planning (RAP) Group, that ultimately held the winning card, for its members owned the land that Formosa needed most. The Whitney Plantation had not given Formosa the land it needed to build a dock. That land ("batture" land) was held by small landholders in Wallace in modest pie-shaped parcels of nine and 10 acres, stretching inland from wide riverbend frontages to narrower road frontages. Formosa made repeated offers, found a few takers, and then hit two brick walls named Wilfred Greene and Samuel Jackson. Between Formosa and the river stood a mere 38 acres in the hands of implacable opponents.

Greene, a feisty, wiry man who bears a vague resemblance to the veteran rock singer Chuck Berry, is a retired school principal. Like

Amos Favorite, he is a strong character shaped by the civil-rights battles that trained many of today's elderly African-Americans in the need to fight for control of their own destinies. Despite his own college education, he was the son of a father who could not read and a mother who could read very little. Having stayed in Wallace when he could have moved to the city, he observes the poverty-stricken families that still surround him and notes, "I stood back because I've had an opportunity to go to school a little bit and look down on him. I sit down and think maybe he would have done as well as I have. . . ."[160]

For Greene, holding on to his property became a form of service to his community, a way of paying back fellow African-Americans who, by virtue of poverty and desperation, were less able than he to resist the Formosa siren song. Those unable to understand such an outlook tended to assume that Greene and Jackson were simply holding out to drive up the price that Formosa would offer. Greene did indeed meet with Matherne and company and parish officials about his property, but he saw little in their offers that he liked. His dedication to the community also enabled him to confront his neighbors' fears and illusions. "The need for a dollar will bring about death," he firmly insisted in an interview with me in New Orleans at the height of the battle. In a community meeting two months before we met, he had confronted a man who suggested that any job was better than none at all. "You don't need a job if you have to give every nickel you make to the doctor—or to the undertaker," he had replied. "You don't want that kind of job."[161]

What Wallace needed, in Greene's view, was access to some sound alternative form of development that would obviate the need ever to deal with the likes of Formosa. Until that happened, he felt, the battle would never truly be over.

In frustration, Formosa at one point suggested it would turn to expropriation through the port commission if Greene did not make a deal. Because the Formosa dock involved no public purpose, Formosa's ultimatum was a hollow one, a fact admitted even by the port's director, Richard Clements. Greene and Jackson, an underemployed, college-educated, young construction worker, stood firm in their resistance.[162] As time ground on, the EPA took a beating over what opponents considered an inadequate preliminary EIS prepared by Walk, Haydel, a New Orleans consulting firm. Critics also demanded that the EIS consider the potential impacts of an additional PVC facility that Formosa had initially promised for the site but then put on hold. The Sierra Club had scored points in the battle by obtaining the preliminary study through a Freedom of Information Act request and then sharing it with the news media.[163]

Key players began to disappear from the scene. Lester Millet, having narrowly won a primary in his bid for reelection, lost the runoff to former parish president Arnold Labat in the fall of 1991.[164] Some of Greene's neighbors sold to Formosa. Greene and Jackson, who had hired the Sierra Club Legal Defense Fund to represent them, refused to budge. One day, they awoke to find out they had finally won.

In October 1992, Formosa pulled the plug on what would have been the world's largest wood-pulp and rayon plant, in part blaming the Evergreen Plantation lawsuit, in part the EPA, in general the delays that whittled away at its desire to locate in St. John the Baptist Parish. Wilfred Greene, the man of the hour, celebrated at the environmental coalition's jambalaya and beer party, held at the Friends of Charity Hall in Wallace. As always, he insisted he had not been fighting the prospect of jobs. "My fight was against equating your life with jobs," he declared. "That's wrong."[165]

For Willie Fontenot, the Formosa fight was gratifying because its resolution was so different from many of the earlier struggles he had helped to organize. The wellsprings of activism he had helped to water across the state were gushing into a mighty stream in a state once nearly devoid of serious environmental pressure groups. Richard Miller, the organizer who had worked with OCAW Local 4-620 during the BASF lockout, perceived advantages in this grass-roots upsurge over states with more well-established and formalized public-interest lobbies. When an issue really mattered, hordes of downhome citizens simply invaded the legislature and made their feelings known, and no public-interest lobbyist could interpret those feelings for them. Mob rule, he said, kept Louisiana's political establishment from co-opting environmental leaders.[166]

But every network eventually needs coordination. As the number of grass-roots groups grew into the dozens, they too sensed that need and created the Louisiana Environmental Action Network (LEAN), the other half of a mutual-admiration society that includes Fontenot. LEAN initially began to come together after a 1986 leadership conference at Louisiana State University in Baton Rouge, attended by Lois Gibbs and other staffers from the Citizens' Clearinghouse for Hazardous Wastes. Those present wanted to retain the sense of community that the conference had fostered.

For two-and-a-half years, the leaders of the new home-grown statewide coalition met and struggled to raise money without a staff. Marylee Orr, who had merely helped to prepare food for the original conference, recalled that at the initial meeting the group decided after a long discussion to choose two co-chairs. With her young son in tow, she raised her hand and volunteered to become a co-chair "if we can hurry up and get out of here!" For those two-and-a-half years, the group continued to meet as a collection of volunteers, often in Orr's living room for eight to nine hours. Eventually, however, during this difficult period of movement growth, Orr came to realize that business skills from her past would help LEAN to marshall the resources it needed to become effective at the state level.

"Business with a heart," Orr called it, bringing a distinctly feminist perspective to the business of political organizing. Orr became the executive director, pulling together the talents of grant writers and the anger of housewives to alter Louisiana's environmental politics for good. Orr decided quickly that traditional public-interest lobbying would disserve her constituency. Taking her cue from Fontenot's style and her own instincts as a single mother whose child suffered from asthma in one of EPA's clean-air nonattainment zones, she shifted LEAN's emphasis to grass-roots power. It is probably this perspective that emboldened Orr to proceed with a project that many middle-class environmentalists feared would alienate the very politicians whose support LEAN needed for effective legislation. In 1988, LEAN published its first environmental scorecard for legislators— and flunked two-thirds of them. This tough tactic, instead of backfiring as more skittish LEAN backers feared, forced many politicians who wanted LEAN's support to come to terms with the coalition's agenda and consider their votes on environmental bills more seriously. LEAN had effectively declared that it would no longer tolerate good-old-boy deception on its issues.

Furthermore, the organization would fight, not beg, for what it wanted. Bringing the people to Baton Rouge to speak for themselves has become the linchpin of LEAN politics. Orr insists that some of the organization's money be set aside to assist needy volunteers with telephone bills and travel expenses. Her job, she explained when we met, is to facilitate people power.

"If they want to go down to the legislature, if they have a problem and they want to bring it to the attention of the legislators, we do everything like tell them where to park. It's very intimidating for rural people to come to the capitol. We meet them at the elevator, we make an appointment with their representative or senator, help them learn how to hand him the green card on the house side or the white card on the senate side and how to lobby the floor. And what's rewarding is, you know, they kind of hang back for the first couple of minutes, but then, pow! They knock you out of the way when we get people over. But then, who can know more about the issue than themselves?"[167]

Ironically, the one-term administration of Governor Buddy Roemer became an object lesson in both the best and the worst ways in which to harness the benefits of this people power, which grew immensely during those four years from 1988 to 1992. On one hand, he hired Paul Templet to lead and expand a Department of Environmental Quality that had been demoralized virtually from its inception because of poor staffing, limited authority, and a lack of support from Governor Edwin Edwards. Templet brought in a brain trust that formed his Office of Policy and Planning and infused the agency with a sense of mission and a long-term perspective. Louisiana made major strides forward in advancing its mission after having languished at the bottom of most environmental indicators for decades.

The extent of Louisiana's progress can be seen, in rough form at least, in the shrinkage of its reported toxic releases into the environment as reported in corporate TRI numbers. In 1987, the year Roemer was elected and appointed Templet as DEQ secretary, the state's reported toxic releases totaled 840 million pounds, easily leading the nation.[168] Only Texas came close; Ohio, in third place, had about half Louisiana's quantity of releases. Louisiana hosted individual companies, such as Shell and American Cyanamid, whose toxic releases within the state actually exceeded the totals for entire industrialized states like New Jersey.[169] Yet by 1989, the state brought its total down to 482 million pounds, falling below Texas for the first time.

There are, of course, some inherent dangers in drawing too many conclusions from such gross numbers. Those who work regularly with TRI data know its many limitations, including the fact that it covers only manufacturing establishments, exempting such commercial and utility sources as dry cleaners, power plants, and gasoline stations. In Louisiana, however, the sheer volume of releases from the chemical industry dwarfs the contributions of all other sectors combined, statistical error notwithstanding. For instance, in 1989, classification of TRI data by the federal Standard Industrial Classification (SIC) code revealed that more than 421 million pounds, or 87 percent, of the state's reported releases emanated from the chemical-products sector. The two closest competitors in pollution were petroleum refining (17.4 million pounds) and paper products (12.8 million).[170] Clearly, there was a primary culprit and a justifiable target for environmental regulatory action.

But in seeking reductions, one must still treat the aggregated data with caution. One key question asks where the toxic releases are going (air, land, or water) and whether reductions in one category merely reflect a transference of the problem to another medium. Even more important is the precise nature of the toxic materials. Although all toxic chemicals have some health impact for humans or wildlife, not all are carcinogens. Some may be neurotoxins, some teratogens, some mutagens, and many have multiple toxic properties. Some are far more potent than others, and there are differences in the pathways by which humans are exposed—through the skin, inhalation, or ingestion, for example. Consequently, a small reduction in volume of a potent toxic may have far greater benefits for public health than a huge reduction of a less dangerous substance. Getting the biggest bang for the state's regulatory buck under the existing circumstances in Louisiana required a level of creativity never before shown by state officials.

Given limited resources and the need for dramatic improvements, DEQ Secretary Templet's most visible approach was disarmingly simple and inexpensive. No corporation likes bad publicity. Templet and his brain trust devised Corporate Response, a challenge to companies to reduce their toxic emissions so as to remove themselves from DEQ's publicly announced list of the biggest polluters in the state. In each of three categories (air, land, and water), DEQ listed the dozen top polluters in the state. Some companies appeared on more than one list. Their "challenge" was to submit a plan that would detail how they would remove themselves from the list. Within those corporations, Templet surmised, pressure would be exerted from headquarters to induce the offending plant to do what was necessary to terminate the firm's negative exposure. From all appearances, it worked. By early 1992, the Woodrow Wilson School of Public and International Affairs at Princeton University had invited Templet (by then out of office) and the heads of three other states' environmental agencies to present their case studies at a symposium on State Leadership in Industrial Pollution Prevention Policy. The others were from New Jersey, Massachusetts, and Washington.[171]

In the search for new ways of cleaning up Louisiana, Templet also began to engineer multimedia negotiations with major firms. Instead of allowing separate permit writers in air-, land-, and water-quality divisions to deal in a compartmentalized fashion with a company's pollution permits, Templet decided that, in major cases, it made more sense to negotiate permit conditions across the board through a cohesive team effort, wherein all the DEQ division representatives could perceive and act on the larger picture. In such an arrangement, pollution prevention would more likely emerge as a strategy, and diversions that simply moved water releases onto the land or into the air would be averted.[172]

One of Templet's major experiments in this area involved Freeport McMoRan, a New Orleans-based producer of fertilizers with phosphate-mining operations in Florida. The company was the biggest phosphate-fertilizer producer in North America; after a joint venture took effect on July 1, 1993, the combined company, Agrico, operated by IMC Company, Freeport McMoRan's joint-venture partner, became the largest phosphate-fertilizer producer in the world. The bulk of its releases involved the permitted discharge of phosphoric acid into the Mississippi River, with smaller releases of sulfuric acid. In DEQ's 1990 summary of corporate responses to its request for waste-reduction plans, the agency deemed Freeport McMoRan's reduction plan for its Faustina facility "marginally acceptable" and the plan for its Uncle Sam facility, which depended entirely on "less rainfall," "unsatisfactory."[173] At least publicly, DEQ and the company seemed to be on a collision course.

In fact, both faced a very difficult problem. Freeport's process involves dissolving phosphate rock in sulfuric acid, yielding an exchange of phosphate and sulfur that leaves behind calcium sulfate, known as gypsum. Because the process uses phosphate mined in open pits in Florida and precipitated from the sea over millions of years, the structure of the gypsum contains both water molecules and trace metals, including minute amounts of uranium and radium. Because of those liabilities, Freeport's daily "waste" yield of 11,000 to 12,000 tons of gypsum was not salable as a construction material. Commercial wallboard gypsum comes almost entirely from "dry" western deposits that are far more pure. The cost of altering the physical structure of Freeport's byproduct to meet commercial standards makes it noncompetitive.

But the two alternatives—discharging it into the river or stacking it on the ground—were also unattractive because of the growing public reaction to industrial pollution. The company had begun to impound the material in the mid-1970s. But without discharge permits from the EPA and DEQ, the company's waste-gypsum stacks could go on forever. By 1992, the company had already accumulated a 100-foot-high stack on 600 acres on one site and a lower stack spread across 1,000 acres across the river. In the late 1980s, it also underwent a punishing public-relations struggle during a long series of hearings "on every aspect of gypsum that you can imagine," according to W. Wayne Forman, the company's director of environmental affairs.[174] The public outcry over the proposed discharge permits effectively produced an impasse that forced Freeport McMoRan back to the drawing board.

But Freeport, according to Forman, had long been aware of its predicament in finding an alternate use for the gypsum. Under a license, it used technology developed by an engineering research firm in Florida that reclaimed the sulfur and produced an aggregate (pebblelike) material usable in construction. Once again, the company faced a problem of economically feasible recycling. Its sheer quantity of gypsum would dominate the aggregate market in the area and undermine prices, yet the company could not profitably produce the material as cheaply as natural aggregate. Some of that natural aggregate production, however, had depleted shells along the shores of Lake Pontchartrain, so the gypsum approach, from an ecological standpoint, actually would be doubly beneficial but for its pricing problems. In its quest to overcome these market difficulties, Freeport McMoRan had also funded an Institute for Recyclable Materials at Louisiana State University to research such market development.

Eventually, these problems drove Forman and Freeport McMoRan to approach Templet with a special appeal, committing themselves to a 75-percent reduction in discharges from the gypsum stacks by the end of 1993, as well as making a number of other improvements, if the DEQ regulators in one division would take proper account of the company's pollution-reduction expenditures in other areas. In effect, they asked for a holistic accounting of the company's overall antipollution efforts. The program cost $30 million in 1992–1993, and would cost $30 million more over the next 10 years.

Templet, enthusiastically eyeing an opportunity to experiment in regulatory procedures, constructed a unified team of permit writers from his various divisions to work with Freeport, with deputy director Joel Lindsey and Forman chairing their respective negotiating teams. By all accounts, the initial sessions were tense and lively, with Freeport seeking to instill in DEQ regulators an understanding of its operations. "We had some meetings, and we talked and did a little hollering, I guess, but the short and long of it is they understood our process, they understood the total commitment we were making, and this was all voluntary," Forman recalled later. The company's commitments, according to Forman, entailed a $50 million investment in new sulfuric-acid plates to reduce two emissions, a new plant whose increased efficiency also reduced sulfur-dioxide emissions by more than 50 percent, and $6 million to spend on ammonia reductions. Methanol emissions were eliminated through process changes.[175]

Despite the pride expressed by both the company and DEQ in the Freeport McMoRan negotiations, Paul Templet suffered from a huge image problem with much of industry, and most of the image problem was manufactured at the Louisiana Chemical Association (LCA). Throughout Templet's tenure, the tension with the LCA was palpable. LCA spokespeople repeatedly tagged him as "confrontational" and, for the most part, despised Governor Roemer for having appointed him. "It's War," declared the headline above a 1990 cover story in *Business Report*, a Louisiana magazine. "The Department of Environmental Quality digs in for a fight as industry launches an assault against policies it claims are killing jobs."[176] Templet, for his part, dismissed such attacks while environmentalists rushed to the defense of the DEQ secretary—and their own hard-won victories.

The battle over the environmental scorecard, spilling over into the gubernatorial election year of 1991, merely fanned the flames of suspicion and distrust on both sides. Templet disputed the notion that industry was locked out of the discussion of environmental policy, noting that on DEQ's advisory committees, "They had enormous representation, but they didn't control committees. . . . When they didn't get what they wanted, they would beat us up that way. They had gotten numerous compromises. They would fight regulations they had agreed to." The bottom-line complaint, as Templet saw it, was that "they didn't control the governor's office."

Indeed, that seemed the problem, and industry had the answer—the political resurrection of Edwin Edwards. Roemer, presumably to cover his flank to the right, switched parties and became a Republican. The switch immediately won him support and contributions from the Bush administration. Fearing the national shadow over the GOP cast by David Duke, who also boasted Republican ties, the

White House was happy to claim a progressive Republican in the Louisiana governor's mansion. In contrast, Democratic former Governor Edwards carried the taint of scandal. The incongruous juxtaposition of Roemer's environmental policies with those of Vice President Dan Quayle, who visited to boost the Roemer campaign, seemed to lose relevance as the politics of opportunity moved to the fore.

What Roemer gained in money and conservative support, however, he lost in the faith of his environmental backers, who harbored doubts about the political transformation they were witnessing. There can also be little doubt that his new Republican affiliation held little appeal for most African-American voters, who could tolerate Edwards but feared Duke with a passion. When Roemer first received, then returned, $15,000 from Formosa Plastics, the doubts grew. The fact that Roemer had succeeded in passing legislation limiting campaign donations and tightening reporting requirements, and that he pledged not to accept money from firms that had permit applications pending, only ameliorated some of those doubts. Still, Roemer was the best thing the environmental movement had going, and it backed him.

But Roemer, who also failed to debate his opponents in person through most of the campaign, seemed to violate every tenet of the Willie Fontenot school of environmental organizing. Fontenot, who for 11 years had been traveling the state, meeting with small groups of citizens, and developing a personal rapport, had become the object of another campaign. His boss, Attorney General William J. Guste, announced that he would not seek reelection. Concern mounted at the grass-roots level that Fontenot might not last beyond Guste's tenure. As those seeking Guste's job campaigned, they were met with a sustained chorus of questions from citizens: "What about Willie?" One by one, they found themselves making pledges to find some way to retain Fontenot in his vital post as the citizens' link to state government on environmental issues. No serious candidate could long avoid the issue of retaining Willie Fontenot.

Roemer, on the other hand, suffered from a retreat into a technocratic personality that failed to touch that deep streak in Louisiana voters that naively seeks entertainment from politicians. Edwards was a colorful figure, and Duke was slick and handsome, giving a smooth edge to the hard-bitten appeal of his racist past. It is hard to know with certainty whether Roemer could have overcome their appeals with a grass-roots campaign that would have touched people Fontenot-style, but it is clear that Roemer's aloof style of technocratic reform failed miserably at the polls. In a multicandidate nonpartisan primary, he placed third behind Edwards and Duke, with 26 percent of the vote. From that point forward, environmentalists' fortunes in the campaign were hitched solely to the reactive appeal of the civil-rights movement, best exemplified in a suddenly popular bumper sticker: "VOTE FOR THE CROOK. IT'S IMPORTANT."

Despite gains in the legislature, the loss of the governor's mansion resulted in a huge setback for Louisiana environmentalists. Edwards quickly rescinded the environmental scorecard. In a move that reeked of cynicism and short-sightedness, he also slated both the Louisiana Geological Survey and the Louisiana Marine Consortium, which researched coastal erosion, for budgetary extinction. Since the savings were minuscule and the survey actually attracted federal money, critics immediately discerned that the issue had nothing to do with fiscal responsibility and a great deal to do with the two organizations' discomfiting honesty about a number of environmental issues of crucial importance to Louisiana oil and chemical producers.[177]

In a process that attracted only a couple of renegade "environmentalists," a new advisory committee appointed by Edwards chose as the new DEQ secretary Kai Midboe, a former oil-and-gas industry lobbyist who had run unsuccessfully for attorney general. To pay off his campaign debts, he held a fundraiser for industry lobbyists at the governor's mansion, producing howls of editorial protest from newspapers around the state. He soon dismantled Templet's Office of Planning and Policy, claiming that the personnel were needed to reduce a backlog of permit processing from the Templet era.

Templet, for his part, decried the removal of the "brains of the agency," noting that it was "unlikely a situation like Freeport McMoRan will ever happen again. Innovation goes out the window. . . . If somebody had told me to make a list of what would make LCA the happiest, it would be doing what they are doing right now."[178]

At the first Earth Day celebration at Southern University after the election, the Reverend Benjamin Chavis, executive director of the United Church of Christ Commission on Racial Justice, spoke to a lightly attended opening rally. It was nearing spring break at the historically African-American college, and Chavis, undeterred by the size of his audience, was trying to inject a sense of rebirth into a struggling African-American environmental movement. Louisiana was vital to the environmental-justice movement Chavis had been trying to lead for a decade. It was a potential model of cooperation between white environmentalists and African-Americans, but it also reflected the deep divisions in American culture. He described the conditions he had seen on tours he had taken of polluted neighborhoods around Baton Rouge.

Then, well into his oration, Chavis began to describe his experience at a North Carolina prison farm following his framed conviction as part of the "Wilmington 10" on charges of setting fire to a grocery during racial tensions in Wilmington, North Carolina, in 1972. (He was released in 1980 by a federal appeals court after witnesses admitted they had concocted their testimony under pressure from local police. On Good Friday, in April 1993, Chavis was chosen as the new executive director of the NAACP.)

"My God did not let me down while I was in prison," he declared. "Sometimes we don't want to turn to or for each other until we're in trouble. Crisis is not enough. Our problem is not coming together but staying together. . . .

"I went to a North Carolina prison farm loaded up with African-Americans. The prison is so big you can't run away from it. There were 600 inmates, mostly black. In February of '76, I was sent to the Caledonia prison farm. There were 54 seats on the bus. They had 78 people on the bus. Of them, the only white person was the driver. The rest were black inmates. As the bus pulled up to the prison, I saw all these brothers, hundreds of them, tilling the soil. I said, Lord, have mercy, slavery is still going on. . . .

"At the prison, they had 20 inmates per gun squad. They gave me a hoe. The bunk beds were stacked eight high—pure warehousing. We marched out to the field with two white prison guards on horses, marching to the field. They said, 'Start hitting.' We hit the ground. I said, 'Give us seeds, don't make us do something for nothing.' The prison guard clicked his gun and said, 'Hit the ground.' You have to do what's logical. I said, 'Lord, this is not the first time we have been told, "hit the ground" when there's nothing to plant.' I started singing 'This little light of mine, all over Caledonia prison, I'm gonna let it shine.' Everybody in our gun squad joined in, then hundreds of brothers began hitting the ground on the same beat."

Chavis was ordered to stop singing. "The prison guard said, 'The problem is you're doing it together,' " Chavis continued.

"The same control factors are in place outside prison as inside. They didn't let me go out in the field anymore. We started organizing in the cellblocks. We stopped prisoners from buying drugs from the guards. Without drugs, we stopped the fighting and cussing. You would have thought the guards would be happy. But they said, 'We can't allow you to take over our prison. . . .' "[179]

Willie Fontenot entered the new Edwards era as an employee of Attorney General William Ieyoub. Despite slight changes in his relationship to the Justice Department, he continued his legendary role with the same freedom he had always enjoyed. It was a hereditary handicap, instead, that began to impose incremental limits. He suffered from retinitis pigmentosa, which steadily narrows one's range of vision, eventually producing near-blindness. No longer could Fontenot drive across the state to act on the latest call. He needed a special magnification machine just to read the daily newspaper.

But he had laid the groundwork, and the movement he played such a large role in building seemed ready to move on despite his new limitations. It was ready to take the hand of its shepherd and lead him through the shadows of the valley of the Edwards years. He had been there before.

APPALACHIA
Defending the Land

The modern stories of working-class and minority people in both Appalachia and southern Louisiana begin with a quest for freedom. In the swamps of Louisiana, the quest for freedom began more than two centuries ago, when both the Houma Indians and the Acadian French sought new lives in exile from their British conquerors. An environment that seemed forbidding to outsiders provided some insulation from the predations of the dominant culture. Ultimately, however, modern industry facilitated the invasion of that environment, both economically and physically.

In the hills of Kentucky and West Virginia, and parts of neighboring states, poor white farmers sought refuge from the political dominance of the landed gentry, the slave-owning planters of Virginia and the Carolina lowlands. They penetrated the Appalachian hills, where the dominant culture largely left them alone. From time to time, escaped slaves joined the exodus, though their plantation masters made repeated efforts to induce the Cherokee Indians to return them for substantial rewards, at the same time pursuing military and social efforts to alienate the two groups from each other.[1] The mountaineers' collective resentment of landed power became manifest when West Virginia, part of Virginia until the Civil War, became the only part of a state to secede from a state that had seceded from the Union. Kentucky, though a slave state, likewise refused to secede from the Union, though in its case a bit of persuasion was applied by the Lincoln administration. Unlike West Virginia,

Kentucky included a sizeable flatland population in its bluegrass country, where rich land supported the plantation lifestyle of slave-owners.

The nature of what people flee shapes their vision at least as much as what they seek, which is generally harder to define. Harry M. Caudill, the Whitesburg, Kentucky, lawyer and author (most famous for *Night Comes to the Cumberlands*), speculated that the feudalism that bound most English peasants to their lower-class status and survived the trans-Atlantic journey in the form of indentured servitude during the colonial period ill prepared them for the unbridled freedom of the wilderness. In his view, old folkways lingered, trapped by the isolation of the hills, and froze their deference to power through the generations.[2] At best, then, this escape from the Old Dominion state became a flight from government as well as from the landed gentry, who were perceived to be one and the same. Beginning with the Whiskey Rebellion during the Washington administration, the yet more distant federal government and its oppressive "revenooers" served to reinforce deeply rooted suspicions that government, rather than being a tool of democratic expression, was primarily the enforcement apparatus for the political wishes of the upper class.

The misfortune of Appalachia was that its wealth attracted precisely those forces that would energetically strive to prove and reinforce that assumption, bringing the interlude of mountaineer freedom to an end. By the middle of the eighteenth century, the barons of the American industrial revolution had discovered the region's coal and began to develop the means to extract it quickly in large quantities. Appalachia's story then became one of exploitation by "outlanders." Those outside forces, including steel companies seeking captive mines for coking coal, often read like a who's who of American industrial wealth. Even the Delano family was involved, organizing the Kentenia Corporation in 1907, and young Franklin Delano Roosevelt spent time in the hills helping his uncle, Warren Delano, Jr., with title work at the county courthouse.[3]

Company towns, with rigged prices in company stores and company-owned rental housing on the only land within reasonable distance of the available jobs, sprang up throughout the region to impose, in corporate form, the very form of indentured servitude the mountaineers' ancestors had sought to escape. But many of their descendants were the victims of their own ecological trap. In love with the land but lacking a well-informed land ethic, they had, over generations, worn out the land they farmed and subdivided it among a burgeoning population of heirs until many found life in the coal towns more attractive than scratching out a living with something less than 40 acres and a mule. Appalachian hill country was not the stagnant, stable society of clans and families that myth has portrayed but a land of mobility and change engaged in an epic struggle for cultural and ecological survival.[4]

Caudill notes often that the rape of Appalachia required the presence of a middle-class "fifth column" that was content to subvert the civic and economic life of its own communities for personal gain. By co-opting and enlisting the aid of this collaborative middle class, the industries of the North stripped Appalachian communities of the very leadership most capable of speaking for the interests of the commonwealth. These native barons of coal, like John C.C. Mayo, provided Caudill's most colorful profiles in *Theirs Be the Power*, his story of the forceful men whose schemes and shenanigans shaped coal development in eastern Kentucky at the turn of the century. Often, these self-made men amassed land and fortunes by employing their wiles and their education at the expense of poorly educated neighbors. Mayo became the king of this genre as the inventor of the infamous broad-form deed. Such deeds essentially left the surface rights to the land in the hands of the mountain dwellers, while transferring broadly defined rights to the subsurface minerals to the mining companies, who were free to extract those minerals, usually coal, in whatever way they found appropriate. From that point forward, the surface owner had no control over the company's mining activities. Mayo was also the mastermind of a quietly engineered 1906 state law that allowed any "adverse claimant" to acquire old Virginia land grants from their original owners by paying their delinquent taxes if they had failed to pay them for any three years from 1901 to 1905. Vast acreages fell into this category, and with the help of a supportive state high-court decision a year later, the coal companies went about the business of dispossessing the heirs of historic Virginia land grants dating back to the American Revolution.[5]

Oral history and other sources support Caudill's picture of how these operators acquired the mineral rights beneath the land, large portions of which are held in separate deeds apart from the small landholders' surface rights. The Appalachian Land Ownership Task Force, for instance, funded by the Appalachian Regional Commission in the late 1970s to study land-ownership patterns, noted that the mineral holdings of the Cotiga Development Company in West Virginia's Mingo County "were acquired by an enterprising sewing-machine salesman who traveled the hills of the county early in the century trading sewing machines for land." As of 1980, Philadelphia-based Cotiga owned 25,081 surface acres and 39,648 mineral acres in Mingo County.[6]

More than a few native writers have described the resulting subjection and destitution that have plagued Appalachia, but few have done it more eloquently than Caudill. Despite his frequent tone of condescension toward regional folkways that he perceives as impeding social progress and governmental improvement, Caudill clearly finds the history of Appalachia's despoliation painful and wishes it had been otherwise. The grim toll taken by the area's economic colonization by extractive industries is the focus of most of his writings. Workers were the object of such contempt by coal-company management that their very lives were worth less than pennies on a ton of coal. Caudill has noted, for instance, that "miners died by needless thousands in accidents no other industrialized western nation would have tolerated." He compared Kentucky's 1971 death rate of 1.13 per million manshifts underground in large operations and 3.47 in small operations (employing 15 or fewer) to a national death rate of 0.84 even in 1952, which already compared poorly to European death rates by the early 1950s of between 0.24 and 0.66. With acrid bitterness, Caudill was driven to conclude, "Slave miners in Hitlerite Germany worked under better safety conditions than prevailed in a large sector of the Kentucky coal industry twenty-six years after the collapse of the Nazi empire."[7]

This atmosphere of contempt for human life and the welfare of working families inevitably led miners to rebel. The Harlan County strike of the 1930s gained national notoriety, but numerous other labor struggles poisoned the landscape for decades. The secretive

Irish organization, the Molly Maguires, inspired terror among coal-company owners. Labor struggles in the coal mines became a persis-tent magnet for muckraking reporters spelunking the darker sides of American culture. In 1923, for instance, James M. Cain, in the *Nation*, published "A Mine-Field Melodrama." The article described a series of brutal confrontations in West Virginia, in which union sentinels on one side demanded of entrants to their compound the pass-word, "I come creepin'," while coal-mine boss Don Chafin (of whom the miners sang "Hang Don Chafin to the sour-apple tree") imported airplanes to bomb the union positions for three days until federal troops arrived. The aftermath, according to Cain, was pure back-woods courtroom spectacle as a grand jury indicted "whole payrolls" on such outlandish charges as treason.[8]

These explosions of worker anger may well have been more the exception than the rule, but they illustrate that, notwithstanding many popular stereotypes about passive, fatalistic "hillbillies," the quest for freedom and justice has deep roots in Appalachia. The in-herent potential for renewal through channeling such anger was, of necessity, more apparent to such radical organizers and teachers as Myles Horton, the founder of the Highlander Center in Tennessee, than to a liberal middle-class professional like Caudill. Both knew that Appalachia's land and people deserved a better fate than his-tory had dealt them. But Horton, who founded his school in the 1930s and fended off attacks by the Ku Klux Klan and red-baiting state and county officials, knew that Appalachia's people—white, African-American, and Native American—held deep within them-selves the seeds of pride and courage that would support a demo-cratic renewal. But like any endangered culture, they needed to tackle the reclamation of Appalachia on their own terms.[9]

The great irony of Appalachia has been its poverty amid an abun-dance of natural resources. A wooded hill country that should be as rich as Switzerland has instead been systematically stripped of for-ests, pride, energy resources, education, and good government. The region's culture and heritage have at times clung to life by the slen-derest of threads. Most of Appalachia either sold or forfeited the birthright of its natural resources before ever truly accounting for what was missing. What was left was often stolen through the crudest forms of fraud and trickery.

At a time when the hill people had yet to build an educational system of any consequence, industry gained a stranglehold on their state governments, from Pennsylvania to Alabama. Mark Twain once observed that John D. Rockefeller had done everything to the Pennsylvania legislature but "refine it." He could easily have said the same of the coal barons in Kentucky, who above all else ensured that mineral rights would be taxed at the lowest possible rate, even though it meant beggaring the state treasury for generations to come. In a state where coal was the primary source of the mother's milk of politics, the coal interests could squash the careers of any politicians who threatened a populist uprising or even a thorough investigation. Alben Barkley, later Harry Truman's vice president, learned that lesson during a gubernatorial campaign in the 1920s. His promise to deliver Kentucky's state finances from the stranglehold of coal nearly earned him a ticket to political oblivion.[10]

The result throughout Appalachia was that the coal industry literally stripmined the tax system, destroying its ability to underwrite basic services like education. In the late 1970s in Morgan County, Tennessee, for instance, poorly assessed mineral rights contributed to a situation in which students wore overcoats because of decrepit, poorly heated school buildings and bus drivers struck because of low wages. The school system in Alabama's largest coal producer, Walker County, was perennially borrowing money in the 1960s and 1970s and paying its teachers late.[11] While the people of the hills sweated to excavate the mineral wealth beneath their lands to earn a living, the powers that be were truly keeping them "barefoot and pregnant." As in Louisiana, the ability to deprive the public of the means to educate its children is the ability to deprive future generations of the knowledge they need to challenge the status quo. That simple fact made Horton's Highlander Center a subversive threat.

Once the politicians of Kentucky, West Virginia, and Tennessee had been bought and sold, the means of securing mineral wealth from the attack of the tax system were disarmingly simple. The first and fundamental rule was to avoid bringing into the light of day the potential for tax revenue that lay beneath the land. Inadequately funding and staffing revenue departments was key to maintaining the obscurity of this information. More than 20 years ago, one Kentucky tax commissioner explained that "the coal companies pretty much set their own assessments. . . . We have no system for finding out what they own."[12] The Appalachian Land Ownership Task Force noted the consequences of an absurd 1978 state law that established a uniform rate of one-tenth of one cent per $100 value on Kentucky's unmined coal. In the state's largest coal-producing county, Martin County, Pocahontas-Kentucky owned more than 81,000 acres of mineral rights, or an area equivalent to 55 percent of the county's surface, and paid $76.05 in property taxes on its coal reserves.[13]

The consequences of inequitable taxation in Tennessee were equally dismal. A 1971 study by three Vanderbilt University students of five major coal-producing counties found that 34 percent of the land surface and 80 percent of the coal wealth lay in the hands of nine large companies that, in 1970, yielded less than four percent of the counties' property-tax revenue.[14] Throughout the region, study after study has documented the same pattern. Nearly exempting such large absentee land and mineral owners inevitably placed the tax burden on small landholders and kept public services hopelessly underfunded. The result is a needless dependency on federal and state welfare funds and revenue sharing, despite the fact that reasonable taxation of the underlying wealth would be the single most effective economic-development tool these counties could ever devise. For many of the petty political machines that infested places like eastern Kentucky, however, such a logical goal was not even on the agenda. Voters are easier to control when they need jobs.

If there is a parallel to the recent development of a grass-roots environmental network of working and poor people in Louisiana, it is the even more mature growth of Kentuckians For The Commonwealth, which grew out of the mountain people's defense of their land beginning in the early 1980s. The organization began life in the eastern hills as the Kentucky Fair Tax Coalition (KFTC), and its evolution and name change clearly indicate that, in Kentucky, environmental and economic issues are thoroughly intertwined. The systematic rape of the land would not have been possible without the economic victimization of its people. What is impressive about KFTC is that its growth has emanated from its contention that the people it represents do not need an advocate, as prior Appalachian reform efforts have assumed. They speak for themselves.

KFTC traces its origins to fierce flooding that afflicted the eastern counties during the spring and fall of 1977. For years, residents had objected to stripmining, which began in earnest as an alternative to underground mining around 1960, largely due to the shifting economics of coal mining. By the late 1970s, it was becoming the dominant mode of extraction, rising from 13 percent of Kentucky production in 1960 to more than half by 1975, and well over two-thirds in seven counties by 1977.[15] While the environmental impacts of underground mining can be serious, including land subsidence and groundwater contamination (not to mention worker-safety issues), the immediate impact of stripmining is often horrendous. Coal runs through the land in seams of varying depth and length, and stripmining reaches those seams by tearing away the overlying topsoil and vegetation, as well as any other geologic obstacles like clay and gravel. The result can be massive soil erosion, particularly as heavy rains wash down steep slopes, and that soil and clay can clog the very streams and rivers that might otherwise handle the flow of normal loads of sediment. Various studies in the 1970s estimated that active strip mines increased sedimentation from 1,000 to 2,000 times over unstripped forest land.[16] In the worst scenarios, flash floods have swept whole communities before them, costing lives and millions of dollars in property damage.

That is precisely what happened in the Big Sandy valley in April 1977. As residents of the area waited for newly elected President Jimmy Carter to win passage of, and sign, a stripmining regulation bill that Presidents Nixon and Ford had vetoed in earlier years, a major storm hit, dumping nine inches of rain on eastern Kentucky. Coming atop a heavy winter snow melt, the waters quickly stormed out of their clogged banks and flooded all of downtown Harlan and Pineville, and large parts of several other communities. Four people were dead and hundreds were suddenly homeless. Moreover, in the aftermath, people learned that efforts to relocate outside the floodplain were complicated by the fact that most undeveloped land was in the hands of coal companies, which did not want the inconvenience of allowing housing on land they might wish to mine in the future. The companies' unwillingness to alleviate obvious human suffering served to draw attention to the issue of land ownership and control.[17]

As a result, a series of grass-roots community groups began to spring up in small towns in Martin and Harlan counties, which suffered the greatest damage. For the most part, these were "kitchen table" organizations, formed during long, informal conversations over a pot of coffee in someone's home. One of those organizations, in the small Martin County town of Beauty, soon discovered that county officials had applied for a federal Community Development Block Grant (CDBG) to relocate the entire town. Moreover, it had falsely claimed that citizens had participated in development of the grant application in order to meet one of the requirements of federal block grants. The members of the new Concerned Citizens of Martin County, who learned about the CDBG application from a newspaper in Ashland, 50 miles away, began to suspect that the real reason for seeking to relocate the 108 affected families related to plans to mine the land beneath the town.[18] This brush with government by secrecy reinforced another tenet of KFTC and Appalachian organizing: There can be no real environmental protection without real democracy. Citizens would have to demand an end to the nepotism, corruption, and back-room deals that had facilitated the very sorts of environmental calamities they were now trying to prevent.

The Martin County group mustered support against the usual backdrop of intimidation, including local officials who organized their own "Concerned Citizens of Martin County" to confuse the issue. The group even raised money to pay for long-distance phone calls from a supportive local general store so that people who could not afford to make their own calls to federal and state officials could use its telephone. Eventually, the federal Department of Housing and Urban Development issued a notice of disapproval for the block grant.[19]

Spurred by that fight, the citizens group went on to investigate property taxation in the county, finding that coal companies received agricultural tax rates without ever proving they qualified for them. The group demanded and won reassessments. They went further. In the aftermath of the 1977 floods, the time was finally ripe for an alliance of the dozens of local grass-roots groups that had routinely sprouted in the hills since the advent of President Lyndon Johnson's War on Poverty. Many of these groups, for lack of a larger movement to support them, had faded quickly and died. But the floods spurred them to organize the Appalachian Alliance, which in turn organized a Task Force on Land Ownership and Taxation, which succeeded in winning funding from the besieged Appalachian Regional Commission to perform a study of land ownership and taxation. The result was the publication in 1981 of the land-ownership survey of 80 Appalachian counties in six states, largely conducted by grass-roots volunteers organized by the Alliance. For the first time in the region's history, its widespread patterns of wholesale resource exploitation at the expense of local communities were laid bare, yielding many of the examples of tax inequities cited above.[20] Widespread coverage of the survey in newspapers like the *Louisville Courier-Journal* helped to ensure that the study would generate long-term political repercussions.

Joe Szakos, who had worked for a local non-profit housing organization but had become a reporter for the *Martin Countian*, convinced his editor at the newspaper to run the land-ownership study as an extended series. The interest and letters it generated led to a new meeting held in Berea, where a group of activists decided to organize an unnamed coalition around the taxation issue. At a later meeting in Hazard in August 1981, they chose their name: Kentucky Fair Tax Coalition. The Appalachian Alliance, which had hired Szakos, made him available to the infant coalition as an organizer. One of KFTC's first aims was to win passage of a significant tax on unmined minerals, as well as the repeal of a 1979 law that had placed a four-percent cap on annual increases in state revenue, thus ensuring that state services that were already underfunded would remain that way.[21]

The ludicrous 1978 law that reduced the assessment on unmined minerals to one-tenth of one cent per $100 value had been the product of political horse trading between the General Assembly and Governor Julian Carroll, who had wanted to raise the severance tax (the tax charged for coal that is "severed," or removed, from the ground) from 4 to 4.5 percent. But the 1976 General Assembly had directed the Revenue Cabinet,[22] made up of the governor's cabinet officers concerned with revenue matters, to consider the issue of unmined minerals taxation. The Revenue Cabinet turned in a lack-luster performance on the issue, triggering the legislature's decision to lower the rate from its previous, and already low, 31.5 cents per $100 of assessed value.[23] The result was a system in which the owners of coal, who often leased their coal to mining companies, virtually escaped taxation while local communities and school districts were deprived of badly needed revenue.

The new KFTC met in Hazard the first week of January to set its agenda for the 1982 legislative session. (The Kentucky General Assembly meets only in even-numbered years for 60 working days.) It chose three priorities: the unmined-minerals tax; a modest increase in the coal-severance tax; and changes in the revenue-cap bill that would allow the unmined-minerals tax to be treated as new property-tax revenue.[24] Governor John Y. Brown quickly scuttled the second goal by promising to veto any increase in the severance tax.[25]

KFTC quickly refocused on the unmined-minerals tax almost exclusively. The group co-sponsored a January 26 rally with Kentucky Action for Human Needs, which was pushing for greater funding of social services (because of President Reagan's policies of shifting the burden to the states), and KFTC chairperson Gladys Maynard, of Martin County, presented Governor Brown's aide a wooden set of "scales for justice," designed to symbolize the imbalance in the system between the tax burdens of homeowners and those of industry. The scales became both the group's logo and the name of its newspaper. When the original sponsor of the tax-reform bill withdrew, the group quickly signed up two other sponsors who have become stalwart supporters of the KFTC program, Representatives N. Clayton Little and William Donnermeyer.

But the coal industry was about to strike back. In the February issue of the *Kentucky Coal Journal*, an unsigned editorial attacked "an assortment of sap-heads" who were seeking to persuade the legislature to "inflict on this industry an assortment of tax increases that would replace federal budget cuts in other services, enlarge the bureaucracy and enhance the comfort of all Kentuckians from cradle to grave."[26]

If the editorial was a sign of concern, the worries were overblown. Friends of the industry, who included House Speaker Bobby Richardson, a partner in a Glasgow law firm that represented a major mining company, knew how to kill unfriendly legislation. After the House Appropriations and Revenue Committee approved the bill with one dissenting vote, the House Rules Committee, chaired by Richardson, sent it to a slow death in the Agriculture and Small Business Committee. On March 23, about 40 KFTC members descended on Richardson's capitol office and refused to leave. After about an hour, Richardson decided to meet with them. In that 15-minute session, the citizens learned that Richardson knew little about the bill and had made little effort to learn, causing the *Lexington Herald-Leader* to refer to the entire episode as "a sorry spectacle in Frankfort."[27]

While they waited two years for another opportunity, KFTC members adopted another organizing approach on the issue. In Martin County and then elsewhere, they began systematically to challenge underassessments through appeals to the county Board of Assessment Appeals and subsequently to the Kentucky Board of Tax Appeals. Other county chapters followed suit, as citizens engaged the coal companies in a series of legal battles, winning a March 1983 state tax-board decision that held that the companies had to cooperate in providing records of the true extent of their land holdings. Only after the board's chairman resigned, and Governor Brown replaced him with a lawyer with various energy-company ties, did the Board of Tax Appeals reverse course and rule that individual property owners lacked standing to file third-party tax-assessment appeals. Among those individuals were Maynard and the Concerned Citizens of Martin County, whom the board labeled "unhappy people."[28]

The tax battle dragged on with little real headway for KFTC. In 1984, the group released a study showing that the impact of an unmined-minerals tax would be less than claimed by the coal companies, a conclusion backed by the Legislative Research Commission. But in February, KFTC members from six counties filed a federal class-action suit claiming that the unfair tax burden for ordinary Kentuckians violated the U.S. Constitution's Fourteenth Amendment, which guarantees equal protection of the law. House Speaker Pro Tem David Thomason cited the suit as an excuse to table the unmined-minerals tax bill.[29] Two years later, the House Rules Committee again thwarted KFTC by killing a bill that would have clarified the standing of citizens to file third-party tax appeals.[30] Clearly, Kentucky's tax system was more resistant to reform than KFTC leaders had at first envisioned.

It took until March 1988 for KFTC's case, after being rejected in federal court, to make its way to the Kentucky Supreme Court, where a historic ruling held that coal should be taxed no differently from other real property and that the legislature's near exemption of unmined coal was, therefore, unconstitutional.[31] Even that victory, however, required further legal embellishment as the Revenue Cabinet delayed administrative efforts to establish a system for assessing mineral wealth. Two years later, after a judge threatened to take over the assessment program himself, the state finally began to do its job. Finally, in May 1991, Pocahontas-Kentucky, which once had paid $76.05 in taxes on its unmined coal, delivered a check to the Martin County courthouse for $296,000, paying 57 cents per $100 of assessed value.[32]

Win or lose, however, the previously dour Harry Caudill had finally become a happy man. Seeing the newly coordinated activity, Caudill took heart at the change in Kentucky and declared, at the October 16, 1982, KFTC annual meeting that the organization, which had dropped its coalition format and became a grass-roots membership-based group with chapters, "had long been needed."[33] Wendell Berry, a well-known author, social critic, and Kentucky farmer, was later moved to say there had been "nothing like it" in Kentucky's history.[34]

Berry's assessment was never made more true than in the epic political battle over broad-form deeds. KFTC has buried that instrument of exploitation for eternity.

Thanks to the Kentucky Supreme Court, the broad-form deed allowed coal operators who held the mineral rights beneath the sur-

face of another owner's land to extract it "by any method convenient or necessary."[35] While underground mining prevailed, this generally meant that the coal companies drove holes into the sides of
mountains (or shafts downward from the surface). Depending on the
care with which the mining was conducted—always a problematic
matter given the laissez-faire attitudes of state officials—this could
either leave the surface owner relatively safe or lead to subsidence of
the overlying soil and rock strata. Even today, subsidence remains a
problem at abandoned mine sites, especially where long-smoldering
fires have taken hold in remnant coal seams.

But with the advent of large-scale surface mining, with the largest
operations consuming tens of thousands of acres of valleys and hilly
forest lands, the broad-form deed produced a first-class environmental and social-justice wake-up call for Kentucky. Suddenly, for rural
homeowners often caught unaware of the very existence of a broad-
form deed applying to their land, the arrival of any kind of explor-
atory team was the prelude to total dispossession. Once the bulldozers
arrived, free to strip the land to mine coal "by any method convenient or necessary," saving the site for a home was a lost cause. Moreover, the off-site impacts of surface mining, including poisoning
downstream waters with acidic runoff, despoiled more than just the
immediate property on which it was conducted. The sheer tension
produced by these rude awakenings often led to physical confrontations. The newly coined phrase, "You've been broad-formed," had a
distinct ring of obscenity in the ears of most eastern Kentucky hill
people.

One of those people was Mary Jane Adams, until 1976 a Leslie
County housewife with no political pretensions. She and her husband Raleigh were "broad-formed" by the Kentucky–West Virginia
Gas Company, which had decided to drill on their property. Mary
Jane visited a lawyer who told her there was nothing she could do.
On the next visit, she refused to talk to a gas-company official who
parked behind her in her driveway. Instead, she drove around him
and blocked the road below their house while a neighbor pulled in
behind the company car. After some more confrontations, the company sought a restraining order in court, but the part pertaining to
her was lifted when company officials failed to show up for the hear-

ing. Eventually, the company gave up, but Mary Jane Adams did not. Within a few years, she was the vice chairperson of KFTC, visiting the state capital with regularity and lobbying persistently for reform.[36]

Sidney Cornett, of Dwarf in Perry County, returned to his family's land in 1974 after a 20-year stint in the military that included two tours of duty in Vietnam. In that same year, Kentucky passed a new law making the landowner's consent necessary for a stripmining permit, but the Kentucky Supreme Court declared it unconstitutional a year later. Meanwhile, Falcon Coal, which held a broad-form deed, worked out an agreement with Cornett to mine just one seam of coal at the edge of his property. By 1981, however, Falcon sold its permit to Vegas Coals, a local firm operated by a Hazard banker. Alerted by a neighbor one day, Cornett discovered that the firm had stripped between 10 and 15 acres of timber and pastureland well beyond the seam for which it had a permit. Cornett, like Adams, found that direct personal action was more immediately effective than turning to the slow-moving forces of Kentucky law enforcement. A resulting newspaper story led Adams to Cornett, and thus led Cornett to KFTC, generating a new KFTC chapter in Perry County with more than 100 members. Other local property owners, it seemed, were also being "broad-formed."[37]

Ten years and many protests later, Cornett was still fighting for the reclamation of his land. In the spring of 1993, the former chairperson of the Citizens Coal Council[38] was still seeking justice, hoping that the federal Office of Surface Mining (OSM), which is responsible for overseeing state regulatory agencies, would at last respond to his complaints. No one had yet reclaimed his land. The local OSM inspectors, Cornett said, were trying to do their jobs, but somehow the agency itself never followed through.[39]

By 1984, like a series of creeks and streams flowing into a mighty river, the complaints about broad-form deeds reached Frankfort in a torrent that swept the broad-form deed into history. Almost.

The bill said that only the method of mining common at the time the deed was executed could be used. Simply put, no stripmining permit could be issued without the surface owner's consent. Despite signing the legislation, Governor Martha Layne Collins failed to bring her Natural Resources and Environmental Protection Cabinet to heel on meeting the conditions of the law. KFTC soon found a test case to force the issue through the courts. Elizabeth Wooten of Perry County had been seeking to stop Marandco Coal from stripping her property. In April 1985, Judge Calvin Manis ruled in her favor, upholding the constitutionality of the new law, which Marandco had challenged.

Another group of KFTC members successfully sued the cabinet over its failure to enforce the new law, with federal Judge William Bertelsman ruling that mining permits issued in violation of the 1984 law could be invalidated at the landowner's request. On appeal, the Kentucky Supreme Court agreed to consolidate both cases. Two years later, on July 2, 1987, a divided high court overturned the 1984 law—three for, three against, and one judge affirming the ruling without judging the law's constitutionality.[40] For KFTC, it was a declaration of political war.

The advice from Representative Little was that the only route left was to amend the state constitution in a way that no judge could misinterpret. KFTC members were prone to complain of democracy itself being stymied by four old men.[41] The alternative was to place the amendment on the ballot by a two-thirds vote in each chamber of the legislature. Kentucky had become the last bastion of the broad-form deed, which had at one time been in use in several surrounding states. Tennessee, for instance, had already passed the Surface Rights Act, which the Tennessee Supreme Court had upheld.[42] And no other state's courts had interpreted the rights of mineral-rights owners so broadly as had those of Kentucky.

KFTC geared up for the campaign of its organizational life. Herb Smith, a member from Letcher County, organized the Citizens Against Broad-Forming (CAB) Team, whose job was to use direct action to block stripmining wherever the KFTC leadership should send it. It was never mobilized, but it did introduce civil-disobedience principles and training into the organization's repertoire of skills. Members also poured into the capitol to lobby and kept legislators' telephones busy. The full-court press paid off. Both houses referred the measure to the November 1988 statewide ballot on unanimous votes.[43] The new constitutional amendment, stripped of its legal jargon, asked voters whether coal companies should have to reach an agreement with the surface owner before getting a strip-mining permit and whether they should be required to pay for damages their mining caused.

The real campaign had just begun. From fair booths to door knocking, KFTC mobilized its members, and recruited new ones, as never before. The campaign to pass Amendment #2 became the campaign that forged the unity in a statewide organization that had previously engaged its members in a multiplicity of local causes ranging from stopping incinerators to cleaning up local water supplies to appealing unfair taxation. The broad-form-deed campaign forged bonds that have strengthened the organization for the long haul. Members raised money for TV and radio ads and adopted the slogan "Save the Homeplace" to sell the amendment to fellow voters. Supportive journalists and radio announcers helped to produce advertisements. County coordinating committees posted yard signs and staffed phone banks. On election night, KFTC emerged as an acknowledged force in Kentucky politics, an ersatz "third party" as Wendell Berry was wont to put it (to the dismay of some members). The broad-form-deed amendment won the support of 83 percent of Kentucky voters, a smashing repudiation of the state supreme court's obeisance to King Coal.[44] On July 15, 1993, by a 4-to-3 margin, the Kentucky Supreme Court finally bowed to public opinion by upholding the broad-form-deed amendment against the legal challenge by the Lash Coal Company of Virginia, which had charged that the amendment was an unconstitutional taking of private property.[45]

If anything served to add insult to environmental injury in eastern Kentucky, it was the threat of stripmine operators turning unreclaimed pits into garbage dumps. In February 1988, that threat was enough to draw 350 people to the organizing meeting of Greenup Residents Opposed to the Waste Landfill (GROWL). As Janet Brown, one of the organizers, recalled, they also tossed $850 into the hat to launch the new group, which also formed the nucleus of a new county KFTC chapter during the summer. In addition, lawyers in the audience that night volunteered their assistance. "I thought there was some other meeting," Brown said.[46]

The proposal that stirred up a hornet's nest, particularly among

Greenup County's senior citizens, who regularly turned out in force to support GROWL, came from Addington Resources, the state's largest independent coal producer and the owner of Green Valley Environmental Corporation, the applicant for the landfill permit. Addington owned some 22,000 acres in the area. The landfill, planned for 937 acres near the town of Argillite, was actually what has come to be known as a "mega-fill," an unusually large landfill drawing waste from a multi-state area. GROWL wasted little time in contacting KFTC, whose staff suggested ways in which members could research the company and the Addington brothers who owned it. The research soon showed that no state engineer had inspected the proposed site. They also learned that, despite company claims that the landfill would use a synthetic liner to prevent leakage into underlying groundwater, the permit application contained no such provision. Instead, the official plans involved the use of a two-foot clay liner, generally regarded by engineers as more vulnerable to leakage. These concerns were particularly important in light of the fact that several year-round streams flowed through the heart of the lofty site, eventually draining into the Ohio River, as well as the fact that, as in most parts of rural Kentucky, most residents relied on clean groundwater for their drinking water.

Moreover, they learned from a *Louisville Courier-Journal* article that Governor Wallace Wilkinson had received more than $220,000 in campaign donations from the Addingtons and affiliated donors. For GROWL members, the landfill suddenly raised the specter of big money and greased skids. Indeed, that summer Don Harker, director of the state's Division of Waste Management, admitted in a newspaper interview that the permit application was "fast-tracked." (The following year, the day before Thanksgiving, Harker was fired.)[47]

By summer, the state had held an administrative hearing and granted a construction permit. The following March, Green Valley began construction of the landfill, a period that triggered serious annoyance for Becky Harris, another GROWL activist:

> They were stripmining and blasting, cracked the ground, and the septic tank leaked 90 feet down into the water. Our well water. I had bladder surgery over it. We had a meeting with Addington, and they asked how they could help us. I mentioned the fireplace being useless because it was

cracked. They held this over our heads for four months. Robert Addington, the president of the company, said, "Don't worry, we'll take care of all expenses." They offered to buy our house. The Addingtons were running a recycling center and dumping garbage on top of the hill. Addington called after we did a demonstration and said, "You had no business up there, and our offer to buy the house is off."

Harris also complained that trucks occasionally ran her off the narrow landfill road. Meanwhile, according to Brown, Jack T. Baker, the president of Green Valley and Addington's attorney, said that it was a shame that a handful of ladies was keeping a state-of-the-art landfill out of Greenup County. By the fall of 1989, Green Valley had its operating permit from the state. The permitted acreage had grown to 1,665 acres.

The Greenup County controversy became symbolic of the new trend in Kentucky resource management—opening up the state's gaping mine sores for garbage dumps. KFTC attorney Phillip Shepherd filed suit in March 1989 to invalidate the Green Valley permit, and in September filed more suits against both the operating and construction permits. Somehow, over the next few years, GROWL managed to raise tens of thousands of dollars to maintain its lawsuit, including $1,000 from the local Farm Bureau. Meanwhile, GROWL and KFTC members launched a political counterattack against the process that had allowed the permits to be issued. On May 31, a group of 70 mourners showed up at the state capitol in Frankfort to conduct a funeral for Kentucky. As the cortege marched a coffin into the rotunda, members solemnly peeked out from behind black veils, and two KFTC clergymen presided over the ceremony, reading Bible passages and a eulogy. They later went to visit a governor who, they learned, was not available.

In fact, neither Natural Resources and Environmental Protection Cabinet Secretary Carl Bradley nor Governor Wilkinson was available for nearly 18 months from the onset of the GROWL campaign. To "find" Bradley, KFTC members finally decided to distribute "WANTED" posters that described him as "deaf to the calls of citizens" and "blinded to the facts" and blamed him for a rash of permits being granted for the dumping of out-of-state garbage.[48]

Within days, Bradley met with KFTC members. Susan Shoulders, a member from Louisville, gave him a 10-point plan for recycling drawn up by KFTC, with the intent of obviating the need for large dumps or incinerators. But the group's major victory in the case came not on the streets but in court. On November 30, Judge Ray Corns ruled the permits void because the cabinet had not given public notice of its decision and allowed changes in the construction plans without public comment. The decision struck a blow for democratic process in environmental decision making in Kentucky.[49] Little more than a year later, GROWL won again when an appeals court upheld the decision.[50]

Eventually, GROWL's stubborn insistence that any permit be done right brought Green Valley to the negotiating table. GROWL did not completely stop the landfill, but Addington settled for far less than it had originally sought, reaching an agreement with three GROWL plaintiffs and KFTC on September 21, 1992, about five years after it first proposed its project. Starting with a 37-acre section, the company could eventually develop a 138-acre landfill. No longer would it advertise for garbage from throughout the East Coast; it would now serve a 38-county area that included small portions of Ohio and West Virginia. The firm agreed as well to most of what GROWL and KFTC asked, including an extra liner, nine new monitoring wells, and replacement of any damaged drinking water.[51]

Farther south in Lawrence County, two waste projects met a less happy fate at the hands of KFTC activists. The first was an incinerator called PyroChem; the second was a landfill called Roe Creek. Both became object lessons in KFTC's persistent style of people power.

"In 1982, these fellows came into our fiscal court [Kentucky's equivalent of a county board] and said they wanted to build a recycling plant in our county," recalls Patty Wallace, a grandmother turned activist who lives in a country home in Louisa, the Lawrence County seat. "They were going to burn toxic wastes."[52]

It was actually Bruce Short, an engineer who lived across the street from the proposed site in Richardson, on the Martin County border, who learned the nature of the facility through an inquiry to the Natural Resources and Environmental Protection Cabinet. He learned that PyroChem, Inc., based in Louisville, was planning another hazardous-waste incinerator. Short quickly spread the word, and by May 1983 Lawrence County Concerned Citizens was born. It quickly garnered staff and moral support from KFTC's Martin County chapter.[53]

The new group called an open public meeting with PyroChem officials to discuss the facility. PyroChem officials, including company president James Neel, arrived to reassure the crowd. But they failed. Wallace remembers exactly what stirred her deepest suspicions.

"I have a tape of somebody talking to [Neel]," she says. "They asked what they would do if there were an accident. He said it would be handled in an appropriate health-and-safety manner with soap and water. In a few months we knew how little he knew about incinerators."

Wallace's distrust sent her to Louisville to search old clippings at the *Louisville Courier-Journal*. She soon learned, she says, that "Neel had been involved with the Maxie Flats radioactive waste dump near Morehead, Kentucky, and a dump in Sheffield, Illinois, that's now leaking plutonium and radiation. He had a poor track record and moved to different companies." Other KFTC researchers learned that PyroChem's proposal had been turned away by four other Kentucky counties, all of which had zoning ordinances, unlike Lawrence and some other eastern Kentucky counties.[54] She and her friends took their findings to the state Division of Waste Management.

In August 1983, PyroChem announced it would accept job applications. It was a shrewd move, for residents of Lawrence County had been anxious for a new employer to locate there since the coal industry had begun to decline. Applicants lined the streets. There was a catch. To receive a job application, applicants needed to sign a petition supporting the new incinerator and opposing county zoning.

It was the opening bell in a political war designed to drive a wedge through Lawrence County's electorate. Zoning, which had been on the fiscal court's agenda, had never been a popular idea in eastern Kentucky. In the 1985 county elections, PyroChem exploited traditional distrust of such government intervention by aiding candidates who opposed zoning in order to dislodge the county officials who supported zoning, a legal weapon that could be used against

PyroChem. The strategy backfired. Although the incumbents lost, fear of PyroChem won, and the new fiscal court enacted countywide zoning as the lesser of two evils, designating the new proposed incinerator site near Louisa as agricultural and thus not available for heavy industry.[55]

PyroChem fired back. In the summer of 1985, a large delegation of supporters had received encouragement during visits with Governor Martha Layne Collins and her environmental cabinet secretary.[56] Bolstered by apparent state support, PyroChem filed suit in Lawrence Circuit Court to overturn the new zoning ordinance and an ordinance banning hazardous-waste incineration. The court granted a restraining order, which it lifted in May 1987, at the same time that it dismissed the suit. On appeal, PyroChem won an order sending the case back to the lower court to be heard on its merits. On its merits, the lower court upheld the zoning ordinance and rejected PyroChem's claim of discrimination.[57]

But KFTC was never content to let its case rest with the courts. Applying the usual full-court press, KFTC members had by 1986 developed a statewide strategy around toxic-waste issues that included a state law granting local control over hazardous-waste management issues. The bill, which failed to pass in the 1986 session, would give local communities veto power over the siting of facilities like PyroChem. KFTC had taken notice that landfills were not the only new proliferating land use on the Kentucky landscape. Another troublesome facility in Calvert City, on the western end of Kentucky, had already drawn the attention of chemist-activist Paul Connett and a Public Broadcasting System documentary crew.[58] Other companies were now eyeing a state where regulation was loose and zoning sometimes was nonexistent.

By the fall of 1987, the citizen lobbying took its toll on PyroChem's credibility. In November, the state environmental cabinet denied the firm's application to build the incinerator in Lawrence County, partly because it conflicted with local zoning and partly because of the evidence KFTC had mustered on the track record of the company and its president.[59] By the following year, the incinerator was dead. Citizens in a packed room erupted into applause when, in

April 1988, the county fiscal court stood its ground in the face of PyroChem's legal actions and voted to ban the incinerator.[60] Two years later, with the nails already firmly embedded in the coffin, PyroChem finally withdrew its application.[61]

For the Lawrence County Concerned Citizens, however, the victory was just a prelude to another fight. Wallace, who had become the state KFTC chairperson, once again had to postpone any visions of leisurely grandmotherhood to lead an environmental fight. The Roe Creek landfill introduced the group to much more questionable operators in a company called Invesco International. This time, the *Louisville Courier-Journal* took on the task of investigation and discovered what it headlined "environmental 'bad apples.' " Invesco's stripmining record had left a trail of bad memories from Alabama to Indiana. Milton McCarthy, the general counsel for the Alabama Surface Mining Commission, hung the "bad apple" label on the firm. Invesco had mined about 1,500 acres in some two dozen sites between 1972 and 1982, forfeiting a $1.8 million reclamation bond with a bonding company that had itself gone bankrupt. The article detailed, moreover, that the company's unpaid civil fines issued by the federal government totaled $76,700, and it also had never paid $363,000 in abandoned-mine land-reclamation fees. It had forfeited reclamation bonds in West Virginia and elsewhere in Kentucky itself. And in Indiana, where Wallace said the firm stripped Amish farmers' land and left, it had forfeited $2.9 million in reclamation fees that could no longer be collected due to bankrupt bonding firms, and never paid $476,950 for 50 penalties. As a result, the firm was under a nationwide ban for new stripmining permits.

Nonetheless, Kentucky's landfill-permit regulations did not force a background check of the company, which became National Waste, Inc., under a stock buyout. Don Harker, the fired waste-division director who had become a critic of the state's laxness, noted that state law, which did not require a background check in the event of a stock buyout of a firm operating a landfill, had a "loophole big enough to drive a convoy of garbage trucks through."[62]

Forced to rely on vigilance to uncover the truth, Patty Wallace and her niece, Ruth Colvin, hid behind trees to count the trucks entering the landfill and to record their names and numbers. They soon found they were counting asbestos trucks, as that hazardous substance was hauled to the site. The two women did not trust that the numbers of trucks would match the volume of garbage the company said it was receiving. They also did not trust for their own safety; Colvin carried a gun. The women began to film the illegal asbestos dumping, taking their videotapes to state officials. Also, Wallace noted, the *Ashland Daily Independent* published an article accompanied by aerial photos. The women were to appear on an investigative television news show called "Expose" just after the state granted the firm permission to bring automobile fluff (shredded seat material and the like) into the landfill. Finally, again pressed by citizens to respond, the environmental-protection cabinet in April 1991 ordered the Roe Creek landfill closed, charging in part that the company had violated its permit by dumping outside its permitted boundaries.[63]

For Patty Wallace, vindication by the state government, whose officials undoubtedly had once viewed her as a crank, came some 10 years after she first girded for battle against PyroChem. On March 9, 1993, Governor Brereton Jones named her to the Kentucky Environmental Quality Commission (EQC) for a four-year term. The EQC is strictly an advisory body, but the placement of an activist on the council was for KFTC a sign of genuine progress. Its leaders had not always been so welcome.[64]

Moving into its second decade, KFTC was showing other signs of a growing political maturity while maintaining its clear vision. With the passage of Senate Bill 2 in a special 1991 legislative session, it had finally convinced the state to establish a meaningful statewide policy on solid waste. The new law's solid-waste-reduction goal of 25 percent by July 1, 1997, while not as ambitious as those in some other states, at least set Kentucky down a path that contemplated reduced needs for the landfills and incinerators that stirred so much controversy and invited others to turn the state into a cheap dumping ground. Moreover, the law for the first time required local solid-waste plans with which any future projects would have to be consistent. Kentucky, in short, had been dragged into the era of modern environmental planning, and there is good reason to doubt whether it would ever have arrived at that point without the active grass-roots movement that became KFTC.

KFTC, at the same time, was mature enough to reexamine shortcomings in its own origins. The white, often poor, rural Appalachian citizens who had formed its base had accomplished a great deal in making Kentucky a more environmentally and economically progressive place, but the organization realized that it could progress only if it reflected the real diversity of its ideal organizing base. Certainly, the organization had had strong female leadership from the outset, but even a progressive grass-roots coalition could not avoid all the impacts of Kentucky's history of race relations. In Louisville, for example, despite the defeat of a municipal solid-waste incinerator and an emphasis on utility issues among low-income consumers, organizers admitted they had not really achieved an optimal level of involvement within the African-American community.[65] In the spring of 1992, the KFTC board undertook a new program called "Bridges and Barriers" to examine the diversity of backgrounds within its own leadership and seek ways of expanding and diversifying the ethnic, racial, income-level, and gender makeup of the organization. As for its socioeconomic composition, however, its poetic voice, Wendell Berry, seemed unconcerned. In its tenth-anniversary videotape, he praised the organization for its "poverty," which in his view meant that it could be trusted to represent the people of Kentucky.[66]

There remained, however, some corners of the Bluegrass State where environmental law enforcement still bore a resemblance to the Wild West. In Ashland, in the tri-state corner where Ohio, West Virginia, and Kentucky meet along the Ohio River valley, a home-grown company still seemed above the law to most local citizens. Members of the Ohio Valley Environmental Coalition (OVEC) on all sides of the border had complained for years about air pollution from the Ashland Oil Company refinery in Catlettsburg to no avail. At first, they said, company officials tried to discredit them as unemployed and illiterate people who had no idea what they were talking about. When visiting state inspectors learned that the complainants, most of whom were intelligent, working-class women, fit no such welfare stereotypes, the company toned down the criticism. But still nothing happened.

The simple tactic that eventually brought Ashland Oil to heel took root when George Hockley, an engineer in the Ashland branch office of the Kentucky Division of Air Quality (DAQ), visited the hillside home of Barbara Christian, then a telecommunicator for the West Virginia state police, and her husband, a long-haul truck driver. Christian recalls that she became involved in the issue because of continuing health problems and paint damage to their vehicles and their house. In August 1987, she said, "It looked like snow in August, our cars and porches were covered with a white granular substance. We had problems with our skin. We had been having really bad odors that burned our eyes, nose, and throat." Yet calls to the U.S. EPA only drew denials from the company that anything was happening.

As Hockley stood on Christian's porch just over the border in Kenova, West Virginia, he offered a suggestion. He observed that one could do some very good filming from the Christians' vantage point. Barbara needed no further cues. Soon state and federal air-quality officials were receiving dated copies of videotapes to prove that the company's denials were disingenuous.[67] Later, other volunteers would also begin videotaping from hillsides and streets near the refinery. The women involved said they received threatening telephone calls. One of them, Diana Bowen, was shot at on one occasion by two men who hopped out of a two-tone blue car. While she did not dare to turn her camera toward them, her videotape nonetheless captured the shots, one of which took a limb off a nearby tree.[68]

It was soon clear from the films that the plant suffered frequent "upset" conditions in which more than normal emissions erupted from the smokestacks. The question was: What was coming out of the stacks?

According to Dan Kash, the chief of the Ashland DAQ office, Ashland Oil built a reduced-crude conversion system (RCCS) that started up in the spring of 1983. The company injects the boilers with limestone, which reacts with sulfur to allow the company to refine low-grade crude oil. Using the dirty crude that most refineries would not accept required the removal of sizeable quantities of heavy metal pollutants, such as lead and arsenic. One day, Kash recalled, a gigantic white cloud appeared at the top of the RCCS unit, prompting Hockley to observe that "you could walk two miles on it." The problem, Kash said, was that Ashland Oil had built the RCCS with two bypass units that were never listed on its air-quality permit application. Despite this breach of honesty, he noted, the state eventually "codified the fact that they could use those bypass stacks and did nothing about it." Nonetheless, "At first we thought it was a dust." Later Hockley hypothesized that it was actually calcium oxide, a caustic substance used as an industrial alkali.[69]

The suspicious and accumulating medical impacts also began to suggest that the "dust" was not mere dust. Bowen, a human-services worker who suffers from acute bronchitis, knows when the plant is suffering upset conditions. "Upsets over there give me trouble breathing," she said. "Sometimes I have to go to the hospital and have breathing treatments." She also had problems with her eyes. "A couple of years ago they had a bad fallout, and it burned my eyes. I had extensive damage to my eyes. My optometrist said it was a chemical burn." Then she learned about the company's pervasive influence as a major local employer. When she sought his cooperation in providing evidence, "The optometrist said he didn't want to get involved in this."[70]

Barbara Christian's family paid an even higher price, being driven from the area for three years to allow her son to recover from what doctors diagnosed as toxic chromium poisoning. A chromium unit at Ashland Oil had shut down in May 1989. The family's pediatrician, she said, told them it was imperative that they move their son because of his sensitivity to the pollution. Because of his illness, Mark, then 17, was hospitalized while the family rented a home in Huntington, West Virginia, where Barbara took a new job as a secretary at Marshall University. As of the spring of 1993, the Christians had their hilltop home on the market, and Mark, 21, was attending West Virginia University in Morgantown. When he returned home, she said, his nosebleeds started again. "I don't want to live here at all," she concluded.[71]

To support its members' contentions that Ashland Oil's air pollution was excessive and unnecessary, OVEC compared emissions from other refineries across the country, using conservative assumptions that favored the company in order to control for differences in refinery size. It was a classic case of the power of information through public access, for the basis of the study was the federal Toxic Release Inventory information that most manufacturing enterprises must provide to the U.S. EPA. In January 1992, OVEC released its report, showing that Ashland's Catlettsburg refinery compared poorly to other refineries of its size and very poorly to state-of-the-art refineries (an indictment of its unwillingness to modernize its pollution controls) of its size. Virtually across the range of pollutants, Ashland was well above both sets of averages—sometimes by ridiculous margins, such as for benzene, where its emissions were nearly four times the overall average and eight times the average for the state-of-the-art refineries surveyed.[72]

The sacrifices of the members of OVEC did not prove futile. More than 700 local residents had filed damage claims against the company while waiting for the ponderous bureaucracy of the state of Kentucky to respond to the complaints being written in Dan Kash's office. Kash's engineer, George Hockley, moved on, possibly because he had received death threats, the last of which promised to kill his wife and children, according to Kash. Tensions rose as the suits dragged on, for Ashland Oil employs more than 2,500 people in the area, most at its refinery but about 1,000 at its headquarters. By the time one accounts for the secondary economic impacts of such a large labor force, it is not hard to imagine why many citizens feared that the controversy would hurt the community. Thus, when four residents won a $10.3 million jury award in July 1990, others feared they were simply becoming wealthy at the expense of the community's future.[73] Most, however, settled for far less two-and-a-half years later when their lawyers concluded they could no longer sustain the case in the face of mounting expenses and time commitments.[74]

In the end, it was the state's legal action, pushed by vigilant citizens, that forced a settlement. Ashland Oil had operated for years on interim agreements for lack of an air-quality permit. Perhaps recognizing its slipping credibility and the need finally to get a permit, the company swallowed a bitter pill and reached an $8.5 million settlement to resolve outstanding fines and violations and guarantee future compliance.[75] It was the twelfth agreement in 13 years, dating back to 1980. But this time, it included a $7.7 million commitment to environmental improvements in the plant.[76] As part of the settlement, it also agreed to pay for the nation's first state-installed, round-the-clock, in-plant video-monitoring system to track pollution incidents.[77] Equipped with battery packs to keep it operating in the event of a power cutoff, it is wired directly to screens in the Ashland DAQ office, where Dan Kash and his staff can pick up the task that OVEC had begun.[78]

On the surface, it seems hard to argue the case for the existence of environmental racism in Appalachia. The overall damage to all the land and all its people has been so severe for so long that identifying a disproportionate impact on any racial minority seems like an exercise in splitting hairs. Indeed, some Appalachian activists have argued that poor Appalachian whites have been treated as the functional equivalent of "mountain niggers" because of their lack of education and relative powerlessness. While true to an extent, that analogy may also miss a crucial element in the dynamic of racism. The use of such insulting phrases as "white trash" has always carried the implication that racism maintained its hold on the rural South by enforcing a strict caste system within the white community. In order to hold a man down in the gutter, Booker T. Washington once said, you have to crawl in there with him.

The history of the mining camps do provide evidence that some men were held in the gutter on the basis of race. Certainly, it is clear that coal-mine employers, like those in many other turn-of-the-century industries, often exploited racial differences in the makeup of their workforce as a convenient, though not always successful, union-busting tactic. Still, historian Crandall Shiflett has noted that, considering the urgent need for labor during boom periods in the industry's recurrent boom-and-bust cycles, it is unsurprising that employers aggressively recruited both immigrants and southern African-Americans to work in the mines. The latter, who constituted overall about 10 percent of the coal-mining workforce, generally found coal mining a better-paying alternative to the grinding poverty of sharecropping. But they also tended to be assigned to the dirtiest, hottest, and toughest jobs in the coal camps, particularly the coke ovens, where they often were the majority of the workforce.[79]

During World War I, a concentration of chemical industries began to emerge in the Kanawha River valley in central West Virginia, capitalizing on advances in synthetic chemistry and the local abundance of raw materials. The war provided the initial impetus because Germany had been a key supplier of chemicals. The Union Carbide Corporation established early roots in the area, building the nation's first petrochemical plant near Institute in 1920. During World War II, the federal government built a synthetic rubber plant in Institute, which it afterward sold to Union Carbide, creating the primary base of the current facility. By the mid-1980s, Union Carbide ranked as one of the state's major employers with a payroll of 7,000 people. Other companies that built chemical plants in the area include DuPont, FMC, and Occidental.

Unfortunately, as the company built its empire in the state, it demonstrated the same lack of concern for human life that had plagued the coal industry. The most dramatic illustration of this callousness occurred during the construction of the Hawk's Nest Tunnel, part of an effort to develop hydroelectric power along the New River for a new metallurgical complex in Alloy, about 30 miles southeast of Charleston. During construction, which was contracted to the Virginia firm of Dennis and Rinehart, the company discovered a high-content silica deposit and expanded the size of the tunnel, mining the silica for its nearby plant. But the entire project proceeded on a hurried schedule, starting in 1930 and reaching completion within a year and a half. The mining, it seems, was illegal and never properly reported to federal authorities, and Union Carbide also feared that federal authorities would block construction of the hydroelectric facility unless the company presented a *fait accompli*. (Indeed, after a 30-year legal battle, the Federal Power Commission won a case against the company, retaining the right to buy the complex.)

Union Carbide's haste made human waste. Despite the fact that medical science had established a link between silica dust and silicosis more than two generations earlier, many of the most obvious known safety precautions, like wet drilling to control dust or the use of respirators, were often ignored. There was also obvious racial discrimination, with African-Americans comprising nearly three-quarters of those who worked strictly inside the tunnel, where the highest occupational exposures occurred. In contrast, the outside-only workers were about evenly divided. The human toll was predictable, resulting in a congressional investigation in 1936. Depending on the source used, anywhere from 65 to 2,000 of the men eventually died of silicosis. Pinning down the numbers is problematic both because of sloppy company records and the fact that all documents became the exclusive property of Union Carbide in an out-of-court settlement. (Union Carbide had shielded itself from liability in the construction contract). High turnover and the rapid dispersal of a temporary workforce helped to skew the body count in the company's favor. White plaintiffs who had sued the contractor received a maximum settlement of $1,000 apiece, and African-American workers generally received considerably less.[80]

It is against that historical backdrop that the case can be made for the existence of environmental racism in Institute, West Virginia. In the heart of the Kanawha River valley six miles west of Charleston, this small unincorporated town of 1,500 people has hosted Union Carbide's U.S. equivalent of its Bhopal, India, pesticide plant, whose leak of methyl isocyanate (MIC) gas killed somewhere between 2,000 and 10,000 residents in December 1984.

Institute just happens to have a predominantly African-American population and the state's only historically African-American institution of higher education, West Virginia State College. It also sits at the bottom of a valley surrounded by steep mountains with limited access from the outside. Many of the homes are frighteningly close to the plant boundaries, so close that local activist Mildred Holt wondered whether the company "would have done this in a white neighborhood. Maybe a poor white neighborhood, but not one of affluence."[81] Many residents are elderly, and the town also hosts the West Virginia Rehabilitation Center, which houses a number of physically disabled persons. A Bhopal-type leak would unquestionably produce massive human tragedy. After first reassuring India that its plant had all the safety features of the U.S. plant, Union Carbide's response to American concerns was, in effect, to say that it can't happen here.[82] "Our employees have been manufacturing MIC in an effective and safe manner for 17 years," plant manager Hank Karawan told an outdoor press conference on December 11, 1984.[83] The year after the Bhopal disaster, it almost happened here.

In the immediate aftermath of Bhopal, Union Carbide shut down its MIC unit in Institute and installed a $5 million safety system. It reopened after federal inspectors declared it safe. But on the Sunday morning of August 11, 1985, a plume of poison gas escaped over the skies of Institute and sent 135 people to the hospital. The gas was aldicarb oxime, used in the production of Temik, a pesticide used on potatoes and other crops.[84] It was a pesticide that already had a history of regulatory sanctions because of groundwater contamination in the farmlands of Wisconsin, Florida, and Long Island.[85] Now a 15-minute leak was sending local residents into spasms of breathlessness, burning their eyes, and producing headaches, nausea, and dizziness. Some 500 gallons of the material in a tank had overheated, causing three gaskets to fail and allowing the gas to escape.[86] Because of shortcomings in the new safety system, it was twenty minutes after the leak began before company officials notified the public of an emergency. By that time, sirens were wailing and the ambulances were arriving. Later, a U.S. EPA investigation would show that this had been actually the sixty-first such leak in the past five years, the others ranging from one to more than ten pounds.[87]

Bhopal alone had been sufficient to spur the creation of a new organization in Institute called People Concerned About MIC, led by Edwin Hoffman, a history professor at the college who later moved to California. The group had laid out three simple goals: organizing the community; establishing evacuation routes; and getting a reliable alarm system. One week after the accident, more than 300 protesters marched against the plant, demanding the truth about earlier assurances that such an accident would not happen.

Union Carbide officials responded with some familiar bromides that just would not sell any longer. Karawan found "no reason to believe there will be any long-term damage from the exposure." Union Carbide CEO Warren Anderson, who had been sent packing by Indian officials when he tried to visit their country after the Bhopal accident, tried to be more philosophical but sounded inane: "Someone has sold the bill of goods that this is a zero-risk world. . . . I doubt that you could get the pencil introduced in the market today." And supportive politicians came to the company's defense. Kanawha County Commissioner E. Douglas Stump opined that there were "two ways to die in this valley, chemical or starvation. Starvation is a slow process."[88]

Stump's hyperbolic approach to the issue had dominated the state's environmental discussion for a long time. With high unemployment and frequently poor education levels, West Virginia had long been one of the states prone to sigh, "Thank God for Mississippi," whenever it avoided ranking fiftieth on a key statistic.

But the discussion reached a turning point at a meeting of People Concerned About MIC to which Hoffman had invited Robert Kennedy, the president of Union Carbide Plastics and Chemicals Company, a Union Carbide subsidiary. Kennedy listened with reddening face as speaker after speaker harangued the company.

One speaker noted that the birds "stopped singing on Sunday morning" and only returned on Wednesday after the leak. Another told Kennedy and the company simply to "get out." Cheryl Whiteside, a white resident who was two months pregnant, complained that she had called "everywhere to find out the long-term effects" and could not get any information. She said she had been reassured that the gas was only a Class-I chemical, only to learn later that it was actually a far more dangerous Class-IV chemical. After listening to other emotional testimony, Kennedy finally responded.

"We can shut down," he announced. "It would in some ways be simpler for us to cut our economic losses . . . and walk away from the terrible publicity we have received. . . . I don't think we're an organization of quitters. I don't think we want to admit that we can't manage our affairs. . . . That's why we shouldn't shut down. If we don't make those chemicals, someone else will."

Then, drifting off into an anecdote whose point was not immediately clear, he said, "I had a dog who bit a mailman once. . . ."

"We don't care about your dog," a Union Carbide employee yelled from the back of the audience. Standing to shout and pointing at

Kennedy amid enthusiastic applause, he announced his payroll number and said, "You can have it if you want. I'm not going to quit. I'm
going to make sure you hold to those safety rules."

Clearly, whatever solid wall of labor silence Union Carbide had
been able to enforce previously had begun to crack. It had lost the
community's trust. One African-American woman crystallized that
anger when she told interviewers during the taping of a PBS documentary, "They killed the Indians. Now they're killing the hillbillies."[89]

Previously, union members' fears about protecting their jobs had
been a major deterrent to community organizing around safety issues. Many residents, if not employed at the plant, at least had relatives or friends who worked there. But as worker-safety and
community-safety issues began to converge, a new cooperation
emerged. Mildred Holt and Pamela Nixon, two leaders of People
Concerned who became involved in lobbying at the state capitol on
clean-air issues, noted that they increasingly found themselves in
tune with lobbyists for the steelworkers, the AFL-CIO, and the International Association of Machinists, which represented the Union
Carbide workers. On the fifth anniversary of the Bhopal disaster,
Nixon proudly noted, she was an invited speaker at a rally in Charleston hosted by the state's labor unions.[90]

The new cooperation helped People Concerned advance its
agenda, but the problems facing Institute have been much too tick-
lish to yield to easy solutions. Despite Kennedy's bravado at the
organization's public forum, Union Carbide had been looking for a
buyer for its Institute facility and found one. French chemical conglomerate Rhone-Poulenc acquired the company's agricultural-
chemicals division, although Union Carbide retained ownership of
some units within the Institute plant. Despite new management, the
challenges remained.

As far back as 1952, the Kanawha Valley Emergency Planning
Council had been organized. Until the emergence of People Concerned, it had functioned as the only organizational voice for concerned citizens in the vicinity of Institute. It had never, however,
been able to organize a test drill to see whether, in fact, it was feasible to evacuate the community in the event of a major accident.

Finally, in April 1988, under pressure from community groups, county emergency officials staged a drill that satisfied no one.

Residents say the alarms went off 15 minutes late. The wrong alarm went off—the fire alarm rather than the evacuation alarm. Despite the need to test whether a crowded campus could be evacuated during school hours, the college canceled classes for the day. School buses were already parked at nearby Shawnee Park waiting for the drill, an unlikely contingency in the event of a real emergency. The potential for panic during an evacuation along the town's few clogged arteries prompted discussion of "sheltering in place" as an alternative to fleeing the community.[91]

While People Concerned ridiculed the inadequacies of the long-awaited drill, the potential for disaster remained no laughing matter. On a slow Saturday morning that August, the roar of an explosion ripped through the town, which awoke to 25-foot flames leaping into the air. Hearing no warning sirens, Estella Chandler, a professor who teaches architectural technology at the college, called both the plant switchboard and 911 only to be told that the "minor emergency" did not affect the community. But outside her window, people were already scrambling to find a way out of town. By the time the company decided to share information about the incident with the public, the national news media had had enough time to reach Institute once more.[92]

One push by the residents did result in a strange sort of partial victory. People Concerned member William Anderson said that the group "had to prevail on the highway department to build ramps, some kind of ramps," to facilitate evacuation from Route 25, the main route through the community, to Interstate 64. There is only one ramp from Institute to the interstate—and it leads past the very plant whose fumes people would be trying to escape. When the highway department relented, it created a new emergency ramp from one back road to the interstate, but barred it for normal use with a locked gate. In the event of an emergency, someone from the maintenance department must arrive to open the gate.[93]

Still, the Institute activists have helped to generate real change. Plants throughout the Kanawha Valley have spent millions of dollars to upgrade safety and warning systems. Political attitudes have begun to change, even in subtle ways. Drawing some connections to larger issues of the end use of Rhone-Poulenc's products, People Concerned members told me that they no longer "automatically start spraying or powdering our vegetables." Their gardens, it seems, have become organic.[94]

The change in West Virginia is coming about, said Norm Steenstra, because People Concerned About MIC is a microcosm of a new awareness across the state. Steenstra is the executive director of the West Virginia Citizen Action Group (WVCAG), a Ralph Nader-inspired advocacy group launched in the 1970s. When I interviewed him at the basically furnished WVCAG office in Charleston in the summer of 1991, he noted that only three staff people were working on salary for citizen groups in West Virginia.

Nonetheless, he noted, "Maybe because we started later as an environmental group, we have had some success in blending collars. We have tried to get this coalition to be broad, cutting across group lines, class lines, and race lines."

There was another element adding to the citizen coalition in West Virginia. "In every county in this state during the mid-1970s to the mid-1980s, hippies moved down. Many are artisans or subsistence farmers. They are educated, yet they live in these rural areas and have become the core of citizen activism on rural issues. We have two goat farmers on our board and some housewives. . . ."

One of those housewives is Martha Huffman of New Martinsville. Actually, she is fondly known as the "housewife from hell," a nickname that has started to attach to other Appalachian women who have empowered their communities. In Martha's case, the issue is little different from the one that empowered numerous angry women across Kentucky—garbage. Like Kentucky, West Virginia became the target of garbage haulers seeking cheap land and lenient regulations to establish landfills that could host a lucrative business in fugitive East Coast trash.[95]

Huffman, who became a full-time activist in her fight to block out-of-state garbage in New Martinsville, succeeded in leading her newly organized Halt Out-of-state Garbage (HOG) to victory on fronts that West Virginia's good old boys had never even contemplated as likely battlefields. Two of three county commissioners were defeated as a consequence of their willingness to host the expanded landfill, purchased by a Pennsylvania firm. A new environmental candidate won the mayor's office by a landslide. And Wetzel County wrote stiff new landfill regulations in a state that had no state landfill inspectors when Huffman launched her crusade. The regulations pushed the state to follow suit. Huffman herself was appointed to the county waste authority, only to become president of the West Virginia Association of Solid Waste Authorities.

The mother of two girls and wife of a chemical engineer became a model for dozens of "housewives from hell" throughout West Virginia and Appalachia in the fight for control over the flow of waste into landfills and incinerators. To the east, for instance, Faith Reilly of Berkeley County led blue-collar resistance to the Chambers landfill in West Virginia's Eastern Panhandle. It is all part of Norm Steenstra's environmental vision of a patchwork hillbilly quilt: "Get the garbage crazies working with the coal crazies working with the air toxics crazies and Save the Mountain." Together, the housewives, the blue-collar workers, and what Steenstra likes to call the "grey collars" in what he also likes to call a "no-collar" movement have pushed the state to pass some remarkable legislation, including a ban on incinerators and a law that allows citizens to petition for a referendum to overturn landfill approvals granted by county commissions or solid-waste authorities—the very entities Huffman represented.[96]

Once stifled by the relentless need for jobs in a region of grinding poverty, environmental politics underwent rapid change in Appalachia and the rural South throughout the 1980s. As a new century approaches, old-style politicians will find it increasingly difficult to rely on economic blackmail to silence the growing movement for change. Though the strength of the grass-roots environmental movement remains spotty, it has built sizeable pockets of great strength where old arguments against the new environmental ethic will no longer sell.

It was North Carolina that hosted the nation's first major civil-disobedience action by African-Americans and other minority activists against what they deemed environmental racism. The year was 1982. The target was a PCB landfill slated for predominantly African-American Warren County. The issue was not merely the

fact that the county happened to have a low-income, minority-domi-
nated population, but the fact that all evidence pointed to its selection on that basis. U.S. EPA regulations required that the bottom of
such a landfill be at least 50 feet above groundwater. State officials
chose a site that would lie just seven feet above groundwater with
permeable soil instead of clay.[97]

The persistent protests in Warren County, though they failed to
block the PCB dump, acted as a trigger to ignite the environmental
movement among people of color in North Carolina and the Deep
South. Bill Holman, a lobbyist for the Conservation Council of
North Carolina, credits that uprising and the increasingly visible protests of other blue-collar and minority groups across the state with
shocking an otherwise complacent legislature and state government
and turning the tide toward pollution prevention instead of landfills
as the solution to the state's hazardous-waste problems. Many of these
people were from rural areas whose legislators had not previously
voiced environmental concerns. But as GSX Corporation sought to
build a hazardous-waste treatment facility in Scott County, it inad-
vertently activated a tri-racial environmental coalition of Lumbee
Indians, African-Americans, and whites. Another hazardous-waste
proposal triggered a public reaction that made Anson County's state
representative a leader in the fight for pollution-prevention programs.[98] Radioactive-waste storage activated constituencies in the
western mountains.[99] In the span of a decade, a state whose environmental officials had effectively envisioned it as a dumping ground
has spawned a grass-roots network so powerful and so insistent on its
pollution-prevention goals that the North Carolina Waste Awareness and Reduction Network (NC-WARN) has literally chased a
German incinerator company, ThermalKEM, Inc., back and forth
across the state in its futile attempt to find a welcome sign for its
operations. While it strives patiently to persuade the state that there
is a better way, NC-WARN pumps out a steady stream of analyses of
how that better way might work.[100]

In short, due to the rainbow environmental coalition that
sprouted from the once-powerless grass roots during the 1980s, environmental politics in Appalachia and the Deep South will never be
the same again.

INDIAN COUNTRY

Defending
Mother Earth

In the years following World War II, a government-sponsored energy boom swept the Colorado Plateau. Throughout the hills and mesas stretching from the Four Corners area, where the states of Colorado, New Mexico, Utah, and Arizona meet at the northeastern edge of the Navajo Nation, north to Grand Junction, where the Uncompaghre River meets the Colorado, hundreds of small uranium mines punctured the sides of mountains in a lucrative quest to feed the new atomic monster created by the Cold War. There was only one buyer for the product, the U.S. Atomic Energy Commission (AEC). But there were dozens of resourceful entrepreneurs and prospectors who made and lost fortunes extracting the raw material the AEC needed for bombs and nuclear power plants.[1]

The fortunes were reserved for those who truly understood the significance of uranium in the post-war world, and who had the moxie and the venture capital to engage in finding and developing it. Inevitably, these people, and the companies they created or financed, needed an army of workers whose primary concern was feeding families and, if they were lucky, making an education possible for their children. Living in hastily constructed mining camps, these workers lived at the base of the mountains, sometimes hiking to work if the terrain was too rugged for vehicles or if, like many Navajos, they simply did not own one. Many would hike up steep mountain-sides two, or three, or even five miles from their camp homes. At their busiest, the mines ran three shifts, so that some men were finding their way down the hills in the dark of night.

Phillip Harrison, Jr., grew up in the mining camps in the 1960s. His father, one of perhaps 3,000 Navajos recruited to work in the uranium mines beginning in the late 1930s, worked in southeastern Utah at the Mesa One mine, one of the largest in the area. Many of the Navajos were desperate for work, having reluctantly entered the white man's world of wage labor. Once proud sheepherders, many had become surplus pastoral labor in the course of the federal government's efforts to reduce the Navajos' grazing herds during the 1930s and 1940s. The stock-reduction plan had arisen from Bureau of Indian Affairs (BIA) fears that Navajo overgrazing was damaging the land and leading to massive soil erosion. But the Navajo shepherds had nowhere else to go—until the mines came along.[2]

In his earliest years, Harrison recalled, he lived in the camps with his family, in worker-built housing constructed of Celotex with corrugated metal for a roof atop a wooden frame. In other camps, whole families lived in tents. The mining companies, he said, often built sturdier company housing elsewhere for the Anglos, particularly the company brass, but the Navajos were left to fend for themselves. "It was a shack, actually," Harrison said. "As long as it had a roof, that's what counted."[3]

Now in his forties, Harrison retains photographs taken during his childhood, showing the adit blown into the side of the mountain. Small steel carts carried workers inside the opening to their worksites.

The company blasted holes in the mountain and extracted the uranium through the horizontal shaft. Workers often were sent into the mines, he recalled, just minutes after the company dynamited a new section, when the air was still thick with what he now knows was radioactive dust. Although respirators were available in some other mines, the Navajos never enjoyed the benefit of such equipment. They were expendable, he says now.

Never having been apprised of the dangers of the dust, the workers ate their lunch in it, and, often lacking showers, wore their work clothes on the way home, where wives and children hugged them and washed those uniforms with the rest of the family clothing.

Later, however, Harrison spent only his summers in the camps. The rest of the year, he lived away from his struggling family, attending a boarding school. His father, he says, worked hard to ensure that his children would be able to make a good life for themselves. "Our family was fortunate enough to finish school," he said in his modest office at Harrison Construction Company, the firm he owns in Shiprock, New Mexico, on the Navajo reservation. He earns a precarious living because, in addition to his occupation, Harrison has a lifelong preoccupation.

He wants justice for the men who worked in the uranium mines and mills, and for their families. "There was no justice for those men," he declared softly. "They thought they were doing a favor for their country." At the peak of the Cold War, supplying fuel for the nation's defense seemed a high calling. Some of the miners were veterans of World War II, including Navajos who had constituted the famous Code Talkers units in the Marines. Speaking in a code within the Navajo language, a tongue virtually unknown to Japanese cryptographers, theirs was the only code the Japanese never broke during the war. One Marine signal officer credited these proud men with American success in taking Iwo Jima.[4]

Harrison's own father left him too soon. In 1971, lung cancer reduced him from a strong man, five feet, eight inches tall and weighing 160 pounds, to "nothing but skin and bones." When he died after a struggle of several months, he weighed just 80 pounds. As a young man still completing his education, Phil Harrison watched his father shrivel and die before his eyes. Afterward, Harrison was determined to complete the education his father had desired for him.

It took several years before he realized that what had happened to his own father was happening not only to other relatives—he now counts five uncles as victims—but also to hundreds of other families throughout the Four Corners area of the Navajo Nation. By the early 1980s, it became a cause, and Harrison formed the Uranium Radiation Victims Committee to fight for compensation for the dying men and their families. In a struggle that has lasted more than a decade, Harrison has learned much that he never wanted to know about the quality of justice for Native Americans and workers in America.

He has learned that the government understood the impacts of radiation exposure long before it finally required the mining companies to take preventive measures. As early as 1949, Ralph Batie, chief of Health and Safety for the AEC's Colorado Raw Materials Division, was fighting a lonely bureaucratic battle to win attention for ventilation and exposure problems in the relatively new western uranium mines. With the help of Duncan Holaday, an industrial hygienist with the Public Health Service, he sounded the alarm about repeating the "European experience," where extensive studies that documented the adverse health impacts of uranium mining dated back to the 1920s. Hundreds of miners in the Erz Mountains of Germany and Czechoslovakia had died from lung cancer induced by exposure to radon in the course of extracting pitchblende, the most common form of uranium ore. Area residents were aware of the disease, although not of its cause, as early as the 1500s.[5] In 1952, a U.S. Public Health Service report noted that the European studies had found that 50 to 70 percent of all workers in those mines had died of some variety of respiratory cancer. Federal inspectors concluded on three separate occasions that the mines in the Four Corners area needed better ventilation because of hazardous levels of radon gas.[6] Despite the alarms, and the fact that the AEC could easily have mandated safety precautions and even paid for them, mining companies largely refused to install ventilation equipment unless mandated, and nothing was done.[7] One Navajo supervisor indicated later that, in his training to become a foreman, he had been informed about the dangers of radiation but was instructed not to share that information with the workers he was supervising.[8] Only in 1969, with the advent of the federal Mine Safety and Health Administration, did the Navajo workers finally begin to receive protective equipment and the benefit of ventilation.[9]

The process of uncovering and fighting such blatant injustice has been more than depressing for Harrison. It has been a long-term strain on his family and on his small business, which builds affordable homes for Navajos. Harrison Construction operates out of modest quarters in an inauspicious building near an old bridge that spans the San Juan River. The building also houses a law firm that represents many Navajo miners. Harrison probably spends as much time interviewing and assisting miners as he does managing his business.

Despite the hardships and the financial burdens, he has a special motivation. "My family often asks, 'Why are you doing this to yourself? You're running yourself down,' " he noted. Death is not an easy topic for Navajos, who traditionally abandoned a hogan, their earthen home, when someone died inside, in order to avoid the contamination of death. Those traditional beliefs are still strong and have served as a barrier to discussing the plague that has affected the uranium miners, many of whom still attribute their illnesses to spiritual imbalances. But when Harrison gets depressed, he thinks about his father, and the anger burns inside him.

"They killed my father and my relatives," he said. "I lost my father 22 years ago. It won't happen again. I don't want this to happen again to anybody. These guys work 20 years to provide clothing and school for their kids, and yet they did not know this was killing them."

Harrison now travels to lobby for the former Navajo miners and to speak to other Indian nations whose lands are threatened by potential uranium mining, to tell them of the plague that has afflicted the Navajo Nation. As we discussed his plans in the spring of 1993, he was prepared to travel to Washington, D.C., to meet with officials of the U.S. Justice Department. He also had airline tickets for a trip to Saskatoon to speak to what he called the Northern Dené, Athabaskan tribes whom anthropologists have linked to the Navajos and Apaches of the American Southwest.[10] Uranium has been found on Indian lands in western Canada. To combat the preoccupation with death that this activist burden entails, Harrison carries a traditional Navajo herb, sage, for the purpose of having ceremonies conducted to purify his soul of this contamination.

"The elders say the uranium should not have been mined, it should have been left alone," he noted. "They woke up the monster in the rocks."[11]

Harrison's meagerly funded, ragtag band of seekers after justice is no longer fighting alone. In 1990, they won a major victory when the U.S. Congress enacted the Radiation Exposure Compensation Act (RECA), in which the federal government formally apologized not only to the Navajo miners but to the "downwinders," those people in places like southern Utah who lived in the path of the atmospheric fallout from nuclear bomb tests in the Nevada desert. Many of these people also developed patterns of lung cancer despite the predominance of a Mormon population whose vices had never included smoking. The act provided for "compassionate payments" to both groups up to a maximum of $100,000 per person.

About 100 miles south of Shiprock, another Navajo community has paid a high price for the nation's cavalier dalliance with nuclear power. On July 16, 1979, just a few months after the nation's attention was riveted by the accident at the Three Mile Island nuclear plant in Pennsylvania, a much larger radiation release occurred near Church Rock when an earthen dam collapsed near the United Nuclear Corporation (UNC) mill. Into the Rio Puerco flowed 94 million gallons of radioactively contaminated materials and toxic chemicals, poisoning the river for more than 100 miles downstream into Arizona.[12] One Navajo woman and some animals wading in the water when the putrid yellow flood rushed by developed burns on their legs and later died. Environmentalists pointed fingers at New Mexico state officials, who denied responsibility, though the Southwest Research and Information Center (SRIC) reported that the license for the facility may have been granted hurriedly to beat the effective date of new state groundwater regulations.[13] In any event, some 10,000 Navajo residents of the valley lost all use of the Rio Puerco as signs were posted in Navajo, English, and Spanish warning of the dangers of allowing humans or animals to drink the water.[14] Even that notice may have been problematic for some because the Navajo language contains no word for radiation.[15] Ten years later, the U.S. Geological Survey was still finding radiation levels up to 100 times the maximum allowable level under Arizona regulations, which were stricter than those in force in New Mexico.[16] In the meantime, residents had to seek alternate sources of water to supplement the inadequate supplies from UNC and the tribe. With the help of both SRIC and DNA–People's Legal Services, a Navajo legal-aid group, they sued and won an out-of-court settlement for $525,000 in Benally v. UNC.[17]

Today, another Benally activist, Timothy Benally, works in Shiprock, the site of a giant covered pile of uranium mill tailings from the nearby mill that once processed uranium from Four Corners mines. He is the director of the Office of Navajo Uranium Workers, which helps former uranium workers apply for federal compensation under the terms of RECA. Despite the promise of that legislation, won after years of struggle and the insistent persuasion of skeptical members of Congress, the regulations implementing it have erected new obstacles to justice. The office Benally heads was created by the Navajo Nation in 1990 when it anticipated the passage of RECA. It has five functions: recordkeeping, developing legal records—and medical records—for the miners, arranging for medical services, and researching the history of families of affected uranium workers. Its services are free to Navajo people.

As of May 1993, according to Benally, the office had registered almost 2,000 former uranium miners, though "documents that we see say that we probably had some 3,000 uranium workers from 1947 to 1971," when the last mine closed. But identifying the workers is only the beginning of the task. In order to help them (or their widows or children) qualify for the benefits, which have a $100,000 ceiling, the office must establish a dossier that includes work records, the nature of the exposure, and medical records documenting that the worker suffers from one of the specific respiratory or related diseases listed in RECA. For many, particularly illiterate or poorly educated Navajos who may not have kept pay stubs dating back more than 40 years, these can be daunting obstacles. Old medical records that became inactive often have disappeared. Public Health Service records transferred to storage centers can take months or years to retrieve, according to Benally.

For miners' families, matters can be even more complicated, for the regulations also require proof of marriage. Many older Navajos have no such proof because they were married in traditional ceremonies involving the use of witnesses and wedding baskets but no written records. Marriage licenses were not legally required for Navajo marriages until 1958; only recently, the tribe passed new legislation providing for the legitimation of traditional unlicensed marriages if the family could provide witnesses. But, Benally notes, "Whether the government recognizes that, we don't know yet."

Benally readily admits that the whole process, which will probably exclude many sick and dying Navajo miners from ever receiving the benefits they were promised, "gets depressing. Sometimes it seems hopeless to pursue what they want us to pursue." So the office has been forced to pursue political routes, meeting with the Navajo and Arizona congressional delegations to seek ways to liberalize the regulations before time runs out.[18]

To its credit, Navajo government had been raising the issue of uranium mill-tailings impacts as well for several years in the face of a fair amount of congressional and U.S. EPA indifference. Navajos, after all, not only had to contain the mill-tailings pile that was left on the ground in Shiprock near the San Juan River, but many also had to live with the contamination at home. Unaware and uninformed about the long-term radiation hazards, many had used the tailings and mine wastes over the years as a cheap source of building materials in their homes. Approximately 220 acres of land in the Four Corners region were contaminated by mill tailings.[19] Despite the passage in 1978 of the Uranium Mill Tailings Radiation Control Act, the Navajo Nation in the 1980s was forced to plead with Congress for additional funds to undo the continuing health damage this was doing to Navajo families, especially children.[20]

The Office of Navajo Uranium Workers faces the unenviable task of trying to document those family exposures that in turn caused more needless deaths and suffering. But it has at least lifted part of one burden from Harrison's shoulders. Before 1990, before RECA and the creation of the office, Harrison's committee had lobbied virtually alone for justice for a constituency that was often too sick, too poor, and too isolated in rural communities to speak for itself.[21] In spite of those hurdles and the Bush administration's opposition to the compensation bill, the committee helped win the passage of RECA.[22] Now it lobbies for liberalization of the regulations that implement RECA. It also has taken on another unenviable task— amending RECA to include the uranium millers, left out of the law, who often suffered equal or greater exposure in the mills where the mined uranium ore was processed. Other groups, such as the World Uranium Hearing and the Southwest Indigenous Uranium Forum, are also beginning to organize Indian miners from Laguna Pueblo, according to Chellis Glendinning, a Santa Fe psychologist, author, and activist on uranium issues. The Laguna workers were not covered because the Jackpile-Paguate mine is an open pit, and the law covers only underground miners.[23]

Meanwhile, Harrison's committee continues to educate and organize around the other impacts of the uranium fiasco. Harrison himself was recently elected vice president of the local Red Valley chapter of the Navajo Nation. (Chapters are the local organizational unit of the Navajo Nation.) In that capacity, Harrison worries about the social damage the entire affair has caused to a traditional community. The deaths of hundreds of miners, Harrison said, has depleted the local villages of a supply of elders to guide the training of the young. With widows heading poverty-level households, too many young, he says, lack adequate guidance and become delinquent. A whole generation of leadership is sick or dying, and the leadership of the chapters in the Four Corners area has fallen prematurely to men of his age when they should be raising the next generation. In social terms, the impacts of this ordeal are being visited on future generations and on the future of the Navajo Nation itself.[24]

In the face of despair, however, there are positive impacts. If environmental democracy is blossoming in Navajo country, it is due in large part to Harrison's pioneering role model. Susan Dawson, a sociologist at Utah State University who has interviewed and written about the Navajo miners, noted that the challenges in organizing such a constituency on the Navajo reservation seem enormous. There are only 2,000 miles of paved roads on a reservation the size of West Virginia.[25] Three-fourths of Navajo homes lack telephones. Access to newspapers is sometimes limited. Yet one meeting she attended at a chapter house drew more than 300 people, who sat outside for most of the day. Obviously anticipating a crowd, she noted, the organizers had set up a public-address system outside the chapter house before the people ever arrived.

Perry Charley, a Navajo activist who now heads the tribe's Abandoned Mines Program, shared the secret with her. "You must use the radio," he told her. "Every house has a radio."[26] Indeed, the visitor to the Shiprock area who tunes in to bilingual Navajo radio will notice such announcements throughout the day, whether or not he or she understands Navajo. After a long, dark history of secrecy and deceit, grass-roots environmental democracy is in the air.

Democracy has been missing from Native American affairs in the United States for a long time, but not because it was foreign to the culture. Before European civilization intervened in their affairs, many native nations functioned by consensus and were highly egalitarian and communal in nature. Although there were exceptions, Native American tribal leaders generally did not inherit their leadership. They earned it. In the nations of the Iroquois confederacy, for example, women met to choose the warrior chiefs who would lead their people. In those matriarchal societies, women also retained ownership of their families' belongings while men took responsibility for hunting and defense. Among the Navajos, individual bands chose their headmen largely on the basis of their skills and persuasive abilities, making leadership a function of one's utility to the band's needs at a given time. The Navajos, who called themselves Diné (meaning "the people"), gathered both male and female adults to choose someone (who could also be male or female) in whom they could place their confidence.[27] The Navajos also observed a matriarchal line of descent; a husband joined his wife's clan. And among the Sac and Fox, consensus was taken for granted as the way to make decisions.[28]

In determining how energy development and its attendant problems have evolved on Indian reservations, then, it is essential to trace the loss and reassertion of tribal sovereignty and of the tribal democracy that is central to the exercise of that sovereignty. The experience of the Navajos is a particularly enlightening case because it illustrates the degree to which the very concept of "chiefs" as powerful, autocratic leaders was superimposed on Native American culture by whites. The Navajo Nation, until the twentieth century, did not exist as a nation in the sense in which white Americans and Europeans use the term. The nation consisted of numerous, largely autonomous bands that occupied a wide swath of territory in parts of what are now Arizona, New Mexico, and Utah, and occasionally southern Colorado. Bound largely by a shared culture and a common language, they evolved together over centuries after their first known appearance in the Southwest. From the Spanish, who arrived in the 1540s, they gained horses and sheep, becoming excellent sheepherders and regarding their growing horse herds as a form of wealth. Living in more barren land than the neighboring Pueblos, they began to raid Pueblo and Mexican communities for flocks of sheep, horses, and captives. The Spanish found it impossible to missionize or convert them or to identify any leader who could make peace. No such leader existed. The peace that was made with one leader might hold for his band while he remained a leader, but had no moral or legal force among other Navajos.

Americans who arrived during the Mexican–American War repeated the Spanish mistake of seeking to make peace with "chiefs" whose authority to enforce agreements proved extremely limited. In frustration, and anxious to end the raids and impose their own brand of order and authority on the newly conquered Mexican territories, the Americans turned to an itinerant Indian agent named Kit Carson. In the midst of the Civil War, Carson marched against the Navajos with a motley but devastatingly effective crew of whites plus those Indians who wanted revenge against a traditional enemy. And, in the first hint of the coming struggle over Navajo mineral resources, General James H. Carleton, who commissioned Carson, seems also to have had his eye on the potential for gold and silver in the Navajo hills.[29]

With the help of Zuni scouts, Ute warriors, and American soldiers, Carson inaugurated in 1863 one of the saddest chapters of Navajo history. It was a turning point that changed Navajo life forever. Carson's troops chased the Navajos deep into their own lands, forcing them to forego even their winter campfires as they hid in cold mountain caves in their sacred Canyon de Chelly in eastern Arizona. Determined to starve them into submission, Carson rounded up their herds, destroyed their corn and wheat crops, and oversaw the destruction of whole groves of peach trees that the Navajos had long ago planted in the valley.[30]

Slowly, various bands surrendered to Carson until thousands were being marched eastward across the New Mexico desert to the broiling flatlands of Fort Sumner, where they stayed for several years in one of America's first large-scale concentration camps. Amid inadequate provisions and forced farm labor, they drank rancid water that turned their stomachs and lined up daily in corrals to be counted for their ration distributions. There General Carleton began the first of many American efforts to reshape Navajo leadership patterns into a form that federal officials could find acceptable. With more than 8,000 Navajos at Fort Sumner at the end of 1864, Carleton decided to have them settle into 12 villages a half-mile apart, each under a chief responsible to an army officer and appointed by Carleton. Below them would be one subchief for each 100 Navajos. Each village would include a farm, for Americans had long nurtured the idyllic misconception that Indians would become "civilized" and Christian if taught to till the soil.[31] (The Navajos, of course, had long before learned to till the soil. The real question was whether they wanted to till the sterile soil of southeastern New Mexico just to please Carleton.)

For four years, amid mounting expenses, Carleton's containment experiment lasted, with steadily dwindling numbers of Navajos, until federal authorities declared it a massive failure. On June 1, 1868, following negotiations in which the Navajos refused relocation to the Indian Territory, which later became Oklahoma, a peace treaty was signed by two federal commissioners and a dozen headmen. The Navajos could return to their homeland, with a reservation in Arizona of more than three million acres set aside for their use, and with new sheep provided by the federal government. It was a treaty negotiated with the help of Spanish–Navajo interpreters in the absence of anyone who could handle a direct translation into English.

Not knowing or particularly caring about the precise boundaries described in the treaty, the Navajos largely returned to whatever lands their own band had occupied before. For the most part, they resumed their own indigenous pattern of government and let the BIA agents take care of relations with Washington. There was no central tribal leadership. When an issue arose that required a decision of the people, the Diné of the affected area simply would gather to debate the issue. At the turn of the century, one Catholic priest living among the Navajos commented in his writings on the remarkable efficiency of Navajo self-governance:

> Civic organization there is absolutely none. They have neither Chiefs who could be compared with the Governors of the Pueblos or the Chiefs of other Tribes, nor lawmakers, nor any other kind of public or civic officials with authority of enforcing any traditional or unwritten laws. Everybody lives and lets live, and they get along with more law and order so far as peaceful juxtahabitation and social benevolence is concerned than White communities with all their civil authority, criminal courts, jails, etc. Although in each locality there are so-called headmen or chiefs, yet they do not represent what the word Chief signifies according to general acceptation where applied to head or leader of Indian tribes. They have no coercive authority whatever over their fellow tribesmen, but they exercise a certain amount of influence which is greater or lesser according to their age, courage, oratory and their supposed wisdom and influence with the Agent. Their opinion is sought in cases of doubt, differences and difficulties—their words are listened to with deference and their counsels usually followed.[32]

Despite the frequent failure by federal agents to live up to treaty promises concerning food and other supplies, the Navajos prospered, greatly expanding both their numbers and their herds of sheep, goats, and horses in the decades after their return. By the turn of the century, their numbers had grown to 20,000, and their herds were estimated to include one million sheep, 250,000 goats, and 100,000 horses.[33] A clearly resourceful people had restored its ties to the land, and over time U.S. presidents added land to the reservation by using executive orders to transfer parts of the surrounding public domain. For the most part, however, these transfers involved land already occupied by Navajos. Eventually, the reservation grew to the 17 million acres Navajos occupy today, slightly larger than West Virginia.[34]

Despite their clear aptitude for learning, the Navajos generally resisted the education that the treaty had promised and that federal officials "offered" their children. The larger issue, however, was not about the Navajos' interest in education but about the cultural milieu in which education was to be delivered.[35] In their zeal to overcome the obstacles to education posed by the Navajos' migratory sheepherding lifestyle, and in some cases to appease the missionary desires of Christian denominations, federal agents often rounded up children and shipped them off to boarding schools far away from the reservation, not always taking the time to inform parents of where their children had gone. More than a few Navajo children ran away and somehow found their way back home. Tensions boiled over briefly in 1892 when Black Horse, a local headman, led a rebellion against a federal agent over his practices of kidnapping children for school.[36]

Similar practices on other reservations also created bitterness among parents deprived of a voice in determining their own children's future. Oglala medicine men, for instance, took note of the absurdity of Indian boarding schools that required students to cut their hair while showing them pictures of a long-haired, bearded savior and his hirsute disciples.[37] A more lasting consequence was that the boarding schools launched a steady flow of returning students maladapted to the realities of life on the reservation. Many returned as "strangers" to their parents, who were not generally prepared to handle the newfound sophistication of their children.[38] The tensions this generated within the reservation community were noted by Elizabeth W. Forster, a Public Health Service nurse who worked among the Navajos in the 1930s, when she wrote this:

> It is distressing to see their partly educated youth returned to their home entirely out of tune and sympathy with the only life which circumstance offers. If this continues, what can the future hold for the race? It is a keen interest in their development which makes me loath to leave them. My small contribution to their comfort does not really matter. Individuals are born, suffer and die and the life of a race is not much affected by the alleviation of suffering in a few or the saving of a few lives. It is education which vitally affects the future, and one wishes it might be more intelligently directed.[39]

In the drive to bring about development on the Navajo and other reservations, the white man's government in far-off Washington did not attempt to learn what the Navajos and other Indians obviously wanted to share concerning their own culture. It simply imposed its own brand of education, tried to impose its own religious traditions upon Indian children, and, in the end, imposed its own form of government.

Navajo needs at the turn of the century did not include a strong central government. What few needs did exist in that direction seem not to have received any consistent support from Washington, which in 1870 authorized a Navajo police force headed by Manuelito, a respected warrior. The force did an excellent job of retrieving stolen cattle, only to be disbanded a year later when Congress chose to cut off its funding.[40] For the most part, Navajos still handled their own internal governance according to time-honored traditional methods, no matter how much their decentralization frustrated the efforts of federal agents to organize affairs through "chiefs." For all practical purposes, however, the only autocratic authority that existed on the reservation was that of the area Indian agents, who controlled all the Navajos' relations with the U.S. government. Given their frequent replacement amid the political spoils of new administrations in Washington, it is an open question whether the Navajos would have benefited from greater consistency. What is clear is that beginning in 1871 federal policy toward Indian nations began a century-long series of philosophical zigzags that have impaired native sovereignty and development and created a mishmash of contradictory results.

In that year, while still in the midst of Reconstruction after the Civil War, Congress responded to the jealousy of its lower house over the Senate's exclusive treaty-approval powers by ending the power of the President to make treaties with Indian nations. For more than 80 years, the young nation, despite its relentless drive to acquire new lands, had at least officially respected the notion that Indian nations were nations, sovereign entities within the lands claimed by the United States, whose written consent in a signed treaty was necessary before they could "cede" their lands. This legal theory undergirded legislation dating back to the Continental Congress that had prohibited any land transactions between those nations and the individual states, reserving such powers to the federal government. Of course, the same federal government often resorted to war and deceit to achieve its own land-acquisition aims, but with the 1871 act, even the fiction that a treaty was needed to settle such claims was stripped away. Indian land could now be taken simply because Congress wanted to take it. That same logic also led some in Congress to question repeatedly the authority of the executive branch to add land to the Navajo reservation through executive orders. By 1918, Congress disallowed such public-land withdrawals in Arizona and New Mexico without its permission, and a year later it extended the prohibition to the entire nation.[41]

The Navajos had already executed a treaty with the United States before that date, and such treaties necessarily remained in effect, although many promises were observed largely in the breach. The Navajos were affected far more by other federal initiatives in the following years. One that affected them only marginally, however, was the General Allotment Act of 1884, sponsored by Senator Henry Dawes, a man whose presumed knowledge of Native American development needs stemmed from his representation of the state of Massachusetts. Drawing upon this limited exposure to indigenous culture, Dawes concluded, with the backing of many religious denominations, that Indians would become good Christian farmers if allowed to homestead their lands instead of owning them communally through tribal treaty rights. The act actually followed practices begun years earlier with such tribes as the Omaha, Otoe and Missouri, Quapaw, and the Oneidas of Wisconsin, who kept their political identity while losing lands to allotment beginning in the 1850s.

The Dawes Act, passed in 1887, offered each Indian family head a 160-acre tract of farmland, augmented by 80 additional acres for each family member under 18 years of age. The patent to the land in fee simple was to be held in trust by the federal government for 25 years, during which time it could not be affected by any liens or sales. Among those tribes to whom the law was applied, members would have four years to choose their plot of land, after which certain lands could be allotted to them by the Secretary of the Interior. As an inducement to comply, the Congress offered to confer citizenship on those who abandoned traditional tribal lifeways in favor of allotment. At the time, Native Americans did not yet enjoy automatic privileges of American citizenship, regarded as they were as citizens of alien nations.

There was, of course, one legal nicety standing in the way of implementation of the Dawes Act—the preexisting treaties that had conferred ownership of tribal lands on those Indian nations that had made the treaties. Thus, federal agents and commissioners had to set about the task of "persuading" various supermajorities of tribal elders or males or adults, as designated by the treaties as necessary to approve future agreements, to accept what Congress had wrought. Needless to say, a fair amount of duplicity generally entered the negotiations over such issues as allotments. One common mode of persuasion was for federal officials to fall down on the job of providing the annuities, as well as food and provisions, that the treaties had offered as compensation for the ceding of Indian lands for white settlement. Starving Indians tended to be more complicit with white demands. The Sioux, in particular, were major customers of this kind of salesmanship, accompanied by a good deal of fraud, all ratified in due course by Congress and later upheld as valid by the U.S. Court of Claims.[42]

There can be little doubt that the main goal of federal policymakers of the period was to use such instruments as the Dawes Act to subvert the very notion of Native American sovereignty and tribal existence. In 1889, T.J. Morgan, the commissioner of Indian affairs, made this explicit in his annual report, noting six points: first, that the reservation system must come to an end; second, that Indians must be absorbed into the national life as American citizens; third, that Indians must eventually relate to the government solely as individuals; fourth, that Indians must "conform to the White man's ways," forcibly if necessary; fifth, that compulsory, comprehensive education for Indians must be developed as quickly as possible; and, sixth, that the autonomy of individual Indians should be substituted for tribal relations, which were to be "broken up." Morgan later summarized his goal as one of turning the American Indian into the "Indian–American," in effect, just one more set of hyphenated elements in the great American melting pot.[43] President Theodore Roosevelt, never known for his mild-mannered rhetoric, later put it all more forcefully and succinctly when he extolled the Dawes Act as "a mighty pulverizing engine to break up the tribal mass."[44]

Those Native Americans who willingly accepted the inducement of citizenship for the sake of their families and children, however, need not have bothered. The advantages so acquired lasted little more than a generation. Despite their treatment at the hands of the federal government, Native Americans contributed far beyond their numbers to the American effort in World War I. This tendency, which included the Navajos, has repeated itself throughout the twentieth century, in part because military service provides a break from the tedium of reservation life, and in part because, for some, warrior traditions of the past combined with a brand of patriotism tied to the land that many whites still find hard to understand. At any rate, a grateful Congress took note of this contribution in 1924 by granting citizenship to all Indians living in the United States.

One thing it continually failed to do, however, was recognize those same peoples' persistent desire to maintain their cultural integrity. The military in which they served, which at the time was segregating African-Americans and Asian-Americans, refused to allow separate units for Native Americans. White America was still bent on injecting into the melting pot those cultures that sought autonomy even as it imposed separation on those nonwhites who sought access to the mainstream.

In the Southwest, the Navajos suffered fewer of the melting-pot pressures both because of their relative isolation and because the arid nature of their lands made allotment such a ridiculous proposition that, for the most part, the federal Indian agents in the area never even attempted to suggest it. A 160-acre plot in short-grass South Dakota was a marginal proposition at best for the Sioux, who at the turn of the century showed considerable skill at cattle ranching (before being "persuaded" to sell most of their herds), a decidedly large-lot operation. But due to the southwestern climate, allotment would have constituted the height of cruelty if imposed on the sheepherding Navajos. Most eastern congressmen in the late nineteenth century clearly had no firsthand awareness of how utterly impossible it would be to raise adequate crops for even one family on such a small fixed acreage in Arizona.

If the Dawes Act in its application often defied common sense, it nonetheless served a purpose for land-hungry whites, who managed to acquire large tracts of what were deemed "surplus" lands, those left over after allotments had been made to an Indian nation's members. White farmers also managed to acquire many of the allotments themselves as Indians became encumbered with debts, failed to pay taxes, or lost their lands through any number of other means whose legal significance was more apparent to whites and their attorneys. The Dawes Act also imposed on reservations the infamous checkerboard pattern of interspersed Indian-owned and white-owned tracts of land, much of which was deliberately designed to provide the new Indian farmers with white neighbors from whom they could "learn." The result ever since has been a land-use-planning nightmare for tribal planners and a maze of jurisdictional issues that complicate the exercise of native sovereignty to this day.

The Navajos, at the outer edges of their reservations and in the vicinity of certain railroad land grants, do suffer from some of the same checkerboard patterns, but the core of their reservation remains intact. That fact alone probably facilitated one governmental accommodation to indigenous culture that might have had less chance to survive elsewhere—the chapter system. It is a system embedded within another system which had to be grafted onto Navajo life to make it work—the tribal council.

The evolution of Navajo government is almost entirely traceable to external influences. In the early reservation period, Navajos conducted business with the white Indian agents and federal officials through "councils," which included representatives of various sections of the reservation designated to deal with issues that ranged beyond the concerns of individual Navajo communities. The government retained its autocratic control over the reservation and treated these councils largely as advisory bodies, choosing to accept their positions on some occasions and not on others. Most of the time, the councils consisted of chiefs appointed by the agents themselves.[45] Indian agent D.M. Riordan appointed Henry Chee Dodge head chief of the entire tribe largely because he was one of very few Navajos who could speak English—due to his partially Anglo upbringing—although noting this circumstance is not at all meant to diminish his considerable historic importance in the development of the Navajo Nation.[46]

The Navajos fell gradually under the influence of events far from their homes. Interest in prospecting on American Indian lands for precious metals built steadily after the Civil War and became hopelessly intermingled with a larger debate over the development of mineral and energy resources on public lands. Legally, mining on federal lands and Indian lands were two separate issues, one involving the sovereignty of the United States government, and the other that of Indian nations. But in the minds of congressmen bent on exploiting the nation's natural resources, the line began to blur, particularly when it concerned new reservation lands established by executive order of the president.

Step by step, the outside world closed in on the Navajos. In 1870, the Placer Act authorized prospectors for minerals such as gold and silver to stake claims. (This mining law is still the subject of controversy today and the target of criticism by conservation groups.) This law was later refined in 1897 to make it specifically applicable as well to petroleum, relieving the growing oil industry of a great deal of legal uncertainty that had developed over the interpretation of the 1870 act. But, because the Navajo reservation was not known to contain any valuable deposits, the tribe was spared the kinds of major trespassing that sparked the Sioux wars over the Black Hills. Nonetheless, Navajo country was the scene of a few unfortunate encounters between residents and uninvited prospectors.[47]

The legal trappings of future Navajo energy development moved forward another notch in 1891, when Congress passed the first law allowing the Secretary of the Interior to authorize leases for mineral development on Indian lands while specifically exempting executive-order reservations from the law's application. Of course, the Secretary was obliged, as with other such matters, to authorize these leases with the "permission" of the affected tribe. But the executive-order exemption invited mischief from the start. By 1900, Texas Representative John Hall Stephens was already introducing legislation "demanded by the people of the West" to declare both treaty and executive-order reservations subject to the leasing laws that applied to the public domain. His bill also would have made allotment mandatory as an obvious means of expanding the quantity and availability of "surplus" lands. This obvious land grab was so crude and devoid of legal merit that it consistently received the quick burial it deserved.[48]

But others with their eyes on the prize of Indian mineral wealth were more sophisticated than Stephens. With the arrival of statehood for Arizona and New Mexico, the Navajos' Anglo neighbors, many of whom were steadily closing in on the reservation, had a team of voices in Congress. They immediately went to work representing those interests but had to contend with a complicating factor introduced by President William Howard Taft.

In 1909, Taft evinced the growing power of the new conservation movement ushered into the White House by his predecessor, Theodore Roosevelt, by withdrawing substantial areas of the public domain in Wyoming and California from public entry for mining purposes. Over the following year, he continued to establish further withdrawals by executive order. Part of the rationale was to ensure a fuel supply for the U.S. Navy by reserving oil-bearing lands for its use. The oil industry predictably lobbied both Congress and cabinet officials to rescind or modify the orders, but in 1915 the U.S. Supreme Court upheld their validity. This victory for the conservation movement set off another round of debate concerning its proposals for legislation requiring that mining on public lands take place under the provisions of leases from the federal government.

Meanwhile, the Arizona and New Mexico delegations sought to open the Navajo lands to prospecting, mining, and oil drilling. The first bill came from Arizona's Senator Henry Ashurst, who sought to apply the 1891 Indian leasing law to executive-order reservations while ensuring affected tribes of some portion of any proceeds. The measure was backed by Senators Albert B. Fall of New Mexico and A.J. Gronna of North Dakota. In 1916, Representative Carl Hayden (later to be President Pro Tem of the Senate during the Kennedy administration) introduced a bill that authorized a leasing system that would apply to unallotted lands on any reservation in Arizona that was not previously subject to entry—in other words, the executive-order reservations. The bill, after being amended in the House Indian Affairs Committee, provided royalties to the tribe of five percent of the net proceeds—in other words, the bill explicitly recognized Indian ownership.

That concept did not last, however. A year later, the nation was at war in Europe, and the members of Congress were concerned more about defeating the Kaiser than about Indian rights, arguing that the minerals on Indian lands were needed for the war effort. Oddly enough, the war was over when the Hayden-Ashurst bill finally reached the House floor for final approval. Hayden simply argued that providing tribes with a source of income from mineral royalties would relieve Congress of some of the burden of supporting them, thus freeing money to pay the huge debts incurred in winning the war. Thus Congress passed the Metalliferous Minerals Leasing Act of 1919.[49]

A year later, Congress also passed the General Leasing Act, a triumph for conservationists who had argued that the federal coffers should benefit from the private exploitation of mineral and energy wealth on public lands. Western senators had fought the bill fiercely, charging that the notion of leasing mining rights on public lands smacked of socialism and would retard the economic development of the West.[50]

The Navajo lands, however, at least by any reasonable interpretation, fell within the domain of the 1919 law and were completely unaffected by the 1920 law. Or so it seemed.

But Albert Fall, appointed Secretary of the Interior in March 1921 by incoming President Warren G. Harding, decided that executive-order reservations somehow fell under the public-land provisions of the General Leasing Act. His logic was that the United States, not the Indians, owned the land. He issued an administrative decision in June 1922 to implement this new policy.[51] Less than a year later, he resigned under the cloud of the Teapot Dome oil scandal, a matter involving public lands in Wyoming.

Then on September 24, 1922, the Midwest Oil Company struck high-grade oil in a northeastern portion of the Navajo reservation called the Hogback. It followed leasing arrangements made in the San Juan agency, which governed the reservation's Four Corners area, after a general council of the Navajos in the area approved a lease of 4,800 acres to Midwest in August 1921. But relations with Midwest had soured as it sought additional leases for allied companies on adjoining acreage. Midwest found its oil shortly after the Navajos in another general council granted a lease to a competitor in the Tocito Dome, 15 miles from the Hogback. In little more than a week, headlines were spreading the news. The Navajos needed something more than temporary councils to cope with the problems that resulted. Whiskey flowed in abundance, and fly-by-night operators and speculators swarmed over the Shiprock area. Times had changed suddenly, and the Navajos were virtually powerless to put the genie back in the bottle.[52]

It is necessary to backtrack temporarily to trace one of those parallel events in the lives of another people in order to understand adequately the dynamics of the events that overtook the Navajos.

The neighboring Pueblos of New Mexico had long enjoyed a unique status among American Indian populations. Even today, each individual Pueblo nation retains a cane originally granted by the king of Spain as a symbol of its authority to govern its own affairs. (The Spanish never really left the Pueblos alone, but that is another story with a long, sad history.) Later, the Pueblos found themselves inside the newly proclaimed Republic of Mexico and then within the United States. But President Abraham Lincoln renewed those canes of authority on behalf of the United States government, and the terms of the 1848 Treaty of Guadalupe Hidalgo, ending the Mexican–American War, guaranteed that autonomy. In 1871, the U.S. Supreme Court reasserted this position, stating that, unlike other Indians, the Pueblos were not wards of the federal government and had total control over their own lands. Over the years, the Pueblos sold or leased some of those lands to various non-Indians.

Then, in 1913, the Supreme Court reversed its own position on the matter, suddenly ruling that the Pueblos had been wards of the federal government all along. If it seems illogical to apply that ruling to the period between the two decisions, welcome to the world of federal Indian policy. The new ruling placed a cloud over the title to lands belonging to nearly 3,000 people and led to the introduction of a bill by Senator Holm O. Bursum, who had taken Fall's seat upon his appointment to Harding's cabinet. The Bursum bill sought to clarify the status of these land titles, but reversed longstanding precedent concerning Indian land disputes by placing the burden of proof of title on the Pueblos. Further, the bill placed Pueblo waters under the jurisdiction of the state of New Mexico, a clear threat to Pueblo interests. When Bursum then had the audacity to announce

on the Senate floor that the Pueblos supported him, a political rebellion erupted.

In November 1922, with the help of former New York social
worker John Collier, the Pueblo Indians met in Taos to form the
Council of All the New Mexico Pueblos, whose first mission was to
oppose the Bursum bill. The bill eventually died, but the council
lived on despite the BIA's attempt to form its own Pueblo council in
an effort to undermine an institution created by the Pueblo nations
themselves in opposition to government policy.[53]

In this atmosphere, and with Fall still in office, the BIA created
the Navajo tribal council to govern affairs concerning the entire
Navajo Nation. With the increasing outside interest in oil leases,
the BIA faced a daunting legal problem. The 1868 treaty required
the consent of three-fourths of the adult males of the tribe, an arrangement that was virtually impossible to execute. The BIA's practice of using general councils from the immediate area stood on shaky
legal ground. But a duly constituted council of the entire tribe might
pass muster as being sufficiently representative.

From the beginning, however, the BIA sought to use the council
not as an autonomous body but as a rubber stamp. No headmen or
other leaders were consulted as to whether the Navajo people desired such a council.[54] When the Navajo council members raised objections or questions, they were, for the most part, ignored. The
council could not meet without the newly established commissioner
to the Navajos in attendance. Under the original proposed rules, the
Secretary of the Interior could remove council members for cause (a
provision removed in the final regulations). The Secretary could also
appoint a council member to represent any jurisdiction that failed to
elect one.[55] Most important, the government maintained control of
the new council's agenda with a provision that the council would
deal with "all matters coming before it."[56]

In short, stung by what he viewed as the audacious independence
of the Pueblos, BIA Commissioner Charles H. Burke was not inclined to let Indian autonomy get out of hand on the Navajo reservation. The Navajos had already shown significant signs of
independence, and there were hints that those in the San Juan
agency might boycott the new council.[57] One of the government's

first moves was to win tribal council approval to transfer power of attorney for the tribe to the commissioner to the Navajo tribe, an action that the council revoked 10 years later.[58] The Secretary of the Interior also assumed authority to approve leases of up to 4,800 acres on the reservation without advertisement.[59]

Throughout this period, Navajo resentment continued to boil. For lack of day schools on the reservation, Navajo children were still being forced either to attend boarding schools or forego an education. Supplies and conditions were often grossly inadequate.[60] Congressional penny-pinching in the matter of funding Indian schools forced the BIA to fill its boarding schools by hook or crook—or lose the funds in the following fiscal year. Within a tribal council that Washington officials had expected to be compliant, the host of abuses by BIA staff produced fierce criticism including accusations that BIA officials favored the leadership of the returned students.[61] In Washington, what appear in retrospect to be profoundly silly debates about Indian policy left the BIA staff woefully inadequate, demoralized, and suffering from high turnover throughout the 1920s.[62]

The one institution of Navajo governance that did take root quickly was the only one that responded to traditional patterns of self-governance. In 1927, John Hunter, superintendent of the Leupp agency in the southwestern corner of the reservation, introduced the notion of a chapter system. In reality, the idea was built upon the solid foundations of traditional community meetings held by headmen to discuss the problems affecting bands in local areas, and the Navajos quickly and enthusiastically spread the practice across the reservation. The new chapters allowed settlement of local disputes and reintroduced an element of grass-roots democracy to a people whose thirst for such strategies had not been slaked in nearly three generations. Within the first few years, more than 100 chapters were organized, and the Navajos used development funds to build chapter houses throughout their land.[63] In the view of a number of scholars of Navajo history, the chapters could have been the basis for implementing a much more traditional pattern of democracy on the reservation. Instead, by the mid-1930s, they began to suffer official neglect. Meeting houses began to suffer disrepair, and local leaders vainly sought reassurances that the chapters really mattered.[64]

Among the BIA's fiercest critics during the period preceding the New Deal was John Collier, whom BIA officials regarded as the architect of the Pueblo rebellion. Collier may well have had personal motives for his involvement, but the officials' dislike for Collier caused them to lose sight of the fact that the Pueblos were capable of articulating their own grievances. After working with the Pueblos, Collier returned to Washington as secretary of the American Indian Defense Association.[65] With the election of Franklin Delano Roosevelt as president, the tables were turned. Backed by Secretary of the Interior Harold Ickes, Collier won confirmation as the new, reformist commissioner of the BIA in 1933.

Collier was a man with a purpose. One of the first efforts to which he harnessed his energies was the passage in 1934 of the Indian Reorganization Act (IRA), which reversed a half-century of trends toward transformation of Indians as newly minted American citizens and proclaimed a new basis for tribal sovereignty. It was, of course, a bit much to expect that any one piece of legislation would undo four centuries of accumulated damage to Indian rights, if for no other reason than that white officials—whose attitudes could not be expected to change quickly—had to implement the law. But since the IRA became and remains the predominant organizing principle for tribal governments, its provisions are worth considering for a moment.

First, the draft of the IRA legislation prepared by Collier offered a new charter to tribes that wished to organize under its principles. Tribes would gain some control over funds previously entrusted to the federal government. Indian culture and traditions would be promoted through special appropriations. Another provision abolished the allotment system and provided for restoring "surplus" lands to the tribes, allocating $2 million yearly for land purchases (actually a paltry sum when spread across the country, even by New Deal standards—but better, perhaps, than nothing). A final section of the bill proposed to create a court of Indian affairs as a court of original jurisdiction for cases involving Native Americans or their tribes.[66]

Like most attempts at reform, Collier's proposal drew fire from several directions at once and not necessarily because it was too perfect a solution to survive politics. On one hand, some missionary groups who opposed his longstanding support of religious freedom for Indians attacked the revival of Indian culture that the bill promised.[67] Naturally, the backers of assimilation and allotment were opposed. But there were also legitimate concerns among Native Americans, many of whom did not fully understand a bill whose original text was 48 pages long. To enlist their support, Collier held dozens of congresses for American Indians across the nation, most of which he attended personally to explain the bill's provisions. Collier was determined to bring an end to the allotment period and install his vision of restored Indian self-determination.

But Collier, for all his advocacy, was also a product of Anglo-Saxon culture as were his white critics, and he could be just as paternalistic as they had been in "solving" Indian problems. His design for tribal government was not nearly as well founded in indigenous patterns of self-governance as he would have liked to believe, for the fundamental premise involved tribal organization through an elected council that basically followed the Anglo-American model of political organization. Probably nothing more radical could have passed the Congress, but the model was nonetheless grafted onto traditional cultures that had generally organized more along the lines of the bands that formed the basis for Navajo chapters.

Native Americans at the congresses voiced other concerns as well, objecting to provisions that would have required allotted lands to revert to tribal ownership upon the owner's death. One of nearly 40 amendments eventually tacked on to the IRA proposal left this to the discretion of the individual landowner. Although many amendments arose from Native American objections to specific provisions of the bill, others came from various factions in Congress that sought to weaken its provisions. The most obvious case in point was an amendment backed by an Oklahoma senator that excluded the Oklahoma tribes from the law's coverage.[68]

Nonetheless, Congress ultimately passed the IRA in the summer of 1934. Individual tribes then had two years within which to vote on accepting the IRA as the basis for a new tribal government with the attendant benefits the act provided. Nine tribes that failed to hold such an election fell automatically under its provisions. About two-thirds of all tribes voted to accept the IRA, but the crowning blow for Collier came from the Navajos, the largest tribe in the nation. Moreover, Collier set the stage for Navajo rejection of the IRA with a program of his own making.

The 1930s were the era of the Dust Bowl, and Secretary of the Interior Ickes was a devotee of new programs for soil conservation. Collier, as BIA commissioner, sought to bring those concerns to tribal lands. New Deal zeal on conservation was heightened by a powerful sense that time was running out. Only later would hindsight indicate that the Roosevelt administration would have 12 years in which to implement its programs.

Collier's solution struck at the very heart of traditional Navajo culture. He proposed to a reluctant tribal council a program for reducing the livestock herds to levels federal experts deemed the Navajo reservation lands capable of supporting. Yet sheepherding and raising ponies virtually defined what it meant to be a traditional Navajo. The people made it their life's work to breed and tend their flocks, and most had known no other livelihood.

But Collier's concerns about soil conservation on the Navajo reservation had some basis in both the physical deterioration of the land and in statistical indicators, as shown by the large increases in herds cited earlier. The Navajos were facing an unprecedented problem in their own history, the expansion of their numbers being largely unaccompanied by the expansion of their land to accommodate larger herds. As noted above, the previous expansions of the Navajo reservation usually encompassed areas already settled by Navajos anyway. By the 1930s, however, white ranchers and farmers were ringing the reservation, and there was no prospect that these settlers would agree amicably to an expansion of Navajo lands. Collier made the mistake of promising new land acquisitions to the east in New Mexico if the Navajos agreed to reduce their herds. In the first program of stock reduction in 1934, they did so, only to see the New Mexico congressional delegation thwart Collier's promise. Perceiving him as either a liar or incapable of delivering, the already restive Navajos took umbrage at Collier's further plans for stock reduction.[69]

But Collier's program suffered from more than just his inability to deliver more land. For one thing, Collier was every bit as prone to use the tribal council to push his own programs as his predecessors had been. In the process, he succeeded largely in mortgaging the tribal council's credibility with its own people, even as its members raised their own objections and concerns about the implementation of the stock-reduction program. He also failed to pursue what might have proven a more effective route, that of working through the local chapters to promote discussion of the aims of the program and achieve solutions acceptable to the Navajos themselves. The program generally failed to recognize that the government and the Navajo people were working from two fundamentally different premises. Collier saw the program as protecting the quality of rangeland. The Navajos, who view their sheep and horses as gifts from the Holy People, saw their care of their livestock as the means to win blessings that included rain. The entire confrontation thus became a vicious circle that ended in highly authoritarian measures. Hundreds of Navajos still tell tales of their trips to jail because of their resistance to livestock-reduction measures.[70]

It is tempting for many whites to regard the Navajo view as "primitive." It is worth recalling for comparison that just a generation earlier, many white settlers had moved westward through the High Plains with the naive notion that "rain follows the plow." Greedy land developers and railroad agents played a role in purveying that notion, but the fact remains that white farmers who believed it, or wanted to believe it, ignored advice from High Plains Indians about the limitations of the short-grass prairie and thus contributed mightily to the 1930s Dust Bowl phenomenon. For the white farmers, however, the New Deal offered largely voluntary soil-conservation programs, most of which gained legal teeth only as late as 1985 with the passage of the Food Security Act. That act, which reauthorized the nation's farm-subsidy program for five years, also for the first time tied those crop subsidies to compliance with soil-conservation goals and created a Conservation Reserve that paid farmers to retire highly erodible land from agricultural use. On that purely objective basis, the Navajos have some justification for feeling that they were singled out unfairly.

Furthermore, by treating the problem as tribal rather than local, the stock-reduction program tended to ignore major differences in range capacity among the different parts of the reservation, which vary significantly in altitude, rain patterns, and vegetation. Moreover, the plan at times was implemented with across-the-board percentage cuts in stock that left larger owners relatively well off but punished the owners of smaller herds by destroying their economic viability. When resistance to the program began to build, federal agents used increasingly arbitrary and harsh methods to enforce reductions on owners who increasingly took to hiding their sheep in the hills to avoid compliance. Federal officials dickered with the tribal council over the allocation of development funds in desperate efforts to win cooperation. Meanwhile, in the checkerboard area to the east of the reservation boundaries in New Mexico, where white farmers' land was interspersed with Navajo holdings, some subsistence Navajo herders lost claims to grazing ranges after selling their stock to federal agents. They then watched helplessly as white ranchers expanded into the very range they had vacated. The ultimate blow, however, must have come when Depression-era prices fell so low that government agents abandoned attempts to find buyers for the stock they had purchased from Navajo farmers. J.C. Morgan, a tribal-council member who led the opposition to stock reduction, had urged that the meat from the reduced stock at least be given back to the people for food.[71] When, instead, the range riders shot goats and left the carcasses to rot, the struggling Navajos lost all patience with what they viewed as "inexcusable waste."[72]

Ironically, Collier had bungled a major BIA program in much the same way for which he had excoriated his less progressive predecessors. In the face of all the improvements he had dreamed of making, Collier's alienation of the Navajos produced for him a setback of major proportions.

The program lost all credibility in the eyes of Navajos, who associated both stock reduction and the IRA with John Collier. The IRA suffered badly from the association, and the largest Indian nation in the United States narrowly rejected its acceptance as the basis for reorganizing tribal government. Just two of the six agency areas voted against it, but the northern and eastern portions of the reservation contained the largest populations and needed new land the most.

One major consequence of stock reduction was that a growing

number of Navajos found that their labors on the land had become superfluous. Forced out of subsistence farming into the wage economy without adequate economic development to absorb them, some of them took whatever jobs were available. With the onset of World War II, some joined the military. Others found work in the newly opened uranium mines, digging hard rock from the insides of mountains in Monument Valley. Today they and their children are still paying the price.

The shadows of the past continue to haunt the Indian present in other ways. Nowhere in the Southwest is this more clear than in the so-called Hopi-Navajo land dispute.

Whether the boundaries of reservations were set by Congress or the President, they were essentially arbitrary lines drawn by a colonial power, differing little in their impact from lines drawn in the shifting sands of the Middle East or through the tropical rainforests of central Africa. Many of those African and Asian boundaries have led to tragic civil wars and international disputes because they generally bore little relation to the real needs or the true historic occupancy patterns of the people whom they most affected.

For the Navajos, the most classic case in point involves a line proposed to the administration of President Chester A. Arthur by J.H. Fleming, the Indian agent to the Hopis. Amid some minor concerns about the proximity of Navajo and Mormon settlers to the Hopi mesas in east-central Arizona, Fleming largely instigated the creation of the Hopi-reservation boundary lines by executive order in order to rid the Hopi community of two Anglo intruders whom he regarded as nuisances. Paying no known regard to traditional land-use patterns, Fleming drew some neatly symmetrical lines on a map, and President Arthur signed an order authorizing a reservation for the Hopis "and such other Indians as the Secretary of the Interior may see fit to settle thereon." The new reservation encompassed some 1.2 million acres. Several hundred Navajos already lived there, and at least some Navajo presence in the area dated back to 1629.[73]

Unfortunately, this cavalier approach created the legal foundations for the current dispute. The boundaries for this reservation included not only the mesas where Hopis traditionally had lived, but vast areas of flatlands below them. The Navajos and their sheep were traditionally more suited for occupying the dry plains. The mixed uses of the two groups for sacred and agricultural functions had coexisted to various degrees for generations. While that history is too complex to render here, the important point is that the Hopis and Navajos had worked out their own mutual accommodations over that time, sometimes pleasantly and sometimes not so pleasantly, but very clearly without the aid of white authorities. Even more important, neither nation had any input into the plan drawn up by Fleming, nor were they consulted prior to its acceptance by President Arthur. Until the advent of modern tribal government under federal auspices, the white man's lines on a map were of no particular significance to either people.

Both, in fact, maintained a decentralized style of self-government. Like the more numerous Navajos, the Hopis shared ties of religion, culture, and language, but desired no central authority. Their pueblo-style villages each followed the direction of a *kikmongwi*, a religious and hereditary chief. Even when the Hopis, under federal pressure, finally agreed to create a tribal council in 1936, their constitution specifically permitted individual villages to opt out of participation in favor of the traditional leadership of the *kikmongwi*.[74] For years thereafter, the council struggled to establish its legitimacy in the face of traditional indifference. All the while, however, under federal law, the council was empowered to act on behalf of the nation, creating a political dynamic with highly regrettable consequences for Hopi unity. The arrangement created an inevitable tension between the elected leaders of the tribal council and the customary respect of most Hopis for their traditional elders.[75]

Not surprisingly, noted journalist Jerry Kammer in *The Second Long Walk*, a 1980 book examining the land dispute, "An anticouncil faction still scorns the council as an illegitimate artifice superimposed by Washington to speed their assimilation into American society and alienate them from the land so that energy companies can take Hopi mineral resources."[76] For the last half-century, in other words, the Navajo and Hopi tribal councils have waged legal and political war in a dispute made possible only by the existence of a tribal council many Hopis never wanted. The Hopi council, led by the Americanized faction of the Hopi people, has prosecuted its case for partitioning the Joint Use Area (JUA) created by Congress, with the end result of steadily displacing thousands of Navajos whose primary crime was to be found living on the wrong side of an arbitrary boundary rooted in a bureaucratic decision that is now more than a century old. Millions of federal dollars are being spent to implement congressional legislation and a legal decision that splits the JUA and forces the relocation of many elderly Navajos whose traditional pastoral skills have provided the only livelihood they have ever known. The relocation is being forced upon a people whose attachment to the land is so deeply spiritual that they cannot conceive of living anywhere but in the land they have known since birth.

"This is not just a matter of cultural survival," noted Lila Bird, the executive director of the Albuquerque-based Water Information Network (WIN). Bird, who is herself a Pueblo, added that, as the coal company draglines approach Indian homes, "It is simply a matter of survival."[77]

Why does pursuing this dispute matter so much? There are a number of possible explanations. Kammer noted that the extended family of Abbott Sekaquaptewa, former president of the Hopi tribal council, may have sought much of the land for cattle ranching, a lowland activity of no interest whatsoever to traditional Hopis. Kammer also noted the personal animosity toward the Navajos by Abbott's brother Wayne, the publisher of the Hopi newspaper, *Qua Toqti*, which often darkened the tone of the dispute through its antiNavajo and antitraditionalist editorials. Kammer interestingly observed that Wayne Sekaquaptewa treated his undeniable business success as "proof of the Mormon doctrine that promises earthly blessings to members of the priesthood." Traditional Indians of all tribes find the Mormon faith virtually anathema because its teachings include the belief that Native Americans are descended from a Hebrew, Lehi, who sailed to America just before the Babylonian destruction of Jerusalem. As his people later lost faith, *The Book of Mormon* relates, their skin darkened as a punishment from God. They could regain their whiteness by regaining their faith, a notion that Church of Latter Day Saints President Spencer W. Kimball interpreted as literal truth, noting that Indian children placed with Mor-

mon families in Utah became visibly lighter. Kammer noted that
non-Mormon Indians angrily "point out that children on placement
in Utah spend less time in the sun than when they are at home on
the reservation."[78]

Church affiliations, personal and factional animosities, and cattle
raising aside, one fact does remain true. In the midst of the Joint Use
Area that the Hopi tribal council succeeded in getting partitioned,
rising above Navajo and Hopi houses alike, sits Big Mountain, the
home of a huge strip-mining operation run by the Peabody Coal
Company. The company first arranged a lease with the Navajo Nation to mine coal on Big Mountain (also known as Black Mesa) in
1966.[79] Within the JUA, Peabody also has a joint lease with both
the Hopi and Navajo councils. In the late 1970s, at the height of the
fierce lobbying in Congress over the Hopi-Navajo land settlement,
the economically recoverable reserves in the joint lease area were
estimated at 340 million tons. Another 400 million tons lay in the
area strictly under the Navajo lease. Moreover, it was the best coal
on the reservation, averaging just 0.5-percent sulfur content, with a
fuel value of 11,000 British thermal units (BTUs) per pound.[80]

Moreover, as Philip Reno, an economic-development adviser to
then tribal chairman Peter MacDonald, noted, Navajos paid a price
for the royalties the tribe was earning from the leases. Tests had
shown the groundwater in the area to be of the highest quality on
the reservation, yet the aquifer was being pumped by Peabody for
slurrying coal to the Mojave electricity-generating station on the
Colorado River. The result, Reno suggested, was that many Navajos
were drinking poorer-quality water heavily laden with salts, with
whatever health costs that entailed, while their best water was being
"mined and shipped away" if the aquifers did not recharge sufficiently
to allow any uses other than sluicing coal.[81]

How did this fit into the land dispute? More than a few traditional
Hopis and Navajos alike in the Big Mountain area saw the hand of
Peabody somewhere in the actions of the Hopi council. Partitioning
the JUA would give each tribal council a clear right to lease its own
section unilaterally instead of negotiating the type of joint lease then
in existence. Navajo Chairman Peter MacDonald had, in the mid-
1970s, been a major force along with other American Indian leaders,

such as LaDonna Harris, the executive director of Americans for Indian Opportunity, in forming the Council of Energy Resource Tribes
(CERT). MacDonald injudiciously compared CERT to the Organization of Petroleum Exporting Countries (OPEC). The idea of negotiating with the head of an ostensibly domestic OPEC who was also
at least threatening to build a Navajo tribal capacity for strong environmental enforcement must have made unilateral negotiations with
the Hopis look like a much more appealing alternative to Peabody
executives.

Whatever combination of motives lay behind the land dispute,
the fact remained that many traditional Hopis apparently took a dim
view of their tribal council's efforts. Six of them, in fact, had joined
80 Navajos in a lengthy cross-country bus tour in 1974 to lobby Congress for a settlement that would leave their neighbors on the land,
living in their traditional ways, as they had done for generations.[82]

Like bookends in time, another combination of Diné and Hopi
delegates arrived at the United Nations in December 1992 as part of
the International Year of Indigenous People. They sought international aid in their persistent quest to block forced relocation. Thomas Banyacya spoke of Hopi prophecies concerning the end of the
world, warning that "human beings are destroying our Mother Earth
in pursuit of money and greed."[83]

About the time the Hopi-Navajo debate was in high gear in Congress, Indian nations were rapidly reaching two conclusions—that
they had not been getting the best possible deals in BIA-supervised
leases with energy companies developing natural resources on their
reservations, and that they needed to develop the internal and collective capacity to change those leases for the better. CERT became
that mechanism. Many Native American activists think that, like
many other attempts to right historic wrongs in Indian country, it
has somehow gone awry. Its history, too, merits a brief examination.
Equally important is its context.

Every reservation works out its own accommodation with the
pressing need for economic development in its own way. It is naive
for outsiders to think that a tribe should forsake any impact on its
environment while its people languish in poverty. Consider the sta-

tistics facing Native American planners after the 1980 census. Of males between 20 and 64 years of age living on reservations, 58 percent were unemployed. Forty-one percent of reservation dwellers were in households living below the poverty level. Nearly one-fourth of families received public assistance, and fewer than half had telephones.[84]

At the same time, consider that LaDonna Harris was announcing that tribal lands contained one-third of the nation's low-sulfur coal, 37 percent of its uranium, and substantial deposits of oil and gas.[85] Most of the uranium was on land belonging to the Navajo Nation and the Laguna Pueblo.[86] For most tribes, the issue was not whether but how to develop those resources to advance their members' economic welfare. Having also been historically disserved by the BIA, which made little effort to ensure that Native Americans had adequate technical expertise at their disposal when negotiating with large energy companies, Harris and other Native American leaders in 1975 founded CERT.[87]

Coming both at the high point of American Indian Movement militancy and in the aftermath of the 1973 Arab oil embargo that launched OPEC as a major force in world trade, the new Indian organization predictably created fears. Sober officials in the Federal Energy Administration saw its value, however, and funded some of its efforts. Others who were aware that CERT members had legitimate concerns about negotiating fair energy-development deals also supported its creation. Both the Federal Trade Commission and the private Council on Economic Priorities issued studies that criticized BIA ineptitude in accounting for tribal royalties on mineral and energy development and suggested that a purely Indian-run association could eventually obviate the need for BIA involvement by replacing its functions.[88]

Nonetheless, MacDonald, the volatile and colorful first chairman of CERT, fueled the public-relations fire by declaring that CERT would become, in effect, a domestic OPEC. The fact that CERT had hired as its economist a former Iranian energy official, Ahmed Kooros, gave facile credence to this notion in the public mind. It also conjured up an erroneous image of Native American affluence that was hopelessly detached from reality.[89] The catchy phrase drew news-media attention but also constituted a badly flawed analogy. CERT's primary value was not to function as a cartel, a ridiculously infeasible role in any event, but to provide the technical assistance and unity that the reservations sorely needed if they were to make economic self-determination a meaningful concept.

Along the way, CERT also had to shed its image, even among Native Americans, of harboring desires for energy development on reservations at any cost. To some extent, MacDonald's rhetoric and practice on the Navajo reservation helped sustain that image. With the hiring of A. David Lester, a Creek from Oklahoma, as CERT's new executive director, and MacDonald's departure in 1982 after his defeat as Navajo tribal chairman, that image began to change. CERT has since grown to include more than 40 tribes as members.[90] On the Navajo and other reservations, new environmental agencies have come into being, using native resources and personnel to enforce tribal and federal environmental regulations. Most need more resources and greater authority. Noting that the U.S. EPA has long provided grants-in-aid to state environmental agencies to support essential programs, Tom B.K. Goldtooth, a natural-resources specialist for the Red Lake Band of Chippewa Indians in Minnesota who serves on the board of the nationwide Indigenous Environmental Network (founded in 1990), perceives a pattern of environmental racism in the EPA's historic failure to use similar grants to build similar regulatory expertise within tribal governments.[91] The U.S. EPA could undoubtedly provide more assistance to tribal agencies than it has to date, but progress is being made.

In an essential way that non-Indian environmentalists in the United States must soon come to understand, the impetus for stronger environmental regulation on Indian reservations is stemming from a powerful and growing movement for grass-roots environmental democracy. This movement is rooted in deeply held values of the people themselves. Its activists are quickly coming to terms with the necessity for spiritual values to shape political programs to transform the development priorities of Indian nations. It should not be very hard for the rest of the environmental movement to understand this. The main obstacle to date has been ignorance of Native American culture and governance.

What is more problematic for most whites, environmentalists included, is contemplating what it really means to be indigenous. In a movement that has traditionally been dominated by middle-class whites, it is particularly hard to understand the indignity and emotional pain that the dominant culture has inflicted on people whose civilization is generally viewed as primitive or less advanced. Western civilization tends to view the advancement of civilization in technological terms. We have telephones; they don't. We have computers; they don't. Therefore, we are more advanced. For indigenous peoples, this is not the issue. More, perhaps, like the Amish, but with radically different philosophical roots, they are prone to question whether a technical innovation is necessarily an advancement if it wreaks havoc upon the earth. Who is more morally advanced? Where is the moral judgment behind such awesome inventions as the atomic bomb? And can the moral degradation of the bomb be legitimately offset by the peaceful uses of the atom? Of course, white environmentalists tend to ask some of these questions. But as Jerry Mander, the author of *In the Absence of the Sacred*, notes, they still tend to do so in the context of assuming that technology itself is neutral and that its use and control are the central issues.

As a result, middle-class environmentalists view Native American warnings about the damage we are doing to Mother Earth as useful to the cause but still somehow a little quaint. It has been, however, somewhat easier for those nonwhite and working-class environmentalists who are more accustomed to second-class status in the movement to take the Native American message seriously. There is some kinship in being low in the pecking order of power, and there can be little doubt that the environmental movement has had its own pecking order.

Quaint or not, Native American spiritual feelings for the land run deep. In a sense, it does not matter whether archaeologists think these people arrived 5,000 or 10,000 or even 20,000 years ago from another continent, or whether they have been here from time immemorial. Like other indigenous nations in Malaysia, the Philippines, or Siberia, their ancestral roots extend beyond recorded time. They worked out a host of microadaptations to their environments in which they have learned to listen to the land, to know the natural curative power of the herbs that counterculture whites now crave, to sense the movements of birds and small animals and the wind, to honor the animals they kill by using them fully and efficiently, to sense the power and presence of the Creator in both the magnitude of the open sky and the rustling of the smallest leaves — in essence, to become so much a part of the land that it is no longer possible to view it as a mere commodity, to be bought and sold and abused as one pleases. In the context of this attachment, the Lakota people of the High Plains could hardly have seen the destruction of the vast buffalo herds within the span of a decade as the achievement of an advanced civilization, but rather as an act of virtual genocide by a morally debased civilization devoid of even the Christian spiritual values it claimed to espouse. It is small wonder that a century later the Lakota still find it unspeakably painful to reconcile themselves to this dominant culture.

Virtually by definition, non-Indians seem to be excluded from the real meaning of the word "indigenous" as it applies to those who now occupy the Western Hemisphere. Yet, this exclusion is as much psychological and spiritual as it is geographical and historical. At this stage of U.S. history, probably no group would more like to see its "visitors" become indigenous in spirit than Native Americans. There are some hints that this conversion is possible, for there are some interesting examples of non-Indian groups that have reached accommodations with their own bioregional environments in relatively modern times. The sad part is that they, too, are losing some of the land-revering heritage they had started to build. Their indigenous culture is being strangled in its infancy.

One of those cultures is the transplanted Acadian culture of Louisiana, whose original name, drawn from the area of Canada from which French colonists were exiled, has over time been corrupted to "Cajun." Undoubtedly with the help of Native American nations already indigenous to the coastal wetlands of Louisiana, these people over two centuries established a remarkable and unique adaptation to the swamps in which they became sustainable harvesters of the local shellfish, deer, and fish that nature made available. Their primary crime, for which they suffered more than a little bit of Hollywood-style defamation like Native Americans, was that they adapted so well that they no longer fit easily into the dominant Anglo culture that eventually overtook Louisiana. But the dominant culture's steady degradation of the Louisiana coastal wetlands has steadily driven many of these people into the arms of industry in order to survive. Their fishing grounds—and those of the Chittimachas and Houmas who occupied the area before them—are slowly being destroyed.

A more lucrative, but no less painful, fate is overtaking the African-American residents of the coastal barrier islands of the Carolinas. There, the villain is expensive resort development at locations like Kiawa and Hilton Head Island. These former slaves had developed a largely self-sufficient coastal economy based on fishing and agriculture whose viability is declining rapidly as high-income, gated communities envelop the islands and displace their long-time natives. Interestingly, noted Hilton Head Island's community-development director, Stephen G. Riley, many of the newcomers find it impossible to understand what injury they could possibly have done to people who were paid handsomely for their land. It is incomprehensible to them that the African-American natives of the islands, who often sell out simply because they can no longer keep up with their new tax burden while retaining their land for traditional uses, simply do not view the land as a commodity. They have developed a spiritual and emotional attachment that is being severed relentlessly, and it seems there is no turning back. They, at least, understand the sense of loss of Native Americans who discover that they cannot go home again.

With that in mind, it is worth reviewing a few historical examples of Native American environmental concerns to set the stage for the epic battle of the 1990s.

Tribal judge Louis Hawpetoss was blowing up balloons on a blustery April Saturday morning beneath a tent while children dashed around him, chasing a young man in a raccoon costume. In the middle of the Warrington Addition, a housing subdivision in Keshena, Wisconsin, the Menominee County seat and the home of the tribal government, Hawpetoss was helping children and families to celebrate Earth Week 1993. To regain a sense of traditional values within the subdivision, the Earth Week celebration focused on tree planting. Throughout the week, tree planting moved to various parts of the reservation, with seedlings distributed for planting in people's backyards.

Hawpetoss wears many hats on the reservation. Besides being a tribal judge, a position in which he mixes a knowledge of the law and of tribal traditions, Hawpetoss is also a cultural advisor to the Menominee planning department, serving as a link between the largely non-Indian or at least nontraditional planners and the traditional elements of the tribal population. The link is crucial, as even the existence of Warrington Addition shows. Between the largely treeless individual lots surrounding the tract housing stood wooden fences. Fences, Hawpetoss noted, are alien to Menominee tradition. So is tract housing. The Menominee are historically a communal civilization. But in order to get the housing grant the tribe needed from the U.S. Department of Housing and Urban Development to upgrade the living conditions of its people, it had to agree to spend money on fences because the reservation was deemed a "high-crime" area. As in its termination battle, the Menominee had once again been caught in the vise of competing cultural values.

It may seem that Congress and the federal government had conducted enough social experiments on reservations by the time the Collier era brought allotment to a close. Certainly, the Native American contribution to Allied victory in World War II would seem to have merited the same gratitude that prompted Congress to pass the Indian citizenship laws of the 1920s. Instead, it led some in Congress to the conclusion that Indians were "ready" to become part of American society. The way to make that happen, they decided, was to terminate the tribal status of at least the more prosperous Indian nations. The Menominee appeared to be prime candidates for this transition—willing or not.

Hawpetoss recalled a stirring day in his childhood that he thinks may have influenced Congress's termination of Menominee tribal status in the 1950s. When he was eight years old, he said, a Catholic priest on the reservation began a march around the reservation by banging on a large Indian drum. Mormon missionaries had arrived on the reservation, and the priest wanted to alert the people to their presence. Gradually, throughout the day, hundreds of Menominee joined the march as they learned its purpose. Before they were through, it became clear to the missionaries that their presence was unwanted, and they left. Hawpetoss speculated—he admitted that no one can ever know for certain—that Utah Senator Frank Watkins, the Republican chairman of the Senate Indian Affairs Committee, took umbrage at this attitude among the Menominee and targeted them for termination.

In the 1950s Watkins led a drive to terminate the tribal status of some of the more economically successful Indian nations that he deemed ready to join the American mainstream. Basically, this meant that all the trappings of tribal government would disappear, and reservation land would simply fall under standard local governance under state law. Tribal membership would cease to serve any legal purpose as such. Watkins never consulted with the tribes on what they thought of his proposition, which he deemed the Indian equivalent of the Emancipation Proclamation. Ironically, Watkins, a Mormon who must have been aware of the Mormons' use of cooperatives to serve the needs of their own community, felt that what Native Americans needed most was freedom from their own tribal governments. It was a complete, and once again tragic, misreading of Native American culture and values.

Termination was imposed on the Menominee, the Klamath (of Oregon), and four other relatively prosperous tribes against their will. In the case of the Menominee, their reservation became Wisconsin's newest county despite the almost total lack of any tax base.[92] The thriving business cited in determining their readiness for termination was the tribal sawmill, the center of a thriving collective enterprise. That business enterprise became the only remnant of tribal government to which the Menominee could cling as they struggled to make their county economically viable. Even the mill was largely under the influence of its creditors.[93] Its viability increasingly became a matter of selling key assets piece by piece, including a plan for developing vacation homes for affluent Wisconsin whites on tribal land.[94]

In time, faced with a series of increasingly unpalatable choices to support their thinly populated, underfinanced county, the Menominee were driven to fight back. A new group, Menominee DRUMS, led a series of successful legal and direct-action attacks on the land-sale policies to highlight the disastrous results of the termination policy.[95] Ada Deer, a key DRUMS organizer, led a drive for reinstatement of tribal status that finally succeeded in 1974, nearly 20 years after Watkins succeeded in passing his termination bill.[96] Deer, who remained active in Native American and Democratic Party causes, in May 1993 became President William Clinton's nominee to head the Bureau of Indian Affairs, winning Clinton considerable support in Indian country.[97]

Ironically, the Menominee forest created the very prosperity that made the tribe a target for termination and "transition" to "normal" American life. What termination advocates never understood—or chose to ignore—was that the wealth created by Menominee forestry is intimately tied to that communal vision. It is not a resource for short-term, private exploitation.

Drive through northeastern Wisconsin and you will notice immediately that something has changed when you enter Menominee County. Flat, open farmland dotted by trees suddenly gives way to the last expansive tract of virgin hardwood forest, nearly a quarter-million acres in size. Along the back roads, houses and trailers are hidden beneath the canopy in small clearings. The forest is not untouched, however. It is not a park but a working piece of industrial land. Small logging roads wind away from the paved county road, and piles of cut lumber sit atop the ground, waiting for delivery to the sawmill. Drive through the reservation to Neopit and you will see that the other key town on the reservation hosts a sawmill beside the Fox River, bearing the words "Menominee Tribal Enterprises."

For nearly a century and a half since they agreed that it would become their reservation site, the Menominee have cultivated this forest, using a system of marking and cutting mature trees that has allowed crews to complete almost five cutting cycles of 30 to 40 years each while enhancing its natural wealth. "There are more trees in the forest now than when we started," Hawpetoss noted. "Our elders who devised this system showed great foresight."[98]

The lumber business has by no means solved all the economic-development problems of the Menominee reservation, but it most assuredly will provide jobs for as many generations as follow the wisdom of their elders. At the southern boundary, a gambling casino provides a new source of tribal income and employment. But in a time when loggers in the Pacific Northwest fear for their jobs and the very future of their communities, and environmentalists wage holy war against logging companies that clearcut forests and ship raw logs to Japan, the Menominee seem to know something that others have not yet learned. Some are trying to learn, said Hawpetoss; visitors have come from as far away as Sweden to study the Menominee methods of sustained-yield forestry.

Wisconsin underwent an intense debate about logging about a century ago. The careless forestry of the time stripped the state bare, and along the way helped to produce a number of major firestorms that swept through logging country. The fire that began in Peshtigo, Wisconsin, in 1871 killed 1,500 people and gave us the term "firestorm" to describe its intensity. By 1918, a dozen more such fires had raged through the forests of the Upper Great Lakes region.[99] Today, virtually all the forest outside the Menominee reservation is second growth. Over time, this stripmining of forest land has facilitated extensive soil erosion and reductions in wildlife population.

Indian country, of course, is not immune from resource-exploitation disputes, but sometimes the way in which they are handled offers the rest of the United States a way out of its environmental dilemmas. Diné Citizens Against Ruining Our Environment (Diné CARE) in the summer of 1993 was pioneering a path to reconciliation over forestry issues that provided a glaring alternative to the feuding between environmentalists and loggers that had infested the Pacific Northwest. Diné CARE's concern involved the logging practices of Navajo Forest Products Industry (NFPI), a tribal enterprise that harvests timber from the three percent of the Navajo Reservation that is heavily forested.

Logging on the reservation dates back to 1880, but NFPI came into being by action of the tribal council in 1958. The Navajo Nation and the BIA adopted a 10-year management plan for the Navajo forests in 1983 that divided the Defiance Plateau and the Chuska Mountains, in the northeastern corner of Arizona, into 63 timber-cutting departments. In 1991, the Navajo Nation proposed to sell 23.6 million board feet of timber from four compartments that made up the Ugly Valley–Whiskey Creek area, a plan that was approved by the Navajo Area BIA director on a finding of no significant impact, in other words, a ruling that no environmental impact statement was needed because the sale would not materially affect the quality of the human environment.[100]

Diné CARE was founded on the reservation in 1988 at Dilkon, Arizona, with the original objective of fighting a hazardous-waste incinerator proposed by a subsidiary of Amoco. It succeeded in reversing the Navajo council's endorsement of the $40 million project. Diné CARE went on to block an asbestos waste dump.[101] The group objected to the forest-management plan on the grounds that it amounted to clearcutting that would destroy the area for those who lived there. The Tsaile-Wheatfields chapter passed a resolution in October 1991 opposing the sale. The following March, five area residents filed an administrative appeal of the plan with the U.S. Interior Department's Board of Indian Appeals challenging the finding against the need for an environmental impact statement. During this period, according to Lori Goodman, a spokeswoman for Diné CARE, tempers began to flare as the loggers working for NFPI began to express predictable concerns about their own jobs amid a series of legal maneuvers by both Navajo environmentalists and tribal and NFPI officials.[102]

But, Goodman also noted, Navajo traditions helped to defuse the situation. "We greet each other peacefully," she said. In a clan-based society, "It's difficult to yell at your uncle in a public meeting." Quiet discussions about the true nature of the problem, the threat to the land, and the long-term viability of logging jobs in the face of unsustainable forest practices led to negotiations between Diné CARE and the NFPI loggers, who met on the Sunday afternoon of August 15, 1993, in Dilkon. Goodman said they discussed the deforestation of the Chuska Mountains, and the environmentalists made clear their concerns about the well-being of the loggers by vowing to apply for $200,000 in matching federal grants (which required $50,000 from the Navajos) for preservation and restoration of the logged areas—in effect, providing environmentally beneficial work for the loggers.[103] With a less confrontational style than many non-Indian environmentalists might have used, Diné CARE embarked on demonstrating a model of worker-environmentalist cooperation that is often sorely lacking elsewhere.

One of the most moving photographs in Native American history depicts a solemn ceremony in 1948 in which Interior Secretary A.J. Krug signed a contract in which the Fort Berthold reservation sold its best land to the federal government for the construction of the Garrison Dam, part of the Pick-Sloan project that created flood-control reservoirs along the Missouri River in North Dakota and South Dakota. Surrounding Krug were a number of men in dark business suits, most standing politely with their hands folded together in front of them or behind their backs.

One man in a pin-stripe suit, standing immediately to the right of Krug, had his glasses off. His hands obscured his face, where he was wiping a flood of tears from his eyes. His name was George Gillette. He was the chairman of the business council for the Fort Berthold reservation in North Dakota. His reservation, largely against its will, was parting with the richest agricultural land it owned, some 152,000 acres of bottomland along the Missouri River valley that would soon be inundated. It had grown fine crops of corn for the Mandan and Hidatsa tribes for centuries, feeding Lewis and Clark when they wintered there in 1804.[104]

The Three Affiliated Tribes of the Fort Berthold Reservation—the Mandan, Arikara, and Hidatsa—were the big losers in one of the nation's most expensive water-development schemes. Downstream, however, the Yankton, Lower Brule, and Crow Creek Sioux reservations also lost significant river-bottom land. The Pick-Sloan project, a joint effort of the U.S. Army Corps of Engineers and the Interior Department's Bureau of Reclamation, demonstrated that although the frontier Indian wars were over, the days of seizing Native American lands in violation of treaty rights had not yet passed.

While some white farmers also suffered from the Army Corps' high-handed approach to land acquisition for the massive water project, which consumed 1.6 million acres, tribes surrendered most of that land. In spite of treaty obligations, the Army Corps for the most part built the dams first and settled compensation issues with the tribes later, even threatening the use of eminent domain, a right reserved only for Congress in matters affecting Indian lands.

Although most white farmers could take their compensation, just or otherwise, and buy comparable farmland elsewhere, the same was not true for the Indians who farmed the Missouri River bottomlands. They suffered, as often was the case in such situations, the loss of a unique relationship with a very localized ecosystem. They relied on the river bottomlands for shaded pastureland for cattle and for a variety of berries and roots used for medicinal purposes and for an important source of food fiber. Anyone who has driven the vast expanses of South Dakota on a hot summer day can appreciate the value of shade and water. The Sioux and the tribes of the Fort Berthold reservation lost much of this between 1946 and 1960 as the Army Corps presented one *fait accompli* after another while the Bureau of Indian Affairs either failed to notify them of the government's intentions or frustrated their attempts to obtain adequate independent legal counsel. Large portions of each reservation's population were transplanted, often with severe emotional consequences. In the end, forced onto the less hospitable flatlands above the river bluffs, accepting inadequate compensation virtually under the duress of the rising waters behind the dam's closed gates, the tribes once again faced a massive job of adaptation with fewer resources than ever with which to do it. For the Fort Berthold tribes, the experience was nearly fatal. For others, it took years to rebuild any semblance of a viable economic base to replace what had been lost.[105]

The Chemehuevis of Southern California also illustrate the centrality of land to Native American survival. Before the arrival of the Spanish, these cousins of the Shoshones roamed a vast territory from the Tehachapi Mountains near Los Angeles into southern Nevada. Today, their reservation encompasses about 50 square miles of what they deem a desert paradise along the Colorado River. The 36,000-

acre reservation was deeded to them in 1907 by Congress, which presumably assumed that the Chemehuevi Valley was of little interest to anyone but the tribe. The area is south of Needles, the California city that weather forecasters often cite as the hottest in the nation.[106]

During the New Deal, however, the federal government began construction of the Parker Dam, thus backing up Colorado River water to flood the very valley that the Chemehuevis occupied. The local BIA agent persuaded what remained of the tribe to vote to sell the flooded land to the federal government for something in excess of $100,000, held in trust by the federal government. Tribal members then dispersed, and the tribe nearly ceased to exist. Across the river from their nearly unoccupied reservation arose Lake Havasu City, one of Arizona's prime tourist attractions and a popular retirement home for "snowbirds" from the North. The Chemehuevi reservation shrank to its present 28,000 acres, and eventually only one or two tribal members remained on the land.

In time, however, the elders and a new generation of displaced Chemehuevis came to regret their land loss. They petitioned successfully for tribal recognition in 1970 and went about the difficult business of reestablishing their reservation on the remaining land. They discovered that resort development had, in fact, bestowed on them 2,340 acres of shoreline. With a $1 million federal loan, they bought out private improvements made on their land in their absence, as well as the Havasu Landing Resort, which became a tribal enterprise.[107] Today, amid a growing effort to reattract members to the land, they are struggling to balance resort income with ecological concerns in an effort to afford the reconstructed tribe's members an opportunity for economic and cultural survival. A tribe that once numbered in the thousands now has an enrolled membership numbering slightly more than 600 people, of whom a little over one-third live on the reservation.

By 1991, those on the reservation faced another challenge in the form of a secretive and dictatorial tribal leader, Christine Walker. As Walker's followers allegedly blacklisted dissidents from jobs and rigged elections, both tribal members and white residents joined in a bitter protest that lasted 106 days, finally forcing Walker into exile and causing the FBI to seize tribal records in an investigation of corruption. The interim council that took over then had to overcome BIA resistance to recognizing the new tribal constitution that members approved in a referendum. New elections then produced a regular tribal government that replaced the interim body.[108]

Why go back? And why care so passionately about reestablishing what was almost dead? For many it is a process of rediscovery, a Native American version of *Roots*. But it takes on almost mystical qualities. Interim tribal vice-chairman Nicholas Alvarez, whose father served as tribal chairman in the mid-1980s prior to Walker, returned only after his father died. He described his return from his Los Angeles home, where he grew up, as "a calling."[109]

Nowhere is this new activism more evident than in the raging battles over waste disposal, particularly the emerging tendency within the waste-management industry to look for landfill and incinerator sites on reservations where, according to conventional wisdom, tribal sovereignty will shield those firms from stricter state requirements. Although Indian nations are required by federal environmental statutes to uphold minimum federal standards, no doubt there has also been the expectation that actual enforcement will be more lax as well. So far, these assumptions have been big miscalculations for waste-industry officials.

One of those miscalculations involved a proposed nuclear-waste dump that was not even on a reservation, only near it. That technicality was of little consequence to the Chemehuevis, who still saw the dump as a threat to the very tribal homeland they had been working to rebuild.

They were among several California tribes that challenged the California Department of Health Services (DHS) on what has become one of the most controversial environmental issues in the nation—the disposal of low-level radioactive waste. Much of the waste is generated in medical applications and has been piling up at medical facilities for years. A site-selection team chose Ward Valley, near Needles, as the location for a radioactive-waste dump that would use unlined trenches in the desert floor. Residents of the Chemehuevi and Fort Mohave reservations feared that leaks from the facility could endanger water quality in the Colorado River, a source of drinking water not only for five reservations along the valley's Colorado-Arizona border, but also for Los Angeles and other cities.

One issue that troubled tribal interim vice-chairman Alvarez was that the state had chosen U.S. Ecology, Inc., to operate the facility, largely because it was the only firm willing to share financial liability—up to the ludicrously low ceiling of $10 million. Three other contestants for the project refused to share any liability with California taxpayers. Alvarez noted that U.S. Ecology's track record consisted of operating four of the nation's six existing low-level disposal sites. Two of those, in Maxey Flats, Kentucky, and Sheffield, Illinois, had been shut down for violations of EPA regulations and were undertaking remedial action. A third, in Beatty, Nevada, had also been the target of regulatory action because of safety violations by employees.

But Alvarez also noted that California Governor Pete Wilson seemed bent on thwarting public input into the siting process. The site belonged to the federal Bureau of Land Management, which meant that the Department of the Interior had to sell the land to the state before any development could take place. When the state's Lands Commission, which ordinarily must take possession of any new state property, balked over concerns about the environmental assessment, Wilson overrode its objections by arranging for the DHS to take direct possession of the lands instead. After first promising an administrative hearing on the issue—over the strenuous objections of U.S. Ecology, which argued that such a hearing would be unnecessary and illegal—Wilson later changed his mind after the firm won a court decision that merely said that the state was *not required* to hold such a hearing. As of June 1993, the issue was still in limbo, awaiting a possible change of heart by the Department of the Interior. Under President Bush, Interior Secretary Manuel Lujan was prepared to approve the sale of the federal land. It was less clear that President Clinton's Interior Secretary, Bruce Babbitt, would follow through.

The Ward Valley situation was one in which the five tribal governments in the Colorado River valley had no direct authority over the process. Though they saw their interests directly affected, they effectively held no more legal status than other communities, like the city of Needles, and had to rely on procedural challenges and political alliances with non-Indian environmentalists. In this, they showed considerable savvy, forging cooperative efforts with groups like the national Nuclear Information and Resource Service and the Committee to Bridge the Gap, a coalition of opponents of the Ward Valley dump.[110]

In Oklahoma, another coalition, largely composed of Native Americans, fought a long but successful battle to shut down a nuclear-fuel facility not coincidentally named after the Cherokee Indian leader Sequoyah. Originally a subsidiary of the Kerr-McGee Corporation, Sequoyah Fuels was sold in 1988 to General Atomics. Under either company, for nearly a decade it was the steady target of Native Americans for a Clean Environment (NACE). The grass-roots organization of Eastern Oklahoma Cherokees, Creeks, other tribes, and a few white farmers and ranchers at the base of the Ozark Mountains grew out of local frustration with what executive director Lance Hughes called "seventeen years of contamination." Among the sources of that contamination, according to Hughes, was the company's underground injection well for the disposal of radioactive waste. The company also developed a history of accidents and nearly 1,500 violations, Hughes said.

The prospects for battling the facility must have seemed bleak when a dozen activists organized NACE in 1985. They seemed even bleaker five years later when a nearly broken and demoralized organization hired Hughes, a half-Creek, half-white, former Census Bureau liaison to Indian tribes and research analyst for the Cherokee Nation who "was trying to take a break from life."[111]

Undaunted by the task, Hughes insisted that the organization put all its efforts into shutting down Sequoyah. He kept at it seven days a week, keeping the story before the news media, intervening in Nuclear Regulatory Commission (NRC) licensing hearings, and hiring the best management consultants with a string of grants he mustered from various foundations and church groups. Diane Curran, a leading national attorney on nuclear issues who had fought the Seabrooke nuclear-power plant in New Hampshire, agreed to represent NACE.

In the process, Hughes borrowed a new term of art from one of the scientists who had contracted with NACE—"technical militancy." In Hughes's view, the phrase means "the new professional capacity of citizens' groups to develop the technical capacity to take these people on. We walk into the courtroom and argue against their positions. The more successful we get, the more the government tries to keep us out." In the past, Hughes said, grass-roots citizens groups often lost because they failed to lodge substantive challenges.

None of this technical militancy, however, came through major environmental groups, according to Hughes. "We have no relation with big environmental groups, and they have never helped out," he said, adding, "and I guess they never will. Now they say we have to help you. We'll help ourselves now, thank you." The consultants whom NACE hires, he said, are contracted as individuals, not as representatives of national groups.

There is no question about whether or not the strategy succeeded. The NRC first shut down the plant for several months. Later the company agreed to a permanent closure.

The issue of waste disposal—nuclear, toxic, or otherwise—has undoubtedly done more to galvanize Native American environmentalism than any other single question, according to WIN's Lila Bird. The organization's name belies its expansion into a number of environmental issues besides water on behalf of its southwestern constituency of small farmers, Hispanics, and Native American communities. Of late, her organization has been helping tribal members fight off attempts to site radioactive waste dumps on reservations.[112] Other Native American grass-roots networks, such as the relatively new Indigenous Environmental Network, and two Native American organizers hired by Greenpeace (Nilak Butler in San Francisco and Jackie Warledo in Tulsa) have also been involved.

Still, most of the fights originate at the grass-roots level, and outside help is sometimes almost an afterthought. There is something almost instinctively insulting to most Native Americans about the very idea of leasing their land for any sort of garbage disposal, aside from the profound moral objections they naturally feel about the abuses the earth is likely to suffer from most of the waste operators who come knocking on tribal councils' doors. Even when tribal-council members, pressed for viable economic-development options, have shown an interest in such proposals, tribal members have usually forced a showdown on the issue. Although there are literally dozens of examples of Indian nations that have entertained and then rejected lucrative offers to place landfills or incinerators on their reservations, two in particular will serve to illustrate the spontaneous power of the grass-roots movement.[113]

On the Rosebud Sioux reservation in South Dakota, the tribal council signed an agreement in November 1990 with RSW, Inc., a waste-disposal firm, for the development of a landfill for municipal solid waste (although the contract also allowed some medical and hazardous waste). At the time, the tribal council was facing the need to upgrade its existing small tribal landfill to EPA standards but had little money to do so.[114] RSW sweetened the pot by offering $75,000 for the cleanup of existing dump sites, but the contract took that sweetener away in the same sentence with the words, "*provided* further that RSW shall recoup the amount of any such reimbursement from the amounts owed to the Tribe under paragraph 12 (b)."[115] That paragraph provided the tribe with four percent of the gross revenues for the first three million tons dumped per year, rising to eight percent for quantities above that amount. Whether such sums would be adequate to monitor an operator whose track record was questioned by tribal environmental activists was unclear.[116]

Those are, of course, large amounts. The developer of the planned 5,700-acre landfill near White River was busy pitching the advantages of his disposal site to officials in such garbage-rich metropolises as Minnesota's Twin Cities, where county officials were searching for ways to dispose of 250 tons per day of incinerator ash.[117] That sales pitch prompted Native American activists and environmentalists to demand promises from county officials that they would not dump incinerator ash on reservations.[118]

Meanwhile, Christine and Ronald Valandra and their friend, Cheryl Crazy Bull, organized a rebellion that became known as the

Good Road Coalition, named after the road near a tribal cemetery where the landfill would have been located, uprooting the dead. Coalition members rounded up petition signatures and forced the tribal government to back out of the agreement.[119] In the ensuing tribal election, Ron Valandra lost in a bid to become tribal chairman, but the incumbent lost by an even wider margin, clearing the way for Alex Linderman's victory. Under Linderman, the tribe engaged Burl Self, an urban-planning professor at Southwest Missouri State University and an Oklahoma Choctaw, to draft a reservation zoning ordinance, which the tribal council later approved. According to Self, the zoning ordinance "effectively shut down dumping."[120] A desperately poor reservation with 85-percent unemployment had decided there still had to be a better way.

On the Choctaw reservation in Mississippi, authoritarian tribal chairman Phillip Martin had long been credited with significantly advancing his people's economic conditions, reducing unemployment to about 20 percent from three or four times that level.[121] No one minded the manufacturing jobs, but when rumors circulated in January 1991 that a six-month-old waste-disposal firm from Jackson was getting approval to locate a disposal facility of an unspecified nature on the reservation, reaction was swift. Linda Farve, president of the Pearl River Development Club, organized a community meeting and attracted some outside environmental activists and experts to speak to the crowd.[122] Nearly 100 people questioned six tribal-council members who attended.

It soon became apparent that National Disposal Systems, Inc., had offered the tribal council $500,000 to consider the company's proposal. The tribe was also to take jurisdiction over 483 acres of nearby land to be acquired by the company and given to the Choctaws to be placed in trust, insulating any facility on the land from state regulation through tribal sovereignty.[123] The tribe had already received the money, and tribal development officials had been working on the plan for more than a year, but the tribal officials and the company had agreed not to discuss the nature of the facility yet.[124] Company officials later specified that the plans included a hazardous-waste landfill.[125] However, proponents noted that the land contained the same hard-clay formation, considered ideal for such purposes, that underlay the Chemical Waste Management landfill in Emelle, Alabama. That facility, however, had been the target of local environmentalists there, in part because of leaks into the underlying Selma chalk formation.[126]

At any rate, the battle was afoot, with Farve soon circulating petitions seeking a tribal referendum on the dump agreement.[127] Martin responded somewhat hyperbolically, charging that such a referendum would break tribal efforts at economic self-determination and deter other businesses from locating on the reservation.[128] Despite the chief's warning, more than 1,100 people signed within a month, far more than the 800 needed within the 5,000-member tribe.[129]

Farve then upped the ante, organizing a protest march on the reservation, a photograph of which appeared in a *Newsweek* article on the issue of hazardous-waste dumping on reservations.[130] Chief Martin scheduled the petitioned referendum for April 19, 1991.[131] Amid considerable acrimony, the votes rolled in. Chief Martin suffered a rare setback as the Choctaws rejected the proposed landfill by a 3-to-2 margin. The future mattered more than the money, and traditional values triumphed over quick gains. As one elder told the *New York Times*, "We, the old ones and the elderlies, have to do the right thing for the young ones. If they sue us and we have no money, they will take the whole reservation and the young ones will have nothing."[132]

The greatest storm has arisen over a federal search for temporary sites for high-level radioactive waste under a 1987 law that required the U.S. Department of Energy (DOE) to find one by the following year. Five years later, it was still searching. The sites were to consist of concrete bunkers and buildings for short-term packaging and storage of spent fuel rods from civilian nuclear-power reactors. The rods would later be transferred to a permanent site, probably in Nevada. The law also created the Office of the Nuclear Waste Negotiator, headquartered in Boise, Idaho, as an independent agency empowered to find suitable sites, known as "monitored retrievable storage" (MRS) facilities.

Unlike previous searches in which communities near proposed sites had everything to lose and saw nothing to gain from hosting the waste, the new process had a hook: money. Communities that volunteered to study the potential for a nuclear installation were eligible for DOE grants of up to $100,000, no strings attached. Continued cooperation with the process could bring even greater benefits to the tune of several million dollars. At that point, more detailed scientific data were required.

Of the first seven communities to apply, five were Indian reservations—the Yakima Nation in Washington, the Mescalero Apache in New Mexico, Prairie Island in Minnesota, and the Sac-and-Fox and Chickasaw nations in Oklahoma.[133] By May 1, 1993, nine tribes had advanced to the second-phase studies.[134]

Understandably, some tribal officials apparently saw the process as a chance not only to obtain badly needed money but to gain scientific expertise that their tribal governments were sorely lacking. The Yakima, for instance, have been forced for the last half-century to accept the nearby presence of the Hanford nuclear facility in eastern Washington. Would they now be able to gain expertise to cope with this undesirable deprivation of lands they had traditionally used, including Gable Mountain, where they had gone to see visions and talk with the Creator?[135]

Just as predictably, however, a firestorm of criticism broke out within many Native American communities. Wendell Chino, the Mescalero Apache tribal chairman and an outspoken advocate of the program, drew some of the fiercest criticism for his stance. Descendants of the famed Apache warriors Cochise and Geronimo lined up for and against the proposed nuclear dump as the Mescaleros advanced through the study process.[136]

Grace Thorpe, the daughter of the late Olympic athlete Jim Thorpe, first convinced her own Sac-and-Fox tribe to withdraw its application, and then spent her time crisscrossing the country to persuade members of other tribes either not to apply for the grants or to challenge tribal governments that did.[137] Thorpe's story is perhaps the most enlightening with respect to the capacity of the MRS issue to revive seemingly dormant environmental activism among Native Americans. Thorpe, already retired from a career with the National Congress of American Indians (NCAI) and the House Subcommittee on Indian Affairs in Congress, was simply enjoying her retirement and her garden when she learned that her tribe had applied for an MRS grant. The revelation reached her through an article in the *Daily Oklahoman* in January 1993.

"What's happening to our people?" she recalled asking herself. "Have we sunk so low seven generations after the Black Hawk War in 1832?" At that time, Black Hawk, a Sauk chief, objected to the whites' insistence that his tribe move west of the Mississippi. When he led a band of about 500 back into Illinois at what is now Rock Island, a war ensued in which his people were chased northward until 250 men, women, and children were massacred. This proud nation was later relocated to the Indian Territory in present-day Oklahoma.

Armed with the moral indignation of her people's history, Thorpe asked questions. The tribal-council members "said they weren't going to put the waste there. They were just going to take the money and not do anything with it. I didn't like the idea of the tribe even being involved. We're supposed to be the protectors of the land," she recalled.[138]

Schooled in the ways of law and politics, Thorpe studied the MRS issue and the tribal constitution. She discovered that 50 signatures on a petition would suffice to call a general meeting of the tribe's 2,100 members. Thorpe collected more than 80. The provision stems from an amendment to the tribe's IRA-style constitution that aimed to bring the tribe closer to its traditional decision-making gatherings. An annual tribal meeting (loosely akin to a New England town meeting) occurs in August, but Thorpe said the prospects of more frequent general meetings have served recently to keep the tribal council in touch with the people it represents. At the meeting in February 1992, 75 members attended. Thorpe moved the issue of rejecting the MRS grant; another elder, June Stevens, seconded it, and 70 hands were raised in favor of the motion. Only five people supported the grant. All were members of the tribal council.[139] The DOE check for $100,000 was returned uncashed. It is the only such check returned to date, according to Lila Bird.[140]

That did not end Thorpe's involvement. A Chicago firm contacted the tribe about a proposed scheme in which it would donate a gravel pit near the small town of Marseilles, Illinois, if the Sac and

Fox would place the land in tribal trust and allow the firm to operate a waste dump. Again there was an incentive for the tribe, and again Thorpe was incensed.

One tribal council member, she said, asked her, " 'Why did you vote against the one in Illinois? It doesn't affect us.' I said, 'It has to do with the land. I can't believe you're saying this.' "

That still did not end Thorpe's new activist career. She began to receive telephone calls from Indian activists across the country faced with similar problems. The Indigenous Environmental Network called later in the spring, asking her to serve as a keynote speaker at its third annual gathering in The Dalles, Oregon, that June. Puzzled as to the source of the invitation, she was told that members wanted to learn how she had defeated the MRS proposal among the Sac and Fox. Later, she says, she became a consultant on the issue to the Sierra Club as well as a frequent speaker at Native American environmental meetings.[141]

One of the issues that most concerned the grass-roots opponents of the MRS site search was that DOE had become an essential source of funding for the National Congress of American Indians (NCAI), an organization established in the 1920s. DOE had begun to provide grant money to NCAI in 1984, under a cooperative agreement that would help educate tribal leaders about the cleanup, handling, and storage of spent nuclear fuel. On one level, there was nothing unusual about such an arrangement, for federal energy agencies had previously assisted CERT in establishing its mission and organizational structure. But when NCAI and DOE renewed the agreement for five more years as of January 1993, providing a cash-strapped national Indian voice with a total of $1.8 million spread over that period,[142] the activists turned suspicious, sensing that NCAI was being badly compromised in the deal.

They decided their suspicions had been confirmed when NCAI met at the Aladdin Hotel in Las Vegas on March 15 to 17, and the DOE took members of its Nuclear Waste Policy Advisory Group on a public-relations tour of the Yucca Mountain site in Nevada, which was intended as the final repository for high-level radioactive waste.[143] Forty of the grass-roots activists, though uninvited, joined the tour.[144] When the NCAI agenda failed to include any opportunity for opposition voices to be heard, the activists decided to seize the moment and force the issue. Convincing some NCAI delegates to yield their time, they paraded a short list of spokespersons to the microphone to explain their opposition and to demand that NCAI listen to grass-roots voices.[145]

It was not the only opportunity that DOE and Nuclear Waste Negotiator David Leroy enjoyed to make their case to Indian nations about the economic advantages of hosting radioactive waste, which included an estimated 700 to 800 jobs in construction and perhaps 200 to 400 in monitoring the waste.[146] CERT also sponsored meetings that facilitated discussion between tribal officials and Leroy's office concerning applications for MRS study grants. CERT held one meeting in Colorado Springs in April 1992 under the curious title "Dialogue on Tribal Perceptions of the Ethical and Moral Bases of Nuclear Energy and Radioactive Waste Management." CERT executive director A. David Lester faced an interesting challenge in bridging the gap between federal radioactive-waste storage needs and the land ethic of American Indian spirituality. As tribal and federal officials groped toward a mutual understanding with varying degrees of success, Joseph Campbell, representing the environmental-protection committee of the Mdewakanton Sioux of Minnesota, who already lived near the Prairie Island nuclear-power plant, challenged the very notion of morality as posited at the meeting.

> And the way the Indian people told their stories set down a set of rules that were followed [he noted, concerning Indian stories]. . . . and those rules were followed for centuries and centuries and centuries. And because of the way that they were taught, this word that you have here on paper, "morality," is not a word that I know of. It's not even in our language.
>
> So when you ask our people here to answer a question about something that we have no ability to even understand, we can't answer that. But when we tell about our stories and the way that our people treated the living things around them, and those stories were told and taught to the younger people, and anyone that would come and ask to know about those things would be told those things, they would learn.
>
> And through that system, there never was a question of the other word that's on this paper: "ethics." Because ethics are something that

have to be written down by a society in order to guide them on that path to morality. And the Indian people just didn't have it and don't have that to go by.

We know and we realize from our stories that the Creator handed down to our older people through dreams and visions that we have to protect everything that lives around us, including the earth, more so than anything else, because everything comes from the earth.

And only until recently in the '40s did something come to this planet that could threaten everything that ever lived on this planet. It was created by a society that neither has ethics nor morality, and I think that's what we're here to discuss, aren't we?[147]

In the face of such spiritual values, not to mention the history of federal government–Indian relations, later observations by federal officials that the earth is "bathed in radioactivity"[148] seemed like feeble responses to a searing indictment of the political process that had brought American society to its current waste-disposal impasse. Nonetheless, although it certainly became clear that Lester and CERT were out of touch with much of the grass-roots sentiment in Indian country, Lester's view of the issue cannot simply be dismissed out of hand. For one thing, it still carried significant institutional weight. For another, it represents a certain evolution of logic among some national Indian leaders.

Lester made some of his views clear in October 1991 at the first conference of the Society of Environmental Journalists in Boulder, Colorado. Speaking on a panel discussing "People of Color and the Environment,"[149] he noted that "we do not have the dichotomy of polarized development versus the environment. We must have both." While observing that these were apparently diverging or opposing principles in white society, he added, "We cannot protect our environment unless we develop. We cannot afford with the current state of our economies the environmental management that is required."

Inevitably, especially considering Robert Bullard's presence on the panel, a number of journalists in the audience raised questions about the siting of various kinds of waste dumps on reservations. In response, Lester noted that, with increasingly tight federal standards, "very few if any rural communities will be in compliance." The problem of either spending large sums to bring local waste disposal into compliance or to ship tribal waste somewhere else "requires a balance of interests at the local level." Because Indians did not have the option of moving when they were dissatisfied, he reminded the audience, "tribal government takes on a much more heavy burden in not only space but time," ensuring that future generations would be able to live on the reservation.

Still, as the questions persisted, Lester became somewhat testy. He reminded Bullard, a critic of waste-dump siting practices, that "we also have to know that there's no economic activity that does not produce waste." Even tourism, he added, "creates the same inequities as industry that Bob described." In short, in Lester's view, the critics were being simplistic. The role of leadership was to cultivate the new development that would pay for the environmental protection that the critics demanded. Earning money through waste dumps might be the price a tribe would pay to achieve that benefit, although he also pointedly noted that "not one" proposal for a garbage dump had to date been accepted.

Activists like Grace Thorpe and Lance Hughes took a dim view of the outlook that was emanating from NCAI and CERT. Hughes sarcastically noted that some NCAI officials were prone to suggest that their critics were "all working for Greenpeace or something. Stupid, dumb Indians in Washington don't even know when we can take care of our own, as if we don't have a mind of our own, a brain in our head." In the aftermath of the NCAI gathering in Las Vegas, Thorpe and Hughes sought a new way to consolidate Native American efforts against the MRS siting process. The result was the birth of the National Environmental Coalition of Native Americans (NECONA).[150] Grace Thorpe, the bulldog who had forced the issue into the limelight, became its first president.

The MRS issue is likely to be an ongoing concern for years in Indian country despite the setbacks to the siting process envisioned by DOE. But it raises a troubling question that Congress has failed to answer. It was a predictable result of the congressionally mandated process that a racial minority that now controls only three percent of the

U.S. land base was most likely to be desperate enough to accept money to consider hosting spent nuclear fuel. It was also clear from prior failed siting efforts that more affluent communities had been totally unwilling to host such facilities. Given the propensity for legions of conservatives to deny the very existence of environmental racism, one must ask: If the MRS process did not constitute environmental racism, what did?

It could not be enough to answer that the existence of such racism was obviated by the economic opportunities that federal inducements provided, for that had been the history of many previous environmental tragedies, ranging from sharecroppers' needs to work in unsafe Appalachian coal mines to Chicano workers seeking a better life in pesticide-ridden farm fields in California. To top it off, the Navajo uranium miners' tragedy was still unfolding as the search for MRS sites on Indian lands got underway. Furthermore, the MRS issue could not be viewed out of context. It was part of a broader trend toward attempting to use Native American lands as dumping grounds for all sorts of waste, and that in itself was part of an even broader tendency of the dominant culture to lay waste to those lands—and the continent—in many other ways.

The grass-roots activists of Indian country undoubtedly wanted the people of the United States to do some soul searching. It was not at all clear that most American citizens understood the gravity of the history that preceded the latest attempt to use Indian lands to solve the problems of a society that would not come to terms with its own legacy of waste.

A Place at the Table

Their time in the national limelight had come. More than 600 delegates, participants, and observers arrived in Washington, D.C., during the third week of October 1991 for a conference that, a few years before, veteran environmentalists might have assumed could figuratively be held in a telephone booth. They would have been wrong, but that is part of the story.

The First National People of Color Environmental Leadership Summit made headline news, declaring that a movement was staking its claim on the American political scene. Representing almost as many grass-roots groups as there were people, the summit drew Native Americans from tribal organizations, Hispanics and African-Americans from both inner-city and rural areas, Asian-American electronics workers from the Bay Area, Pacific Islanders, and a contingent of white supporters from allied networks like the Citizens' Clearinghouse for Hazardous Wastes and the Institute for Local Self-Reliance.

The summit had been made possible by the United Church of Christ (UCC), whose Commission for Racial Justice (CRJ) supplied two of its key organizers—Charles Lee, a Chinese-American who directed its Toxics and Minorities Project, and the Reverend Ben Chavis, the CRJ's executive director, who a year and a half later became the executive director of the National Association for the Advancement of Colored People (NAACP). For speakers, it attracted stars of the civil-rights and environmental movements like the Reverend Jesse Jackson, but the real stars of the conference were lesser known people like Gail Small, the director of Native Action, and Robert Bullard, the author of *Dumping in Dixie*, a book examining racial discrimination in the siting of environmentally hazardous facilities. Given the potential divisions beneath the newly emerging environmental rainbow, the summit's signal achievement was to bring about unity and harmony in less than 100 hours.

Bullard recalled later how his own African-American delegation had met with Native Americans to exchange views and experiences. While the Native Americans began to appreciate the intensity of the urban environmental stress inflicted upon African-Americans, he said, his African-American friends learned to place new value on Mother Earth and the animals.[1] The mutual willingness to listen drew its strength from the shared sense of loss and struggle that each party brought to the table.

Many of the activists enriched their grass-roots perspectives by hearing voices and views to which they had not previously been exposed. Mililani Trask, a native Hawaiian attorney, told of an effort by her people to declare a sovereign nation where none had existed for a century. Within a generation of the arrival of Captain James Cook in 1778, she said, a thriving, self-sufficient population of 800,000 had lost 770,000 people to disease, much as the native populations of Mexico, the Caribbean, and other parts of the New World had been decimated. Nonetheless, the islands had grown again to maintain 20 international treaties until U.S. Marines subverted the Hawaiian government in 1893. Later, she said, prior to statehood in 1959, there had been great debates about the wisdom of incorporating a state where whites would be a minority. When it joined the union, Hawaii became the only state where lands were not reserved by the federal government for indigenous people, but instead were placed in trust with the state government.

Trask went on to detail the environmental damage beneath which the Hawaiian islands groaned. "Tourists," she said, "need golf courses, golf courses need tons of pesticides, herbicides, and millions of tons of water." The rains percolate through the lava of the islands, she added, bringing with them "all the herbicides and pesticides that have been used for years by agribusiness, King Cane, Dole Pineapple, United States military. . . . Nobody in the state of Hawaii or the Hawaii Visitors Bureau is going to tell you that at the present time there are 30 contaminants in the drinking water in the state of Hawaii." Trask related the perils associated with development of the islands' geothermal resources, the loss of native rights to worship in Wao Kele o Puna Forest, where geothermal development was taking place, and the depletion of native fisheries.

What was needed to respond to this crisis, Trask declared, was a new way to perceive justice. Recalling the images of law school, she declared, "Environmental justice is not a blindfolded white woman. Environmental justice is everybody that is sitting right here." Many attorneys sitting in the audience were working on environmental cases, she noted. "I support them. But do not put your eggs in the basket of the blind white lady. We must try other approaches."[2]

In a more figurative way, the issue of sovereignty dominated the People of Color Summit. With few exceptions, the participants had not arrived to seek a voice within the major national environmental organizations, though they certainly directed some criticism toward them for what appeared to be policies of benign neglect, to borrow the phrase coined by Senator Daniel Patrick Moynihan. They had come to speak for themselves, using their own networks, their own organizations, and their own media of expression.

They had all come a long way, both in a short time and over the course of centuries. In a few short years, their organizations responding to the national and international environmental crisis had blossomed, not by tackling large, amorphous issues like global warming and the depletion of the ozone layer, but by responding to threats in their backyards, where their own people were suffering and dying from environmentally related illnesses. Their people had been doing this for a long time, actually, but they had only recently begun to see it as "environmental" in nature. The word, until lately, had seemed the relatively exclusive property of the largely white, middle-class conservation movement, which had focused on issues like national parks, saving whales, and preserving endangered species. The movements among people of color saw nothing wrong with those efforts as such, but for too long they had sought a voice for other concerns and been denied. Now they would speak for themselves.

And they would broaden steadily the definition of environment.

In the inner city, it would also include the invasion of drugs, the inadequacy of housing, the atmosphere of violence. In rural areas, it would include the lack of jobs, the deprivation of educational opportunity, and the stultifying impact of political corruption. It would include those things that cheapened and degraded the future of the children of color and of low-income families of all colors.

Around the country, the new environmental voices from the grass roots repeated stories of their difficulties in making these equity-based concerns heard in the larger coalitions that had been dominated by the established environmental organizations. In southern Florida, Oannes Pritzker noted that the indigenous tribes, the Miccosukee and Seminoles, had sought participation in the Everglades Coalition when it began formulating its initiatives but met resistance. Usually, he said, the indigenous groups were merely asked to lend their names to projects and programs that the coalition had already worked out, despite the obvious stake they have in the precarious future of their ancestral homelands.[3]

In Los Angeles, Concerned Citizens of South Central and the Mothers of East L.A. had at times fought their own battles and protected their own neighborhoods without the support of mainstream environmentalists, although that was changing, slowly. But there was still significant distrust between the two camps, and a long learning curve.

In Chicago, Greenpeace organizer Sharon Pines shook her head in disgust as she watched the drama of Earth Day 1990 unfold with no significant Hispanic or African-American leadership. The author, asked to attend an Earth Day planning meeting that spring, noted that, of 50 people gathered in an office in the posh North Pier, only one was African-American. The rest, who seemed to have no sense that anything was missing, were almost entirely young and white. Environmentalism for them was a yuppie affair. They had, to be sure, invited some African-American and Native American speakers. It just had never occurred to them to reach out to the people in Robbins or Altgeld Gardens or even to local labor unions.

In New York in the fall of 1990, Peggy Sheppard of the West Harlem Environmental Action Coalition (WHEACT) also complained of difficulty in winning support or involvement from a citywide coalition called Environment '90 for issues of concern to New York's African-American community. The coalition, whose name had been Environment '89 during the mayoral campaign in which it supported David Dinkins, had just drafted a letter to Dinkins outlining a series of development issues where it felt he had not been supportive of the environmental viewpoint. A year before, Sheppard and others from nonwhite communities (we will not here call them minorities since everyone is part of a minority today in New York) had introduced the coalition's members to the term "environmental racism." Their mere shock upon hearing those words, she said, produced a long string of invitations to discuss the issue, often at the expense of attending to matters in her own backyard. Nonetheless, Sheppard said, when she attempted to add one of her group's priorities in the letter to Dinkins, the coalition leaders refused.

The upshot, Sheppard added, was that her members had to face a basic decision. Were they going to "waste all that time running to everybody else's meetings, trying to educate them, or are we going to put our attention on getting our own selves together? So we started a group called New York City Coalition for Environmental Justice," consisting of groups like the Toxic Avengers, a Hispanic youth group in Brooklyn, and the Harlem organizations, to pursue environmental concerns in communities of people of color.[4]

The issue of environmental sovereignty and mutual respect arose at the national as well as local level, and among white working-class people as well as people of color. At the Citizens' Clearinghouse for Hazardous Wastes (CCHW), executive director Lois Gibbs, the housewife-turned-organizer who had fought to evacuate the citizens of the Love Canal area, had a beef with the Environmental Defense Fund (EDF) over the clamshell containers used to hold Big Macs. The grass-roots movement for which CCHW functions as a network, she said, had initiated and moved forward the issue of disposable foam packaging by targeting McDonald's with a boycott and an organizing campaign called McToxics. The local organizations that turn to CCHW for help had questioned such packaging because they had recognized it as a factor in the drive to develop new landfill space, almost always in their backyards. Yet in the end, she charged,

EDF executive director Fred Krupp had appropriated the issue after accepting a last-minute invitation to join a McDonald's task force, then seizing the credit when the firm at last abandoned the use of the foam packaging. For Gibbs and the grass-roots constituency of CCHW, the bridge of trust with EDF had been breached.[5]

Unquestionably, however, the single most stirring challenge to traditional environmentalism came in a letter drafted by a group of activists led by Richard Moore, the executive director of the Southwest Organizing Project (SWOP). Sent to the so-called "Big Ten" environmental groups, and signed by more than 100 organizations, it accused them of failing to hire or recruit adequate numbers of minority-group staff members. (The "Big Ten," or "Group of Ten," according to a SWOP briefing paper, included Sierra Club, National Wildlife Federation, Natural Resources Defense Council, Environmental Defense Fund, Environmental Policy Institute/Friends of the Earth, Izaak Walton League, National Audubon Society, Wilderness Society, National Parks and Conservation Association, and Sierra Club Legal Defense Fund [a separate entity from Sierra Club itself.] The briefing paper also suggested that the Nature Conservancy and some other "conservation" and "land trust" organizations could qualify for this elite grouping.[6]) The letter cited a study by the CEIP Fund, Inc., that found "only six minority persons serving on the boards and only 222 (16.8%) minorities employed out of a total of 1,317 staff members. Only 24 (1.8%) of those were professionals."[7] The study created an immediate stir, gaining publicity in the *New York Times* and an op-ed piece by columnist Clarence Page in the *Chicago Tribune*,[8] and led to a broader focus on the role of minorities in environmental issues throughout the preparation for Earth Day 1990, the twentieth anniversary of the first Earth Day.

Despite the attention drawn to the issue at that time, some mutual tension and suspicion have continued between the Big Ten and the environmental-justice movement. Inevitably, some of this emerged almost as soon as both wings of the environmental movement realized that the new Clinton administration presented opportunities for redirecting national policy. Obviously, Clinton was expected to be more receptive to movement suggestions than either Bush or Reagan. But as early as November 6, 1992, SWOP issued a

memorandum, co-signed by several grass-roots leaders, to seven national groups, accusing them of having "entered into negotiations
with the transition team" while "[w]e have been shut out of this process." Moore demanded that the groups "cease making decisions
which affect our well-being without our being full partners in the
process." Within days, memos, letters, and telephone calls were crisscrossing the country, attempting to clarify just who was doing what
on behalf of whom. Ultimately, Moore sent a letter to Clinton on
behalf of the grass-roots groups outlining their concerns that environmental justice be incorporated into the new administration's
agenda at the earliest opportunity.[9]

Few people enjoy being labeled racists, even if the implication is
strong that their racism may have been the product of neglect or
ignorance rather than intention. The reactions among leaders of
mainstream environmental groups ranged from anger to mild *mea
culpas* to sincere attempts at outreach. And, as both Gibbs and Moore
are quick to point out, the accusations arose not out of a desire to
attack other elements of the environmental movement, but out of
the frustration felt by grass-roots groups trying to work creatively and
productively with their better-funded, more well-established breth-
ren. Gibbs noted that the environmental movement needed the Big
Ten's strength and presence on Capitol Hill, but needed it used for
the benefit of the people most at risk from modern industrial poisons. To her mind, the distinction between the two wings of environmentalism was one of controlling pollution versus preventing it,
a point also made by Barry Commoner in *Making Peace with the
Planet*. Gibbs felt that the major environmental groups had lost touch
with the poor, working-class victims of pollution who suffered from
the impacts of scientific approaches to pollution control that sought
proof of harm before imposing limits on pollutants. The issue for
Gibbs has long been that chemicals "ought to be presumed guilty
until they are proven innocent."[10]

    That was not the *only* issue for others like Moore and Chavis, who
also saw the need to address the disproportionate patterns of siting of
facilities handling toxic waste, and therefore saw a need for government and the environmental movement to address the land-use is-

sues of siting equity. But together, the issues of prevention and equity constituted essential questions.

Bullard and Dana Alston, of the Panos Institute in Washington, D.C., drafted a position paper for the summit, which outlined what they deemed to be three issues that needed to be addressed by both the environmental movement and the larger society: procedural equity, geographic equity, and social equity.

Procedural equity involves the access of all people to participation in the decision-making process. Efforts to quell participation, to locate hearings away from disadvantaged populations, and the use of English-only communications (as in Kettleman City, California) were examples of violations of procedural equity. Procedural equity would also include adequate representation for disadvantaged communities on decision-making boards.

Geographic equity quite obviously deals with the disproportionate burdens imposed on areas like South Central Los Angeles or the Calumet region of Chicago and Northwest Indiana. It involves attempts to redress the inequity of some communities being forced to host other people's dangerous wastes without receiving appropriate reciprocal benefits.

Social equity deals with the human impacts, in terms of race, income, and other cultural factors, of the inequitable distribution of environmental burdens. Social equity initiatives would, for example, call upon the nation to expend far more resources on such health burdens as lead poisoning of children from contaminated soil and paint in inner-city neighborhoods. Social inequity in an environmental context can even take the form of systematic neglect of garbage collection and other essential services in poverty-stricken neighborhoods. Bullard and Alston noted that the Kerner Commission in the 1960s had found that such neglect had contributed to the feelings of deprivation that led to the 1960s riots.

Like water dripping on a rock, the onslaught of criticism has slowly brought about changes in the major national environmental organizations. They are still evolving, and undoubtedly, each in its own way, will continue to respond to these issues well into the next century. The Natural Resources Defense Council, which had at least been making some of its regional-office attorneys available to groups like WHEACT and Concerned Citizens of South Central, was stepping up the pace and discussing the issue in its newsletters and publications. The Sierra Club Legal Defense Fund had taken up the cause of the opponents of Formosa Plastics in southern Louisiana. And Sierra Club executive director Michael Fischer, on the club's 100th anniversary in 1992, boldly called upon minorities to take over the Sierra Club by joining its many chapters and redirecting its priorities from the grass-roots level. Richard Moore, in fact, indicated that he held greater hope for the Sierra Club's future precisely because its chapter structure facilitated such participation.[11]

In many cases, however, taking over a Big Ten organization, chapter by chapter or nationally, was not what the blue-collar or people-of-color constituents wanted or sought. Driven largely by the necessity to speak for themselves, they had developed their own networks, which had come together in such forums as the People of Color Summit. Vastly underfunded in comparison to the major national groups, however, they needed resources and support to fight some of the most difficult environmental battles in the nation. The tendency of established groups was to offer such resources with the proviso that they would control the agenda.

It was a compromise that the grass-roots activists could not afford to make for reasons deeply embedded in the history of racial and class relations in America. What the major groups needed to learn was the value of welcoming their new partners as equals in effective new coalitions. Money and staff are important instruments of political power, but in the absence of strong grass-roots involvement, they are hollow reeds in the face of the greater money and staff of the environmentalists' traditional adversaries. Lois Gibbs has been adamant that without the people power of grass-roots organizing even the Big Ten are sorely overmatched by the resources of industries like coal, oil, chemicals, and steel, which have fought pollution control and prevention initiatives with depressing regularity.

In short, the grass-roots groups brought to the table another set of resources inadequately valued by the environmental attorneys and lobbyists who had learned so well the battle tactics of conventional politics. They brought commitment, a willingness to get arrested in outrageous situations, and a newfound solidarity often lacking in more affluent constituencies.

In the face of urban tensions sweeping across America at the dawn of the twentieth century's last decade, solidarity was the final major asset the new movement offered the nation as a whole. In Los Angeles and New York, tensions had flared needlessly between African-Americans and Korean-Americans; in Chicago, another layer of aggravation was sometimes added when African-Americans confronted Arab-American store owners in the inner city. The People of Color Summit tried to calm those troubled waters, noting that all these groups faced similar problems of survival that they could address together. It would not always be easy, but it was necessary.

And it was beginning to happen, again like water slowly making its indentation in a rock. In New Orleans, African-American civil-rights activists met in the spring of 1992 with members of the Vietnamese-American Voters Association to discuss common problems with a landfill siting process that threatened to dump a landfill in the largely Vietnamese east end of the city. In a city with an African-American majority and an African-American mayor, this could easily become a sad case of one minority group perpetuating the process of discrimination by dumping on another, a potential scenario in dozens of U.S. cities in coming decades. It was made worse in New Orleans by the fact that, as Louisiana Geological Survey geologist Brad Hanson noted, there was no suitable location for a landfill in southern Louisiana. Any landfill would eventually cause problems. The obvious solution was for the city to undertake a massive recycling program to avert the need to burden any of its populations with such a facility. Both sides recognized that, but most important, they *met*.

The fact that such cooperation was taking hold became more evident later that year. While the attendance at the People of Color Summit was impressive, the attendance at the Southern Organizing Conference for Social and Economic Justice, held in December in New Orleans, simply stunned many veteran observers of politics in the Deep South. More than 1,500 people, largely from eight south-

ern states stretching from Florida to Oklahoma, arrived to participate in a full weekend of activities focused on environmental issues
in disadvantaged communities. Organizers like Damu Smith, from
Greenpeace, had trekked across the southern countryside for months,
finding and enlisting the support of grass-roots community organizations for this historic initiative.

The new movement had won a place at the table. The Deep
South, the nation, would never discuss environmental issues in the
same way again.

Detoxifying America

Pollution, Barry Commoner used to say, is a resource in the wrong place. The United States is a nation rich in both waste and wealth. The point of the environmental-justice movement is that as one descends the economic ladder the burdens of waste increase just as surely as the luxuries of wealth decline. America is an environmentally stratified society.

The issue, however, is not simply one of redistributing environmental burdens so that the wealthy suffer along with the poor. Nor is it, as many in industry are suggesting, simply a matter of present-day pollution reflecting historical patterns of land use that clustered low-income, working-class people around the industrial areas that provided jobs. As many of the cases examined in earlier chapters illustrate, there has been all too much willful neglect of the environmental quality of such communities to allow this easy excuse to be viable.

The issue is that the American industrial sector remains unnecessarily wasteful, often in ways that hurt its own long-term bottom line. American industry, with insufficient exceptions, has failed to take seriously the implication of Commoner's maxim—that there is wealth in the recovery of the very materials that now constitute pollution. Moreover, there is even more wealth to be found through energy and manufacturing-process efficiencies that would avoid creating much of this pollution in the first place.

That industry is capable of major improvements is evident from the steady reductions in Toxic Release Inventory (TRI) numbers ever since the public availability of these data began to put the worst companies in the public spotlight. Until the creation of TRI within the framework of the 1986 Emergency Planning and Community Right-to-Know Act (EPCRA), the standard operating assumption was that a company needed to implement whatever controls would bring it into compliance with current pollution-control requirements, but no more. With the spotlight of the TRI, however, companies found new ways to improve and made them happen. The purpose of this chapter is to shine that spotlight on the best positive examples of what can happen to help American industry clean up its act.

As the stories from places like Cleveland and the Calumet region demonstrate, the minority communities and blue-collar workers most affected by industrial pollution are seldom purist or unreasonable in their expectations. They have, for the most part, lived with some of the most difficult economic tradeoffs any group should have to face, at times when many affluent suburbs could avoid such choices simply through exercising the land-use planning discretion that accompanies wealth and power. These groups simply want industry to become a good neighbor, sincerely committed to doing the best job possible within the broad meaning of environmental justice. It is, of course, perfectly natural in view of past history that suspicions often run high. Some industries still have a lot of explaining to do. But blue-collar and minority communities have a right to expect that their jobs and tax base will not come at the expense of their own lives or their children's future.

Thus, when these communities rise up in opposition to new commercial hazardous-waste incinerators or landfills, they are not trying to shut down American industry. They are, as Lois Gibbs suggests, trying to "plug up the toilet" to force American industry to adopt strategies to reduce its generation of the chemical wastes that find their way into industrial neighborhoods and remote, powerless rural areas.[1]

Although it is difficult to obtain a perfect set of comparative data due to differences in data-collection practices between nations, it is clear that the United States generates far more hazardous waste than is necessary even in relation to its high level of industrial productivity. In their 1990 book, *Prosperity Without Pollution*, Joel S. Hirsch-horn and Kirsten U. Oldenburg compare data from a number of in-dustrialized nations around the world. The U.S., with a high gross national product (GNP) per capita ($17,000)—but not remarkably higher than Japan ($16,000), West Germany ($15,000), and Canada ($14,000)—would need a 90-percent reduction in its 2.3-tons-per-capita annual rate (in 1985) of hazardous-waste generation to bring itself down to the range of other leading industrial nations. Japan's rate, based on 1983 data, was the lowest of the crowd at 0.01 tons per capita. Switzerland, with a higher GNP per capita of $21,000, was still well below the U.S. at 0.05 tons per capita. The closest to the U.S. were France (1988 data) and Austria (1984 data) at 0.4 tons. Clearly, since Hirschhorn and Oldenburg were unable to acquire matched sets of identical data across international lines, there is con-siderable room for interpretation as to the real extent of the differ-ence, particularly since nations vary as to the range of chemicals covered by their regulatory programs. Hirschhorn, formerly with Congress's Office of Technology Assessment (OTA) and now a pri-vate consultant on waste-reduction technologies, and Oldenburg, still with OTA, understand those limitations in the data they used. But this they conclude nonetheless:

> It is doubtful that the broader universe of wastes regulated in the United States alone accounts for the differences between it and the four low-waste industrial nations. More efficient industries which use cleaner technology appear to be an important explanation in some other nations. The other nation that stands out as a high hazardous-waste producer is Taiwan. This finding too is consistent with general observations that Taiwan has been lax about environmental regulations which would pressure industry to practice even simple waste reduction measures, although that condition is changing rapidly.[2]

In the United States, for the last two decades, the operative word in pollution control has been *control*. The operative word in waste management has been *management*. The control-and-manage ap-proach (generally known in the regulatory world as command-and-control) does not challenge the sanctity of existing production methods or product compositions but merely seeks to attack the problem after it has been created. Its failures have led American industry down the primrose path of increasing expenditures on pollution-control equipment and ever-higher costs for waste disposal, fed in part by the public's demands for tighter regulatory controls. Moreover, American consumers and their communities, lured into buying products wrapped in increasingly elaborate and chemically complicated packaging, have likewise faced escalating disposal costs for municipal solid waste. The major service of the grass-roots movement for environmental justice has been to create the groundswell of public opinion, first for the right to know embodied in EPCRA, and second for the shift in thinking toward pollution prevention and waste reduction that only recently has begun to infiltrate the policymaking centers of the Environmental Protection Agency.

In spite of the slowness with which the EPA has come to understand the seriousness of this approach, and the tenacity with which it has clung to the notion of handling the growing volume of hazardous waste with treatment, storage, and disposal facilities, there have been remarkable examples of progress—and of what could be happening on a wider scale with different policy incentives.

Some states and some elements of private enterprise have proven faster on the uptake. In California, one county even led the parade. Ventura County, threatened with a series of job losses, launched a waste-minimization program in 1984 as part of a creative bid to retain local businesses. County inspectors who helped businesses identify waste-reduction opportunities found that 95 percent of the county's generation of hazardous waste came from 75 companies. The program concentrated technical assistance on those firms and, within two years, had reduced their output of waste by 70 percent, a figure it derived from examining the firms' waste manifests, required by the Resource Conservation and Recovery Act (RCRA). In the process, many of the companies saved money. Based on that experience, California passed statewide legislation. Every county and municipality must now produce a hazardous-waste-reduction element as part of its comprehensive plan.[3] California law also requires plans for managing and reducing household hazardous wastes.[4]

Around the country, the number of states with some sort of toxics-use reduction program for business is in the dozens and growing. Among the major initiatives are Massachusetts's Toxics Use Reduction Act and the Minnesota Technical Assistance Program. Still, as

Scott Bernstein, president of the Chicago-based Center for Neighborhood Technology (CNT), has noted, most are woefully underfunded and pose weak alternatives to the dominant regulatory mode of pollution control. Only a handful offer financial as well as technical assistance for small businesses. Thus, the potential reduction in America's industrial load of hazardous wastes goes largely unrealized.

Still, a growing body of experience and technical literature indicates that substantial reductions are both feasible and generally helpful to industry's bottom line. Hirschhorn and others, including Joel Makower (author of The E Factor), have treated some of these issues in greater technical depth, so this book will not attempt to replicate those efforts. But a few brief case studies will help to illustrate how some manufacturers have succeeded in achieving significant reductions in toxic pollution and hazardous waste.

Fisher Controls International, located in Marshalltown, Iowa, employs 2,100 people in manufacturing control valves for the pulp-and-paper and chemical industries. The process involves spray-painting and machining operations, both of which used to generate significant pollution, particularly in volatile solvents. Around 1987, the company began to examine how RCRA was affecting its costs for disposing of hazardous waste and found that they were rising rapidly.

"We saw it coming pretty fast," noted Dennis Swanson, the company's pollution-prevention specialist. "I wrote an analysis for the company of where we would be in five or ten years if we didn't change."

The goal in Swanson's resulting proposal: zero emissions. The company changed the way paint guns were cleaned in order to reduce waste generation. Water-soluble operations were substituted for vapor products in cleaning machining operations, reducing air emissions by 86 percent. In 1987, the company's toxic air emissions, consisting of xylene, toluene, and 1,1,1–TRI, totaled more than 100,000 pounds. The xylene and toluene comprised about three-fifths of the cleaning solvent the company was using. By 1992, the company reduced the total volume of those emissions by more than 95 percent and was still driving for its ultimate goal of zero.

The company also did its employees a favor by improving the quality of indoor air in its plant. The primary method for accomplishing this was disarmingly simple and applicable to thousands of shop floors across the country. It completely eliminated the generation of 235,000 annual pounds of hazardous waste by ceasing the use of "Floor-Dry," an absorbent material spread on factory floors to soak up oil and liquid waste. The new cleanup method is an old-fashioned one: mops and brushes. No longer is the air inside the plant laden with toxic dust. Swanson noted, "The air you breathe in the shop becomes better, and the Floor-Dry is not tracked on tires and shoes." Going further, the company has also reduced cardboard and paper waste headed for landfills by 60 percent. And no hazardous substance may be accepted at the company's loading docks unless it is on an approved list, according to Swanson. These efforts have won Fisher Controls the kind of public relations other companies may envy. The firm has received both the Iowa Waste Reduction Award and the Iowa Energy Leadership Award.

What is particularly intriguing about the Fisher Controls program is that it is not purely leadership driven, though leadership is obviously essential to its success. Employees have a vital role to play. Responding to Swanson's 1989 proposal, the company created eight committees with specific assignments to research and implement waste-reduction solutions. Such committees are not risk free; people vary in their response to such challenges. Swanson noted that two were "somewhat successful," and two others were "very successful." The important factor is that the whole program is producing a change in the corporate culture.

"People could see that they could affect the changes we were trying to make," Swanson said. "Everyone on the shop floor is looking for changes to make now."[5]

Employee involvement is precisely the lesson that 3M Corporation learned long ago in its Pollution Prevention Pays (3P) program. As author Joel Makower notes, "The idea of having hundreds or thousands of pollution preventers, waste watchers, and energy savers in every department and facility can't help but have a salutary effect on the bottom line." Makower describes the pervasive 3P program as, at its simplest, a "glorified suggestion box." But these suggestions, when accepted by management, bring cash awards. An idea that *pre-*

vents rather than controls pollution, and that involves a technical accomplishment, unique design, or innovative approach, can earn the creative employee a $500 gift certificate. By 1993, the company estimated that, since the program's inception in 1975, it had produced cumulative savings of $575 million and cut pollution in half.[6]

Finally, one other company that revolutionized its production process in order to eliminate its own pollution—in the face of a 1987 water-pollution lawsuit by the Massachusetts Public Interest Research Group—is the Robbins Awards Company in Attlesboro, Massachusetts. The firm manufactures jewelry and custom-designed awards, such as plaques and trophies. Metal plating and etching necessarily involve the intensive use of highly acidic chemicals, which had been part of the company's discharged wastewater. The firm was using more than 100,000 gallons of city water daily until it engineered a complete closed-loop system for managing and recycling its heavily contaminated wastewater.

The system, never before designed for use in that industry, involves both wastewater purification and recovery so that, essentially, the same water is reused almost endlessly with continual cycles of treatment. The water used in the firm's manufacturing process is now almost 40 times purer than the city water it previously used, producing improvements in the quality of the firm's products while eliminating the company's dependence on outside water supplies. That latter freedom was handy when a water-main break shut down city water supplies in 1989. Robbins Awards kept operating.

The entire system has cut water use by 48 percent, chemical use by 82 percent, and toxic-waste generation by 89 percent, while virtually eliminating metal hydroxide sludge as a byproduct. The firm's $220,000 investment in the system retrieved an ongoing yearly savings of $71,000, a three-year payback.[7]

If firms that have taken the pollution-prevention route can achieve such results, why do more firms not take up the cause? First, it is important to note that even these firms are not environmentally perfect. In all likelihood, no manufacturer ever can be, particularly if one begins to examine the environmental impacts of product inputs over which their control may be more marginal. Thus, environmentalists who might criticize such examples by noting that the companies involved are "still not perfect" are both correct and missing the point, for modern society itself is incapable of environmental perfection, presuming that such perfection is even susceptible to definition. The assumption that nothing a company can do will ever satisfy environmentalists is undoubtedly a partial motivator in the minds of more intellectually lazy corporate executives.

More important, however, company executives cannot lead unless they know where they are leading. In order to know the impact of a firm's hazardous-waste generation on its bottom line, on the health of its workers, and on the surrounding community, one must choose to know. All too often, these impacts have been the object of willful ignorance, and once a firm's leadership chooses the three-monkeys approach, there is precious little chance that most lower-level executives, or even most employees in the absence of a strong, environmentally conscious labor union, will pursue a more enlightened course. Makower, for instance, notes that "more than one CEO has said that until the TRI data were released, he had no idea how much waste his company was generating in the form of pollution."[8] That simple fact alone was what made Paul Templet's corporate-challenge initiative, while he headed the Louisiana Department of Environmental Quality, such a powerful tool for achieving TRI reductions. By putting the worst companies' emissions under the glare of media publicity, it forced corporate executives to take notice of their own TRI data. Most responded accordingly. Templet noted in an interview that one plant indicated that it had been trying to get the attention of its head office for years with regard to pollution-abatement equipment. The corporate challenge and threatened loss of tax benefits finally spurred that attention.[9]

At the core of the corporate-leadership problem is the matter of accounting for pollution impacts and costs. More than a few ecological economists have noted that conventional economics has done a poor job of accounting for the true costs of pollution. Herman Daly and John Cobb, in *For the Common Good*, have discussed extensively new public-accounting mechanisms for adjusting our measures of economic growth, which now count the cleanup expenditures for the Exxon *Valdez* as being every bit as valid a contribution to the

Gross National Product (GNP) as investments in new plant and equipment. Yet it is obvious that, had the *Valdez* accident never happened, vital resources would have been used in ways that would have improved our quality of life, rather than merely remediating it. For nearly 20 years, environmentally conscious economists have been working on various new social accounting schemes that would more accurately reflect the sustainable social welfare of the society, rather than treating all money changing hands as if it were equally productive of human benefits.

Corporations need to reexamine their internal accounting just as society does. Of course, there can be major differences between short-term cash-flow benefits and long-term sustained economic health. The short-term focus of many corporations and executives has been the subject of a great deal of legitimate social criticism in the United States as well as a concern affecting our international competitiveness. Again, Makower notes, there is gain in moving ahead of the typical learning curve:

> There is a small but growing body of empirical evidence showing that companies with the most proactive policies are also among the most profitable, as measured by a variety of standard measures of economic performance.
>
> One obvious reason is that many of the efficiency measures save money. Another reason is that a leading-edge company often becomes the standard against which all companies in its industry are measured. When those measures are being taken by federal and state regulators, that can result in a company leading regulators rather than following them. More than one progressive company has stated, privately as well as publicly, that remaining far above compliance is for them a competitive advantage.[10]

It is easy to be skeptical about such logic, of course, especially when one has been trained to think in the most purely objective terms about the bottom line. In talking to executives and company environmental officials who have gone down this path, one senses a distinct difference in culture and life outlook from those who remain doubting Thomases. Not every investment in pollution prevention has a payoff, yet those committed to this route often pursue the less lucrative options in the belief that it is simply the right thing to do.

And the last decade has seen the rapid growth in firms that deliberately tout (and, we hope, practice) their environmental consciousness as a means of endearing consumers. At least a part of this leap of faith is intuitive, a product of new thinking and training that is only beginning to penetrate many business and engineering schools. Makower, for instance, raises the intriguing—and largely unanswerable—question of the value of trees in a forest if they go unharvested. It is small wonder that, as Louis Hawpetoss pointed out, foresters from around the world have been visiting the Menominee reservation.[11] Untrained in modern business methods, the Menominee elders of the mid-eighteenth century seemed intuitively to know something very valuable about the relationship of their forest to the future economic welfare of their people. That they never lived to see the world come to value their legacy in no way diminishes their achievement. They have proven that they understood far more than all the logging companies surrounding their reservation, who stripped Wisconsin bare.

As accountants and economists strive to emulate the Menominee wisdom with the help of modern mathematics, it is useful to remember that such advanced computational techniques as life-cycle analysis are, at their roots, driven by a very human, intuitive sense that our management of the environment has gone sadly awry. Neither in corporate accounting nor in economic analysis is there such a beast as value-free methodology.

Armed with the knowledge that substantial pollution reductions are not only possible but often beneficial even to the company pursuing them, there remains the question of how communities can act to bring about desired solutions to longstanding problems of environmental pollution and inequities. The issue is, at bottom, one of knowledge and political will. As with corporate executives, public officials must be willing to see what they need to see, irrespective of what they may consistently be told by the more recalcitrant special interests and trade associations. Much of the frustration of the environmental-justice movement stems from repeated experiences of failing to stir such consciousness in skeptical public officials at all levels. Yet even here, there are examples of communities that have demon-

strated significant gains from taking the initiative. Paul Templet, returning to his post as professor in the environmental-studies program
at Louisiana State University, has undertaken a series of studies of
the relationship between environmental quality and economic development. His findings are a startling lesson for those who believe
it is necessary to trade one for the other. In effect, he has found, poor
environmental quality drives out quality economic development, resulting in the impoverishment of public services, education, health
care, and other elements that make up quality of life.[12]

Governments themselves can be major polluters, and they often
use the same economic excuses that corporations do—excuses that
they often would not accept from private industry in regulatory disputes. Yet, cities in particular, with their operation of sewage-treat-
ment plants, a large fleet of police and emergency vehicles,
water-purification systems, and other major utilities, can take the
lead in demonstrating a commitment to the same sort of environmentally conscious thinking that consumers are now demanding of
corporations. San Jose, California, for instance, created an Office of
Environmental Management to coordinate and encourage energy-
efficiency and pollution-prevention initiatives within city government.[13] The city hiked its percentage of recycled solid waste from
under 15 percent in 1986–1987 to nearly 40 percent in 1992–1993.[14]
The Institute for Local Self-Reliance (ILSR) has published an entire
volume of case studies titled *Beyond Forty Percent*, examining how
some cities achieved even higher recycling rates in a drive to avoid
landfill costs. And, as ILSR is fond of pointing out, many of these
cities are, in turn, discovering that those recovered goods are a form
of "urban ore" that can be a resource for further economic development. Other forums and studies by the National Council for Urban
Economic Development and California's Local Government Commission have begun to detail how cities can mine the entire area of
environmental services, including but hardly limited to recycling, as
a new means of reconciling concerns about job creation and environmental protection.

Two areas that merit a brief review are energy efficiency and municipal approaches to pollution prevention, for they are areas where
local environmental activists can have direct and noticeable impacts.

They have also been sorely neglected amid the discord over environmental racism.

On the first matter, it is unarguable that communities that own their own electric-power companies maintain far more potential control over their own economic and environmental fate than do those that do not. This is not to deny that there are some progressive public utilities such as Pacific Gas and Electric. But cities in control of their own power need not rely on the beneficence of enlightened corporate management. In cities like Chicago, under the sway of highly conservative Commonwealth Edison Company, the lack of such control has provided many bitter lessons for community organizations seeking to influence local and state energy policy.

One of the favorite examples of Amory Lovins and the Rocky Mountain Institute, which he founded and which works with communities on developing energy-efficiency projects, is Osage, Iowa (pop. 3,500). Its now-retired municipal utility director, Wes Birdsall, was a veritable prophet of energy conservation, supplying the utility's customers with free caulking guns, insulation, high-efficiency light bulbs, and a copious dose of education to forestall any need for expanded power capacity. The result, according to Lovins, has been that this tiny farm town keeps an additional $1.5 million in its local economy, a tidy sum that equals $1,000 per household. Moreover, the profitable municipal entity is able to use some of its savings to support other municipal needs. One can only imagine what savings much larger cities could achieve with similar evangelism.[15]

Lest it be unclear that such municipal innovation has serious environmental consequences, let us first note the efforts of another municipal utility, in Rocky Mount, North Carolina. According to Marie Swindell, the city's utilities-marketing coordinator, the utility set out in 1992 to plant 27,000 trees, one for each of its customers. This, too, was aimed at forestalling the need for new power capacity, this time through tree shading, which can cut summer air-conditioning loads by 15 to 35 percent, and sometimes more. In the bargain, it should be noted that, to varying degrees depending on the species planted, trees also have known pollution-absorption values, helping to cleanse urban air (so long as that capacity is not overtaxed).[16]

Every kilowatt-hour of electricity saved by any of these means has a direct effect at the power plant by reducing pollution from the burning of coal, oil, or other fuels. It is by now an indisputable fact that the nuclear-power trend of the 1970s died an agonizing death more because of a slackening of consumer demand for electricity than because of antinuclear protests, important as they may have been in shaping environmental policy. Hirschhorn and Oldenburg noted that, due to technological improvements in lighting, an 18-watt fluorescent bulb now produces as much light as a 75-watt incandescent. (Actually, continuing advances in lighting technology have made even that statement obsolete.) They noted that using the fluorescent bulb (which now generally would have a useful life several times that of most incandescents) "prevents the burning of 400 pounds of coal, forestalling the release of an enormous quantity of air pollutants, including about 700 pounds of carbon dioxide and twelve pounds of sulfur dioxide."[17]

To get an idea of the cumulative impact of programs to institute such efficiencies, consider the case of one inner-city church in Chicago, renovating its lighting with assistance from a synodical energy-conservation project. Augustana Lutheran Church replaced a bank of 45 75-watt incandescent bulbs in its sanctuary with 13-watt compact fluorescents that actually produce better lighting and last 10,000 hours instead of 1,500, thus eliminating a good deal of bulb waste. Job Ebenezer, the Evangelical Lutheran Church in America's environmental stewardship director, has calculated Augusta's yearly pollution reduction at 19,282 pounds of carbon dioxide, the equivalent of taking 10 cars off the road. It also averts the generation of 214 pounds of sulfur dioxide and 94 pounds of nitrous oxide. It will recover its $3,000 investment, which covers a number of other areas of the building as well, in two and a half years. It is, of course, only one of thousands of churches in the metropolitan area capable of making such improvements.[18]

Cities can implement such efforts through regulatory as well as direct programmatic means. Indeed, that is the point of the remainder of this chapter. City officials are not nearly as powerless to effect meaningful environmental improvement as many would claim. Lovins notes that municipalities not only can reduce their own energy use by a variety of means, but they can also institute energy-efficiency codes that will bring down the cost of heating, cooling, and operating new buildings. The California Energy Commission, for example, estimates that state codes instituted since 1977 will save $700 million in electricity and $524 million in natural-gas costs throughout the state, again entailing major reductions in pollution from power plants. Cities can also take nonregulatory steps to improve energy design, such as San Jose's Innovative Design and Energy Analysis Service (IDEAS), which one client found reduced energy use in his development project by one-third. Other municipalities have used zero-interest revolving loan funds to spur such improvements.[19]

The mechanism for implementing many of the energy codes is one very familiar to urban planners and zoning administrators: site-plan review. A developer seeking a permit submits its plans for review to determine compliance with municipal zoning, landscaping, subdivision, and other ordinances. Although this review is generally administrative in nature, it often offers opportunities for public comment, particularly if it involves any sort of rezoning or special- or conditional-use permit, which usually is approved by a zoning board of appeals or similar appointed body.

Herein lies a strategy many community organizations have learned to use, particularly in suburban areas where people generally feel a greater sense of control over the affairs of local government. Planners can use site-plan reviews of proposed industrial facilities to induce corporate attention to environmental efficiency. Such reviews can be built into the industrial-performance standards in a city's zoning code if it has such standards. Unfortunately, industrial-performance standards, a serious trend in the planning field in the late 1950s, have become one of the most sorely neglected regulatory tools in the planner's arsenal. As a result, cities across the country are losing vital opportunities to achieve major gains in environmental equity, given the historical fact that the neighborhoods most proximate to industrial districts tend to be populated by low-income and minority people.

Just as it is possible to perform energy audits in buildings to determine their potential for energy savings, it is also possible to conduct engineering audits of industrial operations for their efficiency in the use of toxic chemicals. Indeed, that is the object of many of the state technical-assistance programs aimed at toxics-use reduction. But most of these programs, as noted earlier, remain both voluntary and underfunded, and thus underutilized as well. Municipalities can begin to change that by making such audits a requirement for site-plan reviews of new facilities, and even a periodic requirement for existing businesses. It is only fair to warn, however, that the subject of toxics-use efficiency and pollution prevention is considerably more complex than that of energy efficiency, where the nature of the uses and of the audits is much more standardized. Pollution prevention, as Hirschhorn noted, is a strategy of considerable subtlety and often involves insights into proprietary processes. The sanctity of corporate control over the production process in the free-enterprise system, while slowly yielding ground under the assault of the environmental-justice movement, nonetheless is sufficient to spur many companies to resist any such intrusion on their freedom to operate, irrespective of the touted benefits. Fighting for such mandatory review of companies' pollution-prevention practices may be a significant struggle in many communities. It is also a struggle that is only beginning to make a dent in federal environmental policy.[20]

There are a number of other areas in which the United States can begin to detoxify its economy and produce short- and long-term benefits in its citizens' health and quality of life. The National Academy of Sciences, for instance, has published an extensive study of sustainable agricultural techniques, showing that they are often at least as productive as chemical-intensive agriculture while they reduce farmers' input costs and restore the nutrient value of the land. Consumers can drive many changes in corporate culture by insisting on better information about the contents of the products they buy and making appropriate substitutions for those that do not meet their expectations. But in some areas, government and the environmental-justice movement need to consider obstacles to progress on all these fronts.

For the most part, major national and international corporations like 3M have the means and the personnel to institute serious pollution prevention once they establish a corporate culture of support for such efforts. But many small businesses, like many smaller municipalities, may lack the expertise and the financing to implement valuable changes.

It is in this area that environmentalists may need to think seriously about their priorities and strategies. Many groups have been born of struggles against large corporations, and such struggles breed a distrust of industry as the enemy. But the Center for Neighborhood Technology, noted for its advanced strategic thinking on environmental issues, has shown that a helping hand for smaller manufacturers may be more helpful in solving real problems than confrontation. For several years, it has been conducting an ongoing experiment in working with Chicago's electroplating industry, which is dominated by small, often marginal and family-owned, enterprises. For the most part, they did not feel challenged, but instead threatened, by new regulatory requirements that they could not afford to meet. Often, when regulations are written by federal and state environmental agencies, they are written with the larger firms in mind.

CNT embarked on a plan of consultation and communication, overcoming barriers to productive relationships. It helped to demonstrate to policymakers and the companies that what was needed most for these companies to comply effectively with pollution-control regulations was an opportunity to pool their resources by using common hazardous-chemical treatment facilities that none could individually afford. The step facilitated the retention of thousands of jobs among dozens of employers in an industry where the use of *some* toxic chemicals was unavoidable. Those jobs were almost entirely in the inner city and belonged to the very people the environmental-justice movement is seeking to protect.[21]

There, too, lies a lesson for state and federal policymakers. With a modest amount of imagination, it is possible to construct win-win scenarios.

The Future of
the Movement

Despite the many win-win scenarios described in the previous chapter, there will be losers in the battle for environmental justice. Should the struggle for pollution-prevention succeed, these losers will largely be found in the chemical and waste-management industries. Many companies involved in the latter, if they are smart, will move into environmental-cleanup and pollution-prevention consulting, leaving the dinosaurs of the waste business to feast solely on what surely will remain a sizeable mountain of garbage for some time to come. There is abundant evidence that large waste firms, such as BFI and WMX (the new corporate name for Waste Management, Inc.), have already read the handwriting on the wall and are moving into areas such as recycling and the cleanup of contaminated sites (sometimes even earning money for cleaning up sites that they helped to contaminate). Those in the chemical industry will most likely strive simply to find new ways to sell us on a better life through chemistry, whether we need it or not.

But the struggle for environmental justice will not be won easily, and it is worth looking into the crystal ball to divine the future of this movement, even if its progress remains somewhat hazy.

First, it is clear that America's racial and ethnic minorities, with few exceptions, contain disproportionate numbers of blue-collar workers whose jobs are often found in the very industries that are creating problems the environmental-justice movement is seeking to address. Even where that is not the case, blue-collar workers of all types, particularly those who are unionized, represent valuable real or potential allies for the movement. Since movements for social justice can seldom afford to squander potential alliances, this movement must pay close attention to the issue of jobs.

Fortunately, one strong point of the environmental-justice movement, particularly in comparison to some middle-class environmental movements, is that, for the most part, its constituency is already highly sensitized to the issue of job creation and preservation. The issue is simply the types of jobs that are being created.

Thus, it is worth noting that a major consideration for this movement, in light of the likely dislocation of petrochemical-industry jobs if other goals are achieved, is the future of the workers in that industry. The Oil, Chemical, and Atomic Workers International Union (OCAW), one of the most progressive unions in the AFL-CIO, has already come to grips with the issue of job dislocation due to the detoxification of American industry. Largely under the leadership and prodding of vice president Tony Mazzocchi, the union has devised a plan that it calls the "Superfund for Workers." Environmentalists would do well to note that the logical alternative to thinking about the future in this way is to adopt the usual tactic of stonewalling change in order to preserve jobs in a threatened industry. The idea behind the plan is that the workers in the chemical industry deserve at least as much respect and funding as the federal government has lavished on the contaminated sites industry has helped to create. The fund would be used to help educate displaced workers for new careers in much the same fashion that America once enabled its veterans to gain an education through the GI Bill.

In the absence of such an initiative, as recent events in the Pacific Northwest have shown in the case of loggers, the fear and anger that result when workers feel used up, useless, and irrelevant can only spawn an antienvironmental backlash that will severely retard the growth of the environmental-justice movement. Conservative forces, including the so-called wise-use movement that opposes government-defined environmental constraints on land use, know this and exploit such divisions to the hilt.

It is also not enough, as advocates of OCAW's plan note, to argue that pollution control and environmental cleanup create more jobs than are being lost. After all, most jobs in recycling are likely to be low-paying for the foreseeable future, and many of the sophisticated, well-paid jobs in environmental careers will require college degrees. Before people in the environmental movement make such arguments, they must first ask whether the jobs being created are desirable, accessible, and adequate in number to absorb the displaced workforce. Unless they can answer yes on all counts, the alternative being proffered to displaced workers is merely going to intensify the insecurity, and potentially the bitterness, they likely will already feel.

It is important, therefore, that a movement based on expanding the nation's dialogue on environmental issues maintain a serious, open, and ongoing dialogue with the labor movement over issues of worker displacement. It is already clear that the environmental-justice movement is incorporating concerns about worker safety, so this next step should not be difficult. Moreover, OCAW does not have an exclusive claim to this issue. Obviously, its plan has roots in the concept of conversion to a peace economy. OCAW has merely developed a prototype for application in many similar situations as the nation moves toward an ecologically sound economy.[1]

Second, in order to overcome the ready arsenal of money, expertise, and political clout of the industries that will be at odds with the environmental-justice movement, new resources must be available to grass-roots groups. As noted in Chapter 9, it behooves the major environmental groups to make such resources available on a basis of mutual respect for the grass-roots energy that the smaller groups bring to the table. Moreover, the degree of expertise that many of the most committed activists have achieved through diligent study of the issues, combined with their common sense derived from real-life experience, signifies that they often have overcome a long learning curve that, in many cases, has made them the well-informed terror of their opposition.

It is entirely possible that the mainstream environmental movement might now be suffering some degree of intellectual stagnation if it had not been supplemented in recent years by these so-called newcomers. There is no shame in recognizing this. The environmental movement has won many victories over the years, but movements that do not undergo periodic renewal tend to fade into irrelevance.

Nonetheless, an ongoing problem for many of the grass-roots networks has been their difficulty in raising funds. Too often, foundations that readily fund the major national groups with whom they have established relations have had difficulty in comprehending the historic importance of this grass-roots renewal. Sometimes, when they have, they have been inclined to fund the major groups for outreach campaigns rather than funding the groups that need to be reached. This has been a source of frustration for many elements of the environmental-justice movement and poses an obstacle that it must somehow overcome if it is to have major input into the development of policies that address the issues it has raised.

Finally, in this regard, the nation's educational institutions, including its universities and extension services, must prove their commitment to environmental equality by making expertise available to grass-roots groups. They should regard it as part of their commitment to open debate in a free and open society. Some, like the UCLA urban and regional planning program, have already done this. But too many others have been indifferent or actually hostile to such movements.

Third, despite the unquestionable value of such right-to-know victories as the passage of the Emergency Planning and Community Right-to-Know Act (EPCRA), there are still major problems in the area of procedural equity outlined by Bullard and Alston. These problems are both of a local and a state and federal nature.

Locally, as many of the stories outlined throughout this book testify, many citizens still must fight local officials for the right to even basic information about the impacts of industrial development on their lives and health. During the late stages of the Robbins battle, for instance, the village board of nearby Summit, Illinois, approved a proposed new incinerator after hearings that effectively shut out any meaningful citizen participation. Opponents, for example, claimed that they were denied access to public documents concerning the project. Citizens then had to engage in a legal challenge before the Illinois Pollution Control Board to overturn the approval on grounds that basic rules of fairness had been violated in the hearing process.[2] These types of stories are not at all unusual, have a great deal to do with the types of tactics many groups undertake, and do not always reach the same successful resolution that Summit residents were able to achieve. The environmental catastrophe in the former Communist-bloc nations should be sufficient to demonstrate that stifling public debate and participation is the path to ecological suicide.

But there are more serious, and less easily resolved, issues of access to information that the movement must continue to address. Already, some groups are lobbying for what they call "right-to-know-more" legislation. The Toxic Release Inventory, for instance, provides no ranking whatsoever of the relative toxicity of the chemicals on the list. Thus, the prospective addition by EPA of new chemicals to those already listed poses as much potential for confusion as it does for enlightenment. While any comparative ranking must necessarily involve value judgments, it should be possible for EPA, if it truly wishes to enhance the public's right to know, to use the services of credible toxicologists to develop such a ranking.

Moreover, releasing TRI data in a way that readily links the specific chemicals to their known health effects would go far toward furthering public understanding of the relative significance of various toxic threats. Not every TRI-listed chemical is a carcinogen, for instance, and most do not randomly cause just any cancer but are either agents or promoters of specific types of cancer. Before experts condemn the public's ignorance in such matters, it would be appropriate for the EPA and academic experts to make TRI and related public information intelligible and readily useful to the average citizen.

Finally, Dr. Samuel S. Epstein, the author of *The Politics of Cancer* and a professor of occupational and environmental medicine at the University of Illinois in Chicago, noted that the United States has no central registry that monitors most environmental exposures by socioeconomic class. The excuses for not doing so are flimsy, he said, noting that the United Kingdom, with fewer economic resources, has long maintained such a registry for cancer and a wide range of other diseases. "There's a total dependency in this country," Epstein said, "on case reports and studies of an idiosyncratic nature funded by idiosyncratic agencies." But cancer, he notes, is a good surrogate for a wide range of other toxic-induced diseases because most carcinogenic agents also induce other environmental diseases. There is, however, a great deficiency in cancer data in the lack of a breakdown in cancer incidence by socioeconomic group. "If this was done," Epstein says, "this would create the most powerful indictment of planning, ethical, and scientific approaches to these areas. This change in reporting alone would have a dynamic effect on decision making." Already, he notes, we know that there is a 50-percent five-year survival rate for cancer among whites, but only a 38-percent rate for African-Americans.[3] The socioeconomic breakdown would be the right-to-know nail in the coffin for arguments that environmental racism was a figment of the civil-rights movement's imagination.

Fourth, the environmental-justice movement will most certainly continue to work on building bridges of interethnic cooperation. As this topic was already discussed in Chapter 9, we will merely note here that, in the face of social pressures from immigration and the tendency of ethnic minorities to be pitted against one another, this is likely to be a high and lasting priority for this movement if it is to succeed.

Fifth, the movement must find creative ways to deal with two closely interrelated land-use issues that have reappeared as themes throughout this book. Southeast Chicago, which the Reverend Ben Chavis, in his new role as executive director of the NAACP, has chosen to highlight as an example of environmental racism, in fact embodies the dilemma: an area peppered with historically detrimental land uses that stymie welcome development but attract the very kinds of noxious industries that foreclose the region's opportunity for a more environmentally benign future.

One key task in this area that the environmental-justice movement will have to face is finding ways to clean up highly contaminated areas. Without cleanup, they simply have no future because current federal and state hazardous-waste laws—RCRA, CERCLA, and SARA—impose liability on the owners and purchasers of contaminated sites that no new industry would want to assume. As Steve Hiniker, the environmental-policy coordinator for the city of Milwaukee, notes, a map overlay of his city's poor and minority-populated areas would virtually match the map identifying its contaminated sites.[4] But the city has been relatively powerless to alleviate the deterioration caused in those neighborhoods because it, too, would be liable for cleanup costs if it condemned abandoned sites through such means as tax foreclosure. The city learned that bitter lesson after acquiring a tax-delinquent metals-plating facility in 1986. The Wisconsin Department of Natural Resources required a city cleanup costing some $300,000 for a property that, Hiniker estimates, is still barely worth $30,000.[5]

Hiniker's solution to the most immediate problems facing the city has involved work with a state legislative committee. The committee drafted a bill to create an industry-funded pool for subsidizing cleanup of sites. The hope is that Wisconsin cities will be able to attract new development by firms willing to pay a finite sum to underwrite cleanup in order to take advantage of the existing city infrastructure. Not only does this create inner-city jobs, Hiniker emphasized, but it deters urban sprawl through industrial flight to the suburbs. Given the stigma attached to contaminated areas now, it is an ameliorative measure that grass-roots environmental groups should take seriously. Moreover, as grass-roots interest (at least in the Calumet region) in a similar federal measure sponsored by the Northeast-Midwest Coalition attests, it is a subject of great urgency for many of the neighborhoods that produce environmental-justice activists.

In short, many of the areas that have become focal points for the environmental-justice movement are the victims of longstanding waste-disposal practices that have dotted their landscapes with Superfund and other contaminated sites. One initial response of this movement, in the aftermath of the People of Color Summit, was to support legislation first introduced in 1992 by Senator Al Gore as the Environmental Justice Act. Its basic aim was to steer land uses with heavy environmental impacts away from those areas that are already heavily affected. In effect, the bill says of those areas, "enough

is enough." The bill, reintroduced in 1993 by Representative Cardiss
Collins, a Chicago Democrat and member of the Congressional
Black Caucus, would not prohibit such new facilities outright but
would ensure new rights for area residents to raise legal objections to
them on the basis that the area had been designated as a high-im-
pact zone.

That concept serves a purpose as far as it goes, but it is hardly
enough. In the larger sense, the only way to "plug the toilet" is to
work hard at all levels and in all opportunities to reject waste-management options that foreclose realistic pollution-prevention options. Since it is obvious that much of the successful siting of noxious
facilities is taking place in these highly polluted areas, regional bodies and state governments must be forced to come to grips with the
differential impacts of current siting patterns. So long as there is a
Robbins prepared to accept an incinerator as a path to economic
development, even the Collins bill may not succeed. Many African-
American politicians in Chicago, some no doubt influenced by
waste-industry contributions, supported the village's desire to site the
Reading Energy incinerator. It was the only economic development
the village had been able to attract in 15 years.

This poses a moral challenge of the highest order to mainstream
environmentalism. Unless most white environmentalists are prepared to confront the challenge of offering viable economic-development alternatives to villages like Robbins, there is no way they
will ever halt the juggernaut of the waste-disposal industry. The economic disparities that produced the Robbins controversy cannot be
dismissed as being outside the arena of environmental issues. The
Robbins incinerator controversy is the ultimate proof that poverty
and the disparities of wealth in America are the most powerful environmental issues that exist today.

Furthermore, they are a small window through which middle-class
environmentalists can come to understand the dynamics of the international environmental crisis. Massive disparities in wealth and
privilege underlie the destruction of the rainforest, and no debt-for-
nature swap will save the rainforest in the absence of that understanding. Massive disparities in wealth and privilege lie at the heart

of environmental concerns about the North American Free Trade Agreement (NAFTA), and no tinkering with NAFTA's provisions will cure its deficiencies in the absence of that understanding.

As always, the central issue in human affairs is social equity. The environmental equity sought by the environmental-justice movement is now, and always will be, a part of that larger framework.

Finally, the grass-roots environmental movement faces a challenge that we shall here call indigeno-feminization. I coin this new hyphenated term with some trepidation for fear that its meaning will be diluted and the very label oversimplified and exploited, as so many other ideas have been in the past. In combining two fundamental ideas—that of the sacred relationship to the earth of indigenous peoples and that of the matriarchal leadership patterns that are already evident in this young movement—I am merely recognizing a synthesis that is already apparent to sensitive observers. It is not at all new to Native Americans. There is a close tie in many of their cultures between matriarchal patterns of social organization and the equality of their reverence for nature. It is a pattern that has also been apparent throughout the world in many other indigenous cultures. The inability to understand such leadership drove white Americans for centuries to search for powerful "chiefs" among Indian nations in the hope that some autocrat could both make peace and lead his people into the white man's world. That Native American culture survives in its wonderful diversity is a testament to the power of the indigenous way of looking at the world.

White, African-American, Hispanic, and Asian-American working-class people involved in the grass-roots environmental movement have rediscovered some small portion of the magic of this indigeno-feminist relationship with the earth. It is, in many ways, no accident that so many women, including Appalachian "housewives from hell" and Chicano "mothers of East L.A.," have taken the helm of this movement, for the values that have driven them have involved the protection of home and family. The protection of the earth, the larger sense of values that Native Americans have tried to share with their guests in the Western Hemisphere for centuries, is but one long, reflective moral step away from this basic starting point. And it is little surprise that even middle-class white activists like Terri Swearingen find themselves in profound sympathy with Native American environmental and spiritual causes once they have received their baptism by ordeal in the new movement.

The danger for this movement is that every movement, as it has become more firmly established in the American political firmament, has been slowly drawn into the exploitive, male-dominated, hierarchical leadership style of the dominant culture with which it is doing battle. The transformation is seldom blatant; often it is subtle and gradual. It may involve accommodation to the values of philanthropic foundations that begin to take an interest in a new form of social change but do not fully understand the moral and cultural underpinnings of their beneficiaries. It may involve increasing degrees of acculturation to a political system that transforms the very reformers who facilitate its periodic renewal. And, at its worst, it may attract leaders, male or female, whose sense of defiance of the establishment overtakes or obliterates the movement's central values in favor of a machismo that erodes the very core of the participatory democracy such leaders—sometimes known among Native American activists as "Lone Rangers"—profess to foster.

This very issue of leadership style is at the core of current disputes between the mainstream environmental organizations and the grassroots movement. To the extent that elements of the grass-roots movement undermine their own indigeno-feminist leadership (which itself is a function not of gender but of values), they undermine the power and sanctity of their own message. It is, of course, impossible for any movement to remain "pure" in this regard since we are talking about positions on a spectrum of values and about values that are the product of experiential learning. But the challenge to the new movement remains. It has a chance to contribute a perspective both new and very old that the world, in its current environmental crisis, sorely needs. If we listen to each other, we may once again learn to listen to the earth.

Record of Interviews Conducted and Meetings/Conferences Attended

Author's note on sources: In a book of this type, oral sources and in-person interviews take on a far more significant dimension than in an ordinary work of scholarship. Much of the information would not be nearly as fresh or incisive without the benefit of such interviews. The list below indicates all those people who served as interview sources, either by telephone or in direct, face-to-face interviews. In some cases, people were interviewed in groups; in one case in New Orleans, they allowed me to sit in on a small-group discussion of a problem pertaining to a landfill, and I was able to ask questions throughout the discussion. In all cases, I wish to thank these people for taking the time to share their insights and knowledge, especially any who may disagree with some or all of what I ultimately chose to say on the topic that we discussed. Their ideas still sharpened my perspective and forced me to reconsider some aspects of the subject matter.

The second list derives from the fact that, again for a book of this type, public meetings and conferences are an important means of absorbing the ethos of a movement and gaining access to the network of activists about whom one is writing. Thus, listing the gatherings attended during the course of work on this book provides the reader with additional insight on source material.

Individuals Interviewed for this Book

Joy Allison, Tri-State Environmental Council, Chester, WV

Roger Allison, Missouri Rural Crisis Center, Columbia, MO

Nicholas Alvarez, Chemehuevi Indian Nation, Havasu Lake, CA

Paul Anderson, Ohio Environmental Protection Agency, Twinsburg, OH

William Anderson, People
Concerned About MIC,
Institute, WV
Carol Andress, Northeast-Midwest
Institute, Washington, DC
Michael Aniol, Hegewisch
Chamber of Commerce,
Chicago, IL
Thomas Atkins, Environmental
Action, Washington, DC
Rose Marie Augustine, Tucsonians
for a Clean Environment,
Tucson, AZ
Elizabeth Avants, AWARE,
Plaquemine, LA

Dianne Bady, Ohio Valley Envi-
ronmental Council,
Proctorville, OH
Alex L. Bailey, South Coast Air
Quality Management District,
Diamond Bar, CA
Betty Balanoff, Hammond, IN
State Representative Clem
Balanoff, Illinois General
Assembly, Chicago, IL
James Balanoff, City Council,
Hammond, IN
Guy Barone, Dow Chemical USA,
Plaquemine, LA
Reverend Joseph Bartlett,
Sulphur, LA
Timothy Benally, Office of Navajo
Uranium Workers, Shiprock, NM
Laberta Benoit, Sulphur, LA
Wilbert Benoit, Sulphur, LA
Robert Bergsvik, *Southtown
Economist*, Chicago, IL
Alan Bernard, Injured Workers
Union, New Orleans, LA
Scott Bernstein, Center for
Neighborhood Technology,
Chicago, IL

James F. Berry, Biology Depart-
ment, Elmhurst College,
Elmhurst, IL
Lila Bird, Water Information
Network, Albuquerque, NM
Nedra Bonds, Quindaro Township
Preservation Society, Kansas
City, KS
Fred Bosselman, Illinois Institute of
Technology–Kent Law School,
Chicago, IL
Lee Botts, Environmental Consult-
ant, Miller, IN
Mark Bouman, Geography Depart-
ment, Chicago State University,
Chicago, IL
Diana Bowen, Ohio Valley
Environmental Coalition,
Kenova, WV
La Ronda Bowen, South Coast Air
Quality Management District,
Diamond Bar, CA
Irene Brodie, Mayor, Robbins, IL
Janet Brown, GROWL,
Greenup, KY
Thomas Brown, South Suburban
Solid Waste Agency,
Homewood, IL; Village Presi-
dent, East Hazel Crest, IL
Pat Bryant, Gulf Coast Tenants
Organization, New Orleans, LA
Robert D. Bullard, Sociology
Department, University of
California, Riverside, CA
Charlotte Bullock, Concerned
Citizens of South Central, Los
Angeles, CA
Nilak Butler, Greenpeace, San
Francisco, CA
Marian Byrnes, 35th District
Environmental Task Force,
Chicago, IL

Eugene F. Calafato, South Coast Air Quality Management District, Diamond Bar, CA

Dr. Tom Callender, MedHealth Clinic, Lafayette, LA

Robin Cannon, Concerned Citizens of South Central, Los Angeles, CA

Ruth Caplan, Environmental Action, Washington, DC

Dorreen Carey, Grand Calumet Task Force, Whiting, IN

Mick Casey, Tri-State Environmental Council, Wintersville, OH

Lisa Casini, Southeast Clevelanders Together, Cleveland, OH

Robert Castro, Citizens to Bring Broadway Back, Cleveland, OH

Katherine Chaney, POWER, Cleveland, OH

Robert Chaney, POWER, Cleveland, OH

Robert Childers, Gwich'in Steering Committee, Anchorage, AK

Barbara Christian, Ohio Valley Environmental Coalition, Kenova, WV

Renee Cipriano, Illinois Attorney General's Office, Chicago, IL

Henry Clark, West County Toxics Coalition, Richmond, CA

Mark Cohen, Center for the Biology of Natural Systems, Queens College, New York, NY

Luke Cole, California Rural Legal Assistance, Bakersfield, CA

Reverend Adolph Coleman, South Cook County Environmental Action Coalition, Robbins, IL

Barry Commoner, Center for the Biology of Natural Systems,

Queens College, New York, NY

Paul Connett, Work on Waste USA, Canton, NY

Charlie Cray, Greenpeace, Chicago, IL

Helen Cuprisin, South Cook County Environmental Action Coalition, Evergreen Park, IL

David Czernik, Louisiana Consumers League, Baton Rouge, LA

David Dabertin, Indiana Department of Environmental Management, Gary, IN

Cynthia D'Agostino, GSX Coalition Community Group, Cleveland, OH

Charles Dang, Vietnamese American Voters Association, Metairie, LA

Larry Davis, United Steelworkers Local 6787, Wheeler, IN

Sue F. Davis, People Concerned About MIC, Institute, WV

Susan Dawson, Sociology Department, Utah State University, Logan, UT

Sandra L. Demoruelle, Green Sands Community Organization, Naalehu, HI

James Dermody, Federal Aviation Administration, Des Plaines, IL

Janice Dickerson, Gulf Coast Tenants Organization, Baton Rouge, LA

Rosemary Diorio, 35th District Environmental Task Force, Chicago, IL

Niaz Dorry, Greenpeace USA, Washington, DC

Darnell Dunn, Louisiana Environmental Action Network, Baker, LA

Matthew J. Dunn, Illinois Attorney General's Office, Chicago, IL

Annabelle Eagle, Committee for a Better Tribal Government, Southern Ute Indian Reservation, CO

Job Ebenezer, Office of Environmental Stewardship, Evangelical Lutheran Church in America, Chicago, IL

Mary Ellender, Calcasieu League for Environmental Action Now, Sulphur, LA

Billie Elmore, North Carolina Waste Awareness and Reduction Network, Sanford, NC

Dan Emmanuel, Placid Oil Refining Company, Port Allen, LA

Jeanne Englert, Taxpayers for Responsible Water Projects, Denver, CO

Tom Estabrook, Oil, Chemical, and Atomic Workers Local 4-620, Baton Rouge, LA

Cecilia Estalano, Mayor's Office, City of Los Angeles, CA

Audrey Evans, Tulane Environmental Law Clinic, New Orleans, LA

Larry Evans, Oil, Chemical, and Atomic Workers Local 4-620, Baton Rouge, LA

Alex Ewen, Solidarity Foundation, New York, NY

William Eyring, Center for Neighborhood Technology, Chicago, IL

Tyler Fairleigh, Kentuckians for the Commonwealth, Louisville, KY

Linda Farve, Concerned Citizens, Choctaw Indian Nation, Philadelphia, MS

Amos Favorite, Ascension Parish Residents Against Toxic Pollution, Geismar, LA

Lynn Feakin, East Chicago, IN

Sharon Fields, University Settlement, Cleveland, OH

Jason Finkelstein, The Advance Group, Inc., New York, NY

Bernice Fintel, Environmental Task Force, Evangelical Lutheran Church in America, Byron, NE

Willie Fontenot, Citizens Access Unit, Division of Land and Natural Resources, Louisiana Department of Justice, Baton Rouge, LA

Peter Foote, Calumet Area Industrial Commission, Chicago, IL

Robert L. Ford, Center for Energy and Environmental Studies, Southern University, Baton Rouge, LA

W. Wayne Forman, Freeport-McMoRan, Inc., New Orleans, LA

Craig Francisco, New Orleans Landfill Siting Process, New Orleans, LA

Peggy Frankland, Calcasieu League for Environmental Action Now, Sulphur, LA

Ada Mae Gaines, VOTE United, Port Allen, LA

Brian Gallagher, student, John Carroll University, University Heights, OH

Anupom Ganguli, South Coast Air Quality Management District, Diamond Bar, CA

David Gardner, Exxon Corporation, Baton Rouge, LA

Lois Gibbs, Citizen's Clearinghouse for Hazardous Waste, Arlington, VA

Robert Ginsburg, environmental consultant, Chicago, IL

Chellis Glendinning, World Uranium Hearing, Santa Fe, NM

Judith Goldsworth, *The Neighborhood News*, Cleveland, OH

Tom B.K. Goldtooth, Red Lake Band of Chippewa Indians, Red Lake, MN

Robert J. Golec, City Council, Hammond, IN

Jean Golf, Concerned Citizens Against Incineration, Crestwood, IL

Charles Goodmacher, Albuquerque, NM

Lori Goodman, Diné Citizens Against Ruining Our Environment, Durango, CO

Robert Gottlieb, Graduate Program in Urban and Regional Planning, University of California, Los Angeles, CA

Harold Green, Southern Christian Leadership Conference, New Orleans, LA

Kevin Greene, Citizens for a Better Environment, Chicago, IL

Wilfred Greene, River Area Planning Group, Wallace, LA

Susan Greer, People Against Hazardous Landfill Sites, Valparaiso, IN

Esnard Gremillion, Oil, Chemical, and Atomic Workers Local 4-620, Baton Rouge, LA

Marge Grevatt, Center for Cooperative Action, Cleveland, OH

Juana Gutierrez, Mothers of East L.A., Los Angeles, CA

Ricardo Gutierrez, Mothers of East L.A., Los Angeles, CA

Gilda Haas, Graduate Program in Urban and Regional Planning, University of California, Los Angeles, CA

Brian Hagenbusch, West Virginia Environmental Council, Huntington, WV

David L. Haley, First United Methodist Church, West Chicago, IL

Gay Hanks, Vermilion Association for Protection of the Environment, Kaplan, LA

Ledell J. R. Hannon, Garden City Community Alliance, Baton Rouge, LA

Jeffrey Hanor, Geology Department, Louisiana State University, Baton Rouge, LA

Brad Hanson, Louisiana Geological Survey, Baton Rouge, LA

Keith Harley, South Chicago Legal Clinic, Chicago, IL

Becky Harris, Greenup Residents Opposed to the Waste Landfill, Argillite, KY

Phillip Harrison, Jr., Uranium Radiation Victims Committee, Shiprock, NM

Louis Hawpetoss, Menominee Indian Nation, Keshena, WI

Tony Henderson, Black Environmental Action, Bethesda, MD

James Hendrick, Jackson, MS

Mary Hendrick, Jackson, MS

Paul Hill, National Institute of Chemical Studies, Charleston, WV

Stephen J. Hiniker, Environmental Policy Coordinator, City of Milwaukee, WI

Robert Hodanbosi, Ohio Environmental Protection Agency, Columbus, OH

Mildred Holt, People Concerned About MIC, Institute, WV

Charles W. Howe, Environment and Behavior Program, University of Colorado, Boulder, CO

Lance Hughes, Native Americans for a Clean Environment, Tahlequah, OK

Syed Y. Huq, Rosebud Sioux Tribe Water Resources, Rosebud, SD

Bernadette Jackson, Shrewsbury Neighborhood Association, Metairie, LA

Samuel Jackson, River Area Planning Group, Wallace, LA

Shelby Jackson, Ohio Environmental Protection Agency, Columbus, OH

Sarah James, Gwich'in Steering Committee, Arctic Circle, AK

Hazel Johnson, People for Community Recovery, Chicago, IL

Dan Kash, Kentucky Division of Air Quality, Ashland, KY

Karen Katzman, St. Clair–Superior Coalition, Cleveland, OH

Hugh Kaufman, U.S. Environmental Protection Agency, Washington, DC

Sandra Kaufman, College of Urban Affairs, Cleveland State University, Cleveland, OH

William J. Kelly, South Coast Air Quality Management District, Diamond Bar, CA

Paul Kemp, Coalition to Restore Coastal Louisiana, Baton Rouge, LA

Luella Kenny, Love Canal Medical Fund, Grand Island, NY

Sara Jane Kinoy, Greenpeace, Chicago, IL

Richard Kleiner, Louisiana Chemical Association, Baton Rouge, LA

Reverend Robert Klonowski, Lebanon Lutheran Church, Chicago, IL

Robert Kneisel, South Coast Air Quality Management District, Diamond Bar, CA

Robert Kochtitzky, Eco-Mississippi, Jackson, MS

James E. Landing, Geography Department, University of Illinois, Chicago, IL

Charles Lee, Commission on Racial Justice, United Church of Christ, New York, NY

Dr. Marvin S. Legator, Toxicology Department, University of Texas Medical School, Galveston, TX

Greg LeRoy, Midwest Center for Labor Research, Chicago, IL

David Levine, Learning Alliance, New York, NY

Paula Levy, South Coast Air Quality Management District, Diamond Bar, CA

Jerry Liang, Vietnamese American Voters Association, New Orleans, LA

John Liebman, Greenpeace, Kenner, LA

Ed Lim, Ohio Environmental Protection Agency, Columbus, OH

Judy Linkowski, U.S. Representative George Sangmeister's Office, Washington, DC

Brian Lipsett, Citizen's Clearinghouse for Hazardous Waste,
Arlington, VA

David Lopez Lujan, Tonantzin Land
Institute, Albuquerque, NM

Darryl Malek-Wiley, Sierra Club,
New Orleans, LA

Eric Mann, Labor/Community
Strategy Center, Van Nuys, CA

Lou Marchi, McHenry County
Defenders, McHenry, IL

Mary Martin, South Cook County
Environmental Action Coalition, Chicago, IL

Barbara Masters, Hazardous
Materials Commission, Contra
Costa County, CA

Ruth Matkaitis, South Cook
County Environmental Action
Coalition, Oak Lawn, IL

Ramona Mattix, PBR Hawaii,
Honolulu, HI

Zeb Mayhew, Oak Alley Plantation, Vacherie, LA

Mary McCastle, Coalition for
Community Action, Alsen, LA

Roy McCastle, Coalition for
Community Action, Alsen, LA

Chuck McDermott, Waste Management, Inc., Washington, DC

Randall McDougall, John Deere,
Inc., Waterloo, IA

Kai Midboe, Louisiana Department
of Environmental Quality,
Baton Rouge, LA

Fred Millar, Friends of the Earth,
Washington, DC

Louie Miller, Sierra Club,
Canton, MS

Richard Miller, Oil, Chemical, and
Atomic Workers International
Union, Holyoke, MA

Peter Montague, Environmental
Research Foundation, Washington, DC

Marjorie Moore, Community
Environmental Health Center,
Hunter College, New York, NY

Richard Moore, Southwest
Network for Environmental
and Economic Justice, Albuquerque, NM

Terri Moore, Center Point, IN

Ward Morehouse, Council on
International and Public Affairs,
Croton-on-Hudson, NY

Janet Muchnik, City Manager,
Country Club Hills, IL

Mary Murphy, Recycling Coordinator, Village of Evergreen
Park, IL

Ervin Nakai, Uranium Radiation
Victims Committee, Ship-
rock, NM

Zack Nauth, Louisiana Coalition for
Tax Justice, Baton Rouge, LA

Mark Navarre, Ohio Environmental Protection Agency, Columbus, OH

Barry Neal, Reading Energy
Company, Philadelphia, PA

Reverend Peter Neuman, Vietnamese American Voters Association, New Orleans, LA

Minh Nguyen, Vietnamese
American Voters Association,
New Orleans, LA

Daniel Nicholai, National Toxics
Campaign, Baton Rouge, LA

Pamela Nixon, People Concerned
About MIC, Dunbar, WV

Kathleen Norlien, Project Environment Foundation, St. Paul, MN

Ronald L. Novak, Department of

Environmental Management,
Hammond, IN

Paul Nuchims, People Concerned
About MIC, Institute, WV

James O'Byrne, *New Orleans
Times-Picayune*, New
Orleans, LA

Mary O'Connell, Center for
Neighborhood Technology,
Chicago, IL

Richard Olguin, Isleta Pueblo,
Isleta, NM

Kees Olie, University of
Amsterdam, Netherlands

Marylee Orr, Louisiana Environmental Action Network, Baton
Rouge, LA

Maria Ortega, Santa Ysabel, CA

Mimi Pickering, Appalshop,
Whitesburg, KY

Stephanie Pincetl, Graduate
Program in Urban and Regional
Planning, University of Califor-
nia, Los Angeles, CA

Sharon Pines, Greenpeace,
Chicago, IL

William J. Plunkett, Waste
Management, Inc., Oak
Brook, IL

Natalia Porche, South Coast Air
Quality Management District,
Diamond Bar, CA

Oannes Pritzker, Yat Kitischee
Native American Center,
Naples, FL

Frank Propotnik, Ohio Environmental Protection Agency,
Twinsburg, OH

James Quigley, Center for the

Biology of Natural Systems,
Queens College, New York, NY

Annette Rasch, Wisconsin
Conservation Corps/Oneida,
Seymour, WI

Tawny Ratner, FITE, Shaker
Heights, OH

William Redding, Sierra Club,
Madison, WI

Melanie Rees, RRC Consultants,
Boulder, CO

Douglas Remington, Committee
for a Better Tribal Government,
Denver, CO

Sally Riley, Mayor, Chester, WV

Stephen G. Riley, Town of Hilton
Head Island, SC

Farella E. Robinson, U.S. Civil
Rights Commission, Kansas
City, MO

Florence Robinson, Biology
Department, Southern University, Baton Rouge, LA

Marvin S. Robinson, Quindaro
Township Preservation Society,
Kansas City, KS

Johna Rodgers, *Meridian Star*,
Meridian, MS

Anna Rondon, Southwest Indigenous Uranium Forum,
Gallup, NM

Mary Ryan, Waste Management,
Inc., Oak Brook, IL

Edward Rybka, City Council,
Cleveland, OH

Richard Sahli, Ohio Environmental Council, Columbus, OH

Rodolfo N. Salcedo, Department of
Development, City of Milwaukee, WI

William Sanjour, U.S. Environmental Protection Agency, Washington, DC

Michael Savage, Ohio Environmental Protection Agency, Columbus, OH

Mark Schliefstein, *New Orleans Times-Picayune*, New Orleans, LA

Debra Schwartz, freelance writer, Highland Park, IL

Gloria Scott, South Cook County Environmental Action Coalition, Robbins, IL

Steve Sedam, Audubon Society, Columbus, OH

Neil Seldman, Institute for Local Self-Reliance, Washington, DC

Burl Self, Urban and Regional Planning Department, Southwest Missouri State University, Springfield, MO

Michael Shapiro, Ohio Hazardous Waste Facilities Board, Columbus, OH

Bridget Shea, Clean Water Action, Austin, TX

Ruth Shepherd, Calcasieu League for Environmental Action Now, Sulphur, LA

Laverne Sheppard, Native American Journalists Association, Boulder, CO

Peggy Sheppard, West Harlem Environmental Action, New York, NY

Susan Shoulders, Kentuckians for the Commonwealth, Louisville, KY

Damu Smith, Greenpeace USA, Washington, DC

Thomas Smith, Planning Department, City of Chicago, IL

Tom Smith, Public Citizen Texas, Austin, TX

Wilson Smith, Concerned Citizens of South Central, Los Angeles, CA

Gerson Smoger, Gerson Smoger & Associates, Walnut Creek, CA

David Soileau, Louisiana Department of Natural Resources, Baton Rouge, IL

Alonzo Spencer, Save Our County, East Liverpool, OH

John Spinks, U.S. Fish and Wildlife Service, Denver, CO

Norm Steenstra, West Virginia Citizen Action Group, Charleston, WV

Connie Stein, Tri-State Environmental Council, Wheeling, WV

Ramona Stevens, Ecology Consulting Services, Prairieville, LA

Steve Swanson, Fisher Controls International, Marshalltown, IA

Terri Swearingen, Tri-State Environmental Council, Chester, WV

Jack Swenson, Planning Department, City of Chicago, IL

Joe Szakos, Kentuckians for the Commonwealth, Prestonsburg, KY

Jeffrey J. Tangel, South Cook County Environmental Action Coalition, Chicago, IL

Bill Temmink, Loyola Labor Institute, New Orleans, LA

Paul Templet, formerly Louisiana Department of Environmental Quality; now Environmental Studies Program, Louisiana State University, Baton Rouge, LA

Janis Terrell, Fairlea Residents
Opposed to Noise and Pollu-
tion, Port Arthur, TX
Tony Thaxton, Jr., New
Orleans, LA
Dominic Anh Thien, Vietnamese
American Voters Association,
Chalmette, LA
Grace Thorpe, National Environ-
mental Coalition of Native
Americans, York, OK
William Thrift, Louisiana Coali-
tion for Tax Justice, Baton
Rouge, LA
Gerald Tillman, Louisiana Workers
Against Toxic Chemical
Hazards, Baton Rouge, LA
Jim Toler, *Charleston Gazette*
columnist, Belle, WV
Louis E. Tosi, attorney, Fuller &
Henry, Toledo, OH
Alina Tugend, *Orange County
Register*, Santa Ana, CA

Christine Valandra, Good Road
Coalition, Rosebud, SD
Ronald Valandra, Good Road
Coalition, Rosebud, SD
Joan Van Haren, Suburbs United
to Reclaim the Environment,
Calumet City, IL
Lupe Vela, Integrated Solid Waste
Management Office, City of Los
Angeles, CA
Kirby Verret, Houma Indian
Nation, Dulac, LA
Turk Vincent, Sulphur, LA

Patty Wallace, Lawrence County
Concerned Citizens, Louisa, KY
Jackie Warledo, Indigenous Envi-

ronmental Network, Tulsa, OK
Otmar Wasserman, Toxicology
Department, University of Kiel,
Germany
Dale L. Watson, City Planning
Department, Port Arthur, TX
Lori Weahkee, Tonantzin Land
Institute, Albuquerque, NM
Tom Webster, Center for the
Biology of Natural Systems,
Queens College, New York,
NY
Henry W. Wedaa, Board of
Directors, South Coast Air
Quality Management District,
Diamond Bar, CA
John Wells, Ohio Environmental
Protection Agency, Columbus,
OH
Kenneth Westlake, U.S. Environ-
mental Protection Agency,
Chicago, IL
Chas Wheelock, Oneida Nation
Planning Department,
Oneida, WI
Anne Whitcomb, Jefferson County
Planning Department,
Brookville, PA
Charles White, People Concerned
About MIC, Institute, WV
Corinne Whitehead, Coalition for
Health Concern, Benton, KY
Ed Wojciechowski, U.S. Environ-
mental Protection Agency,
Chicago, IL
Mike Wright, Safety Department,
United Steel Workers of
America, Pittsburgh, PA
Robin Lee Zeff, Environmental
Research Foundation, Annapo-
lis, MD

Meetings and Conferences Attended

1. Chicago Earth Day Committee planning meeting, Chicago, IL, March 21, 1990

2. South Cook County Environmental Action Committee rally, Blue Island, IL, April 7, 1990

3. Seeds of Peace Conference (interdenominational social activism), Milwaukee, WI, April 26–28, 1990

4. Environmental Planning Lobby conference, Albany, NY, September 22–23, 1990

5. Thirty-Fifth District Environmental Task Force meeting, Chicago, IL, October 25, 1990

6. University of Illinois Energy Resources Center Conference: Energy Aspects of Solid Waste Management, Chicago, IL, October 29–30, 1990

7. Grass-Roots Solutions to Solid Waste Conference (Institute for Local Self-Reliance), Indianapolis, IN, November 2–4, 1990

8. South Cook County Environmental Action Coalition media briefing and reception for Dr. Paul Connett, Oak Lawn, IL, January 18, 1991

9. Oak Lawn Village Board hearings on proposed Reading Energy waste-disposal contract, Oak Lawn, IL, January 28–29, 1991

10. Interfaith IMPACT Briefing, Washington, DC, March 16–19, 1991

11. Chicago Recycling Coalition meeting, Chicago, IL, April 1, 1991

12. Teaching the Care of the Earth conference (Evangelical Lutheran Church in America Campus Ministry), Sinsinawa, WI, April 19–21, 1991*

13. Earth Day rally, Livingston, LA, April 27, 1991

14. Center for Energy and Environmental Studies, Southern University, Brown Bag Seminar, Baton Rouge, LA, April 30, 1991*

15. South Cook County Environmental Action Coalition, speech by Robert Gottlieb at St. Xavier's College, Chicago, IL, August 5, 1991

16. Citizens' Conference on Dioxin, Chapel Hill, NC, September 20–22, 1991

17. Society of Environmental Journalists conference, Boulder, CO, October 3–6, 1991

18. University of Illinois Energy Resources Center, Clean Air Act Conference, Chicago, IL, October 11, 1991

19. Illinois Environmental Regulation Conference, Illinois Environmental Protection Agency, Rosemont, IL, October 15–16, 1991

20. First National People of Color Environmental Leadership Summit, Washington, DC, October 25–27, 1991

21. The New Dioxin Debate, sponsored by Greenpeace, DePaul University, Chicago, IL, February 8, 1992

22. Farmers Union National

Convention, Des Moines, IA, March 2, 1992

23. Panel Discussion on Environmental Racism, sponsored by ECO, University of Chicago, Chicago, IL, April 20, 1992*

24. Earth Week Rally, Southern University, Baton Rouge, LA, April 26, 1992

25. Geismar/Dutchtown Residents for Clean Water and Air, community meeting, Dutchtown, LA, April 29, 1992

26. Vietnamese-American Voters Association, joint meeting with African-American environmental activists, New Orleans, LA, May 2, 1992

27. Fourth North American Symposium on Society and Natural Resource Management, University of Wisconsin, Madison, WI, May 20, 1992*

28. Environmental Law Institute Seminar on Great Lakes Water Quality Agreement, Chicago, IL, September 18, 1992

29. Urban and Regional Planning Department Seminar, University of Iowa, Iowa City, IA, September 24, 1992*

30. People for Community Recovery conference, Chicago State University, Chicago, IL, October 24, 1992

31. Society of Environmental Journalists conference, Ann Arbor, MI, November 5–8, 1992

32. Southern Organizing Conference for Social and Economic Justice, New Orleans, LA, December 4–6, 1992

33. Robbins Village Board hearing on siting of Reading Energy incinerator, December 22, 1992

34. Second Native American Symposium on Housing and the Environment, Green Bay, WI, January 24–25, 1993

35. Alliance for a Sustainable Materials Economy, planning meeting, Chicago, IL, January 29–30, 1993[†]

36. American Planning Association annual conference, Chicago, IL, May 2–5, 1993[††]

---

*Author served as speaker at this event
[†]Author served as official representative of American Planning Association at this meeting
[††]Author served as panel moderator for a session at this event

Bibliographic Guide

This listing does not intend to follow the practice in many books of listing all the author's sources, which would add a substantial number of pages to this book. It is instead a briefer guide to key sources directly touching on the main theme, the emergence of a national movement of blue-collar people and people of color for environmental justice.

I. Blue-Collar and Minority Environmentalism

A. BOOKS AND REPORTS

Alston, Dana. *Taking Back Our Lives.* (Washington, DC: Panos Institute, 1990).

Alston, Dana, ed. *We Speak for Ourselves: Social Justice, Race and Environment.* (Washington, DC: Panos Institute, December 1990).

Ambler, Marjane. *Breaking the Iron Bonds: Indian Control of Energy Development.* (Lawrence: University Press of Kansas, 1990).

Appalachian Land Ownership Task Force. *Who Owns Appalachia? Landownership and Its Impact.* (Lexington: University Press of Kentucky, 1983).

Blumberg, Louis, and Robert Gottlieb. *War on Waste: Can America Win Its Battle with Garbage?* (Washington, DC: Island Press, 1989).

Brion, Denis J. *Essential Industry and the NIMBY Phenomenon.* (New York: Quorum Books, 1991).

Brown, Phil, and Edwin J. Mikkelsen. *No Safe Place: Toxic Waste, Leukemia, and Community Action.* (Berkeley: University of California Press, 1990).

Bryant, Bunyan. *Environmental Advocacy: Concepts, Issues, and Dilemmas.* (Sacramento: Caddo Gap Press, 1990).

Bryant, Bunyan. *Social and Environmental Change: A Manual for Advocacy and Organizing.* (Sacramento: Caddo Gap Press, 1991).

Bryant, Bunyan, and Paul Mohai, eds. *Environmental Racism: Issues and Dilemmas*. (Ann Arbor: University of Michigan Office of Minority Affairs, 1991).

Bryant, Bunyan, and Paul Mohai, eds. *Race and the Incidence of Environmental Hazards: A Time for Discourse*. (Boulder, CO: Westview Press, 1992).

Bullard, Robert D. *Dumping in Dixie: Race, Class, and Environmental Quality*. (Boulder, CO: Westview Press, 1990).

Cohen, Gary, and John O'Connor, eds. *Fighting Toxics: A Manual for Protecting Your Family, Community, and Workplace*. (Washington, DC: Island Press, 1990).

Commission for Racial Justice, United Church of Christ. *Toxic Wastes and Race in the United States: A National Report on the Racial and Socioeconomic Characteristics of Communities with Hazardous Waste Sites*. (New York: United Church of Christ, 1987).

Epstein, Samuel S., Lester O. Brown, and Carl Pope. *Hazardous Waste in America*. (San Francisco: Sierra Club Books, 1982).

Gibbs, Lois Marie, as told to Murray Levine. *Love Canal: My Story*. (Albany: State University of New York Press, 1982).

Gottlieb, Robert. *Forcing the Spring: The Transformation of the American Environmental Movement*. (Washington, DC: Island Press, 1993).

Hall, Bob, ed. *Environmental Politics: Lessons from the Grass Roots*. (Raleigh, NC: Institute for Southern Studies, 1988).

Kazis, Richard, and Richard Grossman. *Fear at Work: Job Blackmail, Labor, and the Environment*. (New York: Pilgrim Press, 1982).

Kickingbird, Kirke, and Karen Ducheneaux. *One Hundred Million Acres*. (New York: Macmillan Publishing Co., 1973).

Lawson, Michael L. *Dammed Indians: The Pick-Sloan Plan and the Missouri River Sioux, 1944–1980*. (Norman: University of Oklahoma Press, 1982).

Lazarus, Edward. *Black Hills, White Justice: The Sioux Nation Versus the United States, 1775 to the Present*. (New York: HarperCollins, 1991).

Levine, Adeline Gordon. *Love Canal: Science, Politics, and People*. (Lexington, MA: Lexington Books, 1982).

Mandell, Daniel, and Sanford J. Lewis. *The Formosa Plastics Story: A Report to the People of St. John the Baptist Parish*. (Boston: National Toxics Campaign Fund: 1990).

Mander, Jerry. *In the Absence of the Sacred: The Failure of Technology and the Survival of the Indian Nations*. (San Francisco: Sierra Club Books, 1991).

Mann, Eric. *L.A.'s Lethal Air: New Strategies for Policy, Organizing, and Action*. (Van Nuys, CA: Labor/Community Strategy Center, 1991).

Nabokov, Peter, ed. *Native American Testimony: A Chronicle of Indian-White Relations from Prophecy to the Present*. (New York: Viking Penguin, 1991).

Nelkin, Dorothy, and Michael S. Brown. *Workers at Risk: Voices from the Workplace.* (Chicago: University of Chicago Press, 1984).

Proceedings: The First National People of Color Environmental Leadership Summit. The Washington Court on Capitol Hill, Washington, DC, October 24–27, 1991. (New York: United Church of Christ Commission on Racial Justice, 1992).

Reich, Michael R. *Toxic Politics: Responding to Chemical Disasters.* (Ithaca, NY: Cornell University Press, 1991).

Reno, Philip. *Mother Earth, Father Sky, and Economic Development: Navajo Resources and Their Use.* (Albuquerque: University of New Mexico Press, 1981).

Ringholz, Raye C. *Uranium Frenzy: Boom and Bust on the Colorado Plateau.* (New York: W.W. Norton and Co., 1989).

Rosner, David, and Gerald Markowitz, eds. *Dying for Work: Workers' Safety and Health in Twentieth-Century America.* (Bloomington: Indiana University Press, 1987).

U.S. Environmental Protection Agency, Office of Policy, Planning, and Evaluation. *Environmental Equity: Reducing Risk for All Communities.* (Washington, DC: U.S. EPA, February 1992).

U.S. Environmental Protection Agency, Office of Policy, Planning, and Evaluation, Region V. *Tribes at Risk: The Wisconsin Tribes Comparative Risk Project.* (Washington, DC: U.S. EPA, October 1992).

U.S. General Accounting Office. *Siting of Hazardous Waste Landfills and Their Correlation with Racial and Economic Status of Surrounding Communities,* Pub. No. B–211461. (Washington, DC: U.S. General Accounting Office, 1983).

Whaley, Rick, with Walter Bresette. *Walleye Warriors: An Effective Alliance Against Racism and for the Earth.* (Philadelphia: New Society Publishers, 1992).

Wykle, Lucinda, Ward Morehouse, and David Dembo. *Worker Empowerment in a Changing Economy: Jobs, Military Production and the Environment.* (New York: Apex Press, 1991).

Zuercher, Melanie A. *Making History: The First Ten Years of KFTC.* (Prestonsburg, KY: Kentuckians for the Commonwealth, 1991).

B. ARTICLES

Ambler, Marjane. "On the Reservations: No Haste, No Waste." *Planning* (November 1991), pp. 26–29.

Beasley, Conger, and JC Leacock. "Of Pollution and Poverty." Three-part series in *Buzzworm* (May/June, July/August, and September/October 1990).

Chittum, Samme. "The Politics of Pollution." *City Limits* (November 1992), pp. 18–22.

Colquette, Kelly Michelle, and Elizabeth A. Henry Robertson. "Environmental Racism: The Causes, Consequences, and Commendations." *Tulane Environmental Law Journal* (1991, Vol. 5), pp. 153–207.

Davis, Tony. "Uranium Has Decimated Navajo Miners." *High Country News* (Vol. 22, No. 12, June 18, 1990), pp. 1, 10–12.

Fox, Steve. "Taking Us Down to the River: An Indian Pueblo Challenges Upstream Polluters." *The Workbook* (Vol. 17, No. 4, Winter 1992), pp. 146–155.

Gorisek, Sue. "Ohioana: A Town Divided." *Ohio Magazine* (March 1987), pp. 20–22, 85–91.

Hurley, Andrew. "Challenging Corporate Polluters: Race, Class, and Environmental Politics in Gary, Indiana, Since 1945." *The Indiana Magazine of History*, LXXXVIII (December 1992), pp. 273–302.

LaDuke, Winona. "Whitewashing Native Environmentalism." *News From Indian Country* (Vol. VII, No. 8, Late April 1993), pp. 1, 7–8.

Schwab, Jim. "Blue-Collar Groups Are Saying, 'Not in Our Backyard.'" *Planning* (October 1991), pp. 8–11.

Schwab, Jim. "Toxic Buyouts: You Can't Go Home Again." *The Neighborhood Works.* (August-September 1991), pp. 5–9.

Taylor, Dorceta. "Blacks and the Environment: Toward an Explanation of the Concern and Action Gap between Blacks and Whites." *Environment and Behavior* (Vol. 21, No. 2, March 1989), pp. 175–205.

Tomsho, Robert. "Dumping Grounds: Indian Tribes Contend with Some of America's Worst Pollution." *Wall Street Journal* (January 29, 1990), pp. A1, A7.

Verhovek, Sam Howe. "Power Struggle: Flooding Quebec to Light New York." *The New York Times Magazine* (January 12, 1992), pp. 16–21, 26–27.

White, Andrew. "Small Beginnings: The Birth of Environmental Activism in Fort Greene's Housing Projects." *City Limits* (April 1992), pp. 12–16.

C. PERIODICALS

Balancing the Scales. Monthly. Kentuckians for the Commonwealth, P.O. Box 864, Prestonsburg, KY 41653.

The Community Plume. Quarterly. Friends of the Earth, 218 D St. SE, Washington, DC 20003.

The Egg. Quarterly. Eco-Justice, Center for Religion, Ethics, and Social Policy, Anabel Taylor Hall, Cornell University, Ithaca, NY 14853.

Environics. Bimonthly. P.O. Box 322, Okemos, MI 48805.

Everyone's Backyard. Monthly. Citizen's Clearinghouse for Hazardous Waste, Inc., P.O. Box 6806, Falls Church, VA 22040.

The Neighborhood Works. Bimonthly. Center for Neighborhood Technology, 2125 W. North Ave., Chicago, IL 60647.

The PAHLS Journal. Monthly. People Against Hazardous Landfill Sites, Box 161, Wheeler, IN 46393.

Race, Poverty, and the Environment. Quarterly. Earth Island Institute, 300 Broadway, Suite 28, San Francisco, CA 94133–3312.

Rachel's Hazardous Waste News. Weekly. Environmental Research Foundation, P.O. Box 5036, Annapolis, MD 21403–7036.

Toxics in Your Community Newsletter. Quarterly. Citizens' Environmental Coalition, 33 Central Ave., Albany, NY 12210.

Voces Unidas. Quarterly. Southwest Organizing Project, 211 10th St., S.W., Albuquerque, NM 87102.

Waste Not. Weekly. Work on Waste USA, Inc., 82 Judson, Canton, NY 13617.

The Workbook. Quarterly. Southwest Research and Information Center, P.O. Box 4524, Albuquerque, NM 87106.

II. Local Newspaper Investigations of Toxic-Pollution Issues

A number of local newspapers have published investigative series looking at local toxic-pollution problems and the impacts that these have had on the most vulnerable populations, usually the low-income, working-class, and minority populations living near the types of facilities generating such pollution. This bibliography is a brief guide to such series.

Baton Rouge Morning Advocate, "Just Beyond the Fence," May 10–13, 1992. Reporters: Bob Anderson and Steve Culpepper. Focus: The problems caused in Louisiana by allowing chemical industries to locate near residential communities.

Boston Herald, "Ill Wind," May 13–16, 1991. Reporters: Alan Levin and Nick Tate. Focus: Airborne toxics in Massachusetts.

Detroit News, "Poison on the Riverfront," 1991. Reporters: John T. Wark, Angele Harpole, and Bob Meadows. Focus: The legacy of toxic pollution along the Detroit River left by a century of heavy industry.

Gary Post-Tribune, "Poisoning the Region," December 6–9, 1992. Reporters: Chris Isidore, John Ellis, Kerry Taylor, Erin Kennedy, Kim Steele, and Matthew Tully. Focus: The environmental price Northwest Indiana has paid for industrial progress.

Los Angeles Times, "Southern California's Environment: At the Crossroads,"

December 10, 1989, special report. Reporters: Maura Dolan, Larry Stammer, and Mark Stein. Focus: Detailing the pollution problem facing Southern California and the prospects for the region's future.

Macon (Georgia) *Telegraph*, "Unchecked Toxins," March 17–18, 1991. Reporter: Stuart Leavenworth. Focus: Toxic pollution in Georgia.

New Orleans Times-Picayune, "Louisiana in Peril," February 17–20, 1991; March 24–26, 1991; and May 12–15, 1991. Reporters: James O'Byrne and Mark Schliefstein. Focus: The toxic toll taken on Louisiana's environment by the petrochemical industry.

News/Sun-Sentinel (Orlando, Florida), "The Titans of Trash," December 6–10, 1987. Reporters: Fred Schulte, Robert McClure, Rick Pierce, Keith Hadley, and Jeff Jamison. Focus: Waste Management, Inc., and Browning Ferris, the two largest waste handlers in the nation.

Newsday, "Rush to Burn," reprinted in book form by Island Press, 1989. Reporters: Richard C. Firstman, Irene Virag, Ford Fessenden, Thomas J. Maier, William Bunch, Adrian Peracchio, Michelle Slatalla, Marie Cocco, Ron Davis, Barry Meier, Alvin E. Bessent, Mark McIntyre, Walter Fee, Bob Porterfield, Robert E. Kessler, Jim Mulvaney, William Sexton, Shirley E. Perlman, and Alyssa Lenhoff. Focus: The public policy, pollution, and corruption problems involved in hurried decisions to adopt incineration as the preferred method for handling municipal solid waste.

Pittsburgh Press, "The Burning Question," March 15–18, 1992. Reporter: Don Hopey. Focus: The pros and cons of hazardous-waste incineration, focusing on the WTI controversy.

Providence Journal-Bulletin, "Living with Chemicals," February 1991. Reporter: Bob Wyss. Focus: The impact of toxins in the environment.

San Francisco Examiner, "Toxic Racism," April 7–10, 1991. Reporter: Jane Kay. Focus: The impact of toxic pollution on ethnic minorities in California.

San Jose Mercury News, "Toxic Sieve," March 31–April 3, 1991. Reporters: Christopher H. Schmitt, Pete Carey, and Scott Thurm. Focus: Shortcomings in California state regulation of toxic waste.

III. Videotapes on Blue-Collar and Minority Environmentalism

With the widespread availability of the videocassette recorder, videotapes have come into their own as a primary medium for the exchange of information within grass-roots movements, much as newsletters and other printed documents have been in the past. This list is a short, and by no means complete, guide to some

*videotapes that have played a part in the research for this book. For price informa-
tion, write to the producers.*

Calvert City: One of Kentucky's Best Kept Secrets. Video-Active Productions,
  Box 322, Route 2, Canton, NY 13617. This videotape spurred the later
  production of a PBS documentary, *Who's Killing Calvert City?* Deals with
  the complex of chemical plants and hazardous-waste incinerator in
  Calvert City and the resulting environmental and public health damage.
Chemical Valley. Appalshop Film & Video, 306 Madison St., Whitesburg,
  KY 41858. Aired on PBS; deals with the Union Carbide/Rhone-Poulenc
  plant in Institute, West Virginia.
ELO 33 Trial. Greenpeace, 1017 W. Jackson Blvd., Chicago, IL 60607. Sixteen one-hour tapes of the entire February 1992 civil-disobedience trial
  in East Liverpool, Ohio.
Fighting for Justice: KFTC. Kentuckians for the Commonwealth, P.O. Box
  864, Prestonsburg, KY 41653. The story of KFTC's growth and mission
  as an organization.
The First Citizens' Conference on Dioxin: Overview. Video-Active Productions, Box 322, Route 2, Canton, NY 13617. Highlights of the conference, which was held in Chapel Hill, North Carolina, in October 1991.
Geothermal: A Risky Business in Hawaii's Wao Kele o Puna Rainforest. Video-
  Active Productions, Box 322, Route 2, Canton, NY 13617. Examines
  the problems and feasibility of geothermal development in the Hawaiian rainforest, the target of ongoing protests by native Hawaiians and
  local environmentalists.
Gwich'in Niintsyaa. Gwich'in Steering Committee, P.O. Box 202768, Anchorage, AK 99520. Footage of the historic 1988 gathering of the
  Gwich'in people in Arctic Village, Alaska, to challenge plans for oil exploration in the Arctic National Wildlife Refuge.
Hazardous Waste Incineration: A Scandal in North Carolina. Video-Active
  Productions, Box 322, Route 2, Canton, NY 13617. Examines the physical and emotional health problems suffered by workers and citizens from
  the Caldwell Systems, Inc., hazardous-waste incinerator in Lenoir, North
  Carolina.
Hazardous Waste Incineration in Disguise: Sham Recycling. Video-Active Productions, Box 322, Route 2, Canton, NY 13617. Features problems created by a loophole in the Resource Conservation and Recovery Act that
  was used by two firms in South Carolina and Louisiana.
Injustice in Ohio: WTI. Tri-State Environmental Council, Box 365, Route
  1, Chester, WV 26034. Highlights of the story of the fight against WTI.

Rush to Burn. Greenpeace, 1017 W. Jackson Blvd., Chicago, IL 60607. Examines problems with the strategy of incinerating waste.

Yellow Creek, Kentucky. Appalshop Film & Video, 306 Madison St., Whitesburg, KY 41858. Two-part series on Yellow Creek and the town of Middlesboro, where citizens led a fight to take over city hall on the basis of water-pollution issues involving a local tannery.

IV. Alternatives for the Future

Hart, John. *Saving Cities, Saving Money: Environmental Strategies That Work.* (Sausalito, CA: Resource Renewal Institute, 1992).

Hirschhorn, Joel S., and Kristin U. Oldenburg. *Prosperity Without Pollution.* (New York: Van Nostrand Reinhold, 1990).

Local Government Commission. *Capturing the Local Economic Benefit of Recycling.* (Sacramento, CA: LGC, 1992).

Makower, Joel. *The E Factor: The Bottom-Line Approach to Environmentally Responsible Business.* (New York: Tilden Press, 1993).

Malaspina, Mark, et al. *What Works Report No. 1: Air Pollution Solutions.* (Washington, DC: The Environmental Exchange, 1992).

McLenighan, Valjean. *Sustainable Manufacturing.* (Chicago: Center for Neighborhood Technology, 1990).

National Council for Urban Economic Development. *Economic Development Opportunities from Recycling and Environmental Technology.* (Washington, DC: NCUED, 1992).

Piasecki, Bruce, ed. *Beyond Dumping: New Strategies for Controlling Toxic Contamination.* (New York: Quorum Books, 1984).

Schwab, James. *Industrial Performance Standards for a New Century.* Planning Advisory Service Report No. 444. (Chicago: American Planning Association, March 1993).

V. Directories of Grass-Roots Groups

Resource Directory. Updated yearly; write for price. Started in 1993, lists Native American environmental organizations. Indigenous Environmental Network, Box 485, Bemidji, MN 56601.

Principles of Environmental Justice

The First National People of Color Environmental Leadership Summit, October 24–27, 1991, Washington, D.C.

PREAMBLE
We, the people of color, gathered together at this multinational People of Color Environmental Leadership Summit, to begin to build a national and international movement of all peoples of color to fight the destruction and taking of our lands and communities, do hereby re-establish our spiritual interdependence to the sacredness of our Mother Earth; to respect and celebrate each of our cultures, languages and beliefs about the natural world and our roles in healing ourselves; to ensure environmental justice; to promote economic alternatives which would contribute to the development of environmentally safe livelihoods; and, to secure our political, economic and cultural liberation that has been denied for over 500 years of colonization and oppression, resulting in the poisoning of our communities and land and the genocide of our peoples, do affirm and adopt these Principles of Environmental Justice:

1. Environmental justice affirms the sacredness of Mother Earth, ecological unity and the interdependence of all species, and the right to be free from ecological destruction.
2. Environmental justice demands that public policy be based on mutual respect and justice for all peoples, free from any form of discrimination or bias.
3. Environmental justice mandates the right to ethical, balanced and responsible uses of land and renewable resources in the interest of a sustainable planet for humans and other living things.

4. Environmental justice calls for universal protection from nuclear test-ing and the extraction, production and disposal of toxic/hazardous wastes and poisons that threaten the fundamental right to clean air, land, water, and food.

5. Environmental justice affirms the fundamental right to political, eco-nomic, cultural and environmental self-determination of all peoples.

6. Environmental justice demands the cessation of the production of all toxins, hazardous wastes, and radioactive materials, and that all past and current producers be held strictly accountable to the people for detoxifi-cation and the containment at the point of production.

7. Environmental justice demands the right to participate as equal part-ners at every level of decision-making including needs assessment, plan-ning, implementation, enforcement and evaluation.

8. Environmental justice affirms the right of all workers to a safe and healthy work environment, without being forced to choose between an unsafe livelihood and unemployment. It also affirms the right of those who work at home to be free from environmental hazards.

9. Environmental justice protects the right of victims of environmental injustice to receive full compensation and reparations for damages as well as quality health care.

10. Environmental justice considers governmental acts of environmental in-justice a violation of international law, the Universal Declaration On Human Rights, and the United Nations Convention on Genocide.

11. Environmental justice must recognize a special legal and natural rela-tionship of Native Peoples to the U.S. government through treaties, agreements, compacts, and covenants affirming sovereignty and self-de-termination.

12. Environmental justice affirms the need for urban and rural ecological policies to clean up and rebuild our cities and rural areas in balance with nature, honoring the cultural integrity of all our communities, and pro-viding fair access for all to the full range of resources.

13. Environmental justice calls for the strict enforcement of principles of informed consent, and a halt to the testing of experimental reproduc-tive and medical procedures and vaccinations on people of color.

14. Environmental justice opposes the destructive operations of multi-na-tional corporations.

15. Environmental justice opposes military occupation, repression and ex-ploitation of lands, peoples and cultures, and other life forms.

16. Environmental justice calls for the education of present and future gen-

erations which emphasizes social and environmental issues, based on our experience and an appreciation of our diverse cultural perspectives.

17. Environmental justice requires that we, as individuals, make personal and consumer choices to consume as little of Mother Earth's resources and to produce as little waste as possible; and make the conscious decision to challenge and reprioritize our lifestyles to insure the health of the natural world for present and future generations.

Adopted, October 27, 1991
The First National People of Color Environmental Leadership Summit
Washington, D.C.

Notes

CHAPTER 1

1. Laurie Goering, "Angry Crowd Faces Off on Robbins Incinerator," *Chicago Tribune*, March 8, 1990.
2. Laurie Goering, "South Suburbs Hope Past Is Future," *Chicago Tribune*, March 7, 1990.
3. Robbins Police Department, Complaint Nos. CC-680-821 and CC-680-822, dated March 3, 1990. The offense listed was "obstruction" under Robbins Village Code §131.010.
4. Direct quotes and recollections are drawn from a personal interview with Gloria Scott, February 2, 1991.
5. Alf Siewers and Charles Nicodemus, "Incinerator Ignites Hopes for Recovery in Robbins," *Chicago Sun-Times*, October 1, 1990.
6. Barry Neal, "Siting the Robbins Facility," in *Energy Aspects of Solid Waste Management: Proceedings of the Eighteenth Annual Illinois Energy Conference*, Chicago, October 29–30, 1990 (Energy Resources Center, University of Illinois at Chicago), pp. 179–193.
7. Collective interview with members of the South Cook County Environmental Action Coalition (Jeff Tangel, Mary Martin, Gloria Scott, Reverend Adolph Coleman, and Helen Cuprisin), May 18, 1991. (SCCEAC interview)
8. From personal observation.
9. Laurie Goering, "Suburbs Offer Hope to Trash Problem," *Chicago Tribune*, January 16, 1989.
10. Laurie Goering, "1,500 Fight Plan for Incinerator," *Chicago Tribune*, March 23, 1990.
11. Michael Allaby, *Dictionary of the Environment*, Third Edition (New York: New York University Press, 1989), p. 122: **dioxin** (2,3,7,8-tetrachlorodibenzo-*p*-dioxin, TCDD; $C_{12}H_4C_{14}O_2$). A by-product formed during the preparation of the herbicide 2,4,5-t, and sometimes produced by the incineration of chlorinated organic compounds. It may also occur naturally and is distributed widely in the environment, except locally in extremely low concentrations. Substantial amounts were released by the industrial accident at Seveso in 1976. Exposure to high concentrations causes chloracne. Although dioxin is suspected of causing more lasting damage, including chromosome malformation, there is no conclusive evidence for this.
12. Ibid., p. 348.
13. Norie Huddle and Michael Reich with Nahum Stiskin, *Island of Dreams: Environ-*

mental Crisis in Japan (Rochester, VT: Schenkman Books, 1987), pp. 102–113.

14. *Rachel's Hazardous Waste News* #291, June 24, 1992. *Rachel's* is a weekly newsletter produced by the Environmental Research Foundation in Washington, DC.

15. F. Slemr and E. Langer, "Increase in Global Atmospheric Concentrations of Mercury Inferred from Measurements over the Atlantic Ocean," *Nature*, Vol. 355 (January 30, 1992), pp. 434–437.

16. Ibid.

17. Testimony of Kevin Greene, Citizens for a Better Environment, in the matter of *Draft Permit for Robbins Resource Recovery MSW Incinerator*, before the Illinois Environmental Protection Agency, Robbins, Illinois, March 7, 1990.

18. Steve Johnson, "Neighbors Rail Against Balefill Plan," *Chicago Tribune*, June 25, 1987.

19. George Papajohn, "E. Chicago Heights Hopes Ford Name Is a Better Idea," *Chicago Tribune*, March 26, 1987.

20. George Papajohn, "Other Suburbs Held Their Noses on Deal for Incinerator Bonds," *Chicago Tribune*, July 7, 1987, and "Incinerator Flap Burns Up Mayor," August 5, 1987.

21. George Papajohn and William Presecky, "Ford Heights Advances on Incinerator," *Chicago Tribune*, January 28, 1988.

22. SCCEAC interview.

23. Kenan Heise and Mark Frazel, *Hands on Chicago* (Chicago: Bonus Books, 1987), pp. 256–257, 260.

24. SCCEAC interview.

25. Personal interview with Matthew Dunn, Chief, Environmental Control Section, Illinois Attorney General's Office, March 15, 1991.

26. Telephone interview with Barry Neal, June 20, 1991.

27. Envirodyne Engineers, *South Suburban Mayors and Managers Association, Municipal Solid Waste Plan: Executive Summary*, January 1991. Final Draft.

28. Telephone interview with Tom Brown, June 25, 1991.

29. In *Philadelphia v. New Jersey*, 430 U.S. 141, 97 S.Ct. 987, 1977, the U.S. Supreme Court held that a New Jersey statute prohibiting movement of solid and hazardous waste into the state (in this case, largely from the Philadelphia metropolitan area) violated the commerce clause of the U.S. Constitution, which reserves to Congress the right to regulate commerce between the states. Other cases since then have continued to uphold the principle that waste is an item of commerce in interstate trade.

30. APHA Policy Statement No. 8911 appears in *American Journal of Public Health*, Vol. 80 (February 1990), pp. 230–231.

31. News release from St. Francis Hospital and Health Center, December 1990.

32. Reading Energy had incorporated provisions in its design for separating one-fourth of the incoming garbage, largely aluminum cans and glass bottles, for recycling before compacting the remainder into refuse-derived fuel, or RDF, pellets for burning. In many respects, this improves the combustible quality of the fuel by eliminating substances with poor thermal qualities. Interestingly, though, the percentage matched that in a U.S. EPA regulation proposed in 1988 (but later aborted) that would have required municipal solid-waste incinerators to recycle 25 percent of their incoming waste. The plant had been planned while that regulation was being debated.

33. Details of the hearings are from personal observation.

34. Laurie Goering, "Incinerator Foes Score Big at Polls," *Chicago Tribune*, April 8, 1991, Sec. 2 South, p. 1.
35. Laurie Goering, "Incinerator a Burning Issue in South Suburban Races," *Chicago Tribune*, March 18, 1991, Sec. 2 South, p. 1.
36. Laurie Goering, "Blue Island Mayor Hits Incinerator," *Chicago Tribune*, April 12, 1991, Sec. 2 South, p. 4.
37. Goering, op. cit., April 8, 1991.
38. SCCEAC interview.
39. Neal interview.
40. Stevenson Swanson, "Federal EPA Upholds State Incinerator OK," *Chicago Tribune*, August 7, 1991, Sec. 2, p. 6.
41. Dunn interview, June 20, 1991.
42. Roland W. Burris, "Law Upheld in Incinerator Lawsuit," letter to the editor, *Chicago Tribune*, January 6, 1992.
43. Neal interview.
44. *Ban the Burn News*, newsletter of the South Cook County Environmental Action Coalition, March/April 1992, p. 1.
45. "Matteson and Oak Forest Receive SCCEAC Awards," *Ban the Burn News*, May/June 1992, p. 5.
46. Ibid., p. 3.
47. Headline, *Ban the Burn News*, November/December 1992, p. 1.
48. All observations concerning the hearing come from my own notes taken while attending the meeting.
49. Marla Donato and Laurens Grant, "Robbins OKs Incinerator Siting a 2nd Time," *Chicago Tribune*, February 11, 1993, Sec. 2, p. 7.
50. I interviewed Irene Brodie during a break in the December 22, 1992, hearing.
51. "Key Official Says NO to Robbins Incinerator," *Ban the Burn News*, April/May 1993, p. 1.
52. "Orland Park Unanimously Passes Resolution Against Robbins Incinerator," *Ban the Burn News*, April/May 1993, p. 1.

CHAPTER 2

1. Eric Mann, with the Watchdog Organizing Committee, *L.A.'s Lethal Air: New Strategies for Policy, Organizing, and Action* (Los Angeles: Labor/Community Strategy Center, 1991), statistics from p. 31.
2. Jane Kay, "Fighting Toxic Racism: L.A. Minority Neighborhood Is the 'Dirtiest' in the State," *San Francisco Examiner*, April 7, 1991, pp. A-1, A-12.
3. All of the personal quotations and recollections cited in this part of the chapter are drawn from a November 17, 1991, collective interview with Charlotte Bullock, Robin Cannon, and Wilson Smith at the office of Concerned Citizens of South Central.
4. Shari Roan, "Air Sickness: Evidence Mounts of Dramatic, Permanent Damage to Lungs of Children," *Los Angeles Times*, March 4, 1990, Sec. E, p. 1.
5. Mann, *L.A.'s Lethal Air*, p. 22.
6. Robert Gottlieb, speech at St. Xavier College, Chicago, August 5, 1991.
7. California's municipal corporation law has allowed the incorporation of a number of "municipalities" with minimal residential populations (usually in the lower three figures) that are virtually mere industrial parks legitimized in their governmental status by highly pro-industrial mayors and councils, among them the City

of Commerce, City of Industry, Vernon, and Irwindale. The last at one point tried to lure the Los Angeles Raiders away from Los Angeles by offering to redevelop an abandoned quarry into a football stadium. These municipal oddities have full taxing and zoning powers, despite their obvious deficits as true "communities."

8. Louis Blumberg and Robert Gottlieb, *War on Waste: Can America Win Its Battle with Garbage?* (Washington, DC: Island Press), p. 161.

9. Gottlieb speech.

10. Blumberg and Gottlieb, pp. 162–163.

11. Gottlieb speech.

12. Blumberg and Gottlieb, p. 163.

13. J. Stephen Powell, Senior Associate, Cerrell Associates, "Political Difficulties Facing Waste-to-Energy Conversion Plant Siting," California Waste Management Board, Los Angeles, 1984.

14. Dick Russell, "Environmental Racism: Minority Communities and Their Battle Against Toxics," *Amicus Journal* (New York: Natural Resources Defense Council), Spring 1989, p. 26.

15. Ibid.

16. Russell, p. 27.

17. Ibid.

18. Kevin Roderick, "UCLA Group Urges City to Drop Lancer Trash Plan," *Los Angeles Times*, June 10, 1987, pp. 1, 3.

19. "Student Projects," *Planning*, American Planning Association, April 1989, p. 32. Rita Calvan, a U.S. EPA official, objected to the award in a "Viewpoint" in the magazine's October 1989 issue. A series of letters to the editor followed for several months thereafter, taking various sides in the solid-waste issue.

20. Victor Merina, "City Politicians Reap Harvest in Bond Sale Field," *Los Angeles Times*, August 11, 1986, p. 1; Blumberg and Gottlieb, op. cit., pp. 166–167.

21. Matthew Reiss, "Garbage Broker: Norman Steisel and the Art of the Done Deal," *Village Voice*, November 26, 1991, pp. 30–39.

22. Russell, p. 28.

23. Kyle Arndt et al., *Improving Environmental Quality: Community Empowerment in East Los Angeles and Santa Fe Springs* (Los Angeles: University of California, 1991), p. ELA-14.

24. Unless otherwise cited, most of the personal recollections included in this part of the chapter are drawn from an interview with Juana and Ricardo Gutierrez at their home, November 18, 1991.

25. See the explanation in footnote 7, above, concerning California's virtually unpopulated, but incorporated, industrial havens. Vernon, with a population of about 100, is one of them.

26. Russell, p. 22.

27. Russell, pp. 22–23.

28. Mann's opinions and recollections here are drawn from an interview at the Labor/Community Strategy Center office in Van Nuys, November 18, 1991.

29. Arndt et al., pp. ELA-43–46, 65–66.

30. John Harte, Cheryl Holdren, Richard Schneider, and Christine Shirley, *Toxics A to Z: A Guide to Everyday Pollution Hazards* (Berkeley: University of California Press, 1991), pp. 415–417.

31. Arndt et al., p. ELA-23.

32. *Final Air Quality Management Plan: South Coast Air Basin*, South Coast Air Quality Management District and Southern California Association of Governments, July 1991, Chapter 2.
33. *Making Clean Air a Priority: A Guide for Planners in Local Governments*, South Coast Air Quality Management District, September 1990, p. 2.
34. Mann, *L.A.'s Lethal Air*, p. 6.
35. Ibid., p. 42.
36. Barry Commoner, "Yearning to Breathe Free," *Nation*, February 24, 1992, p. 242.
37. Mann, *L.A.'s Lethal Air*, p. 31.
38. Paul Ong and Evelyn Blumenberg, "Race and Environmentalism," Graduate School of Urban and Regional Planning, UCLA, pp. 6–7.
39. Ibid., p. 9.
40. See the report of Arndt et al., referenced above.
41. Letter to Kyle Arndt from Alex Bailey, SCAQMD Senior Engineering Manager, August 12, 1991.
42. Telephone interview with Alex Bailey, November 20, 1992. Bailey, who was in charge of this initiative, indicated that it materialized from a suggestion by the author during an interview with Bailey; Eugene Calafato, assistant to Executive Director James M. Lents; and Board Chairman Henry W. Wedaa, January 27, 1992.
43. Mann, *L.A.'s Lethal Air*, pp. 51–53, supplemented by personal interview with Eric Mann.
44. Mann interview.
45. Assembly Bill 939, passed in 1990, set goals for solid-waste reduction and established deadlines for counties and municipalities to submit plans for achieving those goals to the state agency, which has become part of the new California EPA under later legislation that consolidated a number of agencies and programs.
46. Personal interview with Lupe Vela, January 27, 1992.
47. Megan Ryan, "Los Angeles 21, New York 5. . . .," *World Watch*, March/April 1993, pp. 18–21.
48. Mark Malaspina, Kristin Schafer, and Richard Wiles, *What Works Report No. 1: Air Pollution Solutions* (Washington, DC: The Environmental Exchange, May 1992), p. 60.
49. Joel S. Hirschhorn and Kirsten U. Oldenburg, *Prosperity Without Pollution: The Prevention Strategy for Industry and Consumers* (New York: Van Nostrand Reinhold, 1991), pp. 104–105.
50. Telephone interview with Henry Clark, August 22, 1992.
51. Miles Corwin, "A Toxic Issue: Proposed Waste Incinerator Unites Unusual Foes in Kings County," *Los Angeles Times*, February 24, 1991, pp. B1–B5.
52. Julia Flynn Siler, " 'Environmental Racism': It Could Be a Messy Fight," *Business Week*, May 20, 1991, p. 16.
53. Katherine L. Ratcliffe, "Kettleman City Residents Claim 'Environmental Racism'," *Bakersfield Californian*, September 15, 1991, p. B5.
54. "Communities Can Regulate Dumps, Say California Rulings," *MSW Management*, March/April 1992, pp. 64–65.
55. Personal interview with Luke Cole, December 4, 1992.

CHAPTER 3

1. Personal interview with Richard Sahli, June 26, 1992.
2. Mary Beth Lane, "Riffe Linked to EPA Lobbyist's Exile," *Plain Dealer*, February 15, 1989, p. B1. For a more detailed exposition of Riffe's career as a legislative power broker, see Lee Leonard, "Power at the Statehouse: The Riffe Reign," *Columbus Monthly*, August 1989, pp. 54–59.
3. Samuel S. Epstein, Lester O. Brown, and Carl Pope, *Hazardous Waste in America* (San Francisco: Sierra Club Books, 1982), pp. 226–256. In another section, pp. 194–199, the authors note that Congress gave EPA 18 months, or until March 1978, to draft regulations. But industrial interests responded to a December 1978 proposed rulemaking by lobbying Congress for amendments that weakened some sections of the act in its 1980 reauthorization, at a time when EPA had actually gained no real experience with RCRA.
4. From "Ohio EPA Fact Sheet, GSX Chemical Services, Inc., Draft Revised Permit, Ohio Permit #02-18-0602."
5. Sahli interview.
6. Transcript of meeting with Citizens to Bring Broadway Back, called by Richard Shank, March 23, 1989, pp. 24–25.
7. Sahli interview.
8. David Beach, "Not in My Back Yard! A Neighborhood Up in Arms Over a Proposed Toxic Waste Plant," *Cleveland Edition*, April 6, 1989, pp. 1, 6.
9. Ohio EPA interoffice communication from Dave Sholtis through Mike Savage, Manager, Surveillance and Enforcement Section, to Ed Kitchen, Manager, Technical Assistance and Engineering Section, dated November 30, 1987. The three-page memo outlines "a history of noncompliance" for both facilities from 1982 to 1987.
10. Personal interview with Michael Savage, June 26, 1992.
11. United States Environmental Protection Agency, *Public Hearing Re: Issuance of RCRA Permit to GSX Chemical Services of Ohio*, April 29, 1988, Cleveland Public Library, Cleveland, Ohio. Pages in the transcript were not numbered.
12. Telephone interview with Robert Castro, August 2, 1991.
13. Personal interview with Sharon Fields, May 23, 1991.
14. Edward W. Rybka, "City Council Update," *Neighborhood News*, January 18, 1989.
15. Environmental Risk Limited, *Information Submitted on Behalf of GSX Chemical Services of Ohio, Inc. Re: Siting Criteria Demonstration of RC Section 3734.05 (C) (6)*, Submitted to: Ohio Hazardous Waste Facilities Board, ERL Project No. 7350-C42-88, Revised November 1988. The assertion is made twice, on p. 84 and again on p. 90.
16. I can personally verify this because I visited Fields at her home on East 71st Street. Her block is completely residential. Even a cursory test with a street map and a ruler reveals that her home is but a quarter-mile from the facility. My own odometer test from driving through the area, which obviously gives GSX a wider margin of error than a straight-line test, revealed residences closer even in driving distance than .45 miles.
17. California Department of Justice press release, January 23, 1989.
18. Fields interview. The author has a photocopy of this strange note.
19. Personal interview with Edward Rybka, May 24, 1991.

20. Fields interview.

21. Lisa Casini, "Community Unites in Opposition to Chemical Plant Expansion," *Neighborhood News*, February 1, 1989, p. 1.

22. Castro interview.

23. Telephone interview with Tawny Ratner, August 2, 1991.

24. Fields interview.

25. Elizabeth Sullivan, "GSX Officials May Boycott Public Meeting," *Plain Dealer*, April 13, 1989, p. 2-B.

26. Fields interview.

27. Elizabeth Sullivan and James Lawless, "600 Attend Meeting to Oppose Incinerator," *Plain Dealer*, April 14, 1989, pp. 1-A, 4-A.

28. Personal interview with Katherine Chaney and Cynthia D'Agostino, May 23, 1991.

29. "A Cloud Over Toxic Waste," *Plain Dealer*, April 18, 1989, p. 6-B.

30. Edward W. Rybka, "City Council Update," *Neighborhood News*, April 26, 1989.

31. Beach, p. 6.

32. "EPA Reverses Ruling on GSX Request to Treat 83 New Chemicals at Plant," *Neighborhood News*, June 21, 1989, p. 1.

33. Beach, p. 6.

34. Rae Tyson, "S.C. Hazardous Waste Ban Could Fuel Toxic 'Civil War'," *USA Today*, March 1, 1989.

35. "Chemical Fire Ignites at GSX Plant," *Neighborhood News*, July 12, 1989, p. 1.

36. Tom Breckenridge, "GSX Waste Shutdown Ordered," *Plain Dealer*, July 14, 1989, pp. 1-B, 3-B.

37. Tom Breckenridge, "GSX Allowed to Treat Waste," *Plain Dealer*, July 27, 1989, pp. 1-A, 8-A.

38. Fields interview.

39. Judy Goldsworth, "Celeste Says State Will Back Move to Close GSX Chemical," *Neighborhood News*, August 8, 1989, p. 1.

40. James Lawless and Amy Westfeldt, "Violations Continue at GSX," *Plain Dealer*, August 10, 1989, pp. 1-A, 1-B.

41. Press release of Attorney General Anthony J. Celebrezze, Jr., August 15, 1989.

42. Tom Breckenridge, "GSX Burner Ruled in Violation," *Plain Dealer*, August 15, 1989, pp. 1-B, 3-B; also Judy Goldsworth, "Zoning Board Shuts Down GSX Incinerator," *Neighborhood News*, August 16, 1989, p. 1.

43. Judith Goldsworth, "GSX Appeals Zoning Board Ruling," *Neighborhood News*, September 6, 1989, p. 1.

44. Judith Goldsworth, "Crowd Stages Protest Sunday at GSX Site," *Neighborhood News*, October 11, 1989, p. 1.

45. Chaney/D'Agostino interview.

46. Fields interview.

47. "GSX Tank Pops Open, Sprays Solvent on Nearby Building," *Neighborhood News*, March 14, 1990, p. 1.

48. Fields interview.

49. Tom Breckenridge, "Operator of Troubled Waste Plant Changes Name," *Plain Dealer*, April 18, 1990, p. 5-C.

50. "Files Contempt of Court Charges," *Neighborhood News*, July 11, 1990, p. 1.

51. "Revokes Laidlaw Environmental Permit," *Neighborhood News*, July 18, 1990, p. 1.

52. Harry Stainer, "City to Ask Court to Halt Operations at Laidlaw Plant," *Plain Dealer*, August 19, 1990, p. 6-B.
53. Telephone interview with Marge Grevatt, June 18, 1991.
54. Telephone interview with Louis E. Tosi, August 2, 1991.
55. "Laidlaw Found Guilty of Failing to Report Accident," *Neighborhood News*, August 29, 1990, p. 1.
56. Savage interview.
57. Tom Breckenridge and Dave Davis, "Judge Extends Laidlaw Closing Until Oct. 11," *Plain Dealer*, September 5, 1990.
58. "Environmental Group Says 'No' to Laidlaw Concessions," *Neighborhood News*, September 12, 1990, p. 1.
59. "Crowd Hears of GSX/Laidlaw Nightmares in South Carolina at Environmental Conference," *Neighborhood News*, October 17, 1990, p. 1.
60. "Testimonies Cite Employee Ignorance as Possible Cause of Laidlaw Mishaps," *Neighborhood News*, October 17, 1990, p. 1.
61. Consent Judgment, *State of Ohio, ex rel. Anthony J. Celebrezze, Jr., Attorney General of Ohio v. GSX Chemical Services of Ohio, Inc.*, Case Nos. 172743, 98877, and 179969, October 23, 1990.
62. Chaney/D'Agostino interview.
63. Fields interview.
64. Castro interview.
65. Ratner interview.
66. Grevatt interview.
67. Sahli interview.

CHAPTER 4

1. Michael Allaby, *Dictionary of the Environment*, Third Edition (New York: New York University Press, 1989), p. 126.
2. Sue Gorisek, "Ohioana: A Town Divided," *Ohio Magazine*, March 1987, pp. 20–22, 85–91.
3. Gorisek, p. 91, notes that the CECOS landfill had its own problems: "At CECOS, where the deadliest wastes are disposed of—dioxin, PCBs, vinyl/chloride—the operators were caught pumping waste water into a stream that supplies drinking water for the nearby town of Williamsburg. Waste cells that were supposedly lined with impervious clay were found to contain porous sand and gravel."
4. Joint interview with Joy Allison, Alonzo Spencer, and Teresa Swearingen, at the Swearingen home, Chester, West Virginia, December 27, 1991 (Joint interview hereafter).
5. Transcript of Public Meeting, Ohio Environmental Protection Agency, Issuance of Preliminary Staff Determination, Permit to Install No. 17-104, Waste Technology Industries, East Liverpool, Ohio, November 8, 1982, p. 8 (testimony of Stuart Wilson).
6. Ibid., pp. 10–11.
7. Ibid., pp. 12–17.
8. Ibid., pp. 28–29.
9. The regulations can be found in *Federal Register*, May 19, 1980, pp. 33036–33074.
10. Peter Montague and William Sanjour, "The Breakdown of Morality," *Rachel's Hazardous Waste News* #287, May 27, 1992.

11. Ibid.

12. View expressed in joint interview.

13. Gorisek, p. 91.

14. Personal interview with Richard Sahli, June 26, 1992.

15. "City Council Instructs Payne to Cease His Support for WTI," *Morning Journal* (East Liverpool, Ohio), February 15, 1983.

16. Gorisek, pp. 90, 91.

17. "WTI Sold to Illinois Firm," *Salem News*, January 28, 1987.

18. Tom Giambroni, "Company Calls off WTI Purchase," *Morning Journal*, June 10, 1989.

19. For a full account of the company's history in this regard, see *Final Report: Waste Management, Inc.*, March 1992, a report prepared by San Diego, California, District Attorney Erwin L. Miller, Jr. Waste Management, Inc., subsequently sued to force the recall of all copies of the report. Also see *Waste Management, Inc.: An Encyclopedia of Environmental Crimes and Other Misdeeds* (Washington, DC: Greenpeace, 1991).

20. Joint interview.

21. "WTI Gets Financing," *Evening Review* (East Liverpool, Ohio), October 5, 1990, pp. 1, 5.

22. Glenn Clark, "Swiss Company Takes Over WTI," *Evening Review*, August 21, 1990, p. 1.

23. Joint interview.

24. Tom Giambroni, "Regulators Field Questions from WTI Plant Opponents," *Central Shopper*, December 2, 1990.

25. "Birthday Greetings: Message, Anti-WTI Style, Sent to EPA," *Salem News*, December 5, 1990.

26. All of the testimony cited from this point on is drawn from the transcript, before the Ohio Environmental Protection Agency, East Liverpool, Ohio, in *Re: WTI Draft Permit-to-Install Spray Dryer 1 & 2, Public Hearing, Thursday, January 17, 1991*.

27. Pat Costner and Joe Thornton, *Playing with Fire: Hazardous Waste Incineration* (Washington, DC: Greenpeace, 1990), pp. 19–20.

28. John C. Kramlich et al., *Experimental Investigation of Critical Fundamental Issues in Hazardous Waste Incineration* (Springfield, VA: National Technical Information Service, September 1989), pp. 5-1, 5-2.

29. Peter Montague, "New EPA Memo Says All Hazardous Waste Incinerators Fail to Meet Regulations," *Rachel's Hazardous Waste News* #312, November 18, 1992. Unless otherwise cited, all material in *Rachel's Hazardous Waste News* is by Peter Montague.

30. See Alfred Sigg, "Wet Scrubbing System for Waste Incinerators," presented at Air and Waste Management Association, 84th Annual Meeting and Exhibition, Vancouver, British Columbia, June 16–21, 1991 (#91-34.1). A specific discussion of mercury as a "problem pollutant" in spray dryers occurs on page 14, where Sigg notes that "recirculation of the scrubber blowdown to the spray dryer causes mercury to revolatilize," driving emission rates "up to levels similar to the uncontrolled rates." Sigg includes figures showing a 90-percent reduction in mercury emissions with the addition of an activated carbon filter.

31. Telephone interview with Paul Connett, September 14, 1992. An interesting

point here is that, although Connett faxed a copy of his presentation, including visuals and supplemental comments, which themselves included responses to the remarks of Peter Schoener, and then called to confirm that his fax was received by the agency, Ohio EPA officials criticized Connett and McCawley to me in a group interview in June 1992 for failing to supply a written critique of the spray dryer that they could evaluate. It may be that they did not feel that his submitted critique was adequate (though that was not what they said), but that suggestion in itself induced Connett to suggest to me that the agency was operating by a double standard in judging the adequacy of technical testimony.

32. Letter to Honorable Robert C. Byrd from Valdas Adamkus, U.S. EPA Region V, October 15, 1991.
33. Letter to Jane Massey from Valdas Adamkus, U.S. EPA Region V, February 28, 1991.
34. Letter to Honorable Robert C. Byrd from Terri Swearingen, February 7, 1992.
35. It should be noted here that I specifically discussed this issue with Paul Connett in a telephone interview in September 1992, after finding this contradiction in my own notes of a group interview with Ohio EPA officials. Connett's response: "It's hard sometimes to tell where incompetence ends and corruption begins."
36. "Voinovich Won't Interfere with WTI," *Morning Journal*, May 13, 1991.
37. Tom Giambroni, "WTI Making Plans for 2nd Incinerator," *Morning Journal*, June 5, 1991, pp. 1, 16.
38. Rick Armon, "Praying for WTI's Fall: Actor Joins Protest Against WTI Facility," *Morning Journal*, June 3, 1991, pp. 1, 8.
39. It is not clear to the author what difference it would have made if he had. As noted earlier, WTI never responded to the author's requests for interviews, even though I made four attempts to arrange such contact during the spring of 1992.
40. Dennis C. Wise, "WTI Opponents on the March," *Morning Journal*, June 21, 1991, pp. 1, 12.
41. "WTI Opponents Begin March to Rally on Statehouse Lawn," *Salem News*, June 24, 1991, p. 2.
42. "Alphabet Soup: W. Va. vs. WTI and EPA," *Morning Journal*, July 4, 1991, pp. 1, 7.
43. Tom Giambroni, "State Medical Association Joins County Physicians Against WTI," *Morning Journal*, June 4, 1991, p. 1.
44. Resolution adopted by Pittsburgh City Council, June 25, 1991.
45. "WTI Owner Pledges Help for ELO Hospital Project," *Morning Journal*, June 22, 1991, pp. 1, 16. Oddly, this same article reappeared in its entirety, including a posed photograph with Von Roll America's D.J. Blake Marshall handing the check to the hospital's Hannah T. Greenburg, in the *Weirton Daily Times*, August 1, 1991, under the heading, "WTI Donation Boosts Project."
46. Tom Giambroni, "WTI Fights Back: Company Plans to Push Its Own Promo Campaign," *Morning Journal*, June 29, 1991.
47. Giambroni, June 5, 1991.
48. Giambroni, June 29, 1991.
49. Glenn Clark, "WTI Misinformation Draws Accusations," *Evening Review*, August 28, 1991, pp. 1, 5. On August 24, a letter appeared in the *Evening Review* from D.J. Blake Marshall, announcing that WTI was pulling the brochures.
50. Glenn Clark, "WTI Unveils Environmental Slogan," *Evening Review*, August 28, 1991.

51. Glenn Clark, "WTI Permit Changes Tentatively OK'd," *Evening Review*, August 22, 1991, pp. 1, 5.
52. Dennis C. Wise, "Controversy Burns Hotter Than WTI's Smokestacks," *Evening Review*, July 2, 1991, pp. 1, 16.
53. "WTI Incinerator Focus of University of Pitt Study," *Morning Journal*, August 10, 1991.
54. Glenn Clark, "Von Roll Is Pleased," *Evening Review*, September 24, 1991, pp. 1, 5; also Sharon Voas, "Study Calls Incinerator Safe," *Pittsburgh Post-Gazette*, September 24, 1991, p. 7.
55. See *Final Report: Environmental Review of the Waste Technologies Industries Hazardous Waste Incinerator Located in East Liverpool, Ohio* (Pittsburgh: Center for Hazardous Materials Research, University of Pittsburgh Trust, September 1991).
56. Voas, September 24, 1991.
57. Dennis Wise, "Health Department May Conduct WTI Study," *Evening Review*, September 4, 1991.
58. "EPA Plans Yearlong Study of WTI," *Salem News*, September 5, 1991.
59. Tom Giambroni, "Up in the Air: WTI Emissions to Get Long, Hard Look," *Morning Journal*, September 6, 1991, pp. 1A, 12A.
60. Robert E. Miller, "Voinovich Rejects Halting WTI: Civil Disobedience Promised by Foes of Project," *Intelligencer* (Wheeling, WV), pp. 1, 3.
61. Tracy Carbasho, "WTI Officials Are Prepared for Massive Civil Disobedience," *Intelligencer*, pp. 1, 7.
62. Linda Harris, "Incinerator Protesters in Weirton: Claim Voinovich Dug Himself Hole," *Weirton Daily Times*, September 20, 1991, p. 1.
63. Sahli interview.
64. In the interview, Sahli handed me a copy of Ohio Revised Code Section 3734.05, which deals with hazardous wastes. He had highlighted (D)(6)(c) and (d), which read:

   (6) The [hazardous waste facility] board shall not approve an application for a hazardous waste facility installation and operation permit unless it finds and determines as follows:

   (c) That the facility represents the minimum adverse environmental impact, considering the state of available technology and the nature and economics of various alternatives, and other pertinent considerations;

   (d) That the facility represents the minimum risk of all of the following:
       (i)   Contamination of ground and surface waters;
       (ii) Fires or explosions from treatment, storage, or disposal methods;
       (iii) Accident during transportation of hazardous waste to or from the facility;
       (iv) Impact on the public health and safety;
       (v)   Air pollution;
       (vi) Soil contamination.

65. Joint interview.
66. Dennis Wise, "Illinois Legislator Joins Fight Against WTI Operation," *Evening Review*, September 6, 1991.
67. With this author.
68. Telephone interview with William Muno, March 19, 1993.
69. Linda Harris, "Protesters Boycott Meeting," *Weirton Daily Times*, September 25, 1991, pp. 1, 18.

70. Mark Law, "Protesters Refuse to Attend WTI Hearing," *Steubenville Herald-Star*, September 25, 1991, pp. 1, 7.
71. Glenn Clark, "City, WTI Sign $600,000 Payment Plan," *Evening Review*, September 25, 1991, p. 1.
72. Kevin Clark, "WTI Foes Shut Down Hearing," *Morning Journal*, September 26, 1991, pp. 1A, 3A.
73. Thomas Jewell, "Enemies of WTI Protest: Chanting Thwarts Testimony to EPA," *Intelligencer*, September 26, 1991, pp. 1, 2.
74. Clark, September 26, 1991.
75. Joint interview.
76. STC Enviroscience, Inc., and The Castillo Group, Inc., *Recommendations and Background Overview on Waste Technologies Industries and Von Roll Hazardous Waste Facility, East Liverpool, Ohio*, prepared for the City of East Liverpool, Ohio (Cleveland: STC Enviroscience, Inc., September 1991), pp. 6–7.
77. Ibid., p. 14.
78. Ibid., pp. 14–17.
79. Ibid., p. 26.
80. Ibid., p. 36.
81. Ibid., p. 22.
82. Ibid., p. 37.
83. T.C. Brown, "Consultant Questions Data on Incinerator," *Plain Dealer*, October 2, 1991.
84. STC Enviroscience, p. 98.
85. Ibid., p. 38.
86. Ibid., pp. 4–5.
87. Joint interview with Shelby Thurman-Jackson, Paul Anderson, John Wells, Ed Lim, and Robert Hodanbosi at Ohio EPA headquarters, June 26, 1992 (Ohio EPA interview hereafter).
88. T.C. Brown, "Incinerator Permits Outdated, Report Says," *Plain Dealer*, October 15, 1991, pp. 1-A, 10-A.
89. Much of the description is derived from a variety of videotapes acquired by the author, supplemented by comments from the Joint Interview, noted above.
90. Telephone interview with Paul Connett, December 2, 1992.
91. Thomas Jewell, "33 Arrested in Waste Incinerator Protest," *Wheeling News-Register*, October 14, 1991, p. 1.
92. Connett interview.
93. "Voinovich Defends WTI Plant as Protests Continue at Facility," *Steubenville Herald-Star*, October 16, 1991, p. 1.
94. Glenn Clark, "Police Arrest Another Protester at WTI Plant," *Evening Review*, October 16, 1991.
95. Kevin Clark, "WTI: Day 3 of Demonstrations, 2 More Arrested at Gates," *Morning Journal*, October 16, 1991, p. 1A.
96. Kevin Clark, "Strain Starts to Show on East Liverpool Police," *Morning Journal*, October 16, 1991, p. 1A.
97. Tom Giambroni, "Firm Asks Limit on Protesters," *Morning Journal*, October 16, 1991, pp. 1A, 6A.
98. Glenn Clark, "Judge Bars WTI Protesters," *Evening Review*, October 17, 1991, p. 1.
99. John Chalfant, "Foes Want Voinovich to See WTI for Himself," *Morning Journal*, October 23, 1991, pp. 1A, 7A.

100. Glenn Clark, "Governor Won't Visit WTI," *Evening Review*, October 24, 1991, p. 1.

101. T.C. Brown, "Incinerator Opponents Bring Concerns Home to Voinovich," *Plain Dealer*, October 28, 1991.

102. "WTI Opponents Protest at Governor's Mansion," *Evening Review*, p. 1.

103. John Mollo, "Hazardous Waste Law Passed in Chester," *Panhandle Press*, November 24, 1991.

104. T.C. Brown, "EPA Allowed Change Without Hearing," *Plain Dealer*, November 20, 1991, pp. 1-C, 2-C.

105. Mary Beth Lane, "Protests Convince Governor," *Plain Dealer*, December 5, 1991, pp. 1-C, 2-C.

106. T.C. Brown, "Protest Roasts 'Weenie'," *Plain Dealer*, December 10, 1991, pp. 1-C, 2-C.

107. Details were culled from the Joint Interview; T.C. Brown, "State Patrol Arrests 10 During Protest at Ohio EPA Office," *Plain Dealer*, December 18, 1991, pp. 1-C, 3-C; and Mark D. Somerson, "Protesters Handcuff Themselves in EPA Chief's Office," *Columbus Dispatch*, December 18, 1991, p. 7C.

108. Tom Giambroni, "Final Revised Permit Issued for WTI," *Morning Journal*, December 19, 1991, p. 1.

109. "WTI Protests Lead to EPA's Tightened Security," *Morning Journal*, December 30, 1990, p. 1.

110. Mitzi Probert, "Parents Oppose WTI Health Study," *Intelligencer*, December 30, 1991, pp. 1, 8.

111. Linda Harris, "Board to Review WTI Permit," *Weirton Daily Times*, January 6, 1992, p. 1.

112. John Mollo, "New Orders for Order, but WTI Foes Don't Comply," *Morning Journal*, January 7, 1992.

113. Tracy Carbasho, "Review of WTI Is Questioned," *Intelligencer*, January 11, 1992, pp. 1, 6.

114. Theresa Pudik Card, "Judge Refuses to Acquit Sheen of Charges," *Beaver County Times*, February 14, 1992, p. A5.

115. Except where otherwise noted, all descriptions of the trial are drawn from the 16 hours of Greenpeace videotapes, which covered the entire courtroom proceedings.

116. Don Hopey, "The Burning Question: Incinerator Neighbors Mistrust Government," *Pittsburgh Press*, March 18, 1992, pp. A1, A6.

117. Connett interview.

118. Phil Brown and Edwin J. Mikkelsen, *No Safe Place: Toxic Waste, Leukemia, and Community Action* (Berkeley: University of California Press, 1990), pp. 38–40.

119. See John Mollo, "Kaufman: EPA in a Free Fall," *Morning Journal*, February 14, 1992, p. 3A; Glenn Clark, "WTI: Kaufman's 'Out of Touch' with the EPA," *Evening Review*, February 14, 1992, p. 1; Don Hopey, "EPA Engineer Calls Incinerator Permits Illegal, Defends Activists," *Pittsburgh Press*, February 14, 1992.

120. Dennis Wise, "Case Closed: They're Innocent: '. . . We've Proved Our Point'," *Saturday Review*, February 15, 1992, pp. 1, 5.

121. Glenn Clark, "WTI Begins Plan for Citizens Committee," *Evening Review*, March 25, 1992.

122. "Metzenbaum Wants Waste Plant Blocked," *Plain Dealer*, April 25, 1992, p. 1-C.

123. "Clinton Due in Ohio Today, Brown Tomorrow," *Plain Dealer*, April 24, 1992.

124. Keith Schneider, "2 Admit E.P.A. Violated Hazardous Waste Law in Issuing Permit," *New York Times*, May 8, 1992.

125. T.C. Brown, "Senate Panel Wants to Stall WTI," *Plain Dealer*, May 21, 1992, pp. 1-C.

126. John Wagner, "EPA Office Occupied by 20 Protesters," *Washington Post*, July 13, 1992.

127. "EPA Gives Nod to Incinerator Operator; WTI to Move Ahead with Shakedown Burn," *Daily Environment Report*, September 10, 1992, pp. A18–A19.

128. "WTI Protesters Say Quayle Council Involved in Ohio Incinerator Battle," *Daily Environment Report*, August 6, 1992, pp. AA1–AA2.

129. "Ohio Drops Trespass Charge Against WTI Incinerator Protesters," *Daily Environment Report*, September 1, 1992, p. AA1.

130. T.C. Brown, "Incinerator Land Sold to WTI," *Plain Dealer*, August 12, 1992, p. 2-C.

131. Interview with Terri Swearingen and Mick Casey, June 27, 1992.

132. Memorandum in Support of Motions for Temporary Restraining Order and for Preliminary Injunction, Civil Action No. 92-0072-W(S), filed by Mario J. Palumbo, Attorney General of West Virginia, August 26, 1992; and Motion to Intervene, filed by City of Pittsburgh, June 1, 1992.

133. *Waste Not* #215, November 1992. The two-page weekly newsletter is written entirely by Paul Connett.

134. "Study Finds Children with High Lead Levels Already Living Nearby New Ohio Incinerator," *Daily Environment Report*, September 10, 1992, p. A7.

135. Letter from Ted Hill, D.O., to Governor George V. Voinovich, September 14, 1992.

136. Telephone interviews with Terri Swearingen, November 21 and 28, 1992.

137. Personal conversation with Niaz Dorry, December 5, 1992.

138. Swearingen interview, November 28, 1992.

139. Keith Schneider, "Gore Says Clinton Will Try to Halt Waste Incinerator," *New York Times*, December 7, 1992, p. D9.

140. "Please Mr. President-Elect, Give Our Town Hope," advertisement in the *New York Times*, December 15, 1992, p. A17.

141. The editorials appeared on December 30, 1992, and January 6, January 8, January 17, and January 19, 1993.

142. Keith Schneider, "Ohio Incinerator Cleared Over Objection by Gore," *New York Times*, March 18, 1993, p. A9.

143. Keith Schneider, "Agency Head Removes Herself from Decision on Ohio Incinerator," *New York Times*, February 8, 1993.

144. Telephone interview with Connie Stein, March 1, 1993.

145. Memo from Robert A. Olexsey to James Berlow, "Review of Proposed Rule, Land Disposal Restriction Framework and Decision on Solvent and Dioxin Containing Wastes," October 24, 1985.

146. Casey Bukro, "Judge Bars Incinerator Dioxin Burn," *Chicago Tribune*, February 13, 1993, Sec. 1, p. 11.

147. Affidavit of Douglas Crawford-Brown, Exhibit 3a of Plaintiffs' Statement of Issues for the Preliminary Injunction Hearing, *Greenpeace et al. v. Waste Technologies Industries*, Case No. 5:93CV0083, Judge Aldrich, United States District Court, Northern District of Ohio, Eastern Division (Cleveland), January 19, 1993.

148. Memo from Richard Guimond to Carol Browner, "WTI Incinerator Issues," January 22, 1993.

149. "Internal EPA Study Says WTI Dioxin Risk May Be 1,000 Times Above Previous Estimates," *Daily Environment Report*, February 10, 1993, pp. AA1–AA2.

150. "An Update on Two Key Incinerator Battles," *Rachel's Hazardous Waste News* #328, March 11, 1993.

151. Schneider, March 18, 1993.

152. *Rachel's* #328.

153. Schneider, March 18, 1993.

154. Telephone interview with Tom Webster, March 18, 1993.

155. "EPA Announces New Incinerator Policies," *Rachel's Hazardous Waste News* #338, May 20, 1993.

156. Keith Schneider, "For Crusader Against Waste Incinerator, a Bittersweet Victory," *New York Times*, May 19, 1993, p. A7.

157. Keith Schneider, "Administration to Freeze Growth of Hazardous Waste Incinerators," *New York Times*, May 18, 1993, pp. A1, A9; EPA news release, "EPA Administrator Browner Announces New Hazardous Waste Reduction and Combustion Strategy," May 18, 1993 (accompanied by "Statement from Carol M. Browner" and "Environmental Fact Sheet: Source Reduction and Combustion of Hazardous Waste"); "Draft Strategy for Combustion of Hazardous Waste," U.S. Environmental Protection Agency, May 1993; and "Guidance to Hazardous Waste Generators on the Elements of a Waste Minimization Program," EPA 530-Z-93-007.

158. *Rachel's* #338.

CHAPTER 5

1. Lake Michigan Federation, *The Grand Calumet: Exploring the River's Potential* (Chicago: Lake Michigan Federation, 1984), p. 5.

2. Isaac James Quillen, *Industrial City: A History of Gary, Indiana to 1929* (New York: Garland Publishing, 1986), pp. 59–60. The Garland edition is an original publication of Quillen's 1942 doctoral dissertation at Yale University.

3. James E. Landing, *Conceptual Plan for the Lake Calumet Ecological Park: Chicago, Illinois* (Prepared for the Lake Calumet Study Committee, Chicago, Illinois, August 1986), pp. 7–8.

4. Lake Michigan Federation, p. 5.

5. Ibid., p. 5.

6. Ibid., p. 12.

7. Personal interview with the Reverend Robert Klonowski, May 22, 1992.

8. J. Ronald Engel, *Sacred Sands: The Struggle for Community in the Indiana Dunes* (Middletown, CT: Wesleyan University Press, 1983), p. 4.

9. Indiana Port Commission, *Burns International Harbor*, undated videotape.

10. William Cronon, *Nature's Metropolis: Chicago and the Great West* (New York: W.W. Norton & Co., 1991), p. 233.

11. Laurie Goering, "Big Cleanup Makes It Hard to Know Where to Start," *Chicago Tribune*, October 28, 1991, Sec. 2, pp. 1, 4.

12. Kenan Heise and Mark Frazel, *Hands on Chicago* (Chicago: Bonus Books, 1987), p. 8.

13. Quillen, pp. 81–82.

14. Quillen, pp. 52–53.

15. Quillen, pp. 88–91.
16. Quillen, p. 194.
17. Quillen, p. 238.
18. Quillen, pp. 387–388.
19. Quillen, p. 375.
20. Richard M. Dorson, *Land of the Millrats* (Cambridge, MA: Harvard University Press, 1981), p. 39.
21. Burns Harbor videotape.
22. Personal interview with Lee Botts, December 8, 1992.
23. Engel, pp. 9–42.
24. Engel, p. 41.
25. Engel, p. 280.
26. Engel, p. 286.
27. Ibid.
28. Personal interview with Dorreen Carey, January 20, 1993, and Engel, p. 288.
29. Engel, pp. 286–288.
30. John N. Maclean, "A Mighty Engine Expires," *Chicago Tribune*, January 10, 1992, Sec. 1, pp. 1, 14.
31. Jim Schwab, "Airport Siting: The Environmental Challenges," *Environment & Development*, July 1992, p. 2.
32. Kathy Orr, "South Works Site Eyed for Electric Minimill," *Southtown Economist*, January 5, 1993, Sec. 2, pp. 1–2.
33. Lester B. Knight & Associates, Inc., et al., *Steel Industry Marketing Study* (Prepared for the City of Chicago, Department of Economic Development, May 1990), pp. 5–9.
34. John N. Maclean, "Steel Yard Blues," *Chicago Tribune Magazine*, March 29, 1992, pp. 14–21.
35. *Lake Calumet Airport: Crossroads of the Nation . . . Future of the Region* (City of Chicago, December 9, 1991), p. 10/2.
36. Klonowski interview.
37. Donald L. Hey et al., *The Third Airport, Southeast Chicago and Environmental Opportunities: Ideas, Concepts and Suggestions*, November 14, 1991, p. 8.
38. Named, incidentally, after the aforementioned Illinois governor.
39. Mike Ervin, "The Toxic Doughnut," *Progressive*, January 1992, p. 15.
40. Unless otherwise noted, the comments of Hazel Johnson in this section are from a personal interview and tour of the neighborhood conducted September 1, 1990.
41. Patricia Jackson, "Meet the Mother of Our Movement," *F.A.T.E.*, newsletter of PCR, Winter 92–93, p. 1.
42. Telephone interview with Mary Ryan, March 24, 1993.
43. "PCR's Community Health Survey Results," Press release of People for Community Recovery, July, 1993.
44. David Jackson, "City Shuts Landfill After 9-year Battle," *Chicago Tribune*, April 22, 1992, Sec. 2, p. 3.
45. Alton Miller, *Harold Washington: The Mayor, the Man* (Chicago: Bonus Books, 1989), pp. 240–241.
46. "Alderman Kelley Pleads Guilty," *Chicago Sun-Times*, April 26, 1987, p. 1.
47. Matt O'Connor, "Panici Took Bribe, Pal Testifies," *Chicago Tribune*, February 9, 1993, Sec. 2, pp. 1, 7.

48. Matt O'Connor, "Ex-Chicago Heights Mayor Convicted," *Chicago Tribune*, February 23, 1993, Sec. 2, pp. 1, 7.

49. Telephone interview with Marian Byrnes, March 11, 1993.

50. Botts interview.

51. City of Chicago, Department of Planning, *Waste Management Options for Chicago*, February 1985. The two volumes are "Findings and Recommendations" and "Detailed Analysis."

52. Lake Michigan Federation, p. 21; John Harte, Cheryl Holdren, Richard Schneider, and Christine Shirley, *Toxics A to Z: A Guide to Everyday Pollution Hazards* (Berkeley: University of California Press, 1991), pp. 382–385.

53. Deborah Nelson, "Critics Do Slow Burn on S. Side Plant," *Chicago Sun-Times*, September 30, 1990, p. 18.

54. *Fact Sheet, Draft Federal Hazardous Waste Management Permit for CWM Chemical Services, Inc., Chicago Incinerator* (U.S. EPA document).

55. *History of Enforcement and Permitting Actions Regarding Chemical Waste Management's Hazardous Waste and PCB Incinerator, Chicago, Cook County, Illinois*, briefing paper provided by the Illinois Attorney General's Office.

56. Letter of Steven Katich, Chairman, Environmental Committee, Veteran's Park Improvement Association, to Gary Westefer, U.S. EPA, August 10, 1989; Letter of Thomas Bohling, President, Southeast Sportsmen's Club, to Gary Westefer, August 8, 1989; and Letter of State Representative Clem Balanoff to Valdas V. Adamkus, Regional Administrator, U.S. EPA, August 11, 1989.

57. T. Petzinger and M. Moffett, "Burning Issue: Poisonous Wastes Run Into a Host of Problems," *Wall Street Journal*, August 26, 1985, p. 1.

58. Robert Bergsvik, "Incinerator Gets $4.5 Million Fine," *Daily Calumet*, May 18, 1989, p. 1.

59. Personal interview with Clem Balanoff, October 24, 1990.

60. Jeff Bailey, "Tough Target: Waste Disposal Giant Often Under Attack Seems to Gain from It," *Wall Street Journal*, May 1, 1991, pp. A1, A4.

61. Andrew Webb, "Waste Management Cleans Up," *Chicago Magazine*, June 1990, p. 122; Julia Flynn, "The Ugly Mess at Waste Management," *Business Week*, April 13, 1992, pp. 76–77.

62. Robert Bergsvik, "Incinerator Ban Urged," *Daily Calumet*, August 6, 1989.

63. Denial Notice, CWM Chemical Services—Chicago Incinerator, Illinois Environmental Protection Agency, September 29, 1989.

64. History of Enforcement, *supra*; Balanoff interview.

65. Telephone interview with Marian Byrnes, December 13, 1990.

66. Deborah Nelson, September 30, 1990.

67. *Complaint for Injunctive and Other Relief, People of the State of Illinois, ex rel. Roland W. Burris, Attorney General of the State of Illinois, Plaintiff, v. CWM Chemical Services, Inc., and Chemical Waste Management, Inc.*, in the Circuit Court of Cook County, Illinois, County Department, Chancery Division, May 23, 1991.

68. Charles Nicodemus, "Heavy Fine for Waste Site," *Chicago Sun-Times*, June 22, 1992, pp. 1, 20.

69. Jeff Bailey, "Concerns Mount Over Operating Methods of Plants that Incinerate Toxic Waste," *Wall Street Journal*, March 20, 1992, pp. B1, B3.

70. See Robert Ginsburg, *Beyond the Rush to Burn* (Boston: National Toxics Campaign Fund, 1991), for a full treatment of this point.

71. Jeff Bailey, May 1, 1991, *supra*.

72. "Chemical Waste Plant Fined," *Engineering News-Record,* July 6, 1992, p. 18.

73. Personal interview with James and Betty Balanoff, February 12, 1993.

74. Personal interview with Robert J. Golec, March 1, 1993. See Hammond ordinances #7442 and #7508.

75. Linda Schmidt, "Wheeler Hazardous Waste Petition Withdrawn," *Vidette-Messenger* (Valparaiso, Indiana), March 25, 1983, p. 1.

76. Personal interview with Susan Lynch, December 8, 1992; also Sue Greer (now Lynch), "Conduct Your Own On-site Inspection," *PAHLS Journal,* March 1991, pp. 1, 3.

77. Ryan interview.

78. "Fact Sheet: Wheeler Landfill, Porter County," Prepared by the Office of External Affairs, Indiana Department of Environmental Management, May 1992; "Report of Technical Findings: Wheeler Landfill," Indiana Department of Environmental Management," undated.

79. Ryan interview.

80. Webb, op. cit.

81. Laurie Goering, "Judge Voids Indiana Landfill Law," *Chicago Tribune,* December 28, 1990, Sec. 1, p. 1.

82. "River Community Speaks Out for a Clean and Safe Environment," *Grand Cal Currents,* Winter 1992, p. 1.

83. Carey interview.

84. Chris Isidore, "Inland Steel: Continuing to Build on a Toxic Landfill," in "Poisoning the Region," special reprint of the *Gary Post-Tribune,* February 10, 1993, p. 7.

85. Carey interview.

86. John N. Maclean and Janita Poe, "Pollution Case Costs Inland $54 Million," *Chicago Tribune,* March 10, 1993, Sec. 3, pp. 1, 3.

87. Todd Sloane, "Gary, Ind., Defies Court Orders," *City & State,* March 26, 1990, pp. 3, 18.

88. For a brief history of enforcement actions against the sanitary districts and industry alike in the Grand Calumet area, see Michael O. Holowaty et al., "A RAP for the Grand Calumet River," in *Under RAPs: Toward Grassroots Ecological Democracy in the Great Lakes Basin,* John H. Hartig and Michael A. Zarull, eds. (Ann Arbor: University of Michigan Press, 1992), pp. 211–233.

89. Todd Sloane, "Cities, Industry Now Face Mammoth Cleanup Job," *City & State,* March 26, 1990, pp. 3, 19.

90. Holowaty et al., p. 218.

91. James and Betty Balanoff interview.

92. John Ellis, "Family: Toxins Killed Daughter," in "Poisoning the Region," *supra,* p. 12.

93. Chris Isidore, "Lake's No. 8 Worst Polluted County," in "Poisoning the Region," *supra,* p. 4.

94. INFORM, *Toxic Clusters: Patterns of Pollution in the Midwest* (New York: INFORM, 1991), p. 88.

95. Chris Isidore, "Environmentalists: Cancer Rate Tied to Toxins," in "Poisoning the Region," *supra,* p. 12.

96. See, e.g., Patrick C. West, J. Mark Fly, Frances Larkin, and Robert W. Marans, "Minority Anglers and Toxic Fish Consumption: Evidence from a Statewide Survey of Michigan," in *Race and the Incidence of Environmental Hazards: A Time*

for Discourse, edited by Bunyan Bryant and Paul Mohai (Boulder, CO:Westview Press, 1992), pp. 100–113.

97. Carey interview.

98. Personal interview with David Dabertin, March 18, 1993.

99. For an exposition of this period, see Andrew Hurley, "Challenging Corporate Polluters: Race, Class, and Environmental Politics in Gary, Indiana, since 1945," *Indiana Magazine of History* (Volume LXXXVIII, No. 4), December 1992, pp. 273–302.

100. Telephone interview with Michael Wright, February 25, 1993. The 90-percent reduction estimate was confirmed by Kenneth Westlake, EPA Region V state-relations coordinator, in a telephone interview May 28, 1993.

101. Telephone interview with Larry Davis, February 25, 1993.

102. Personal interview with Michael Aniol, May 15, 1992.

103. *Lake Calumet Airport,* p. 7/2.

104. Ben Joravsky, "Trouble in Paradise," *Chicago Reader*, July 26, 1991, p. 20.

105. Schwab, p. 2.

106. Harold Henderson, "Will It Fly: Six Questions That Need to be Asked About the Lake Calumet Airport," *Chicago Reader*, January 4, 1991, p. 12.

107. Henderson, p. 19.

108. Joravsky, p. 21.

109. Henderson, p. 20.

110. Joravsky, pp. 25–26.

111. *Lake Calumet Airport*, p. 10/3.

112. Gary Washburn, "3rd-Airport Studies Rip City's Site," *Chicago Tribune*, Sec. 2, p. 1.

113. *Lake Calumet Airport*, p. 14/7.

114. Hey et al., p. 4.

115. Schwab, p. 3.

116. Rick Pearson and Hugh Dellios, "3rd-Airport Proposal Fails to Get Fast-Track Approval," *Chicago Tribune*, June 30, 1992, Sec. 2, pp. 1, 7.

117. John Kass, "Now It's All Over but the Snarling," *Chicago Tribune*, July 3, 1992, Sec. 1, p. 16.

118. Center for Neighborhood Technology, *Building a Sustainable Future for Chicago's Southeast Side: Is an Airport the Answer?* Proceedings of a Workshop on May 15, 1991, Chicago Academy of Sciences, p. 18.

119. Carey interview.

CHAPTER 6

1. Robert D. Bullard, *Dumping in Dixie: Race, Class, and Environmental Quality* (Boulder, CO: Westview Press, 1990), p. 65.

2. Bob Anderson, "La. Ranks First in Discharging Toxic Pollution," *Baton Rouge Morning Advocate*, April 20, 1990, pp. 1-A, 4-A.

3. Dennis Farney, "Bayou Politics: Election in Louisiana Features Critical Issues and Quirky Candidates," *Wall Street Journal*, Vol. LXXII, No. 228, pp. A1, A3.

4. William Sanjour, "Why EPA Is Like It Is," paper presented to the Coalition for Health Concern, Kenlake, Kentucky, November 17, 1990.

5. The personal history of Willie Fontenot is drawn from a series of telephone and personal interviews with him during April 1991.

6. Coalition to Restore Coastal Louisiana, *Coastal Louisiana: Here Today and Gone Tomorrow?* (Baton Rouge: Coalition to Restore Coastal Louisiana, 1989), p. 7.
7. Telephone interview with Gay Hanks, April 18, 1991, supplemented by interviews with Willie Fontenot.
8. Personal interview with Gerald Tillman, April 29, 1991.
9. Fontenot is hardly the only person to express some disenchantment with the state health department. DEQ officials by then were also expressing considerable annoyance at the agency's refusal to accept their water-testing data as evidence that the department should post various polluted rivers and streams as unacceptable for swimming. The health department, which lacked adequate resources to do its own testing, contended that the testing was not done frequently enough to justify such advisories. Consequently, the no-swimming signs never appeared on bodies of water that probably did pose a threat to human health. See James O'Byrne and Mark Schliefstein, "Rivers, Streams, Bayous Awash in Pollution," *New Orleans Times-Picayune*, May 12, 1991, p. A-14. The article is part of an investigative series, "Louisiana in Peril: Saving the Lake."
10. Personal interview with Mary McCastle and Roy McCastle, April 24, 1991.
11. Separate personal interview with Roy McCastle, same day.
12. Mary McCastle and Roy McCastle interview.
13. Bullard, p. 66.
14. Ibid.
15. Bullard, p. 67.
16. Mary McCastle and Roy McCastle interview.
17. Fontenot's account of the Alsen story comes from a personal interview conducted April 27, 1991.
18. Bullard, p. 68.
19. Mary McCastle and Roy McCastle interview.
20. Bullard, p. 68.
21. Steve Culpepper, "Rollins Hears Few Supporters," *Baton Rouge Morning Advocate*, November 17, 1989, pp. 1B–2B.
22. Steve Culpepper, "OSHA Investigating Accident at Rollins," *Baton Rouge Morning Advocate*, October 26, 1989, pp. 1B–2B.
23. "EPA Suspends Rollins from Disposing of Superfund Waste," *Baton Rouge State-Times*, January 12, 1990. The article notes that EPA had suspended Rollins once before, in August 1986.
24. Marsha Shuler, "State Files Suit to Stop Rollins' Dinoseb Burning," *Baton Rouge State-Times*, January 12, 1990.
25. "Louisiana Protest Stops DOE Waste Shipments," *Engineering News-Record*, June 10, 1991, p. 24.
26. Hearing on Groundwater Contamination, U.S. House of Representatives, Subcommittee on Environment, Energy, and Natural Resources of the Committee on Government Operations, June 22, 1983, p. 37.
27. Joan McKinney, "La. Farmer Creates Stir at Water Hearing," *Baton Rouge Morning Advocate*, June 23, 1983, pp. 1-A, 10-A.
28. Ibid. It should be noted that, with a wry smile, friends note that Rigmaiden is prone to a mild degree of exaggeration in describing his livestock losses. "The numbers change a little," concedes Mary Ellender. None of the activists, however, question the fundamental truth of his tragic experience.

29. Ibid.
30. Ibid.
31. Ibid., p. 66.
32. Ibid., p. 37.
33. Medical Study of Willow Springs, January 1984, supplied by the Calcasieu League for Environmental Action Now (CLEAN).
34. Telephone interviews with Peggy Frankland and Ruth Shepherd, May 13, 1993.
35. Telephone interview with Marvin S. Legator, March 18, 1993.
36. Peggy Frankland escorted me on a tour of the site boundaries on April 26, 1991, during which time we spoke with the neighbors described here.
37. After hiring former U.S. EPA Administrator William Ruckelshaus as its CEO in 1989, BFI made a strategic decision to get out of the hazardous-waste business and concentrate on municipal solid waste.
38. Don Ellzey, "Chemical Waste Threatens Retired Minister's Home," *Lake Charles American Press*, August 12, 1979, p. 66.
39. Personal interview with Reverend Joseph Bartlett and Peggy Frankland, April 26, 1991.
40. Fred Schulte and Robert McClure, "The Trashing of America," *News/Sun-Sentinel* (Orlando, Florida), December 6, 1987.
41. Robert McClure and Fred Schulte, "Laws Fail to Prevent Pollution at Dumpsites," *News/Sun-Sentinel*, December 6, 1987.
42. Personal interview with Jeffery Hanor, May 1, 1992.
43. Personal interview with Brad Hanson, May 1, 1992.
44. Personal interview with Kirby Verret, April 27, 1992.
45. Greg Bowman and Janel Curry-Roper, *The Houma People of Louisiana: A Story of Indian Survival* (Houma, Louisiana: The United Houma Nation, Inc., 1982), p. 1.
46. Vickie Duffourc, *Environmental Racism and the Houma Indians of Louisiana* (College of Urban and Public Affairs, University of New Orleans, Fall 1991), p. 2.
47. Ibid., p. 3.
48. Ibid., p. 3.
49. Ibid., p. 9.
50. Ibid, p. 10.
51. Ibid., p. 11.
52. Ibid., p. 9.
53. The remainder of this story is drawn from the interview with Verret.
54. George F. Lundy and William Temmink, "A Battle on the Mississippi," *Blueprint for Social Justice* (Newsletter of the Institute of Human Relations, Loyola University, New Orleans), Volume XL, No. 8 (April 1987).
55. Telephone interview with Esnard Gremillion. The history of the BASF lockout is derived from this interview unless otherwise noted.
56. Lundy and Temmink.
57. Gremillion interview.
58. Lundy and Temmink.
59. Lundy and Temmink.
60. Vicki Ferstel, "BASF, Union Together, But Apart," *Baton Rouge Morning Advocate*, January 20, 1991, pp. 1B, 6B.
61. Gremillion interview.
62. Lundy and Temmink.

63. Darryl Malek-Wiley, "Stress and Air Pollution in the Mississippi River Corridor: A Case Study," paper presented September 14, 1989, at the Eighth World Clean Air Congress, The Hague, Netherlands.

64. *Louisiana Chemical Industry Emissions Report: A Compilation and Comparison of Toxic Release Inventory Data, 1989–1990* (Baton Rouge: Louisiana Chemical Association, November 1991), pp. A1–A7.

65. Malek-Wiley paper.

66. Conger Beasley, Jr. and JC Leacock, "Of Pollution and Poverty, Part 2: Keeping Watch in Cancer Alley," *Buzzworm*, July/August 1990, p. 39.

67. David Maraniss and Michael Weisskopf, "Jobs and Illness in Petrochemical Corridor," *Washington Post*, December 22, 1987, pp. 1–5.

68. Malek-Wiley paper.

69. Personal interview with Amos Favorite, April 23, 1991. This story has been repeated often and appears in several newspaper stories. There is no reason to believe that their pharmacy failed for any other cause.

70. Maraniss and Weisskopf, p. 2.

71. Favorite interview.

72. Gremillion interview and Lundy and Temmink article, p. 6.

73. Telephone interview with Richard Miller, August 10, 1993.

74. The story of UFCW Local P-9's "adopt-a-family" strategy appears in Peter Rachloff, "Supporting the Hormel Strikers," in Jeremy Brecher and Tim Costello, eds., *Building Bridges: The Emerging Grassroots Coalition of Labor and Community* (New York: Monthly Review Press, 1990), pp. 57–69.

75. Gremillion interview.

76. Gremillion interview and Ferstel article.

77. Mark Schliefstein and James O'Byrne, "Troubled Plant Neighbors Would Like to Breathe Easier," *New Orleans Times-Picayune*, February 18, 1991, p. A8.

78. *Louisiana Toxic Release Inventory 1989* (Baton Rouge: Louisiana Department of Environmental Quality, December 1990), pp. 12–15.

79. Gary Gauthier, "Public Hearing Shows Sentiment Against Rubicon," *Baton Rouge Morning Advocate*, June 26, 1990, p. 3B.

80. Notes from attending a meeting of the Geismar/Dutchtown Residents for Clean Water and Air, April 29, 1992, and BASF Hazardous Waste Injection Fact Sheet, distributed by the same organization.

81. Notes from Geismar/Dutchtown meeting and personal interview with Daniel Nicholai, April 29, 1992.

82. Newsletter, Geismar/Dutchtown Residents for Clean Water and Air, March 25, 1992.

83. Ferstel, January 20, 1991.

84. Personal interview with David Czernik, April 24, 1991.

85. LA-WATCH *"For Safety"* Column, #1, February 1990.

86. Joe Gyan, Jr., "Group Protests on Behalf of Ailing Texaco Employee," *Baton Rouge Morning Advocate*, December 18, 1990, p. 4B.

87. Personal interview with William Temmink and Alan Bernard, April 25, 1991.

88. Personal interview with Dr. Tom Callender, April 30, 1992.

89. The slash between the words coalition and citizens denotes LCTJ's combined constituency of individual family members and organizational backers. As of 1992, it claimed at least 600 families and 33 organizational members.

90. Louisiana Constitution, 1974, Article VII, Section 21.

91. Zack Nauth, *The Great Louisiana Tax Giveaway* (Baton Rouge: Louisiana Coalition for Tax Justice, 1992), p. 11.

92. Nauth, p. 12.

93. Nauth, p. 11.

94. Nauth, p. 12.

95. Nauth, p. 14.

96. Nauth, p. 12.

97. Nauth, p. 21.

98. Fred Kalmbach, "Judge Orders Settlement Payments in '89 Exxon Blast," *Baton Rouge Morning Advocate*, April 30, 1992, p. 17A.

99. Nauth, p. 38.

100. Nauth, p. 42.

101. Nauth, p. 43.

102. Nauth, pp. 43–44.

103. Vicki Ferstel, "Environment Impact, Tax Exemption Link Eyed by Task Force," *Baton Rouge State-Times*, December 21, 1989.

104. "Economics Should Be Factor in Environmental Protection," *Business Report*, March 1990, p. 37.

105. Nauth, p. 45.

106. Nauth, p. 46.

107. Nauth, p. 42.

108. Linda Young, "Group Wants Seven Off Commerce Board," *Lake Charles American Press*, March 29, 1991, p. 1; also see James Gill, "Commerce Board Fends off Roemer," *New Orleans Times-Picayune*, March 29, 1991, p. B-6, a notably sarcastic column that stated that "tarring and feathering would be too good" for the recalcitrant board members.

109. Cyndy Falgout, "Board Approves Revised Tax Policy," *Baton Rouge Morning Advocate*, April 25, 1991, pp. 1C, 4C.

110. Nauth, p. 49.

111. Nauth, p. 50.

112. Telephone interview with Kai Midboe, March 13, 1992.

113. Nauth, p. 37; Cyndy Falgout, "Environment Scorecard Discontinued," *Baton Rouge Morning Advocate*, February 27, 1992, pp. 1F, 2F.

114. Nauth, p. 49.

115. Telephone interview with Janice Dickerson, June 3, 1992.

116. Telephone interview with Ramona Stevens, June 4, 1992.

117. Dickerson interview.

118. Stevens interview.

119. Dickerson interview.

120. Telephone interview with Janis Terrell, February 15, 1992.

121. Telephone interview with Dale L. Watson, February 14, 1992.

122. Terrell interview. Also see: Caleb Solomon, "Big Payoff: How a Neighborhood Talked Fina Refinery into Buying It Out," *Wall Street Journal*, December 10, 1991, pp. A1, A5; and articles in the *Port Arthur News* by Greg Rabel ("Six Changes Made in Fina Buyout Plan," January 14, 1992, pp. 1A, 2A; "Fairlea Residents: Doctors Unwilling to Prioritize Respiratory Problems," February 5, 1992, pp. 1A, 2A) and by Steve Brewer ("Buyout Proposal Surfaces," December

19, 1991, pp. 1A, 3A; "Fairlea Residents Blast Fina," January 8, 1992, pp. 1A, 3A). It should be noted that residents took strong exception to the tone of the article in the *Wall Street Journal* because of the writer's skepticism about their claims.

123. Telephone interview with Guy Barone, June 4, 1992.

124. *Louisiana Chemical Industry Emissions Report*, p. A-22.

125. Barone interview.

126. Telephone interview with Elizabeth Avants, April 30, 1992.

127. Telephone interview with Dale Emmanuel, June 3, 1992.

128. Telephone interview with Ada Mae Gaines, June 3, 1992.

129. Telephone interview with Ledell J.R. Hannon, June 2, 1992.

130. *Louisiana Chemical Industry Emissions Report*, pp. A15–A16.

131. Kalmbach, April 30, 1992.

132. Telephone interview with David Gardner, June 4, 1992.

133. Hannon interview.

134. Testimony of Dan Borne, President of Louisiana Chemical Association, before Louisiana Advisory Committee to the U.S. Commission on Civil Rights, February 20, 1992, pp. 518–559 of transcript.

135. Barone interview.

136. "2,000 Protesters Rally to Halt Chemical Plant," *New Orleans Times-Picayune*, December 2, 1990, p. B12.

137. Daniel Mandell and Sanford J. Lewis, *The Formosa Plastics Story: A Report to the People of St. John the Baptist Parish* (Boston: National Toxics Campaign Fund, 1992), p. 16.

138. James Gill, "Mr. Millet and the Formosa Plant," *New Orleans Times-Picayune*, January 6, 1991, p. B9.

139. Bob Warren, "Sheriff Is Pushing for Jail Expansion in St. John," *New Orleans Times-Picayune*, September 7, 1990, p. B1.

140. Bob Warren, "Political Style Is Top Issue in St. John Race," *New Orleans Times-Picayune*, October 11, 1991, p. A1.

141. Bob Warren, "Protesters Blast Proposed St. John Plastics Plant," *New Orleans Times-Picayune*, April 19, 1990, p. B1.

142. Bob Warren, "Charges Against 21 Pollution Protesters Are Dropped," *New Orleans Times-Picayune*, November 30, 1990, p. B10.

143. James Gill, "Beyond Environmental Unconcern," *New Orleans Times-Picayune*, January 20, 1991, p. B7.

144. Bob Warren, "Rayon Plant OK'd by St. John Council," *New Orleans Times-Picayune*, April 20, 1990, p. A1.

145. Bob Warren, "Formosa Opponents Sue Against Rezoning," *New Orleans Times-Picayune*, May 1, 1990, p. B1.

146. Stephen Casmier, "School Board Gives Formosa Tax Incentive," *New Orleans Times-Picayune*, May 5, 1990, p. B1.

147. Ed Anderson, "Panel Kills Bill Blocking Formosa Plastics Plant," *New Orleans Times-Picayune*, June 15, 1990, p. B2.

148. John Harte, Cheryl Holdren, Richard Schneider, and Christine Shirley, *Toxics A to Z: A Guide to Everyday Pollution Hazards* (Berkeley: University of California Press, 1991), p. 431.

149. Mandell and Lewis, p. 11.

150. Mandell and Lewis, pp. 14–15.

151. Mandell and Lewis, pp. 9–10.

152. Bob Warren, "Formosa Plastics Fined $3.3 Million," *New Orleans Times-Picayune*, February 28, 1991, p. B1.

153. Bob Warren, "Formosa Review to Include Its Record," *New Orleans Times-Picayune*, May 21, 1991, p. B1.

154. Bob Warren, "Plastics Plant Battle Renewed," *New Orleans Times-Picayune*, January 4, 1991, p. A1.

155. Bob Warren, "Formosa Negotiates to Buy Plantation Neighbor," *New Orleans Times-Picayune*, January 5, 1991, p. B1.

156. Tyler Bridges, "Roemer Will Return Three Contributions," *New Orleans Times-Picayune*, May 17, 1991, p. B4.

157. Matt Scallan, "German Coast Pushes for Tourism," *New Orleans Times-Picayune*, August 4, 1991, p. I11.

158. "Formosa Gets New Criticism," *New Orleans Times-Picayune*, August 4, 1991, p. I11.

159. Bob Ross, "Plantation Owner Suing Formosa," *New Orleans Times-Picayune*, May 6, 1992, p. B3.

160. Personal interview with Wilfred Greene, May 2, 1992.

161. Bob Ross, "Rayon Plant Battled by Tough Ex-Principal," *New Orleans Times-Picayune*, February 20, 1992, p. B1.

162. Joe Byrnes, "Formosa Hits Obstacle in Land Purchase," *L'Observateur* (La Place, Louisiana), June 6, 1991, pp. 1, 3.

163. Bob Warren, "Impact Study Downplays Minuses of Formosa Plant," *New Orleans Times-Picayune*, November 5, 1991, p. A1.

164. Bob Warren, "Labat Turns Tables on Millet for St. John Parish Presidency," *New Orleans Times-Picayune*, November 17, 1991, p. A15.

165. Frances Frank Marcus, "A Town Loses Jobs, Then Celebrates," *New York Times*, October 26, 1992, Sec. A, p. 10.

166. Telephone interview with Richard Miller, April 17, 1991.

167. Personal interview with Marylee Orr, April 25, 1991.

168. *Louisiana Toxic Release Inventory 1989*, p. 10.

169. *Corporate Response to DEQ's Request for Toxic Waste Reduction Plans, 1990.* (Baton Rouge: Louisiana Department of Environmental Quality, November 1990).

170. *Louisiana Toxic Release Inventory*, p. 34.

171. Letter to Paul Templet from Brenda S. Davis, Princeton University, February 27, 1992.

172. Personal interviews with Paul Templet, April 25, 1991, and April 30, 1992.

173. *Corporate Response, 1990*, pp. 62–63.

174. The company later separated all of its engineering, technical, and environmental personnel by spinning off a new company called Crescent Technology, for which Forman now works. Its only client initially was Freeport McMoRan, but the separation freed it to contract with other firms.

175. The details of this segment are drawn from personal interviews with W. Wayne Forman, April 29, 1992, and Paul Templet, April 30, 1992, plus a telephone interview with Forman, August 10, 1993.

176. Kelly King Alexander, "It's War," *Business Report*, March 1990, pp. 36–43.

177. Chris Harris, "Louisiana Agencies Fight Budget Cuts," *Environment & Development*, July 1992, p. 4.

178. Templet interview, April 30, 1992.

179. Earth Day keynote speech of Reverend Ben Chavis, Southern University, Baton Rouge, April 25, 1992.

CHAPTER 7

1. Theda Perdue, "Red and Black in the Southern Appalachians," in *Blacks in Appalachia*, William H. Turner and Edward J. Cabbell, eds. (Lexington: University Press of Kentucky, 1985), pp. 23–29.

2. Harry M. Caudill, *A Darkness at Dawn: Appalachian Kentucky and the Future* (Lexington: University Press of Kentucky, 1976), pp. 5–7.

3. Harry M. Caudill, *Theirs Be the Power* (Lexington: University Press of Kentucky, 1983), pp. 87–90.

4. For a well-informed recent treatment of the social and ecological conditions that facilitated the rise of coal towns and their attraction for small-scale Appalachian farmers, see Crandall A. Shiflett, *Coal Towns: Life, Work, and Culture in Company Towns of Southern Appalachia, 1880-1960* (Knoxville, University of Tennessee Press, 1991).

5. Caudill, *Theirs Be the Power*, pp. 77–79.

6. Appalachian Land Ownership Task Force, *Who Owns Appalachia?: Landownership and Its Impact* (Lexington: University Press of Kentucky, 1983), pp. 28–29.

7. Caudill, *A Darkness at Dawn*, p. 22.

8. James M. Cain, "West Virginia: A Mine-Field Melodrama," in *America's Energy: Reports from* The Nation *on 100 Years of Struggles for the Democratic Control of Our Resources*, edited by Robert Engler (New York: Pantheon Books, 1980), pp. 4–8.

9. The story of the Highlander Center is well told in his own autobiography, as told to Judith Kohl and Herbert Kohl, *The Long Haul* (New York: Doubleday, 1990).

10. Caudill, *Theirs Be the Power*, p. 107.

11. Appalachian Land Ownership Task Force, pp. 60–61.

12. Appalachian Land Ownership Task Force, p. 10.

13. Appalachian Land Ownership Task Force, p. 49.

14. Appalachian Land Ownership Task Force, p. 11.

15. Appalachian Land Ownership Task Force, p. 120.

16. Appalachian Land Ownership Task Force, p. 142. Anyone who has driven through eastern Kentucky and West Virginia knows well that, in those few areas untouched by energy development, the hills are and always have been thick with forest cover.

17. Melanie A. Zuercher, ed., *Making History: The First Ten Years of KFTC* (Prestonsburg, KY: Kentuckians for the Commonwealth, 1991), pp. 1–3.

18. Zuercher, pp. 4–7.

19. Zuercher, pp. 6–7. This was the first time HUD turned down a CDBG because of the "lack of citizen participation."

20. Zuercher, pp. 9–12.

21. Zuercher, pp. 13–15.

22. The Kentucky State Constitution creates a number of special "cabinets" of statewide officials for specified purposes, such as the Revenue Cabinet or the Cabinet for Natural Resources and Environmental Protection.

23. Zuercher, pp. 14–15.

24. Zuercher, p. 18.

25. Zuercher, p. 19.

26. Zuercher, p. 20.

27. Zuercher, pp. 20–21.

28. Zuercher, p. 38.

29. Zuercher, p. 40.

30. Zuercher, p. 52.

31. See *Gillis v. Yount,* 747 S.W. 2d 357.

32. Zuercher, p. 141.

33. Zuercher, p. 26.

34. *Fighting for Justice,* a videotape produced by Kentuckians for the Commonwealth.

35. Zuercher, p. 16.

36. Zuercher, p. 25.

37. Zuercher, pp. 68–71; *Fighting for Justice* videotape.

38. The Citizens Coal Council emerged from a Citizens Coal Summit in 1987 in Lexington, Kentucky, co-sponsored by KFTC and Save Our Cumberland Mountains. It initially included eight citizens groups and one Indian nation, lobbying for strong enforcement of the federal Surface Mining Act, among other goals.

39. "Congressional Report Adds Credence to Citizen Complaints About OSM's Performance," *balancing the scales,* Vol. 12, No. 3, April 22, 1993, pp. 1–2. *balancing the scales* is KFTC's newspaper.

40. See *Akers v. Baldwin,* 736 S.W. 2d 294.

41. *Fighting for Justice* videotape.

42. Appalachian Land Ownership Task Force, p. 144.

43. Zuercher, pp. 77–79.

44. Zuercher, pp. 80–85; *Fighting for Justice* videotape.

45. "Deed Amendment Constitutional, High Court Rules," *balancing the scales,* July 22, 1993, pp. 1, 4.

46. Except where otherwise noted in this section, the details in the GROWL story come from a personal interview with Janet Brown and Becky Harris, August 11, 1991. Some material is also drawn from personal notes on dates and events, plus miscellaneous clippings, supplied by Brown and Harris.

47. Zuercher, pp. 110–111.

48. Zuercher, p. 121.

49. Zuercher, p. 122.

50. "GROWL Wins Again in Landfill Fight," *balancing the scales,* Vol. 10, No. 2, February 21, 1991, pp. 1, 7.

51. Thelma Hicks, "Settlement Reached in Greenup County Landfill Controversy," *balancing the scales,* Vol. 11, No. 8, October 8, 1992, pp. 1, 7.

52. Much of the material on Lawrence County is drawn, except where otherwise noted, from a personal interview with Patty Wallace, August 11, 1991.

53. Zuercher, pp. 88–89.

54. Zuercher, p. 91.

55. Zuercher, p. 91; also Lee Mueller, "Lawrence Panel Fights Incinerator Plan," *Lexington Herald-Leader,* April 25, 1986, pp. C1, C2.

56. Gene Marvin, Jr., "PyroChem Application to Be Judged on Merit, Not Politics Says Governor," *Big Sandy News,* July 24, 1985, p. 1.

57. Zuercher, p. 96.

58. Telephone interview with Corinne Whitehead, July 22, 1992.

59. "Sensible PyroChem Decision Is Only First of Many Looming on Toxic Waste Facilities," *Lexington Herald-Leader*, November 30, 1987, p. A12.

60. "Applause Greets Vote to Ban PyroChem," *Ashland Daily Independent*, April 30, 1988, pp. 1, 10.

61. Ruth West, "Focus on: Lawrence County," *balancing the scales*, Special Tenth Anniversary Edition, Vol. 10, No. 11, November 21, 1991.

62. Robin Epstein, "Landfill Operators Had Poor Strip-Mining Record," *Louisville Courier-Journal*, August 23, 1990, pp. A1, A10.

63. Jane Rosko, "Controversial Roe Creek Landfill Ordered to Close," *balancing the scales*, Vol. 10, No. 5, May 23, 1991, pp. 1, 7.

64. "Patty Wallace Named to Kentucky Environmental Quality Commission," *balancing the scales*, Vol. 12, No. 2, March 11, 1993, p. 8.

65. Personal interviews with Tyler Fairleigh and Susan Shoulders, August 10, 1991.

66. *Fighting for Justice* videotape.

67. Telephone interview with Barbara Christian, April 6, 1993. The author personally drove through the area in question in August 1991 during an interviewing tour of Appalachia.

68. Telephone interview with Diana Bowen, April 6, 1993.

69. Telephone interview with Dan Kash, April 8, 1993.

70. Bowen interview.

71. Christian interview.

72. *Air Pollution from the Catlettsburg Refinery Compared to Other Large U.S. Refineries* (Proctorville, Ohio: Ohio Valley Environmental Coalition, January 1992), pp. 5–6.

73. "Citizen Monitoring Spurs State Enforcement in KY," *What Works Bulletin* (Washington, DC: The Environmental Exchange), March 1993. The bulletin is an occasional two-page newsletter devoted to pollution-reduction news.

74. Stephanie Martz, "Ashland Settlement Embitters Plaintiffs," *Charleston Sunday Gazette-Mail*, February 21, 1993, pp. 1A, 4A.

75. *What Works Bulletin*, March 1993.

76. Jim Malone, "Refinery Air Issues Settled," *Ashland Daily Independent*, January 29, 1993, pp. 1, 12.

77. *What Works Bulletin*, March 1993.

78. Kash interview.

79. Shiflett, pp. 73–75; see also Kenneth R. Bailey, "A Judicious Mixture: Negroes and Immigrants in the West Virginia Mines, 1880–1917," in *Blacks in Appalachia*, pp. 117–132.

80. David Dembo, Ward Morehouse, and Lucinda Wykle, *Abuse of Power (Social Performance of Multinational Corporations: The Case of Union Carbide)*, (New York: Apex Press, 1990), pp. 21–31.

81. *Chemical Valley*, videotape produced by Appalshop, Inc., Whitesburg, KY. The hour-long program, directed by Mimi Pickering and Anne Lewis Johnson, aired on the Public Broadcasting System on July 9, 1991.

82. Dembo et al., p. 81.

83. *Chemical Valley* videotape.

84. Robert D. Bullard, *Dumping in Dixie* (Boulder, CO: Westview Press, 1990), pp. 62–63.

85. Dembo et al., pp. 48–49.

86. *Chemical Valley* videotape.

87. Bullard, p. 63.

88. *Chemical Valley* videotape.

89. *Chemical Valley* videotape.

90. Joint personal interview with members of People Concerned About MIC, August 12, 1991. The tape-recorded session at West Virginia State College included Mildred Holt, Pamela Nixon, Paul Nuchims, Charles White, William Anderson, and Sue F. Davis.

91. People Concerned About MIC interview.

92. People Concerned About MIC interview; Norman Oder, "In Case of Disaster," *Environmental Action*, May/June 1989, pp. 17–19.

93. Oder, op. cit.

94. People Concerned About MIC interview.

95. Personal interview with Norm Steenstra, August 12, 1991.

96. Steenstra interview; John E. Frook, "Don't Mess With Martha," *Family Circle*, July 23, 1991, pp. 13–16.

97. Jenny LaBalme, "Dumping on Warren County," in *Environmental Politics: Lessons from the Grassroots*, Bob Hall, ed. (Durham, NC: Institute for Southern Studies, 1988), p. 24.

98. Bill Holman, "Environmentalist in the Legislature" in *Environmental Politics*, pp. 56–64.

99. Edgar M. Miller, "Too Hot to Handle: Where to Put Radioactive Waste," in *Environmental Politics*, pp. 48–55.

100. Two examples available to readers are *The North Carolina Waste Reduction Assurance Plan* (July 1991) and *Analysis of the Regional Agreement States Capacity Assurance Plans* (September 5, 1990), available from NC-WARN, 5301 Rolling Hill Road, Sanford, NC 27330, telephone 919-774-9566.

CHAPTER 8

1. For a detailed analysis of the boom and bust that accompanied the discovery of uranium on the Colorado plateau, see Raye C. Ringholz, *Uranium Frenzy: Boom and Bust on the Colorado Plateau* (New York: W.W. Norton & Co., 1989).

2. Telephone interview with Susan Dawson, May 21, 1993.

3. Personal interview with Phillip Harrison, Jr., April 20, 1993.

4. Jerry Kammer, *The Second Long Walk: The Navajo-Hopi Land Dispute* (Albuquerque: University of New Mexico Press, 1980), p. 207.

5. Ringholz, pp. 37–51.

6. "Experts Knew Miners Were at Great Risk," *High Country News*, June 18, 1990, pp. 11–12.

7. Ringholz, pp. 37–51.

8. Susan E. Dawson, "Navajo Uranium Workers and the Effects of Occupational Illnesses: A Case Study," *Human Organization* (Vol. 51, No. 4, Winter 1992), p. 392.

9. Susan E. Dawson, "Social Work Practice and Technological Disasters: The Navajo Uranium Experience," *Journal of Sociology and Social Welfare*, June 1993.

10. It should be noted that this connection is a modern theory developed in the twentieth century by linguistic scholars and not one that is found in any of the individual tribes' traditional beliefs or creation stories. Consequently, not all Native Americans are prepared to accept its validity.

11. Personal interviews with Phillip Harrison, Jr., and Ervin Nakai, April 20, 1993.

12. Ramona Gault, "Navajos Inherit a Legacy of Radiation," *In These Times*, September 13–19, 1989, p. 6.

13. Marjane Ambler, *Breaking the Iron Bonds: Indian Control of Energy Development* (Lawrence: University Press of Kansas, 1990), pp. 174–175.

14. Gault.

15. Dawson interview.

16. Gault.

17. Ambler, p. 175.

18. Telephone interview with Timothy Benally, May 21, 1993.

19. Dawson, "Navajo Uranium Workers," p. 391.

20. Ambler, pp. 178–179.

21. Harrison interview.

22. *High Country News*, op. cit.

23. Telephone interview with Chellis Glendinning, May 17, 1993.

24. Harrison interview. Virtually all of Harrison's recollections were substantiated without exception in the interviews collected by Susan E. Dawson.

25. Telephone interview with Lori Goodman, August 9, 1993.

26. Dawson interview.

27. Robert W. Young, *A Political History of the Navajo Tribe* (Tsaile, Navajo Nation, Arizona: Navajo Community College Press, 1978), pp. 25–27.

28. Telephone interview with Grace Thorpe, July 2, 1993.

29. Young, p. 33.

30. Ruth M. Underhill, *The Navajos* (Norman: University of Oklahoma Press, 1956), pp. 112–121.

31. Young, pp. 34–35.

32. Father Leopold Ostermann, *The Navajo Indians of New Mexico and Arizona* (Anthropos, 1909), quoted in Young, p. 48.

33. Underhill, p. 215.

34. Philip Reno, *Mother Earth, Father Sky, and Economic Development: Navajo Resources and Their Use* (Albuquerque: University of New Mexico Press, 1981), p. 33.

35. Those who doubt the seriousness of Navajo interest in education would do well to read the account of Navajo educational development by Hildegard Thompson, Supervisor of Education on the Navajo Reservation during the Franklin Roosevelt administration, and later Director of Indian Education in the BIA during the 1950s and 1960s. See Hildegard Thompson, *The Navajos' Long Walk For Education: A History of Navajo Education* (Tsaile, Navajo Nation, Arizona: Navajo Community College Press, 1975).

36. Underhill, pp. 205–206.

37. William K. Powers, *Oglala Religion* (Lincoln: University of Nebraska Press, 1975), p. 115.

38. Underhill, p. 225.

39. Elizabeth W. Forster and Laura Gilpin, *Denizens of the Desert: A Tale in Word and Picture of Life Among the Navaho Indians*, edited and with an introduction by Martha A. Sandweiss (Albuquerque: University of New Mexico Press, 1988), p. 140.

40. Underhill, pp. 161–162.

41. Lawrence C. Kelly, *The Navajo Indians and Federal Indian Policy* (Tucson: University of Arizona Press, 1968), pp. 33–34.

42. Kirke Kickingbird and Karen Ducheneaux, *One Hundred Million Acres* (New York: Macmillan Publishing Co., 1973), pp. 18–21.

43. Garrick Bailey and Roberta Glenn Bailey, *A History of the Navajos* (Santa Fe, NM: School of American Research Press, 1986), p. 106.

44. Kickingbird and Ducheneaux, p. 65.

45. Young, pp. 51–52.

46. Young, pp. 43–45; Underhill, pp. 208–209.

47. Young, p. 53.

48. Kelly, p. 39.

49. Kelly, pp. 39–42.

50. Kelly, pp. 43–44.

51. Kelly, pp. 57–58.

52. Kelly, pp. 53–55.

53. Joe S. Sando, *The Pueblo Indians* (San Francisco: The Indian Historian Press, 1976), pp. 88–99; Kelly, pp. 58–61.

54. Young, p. 58.

55. Kelly, pp. 62–63.

56. Young, p. 60.

57. Kelly, p. 63, footnote.

58. Young, pp. 62–63.

59. Young, p. 62.

60. Hildegard Thompson, op. cit., notes that the daily food budget for the children in her care even later was just 11 cents per child, and that even as late as the postwar years in the 1940s, "the Bureau had insufficient sheets to maintain clean beds for Navajo children housed in the dormitories." This had serious sanitary implications in view of the difficulty health officials faced in dealing with such common and contagious diseases as impetigo.

61. Young, pp. 73–74.

62. Kelly, pp. 142–145.

63. Young, pp. 66–68; Donald L. Parman, *The Navajos and the New Deal* (New Haven, CT: Yale University Press, 1976), pp. 13–14.

64. Young, p. 67.

65. Kelly, pp. 136, 154.

66. Francis Paul Prucha, *The Great Father: The United States Government and the American Indians*, abridged edition (Lincoln: University of Nebraska Press, 1986), p. 321.

67. Prucha, p. 333.

68. Prucha, p. 327.

69. Kelly, pp. 160–161.

70. For a Navajo-sponsored oral-history account of this period, see *Navajo Livestock Reduction: A National Disgrace* (Tsaile Lake, Chinle, AZ: Navajo Community College Press, 1974).

71. *Navajo Livestock Reduction*, p. 48.

72. Kelly, p. 162. For a detailed Navajo perspective on the history of this period, see George A. Boyce, *When Navajos Had Too Many Sheep: The 1940s* (San Francisco: The Indian Historian Press, 1974).

73. Kammer, pp. 26–27.

74. Kammer, pp. 51–52.

75. Kammer, pp. 53–54.

76. Kammer, p. 52.

77. Telephone interview with Lila Bird, June 13, 1993.

78. Kammer, pp. 61–64.

79. Reno, p. 108.

80. Reno, p. 112.

81. Reno, pp. 59, 61.

82. Kammer, pp. 118–119.

83. Valerie Taliman, "Nations Hear Plight of Diné, Hopi People of HPL," *Navajo Times*, December 23, 1992, pp. 1, 12.

84. Ambler, p. 5.

85. Ambler, p. 94.

86. Reno, p. 133.

87. Ambler, p. 75.

88. Ambler, p. 61.

89. Ambler, pp. 96–99.

90. Ambler, pp. 107–117.

91. Telephone interview with Tom B.K. Goldtooth, April 5, 1993.

92. Nicholas C. Peroff, *Menominee DRUMS: Tribal Termination and Restoration, 1954–1974* (Norman: University of Oklahoma Press, 1982), p. 113.

93. Peroff, p. 140.

94. Peroff, pp. 174–175.

95. Peroff, pp. 178–179.

96. Public Law 93-197, the Menominee Restoration Act, was passed by the Ninety-third Congress, First Session, on December 22, 1973.

97. Rogers Worthington, "Woman Picked to Lead Indian Bureau," *Chicago Tribune*, May 20, 1993, Sec. 1A, p. 24.

98. Personal interview with Louis Hawpetoss, April 24, 1993.

99. Jack Weatherford, *Native Roots: How the Indians Enriched America* (New York: Crown Publishing Group, 1992), p. 45.

100. "Navajos Oppose Logging," Fact Sheet of Diné CARE, undated but listing events through August 10, 1992.

101. Michael Williams, " 'Done Deal' Asbestos Dump Undone by Diné CARE," *Everyone's Backyard*, December 1992, pp. 4–5.

102. Telephone interview with Lori Goodman, August 20, 1993, and "Navajos Oppose Logging."

103. Goodman interview.

104. Marjane Ambler, *Breaking the Iron Bonds: Indian Control of Energy Development* (Lawrence: University Press of Kansas, 1990), pp. 204–206.

105. Michael L. Lawson, *Dammed Indians: The Pick-Sloan Plan and the Missouri River Sioux, 1944–1980* (Norman: University of Oklahoma Press, 1982). The account presented here is extracted from Lawson's book, supplemented by information from Ambler, note 23.

106. The single best source of background on the Chemehuevi tribe is Carobeth Laird, *The Chemehuevis* (Banning, CA: Malki Museum Press, Morongo Indian Reservation, 1976).

107. David Pasztor, "The Great Unknown Indian War of 1992," *Phoenix New Times*, p. 22.

108. Pasztor, op. cit.; and personal interview with Nicholas Alvarez, May 17, 1993.

109. Alvarez interview.

110. Personal interview with Nicholas Alvarez, May 17, 1993; Debra A. Schwartz, "Mojave Valley: Radwaste Site?", *Environment & Development*, April 1993, pp. 3–4; Charles McCoy, "Plan for California Nuclear Waste Dump Points to Problems with Federal Policy," *Wall Street Journal*, January 11, 1993; Hugh Dellios, "Brawl Over Nuclear Dump in the Middle of Nowhere," *Chicago Tribune*, January 29, 1993, Sec. 1, pp. 1, 8; Robin Richards, "Is Ward Valley a Dead Issue?", *Needles Desert Star*, April 7, 1993, pp. A1, A3; Letter from Nicholas A. Alvarez to Hon. Bruce Babbitt, February 26, 1993.

111. Telephone interview with Lance Hughes, July 1, 1993.

112. Bird interview.

113. See Mary Hager et al., " 'Dances With Garbage': Reservations as Toxic Dumping Grounds," *Newsweek*, April 29, 1991, p. 36; Robert Tomsho, "Dumping Grounds: Indian Tribes Contend with Some of Worst of America's Pollution," *Wall Street Journal*, November 29, 1990, pp. A1, A7; and Marjane Ambler, "On the Reservations: No Haste, No Waste," *Planning*, November 1991, pp. 26–29.

114. Peter Carrels, "South Dakota's Sioux Debate Huge National Garbage Dump," *High Country News*, June 17, 1991, p. 4.

115. Rosebud Sioux Tribe–RSW Agreement, dated November 14, 1990, provided to the author by Ronald Valandra.

116. Assessment derived from a personal interview with Syed Y. Huq, August 19, 1992.

117. Bob von Sternberg, "City Garbage on Indian Land? Tribes See Some Pros, Some Cons," *Minneapolis Star Tribune*, February 28, 1991, pp. 1B, 7B.

118. Bob von Sternberg, "Don't Dump on Reservations, Activists Urge," *Minneapolis Star Tribune*, August 31, 1991, pp. 1B, 2B.

119. Personal interview with Christine and Ronald Valandra, August 19, 1992.

120. Telephone interview with Burl Self, August 3, 1992.

121. Correspondence from Johna Rodgers, reporter for the *Meridian Star*, April 3, 1992.

122. Johna Rodgers, "Indian Land Eyed for Incinerator?", *Meridian Star*, January 10, 1991, pp. 1A, 13A.

123. Johna Rodgers, "Choctaws: Firm Paid $500,000 for Incinerator Study," *Meridian Star*, January 11, 1991.

124. Johna Rodgers and William Rabb, "Choctaw Disposal Site Could Bring Jobs, Strife," *Meridian Star*, January 27, 1991, pp. 1D, 2D.

125. William Rabb, "Choctaw Leaders Say Landfill Money in Bank," *Meridian Star*, February 4, 1991, pp. 1A, 7A.

126. Johna Rodgers, "Chief Martin Lauds Choctaw Landfill Venture," *Meridian Star*, February 6, 1991, pp. 1A, 7A.

127. Johna Rodgers, "Petition Seeks to Bar Toxic Dump," *Meridian Star*, February 15, 1991, pp. 1A, 9A.

128. Johna Rodgers, "Landfill Vote Bid Could Ruin Tribe, Martin Claims," *Meridian Star*, February 22, 1991, pp. 1A, 9A.

129. Johna Rodgers, "Anti-landfill Choctaws Say They Can Force Vote," *Meridian Star*, March 22, 1991, pp. 1A, 7A.

130. Johna Rodgers, "Choctaws Drum Up Protest of Landfill," *Meridian Star*, March 24, 1991, pp. 1A, 9A. The photo appeared with " 'Dances With Garbage'," *Newsweek*, April 29, 1991, p. 36.

131. Johna Rodgers, "Chief Calls for Vote on Landfill Site," *Meridian Star*, March 30, 1991, pp. 1A, 2A.

132. Ronald Smothers, "Future in Mind, Choctaws Reject Plan for Landfill," *New York Times*, April 21, 1991. Other information for the Choctaw story came from telephone interviews with Linda Farve, April 2, 1992, and with Bob Kochtitzky, April 1, 1992, and from correspondence from Johna Rodgers, reporter for the *Meridian Star*. Rodgers supplied a complete package of news clippings covering this controversy. Attempts to reach Chief Phillip Martin to discuss the controversy drew no response.

133. Linda Lamb, "Can Money Buy a Home for America's Radwaste?", *Environment & Development*, April 1992, pp. 3–4.

134. MRS Grant Applicant List, May 1, 1993, Office of the Nuclear Waste Negotiator, Boise, Idaho. The nine nations included the Mescalero Apache (New Mexico); Skull Valley–Goshute (Utah); Fort McDermitt Paiute Shoshone (Nevada); Ponca Industrial Corporation (Texas) for the Tonkawa Tribe (Oklahoma); Eastern Shawnee (Oklahoma); Prairie Island Sioux (Minnesota); Ute Mountain Ute (Colorado); Miami Tribe (Oklahoma); and Northern Arapaho (Wyoming).

135. Council of Energy Resource Tribes (CERT), "Dialogue on Tribal Perceptions of the Ethical and Moral Bases of Nuclear Energy and Radioactive Waste Management," transcript of meeting held at Cheyenne Mountain Conference Resort, Colorado Springs, Colorado, April 6–8, 1992, p. 18.

136. Paul Salopek, "Mescalero Apaches Wrestle with Notion of Nuclear Reservation," *El Paso Times*, April 26, 1992, pp. 1A, 6A.

137. Telephone interview with Tom B.K. Goldtooth, April 5, 1993; and Winona LaDuke, "Whitewashing Native Environmentalism," *News from Indian Country*, Late April 1993, pp. 1, 7–8.

138. Telephone interview with Grace Thorpe, July 2, 1993.

139. Thorpe interview.

140. Bird telephone interview.

141. Thorpe interview.

142. *Federal Register*, November 2, 1992, p. 49463.

143. Agenda, National Congress of American Indians, "Nuclear Waste Issues: A Tribal Dialogue," March 15–17, 1993, Aladdin Hotel, Las Vegas, Nevada.

144. Personal count by Lila Bird.

145. Elmer Savilla, "Nuclear Waste Storage on Reservation Lands Issue Heats Up," *News from Indian Country*, Mid April 1993, p. 9; Bird and Harrison interviews.

146. CERT, "Dialogue on Tribal Perceptions," comments of Chuck Lempesis, Office of Nuclear Waste Negotiator, p. 77.

147. CERT, pp. 13–14.

148. CERT, p. 67.

149. Comments of A. David Lester, Session on People of Color and the Environment, Society of Environmental Journalists Conference, October 4–6, 1991, Boulder, Colorado.

150. Hughes, Thorpe, and Bird interviews.

CHAPTER 9

1. Keynote speech of Robert D. Bullard, People for Community Recovery conference, Chicago, October 17, 1992.

2. Mililani Trask, "Indigenous Hawaiian Historical and Cultural Perspectives on Environmental Justice," in *Proceedings: The First National People of Color Environmental Leadership Summit*, The Washington Court on Capitol Hill, Washing-

ton, DC, October 24–27, 1991 (New York: United Church of Christ Commission for Racial Justice, 1992), pp. 35–39.

3. Telephone interview with Oannes Pritzker, May 21, 1993.

4. Personal interview with Peggy Sheppard, September 24, 1990.

5. Personal interview with Lois Gibbs, April 5, 1991.

6. "Major National Environmental Organizations and Problems of the 'Environmental Movement,' " Briefing Paper prepared by the Southwest Organizing Project, Albuquerque, New Mexico, February 1990.

7. "The Minority Opportunities Study," The CEIP Fund, Inc., August 1989.

8. Clarence Page, "Minorities 'Going Green' as Ecology Gets Rainbow Voice," *Chicago Tribune*, April 18, 1990, Sec. 1, p. 15.

9. Memorandum from Robin Cannon, Richard Moore, et al., to Environmental Defense Fund, Friends of the Earth, National Audubon Society, National Wildlife Federation, Natural Resources Defense Council, Sierra Club, and Wilderness Society, November 6, 1992; Letter from George T. Frampton, Jr. (Wilderness Society) to Robin Cannon et al., November 9, 1992; Memorandum from Michael Fischer (Sierra Club) to Brooks Yeager (Sierra Club), November 12, 1992; Letter from Jane Perkins (FOE) to Robin Cannon et al., November 16, 1992; Letter from Stephen Viederman (Jessie Smith Noyes Foundation) to Katy McGinty (Senator Gore's office), November 17, 1992; Letter from Richard Moore et al., to President-elect Bill Clinton, November 17, 1992.

10. Gibbs interview.

11. Personal interview with Richard Moore, April 21, 1993.

CHAPTER 10

1. Luncheon speech by Lois Gibbs, Society of Environmental Journalists, Second National Conference, Ann Arbor, Michigan, November 7, 1992.

2. Joel S. Hirschhorn and Kirsten U. Oldenburg, *Prosperity Without Pollution: The Prevention Strategy for Industry and Consumers* (New York: Van Nostrand Reinhold, 1990), pp. 121–123.

3. Valjean McLenighan, *Sustainable Manufacturing* (Chicago: Center for Neighborhood Technology, 1990), p. 11.

4. Jim Schwab, "Avoiding the Sting: Cities and Contaminated Sites," *Environment & Development*, November 1992, p. 3.

5. This case study was previously published in Jim Schwab, *Industrial Performance Standards for a New Century*, Planning Advisory Service Report No. 444 (Chicago: American Planning Association, 1993), pp. 27–28, and in Jim Schwab, "Toxics Use Reduction," *Environment & Development*, March 1993, p. 2. Another source is Mark Malaspina, Kristin Schafer, and Richard Wiles, *What Works Report No. 1: Air Pollution Solutions* (Washington, DC: The Environmental Exchange, 1992), pp. 57–58.

6. Joel Makower, *The E Factor: The Bottom-Line Approach to Environmentally Responsible Business* (New York: Tilden Press, 1993), pp. 62–63.

7. *What Works Bulletin*, November 1992. *What Works* is a two-page monthly newsletter of The Environmental Exchange, Washington, D.C.

8. Makower, p. 24.

9. Personal interview with Paul Templet, April 25, 1991.

10. Makower, p. 26.

11. Personal interview with Louis Hawpetoss, April 24, 1993.

12. Paul H. Templet, "Jobs and a Clean Environment: Having Them Both," *Environment & Development*, October 1993, pp. 1–3.

13. John Hart, *Saving Cities, Saving Money: Environmental Strategies That Work* (Sausalito, CA: Resource Renewal Institute, 1992), p. 13.

14. Hart, p. 28.

15. Amory Lovins and Alice Hubbard, "Community Energy Planning: A Tool for Economic Development," *Environment & Development*, February 1993, p. 2.

16. Jim Schwab, "Urban Trees, Air Quality, and Energy Conservation," *Environment & Development*, March 1992, p. 3. For an excellent source of data and design guidelines on this precise issue, see *Cooling Our Communities: A Guidebook on Tree Planting and Light-Colored Surfacing* (Washington, DC: U.S. Environmental Protection Agency, 1992).

17. Hirschhorn and Oldenburg, pp. 58–59.

18. The author is chairman of the Evangelical Lutheran Church in America (ELCA) Metropolitan Chicago Synod's Environmental Concerns Working Group and has direct experience with the Augustana project. For details on this program, write to Dr. Job Ebenezer, Director, Environmental Stewardship, ELCA, 8765 W. Higgins Road, Chicago, IL 60631.

19. Lovins and Hubbard, op. cit.

20. For a fuller discussion of this whole area, see Jim Schwab, *Industrial Performance Standards for a New Century*, noted above.

21. McLenighan, op. cit.

CHAPTER 11

1. For a full discussion of the Superfund for Workers and related issues, see Lucinda Wykle, Ward Morehouse, and David Dembo, *Worker Empowerment in a Changing Economy* (New York: Apex Press, 1991).

2. Hamid Razik, "Two Sides Vow Summit Burner Fight," *Southtown Economist*, December 12, 1992, pp. 1, 8.

3. Presentation of Dr. Samuel S. Epstein, Environmental Equity Session, American Planning Association Annual Conference, Chicago, May 2, 1993. The author moderated this panel discussion.

4. Personal interview with Steve Hiniker, August 28, 1992.

5. Jim Schwab, "Avoiding the Sting: Cities and Contaminated Sites," *Environment & Development*, November 1992, p. 2; also, presentation by Steve Hiniker at the same session as Dr. Epstein, noted above.

Index

Acadian culture (Louisiana), 359–360
Adamkus, Valdas, 122, 126, 128, 151, 158
Adams, Mary Jane, 296–297
Addington Resources, Argillite landfill, 300–302
Agrico, 276
Air-dispersion modeling, 131, 144–145
Alchem-Tron, 80–86
Alexander, Avery, 265
Allied Signal, 219, 220
Alsen, Louisiana, Rollins landfill, 217–223
Alston, Dana, 390, 413
Alvarez, Nicholas, 369, 370
American Cyanamid, TRI numbers, 274
American Public Health Association, incinerator construction ban, 26, 29
Aniol, Michael, 204–205
Appalachia, socioeconomic history and exploitation, 283–289
Appalachian Land Ownership Task Force, 286, 289, 292
Ascension Parish, TRI figures, 240–241
Ashland Chemical, toxic buyouts, 255
Ashland Oil Company, Catlettsburg refinery, 307–311
Atmospheric inversions and air pollution, 105
Atomic Energy Commission, 167; Colorado Raw Materials Division, 324
Audubon Society, 176, 204, 211

Bailly nuclear power plant proposal, 167
Balanoff, Clem, 9, 127, 177–178, 181, 182, 183

Balanoff, James, 185, 193, 203
Baloney, Carl, Jr., 263, 264
Barone, Guy, 258, 261
Bartlett, Joseph, 227–228
BASF Corporation: BASF Chemicals Division, 235; safety violations, 236; union busting, xviii, 234–236, 239–240
BASF Wyandotte, 218; Geismar chemical plant, 234–241
Bechtel Corporation, 23, 39
Benally, Timothy, 327, 328
Benoit, Wilbert and Laberta, 226–227
Benzene emissions, 258, 259, 310
Berg, Deborah, 84–85
Bernard, Alan, 244
Best Available Control Technology, 22
Bethlehem Steel, 166, 170, 196; safety violations, 193
Big Ten environmental groups, minority involvement, 388–391
Bird, Lila, 353, 372, 377
Blumenberg, Evelyn, 66
Boas, Paul, 142–145, 147
Boilers and industrial furnaces, regulation of, 186
Botts, Lee, 166, 175–176
Bowen, Diana, 308, 309
BP America, 78
Braden, Everette A., 39
Bradley, Carl, 301
Bradley, Tom, 49, 52–53, 54
British Petroleum, 78
Broad-form deeds, 285, 295–299
Brodie, Irene, 1, 40, 41–42
Brown, Don, 105–106
Brown, Janet, 299, 301
Brown, John Y., 293, 294
Brown, Michael, 107, 111

Brown pelicans, effect of pollution on, 212
Brown, Tom, 24–26, 43
Browner, Carol, 156, 158
Browning Ferris Industries (BFI), 44, 223–230
Bullard, Robert, 380, 381, 384, 390, 413
Bullock, Charlotte, 46–47, 50–51, 53, 55
Bureau of Indian Affairs (BIA), 344, 346, 350, 356, 363
Burris, Roland, 38, 39
Bursum Bill, 343–344
Buyouts, See Toxic buyouts
Byers-Emmerling, Melissa, 138, 149
Byrnes, Marian, 175, 178, 181, 183

Cain, James M., 287
Calcium oxide, 309
Caldwell Systems, Inc., 139–140
California: air cleanup,45; farmworkers, effect of air pollution on, 75; waste-minimization program, 397
California Energy Commission, state energy codes, 407
California Integrated Solid-waste Management, 71–72
California Thermal Treatment Service (CTTS), 57–58
Callender, Tom, 245–247, 259
Calumet and Chicago Canal and Dock Company, 162
Calumet region (Illinois): airport plan, 200–206; cancer deaths, 194; economic history and ecology, 161–170, 192–194; toxic wastes, 170
Cam-Or, 190
Campbell, Joseph, 379–380
Cannon, Robin, xvi–xvii, 46–47, 50–51, 55
Cannon, Sheila, 46, 52–53
Carbon monoxide standards, 65
Carcinogens: in hazardous wastes, 141; health effects, 194; occupational exposure, socioeconomic breakdown, 414–415
Carey, Dorreen, 191–196, 206
Carleton, James H., 331, 332
Carnow, Bertram, 33–34, 36, 40
Carolina coastal barrier islands, economic development, 360

Carson, Kit, 331–332
Cassel, Thomas, 27, 31–32, 36
Castro, Robert, 87, 91, 92, 93, 96, 102
Caudill, Harry M., 284–286, 287, 295
CECOS, 226
CECOS International, Clermont County (Ohio) landfill, 107
CEIP Fund, Inc., 388
Celebrezze, Anthony J., Jr., 97, 102, 113
Celeste, Richard, 77, 78, 96, 99, 104, 113
Center for Neighborhood Technology (CNT), 205, 398, 409
Cerrell Report, 49, 50
Chaney, Katie, 88, 92, 95, 98, 101
Chaney, Rob, 92, 94, 95, 98, 101
Chavis, Ben, 281–282, 383, 389, 415
Cheeks, Bob, 106–107
Chemclean, 58
Chemehuevi reservation: nuclear-waste dump, 369–371; Parker Dam project, 367–369
Chemical surrogacy, 155–156
Chemical Waste Management, 8; discriminatory siting practices, 76; Emelle landfill, 375; Kettleman City incinerator, 57, 75–76; permit violations, 181, 184; Southeast Chicago facility, 127, 139, 178–185
Chemical Waste Management, Inc., 111–112
Chevron, pollution-prevention techniques, 74
Chicago: land-use issues, 160–206, 415; waste management, 175–177
Chicago Northwest Waste-to-Energy Facility, 13
Chicago v. Environmental Defense Fund, 13
Choctaw reservation, landfill, 374–375
Christian, Barbara, 308, 309
Chromium emissions, 74, 309
Ciaccia, Carol Redmond, 197
Citgo, 249, 251
Citizens for a Better Environment, 14, 16, 29, 54, 74, 176
Citizens to Bring Broadway Back, 87, 92, 98, 102
Citizens' Clearinghouse for Hazardous Wastes (CCHW), xix, xxiii–xxiv, 113, 158, 223, 272, 387–388

Citizens United to Reclaim the
Environment (CURE), 181, 183
City of Commerce, municipal-waste
incinerator, 48
Clark, Henry, 74–75
Clean Air Act, 180; coke-oven
standards, 196, 199; Prevention of
Significant Deterioration provisions,
110; violations, 193
Clean Water Act, violations, 193
Clinton, Bill, 154, 157, 363, 370, 388
Coal industry, 288–299; broad-form
deeds, 295–299; taxation, 289, 291–
295
Coking ovens, 196–200
Coleman, Adolph, 1, 4, 9
Collier, John, 344, 346–350
Collins, Cardiss, 417
Colorado Plateau, uranium mining,
321–322
Columbiana County Port Authority,
WTI site ownership, 104, 109, 147,
152, 153
Colvin, Ruth, 305–306
Commoner, Barry, 11, 28, 61, 66, 156,
158, 389, 394
Commonwealth Edison Company, 405
Comprehensive Environmental
Response, Compensation, and
Liability Act (CERCLA), See
Superfund
Concerned Citizens of Martin County,
291, 294
Concerned Citizens of South Central
Los Angeles (CCSC), xvi–xvii, 47,
50–55, 57, 67, 70, 71, 386
Connett, Paul, 27–28, 115–117, 119,
121–122, 132–134, 139, 148–149,
153, 304
Contra Costa County, hazardous-waste
management plan, 74–75
Cornett, Sidney, 297
Cotiga Development Company, 286
Council of Energy Resource Tribes
(CERT), 355–357, 378, 379, 380,
381
Crucible Steel Company, 107
Cuprisin, Helen, 16–18
Czernik, David, 242–244

Dabertin, David, 195–196
D'Agostino, Cynthia, 87, 92, 95

Daley, Richard M., 34, 177; Lake
Calumet airport plan, 200–205
Davis, Larry, 196, 199–200
Dawes Act (1887), 336–337, 338–339
Dawson, Susan, 329
Deer, Ada, 363
Delaware Department of Natural
Resources, 266
Delta Iron Works, 230
Deukmejian, George, 52, 56; prison
plan, 55
Dickerson, Janice, 253–256, 259
Diné Citizens Against Ruining Our
Environment (Diné CARE), 364–
366
Dioxins, 10–11, 30, 50; in the food
chain, 156, 157; in incinerator
emissions, 46, 121, 155–156
Donaldson, Francis Richard, 234
Donora, Pennsylvania, air inversions,
105, 144
Douglas Aircraft Company, air
emissions, 66
Dow Chemical: Morrisonville buyout,
257–258; tax breaks, 249
Duke, David, 252, 278, 279, 280

Earth Day 1990, 281, 386; minority
participation, 388
East Liverpool, Ohio, WTI incinerator,
33, 104–159, 138–149
Edgar, James, 201, 205
Edwards, Edwin, 210, 252–253, 273,
278–279, 280
Emergency Planning and Community
Right-to-Know Act (EPCRA), xxv,
194, 395, 413; Toxic Release
Inventory, 208
Energy conservation, 405–407
Envirodyne Engineers, Chicago solid-
waste plan, 23, 24
Environmental Defense Fund (EDF),
387–388
Environmental Elements Corporation,
114
Environmental Elements of Maryland,
111
Environmental Elements (Ohio) Inc.,
114
Environmental Justice Act, 416–417
Environmental justice movement, 281,
385, 388–389, 393, 403, 408, 409;

access to information, 413–414;
   funding, 412–413; indigeno-
   feminization, 418–419
Environmental racism, 171, 197–198,
   230–233, 260–261, 319, 387, 389,
   405, 415; Appalachia, 311, 313;
   grants-in-aid, 357
Epstein, Samuel S., 414–415
Ewell, Catherine, 219, 221
Ewell, David, 214–215, 221
Exxon, 218: Baton Rouge plant, 250,
   259–260; tax breaks, 249; *Valdez*
   cleanup, 401–402

Falcon Coal, 297
Fall, Albert, 341, 342, 344
Families Insisting on a Toxic-free
   Environment (FITE), 91, 102
Farve, Linda, 374, 375
Favorite, Amos, 236, 238, 240, 241
Federated Metals, safety violations, 193
Fields, Sharon, 87–92, 93, 96, 98, 99,
   101–102
Fina oil refinery, Fairlea Subdivision
   buyout, 256–257
Fingerhut, Eric, 91–92
Fisher Controls International, toxic-
   use reduction program, 398
Fontenot, Willie, 209–221, 236, 268,
   271, 272, 279, 282
Ford Heights, Illinois, incinerator
   proposal, 15–16
Ford Motors, Taurus assembly plant,
   202
Forestry, sustained-yield, 364
Forman, W. Wayne, 276–278
Formosa Plastics, 391; PVC facilities,
   266; safety violations, 266–267;
   Taiwanese plants, 261–263; Wallace
   facility, 263–271, 267
Forster, Elizabeth W., 334
Fort Berthold reservation, Garrison
   Dam project, 366–367
Foster Wheeler Corporation, 39
Frankland, Peggy, 225, 226, 227, 228
Freeport McMoRan, 275–278
Furans in incinerator emissions, 10, 11,
   46

Garden City Community Alliance
   (GCCA), 259–260
Garrison Dam, 366–367

Gary, Indiana, industrialization, 164–
   165
Gary Sanitary District, toxic-waste
   dumping, 193
Gary Sanitary Landfill, 189
Gaudet, Kay, 237–238
General Allotment Act (1884), 336
General Atomics, 371
General Motors, 59–61, 65–66, 138
Georgia-Pacific Corporation,
   Reveilletown plant, 254–256
Gibbs, Lois, xxiii–xxiv, 113, 223, 272,
   387–388, 389, 391, 395
Gillette, George, 366
Golec, Robert, 185–186
Good Road Coalition, 374
Goodman, Lori, 365–366
Gore, Al, 154, 157–158, 416
Gottlieb, Robert, 38, 47, 48, 52
Grand Calumet Task Force, 191–192,
   193, 196, 200, 206
Green Valley Environmental Corpora-
   tion, 300–302
Greene, Kevin, 14, 18, 29
Greene, Wilfred, 269–270, 271
Greenpeace, 54, 183; grass-roots and
   minority participation, 372, 386,
   393; incinerator technology studies,
   121; Robbins facility protest, 7–8,
   16; WTI East Liverpool action, 127,
   134, 139, 153, 155, 156, 158
Greenup Residents Opposed to the
   Waste Landfill (GROWL), 299–302
Gremillion, Esnard, 234, 235, 238
Grossman, Richard, 61
GSX Chemical Services, 80; Cleveland
   Bessemer Avenue plant, 81, 85–86
GSX Chemical Services, Inc.;
   Cleveland Bessemer Avenue plant,
   86–102; safety violations, 95–96
GSX Chemical Services of Ohio, 86
GSX Corporation, Scott County
   facility, 320
Gulf Coast Premix, 214
Gulf Coast Tenants Organization, 214
Guste, William J., Jr., 209, 212, 222–
   223, 279
Gutierrez, Juana, 55–56, 66, 67

Haight, Karen, 117, 118–119
Hamilton, Cynthia, 61–62
Hammond, Indiana: Rhone-Poulenc

incinerator, 185–186; wastewater treatment, 193
Hanford nuclear facility, 376
Hanks, Gay, 213–214
Hannon, Ledell J. R., 259, 260
Hanor, Jeffery, 228, 229
Harris, Becky, 300–301
Harris, LaDonna, 355, 356
Harrison, Phillip, Jr., 322–326, 328–329
Hartigan, Neil, 21, 22, 37, 181, 182, 183
Hartsfield, Julia, 1–2, 5
Hatcher, Richard, 196–197
Hawaiian Islands, environmental problems, 384–385
Hawk's Nest Tunnel, 312
Hawpetoss, Louis, 360–361, 364, 403
Hayden-Ashurst Bill (1916), 341–342
Hazardous and Solid Waste Act (1984), 180
Heavy metals: health effects, 194–195; in incinerator emissions, 11–12
Hesse Industrial Waste Company (Germany), 115
Hill, Ted, 153
Hiniker, Steve, 416
Hirschhorn, Joel S., 396, 398, 406
Hockley, George, 308, 309, 310
Hoffman, Edwin, 314, 315
Hooker Chemical Company, 113, 223
Hopis: history and government, 352–353, 354; Navajo land dispute, 351–355
Horton, Myles, 287, 288
Houma Indian Nation, 230–233, 359–360
Huffman, Martha, 318–319
Hughes, Lance, 371–372, 381
Hyon, Inc., 179

IIllinois, Solid Waste Planning and Recycling Act, 23
Illinois Department of Energy and Natural Resources, 170
Illinois EPA, 8, 173; Clean Air Act (1986), 181; CWM permits, 183; Robbins incinerator proposal, 14–15, 20, 21
Illinois International Port District, WTI land ownership, 181
Illinois Steel Company, 168
IMC Company, 276

Incinerators, 49, 79; ash disposal, 13–15, 107, 120, 373–374; automatic cutoff systems, 131; destruction and removal efficiency, 120, 150–151, 155; heavy metal emissions, 11–12; Ohio moratorium, 158–159; pollution-control measures, 13; products of incomplete combustion, 121, 145, 150–151; on reservations, 369; spray-dryer systems, 114, 116–117, 121–122, 131; trial burns, 150–151, 154, 157
Indian Reorganization Act (IRA), 346–348, 350
Indiana Department of Environmental Management (IDEM), 187, 188, 195–196
Indiana Dunes National Lakeshore Act (1966), 167
Indigenous cultures, environmentalism in, 358–360, 386, 418
Injured Workers Union, 242, 244
Inland Steel, 163, 170, 191; Indiana Harbor Works, 192–193
Institute for Local Self-Reliance (ILSR), 404
Invesco International, 305

Jackson, Samuel, 269, 270, 271
Jaxon, Honore J., 166
Johnson, Hazel, 171–173, 181, 183
Johnson, Valerie, 8–9
Joyce, Jeremiah, 20–21

Kammer, Jerry, 352, 353–354
Kash, Dan, 308–309, 310, 311
Kasley, Sam, 124, 128–129
Kaufman, Hugh, 118, 119, 145–148, 150
Kennedy, Robert, 315–316
Kentania Corporation, 284
Kentuckians for the Commonwealth (KFTC), xvii, 289–295, 297–302; Bridges and Barriers program, 307
Kentucky Environmental Quality Commission, 306
Kentucky Fair Tax Coalition, *See* Kentuckians for the Commonwealth
Kerr-McGee Corporation, 371
Kettleman City, California, CWM incinerator, 57, 75–76

Kings County, California, hazardous-
waste incinerator, 75–76
Knotts, A. F., 164–165
Krug, A. J., 366

Labor/Community Strategy Center,
59–60, 66, 68, 69–70
Laidlaw Environmental Services, 80,
81, 99–102
Laidlaw, Inc., Tricil acquisition, 99
Lake Calumet airport proposal, 200–
205
Lake County, Indiana, TRI figures, 194
Landfills: incinerator ash disposal, 13,
107; moratorium; 176; in reclaimed
stripmines, 299–307; on reserva-
tions, 369
Lash Coal Company, 299
Lawrence County, Kentucky,
PyroChem incinerator, 302–305
Lead exposure, 12, 143–144
Lee, Charles, xxv, 383
Legator, Marvin, 225–226, 257
Lents, James M., 64
Leonard, Richard, 235–236, 239
Lester, A. David, 379, 380
Lewis Air Quality Act (1976), 64
Los Angeles: air pollution, 59, 62–63,
64–65, 68; Central and East L.A.
incinerator issue, 61; environmental
activism, 45–55; jobs-housing
balance, 67; landfills, 47–48; prison
plan, 55–56; recycling program, 71–
73
Los Angeles Bureau of Sanitation, 46;
waste-to-energy facilities, 48–49, 50
Los Angeles City Energy Recovery
Project (LANCER), 46–55; advisory
committee, 52
Los Angeles International Airport,
recyling program, 73
Louisiana: coastal wetlands ecology,
211; environmental policy, 247–253,
273–276; industry and ecology, 207–
209, 247–250
Louisiana Board of Commerce and
Industry, 248, 249, 250, 251, 253
Louisiana Coalition/Citizens for Tax
Justice (LCTJ), 247–248, 251, 252,
260
Louisiana Department of Environmen-
tal Quality, 209, 216, 220, 222, 273,
278; Corporate Response program,
275, 401; Office of Planning and
Policy, 280
Louisiana Environmental Action
Network (LEAN), 250, 272–273
Louisiana State University, Institute
for Recyclable Materials, 277
Louisiana Workers Against Toxic
Chemical Hazards (LA-WATCH),
242, 243, 244
Lovins, Amory, 405, 406
Loyola University (New Orleans),
Institute of Human Relations, 242,
244
LTV Steel, 170
Lynch, Susan, 186–190

McCastle, Roy, 217
McCawley, Michael, 118, 119, 122,
144–145
MacDonald, Peter, 354–355, 356, 357
McDonalds, packaging changes, 387–
388
Magnetic Metals, 190
Makower, Joel, 398, 399, 401, 402, 403
Malathion, 58–59, 75
Mann, Eric, 60–62, 69, 70–71
Marathon Oil, 169
Marshall, D. J. Blake, 124, 126, 130,
151
Martin, Mary, 17–18, 19, 20, 25, 29, 35
Martin, Phillip, 374, 375
Massachusetts Toxics Use Reduction
Act, 137, 140, 397
Mather, Stephen, 166
Maya, Esperanza and Joe, 75–76
Maynard, Bob, 110
Mazzocchi, Tony, 61, 411
Menominees: sustained-yield forestry,
364, 403; tribal status, 361–364
Mercury emissions, 11–12, 32–33, 145;
atmospheric sources of, 12; control,
14, 22
Metalliferous Minerals Leasing Act
(1919), 342
Midboe, Kai, 253, 280
Midwest Oil Company, Navajo leasing
arrangements, 342
Miller, Richard, 215, 236, 239, 242,
271
Millet, Lester, Jr., 262, 263–264, 271
Milwaukee, toxic cleanup, 416

Minamata disease, 11–12
Minot, David, 32–33, 40
Mobil Oil, tax breaks, 249
Molina, Gloria, 56
Monitored retrievable storage (MRS) facilities, 375–382
Monsanto Chemical Company, 178
Montague, Peter, 113, 119, 158
Montez, Mary Ellen, 202–203
Moore, Richard, 388–389, 391
Morgan, T. J., 337
Mothers of East L.A.(MELA), 56, 57, 67, 70, 386; malathion protest, 58–59
Mozwecz, Harold, 30–31, 32–33
Muno, William, 97, 127–128
Mustang Fuel of Oklahoma, 111

National Academy of Sciences, 225–226; sustainable agriculture techniques, 408
National Congress of American Indians (NCAI), 376, 381; DOE funding, 378–379
National Disposal Systems, Inc., Choctaw landfill, 374–375
National Steel, 166, 167
National Waste, Inc., 305, 306
Native Americans: economic status, 355–356; education, 333–334, 345; energy and mineral development, 340–343, 356–357; executive-order reservations, 333, 336, 340, 341–342; federal policy, 335–338, 346–348
Native Americans for a Clean Environment (NACE), 371–372
Natural Resources Defense Council, 199, 388, 391
Navajo Forest Products Industry (NFPI), 364–365
Navajos: energy and mineral development, 340–343, 356–357; history and government, 330–345; Hopi land dispute, 351–355; stock-reduction program, 348–351; uranium mining, 322–326, 327–330
Neal, Barry, 3, 23, 37
Needleman, Herbert, 143–144
Nickens, Harold, 234
Nitrogen dioxide standards, Los Angeles, 65

Noise Abatement and Control Act (1973), 145
North American Free Trade Agreement (NAFTA), 418
Northern Indiana Public Service Company (NIPSCO), 167
Northwestern University, Center for Urban Affairs, 175–176

Oak Lawn, Illinois, Robbins facility contracts, 27–34, 36–37, 41
Occupational Safety and Health Administration (OSHA), 222; coke-oven standards, 198
Ogden Martin Corporation, 53, 54
Ogden Martin Systems, Inc., 15–16
O'Hare International Airport, 201
Ohio, "bad boy" law, 112
Ohio Department of Transportation, WTI land sale, 109
Ohio Environmental Council, 77–78, 103, 122
Ohio EPA, 102; Alchem-Tron permits, 82, 83, 84; Environmental Board of Review, 112, 124, 137; GSX Chemical Services permits, 94, 96; WTI permits, 104, 107–109, 114–117, 122, 125–129, 135, 137, 151–152
Ohio Hazardous Waste Facilities Board: Alchem-Tron permits, 83–84; GSX Chemical Services permits, 87–88, 92–94, 98; WTI siting permits, 108, 110–111, 142
Ohio River Valley, air inversions, 105
Ohio Technologies, 123
Oil, Chemical, and Atomic Workers International Union (OCAW), 215, 250; environmental activism, 234, 239; Superfund for Workers, 411–412
Oldenburg, Kirsten U., 396, 406
Ong, Paul, 66
Orr, Marylee, 272
Osage, Iowa, energy-efficiency projects, 405
Ozone levels, Los Angeles, 63, 65
Ozonoff, David, 140–143

Pacific Gas and Electric, 405
Palmer, Lu, 6–7
Palumbo, Mario, 124, 152

Parker Dam, 367–369
Paxton landfill (Illinois), 174
Payne, John, 105–106, 107
Peabody Coal Company, Big Mountain operation, 354
Peloquin, Donald, 36
People Against Hazardous Landfill Sites (PAHLS), 186–190, 196
People of Color Environmental Leadership Summit, xxvi, 383–385, 391, 392; Principles of Environmental Justice, 441–443
People for Community Recovery (PCR), 8–9, 171–174, 183
People Concerned About MIC, 315, 316, 317, 318
Petro Processors, 214, 215, 216–217, 219
Pines, Sharon, 7–8, 9, 16–17, 386
Placer Act (1870), 340
Placid Oil Refining Company, Sunrise buyout, 259
Plant siting, 49, 369, 389–390, 416–417; discriminatory practices, 76; regulation of, 260–261
Pollution prevention, 320; in government, 404–407; in industry, 394–404
Polychlorinated biphenyls (PCBs), 178–179, 182, 185, 319
Port Arthur, Texas, Fina oil refinery, 256–257
Powerine oil refinery, 67
Principal organic hazardous constituents, 155
Pueblos, federal policy, 343–344
PyroChem, Inc., 302–305

Radiation Exposure Compensation Act (RECA), 325, 327, 328
Radiation poisoning, 322–326, 328
Radioactive waste disposal, on reservations, 375–382
Ratner, Tawny, 91–92
Reading Energy Company, Robbins incinerator, 2–43, 413, 417
Reasoner, Stephen, 155, 157
Recycling, 45, 177; curbside programs, 39; economic development and, 73
Reduced-crude conversion system, 308–309
Reilly, William, 22–23, 37, 151
Republic Steel, 169

Resource Conservation and Recovery Act (1976), 13, 48, 146; hazardous waste regulation, 179–180; permit process, 109, 180, 187; reauthorization, 150; tracking requirements, 79; violations, 193
Reveilletown, Louisiana, Georgia-Pacific buyout, 253–256
Reynolds, Baton Rouge plant, 215, 216, 220
Rhone-Poulenc, 185–186, 316, 318
Riffe, Vern, 77–78, 102
Right-to-know legislation, 414
Rigmaiden, Herbert, 223, 224
Rio Puerco River, radioactive contamination, 326
River Services Corporation, 147
Robbins Awards Company, wastewater purification and recovery system, 400
Robbins, Illinois, solid-waste incinerator, 1–43
Rocky Mount, North Carolina, energy-efficiency projects, 405
Roemer, Buddy, 209, 250, 251, 268, 273, 278, 279–280
Rollins Environmental Services, 140; Alsen landfill, 217–223
Roosevelt, Theodore, xxi, 166, 337, 341
Rosebud Sioux reservation, RSW landfill, 373–374
Ross incinerator, Grafton, 135–136
RSW, Inc., Rosebud reservation landfill, 373–374
Rubicon Chemical Company, 241
Ruckelshaus, William, 44
Rust International Corporation, 113
Ryan, Mary, 187–189
Rybka, Edward, 88, 89, 93, 94, 98

Sac-and-Fox Nation, nuclear waste site, 376–378
Safe Drinking Water Act, 193
Sahli, Richard, 77–78, 83, 93, 102–103, 110, 122–123, 127, 136
San Francisco Bay Area, air pollution, 74–75
San Jose, California: Innovative Design and Energy Analysis Service, 407; Office of Environmental Management, 404

Save Our County (SOC), 107, 112, 113, 137
Save Our Selves v. Lousiana Environmental Control Commission, 250–251
Save Our Wetlands, 264, 268
SCA Chemical Services, 179, 180
SCA Services, 101
Scafide, James, 110, 125–126, 138
Schregardus, Donald, 104, 127, 136, 137
Scott County, North Carolina, GSX waste facility, 320
Scott, David, 5–6
Scott, Gloria, 1–2, 4, 5, 21, 30, 40
Self, Burl, 374
Sequoyah Fuels, Nuclear-fuel facility, 371–372
Seveso, Italy, dioxin discharge, 10–11
Shank, Richard L., 77, 83, 94–95, 99, 112
Sheahan, Michael, 19, 20
Sheen, Martin, 122, 130, 132, 133, 138, 139, 149
Shell Oil Company, 249, 263, 274
Sheppard, Peggy, 386–387
Short, Bruce, 302–303
Sierra Club, 54, 70, 271, 388; Lake Calumet airport, 204
Silica mining, 312–313
Smith, Thomas, 91, 92, 93, 96, 97
SONAS, 190
South Carolina, toxic waste disposal, 95, 101
South Coast Air Quality Management District (AQMD), 63–71
South Cook County Environmental Action Coalition (SCCEAC), 17–18, 31, 35, 38–39, 41, 42
South Suburban Mayors and Managers Association (SSMMA), 10, 42; Reading Energy permit, 24, 33; Richton hearings, 25; Solid Waste Agency, 15, 24; waste-management plan, 23–24
Southdown Inc., 123
Southern Organizing Conference for Social and Economic Justice, 392–393
Southwest Organizing Project (SWOP), 388–389
Spencer, Alonzo, 107, 127, 129, 130, 133, 134, 137, 146, 152

Stancik, Ronald, 28, 29–30, 31, 33
Standard Oil Company, 163
Starks, Robert, 7
Stauffer Chemicals, 266
STC Enviroscience, 125, 130
Steenstra, Norm, 318, 319
Stein, Connie, 122, 126, 128, 137, 152, 154
Steisel, Norman, 53–54
Stenzel, Edwin, 235
Stephens Inc., 114
Stephens, Inc. of Arkansas, 111
Stephens, John Hall, 340
Stevens, Ramona, 254–255
St. John the Baptist Parish, Formosa Plastics plant, 261–262
Stripmining, 290, 296, 298; landfills and, 299
Subra, Wilma, 214
Suburban O'Hare Coalition, 201
Superfund (1976), xix, xxiii, 146, 214; technical assistance grants, 214
Superfund Amendments and Reauthorization Act, xxiv–xxv; Toxic Release Inventory, 255
Superfund for Workers, 411–412
Swanson, Dennis, 398, 399
Swearingen, Terri, 114, 122, 126, 128, 129, 133, 134, 137, 146, 149–154, 158, 419

Tangel, Jeff, 19–20, 21, 25, 28–29, 35
Tax breaks: linking with environmental performance, 251–252; for oil-refining and chemical industries, 249–250; for utilities, 248–249
Temik emissions, 314
Templet, Paul, 251, 273, 275, 277, 278, 280, 404; corporate challenge initiative, 401
Terrebonne Parish, Louisiana, hurricane-protection levee, 233
Texaco, 244, 249
ThermalKEM, Inc., 320
Thorpe, Grace, 376–378, 381
3M Corporation, Pollution Prevention Pays program, 399–400
Thurman-Jackson, Shelby, 114, 126, 129, 130
Tillman, Gerald, 215–216, 242, 243
Tobin, Rebecca, 108–109, 134, 137, 146
Tosi, Louis, 99–100, 102

Toxic buyouts, 253–261
Toxic Release Inventory (TRI), 194,
274, 394–395; comparative ranking,
414; Louisiana, 273–276
Toxic Substances Control Act, 180
Toxic waste generation, international
differences, 395–396
Toxics-use reduction, 397; industrial
programs, 398–399; municipal
programs, 408
Trask, Mililani, 384–385
Tri-State Environmental Council,
112–113, 115, 130, 137, 151, 152
Trial burns, 119–120, 150–151, 154
Tricil, Laidlaw acquisition, 99
Tulane Environmental Law Clinic, 250

U.S. Army Corps of Engineers, Pick-
Sloan project, 366–367
U.S. Department of Energy: NCAI
funding, 378–379; radioactive waste
disposal, 375–376
U.S. Ecology, Inc., Ward Valley site,
370
U.S. Environmental Protection
Agency, 127, 151, 158, 397; cancer
risk analysis, 156; coke-oven
standards, 199; CWM permits, 178;
environmental assistance to tribal
agencies, 357; Formosa Plastics
permits, 267; GSX Chemical
Services permits, 96–97; hazardous-
waste law, 84; incineration technology study, 121; levying fines for
violations, 182; National Priority
List, 170–171; Office of Health and
Environmental Assessment, 157;
Office of Solid and Hazardous
Waste, 145–146; Office of Solid
Waste and Emergency Response,
156–157; RCRA implementation,
180, 184; Robbins incinerator
permits, 22–23, 37–38, 222; WTI
permits, 109, 122, 126, 128–129,
150, 154; *See also* Illinois EPA; Ohio
EPA
U.S. Steel: Gary Works, 164–165, 169,
191, 197; South Works, 163, 168,
169
Union Carbide Corporation, 312–317;
Bhopal, India plant, xxiv, 145, 313–
314; silica mining, 312–313

Union Carbide Plastics and Chemicals
Company, 315
United Church of Christ, xxv;
Commission on Racial Justice, xxiv,
281, 383
United Nuclear Corporation (UNC),
326
United Steel Workers of America, 167,
169; environmental activism, 196,
197, 198, 199
University of California, Los Angeles,
planning school, 67
University of Pittsburgh, Center for
Hazardous Materials Research, 125,
150
Uranium Mill Tailings Radiation
Control Act (1978), 328
Uranium mining: health effects, 321–
326; mill tailings, 328–329
USX Corporation, 169; Clairton plant,
199; Gary Works, 170, 194
Utilities, tax breaks for, 248–249

Vegas Coals, 297
Vela, Lupe, 71–73
Velsico Chemical Company, 212
Ventura County, waste-minimization
program, 397
Vermilion Parish, toxic waste dumps,
213–214
Verret, Kirby, 230–233
Vertac Chemical Company, 155
Vertac Site Contractors, 155
Victims of a Toxic Environment
United (VOTE United), 254–255,
259
Vincent, Turk, 227, 228
Vinyl chloride, 266, 267
Voinovich, George, 77, 82–83, 89, 93,
102, 104, 113, 114, 122, 125, 127,
128; moratorium proposal, 134–136;
WTI health study, 125–126, 131,
137
Von Roll, 109
Von Roll America, 124, 151
Von Roll Inc., 131; spray-dryer
technology, 115, 116–117, 131
Von Roll Inc. of Switzerland, 111, 114
Vrdolyak, Edward, 175, 176, 177, 178

W. R. Grace Company, 140
Walker, Christine, 368–369

Wallace, Patty, 302–303, 305–306
Wang, Y. C., 261–262
Ward Valley nuclear-waste dump,
    369–371
Warren County, North Carolina, PCB
    landfill, 319–320
Washington, Harold, waste task force,
    175–177
Waste Management, Inc., 8, 80, 111,
    112, 151, 174–175, 178, 410;
    Calumet River facility, 184–185;
    materials-recovery facility, 177;
    Wheeler landfill, 186–190
Waste Management of North America,
    173
Waste Not, 27, 115
Waste Technologies, Inc., 153; test
    burn permit, 154
Waste Technologies Industries: East
    Liverpool facility, 104–159, 180;
    permit violations, 109

Waste-management industry: import-
    ing out-of-state waste, 189; on
    reservations, 369
Watchdog, *See* Labor/Community
    Strategy Center
Watkins, Frank, 362
West Virginia, landfills, 318–319
Wheeler, Indiana, Waste Management
    landfill, 186–190
White, Leon, xxiv
White, Michael, 89–90, 93
Willow Springs, Louisiana, BFI landfill,
    223–230
Wilson, Pete, 370
Wilson, Sarah, 128–129
Wisconsin Steel, 170
WMX, 410
Wyandotte Chemical Company, 235

Yomtovian, Isaac, 125, 130–132